CW01022822

Lancashire and the New Liberalism

THEIR FINEST HOUR (*see p. 191*)

frontispiece

Lancashire
and the New Liberalism

P. F. CLARKE

Lecturer in History, University College, London

CAMBRIDGE at the University Press 1971

CAMBRIDGE UNIVERSITY PRESS
Cambridge, New York, Melbourne, Madrid, Cape Town, Singapore, São Paulo

Cambridge University Press
The Edinburgh Building, Cambridge CB2 2RU, UK

Published in the United States of America by Cambridge University Press, New York

www.cambridge.org
Information on this title: www.cambridge.org/9780521080750

© Cambridge University Press 1971

This publication is in copyright. Subject to statutory exception
and to the provisions of relevant collective licensing agreements,
no reproduction of any part may take place without
the written permission of Cambridge University Press.

First published 1971
This digitally printed first paperback version 2007

A catalogue record for this publication is available from the British Library

ISBN-13 978-0-521-08075-0 hardback
ISBN-10 0-521-08075-4 hardback

ISBN-13 978-0-521-03557-6 paperback
ISBN-10 0-521-03557-0 paperback

Contents

Contents

Preface

The prevailing historiographical orthodoxy about British politics in the generation before the Great War, as it bears upon the subject of this book, seems to me to be reducible to the following propositions:

That the late nineteenth century saw a form of class politics, but one which was inherently unsatisfactory; so that the Labour party (which represented working-class interests) offered an ultimately irresistible challenge to the Liberal party (which did not). Moreover, that Labour (perhaps in spite of itself) acquired an ideological cutting edge which Liberalism lacked; that Liberalism, resting on *laissez faire* (of which Free Trade was the highest expression), could not come to terms with the modern state; and that the 'new Liberalism' was the pious palliative of a few intellectuals who had no influence on the men of power. That the 'Radicals' failed to shift the party to the left, and instead the 'Liberal Imperialists' kept it to the right; so that, in remaining a bourgeois creed, Asquithian Liberalism lost touch with the workers; and conversely that such popular strength as it could command came from Nonconformity. Hence that the Edwardian Liberal revival was illusory, based as it was upon three freakish election results in 1906, January 1910 and December 1910; but that a disinterested observer could have seen before 1914 that Liberalism was played out and that only with its displacement by the Labour party would class find its proper expression in politics.

This book will suggest that these propositions are at best inadequate and at worst false. In order to make sense of what happened in north west England in the early twentieth century I had to adopt a different interpretative schema. And the argument is less over Lancashire than over a general theory which can subsume Lancashire as a special case. For Lancashire was the cockpit of Edwardian elections. It was, above all, the way north west England voted that kept a Liberal Government in office. Now it is often argued that in so far as the Liberals did well in Lancashire it was for peculiar and unrepresentative reasons; that the cotton bosses were staunch Free Traders and hence Liberals; and so on. I hope to show, however, that Lancashire cannot be explained away in this fashion. I shall argue that what follows cannot be spatchcocked into the conventional interpretation of British politics in this period: that it is not the old story with some modification but a new story altogether.

My indebtedness to two works – Professor Hanham's *Elections and Party*

Preface

Management and Professor Vincent's *The Formation of the Liberal Party* – is so general that it ought to be acknowledged forthwith. The lack of comparable studies for a later period, while it is one that this book cannot adequately remedy, to some extent explains its length. In writing it I have incurred many debts. The help of Dr G. Kitson Clark is now of long standing. I owe thanks to Mr David Ayerst for easing my path in consulting the Scott Papers and for reading a draft of chapter 7. Dr Stephen Koss generously made material from the papers of Sir John Brunner available to me; and to him I am indebted for the references on pp. 113, 205, 214 and 242. Dr Henry Pelling was good enough to read the book in draft and his criticism provoked beneficial amendment. Miss Nazneen Razwi typed the entire manuscript more than once and more than efficiently. What I owe to my wife is no matter for prefaces; and I hope my colleagues at University College, past and present, will allow me a similar reticence over their help.

I make grateful acknowledgement to the following for allowing me access to papers in their keeping or for permission to quote from material of which they hold the copyright: the Rt Hon. the Earl of Cromer; Sir William Erskine Gladstone; Judge J. B. Herbert, Q.C.; Professor Ann K. S. Lambton and Mr Francis Noel-Baker (Viscount Cecil of Chelwood); Mr J. C. Medley of Field Fisher and Co. (Augustine Birrell); Mrs G. A. Morley; Mr A. H. Noble of Haldanes and McLaren, W.S., on behalf of Lady Mottistone (Alexander Murray, Master of Elibank); Miss Juliet O'Hea of Curtis Brown Ltd (L. T. Hobhouse); Marjorie Lady Pentland (Sir Henry Campbell-Bannerman); the Earl of Rosebery; Mr Laurence P. Scott; Mr A. J. P. Taylor on behalf of Sir Max Aitken and the Trustees of the Beaverbrook Foundations (Lord Beaverbrook and Bonar Law), Beaverbrook Newspapers (Lloyd George), the *Spectator* (St Loe Strachey); Mr Ernest Tomlinson on behalf of the City of Manchester Liberal Party (Manchester Liberal Federation). To others whom I have overlooked, or been unable to trace, I extend my apologies.

The frontispiece shows Winston Churchill and C. P. Scott leaving the Manchester Reform Club on 22 May 1909, and is reproduced by permission of the *Guardian*.

Abbreviations used in references

BP	Balfour Papers
CBP	Campbell-Bannerman Papers
CP	Cecil Papers
EP	Elibank Papers
HGP	Herbert Gladstone Papers
BLP	Bonar Law Papers
LGP	Lloyd George Papers
SP	C. P. Scott Papers, British Museum
MGP	C. P. Scott Papers, *Guardian* offices

In the case of British Museum Additional MSS. the number of the volume is cited immediately after the name of the collection

M.L.F.	Manchester Liberal Federation
L.C.L.F.	Lancashire and Cheshire Liberal Federation
Companion	Companion volumes to Randolph S. Churchill, *Winston S. Churchill* (1967–)
C.F.T.	*Cotton Factory Times*
L. Courier	*Liverpool Courier*
Lancs. D.P.	*Lancashire Daily Post*
Liverpool D.P.	*Liverpool Daily Post (and Mercury)*
M. Courier	*Manchester Courier*
M.G.	*Manchester Guardian*
N.D.T.	*Northern Daily Telegraph*

Works listed in the bibliography are cited by short titles only.

To my parents

PART ONE
INTRODUCTION

The politics of change

His wisdom and his eloquence!
Oh, who shall be his heir?
That priceless grand inheritance
'Tis no man's lot to share.
By day and night with eager gaze
The forum's lights we scan,
They are but stars with flickering rays,
Whose sun's the Grand Old Man.

Liberal song, c. 1888

I

The unique personal ascendancy of Gladstone went far towards masking many of the shortcomings and internal tensions of the party he led for so long and in so distinctively personal a style. It was, then, perhaps inevitable that the legacy of Gladstonian Liberalism should be the post-Gladstonian Liberal party. It was exceedingly difficult in the 1890s to strike a resounding positive note about Liberal virtues. The proprietor of the *Manchester Guardian* was reduced to entering minor caveats over the derisive remarks of the Liberal front-bencher Reid which had been reported to him – 'Do you not think he exaggerates matters when he speaks of the party in the House as money combined with intrigue? Of course, the party is practically leaderless and we know how the sheep wander without a shepherd?'[1] The leadership issue was certainly a recurrent problem, but hardly more than one aspect of a more general malaise. There was a marked predisposition towards abdication on the part of all the men whom Gladstone's mantle might have draped. Rosebery was incorrigible in this respect and Harcourt hardly less so; Morley and Asquith for reasons of their own declined to take on more active roles; and Campbell-Bannerman's assumption of the leadership did not presage any sustained initiative from the top. None of the three men who successively led the Liberals in the five or six years after Gladstone's retirement was sanguine about either the prospects of the party or his own ability to affect the course of events.

'We are tossed on the ocean of discouragement just now [wrote Rosebery in 1894], and the judicious mariner however stout-hearted hails every... glimpse of blue sky. I am cheerful enough, because I foresaw all the

[1] J. E. Taylor to C. P. Scott, 31 July 1898, MGP.

difficulties of my position, and, though they may be insuperable they do not come on me with the depression of a surprise.'[1]

The striking Conservative victory in the General Election of 1895 duly confirmed Rosebery's prognostications and left the Liberal party in a state of comprehensive disarray. 'As survivors of the shipwrecked crew', wrote Harcourt to Asquith, 'we shall have to set to work, I suppose, to set up a Robinson Crusoe habitation of some sort about the 12th. I was prepared for the deluge but not for this earthquake.'[2] Harcourt's own brief tenure of the leadership, however, did nothing to make the problems facing the party seem less intractable; Campbell-Bannerman was left to confront the same lack of success in 1900, drawing upon the same metaphors that had solaced his predecessors. 'Now that we have dried our clothes and washed the salt out of our eyes', he wrote to Herbert Gladstone, 'we mariners, survivors of the storm, can communicate with each other in peace.'[3]

The recurrent imagery of shipwreck was deeply appropriate to the state of the Liberal party in the 1890s and it is more than a curiosity that all its leaders indulged in it in a manner that may be termed either stoical or supine. To some extent, obviously, it is true that the Liberals' plight was due to the personal inability of Rosebery, Harcourt or Campbell-Bannerman to measure up to the Gladstonian standard

> That priceless grand inheritance
> 'Tis no man's lot to share.

But Liberalism itself also needed to be reformulated in a sense relevant to a new era. As the *Manchester Guardian* put it after the General Election of 1900:

Liberalism was disorganised by the loss of Mr Gladstone, and more subtly but more completely by its own success. The work of enfranchisement, though not complete, has been carried so far that whole classes have become satisfied with the existing order – that is to say, have become, by natural inclination and in the strict meaning of the term, Conservative. The forces on which the Liberalism of the sixties could rely are no longer at its disposal. Of this its fresh losses in the great centres in this election are but a renewed proof. Hence in domestic politics the problem of social progress has in some respects changed its character.[4]

In short, with the political capital of Gladstonian Liberalism fast becoming exhausted, there was need for a new Liberalism which could more effectively engage the support of working-class voters.

[1] Rosebery to Sir Edward Russell, 8 May 1894, confidential, Rosebery–Russell correspondence.
[2] Harcourt to Asquith, 29 July 1895, Asquith (Oxford), *Fifty Years of Parliament*, I, 245.
[3] Campbell-Bannerman to H. Gladstone, 22 October 1900, HGP 45987 f. 125.
[4] Leader, *M.G.* 17 October 1900 (almost certainly by L. T. Hobhouse).

Ever since the Home Rule split in the party, the situation had been critical. Under Disraeli the Conservative party had already won over enough middle-class support to put it on a parity with the Liberals. Under Salisbury the Unionists became definitively the party of wealth – and thereby gained a decisive advantage under an electoral system that was geared to the representation of the wealthy. This modification of previous lines of political cleavage established the ground-rules of party politics in the period up to the Great War. Prominent Whigs like Hartington had recognised that 'in the long run the active men will have their own way, and the future Liberal party will be Radical'.[1] The emergence and success of Unionism precipitated the question of Liberal viability: clearly the party must consolidate a class basis of electoral support as effective as that of the Tories – or die. Engels observed in 1892 that 'the Liberals know full well that for them it is a question of catching the labour vote if they intend to continue their existence as a party'.[2] But it was equally clear that the Liberal party of the 1890s was incapable of effecting this bold reorientation; and the existence of the I.L.P. was a monument to the disappointment Liberalism had been to many of those who were potentially its warmest supporters among the working class. To a considerable extent the same is true of the foundation of the Labour Representation Committee in 1900.

The existence of a working-class political organisation aiming at parliamentary representation in some ways made the task facing the Liberals more complicated but not necessarily more difficult. Labour shared the spoils when the reaction against the Conservatives eventually came in 1906. Labour pioneers naturally stressed the novelty of this achievement. Mary Hamilton later wrote that, 'What disturbed all calculations was the new spirit animating this group, and the appeal made by that spirit to the workers.' In a similar vein, J. R. Clynes recalled a Labour party which brooked no compromise in its fight for socialism: 'We offered something quite different from the promises of the existing two Parties. We were out with a spiritual appeal, as well as to win material concessions.'[3] The confidence that history was on their side was only natural among Labour leaders who lived to see, if not quite Jerusalem builded here, then at least Ramsay MacDonald as Prime Minister. The history of Edwardian politics seems often to be written under a similar assumption, that despite the apparent revival of Liberalism the Labour party represented an irresistible force which would inexorably displace it.

[1] Hartington to Granville, 3 October 1885, Holland, *Life of the Duke of Devonshire*, II, 73–4.
[2] Engels to A. Bebel, 5 July 1892, *Marx and Engels on Britain*, p. 572. 'Hence', he continued, 'the need of the Liberals to make sham or real concessions to the workers, especially the former.'
[3] Hamilton, *Arthur Henderson*, p. 59; Clynes, *Memoirs*, I, 103.

Perhaps the classical exposition of this view is that of Dangerfield, prescient even about the landslide of 1906: 'But the Liberal Party which came back to Westminster with an overwhelming majority was already doomed. It was like an army protected at all points except for one vital position on its flank. With the election of fifty-three Labour representatives, the death of Liberalism was pronounced; it was no longer the Left.'[1] It is not the purpose of this study to confute the opinions expressed in a brilliant impressionistic book which belongs more nearly in time to the events which it describes than to us. But there is no denying that the interpretation it represents has been influential in moulding preconceptions about the fate of the Liberal party. The result is a sub-Marxian analysis which posits that the change from Liberalism to Labour was determined by a change in the infrastructure of politics. This argument, however, loses its purchase if it can be shown that by 1910 the critical shift had already taken place and that the Liberal party had adjusted to it. This book will argue that in north west England, at any rate, there was a qualitative change in electoral politics in the early twentieth century. This had four main aspects, each of which tends to vitiate one of the commonly advanced analyses of the Liberal downfall. There is the 'sociological' argument, that Labour replaced the Liberals as a result of the rise of the working class. But already by 1910 the collectivities upon which politics were based had changed from communities to classes. Then there is the argument that Liberalism lacked a new generation of leaders – 'the mould was broken'. But the criteria of political leadership were changing; the patriarchal figures of an heroic age of dissent were being replaced by career politicians – and of these the intellectual left was in no short supply. Again, it is often argued that grassroots pressure for independence would prevent the accommodation of Labour within the progressive fold. Yet the whole ambit of politics had changed from the local to the national. Finally, it is sometimes suggested that Liberalism was ideologically bankrupt, on either the theoretical level or the practical level or both. This is to overlook not only the intellectual synthesis of liberalism and socialism as progressivism, but also the fact that the popular issues in elections had changed from those that were at root religious to those that were at root economic. The lines of argument which will be developed here and the evidence that will be adduced do not, of course, preclude the possibility of a Liberal collapse as a result of political crises. (This was substantially what in fact took place.) But they suggest that the change in politics, already substantially complete by 1910, predisposed towards continued Liberal success, if not to the degree of 1906, at least at a level markedly above that of the Gladstonian party.

[1] Dangerfield, *Strange Death of Liberal England*, p. 10.

II

Two important regional studies of electoral politics in this period, of Wales and of London, have been published.[1] A study of the north west has considerable intrinsic attractions, but will be justified here on the grounds of its relevance to forces operative in national politics as a whole. For not only was the electoral history of Lancashire of pivotal importance to the outcome of successive General Elections, but this was recognised to be the case by the respective parties. Indeed it is hardly too much to claim that a central pre-occupation of the Conservative party in the period after 1906, as of the Liberal party in the period up to 1906, was to wrest Lancashire from its opponents: an ambition to which all other aspects of Conservative strategy were subjugated in the General Elections of 1910. The augmentation of the Liberal (or Labour) representation in Parliament by constituencies in the north west was the most important single component in the electoral revolution which kept a Liberal government in power from 1906 until the War. A further point of interest is that in the Labour party's sudden leap to prominence in the 1906 Election, almost half of the M.P.s sponsored by the L.R.C. were elected by constituencies in the north west.

The Liberals increasingly recognised in the 1890s to what extent their possibility of recovery depended upon making inroads upon 'Tory Lancashire'. When, after the General Election of 1895, Lancashire's 58 M.P.s included only nine Liberals, the *Manchester Guardian* delivered a homily:

It is nearly or quite as bad as London, where the Liberals are eight out of 53, and in this election even more clearly than in 1886 London and Lancashire have once more revealed themselves as the two great centres on which Liberal effort must be spent unsparingly if the country at large is to be won from Toryism. So long as the Tories can return a solid phalanx of over 100 members from London and Lancashire alone, no Liberal victory is possible. These are the central fortresses which must be breached at all hazards; and while every Lancashire Liberal will find in the black figures a new incentive to unceasing effort, it may also perhaps be suggested that the Liberal leaders should recognise more fully than they appear to have done hitherto that Lancashire is almost the key to the situation.[2]

While the Liberals engineered minor adjustments in their favour in 1900, it was not until 1906 that they were really able to turn this key.

If the representation of the 460 English seats in the years 1900–10 is investigated,[3] it appears that 110 returned a Conservative and 107 a Liberal

[1] Morgan, *Wales in British Politics*; Thompson, *Socialists, Liberals and Labour*.
[2] Leader, *M.G.* 26 July 1895.
[3] The calculations of this section are based upon the returns given in the *Constitutional Year Book* (1918). The survey deals only with English seats, including Monmouth but excluding the

at each of the four General Elections in this period; hence the remaining 243 made some change of allegiance at some stage. The Liberals held 126 of the 460 seats in 1900. At subsequent General Elections the numbers of seats changing hands was as follows:

	total Liberal gains	total Conservative gains	net advantage
1906	214	2	+212 Liberals
January 1910	8	120	+112 Conservatives
December 1910	24	25	+1 Conservative

The transitory nature of many of the successes which the Liberals achieved in 1906 is apparent; of the 214 seats which they then gained from the Conservatives, they lost half (106) and retained half (108) in January 1910. In December 1910 they lost a further 18 of the 1906 gains, though they won back exactly 18 of the January defectors. The 'permanent' gains made in 1906, therefore, amounted to 108 seats, with whichever of the 1910 elections it is compared.

In many counties the dramatic Liberal victories of 1906 were matched by a Conservative counter-attack in January 1910 which was almost as successful. In the counties of Berkshire, Devonshire, Essex, Hampshire, Herefordshire, Huntingdonshire, Kent, Oxfordshire, Somerset, Suffolk, Surrey, Sussex and Wiltshire, the Liberals made a net gain of 52 seats in 1906; in January 1910 they suffered a net loss of 50. In some cases this picture was modified in December 1910; for instance, the Liberals then won odd seats in Oxfordshire and Suffolk but made a net loss of three further seats in Devon. The conclusion is nonetheless clear that while the political changes in these counties may be very revealing about the exceptional nature of the 1906 Election, that is all. On the other hand, in the counties of Cheshire, Lancashire and Yorkshire, where the Liberals made comparable gains of fifty-six seats in 1906, the Conservatives were limited to a net gain of only ten in January 1910. Little wonder that in private Lloyd George would contrast 'the progressive north' with 'the semi-feudal south'.[1] That this is not entirely a case of rural as against industrial areas, though, is shown by the cases of Nottinghamshire, Warwickshire and Staffordshire where there were sixteen Liberal gains in 1906 and fourteen Conservative gains in January 1910.

Universities. In this and the following section Liberal Unionists and Independent Conservatives are counted as Conservatives; all other M.P.s as Liberals, if only on the grounds that they gave the Liberal Government support. By-elections are ignored.

[1] C. P. Scott's interview notes, 21 June 1911, SP 50901 ff. 17–20.

The seats which most significantly affected the issue were the long-term gains over 1900 which the Liberal party showed after the elections of 1910. After January 1910 the Liberals held 116 seats which had been Conservative in 1900, spread over no less than twenty-nine counties. Thirty-three of them, however, were in Lancashire and Cheshire, 21 in London and 13 in Yorkshire – a total of 67 out of 116, or nearly three-fifths. Similarly, of the 114 seats which had been Conservative in 1900 but were Liberal after December 1910, 25 were in Lancashire and Cheshire, 23 in London and 14 in Yorkshire – a total of 62, or well over half. And although after December 1910 the Conservatives held fifteen seats that had been Liberal in 1900, none was in these counties (though one of them, the High Peak division of Derbyshire, is included within the north west region as defined below). The most impressive changes took place in north west England, where a region that had been heavily Conservative for a generation or more swung decisively against that party. In the seventy-one seats of the region the Liberals (with Labour) showed a net gain in January 1910 of 33 over their position in 1900 and in December 1910 of 24. Since these counted 66 and 48 on a division, respectively, it may be noted that in both Parliaments the progressive majority over the Conservatives was less than this. The north west thus became one of the cornerstones of the Edwardian Liberal revival.

III

It has been natural so far to deal mainly in terms of counties since even the creation in 1885 of what were virtually equal electoral districts was accomplished by a fragmentation of the already partially dismembered ancient counties. The north west region as understood here consists of the counties of Lancashire and Cheshire, together with the High Peak division of Derbyshire. The influence of the two natural hubs of Liverpool and Manchester dictates this extension beyond Lancashire itself, and these boundaries delineate what has many times and for many purposes been defined as a standard region.[1] It was dominated, of course, by two great population centres. The south east Lancashire conurbation around Manchester had reached its present frontiers by the mid-nineteenth century with a population of something over one million; this doubled by 1900. Conurban growth was also pronounced on Merseyside and in a more discontinuous fashion along the northern and western flanks of Rossendale. By about 1880 most of the areas of high population density, based overwhelmingly on cotton, had been

[1] Cf. esp. C. B. Fawcett, *Provinces of England. A study of some geographical aspects of devolution* (1919), pp. 35, 117 ff.; Birch and Campbell, 'Politics in the North West', *Manc. Sch.* XVIII (1950); J. P. Mackintosh, *The Devolution of Power* (Penguin edn 1968), pp. 70–98.

established. Newer towns of mid-nineteenth century origin – like Crewe, Fleetwood, Southport and Blackpool, fashioned in a railway age, and others, like Barrow, St Helens and Widnes, based on new industrial processes – completed a picture that was subsequently to change little.[1]

In the period 1885–1918 the region contained sixty-six Parliamentary constituencies and returned seventy-one M.P.s, five boroughs being double-member seats.[2] These were represented as follows:

	Conservative	Liberal	Irish Nationalist
1885	46	24	1
1886	59	11	1
1892	45	25	1
1895	60	10	1
1900	56	14	1

This is by any standards a strong Tory tradition. Even in the two Liberal victories in the General Elections of 1885 and 1892 the Conservatives won nearly twice as many seats as the Liberals in the north west. After 1906, however, the position was reversed, so that by 1910 the region's political complexion was completely transformed.

	Conservative	Progressive	Irish Nationalist
1906	16	54	1
January 1910	23	47	1
December 1910	32	38	1

The secular trend is to some extent revealed by a comparison of the Conservative percentage of the poll in 1885 and in December 1910.[3] In most seats the Conservative poll was lower in 1910 than it had been twenty-five years previously, the exceptions being, apart from some of the more distinctively residential divisions, most of the constituencies in which there was a strong Irish community. The turnover of Irish votes which might be expected

[1] Cf. L. P. Green, *Provincial Metropolis. The future of local government in South East Lancashire* (1959), pp. 63, 66; Lawton, 'Population trends in Lancashire and Cheshire from 1801', *Trans. Hist. Soc. Lancs. & Ches.*, CXIV (1962), p. 197.
[2] See Appendix A for a map of the constituencies, together with equal-area diagrams of the region which, despite some distortion, are an intrinsically more satisfactory device than a map for showing Parliamentary representation.
[3] See Appendix A, Diagram 3.

on the basis of the well-known injunctions of their leaders to vote Conservative in 1885 and Liberal in December 1910, plainly only adds to the disparity which has to be explained; but the inference that the Irish vote was actually of negative effect in these cases is one which may well come pretty near the truth. In the rest of the region there was a marked decrease in the Conservative vote, suggesting a slackening hold over the period as a whole.

If the Liberal vote of 1885 may be taken as a gauge of the strength of the old Liberalism, the 1892 vote may be taken to measure the flood tide of Home Rule Liberalism. Comparing the two, the Conservatives benefited marginally on balance; they did so heftily in residential Cheshire, markedly in the suburbs of Manchester and Liverpool, and slightly in some of the smaller towns. In many cases a swing to the Conservatives may have been partially concealed by an Irish switch to the Liberals; significantly, in Gorton and Hyde, where it was admitted that the Irish had already been on the Liberal side in 1885,[1] the Conservative poll rose by an exceptional amount. Conversely, the Liberals benefited in most 'Irish' constituencies. Their share of the poll in Widnes increased by over ten per cent and while this was exceptional their position improved considerably if not dramatically in the central Manchester area and most of the larger towns. They also did notably well in Lancaster and, to a lesser extent, North Lonsdale, where the admittedly strong Roman Catholic bodies were not Irish. While these changes, especially the larger ones in both directions, are in many ways revealing, their general significance should not be overrated. In the first place they can plausibly be interpreted as merely the shift of an 'interest'; further, their net effect in the region as a whole was only slight in terms of either seats or the popular vote; and lastly their effect in many constituencies was exceedingly marginal. Perhaps the political revolution of 1886 was more apparent than real, in that the Home Rule party was no different in kind from the old Liberal party, only less successful. At any rate, this would seem to be true electorally.

The Election of 1892 was the only Election in the Home-Rule era of British politics when the Liberal party performed even passably well in the north west. To compare it with the freakish Liberal success in 1906 would be to produce a striking but largely meaningless result. But a comparison of the General Elections of 1892 and January 1910 should provide a fair indication of how far politics had moved on to a new footing in the early twentieth century.[2] In the region as a whole there was a large fall in the percentage Conservative vote between 1892 and 1910.

[1] See Howard, 'The Parnell manifesto of 21 November 1885 and the schools question', *E.H.R.*, LXII (1947), pp. 48–50.
[2] See Appendix A, Diagram 4 and note.

Introduction

(*a*) *In nineteen constituencies this fall was around ten per cent and in some of them nearer fifteen*

This group consisted of the large cotton boroughs like Bolton, Blackburn, Bury and Oldham, together with Clitheroe, a county division dominated by smaller cotton towns. It included, too, the working-class city divisions – Manchester North East, Liverpool East Toxteth and Liverpool Scotland, the last more important, perhaps, as being the Irish Nationalist quarter; and the residential Manchester South. Also in this category of great Liberal improvement were two sets of county divisions: five around Manchester and Liverpool – Stretford, Knutsford, Prestwich, Ormskirk and Wirral – which were mainly rural and residential, though now industrialising; and four in which coalmining was probably most important, Westhoughton, Ince, Newton and Chorley. The remaining constituency in this category was Barrow-in-Furness. These were the areas in which the new Liberalism had made biggest strides. It should be noted, however, that in all of the residential seats except Ormskirk there had been a strong reaction towards the Conservatives in 1892 and the apparent extent of Liberal advance is somewhat exaggerated by this.

(*b*) *In another 25 constituencies the Conservative share of the vote fell by around five per cent over this period*

These were the more mixed city divisions: virtually the whole of Manchester (North, North West, East and South West, Salford West, Eccles) and the Liverpool divisions of Kirkdale and Walton, plus Bootle and Widnes. There were also the urban constituencies of Stockport, Warrington, Chester, Macclesfield, Leigh, St Helens, Wigan and Birkenhead, which were not primarily dependent upon cotton.[1] Six others in this range were cotton seats although they were not such great urban centres as those where the Conservative decline had been heaviest; these were Radcliffe, Hyde, Middleton, Burnley, Rochdale and Accrington. The rural-residential division of Blackpool also showed a shift of this order.

(*c*) *In a further nineteen seats the Conservative vote was either static, or declined by only two or three per cent*

About half of these areas of stability were the remoter county divisions, either in the hills, like Lancaster, Rossendale, Darwen, Heywood and the High Peak, all of which had some cotton interests, or deeply rural like Eddisbury. The other half of the stable seats were urban seats where the Irish influence was strong: five of the Liverpool divisions – Everton, West Toxteth,

[1] In comparison with the 1885 results both Chester and Macclesfield show an actual improvement in the Conservative position by 3–4 per cent.

Abercromby, Exchange and West Derby – plus the North and South divisions of Salford, and Gorton, Preston, Ashton and Stalybridge. In two other county divisions, Crewe and Southport, which were of neither of these types, the Conservative vote also suffered only a slight decline. The Conservative vote in most of these seats emerges as equally stable if 1885 rather than 1892 is taken for comparison. In Lancaster and West Toxteth, however, there was a decline of around ten per cent, while in Southport and Eddisbury they gained by two to three per cent. Gorton was the most remarkable in that the stability of the 1892 and 1910 Conservative votes belied the improvement of nearly ten per cent over 1885.

(*d*) *The three remaining constituencies all showed some long-term increase in the Conservative vote*

In Widnes and North Lonsdale this was in some sense balanced by a deterioration in their position as compared with 1885. But in Northwich, where the increased Conservative share of the poll was admittedly smaller, there was no such compensation, and this was the only constituency in the region where the Conservative vote in January 1910 held up better by a clear one per cent than it had done in either 1885 or 1892.

Now it is true that no scheme of classifying constituencies is entirely satisfactory. But two conclusions are clear. First, that in almost every case the Liberals were more formidable opponents in January 1910 than they had been in 1892, or even in 1885. Second, that the basis of their strength in 1910 was new. The improvement in their position as compared with 1892 had not been uniform. It was *greatest* in the large towns (though not necessarily in the city divisions) and in the cotton and coal areas; and it was *least* in the more sparsely populated areas and in the districts of Irish concentration.

Further amplifications of this tendency become apparent if the pattern of change between particular elections is examined. Thus it is broadly true that in the suburban divisions around the cities there was a steady growth in Conservative support from 1885 to 1900, suggesting a shift in social norms rather than sharp response to any single issue: a trend interrupted but not permanently reversed by a large Liberal swing in 1906. In many of the city seats, on the other hand, the more volatile pattern meant bigger Conservative swings in 1900 as well as bigger Liberal swings in 1906; while the 'Irish' seats which shared this volatility were distinguished by their initial slide towards Liberalism (presumably as a result of Home Rule) and the strong Tory reaction in 1910. Again, there was a distinctive line of development in the typical cotton seat, which made for a peak of Conservative success not in 1900 but in 1895; and some of the less urbanised cotton divisions were notable also for their stability throughout the period.

Introduction

More than one aspect of a constituency's character was politically influential. It plainly mattered a great deal whether a division consisted of one self-contained borough or several scattered communities or one sector of an urban mass; whether it was industrial or rural or residential; whether it was a cotton seat; whether it was an area of Irish settlement; and whether it was within the ambit of Liverpool or Manchester. But as far as their electoral impact upon the Liberal party is concerned, almost all these factors can be subsumed in a single generalisation. With the notable exception of the Liverpool area, what distinguished the progressivism of 1910 from the Gladstonianism of 1892 was the support of the urban working class. It is this fundamental development which the rest of this book will attempt to explain.

IV

André Siegfried long ago pointed to the seemingly immutable political temperament, based on a way of life and a manner of thinking, which underlay the swings in political opinion in the region of France which he studied.[1] It will be suggested here that, for all the variations in party fortunes in the late nineteenth century, popular attitudes as expressed in elections were rooted in a political temperament which was fundamentally stable; whereas change in this temperament itself was the most significant aspect of the Liberal revival after 1906. The stability which obtained can often be seen in the voting, especially in the county divisions where mobility and the vagaries of the register had least effect. The Liberal M.P. for Darwen, where in all the eight General Elections from 1885 the parties were never separated by more than four per cent of the poll, affected to see this as an outward and visible sign of an inward and invisible grace:

There was not a constituency in the country – and he had had the opportunity of conversing with several M.P.'s – where the change was so little and where the pendulum oscillated to such a slight extent. It took as great a sweep to turn over 200 or 300 votes in the division as it took to turn over one or two thousand in the unstable and light-headed constituencies – London for instance (laughter and cheers).[2]

But even where the fluctuations in the vote were much larger it will be argued that, until 1910 at least, this did not reflect a clear qualitative change.

The motivation of individual voters is neither knowable on any large scale nor the essential point here. Some understanding is necessary, however, of the social psychology of voting. A study of electoral behaviour in one town in our region (Stockport) in 1964 found it necessary to distinguish the

[1] André Siegfried, *Tableau Politique de la France de l'Ouest* (Paris, 1913), p. xxvi.
[2] Speech by F. G. Hindle, *Lancs. D.P.*, 28 November 1910.

14

functions of voting for the voter from the functions of election in the political system, and suggested that for individuals the chief functions were emotional or allegiance-maintaining.[1] This is to say, in effect, that if voting is to be understood it must be seen in the context of the voters' world view not the politicians'; and its context and its priority were very different in the two. Not that elections were an unimportant part of people's lives; Charles Masterman for instance, writing in 1905, included among the ordinary pleasures of ordinary people (and it is perhaps the sequence that we should observe) 'the physical satisfaction in food, and the greater physical satisfaction in drink; the delight in the excitement of betting, an election, an occasional holiday'.[2] Partisanship over political parties existed in a world where partisanship over football teams was also common, and either may or may not have stirred a man to the depths.

To assess voting, then, as an explicit demand upon the political system may be to interpret these elections according to the wrong criteria. The novelist Robert Tressell deplored the lack of substantive issues at stake in Edwardian elections:

At such times these people forgot all about unemployment and starvation, and became enthusiastic about 'Grand Old Flags'. Their devotion to this flag was so great that so long as they were able to carry it to victory, they did not mind being poverty stricken and hungry and ragged; all that mattered was to score off their hated 'enemies' their fellow countrymen the Tories, and carry the grand old flag to victory. The fact that they had carried the flag to victory so often in the past without obtaining any of the spoils, did not seem to damp their ardour in the least.[3]

In the most extreme view, then, men did not expect to get anything as a result of an election victory in this period: 'What they primarily hoped to get was the election victory itself, as a visceral thrill, and as an assertion of their proper importance.'[4]

The view taken here does not accord political consciousness so dominant a role in Victorian elections, but does see the social milieu in which people's lives were lived as being central to electoral choice, and would certainly maintain that what men voted for was in many ways less important than whom they voted with. Perhaps this can be reduced to a number of general propositions about electoral behaviour in Victorian England. The first postulate is that voting preferences were a meaningful expression of antecedent social attitudes of some permanence and significance: that they were rooted in something. The fundamental stability of electoral behaviour suggests that it

---

[1] Richard Rose and Harve Mossawir, 'Voting and elections: a functional analysis', *Political Studies*, xv (1967), p. 192.
[2] Masterman, *C. F. G. Masterman*, p. 57.
[3] Robert Tressell, *The Ragged Trousered Philanthropists* (Panther edn 1965), p. 528.
[4] Vincent, *Pollbooks. How Victorians Voted*, p. 47.

was more often based on the habits of a lifetime than on the passing whim of a moment. Next, even though this was so, the rudimentary cares of life do not adequately explain the political concerns of the electorate. So that while sometimes a clash of economic interests underlay political conflict, more often it did not. And in the third place, the importance of religion – not in any narrow sense, and not in a spiritual sense, but *religion in a social sense –* should be stressed. For this was a religious age *faute de mieux*. Its stock of ideas was cast in religious terms, its platitudes were religious platitudes, its clichés religious clichés. At the popular level its whole intellectual orientation was religious. And its divisions were religious. It was, then, a religious infrastructure, reinforced in its cleavages by ethnic factors, upon which popular divisions were based. Perhaps these can best be understood in terms of considerations of status in the sense of Max Weber, for the insistence on the irreducibility of both ideal and material interests which is at the heart of his political sociology is fundamental to the present analysis.[1]

This will appear most clearly as the distinction between classes and status groups. In his interesting study of *How Victorians Voted* J. R. Vincent has sought to demonstrate 'the centrality of class, in a certain sophisticated sense, in rank and file political orientation'[2] by utilising the concepts of Ralf Dahrendorf. In post-Marxian definitions of class, the general problem is that the two basic constituents of Marxian class (materialism and consciousness) are not necessarily reconcilable. Which, then, is the kernel and which the husk? Forced to choose, Dahrendorf prefers to salvage consciousness; hence for him 'classes are social conflict groups the determinant (or *differentia specifica*) of which can be found in the participation in or exclusion from the exercise of authority within any imperatively coordinated association'.[3] It is very doubtful whether class in this sense can be of much help in explaining Victorian elections since insofar as it corresponds to the facts it does not go very far towards explaining them. In short, it tends to become tautologous.[4] Following Weber, it will be accepted here that class differentiation 'is not "dynamic", that is, it does not necessarily result in class struggles or class revolutions'.[5] But the Marxian definition will be retained in the sense that

---

[1] The concepts drawn upon here are treated in Max Weber, *The Theory of Social and Economic Organization*, edited by Talcott Parsons (London, 1964), pp. 407–12, 424–9; and in *From Max Weber: Essays in Sociology*, edited by H. H. Gerth and C. Wright Mills (London, 1948), pp. 180–95.   [2] Vincent, *Pollbooks. How Victorians Voted*, p. 30.

[3] Ralf Dahrendorf, *Class and Class Conflict in Industrial Society* (1959), p. 138.

[4] *viz.* Why do people vote on opposite sides in elections?
Because they belong to classes.
What are classes?
Groups in conflict over power.
How do we know they are in conflict over power?
Because they vote on opposite sides in elections.

[5] *Theory*, p. 425.

'the factor that creates "class" is unambiguously economic interest, and indeed, only those interests involved in the existence of the "market"'.[1]

There is some difficulty, too, about using the term status group since those who have found this distinction most useful have often developed Weber's concept in a somewhat one-sided manner. 'Status' has acquired particular connotations when adapted by sociologists to modern industrial society. W. G. Runciman clearly has this kind of society in mind when, in his perceptive examination of political sociology, he asserts that 'status-*group* is misleading, in the sense that status-*stratum* would be more accurate'.[2] But the opposite approach will prove more useful here: that is, to define the concept not from the point of view of the individual's position in a status hierarchy (as determined by the social esteem in which he is generally held) but from that of group conflict. Though this emphasis is rather neglected in the modern use of the term it was central to Weber's original formulation. Status groups, then, are normally communities; their composition is determined by a social estimation of honour which may be connected with any quality shared by a plurality. Although class situation has now become the predominant factor in conditioning the 'style of life' of status groups, they are *essentially* dependent upon their shared values; hence the independent importance of religious beliefs. For in a society the ideas of which are dominated by religion, it is to be expected that status groups will form around values religious in origin. (So in Victorian England ideal interests were constituted by religion, in a sense running all the way from primary faith to derivative prejudice.) In this context a status group is not a religious group, but a social group whose way of life is informed by values derived from religion. There are two important qualifications. First, that where there are also underlying ethnic differences the social segregation of groups maintaining a distinctive life style is more marked. Second, the status, prestige or honour attaches primarily to the group and only secondarily to the individual.

These economic and social dimensions are distinct from but relate to the political plane. The end for which a party seeks to secure power for its leaders is 'to attain ideal or material advantages for its active members'.[3] Hence parties may represent interests determined through status situation or class situation, respectively. 'But they need be neither purely "class" nor purely "status" parties. In most cases they are partly class parties and partly status parties, but sometimes they are neither.'[4] Although class elements were far from absent in the political parties in Victorian England, status groups, based

[1] *Essays*, p. 183.
[2] W. G. Runciman, *Social Science and Political Theory* (2nd edn Cambridge, 1969), p. 136.
[3] *Theory*, p. 407.
[4] *Essays*, p. 194.

upon a value-orientated sense of community expressed in a whole pattern of living, were the hard core of party. Status politics, or to borrow Richard Hofstadter's term,[1] cultural politics, were predominant. The qualitative change in the Edwardian period already referred to consisted primarily of a reversal of this balance, so that by 1910 the parties were class-based rather than status-based. This change was neither universal nor complete. It was most marked in the big industrial constituencies where the Conservative vote had fallen most heavily by 1910, and it had least effect in the mixed county divisions where voting patterns were hardly disrupted at all. Further, status continued to be at least as important as class where ethnic considerations reinforced religious prejudice in regard to the Irish.

Contemporaries were not unaware of the changes which took place as between Victorian and Edwardian politics. For example, Haslam Mills, the chief reporter of the *Manchester Guardian* and a perceptive observer of political developments in Lancashire, linked the end of the old politics with the Jameson Raid:

Before 1896 politics were concerned very largely with man as an Anglican or Baptist, with man as a teetotaller or not a teetotaller, with man as a single or per-adventure a plural voter. Theology entered very largely into politics. Large masses of people voted one way or the other according as they were or were not of a Puritan strain.[2]

It is not accepted here that the jingoism of the Boer War period was the effective turning point, but the general tenor of his suggestion and the analysis offered in this book are in close harmony.

The ramifications of the argument will be developed at length later but some questions concerning the validity of the general approach can be settled now. The most basic point is whether visible and organised activity at election times bore any relation to the concerns of broader groups in society. It is not claimed here that the whole electorate was partitioned into formally constituted groups, but it seems reasonable to postulate the existence of submerged as well as exposed portions of the icebergs. It may be useful to draw upon the idea of a 'quasi-group'[3] to comprehend entities which are a recruiting field for groups and whose members share to some extent a common character. Thus an organised church body, for instance, may represent an identifiable circle of limited size set within a larger concentric

---

[1] See Richard Hofstadter, *The Paranoid Style in American Politics* (1966), pp. 86–8, where the author offers a considered restatement developing his earlier adumbration of the distinction of status politics from interest politics.

[2] Mills, *The Manchester Guardian*, pp. 131–2.

[3] See Morris Ginsberg, *Sociology* (1934), pp. 40–1; and *Essays in Sociology and Social Philosophy* (Peregrine edn 1968), pp. 20–2; cf. the discussion in Dahrendorf, *Class and Class Conflict*, pp. 179–82.

circle defining all those for whom ties with the church are at least latent. Involvement in politics constrains such an organisation to make hard bargains in the pursuit of limited objectives. In this respect its action is 'associative'; but the social bonds which hold together its following are essentially 'communal'.[1] It is this looser community of feeling which is of most interest – and of most importance in its potential electoral effect.

Even so, it may be objected that associations of the type to be investigated did not impinge upon the life of many of the working class and can hardly have been a factor of decisive importance electorally. But does not this criticism underestimate the extent to which even the most godless sections of Victorian society could not help but come under the pervasive social influence of, at least, denominational prejudice?

In living amongst mill-hands of East Lancashire [wrote the young Beatrice Potter in the 1880s], I was impressed with the depth and realism of their religious faith. It seemed to absorb the entire nature, to claim as its own all the energy unused in the actual struggle for existence. Once the simple animal instincts were satisfied the surplus power, whether physical, intellectual or moral, was devoted to religion. Even the social intercourse was based on religious sympathy and common religious effort.[2]

Furthermore, since it is the behaviour of the electorate which is under examination, it would be as well to be clear that even under the Third Reform Act there was a large helot class in England who were excluded by their poverty and rootlessness from the community of the franchise just as they were for the same reasons excluded from other communities. The voting classes, on the other hand, were well integrated. As illustration, consider the explanation by Sir Max Aitken's local lieutenant of how patients got 'recommends' to Ashton Infirmary.

The subscribers are The Mills – The Unions – The Churches and Chapels and private people. The well to do workers are admitted easily as they can usually obtain recommends from one or other of these sources. The very poor have great difficulty in getting recommends as they are often out of employment, seldom associated with either church or chapel and have no influence with private subscribers.[3]

In short, it is not maintained that status politics of the Victorian type could have existed under conditions of universal suffrage.

[1] Weber, *Theory*, pp. 136 ff. I have attempted to restate this below at the beginning of ch. 10.
[2] Webb, *My Apprenticeship*, I, 187; and see below, pp. 53–4.
[3] J. M. W. Morison to Aitken, 10 December 1911, Beaverbrook P.

V

In testing the foregoing hypothesis against the facts one is faced with the question of whether the available evidence is sufficient either to verify or invalidate it. The analysis of the electorate in terms of, on the one hand, cultural groups, and on the other, social classes is central to the argument of this book, and it is with evidence bearing upon this distinction that it will largely be concerned. Alfred Cobban gave a trenchant warning of the main pitfall endangering this line of historical approach: 'The sociological historian uses his theory as the criterion for the selection of the relevant historical facts, and then on the basis of those selected facts he illustrates and confirms the theory by which they have been selected. Part of the fascination of general sociological theories is that success is built-in.'[1] And it is quite true that there is an inevitable interdependence between the terms of the hypothesis and the methods used to test it.

A great deal of weight is put upon the detailed examination of election campaigns in order to determine the allegiance of some more or less organised active groups. It is a real question, though one more intractable in theory than in practice, how far it is justifiable to infer from the activities of a pressure group the existence of a larger mass of others within the same sub-culture acting in a consonant manner. In fact, the public professions, claims and estimates upon the basis of which these inferences will be drawn were so vulnerable to challenge by other interested parties that it was an important corroboration if they met with acquiescence. This is a sphere of judgement, however, in which the only ultimate guide is an intimate acquaintance with the nuances of a local situation. There is a sense in which the nature of the theory and that of the sources confirm each other, for if the dominant role of social groups were posited *yet there were no obvious groups in evidence at all*, that would be an insuperable objection. The cultural groups with which this book is concerned were essentially communities and their existence and attitudes *ought* to have been knowable and known.

Moreover, because it is held that election campaigns stimulated major cultural groups into making themselves manifest, it is not therefore denied that they encouraged other groups into making themselves a nuisance. Because it is held that the behaviour of some pressure groups in elections was significant it is not denied that the behaviour of others was insignificant. Attention will be reserved for those groups, membership of which represented a whole way of life, at the expense of those which exploited transient or peripheral issues. It is only possible to discriminate here by rule of thumb.

[1] *The Social Interpretation of the French Revolution* (Cambridge, 1964), p. 13. Cf. G. R. Elton, *The Practice of History* (Fontana edn 1969), pp. 52–5.

The examination of constituency voting in terms of social class, on the other hand, must proceed on rather different assumptions since classes were not communities in the sense that the cultural groups were. The political attitudes of organised labour can be assessed in the same way as those of other pressure groups. But since trade-union action was based essentially upon rational considerations of economic benefit, the social relationship of trade unionists remained associative. Institutionalised Labour was never therefore representative of a 'hinterland' beyond its formal membership in the way that the quasi-religious pressure groups were. The correlation of voting patterns with the economic character of a constituency as a whole is one firm guide, though in this the complication of the franchise has to be allowed for. Again, local knowledge, in the press and elsewhere, can be drawn upon. For some county boroughs the census returns of occupations are useful, and the ratio of domestic servants to separate occupiers provides some check on particular areas, though these are not parliamentary constituencies; and within Manchester, for instance, Marr's housing survey of 1904[1] is a good indication of the social character of the separate divisions.

While quantitative material will be drawn upon where it is applicable, much of the evidence must come from the estimates of contemporaries; and these must be subject to critical evaluation. If, under modern conditions, the pundits of press and party cannot be relied upon to sniff the wind and accurately assess the political climate, can it be assumed that things were any different before the Great War? Herbert Gladstone, who should have known, argued in 1924 that they were. 'Up to the War, it was possible, given some shrewdness, to estimate the move of opinion in the electorate. Now it is guess work... In the days when canvassing was thorough, expert officials knew with approximate accuracy the texture and strength of the Parties in the constituencies.'[2]

And at the Conservative Central Office in the 1880s Captain Middleton, the Chief Agent, was noted for the uncanny accuracy of his electoral forecasts.[3] Better organisation in relation to a smaller electorate made it possible for the parties to be well informed, and the workings of the registration system made it necessary. There is reason to believe that canvass reports were a much finer guide than they have proved in a later period. One example will be enough. An hour before the close of the poll in Birkenhead in 1906, James Moon, the Chairman of the Liberal Association, made a forecast of the voting:[4]

[1] *Housing Conditions in Manchester and Salford.* See esp. the excellent map.
[2] Memorandum, 18 November 1924, HGP 46480 ff. 129–37.
[3] Chilston (Douglas), *Chief Whip*, p. 89.
[4] *Liverpool D.P.*, 18 January 1906.

	Forecast	Actual
Vivian (Liberal)	7,237	7,074
Lees (Conservative)	5,132	5,271
Kensit (Protestant)	2,100	2,118
Total	14,469	14,463

Now it is not claimed that this degree of accuracy as to the strength of the vote was commonplace; more important for present purposes was Gladstone's claim that its 'texture' also was known. In Burnley in 1900, far from the result having been accurately forecast, the defeat of the Liberal Philip Stanhope was a great surprise – two weeks before the poll one Liberal had been ready to stake £2,000 on his success. Yet the extent to which leading partisans could reconcile their admitted surprise with a completely unshaken interpretation of how it had come about was striking. A Liberal admitted: 'The canvass was dead against us, and all that we could do was hope that things would turn out all right. But we never anticipated so big a majority for Mr. Mitchell.' And a prominent Conservative went into more detail:

Well, we reckoned things up this way: The temperance vote had always been against us, and we should lose nothing. The Irish vote had been against us always, and we were no worse off in this respect. The Socialist vote we had reason to believe would be equally divided, so that we were equal with Mr. Stanhope in this respect. We knew the English Catholics would go with us on account of their schools, and we had many promises of Liberal votes. But we never, not even the most sanguine of us, expected such a result. The very smallest majority was all that we could expect, and the majority is a great surprise to everyone.[1]

In Burnley, then, although the result itself was unexpected, no one who had been in a position to know imagined that the texture of the respective votes had greatly altered, and these were still confidently explained in terms of cultural politics. 'Reverses', wrote Morley in 1908, 'can only be really understood by wire-pulling experts who know the ground, and analyse the elements of which majorities and minorities are in a given case made up.'[2]

It is true that the overall voting figures provide some confirmation or otherwise of various claims about voting. The electoral complexion of smaller areas within constituencies was also a matter of common knowledge, and there are frequent references to respective districts as 'the Radical Rock', 'the Tory Gibraltar' and the like. To some extent municipal politics, as well as the canvass, provided the evidence for these assertions, but it would be naïve to suppose that the actual state of voting at this level in

---

[1] *N.D.T.*, 5 October 1900.
[2] Morley, *Recollections*, II, 255.

Parliamentary elections remained unknown because of the provisions of a mere Ballot Act. The provision that all the boxes must have arrived and been mixed before counting could begin was blandly ignored. 'The last boxes were not in until ten o'clock', ran a report of the count at Prestwich in 1906. 'At half-past nine the onlookers...heard the word passed "It's all up", meaning that any faint hope of a Unionist win had gone. This was ere the Droylsden or Mossley boxes had come in.'[1] A description of the count at Darwen in 1900 gives an indication of what kind of hard information lay behind the newspaper reports which will be heavily used later:

The clerk whom I chance to be opposite is evidently dealing with a Tory Gibraltar. 'Rutherford', 'Rutherford', 'Rutherford' – there is a deadly sameness about these papers. I ask whence they come. 'Blackburn'.[2] H'm! Blackburn is clearly about four to one in favour of Rutherford. 'Mellor Brook box', whispers a voice, and I turn to another clerk engaged in revealing the electoral wisdom of Mellor Brook. Not much hope for Mr Huntington here, and I make my way to another group dealing with Walton-le-Dale; and Walton-le-Dale is emphatically 'Khaki'. Up comes another box, and a smile of prodigious breadth and length beams on every Tory countenance that is within range. 'Chipping!' It is the Tory tit-bit...I saw three batches of twenty-five each made up, and among these 75 votes two were cast for Huntington! I dislike monotony, so I went elsewhere...Distinctly Great Harwood is not the Radical stronghold one anticipated...[3]

A final illustration of how a constituency worked may serve to show that the type of evidence which largely underpins this study is neither insubstantial nor unrelated to what contemporaries adjudged to be significant. The very full set of constituency papers which Sir Max Aitken kept in the first years of his connexion with Ashton-under-Lyne include frequent letters from his agent, J. C. Buckley, giving advice over the many appeals for subscriptions which he received. Most were from social and sporting clubs, many of which were associated with churches and chapels. If the theory put forward in this chapter is correct, then it would be expected that voluntary social groupings of this kind, outgrowths of religious communities, would have strong and recognisable political leanings. Buckley's correspondence reveals that this was clearly the case and that, with his close knowledge of Ashton, he knew as a matter of course the politics of every football club. The Unitarian Sunday School F.C. was 'Liberal to a man'. Albion Young Men: 'No – you already subscribe to this lot through their Football club – they will work against you to a man next election.' Albion Choir F.C.: 'No – these

[1] *M. Courier*, 22 January 1906.
[2] I.e. from the Blackburn outvoters.
[3] The Tatler, *Blackburn Wkly Telegraph*, 13 October 1900; cf. the report from Accrington. 'In the Padiham Green corner of the Accrington Division there are 300 voters on the list, and of these 270 went to the poll. There is good reason for believing that 196 of these voted for Sir Joseph Leese.' *N.D.T.*, 11 October 1900.

are all Radical lads, and will be against you.' Gatefield F.C.: 'This is one of our own lot. I advise £1. 1. 0.' St. James's School: 'This is all right, a guinea will do a lot of good – they are a loyal lot.' 'The above lot are all Radicals...' 'All the enclosed are a Radical lot.' '1. This is a good Tory boys club, send 10/6. 2. A Radical lot, don't send anything.'[1] In Ashton, even at this late date, it mattered a great deal to a young man's politics where and with whom he naturally spent his leisure. This was *in parvo* the pattern for the evolution of Lancashire politics as a whole in the nineteenth century.

[1] From various letters to Aitken between July 1911 and May 1912, Beaverbrook P.

PART TWO
FORMATIVE INFLUENCES

In order to understand the prevalent political attitudes in late-nineteenth-century Lancashire it is necessary to examine the forces which shaped them. In a political sense the 'Manchester Liberalism' of the mid-century bourgeoisie was succeeded by the 'Tory Lancashire' of the mass electorate. It is tempting to explain the one as a reaction to the other. But Tory Democracy cannot be understood in class terms. Where the workingmen voters were to a large extent Conservative it was because of a social consciousness in which economic considerations did not play a dominant part. Hence the importance of religion in general, and the peculiar nature of Lancashire Anglicanism in particular. In contrast to this, the political influence of the cotton industry was relatively slight. The cotton workers were a representative section of the Lancashire working class and shared its social and religious divisions; they were, therefore, politically impotent. Insofar as the economic position of the cotton trade intruded into politics in the late nineteenth century it did not necessarily divide masters and men. Nor initially did Tariff Reform. But while the Liberals could continue to count on the cotton industry's preference for Free Trade to rally the operatives, it was later far from sure of the employers. There had always been a strong Conservative element among the cotton bosses; and by 1910 many of them were prepared to swallow Tariff Reform, or at least accept the Conservative party, Tariff Reform and all. The divisiveness of these economic considerations marked a break with the political culture of the later nineteenth century, when the Conservatives had been able to work with the grain of social and religious influences.

2 Manchester School to Tory Democracy

I am very well aware that a man may be joined to a 'Radical Association', to the 'Working Man's Association', and to a 'Political Union', and all will be right and square; but only let a man be a member of an Operative Conservative Society, why astonishment is at once excited, and the exclamation made, 'I cannot for the world see why a man is to be a Conservative operative'.

William Paul, 1838

I

To look at Lancashire is to look at the oldest industrial society in the world and at the landscapes of L. S. Lowry. 'Do you know Burnley?' asked H. M. Hyndman. 'If not, don't.' He recalled the impression that this not untypical cotton town made upon him: 'There it lay in the hollow, one hideous Malebolge of carbon-laden fog and smoke, the factory chimneys rising up above the mass of thick cloud like stakes upon which, as I said to my companion, successive generations of the workers and their children had been impaled.' Charles Rowley, who founded the Ancoats Brotherhood in the slums of Manchester and provided a prototype for Toynbee Hall, declared that in Lancashire and the West Riding, 'we have a population of some seven millions, and no tree', but took the view that 'the materialistic advantage is undoubted'.[1] Such considerations of material advantage had played a large, though not always dominant, part in moulding the political consciousness of the region.

The assertion of political rights in the north west began in the 1830s with the first redistribution of parliamentary seats and the incorporation of many newly important towns. Since boroughs in south east Lancashire were often within seven miles of each other, men resident in one might still enjoy full burgess rights in another where they had business interests. Movements for Reform and incorporation throughout the towns were kept on parallel lines since their leadership was knit together in this way, and a habit of cooperation was established. It was especially true in this part of the region that the towns were closely clustered and often adjoined; that they shared a similar industrial base and exhibited no marked differences from one another; and that, achieving civic and parliamentary status at the same time as each other, they were accustomed to act together. It was the Liberals who dominated the politics of these towns. In Manchester itself not only did the Tories oppose

[1] Hyndman, *Further Reminiscences*, pp. 61-2; Rowley, *Fifty Years of Work Without Wages*, p. 4.

the movement for incorporation but they fought the Charter when it had been granted and for several years boycotted municipal elections.[1] The Liberals were associated with Manchester's civic pride, and Manchester in turn gained a reputation as the capital city of Liberalism. The Anti-Corn Law League was peculiarly a Manchester movement even after it had formally moved its headquarters to London. '*My hopes of agitation are anchored on Manchester*', wrote Cobden; and again – 'The League is *Manchester...*' But although the League gave the impression, mainly through assiduous organisation, that it had widespread popular support Cobden would later admit that it was 'one aristocracy pitted against another'.[2] Manchester was a city of class conflict. Chartism and the League fought battles for its control in a more than metaphorical sense.[3]

But however it had been engineered, the repeal of the Corn Laws was indelibly associated with Manchester, and since the Liberal party was forged on the anvil of Free Trade the city had an entrenched position in Liberal mythology. John Bright gave the proposition its classic utterance when, speaking in the Free Trade Hall in 1851, he said: 'Now, we are called the "Manchester party" and our policy is the "Manchester policy", and this building I suppose is the schoolroom of the Manchester school.'[4] Even as he spoke, though, the vision was fading. 'Manchester', wrote Cobden a few years later, 'has never been more than a ghost of its former self in the agitations that have been attempted since the League shut up shop.'[5] Perhaps the League's failure to shut up shop completely was a mistake, for although the rump organisation at Newall's Buildings managed to foist Bright on to the city as one of its Members in 1847, the moderate Liberals were by no means his adherents and in 1857 he met defeat because he talked peace while there was war.[6]

Even the example of this staunchness in adversity would encourage Manchester Liberals at the turn of the century when they were placed in a not dissimilar position; but it was more often the successes of the heroic age of Free Trade which reverberated down the years. Lancashire had shown itself to be the home of liberal statesmen; Peel's name remained indissolubly linked with Bury, Gladstone's with Liverpool, Cobden's with Stockport, and

[1] Simon, *A Century of City Government*, ch. 3; cf. Briggs, *Victorian Cities*, pp. 85–135 for an excellent study of Manchester in this period.
[2] N. McCord, *The Anti-Corn Law League, 1838–1846* (1958), pp. 44, 80; Vincent, *The Formation of the Liberal Party*, p. 32.
[3] See McCord, *op. cit.*, pp. 96–103; Donald Read, 'Chartism in Manchester' in Asa Briggs (ed.), *Chartist Studies* (1959), pp. 29–64.
[4] G. B. Smith, *Life and Speeches of John Bright* (1881), I, 345.
[5] Read, *Cobden and Bright*, p. 120.
[6] See N. McCord, 'Cobden and Bright 1846–1857' in Robson (ed.), *Ideas and Institutions of Victorian Britain*, pp. 87–114.

Bright's with Rochdale. Free Trade was a part of the conventional wisdom of the later nineteenth century, but in the north west its acceptance was so buttressed by local tradition that it was apostasy to question it. The neo-protectionist attempt to force the issue in the late 1870s and 1880s only served to show the solidity of sentiment against fiscal change. It is true that Farrer Ecroyd, a Burnley textiles manufacturer, preached Fair Trade with some success; he twice stood against Hartington in North East Lancashire and in 1881 won a by-election at Preston. In the late 1880s the Fair Traders eventually succeeded in packing a meeting of the Manchester Chamber of Commerce in favour of a protectionist resolution but a poll of the members revealed a solid majority for Free Trade. No further poll was taken until the War.[1]

Free Trade was no mere Liberal shibboleth. The Hornbys, who sat as Conservative M.P.s for Blackburn during most of the nineteenth century, were as firm Free Traders as any Liberals; John Hornby, M.P., helped to get rid of the Corn Laws in the 1840s and Sir Harry Hornby, M.P., refused to accept Tariff Reform in the 1900s. Another pillar of Lancashire Toryism, Sir Francis Powell, claimed when he fought Jacob Bright in Manchester in 1876 to have been a lifelong advocate of Free Trade.[2] The work of the Anti-Corn Law League was a living reality to a number of Lancashire's Liberal M.P.s in the Edwardian period. One of the earliest recollections of Sir William Mather was of 1846 when, as a boy of seven, he had driven all day long with his father, a member of the League, in a large barouche wedged between two large sheaves of corn. Gordon Harvey was another whose father was a member of the League. Sir Thomas Barclay was a reverent Cobdenite; Sir Joseph Leese had made the great man's acquaintance while Cobden was negotiating the Anglo-French Treaty.[3] Leese declared that 'He sucked, so to speak, Free Trade with his mother's milk', while J. E. B. Seely recalled that he had been 'brought up on Free Trade, and believed it to be the ark of the covenant and the foundation of English prosperity and power. Both my grandfathers had been prominent members of the Anti-Corn Law League. I had had tea with Mr Gladstone when I was a boy at Harrow, and had sat on John Bright's knee as a child. The idea of returning to Protection seemed to be positively wicked.'[4]

---

[1] B. H. Brown, *The Tariff Reform Movement in Great Britain, 1881–1895* (New York, 1943), pp. 17–18, 132–4; Redford, *Manchester Merchants and Foreign Trade*, II, 105–7; Smith, *Disraelian Conservatism and Social Reform*, pp. 306–9. Ecroyd himself worked on unrepentantly at his mill in Nelson and, a venerable old man, he issued an address in favour of the Tariff Reform candidate there in 1909. See *N.D.T.*, 13 December 1909.

[2] For John Hornby see *Blackburn Times* 21 November 1896; for Sir Harry Hornby see below, ch. 11; for Powell see Hulbert, *Sir Francis Sharp Powell*, pp. 71–3.

[3] Mather, *Sir William Mather*, pp. 141–2, 246; Hirst, *Alexander Gordon Cummins Harvey*, ch. 1; Barclay, *Thirty Years*, e.g. p. 67; Leese at Green Haworth, *N.D.T.*, 13 January 1906.

[4] Leese at Accrington, *N.D.T.*, 9 January 1906; Seely, *Adventure*, p. 100; and see introduction by Alfred Hopkinson to Hertz, *The Manchester Politician*, p. 5.

II

At the Annual Meeting of the Manchester Liberal Union in 1901 one delegate expressed 'a sense of humiliation at the paralysis which seemed to him to have fallen upon the Liberal party in Manchester' and recalled 'the time when Manchester led the van of Liberalism'.[1] What had caused this decline? When Manchester's first city council met in 1838 it comprised the commercial elite of the town, yet when Beatrice Webb visited Manchester in 1899 it was an assembly of mediocrities. 'The abler among them', she wrote, 'are all old men, a little gang of liberals who are still the salt of the council.'[2] Charles Rowley looked back fondly to the days when Alderman Richard Cobden had lived at his business premises in Quay Street. Already in the 1830s Cobden's neighbours were selling their town houses in Mosley Street for conversion into warehouses and the movement of merchants out of the city gathered pace thereafter. At first it was true suburbanisation – the rise of Rusholme, Broughton and Pendleton, which were soon swallowed up in Manchester's growth. Although Victoria Park retained considerable cachet within the city, when the richer businessmen started to move out as far as Alderley Edge in rural Cheshire their links with Manchester life were becoming more tenuous.[3] Those cotton barons who were 'borne godlike each day to Manchester on a "club" express'[4] from as far away as St Annes, on the Fylde coast, were Mancunians of a newer school. Charles Macara, the *doyen* of the cotton merchants, had by the 1890s linked his house at St Annes to his warehouse by telephone and could thus control his business at a distance.[5] And although Macara actively led the cotton interest in support of Free Trade in the Edwardian period, this is plainly a far cry from Quay Street.

This was not a purely Manchester phenomenon. All over Lancashire proud burghers were succeeded by generations of less committed to the smoky towns. In Oldham by the late 1860s none of the thirty-odd leading cotton magnates remained permanently based in the town. John Platt, the founder of the engineering firm of Hibbert and Platt, lived in the town and was for many years chairman of the Oldham Radical Committee. Later in life he acquired a country house in Wales; only one of his sons lived in Oldham and took an interest in the business; his heir became a Conservative

[1] Speech by Mr Whittle, M.L.U. Minutes, 14 August 1901.
[2] See Simon, *A Century of City Government*, pp. 395–401; cf. Webb, *Our Partnership*, p. 162; Chorley, *Manchester Made Them*, pp. 139–40.
[3] See Rowley, *Fifty Years...*, p. 9; Read, *Cobden and Bright*, p. 11; Davies, *North Country Bred*, p. 88; Chorley, *op. cit.* pp. 136–46; A. J. P. Taylor, 'Manchester', *Encounter*, VII (1957), p. 4.
[4] Bowker, *Lancashire under the Hammer*, p. 10.
[5] *Men of the Period*, p. 39.

candidate in Wales.[1] In 1896 Widnes did not possess a single resident magistrate.[2] Now this trend was neither uniform, nor universal, nor irreversible; but it was persistent. 'We all know', wrote Rowley, 'the old saying, "God made the country, and man made the town"; we may add, "And the Devil made the suburbs".'[3] This process of separating out the classes was completed in a political sense by Gladstone with the partition of the large cities into single-member divisions, a process which left some constituency parties almost entirely lacking in endogenous leadership.

In national terms the self-conscious bourgeoisie of the Manchester School may have been only a narrow section of the Liberal party, but in many Lancashire towns the local Liberal party must have appeared to be the instrument of those who were rich and powerful. In such a context there were more improbable alliances than that between Chartists and Tories. Even in terms of class politics there was a *point d'appui* for working-class Conservativism, if it could but be exploited.[4] In the General Election of 1868 the Conservative party made notable gains in the region and the boroughs of Lancashire – those constituencies in the democratic sector of the constitution – became a Tory bastion. It is clear that the radicalism of John Bright, with its opposition to factory acts and its distrust of trade unions, had little appeal for the operatives. Though it may be incorrect to attribute the Conservative gains to changes in the franchise as such, obviously they could never have been achieved at all but for 'an impressively strong Conservative tradition among the Lancashire working class'.[5] In 1868 and 1874 Conservative candidates scored notable successes in Lancashire by hammering home the message of the importance of the Protestant character of the Church of England and the need for social legislation in the tradition of Shaftesbury; often they supported trade unions and occasionally even the secret ballot. The old Operative Conservative Societies were revived as Conservative Working Men's Associations.

Four men were primarily responsible for building up the Conservative organisation in south east Lancashire: W. Romaine Callendar, John William Maclure, Francis Sharp Powell and, later, William Houldsworth. Callendar was in many ways the most remarkable. Brought up as a Liberal and a Nonconformist, he had become both a Conservative and a Churchman; he was a

---

[1] Williams, 'The Platts of Oldham', *Trans. Caern. Hist. Soc.*, XVIII (1957), pp. 81–8; Foster, 'Capitalism and class consciousness in earlier 19th century Oldham' (Cambridge Ph.D. thesis), p. 184.

[2] Diggle, *A History of Widnes*, p. 99.

[3] Rowley, *Fifty Years of Ancoats*, p. 7.

[4] See William Paul, *History of the Origins and Progress of Operative Conservative Societies* (2nd edn, Leeds 1838).

[5] Vincent, 'The effect of the Second Reform Act in Lancashire', *Hist. Jnl.*, XI (1968), pp. 84–94; cf. Hanham, *Elections and Party Management*, esp. pp. 284–322.

champion of trade unions, cooperative societies and factory legislation. Until his untimely death in 1876 he was virtually the leader of those borough Members in the Conservative party who pressed Disraeli for concrete measures of social reform.[1] Maclure was more easygoing (an opponent recalled him as 'a popular gentleman whom all Lancashire and most of Cheshire knew as "John William"'). He was proud of his part in 'bringing about a change in the political opinions of South Lancashire' but was not always the workingman's friend he seemed. As a railway director he provoked the active opposition of the Railway Servants in 1892 after he had been involved in shameless intimidation.[2]

Of the four, Powell was most like a Tory Democrat. In Parliament he had been the only Conservative to vote for the introduction of the ballot. He was associated at one time with the twin boroughs of Ashton and Stalybridge which probably came as near as anywhere to exhibiting that conflict between bourgeois Liberalism and working-class Conservatism which was the staple of the myth of Tory Democracy. The Liberal millowners there had attempted crudely to impose their will on the town in the 1860s. In the Stalybridge by-election of 1871, when Powell was opposed by a Liberal employer, he apparently carried the vote on the hustings by a large majority but was defeated at the poll. 'In three months time, however', the Conservative chairman warned, 'they would have the ballot (cheers), and then they would not see mill owners bringing up their men to vote.'[3] (Many observers found it difficult to escape the inference that the persistent Conservatism of Ashton and Stalybridge thereafter was a rejection of the politics of the bosses: cotton bosses like Arthur Reyner in the 1890s whose 'position as leader at once of a Liberal organisation which wanted all sorts of democratic changes, and an Employers' Federation which wanted a reduction of wages, was a vexatious inconsistency...'.)[4] When Powell stood against Jacob Bright in Manchester in 1876 his claims to working-class support were vigorously put forward. 'Mr Powell', read one leaflet, 'has fought the battles of the poor when it was unpopular to do so, he has stood on the same platform with Shaftesbury, Feilden, Oastler, and others engaged in the struggle, which has resulted in so many blessings to the working classes.'[5]

The case of William Houldsworth, however, is probably a truer reflection of the dominant trend. Houldsworth was a paternalistic cotton spinner who

---

[1] Hanham, *op. cit.*, pp. 315–16; Smith, *Disraelian Conservatism and Social Reform*, pp. 172–3, 213–14; Feuchtwanger, *Disraeli, Democracy and the Tory Party*, pp. 71–9.

[2] Lord Crewe at Stretford, *M.G.*, 6 January 1906; Maclure at Stretford, *M.G.*, 26 September 1900. For the 1892 election see *M.G.*, 11, 12 July 1892.

[3] Hulbert, *Sir Francis Sharp Powell*, pp. 56–8; cf. Hanham, *Elections and Party Management*, pp. 71–2, 84–5.

[4] Mills, *Sir Charles W. Macara*, p. 88.

[5] Broadsheet in Manchester local collection, f. 1876/1/A.

was first invited to contest Manchester on Callendar's death in 1876 and represented the central business division, Manchester North West, from its creation in 1885. His family had been Liberal but, as a contemporary sketch notes, 'while he himself was disposed to agree with certain of the broad principles of Liberalism, he found himself out of sympathy with the ultra-Radical element, and felt strongly attracted towards that newer Conservatism of which Benjamin Disraeli was the great apostle'.[1] The Disraelian Conservatism which had captured him was no democratic creed but an outgrowth of Palmerstonian Liberalism. 'In the Lancashire manufacturers I see material for Conservative principles to work upon', the future fifteenth Earl of Derby had told Disraeli in 1853.[2] Men like Houldsworth were the living justification of his prescience.

III

In terms of class composition the Conservative and Liberal parties were rather similar in the late nineteenth century. Popular Conservatism in Lancashire was remarkable chiefly because it was strong enough to challenge popular Liberalism. But if this is so, then it is plainly no use looking for the key to party cleavage in terms of a class explanation. Lancashire may have been a class-conscious society in the 1840s but this was not one of its dominant political characteristics a generation later. It may have been that the militancy of working-class movements was softened by mid-Victorian prosperity. (The converse is not the case, however, since the Cotton Famine elicited a docile response.) In their militant phase they had been smashed by force, but the everyday evidence of the late nineteenth century pointed to the fact that the working class had been accommodated within a political structure from which it had earlier been excluded. In the days of its prime Chartism had been bitterly opposed to the Leaguers but in his later years Ernest Jones was groping towards a new Reform alliance, and it was his efforts which led Engels, writing from Manchester, to conclude that 'the English proletariat is actually becoming more and more bourgeois'.[3] To a considerable extent the Chartist tradition flowed into Liberalism, and the party of Reform found it not at all odd to draw upon the mythology of the Charter as well as that of Repeal. In the 1890s subscriptions were successfully solicited from leading Manchester Liberals on behalf of W. H. Chadwick, known in Gorton as

[1] *Men of the Period*, p. 33.
[2] Smith, *Disraelian Conservatism and Social Reform*, p. 22; and see Cowling, *1867. Disraeli, Gladstone and Revolution*, pp. 309–10.
[3] Engels to Marx, 7 October 1858, *Marx and Engels on Britain*, pp. 537–8. For a stimulating analysis of this process in Marxist terms see John Foster, 'Nineteenth century towns – a class dimension' in H. J. Dyos (ed.), *The Study of Urban History* (1968), pp. 281–99. The general argument of this Part runs parallel in many respects to that in Harold Perkin, *The Origins of Modern English Society 1780–1880* (1969), ch. 9.

33

'The Old Chartist', on the grounds that he had 'devoted his life to the advocacy of the principles of Liberalism & of Free Churchism'.[1]

In mid-Victoran Lancashire the more successful party would be that which could unbend most easily towards the working-class sub-cultures which were the world of the new electorate. The Liverpool Liberal William Rathbone was told by George Howell – what he had heard before – 'that everywhere there is less of geniality and *bonhomie* in the treatment of the working classes by the Liberals than by the Conservatives'.[2] When Charles Rowley was elected councillor for the slum area of Ancoats in the 1870s he described it as 'consisting of 60,000 inhabitants, 40 churches, 40 chapels, and 140 public-houses and beer-houses'.[3] These were the constituent elements: the working-class population and the institutions which provided the structure within which their lives were lived. It was with these that the political parties had to establish a rapport.

Drink, which was 'the quickest way out of Manchester', was a social problem and an electoral issue; the public house was not a politically neutral meeting place and its influence was prevalent. 'Why I see that one in every thirty-three houses in Blackburn is a public house!' exclaimed the Bishop of Manchester in 1879; and when A. G. Gardiner was a Liberal journalist in that town in 1900 his observations led him to conclude that 'the cause of progress must not look for assistance from the slums. Slumdom to a man and to a woman is on the side of drink, and therefore on the side of Toryism.'[4] It had been almost a maxim of Disraelian Conservatism in the first exhilaration of leaping in the dark that security lay in 'going lower than the combining class' in order to 'bring other elements into play'.[5] Below the organised artisans was there a stratum of drinking Conservatives? – Conservative because 'no progressive propaganda influences them, and they have no social centre except the public-house'.[6] The social groups whose way of life centred on the pub were offset to some extent, of course, by those who set store by temperance as a life ethic. 'It would be impossible to over-

---

[1] W. Ramage to C. P. Scott, 3 June 1896, MGP. On this development see also P. Hollis and B. Harrison, 'Chartism, Liberalism and the Life of Robert Lowery', *E.H.R.*, LXXXII (1967), pp. 503–35; E. P. Thompson, 'Homage to Tom Maguire' in Briggs and Saville (eds), *Essays in Labour History*, pp. 281–2, 288.

[2] Rathbone to his wife, 13 March 1870, Rathbone, *William Rathbone*, p. 270. Rathbone himself offered generous financial support to the Lib-Lab M.P. Thomas Burt; see article on Rathbone, *Shipping World* (1883–4), pp. 171–5.

[3] Rowley, *Fifty Years of Work without Wages*, p. 196.

[4] Hughes, *James Fraser*, p. 272; 'The Tatler', *Blackburn Wkly Telegraph*, 6 October 1900.

[5] See esp. Gathorne Hardy in Smith, *Disraelian Conservatism and Social Reform*, p. 90 n. 3; Lord Elcho in Cowling, *1867. Disraeli, Gladstone and Revolution*, pp. 51–2.

[6] Villiers, *The Opportunity of Liberalism*, p. 23. But it is noteworthy that Callendar and Birley, the Conservative M.P.s for Manchester, supported the United Kingdom Alliance's legislative efforts in the 1870s.

estimate the importance that was attached to this subject in nonconformist circles between say, 1860, and the start of the First World War', wrote a member of a working-class family brought up in this tradition.[1] When a Liberal club was opened at Waterfoot in Rossendale in 1900 the audience cheered when they were told that no intoxicating liquor would be sold. Respect for this attitude could survive an abandonment of total abstinence for those who passed through the Bands of Hope as children. Perhaps the Warrington Band of Hope, when it sadly admitted that comparatively few members were over 15 years of age,[2] might have taken comfort from the expectation that attitudes had already been moulded.

The drink question inevitably obtruded into the business of running workingmen's clubs. There was always some doubt as to how effective a political instrument the clubs were. If the costs of subsidising them were set against a narrow expected advantage, like that of a supply of free canvassers, then they must often have proved a bad investment. 'Don't you find that the members of these Clubs to a great extent have joined them more for the sake of having a house of call where they can get cheap Billiards refreshments! &c than for any political purposes & are often not very particular about paying subscriptions', wondered one Liberal. But he went on to admit: 'The clubs are however very necessary as rallying places on important occasions.'[3] Wealthy Liberals who had spent a lifetime preaching self-help and temperance were often disinclined to support institutions in which, they suspected, workingmen would drink subsidised beer. If the Tories suspected the same they had fewer temperamental objections to paying up regardless.[4] Charles Schwann, who was at that time one of Manchester's three Liberal M.P.s, closed down the big Liberal club in his constituency when he found that it was 'merely a drinking shop & that the frequenters not only did not pay their subscriptions, but did not even pay for the beer they drank'. He expected it to cost him £1,000 and would not have been unduly distressed if the Conservatives had acquired it.

We have already 5 Tory Clubs in N[orth] M[anchester] [he wrote], but still we beat them & often a club is a source of weakness, as in Cheetham. Perhaps it may prove a mistake to have shut up the Club, but personally if the Tories are determined to buy up Manchester, I don't see how...you are to compete with them. If the working

---

[1] Davies, *North Country Bred*, p. 26.
[2] Warrington Band of Hope *Report* (1903) in Warrington local collection.
[3] Samuel Armitage to C. P. Scott, 26 September 1893, MGP.
[4] Though when Max Aitken was M.P. for Ashton-under-Lyne he refused to help one club on the grounds that it might lay him 'open to the charge that I countenanced late hours, and that which comes after late hours, which sometimes creeps into the best regulated clubs'. Aitken to R. S. Oldham, 28 August 1911, Beaverbrook P. This may not have been the real reason. The club in question was said to be 'a one-man show'.

man can only be kept in good humour by one's paying for his club & *his beer* too, I am afraid he may implement his own salvation.[1]

The Friendly Societies were extremely powerful in Lancashire, and Callendar had urgently warned Disraeli in 1875 that his Government must not offend their members.[2] The two great orders, the Foresters and the Manchester Unity, were non-political but others, like that formed by the Orangemen at Preston, had clear party affiliations and at Rochdale, for instance, the Roebuck Conservative Sick and Burial Society was an integral part of the Tory organisation.[3] There was in the Manchester Unity 'a strong leaning to the usages and tendencies of Freemasonry',[4] and Freemasonry itself, although its extent and activities are difficult to discover, was almost certainly one of these social bonds which helped the Conservatives. When Aitken was Conservative M.P. for Ashton, his constituency chairman thought it was important that he should be initiated.[5]

The influence of the Co-operative movement, however, was not Conservative (although when W. A. S. Hewins was Tariff Reform candidate for Middleton he angled for support on the grounds that it was the Rochdale Pioneers who destroyed the Free Trade system).[6] There were large numbers of members in every Lancashire constituency – 7,500 in Leigh, for example – but their commitment to the wider ideals of the movement cannot be presumed. The leaders, however, were politically conscious in the 1890s. There was a Co-operative Parliamentary Committee with headquarters in Manchester. Its secretary, Ben Jones, a Bury man, was anxious to turn the movement towards Liberalism and considered contesting Bury as a Liberal on the understanding that the Co-operators would support him financially if he got in.[7] But nothing came of the idea and the Co-operative movement did not engage in party politics until after the Great War.

IV

The workingmen of Lancashire were accommodated within the pre-existing political structure because the antagonisms they felt most sorely were not

[1] Schwann to Scott, 2 July 1893, MGP.
[2] His letter is printed at length in Feuchtwanger, *Disraeli, Democracy and the Tory Party*, pp. 75–7.
[3] P. H. J. H. Gosden, *The Friendly Societies in England* (Manchester, 1961), pp. 65–6; *M. Courier*, 13 December 1909.
[4] Baernreither, *English Associations of Working Men*, p. 372; cf. Gosden, *op. cit.* p. 127.
[5] R. Scholes to Aitken, 17 November 1911, Beaverbrook P.
[6] Hewins at Rochdale, *M. Courier*, 1 December 1910.
[7] See Gladstone's diary, 14 November 1899, 10 July 1900, HGP 46483 ff. 47, 72. The Co-operative Society in Bury was clearly a Liberal force, see below, ch. 11. On this type of Co-operation see Sidney Pollard, 'Nineteenth century Co-operation' in Briggs and Saville (eds), *Essays in Labour History*, esp. pp. 90–102; and for some impressions of Lancashire Co-operators just before the Great War see Leonard Woolf, *Beginning Again* (1964), pp. 110–11.

those which united them against their masters. The greatest single mainstay of the Conservative party was the presence in the towns of an Irish immigrant community living uneasily amongst the indigenous population. 'The inroad of strangers introduced a severe competition into the home labour market, and a race prejudice sprang up, which time has not obliterated', wrote one contemporary observer – not Marx nor Engels but Arthur Forwood, the Tory leader in Liverpool.[1] Explicitly religious clashes were not uncommon in localities of Irish concentration, and the fact that the Irish lived in the most squalid districts of the towns was seen as a simple demonstration of cause and effect. The English worker unleashed his prejudices against a way of life which he did not understand; the Irishman in turn had forgiven nothing and forgotten nothing. When Augustine Birrell was naïve enough in the 1880s to mention the names of Cromwell and Pitt before an Irish audience there was a 'yell of fury that rent the conclave' and he 'became aware for the first time what it is to come into collision with a living historical hatred, transmitted from generation to generation'.[2] The rift between the two communities was the most basic and persistent feature of social, and hence political, life in the region. 'This *antagonism*', concluded Marx, 'is the *secret of the impotence of the English working-class*, despite their organisation.'[3] In Lancashire, however, the more immediate effect of such tensions may have been to prevent the strong trade unions there from becoming 'the tail of the great Liberal party' during the nineteenth century.

The Irish question did not emerge in its more naked form until Gladstone took up Home Rule. Although in 1885 the Irish were ordered to vote Conservative, and T. P. O'Connor visited every constituency in the north west on Parnell's behalf, it was admitted that large numbers of them voted Liberal in seven English constituencies, including Gorton, Hyde and Northwich.[4] In the cities, however, Parnell's instructions seem, for one reason or another, to have been carried out, one result being that Jacob Bright who, unlike his brother, was a notable anti-coercionist, lost his seat. 'Manchester with its somewhat evenly balanced English parties, & its Irish party is a difficult place', he wrote ruefully.[5] Bright was less swayed by temporary resentment than men of lesser clay. Told during the campaign that those whose cause he had espoused were deserting him he had merely said, 'Are they? Well, if they are, I think I may say that I will never desert the Irish.'[6] In Lancashire

---

[1] Forwood, 'Democratic Toryism', *Contemporary Review*, XLIII (1883), p. 295.
[2] Birrell, *Things Past Redress*, p. 107.
[3] *Marx and Engels on Britain*, p. 552.
[4] See C. H. D. Howard, 'The Parnell manifesto of 21 November 1885 and the schools question', *E.H.R.*, LXII (1947), pp. 48–50.
[5] Jacob Bright to Scott, 3 December 1885, MGP.
[6] Obit., *M.G.*, 9 November 1899.

most of the Liberals who would desert the Irish had already done so by 1886. All six divisional Liberal Associations in Manchester had passed resolutions warmly supporting Gladstone's Home Rule proposals by the end of April 1886 and there were only a few dissidents when the matter was fought out in the Manchester Liberal Union.[1] It was not Home Rule as such which saw the downfall of Lancashire Liberalism; its position was already weak by 1885. The secretary of the Tariff Reform League, a man who had been an agent in Lancashire for six years, went to some pains in 1911 to measure the impact of Home Rule by comparing the voting figures of 1885 with those of 1886. He found that in the single-member boroughs the Conservative poll declined by 6,304 and the Liberal by 7,022. The Liberals won two seats in Manchester: the Conservatives two in Salford. Three old Liberal M.P.s kept their seats as Unionists at Barrow, Burnley and Bury. In the county divisions which were contested at both elections the Unionist vote was up by 1,494 – but Hartington alone was responsible for a turnover of 1,832. The decrease of 9,106 in the Liberal vote (so he had reason to believe from inquiries) was mainly due to the lack of organisation in new county areas and to lack of vehicles.[2] This is not a disinterested analysis, but it shows that there is a good case to be made against the seismic interpretation of 1886.

When the Chamberlainite M.P. Peter Rylands died in 1887, his former supporters in Burnley could find no Liberal Unionist to succeed him and were forced to accept the scion of a Tory and Anglican family; whereupon they lost the seat. 'Burnley is a bad blow and will make the Gladstonians cocky', noted W. S. Caine, the Liberal Unionist M.P. for Barrow.[3] The Gladstonians duly rallied in the late 1880s and modified their attitude towards the separated brethren. Having at first walked softly they now wielded a big stick. The Manchester Liberals noted with satisfaction in 1888 'that no indications are discernible of any increase in the number or power of the dissentients'.[4] The position of the Liberal Unionists was also weak in Liverpool where, since the Conservative party believed itself to be invincible, they were brusquely ignored.[5] The weakening of the Liberal faith came not so much from the decided apostasy of the Unionists as from the more general lapse into agnosticism which Home Rule encouraged. Soliciting a subscription from an erstwhile supporter, one might find that 'he declined to be known as a Liberal any more than he would be thought a Tory'.[6]

---

[1] M.L.U. Minutes, 29 April, 4, 7 May 1886.

[2] Enc. in T. W. A. Bagley to Law, 9 October 1911, BLP 18/7/195.

[3] See Michael Hurst, *Joseph Chamberlain and Liberal Reunion: the round table conference of 1887* (1967), pp. 346–7.

[4] M.L.U. Minutes, 2 May 1888.

[5] See Chilston, *Chief Whip*, pp. 141–2.

[6] J. B. Fullerton to Scott, 4 December 1893, MGP. This was Frank Spence, 'a Christian & Temperance man'.

Apparently it would have been easy enough to exclude the Liberal Unionists from the Manchester Reform Club but since there was 'a large number of members who are neither Gladstonians or Coercionists' the exercise seemed for the time being unprofitable.[1]

The desertion of the middle classes was what most commonly disturbed the Liberal leaders after 1886. 'Are any Liberal-Unionists-in-black-coats coming back?' Rosebery asked Edward Russell, the editor of the *Liverpool Daily Post*.[2] Yet this trend only overlay the historic weakness of the Lancashire Liberals among the working class. Henry Dunckley, who had edited another Liberal paper, the *Manchester Examiner*, until it had been acquired by the Unionists, was disturbed in his old age at the paradox that by extending the suffrage the Liberals had strengthened the Conservative position in Manchester, so that by 1895 only one of the six divisions was in Liberal hands. 'The working classes were never wholly on the side of Liberalism,' he recollected in tranquillity.[3] In the 1880s and 1890s the Liberals carried the virtue of resignation to the point where they were prepared to write off the boroughs of Lancashire almost as though it were a fact of life that they should be Tory. They attributed this phenomenon not so much to Home Rule (for plainly it antedated 1886) as to some quirk of democracy itself as applied to Lancashire. 'When Manchester was the synonym for all that was progressive', wrote the veteran Isaac Hoyle, 'the middle classes were the backbone of the Liberal party. It seems to me that working men are so largely Conservative *now* that we cannot look to them to turn the scale.'[4]

v

It was upon Lancashire that most of the rhetoric of Tory Democracy was founded. In his prime Disraeli had, at the behest of John Gorst, visited the county to receive homage from the new Conservative fief, and it was recalled a generation later that it was in the Free Trade Hall that he had laid down the policy of 'Sanitas'.[5] There was a mythology of Tory Democracy just as there was a mythology of the Manchester School. It is important to distinguish between the two models to which the term can be applied. It can be used to

---

[1] J. A. Beith to Scott, 23 July 1889, MGP.
[2] Rosebery to Russell, 20 July 1888, Rosebery-Russell corrce.
[3] 'Verax', *M.G*, 23 July 1895.
[4] Isaac Hoyle to Scott, 13 July 1893, MGP. NB Hoyle was probably more of a Unionist than a Liberal by this time.
[5] London letter, *M. Courier*, 19 November 1909. For Gorst and the Lancashire visit see Feuchtwanger, *Disraeli, Democracy and the Tory Party*, pp. 115–20. But the Conservative setbacks in 1880 were blamed by Gorst upon the lack of attention to the social needs of the boroughs by Disraeli's Government. See Trevor Lloyd, *The General Election of 1880* (1968), pp. 80–1; and cf. below, p. 404.

describe the essentially democratic nature of Toryism or the essential Toryism of the democracy. The first model is a deviant form of class politics in which the Conservatives capture the working-class vote by outbidding the Liberals on social policy. The second postulates merely that the Conservative party must not needlessly affront the interests of workingmen predisposed *for other than class reasons* to vote for it. It was unlikely that Lancashire Conservatism could approximate to the first and more ambitious form unless it reached some accommodation with trade unionism. The politics of labour are to this extent a test case of the viability of Tory Democracy under conditions of class politics.

In standing contradiction to labour maxims, the trade union movement in Lancashire was strong but divided. Its divisions were social and political: sometimes industrial too. In the Liverpool docks the coal heavers were organised into two societies, one led by an Orangeman, the other by a Roman Catholic. In the Liverpool transport strike of 1911 it was thought to be a remarkable thing that the (Protestant) carters' union and the (Roman Catholic) dockers' union should cooperate.[1] For the most part, however, an agreement to differ on political questions preserved intra-union peace. In the 1860s there were prominent trade unionists in the Conservative party; S. C. Nicholson and W. H. Wood, the president and secretary of the Manchester Trades Council, gave notable service to the Conservative party in the 1868 elections. Later, Thomas Ashton, the Miners' leader, seems to have been a Tory.[2] Even so, these men were exceptions.

The new socialist movement could not entirely break free from the old loyalties and unite workingmen into a single movement. The Social Democratic Federation found a foothold in Lancashire from the 1880s, and in 1893, when it held its annual conference in Burnley, there were 22 branches in the Lancashire District Council. Several local Fabian Societies were formed following the Fabians' Lancashire campaign of 1890 but only that in Liverpool remained in existence until 1918.[3] More typical was the Blackburn Fabian Society which, formed in 1892, dissolved in the following year to form the Blackburn branch of the Independent Labour Party. At the I.L.P. conference in 1893, 32 delegates out of 120, and in 1895 73 branches out of 305, were accounted for by Lancashire and Cheshire.[4] In the 1890s the north west was the one region where the S.D.F. and the I.L.P. were evenly

[1] Sexton, *Sir James Sexton*, pp. 109–10; Hikins, 'The Liverpool general transport strike, 1911', *Trans. Hist. Soc. Lancs. & Ches.*, CXIII (1961), p. 175.
[2] Hanham, *Elections and Party Management*, pp. 316–18; Arnot, *The Miners*, p. 368; cf. Ashton's endorsement of the Conservative M.P. for Gorton, *M. Courier*, 2 October 1900.
[3] Pelling, *Origins of the Labour Party*, p. 97; Tsuzuki, *H. M. Hyndman and British Socialism*, pp. 54–5, 96 ff.; McBriar, *Fabian Socialism and English Politics*, pp. 167, 179–80.
[4] Blackburn Independent Labour Party, *Bazaar Handbook*; Poirier, *The Advent of the Labour Party*, p. 48.

balanced. Since the S.D.F. most characteristically represented an appeal to
Tory workingmen on secularist terms (as in London) and the I.L.P. to
Liberal workingmen on Nonconformist terms (as in Yorkshire) it is not
surprising to find Lancashire socialism reflecting the region's socio-religious
divisions. The Labour Church movement may have appeared to be the
logical way out of this impasse, and it had some influence. There were
vigorous Labour Churches at Bolton, Hyde and Ashton; that founded at
Stockport in 1904 seems to have flourished and in 1906–7 had average
attendances of 800.[1]

Many able men were associated with different sections of the socialist
movement in Lancashire. H. M. Hyndman, the founder of the S.D.F.,
concentrated most of his electoral efforts upon Burnley; Dr R. M. Pankhurst
was a notable figure in the life of Manchester, moving between I.L.P. and
Liberal circles. Philip Snowden and J. R. Clynes, later two of Labour's
'Big Five', began their parliamentary careers as Lancashire M.P.s. But in the
late nineteenth century the major figure in Lancashire socialism was Robert
Blatchford, to whose influence all shades of opinion testified. First as
'Nunquam' in the *Sunday Chronicle*, then as editor of the *Clarion*, Blatchford
fulfilled his own injunction to 'Make Socialists'. The *Clarion*'s catholic
approach clearly must have enlarged the lives of many 'underdogs'. 'I
speak', he said, 'to the great infant class of undeveloped minds.'[2] There was
enough of the S.D.F. spirit in *Clarion* socialism to make participation in the
Labour party difficult, and after 1907 Blatchford had very little sympathy
for it, working, as he always had, towards some form of socialist unity.

In the General Election of 1900 the *Clarion*'s tone had been generally
hostile to the Liberals (Blatchford was always something of a jingo) and while
in 1906 it supported Labour as well as socialist candidates it could not
stomach any question of alliance with the Liberals. *Clarion* leaflets were in
great demand at this juncture and had to be rationed. The election, however,
probably had more effect upon the *Clarion* than the *Clarion* upon the election;
circulation soared from about 50,000 to over 70,000 in a couple of months.[3]
Blatchford could not share the Labour euphoria which was based, as he
saw it, on a false and therefore temporary confluence of sentiment with the
Liberals. He attempted to deflate this with a front-page article, 'Why the
Socialists Will Fight the Liberal Party'. 'It is not because the Liberal Party
is not prepared to go the whole of the way with us that we are hostile to
them', he explained. 'It is because they are going a different way altogether.'[4]

[1] Stockport Labour Church, *Official Handbook* (1907), pp. 15–21; Mitchell, *The Hard Way Up*
pp. 116 ff.
[2] Thompson, *Robert Blatchford*, p. 48.
[3] *Clarion*, 8 December 1905, 16 February 1906.
[4] *Clarion*, 2 February 1906; cf. 14 January 1910.

And four years later, when Labour seemed to have settled not for socialist unity but a progressive alliance, this article was republished with only minor alterations. In 1910, however, Blatchford was writing about the navy for the *Daily Mail* and could be dismissed by orthodox Labour supporters as a crypto-Tory. The *Clarion* took little interest in the two General Elections. The introverted bitterness of its tone contrasted noticeably with the vigour and resilience of its earlier days when the future had seemed to belong to it and Blatchford's faith in Merrie England had not been dimmed.

In the 1890s almost any development had been possible and the politics of labour were notable chiefly for their confusion. In 1895, for instance, three of the leading trade unionists in Lancashire were at loggerheads during a by-election at Ashton in which James Sexton of the Liverpool Dockers stood as I.L.P. candidate. Sam Woods, the Lancashire Miners' leader, supported his Liberal opponent, while James Mawdsley, the Spinners' secretary, was instrumental in giving Sexton 'Tory gold' when he ran short of funds.[1] Mawdsley was the last and most famous of the prominent Conservative trade unionists, and in 1899 he himself fought a by-election at Oldham in double harness with Winston Churchill; an improbable combination which was the ultimate extension of one line of Conservative development in Lancashire.

The son of Lord Randolph Churchill, consumed with filial devotion to the father he hardly knew, was likely to hold peculiar political views. 'I am a Liberal in all but name', he told his mother in 1897, and but for Home Rule he would be one in name also. 'As it is – Tory Democracy will have to be the standard under which I shall range myself.'[2] It was this young man whom Robert Ascroft, Oldham's Senior Member, approached in 1899 with a view to their becoming running mates at the next election. Ascroft's position as the trusted solicitor for the cotton unions was the secret of his popularity and power in Oldham. It was the reason too for his close association with James Mawdsley, who shared his political outlook, and whom he had sounded earlier about the candidature. The plan was for Mawdsley, or failing Mawdsley Churchill, to succeed Ascroft's sick colleague; but when Ascroft himself died suddenly in June 1899 Churchill and Mawdsley came forward in a double by-election. At first there had been the possibility of a compromise to give an unopposed return to Churchill and to the Liberal Walter Runciman, but, after considering bringing in a Liberal trade unionist, the local Liberal leader

---

[1] See *Ashton-under-Lyne Herald* 6, 13 July 1895; cf. Sexton, *Sir James Sexton*, pp. 146–7 for the information about Mawdsley's role. The story seems credible in that at the end of June it was rumoured that Sexton was about to withdraw; then, suddenly and mysteriously, his problems disappeared.

[2] Churchill, *Winston S. Churchill*, I, 318. Churchill's part in the Oldham campaign is documented in *Companion*, I, 1009–40.

Alfred Emmott was adopted too;[1] so the Tory Democrats took on the son of a wealthy shipowner and a substantial cotton spinner. Mawdsley's candidature was regretted by the Independent Labour men – 'Of course we do not take objection to Mr Mawdsley standing as a Tory instead of a Liberal'[2] – but while admitting that there was a great deal to be said for the I.L.P., Mawdsley thought that 'they would all agree with him that at the present time it was useless for any workman to attempt to get into Parliament on what might be termed independent lines'. Though Labour representatives must choose one side or the other of the House, Mawdsley was emphatic that it did not matter much which. Indeed his reasons for choosing the Conservatives were hard-headed almost to the point of being contemptuous. 'Having had to deal with members of the House of Commons in trying to get working class measures passed, he had come to the conclusion that it was easier – if they would allow the expression – to "squeeze" the Conservatives than the Liberals.'[3] Churchill naturally took a more romantic view of Mawdsley's candidature, as of policy generally, and called it an event of national importance since it marked the birth of the Conservative Labour party.[4] He himself talked mainly about imperialism and would not go as far as Mawdsley in advocating old age pensions. It was Churchill who supplied the rhetoric of Tory Democracy but Mawdsley who had to make the case for the Conservatives as the party of social reform. The claims he made were utilitarian and they were pitched low. 'I am with the Conservative party', he said, 'because I believe, on the whole, that they are the least hypocritical of the two parties. If they don't do as much as the others they are honest enough to do as much as they can, and don't tell us they will do a great deal more (applause).' The case he was really making was that of a socialist who was impatient for the millennium and wanted tactical gains in the present as well.

We are evolving Socialism through co-operation [he said] and through the municipalities taking over gas and water and the control of the streets. We are going still further in the same direction, but for generations to come shall still have employers and workpeople, and I am not going to starve myself, or to ask workpeople to starve themselves, for the idea that their grandchildren might be well off (hear, hear). I want a little of that well-off business myself, and if I cannot get it by any other system I am going to make the best of the system we have (hear, hear).[5]

It was recognised all round that everything depended on how far the contest could be made to turn upon the fulcrum of trade unionism in favour of the Tories. But Churchill and Mawdsley were beaten. 'It has been a

[1] Gladstone's diary, 21–6 June 1899, HGP 46483 ff. 22–3; *Companion*, I, 1028.
[2] *Blackburn Labour Journal*, July 1899; cf. speech by Keir Hardie, *Oldham D. Standard*, 6 July 1899.
[3] Speech by Mawdsley, *Oldham D. Standard*, 4 July 1899.
[4] Churchill's address in *Companion*, I, 1030–2; speech, *Oldham D. Standard*, 30 June 1899.
[5] Speech by Mawdsley, *Oldham D. Standard*, 28 June 1899.

straight fight between Radical and Tory, as proved by the figures, and the Radicals have won', wrote the local Conservative newspaper, making no bones about it. That new party and that strengthening of the friendship between Conservatism and Labour which Churchill had looked for had come to nothing; nor had his own high-flown sentiments met with an encouraging response. 'Altogether', he told Balfour, 'I return with less admiration for democracy than when I went.'[1]

Nowhere had the contest aroused more interest and concern than in the *Manchester Guardian*, where L. T. Hobhouse was commenting on it through the leading articles. The *Guardian* team had considerable respect for Mawdsley, whom they had considered supporting in the event of Runciman fighting on imperialistic lines, and Mawdsley was afterwards said by the Chief Reporter to have been 'delighted because we let him off so lightly'.[2] But though he made no personal attacks, Hobhouse devoted two leaders to exposing (as he saw it) the intellectual inadequacy of the democratic Tory case. 'There is certainly much yet to be done', he admitted, 'in bringing about a better understanding between Liberalism and Labour, or, as we should prefer to say, in fusing what is best in the old tradition of political democracy with what is wise and practicable in the newer movements of social reform.'[3] It was an article of faith for Hobhouse, though, that there was a point of union here in the application of the community's resources, not to imperialism but to domestic problems. Mawdsley's candidature represented 'a deliberate attempt, ingenious of its kind and probably well thought out by others if not by Mr Mawdsley, to unite Conservatism with a certain kind of socialism'. It was the 'practical' argument, from the Conservatives' susceptibility under pressure, which Hobhouse attacked.

It matters a good deal [he asserted] whether the social reforms which we hope and believe will form the backbone of politics in the near future are carried out with regard to principle or to any general conception of social progress...there is all the difference between benevolent officialism setting the world in order from above, and the democratic Collectivism which seeks not to restrict liberty but to fulfil it.

Hence Liberalism and Labour occupied common ground, even though at present their relations were impaired. 'But between these two forces', he concluded, 'union is at bottom natural and in the end necessary. The union of Conservatism and Labour is a monstrosity – and a monstrosity which the Oldham electors have not suffered to live.'[4] For all the strong Conservative tradition of the Lancashire workingmen this conclusion had considerable

[1] *Oldham D. Standard*, 7 July 1899; Churchill to Balfour, 8 July 1899, BP 49694.
[2] See Hobhouse to Scott, n.d. (12 July 1899), MGP.
[3] Leader, *M.G.*, 4 July 1899.
[4] Leader, *M.G.*, 7 July 1899; and see below, p. 173 n. 1.

force. If the politics of the future were to centre on social reform they would raise class issues which the Conservative party would find it impossible to accommodate. Only in a social context where class divisions were overridden in importance by other social conflicts could Tory Democracy survive. It was this second and less ambitious version which continued to dominate the politics of Liverpool.

VI

The tendencies which reinforced the Conservatism of Lancashire in the later nineteenth century had their fullest play in Liverpool. There the Tories had always been predominant and they were to remain so for most of the twentieth century. There were famous Liberal dynasties like the Rathbones, but they were famous chiefly for standing out so staunchly and frequently against the sentiments of their townsfolk. The third William Rathbone who wished to abolish the slave trade; the fourth William Rathbone who denounced war with France; the fifth William Rathbone who campaigned against the corruption of the Liverpool freemen; the sixth William Rathbone who supported the North in the American Civil War – all found themselves in a small and unpopular minority.[1] The traditions of the town were Tory; Irish immigration made it Toryism of a particular kind. The religious clashes of the 1830s and 1840s had the effect of confirming the Conservative party in power for the rest of the nineteenth century. Canon Hugh McNeile, a fiery evangelical preacher, led his forces against the educational policy of a Liberal council which put Protestant and Roman Catholic children side by side in the same schools. The Liberal Edward Russell later recalled 'the extra-ordinary position which Dr M'Neile occupied in Liverpool during the time when he was fixing the political character of Liverpool'.[2] If McNeile was more responsible than anyone else for creating the Protestant Tory party with its mass following it was Arthur Forwood who in the 1880s saw that consequently it must be democratic too. 'My conviction', he wrote, 'is that the working classes must, from the necessity of their position, have a leaning to Conservatism... The worst policy the Conservative party can adopt is to exhibit a want of confidence in the people. Trust them, and they will reciprocate the sentiment.'[3] Forwood insisted that since the democracy was already Tory the Conservative party must take cognisance of the fact.

Forwood was the leading figure in Liverpool Conservatism in the 1880s and 1890s. In his later years he came to work closely with Archibald Salvidge

[1] See Rathbone, *William Rathbone, passim.*
[2] Russell, *That Reminds Me,* pp. 132–8; cf. White, *A History of the Corporation of Liverpool,* pp. 21–3; James Murphy, *The Religious Problem in English Education* (Liverpool, 1959).
[3] 'Democratic Toryism', *Contemporary Review,* XLIII (1883), p. 299. For Forwood, see obit., *L. Courier,* 28 September 1898.

Formative influences

who was ultimately to be his successor. Salvidge's vehicle was the Liverpool Working Men's Conservative Association, an organisation which had existed from 1868 alongside the exclusive Constitutional Association, the official body. Salvidge had joined the Association in 1885 and in 1892 had become its chairman. He built it up so that by 1909 it had 25 branches and over 6,000 members.[1] As Forwood's *protégé* Salvidge maintained a somewhat uneasy peace with the official leadership but after Forwood's death in 1898 an open struggle for supremacy took place.

Protestantism was the issue which Salvidge used to mobilise his working-men. He showed some open-mindedness over labour problems (the social composition of his organisation dictated this) but the essence of his Tory Democracy was that religious unity must mask potential social cleavage. The Constitutional Association contained the fastidious upper crust of commercial Liverpool, the so-called 'currant jelly Tories' who resented Salvidge's up-start organisation and its crude methods.[2] For five years around the turn of the century he fought them in alliance with Austin Taylor, the leading spirit of the militant Protestant Laymen's League. Taylor wished to bring the conflict with the Constitutional Association to an issue because, as he told Salvidge, 'the classes are a complete clog on Protestant assertion and must be shaken off at all costs', but Salvidge himself later claimed that their movement 'had so far suffered because it had been simply a working man's movement'.[3] The reluctance of the respectable old-fashioned Tories to accede to Salvidge's demands was well exemplified by Walter Long, then M.P. for the West Derby division, who would not vote for the League's Church Discipline Bill. 'Poor Long', wrote Salvidge after dining with him, 'I am afraid he will have to quit West Derby.'[4] Moreover, in 1899 Salvidge turned against his party's candidate over the Protestant issue in a by-election at Southport, and was widely held responsible for the Liberal victory; while this flattered his influence it greatly added to the bitterness with which he was regarded.

[1] Report of its A.G.M., *Morning Post*, 26 January 1909. For the Constitutional Association see Feuchtwanger, *Disraeli, Democracy and the Tory Party*, pp. 192–3. There is an excellent biography of Salvidge by his son – *Salvidge of Liverpool*. It is more than a curiosity that in Preston, the borough which most nearly resembled Liverpool in its religious composition, the same kind of Conservative organisation existed. 'From time immemorial', explained the Conservative *Manchester Courier* (30 November 1910), 'there have always been two great sections of the Conservative party at Preston – what may be described as the aristocratic section, with its headquarters at the Guildhall-street club, and the middle and working class section, with headquarters at the Church-street Conservative Working Men's Club.' In 1882 the two had even run candidates in opposition. See Clemesha, *A History of Preston in Amounderness*, pp. 271–2, 284–5; *Lancs. D.P.*, 20 September 1900.
[2] See the survey of Liverpool Conservative organisation, *Liverpool D.P.*, 18 January 1906.
[3] Salvidge, *Salvidge of Liverpool*, p. 30; Salvidge address to the central council of the Laymen's League, *M. Courier*, 19 September 1900.
[4] Salvidge, *op. cit.*, p. 33.

The General Election of 1900 was a full-dress test of Salvidge's power. Long had chosen to abandon West Derby and was replaced by one of Salvidge's nominees, S. W. Higinbottom, who openly approved of the fact that 'in Liverpool political faith had been bound up with the maintenance of the Protestant faith'.[1] Another M.P. who had resigned from the Working Men's Association was forced to rejoin on humiliating terms. Only one of Liverpool's eight Tory M.P.s at first refused to conform on the Protestant issue and Salvidge's efforts were directed to bringing him to heel. Powerful and efficient as the Working Men's Association was, many Conservatives could not stomach Salvidge's methods. 'I begin to doubt', wrote one, 'if these agitators are Conservative at all, except in name. They certainly don't follow the old traditions of the party.'[2] Salvidge, however, was sure that his policy was justifiable. 'Some of the members of their party', he admitted, 'objected to what they called dictation and the pistol-at-the-head policy.' But when the last candidate fell into line he described it as 'the final episode in the struggle with a section of the party in Liverpool, which had thought fit to obstruct the wishes and opinions of the majority of the rank and file of the party'.[3] The policy of making Protestantism the explicit political test had an undeniable logic when most of the working class had their Protestantism daily recalled to mind as they rubbed shoulders with the Roman Catholic Irish. 'A Romanist makes his politics subservient to his religion', wrote one of Salvidge's supporters. 'Why should not a Protestant do the same?'[4]

The General Election had shown how powerful Salvidge had grown, and his brand of Conservatism went on to strengthen its hold. When there was a by-election at East Toxteth in 1902 the divisional Conservative Association promptly selected Austin Taylor as its candidate. It was widely felt that the selection procedure had been manipulated and two of the division's Conservative clubs went into open revolt. Moreover, Councillor Peter M'Guffie, a shipowner who had been displaced as chairman of the Housing Committee by Taylor, gave voice to the opposition to Salvidge which the old-fashioned Conservatives felt. He maintained that the main issue was 'whether the Salvidge clique is to boss the Unionist party of Liverpool' and maintained that the 'talk about "loyalty to the party" coming from the men who betrayed us at Southport is simply sacrilege'. He was joined by another of the old guard who advised electors to vote Liberal in order to show 'that Con-

[1] Higinbottom at West Derby, *Liverpool D.P.*, 20 September 1900.
[2] Letter from 'An Elector', *L. Courier*, 11 September 1900; throughout September the different sections of the Conservative party were sniping at each other in the *Courier* correspondence column.
[3] Salvidge speeches to W.M.C.A. central committee and at West Derby, *Liverpool D.P.*, 18, 20 September 1900; and see below, pp. 263–4.
[4] Letter from F. J. Shaw, *L. Courier*, 20 September 1900.

servatism and Salvidgeism are not synonymous terms'.[1] The revolt, however, proved less effective than had been anticipated when the votes were counted; the Salvidge machine triumphed.

Within three months of Taylor's election there occurred a vacancy in the West Derby division, for which Watson Rutherford, then Lord Mayor, was adopted as candidate. Rutherford was very much one of Salvidge's men: a staunch Protestant and a Tory of quite eccentrically democratic views. Salvidge's organisation was thrown into securing his election. He was opposed by Richard Holt, a scion of one of Liverpool's great mercantile families and just about as good a candidate as the Liberals could hope for. Despite this, and the Government's unpopularity, Rutherford polled over 60 per cent of the votes cast. That it was a victory for Salvidge and Tory Democracy no one doubted. 'We had a splendid band of workers', Holt told Herbert Gladstone, '& the party officials did everything possible, but we made absolutely no impression on the lowest class of electors. Amongst the better educated – clerks – shopkeepers &c we did well & fairly held our own, but the artisans & labourers must have voted five or even ten to one against us.' The result, he added, had by no means pleased 'the better class Conservatives'.[2]

Protestantism had proved a good stick with which to belabour the official leadership. But although by 1903 Salvidge had gained acceptance on his own terms he discovered that the Protestant agitation could not be turned off like a tap. He found himself outflanked on the Protestant issue by a latter-day McNeile, Pastor George Wise. Starting in 1901, Wise built up a following by conducting outdoor meetings at St Domingo Pit, the heart of the Protestant district. These were ostensibly to protest against ritualism but in practice ridiculed 'the lambs of Rome' for letting themselves be fleeced by the priests, who, he maintained, were spending the proceeds on whisky and harlots. These contentions, broadcast in the streets, not unnaturally led to disorder, and Wise was more than once bound over to keep the peace.[3] Wise's followers formed a Protestant party which contested municipal elections with some success against official Conservatives. Salvidge's reaction was to make his peace with the Constitutional Association; he would respect their honorific titles if they would acknowledge the power of 'Boss Salvidge'. The sixteenth Earl of Derby had become president of the Working Men's

---

[1] Letter from M'Guffie, *Liverpool D.P.*, 1 November 1902; manifesto by H. Douglas Horsfall, *L. Courier*, 5 November 1902; cf. that by the officers of the Tagus Street and Toxteth Conservative clubs against Salvidge, *ibid.*

[2] R. D. Holt to Gladstone, 27 January 1903, HGP 46060 ff. 109–10; cf. leader, *L. Courier*, 21 January 1903.

[3] See Head Constable's report, 16 March 1903, City of Liverpool, *Proceedings of the Council* (1902–3), pp. 1159–67.

Association in 1899; his son Lord Stanley became the official Conservative leader a couple of years later and made it his aim to establish close relations with Salvidge. He had intervened at a crucial moment in the East Toxteth by-election, promising to work for 'some understanding between what he was bound to call the two Wings', in order to end the acrimony in the party.[1] On this pledge the election was held to have turned. And although Stanley gave up the leadership on becoming Postmaster-General in 1903 his successors, Sir Thomas Royden and, from 1906, Sir Charles Petrie, made fuller attempts to conciliate the Working Men. In 1909 Salvidge was calling it one of the chief pleasures of his life to work under Petrie's leadership and after the second 1910 election he attributed the Conservative success in Liverpool to 'the absolute unity' between the two sections of the party.[2] Not that this amity was unflawed, or that the social tensions between the two wings were forgotten. The 1911 transport strike, for instance, found Salvidge defending and Petrie attacking the men's right to belong to their trade union. And when Bonar Law became drawn into Liverpool politics he was warned against 'the pushful Alderman A. T. Salvidge' by one of his supporters who was bitterly resentful of 'the way in which the chairman of the Workingmen's Association has systematically sought to set aside his leader and taken to himself and his organization all the credit of the good work done and paid for by the Constitutional Association'.[3]

Salvidge's relationship with Stanley, later the seventeenth Earl of Derby, was an important factor in legitimising his authority. It was also important to Derby. The Stanleys were the only landed family to wield substantial influence in Lancashire, and Lord Derby could claim a considerable social and political position by inheritance. His political weight, however, was greatly enhanced by the fact that through Salvidge he had an intimate knowledge of the inner workings of the Conservative machine. Derby had political views of a studied moderation; but his eagerness to please acquired him a reputation for malleability. (Haig later noted that 'like the feather pillow, [he] bears the mark of the last person who has sat on him'.)[4] He came to act as a two-way channel between Lancashire opinion and the Conservative leadership in London, and his influence was primarily thrown against the policy of food taxes, on the simple grounds that it would lose votes in the north west. While he was later reinforced in drawing this conclusion by Salvidge, this was an issue upon which Salvidge had swung with the wind. In October 1903 he had eagerly welcomed Chamberlain to Liverpool with

---

[1] Stanley at East Toxteth, *L. Courier*, 5 November 1902.
[2] Salvidge at Constitutional Club, and interview, *L. Courier*, 25 November 1909, 7 December 1910.
[3] H. R. Wilkins to Law, 23 October 1912, BLP 27/3/43; cf. Salvidge, *Salvidge of Liverpool*, pp. 114–16.
[4] See Gollin, *Proconsul in Politics*, p. 494; and Churchill, *Lord Derby*.

the result, according to Stanley, who had declined to be involved, that 'Liverpool has gone Joe-mad'.[1] It is true that in later years Salvidge did not abandon Tariff Reform as such – in 1908 the Unionist Free Traders recognised that their whiggish views would not impress Liverpool[2] – but after 1906 he was strongly in favour of subordinating it to Home Rule. The explanation of this inconsistency is that, under threat from the Protestants in 1903, he preferred for once in his life that politics be about economics rather than religion. He reverted to his customary preference once he had reimposed his authority over the Wiseites.

In 1905 there was a by-election in the working-class division of Everton. This was Wise's home ground and the Protestants claimed an electoral strength of two thousand votes. The Conservatives chose a High Churchman, J. S. Harmood Banner, as their candidate and although he promised to support the Church Discipline Bill his selection sparked off a Protestant revolt. Wise held a huge outdoor meeting at St Domingo Pit, at which he advised his audience to support the Liberal, and followed it up with further demonstrations.[3] Salvidge pulled out every stop; in the Government's darkest hour he put Tariff Reform and party loyalty to the fore and Banner was easily elected. The Protestant revolt was over. At the General Election Wise cleared away his 'misunderstanding' with the Conservatives;[4] as a corollary, Tariff Reform was dethroned and Protestantism reinstated in its place. 'It was the tail that wagged the dog in politics', commented the Irish Nationalist M. P. T. P. O'Connor... 'As Colonel Sanderson and the Orangemen ruled the Tory party in Ireland so Geo. Wise and the "no popery gang" ruled the Tories in Liverpool (hear, hear).'[5] The Liberals had no doubt that it was Salvidge's organisation which held the line for the Tories and the period in which the Conservatives were in disarray nationally saw almost his apotheosis as the invincible boss.

Salvidge's Working Men's Association was able to exploit the local peculiarities of Liverpool to perpetuate cultural politics up to and beyond the Great War. When a Labour candidate fought the Kirkdale by-election in 1907 the Conservatives woke up to the danger of their position late in the day. F. E. Smith was hurriedly summoned back from a continental holiday and a virulent attack on socialism was launched in which the atheistic pronouncements of leading socialists were put to the fore. The Labour candidate innocently maintained that 'the electors had not come together to fight over

[1] See Sandars to Balfour, 14 October 1903, BP 49761; Salvidge, *Salvidge of Liverpool*, pp. 47–57.
[2] Memorandum enc. in E. G. Brunker to R. Cecil, 1 February 1908, CP 51072.
[3] *Liverpool D.P.*, 18, 20, 22 February 1905.
[4] See *L. Courier*, 14 December 1905.
[5] O'Connor at Scotland, *L. Courier*, 8 January 1906.

religious questions'[1] – but then he was not a local man. Pastor George Wise rallied to the Conservative cause, and the Conservative leadership put the victory down to 'the efficiency of the strong local organization and to the enthusiasm of the so-called Protestants'. Ramsay MacDonald, who had been assisting the Labour campaign, commented ruefully to Salvidge that: 'It is astounding how in Liverpool, whatever the issue appears to be at the start, you always manage to mobilize the full force of Orangeism.'[2]

Wise was to be responsible for a further crisis which, viewed as a prelude to the General Elections of 1910, strikingly confirms that social tension between different communities was still at least as important in Liverpool as class feeling. Wise had by now gathered a large and enthusiastic congregation at his new Protestant Reformers Church and a bodyguard protected him wherever he went. In May 1909 a Roman Catholic procession resulted in riots and bloodshed when militant Protestants infiltrated the Catholic quarter. When Wise attempted to hold a counter-demonstration in the form of a parade of the 1,200 members of his Bible class in June the Chief Constable, fearful of retaliations, had him bound over. Since Wise refused to give recognisances he was sentenced to four months in gaol and, despite the intervention on his behalf of Watson Rutherford, to prison he went, amidst great popular outcry. At this point a Home Office inquiry was set up with a London barrister, A. J. Ashton, K.C., as Commissioner. The charges which the Protestants had made against the police were dropped and Ashton was left with the problem of apportioning responsibility for the religious riots, eventually deciding in favour of the Catholics.[3]

The elections of 1910, following close on these events, saw Salvidge triumph again. The influence of Liverpool over Lancashire Conservatism had never been so great. Salvidge and Smith went on missionary trips all over the region and in December 1910 Derby took charge of the Conservative effort in Manchester. After December 1910 Salvidge was seized upon by the party chiefs in London as the man who could restore the party's fortunes, but Salvidge himself, though he was flattered by their attentions, saw that he had no panacea for the party as a whole.

They seem to think of me mostly as an organizer [he wrote], but of course I know that organization is only part of the reason for success in Liverpool. Much is due to leadership and the knack of understanding the public mind. I know Liverpool politics like the palm of my hand, but things do not run on the same lines in all

---

[1] John Hill at Kirkdale, *Liverpool D.P.*, 18 September 1907; cf. 19 September for the Conservatives' use of quotations.

[2] J. S. Sandars to W. M. Short, 6 October 1907, BP 49765; Salvidge, *Salvidge of Liverpool*, p. 80.

[3] For this episode see *Liverpool D.P.*, 27, 29 November 1909; Ashton, *As I Went on My Way*, pp. 237–43. A truce was subsequently arranged after a conference under Derby's chairmanship.

parts of the country. A thing I have to remember is that though Liverpool politics are more complicated they are always more alive because of religious feeling and the Nationalist and Orange factions.[1]

The factors which Salvidge so well appreciated prevented Liverpool from following the general pattern of change in the north west in the early twentieth century. One of the leading Liverpool Liberals put the matter more acutely when he attributed the failure of Liberalism there to 'the appeal made by the other side to religious and sectarian bigotry and hatred. When they got rid of that the Liberal party would win in Liverpool, as it won in every other part of Lancashire.'[2] But there was, on the other hand, little prospect of change, for the appeal of Salvidge's type of Tory Democracy was conditioned by the social structure. The career of Pastor George Wise showed that Catholic and Protestant workingmen were fundamentally at odds, and as long as this was so mere political propaganda was inefficacious. 'Liverpool Unionism is a kind of religious faith', C. P. Scott explained to the Liberal Chief Whip in 1911. 'It is really an importation from Belfast and rests on hatred of Rome & of the Irish. That is not a kind of thing which you can affect by speeches or political agitation and the Home Rule Bill will have intensified the feeling.'[3] Through and beyond the period of the Liberal revival, the politics of Liverpool remained notable even more for their conservatism than for their Toryism.

[1] Salvidge, *Salvidge of Liverpool*, p. 106.
[2] Statement by Dr Permewan, L.C.L.F. Minutes, 8 April 1911; cf. Permewan at Walton, *L. Courier*, 6 December 1910.
[3] C. P. Scott to Elibank, 5 December 1911 (draft) MGP; and see report by Walter Long on Liverpool, 8 March 1912, BLP 26/1/76.

3   The Conservative Party at prayer

I do not like that which I find is the accepted maxim in Lancashire, that every Churchman is a Conservative and every Nonconformist a Liberal.

Bishop Fraser

I

In the north west, religion was probably associated with politics even more closely than in other parts of Britain. It is less likely that, when the operatives became voters in 1867 and 1884, they often moved naturally into the Conservative ambit because the Liberals were the bosses' party, than that a large section of the working class were exhibiting Anglican reflexes against Liberal Nonconformity. In its appeal to the urban masses, Lancashire Churchmanship ran a strait and narrow course between the Dissent of the bosses and the Roman Catholicism of the Irish immigrants. It was the strain of fighting Evangelical Anglicanism thus defined which was the peculiar factor in the Conservatives' electoral strength in the region.

It is only necessary to compare Victorian England with the secular society which emerged from it to see that in social terms the nineteenth century was an age of faith. When religious feeling reinforced political allegiance it enshrined a pattern of behaviour which was often broken only by a twofold – or manifold – transfer of allegiance. Two figures mentioned previously exemplify this. W. Romaine Callendar, the eminent Conservative and Churchman, came from a family that was Liberal and Nonconformist; W. Farrer Ecroyd was brought up as a Quaker and a Liberal, but became a Churchman and a Protectionist M.P. It may be that all political behaviour is rooted to an extent far greater than is at first apparent in a complex of habitual responses. If there is a habit of voting, there is also a habit of voting Conservative or voting Liberal. Often religion was the cement which fixed lifelong party loyalties. For instance, it seems that in 1951 religion was still the 'key factor' in explaining the Conservatism of the workers in Glossop, where religious affiliation and voting had been closely linked before the Great War.[1]

It was particularly true in an industrial area that not all men were religious. In the 1840s Engels thought that the workman's faulty education accounted

[1] Birch, *Small Town Politics*, ch. 2; cf. Birch, 'The habit of voting', *Manch. Sch.*, XVIII (1950). For an excellent survey of the process of secularisation see Bryan Wilson, *Religion in Secular Society: a sociological comment* (1966), Pt. I.

53

for his knowing 'nothing of the fanaticism that holds the bourgeoisie bound'; and such ignorance and apathy seem to have been widespread.[1] Churchmen admitted as much.

It is asserted [said Bishop Fraser of Manchester in 1874], that the working classes are not under the influence of the Church of England, and perhaps not under the influence of any religious body outside. It is said that the Church of England possesses the wealthy classes; the Nonconformists the tradesmen; and the artizans and mechanics stand outside of all religious agencies. This ought not to be...[2]

Dean Oakley of Carlisle, who had been one of Fraser's canons, once heard Carlisle described as 'the most godless city in England' and 'drily replied that he perhaps might have been more of that opinion if he had not formed the acquaintance of Manchester'.[3] A Lancashire person, writing at the turn of the century of the need for more pastoral work in such areas as Ancoats and Oldham, countered the squeamish objection that Lancashire was 'hopelessly Protestant' with the blunt assertion, 'It is semi-pagan'.[4]

The problem of maintaining religious life, especially in large towns, was not helped by contemporary social developments. When the prosperous moved out of the areas where their prosperity had been created, the chapels they had built were left behind them. 'Go into many of the churches in the lower part of the town', enjoined William Rathbone of Liverpool, 'and you will find the clergyman left almost unsupported by the sympathy and assistance of men of his own class and education, and struggling almost hopelessly with the mass of poverty, recklessness and unbelief around him.'[5] Bishop Fraser deplored the effects of this trend which in practice meant the greater social segregation of towns and denuded the central areas of religious as of political leadership. Here lay one of the great arguments for an Established Church, in its ability to apply the resources of the Church as a whole to needy areas. The idea that the Church of England had special obligations in attending to the religious life of the people – Bishop Knox was to call it 'a sense of responsibility to the nation'[6] – was still powerful. In Lancashire the Church met that responsibility more fully than elsewhere.

Lancashire had become thought of as the centre of Nonconformity in the days of the Manchester School. But just as the leadership of the Liberal party effectively passed to Birmingham in the 1860s and 1870s, so Birmingham

---

[1] *Marx and Engels on Britain*, pp. 158–9; cf. E. R. Wickham, *Church and People in an Industrial City* (1957); Pelling, 'Popular attitudes to religion', in *Popular politics and Society in Late Victorian Britain*, pp. 19–36.
[2] Fraser's speech at the Diocesan Synod, Diggle, *The Lancashire Life of Bishop Fraser*, p. 162.
[3] Russell, *That Reminds Me*, p. 308.
[4] Smith, *Parsons and Weavers*, p. 60.
[5] Speech to the Domestic Mission, 1874, Rathbone, *William Rathbone*, pp. 436–41.
[6] Knox, *Reminiscences of an Octogenarian*, p. 117.

also assumed the mantle of Free Church leadership. In Lancashire Methodism was the strongest Free Church. It was indeed the great rival of the Church of England, except in Liverpool and those other towns in the western part of the county where the main challenge to the Church came from Roman Catholicism. It may have been that the system of organisation adopted by the Congregationalists, Baptists and Presbyterians was best adapted to compact towns, and more to the middle-class parts than the industrial parts of urban areas. The Methodist circuit system, on the other hand, was quite capable of maintaining chapels in villages. In the cotton districts, where a large number of smaller textile centres were often grouped round a larger town, Methodist chapels could be served by ministers living in the important centres.[1] In an industrial village the resident Methodist employer might perform the roles undertaken in an agricultural village by a squire. The velvet glove of paternalism no doubt mitigated class antagonism, but it was impossible not to notice the iron fist of social control – 'Methodist workmen were apt to be promoted, became tacklers, overseers and foremen'.[2] Philip Snowden gave a picture of Cowling, a textile village not far from, and similar to, those of North Lancashire. The Anglican vicar there was personally popular as 'a teetotaller and a yoller' (a Liberal), but he had no congregation and in his later years visited his parish only at weekends 'in case anybody should turn up for the Sunday service'.[3] Wesleyanism, with its close ties with the Established Church, had had a Conservative tradition in the mid-nineteenth century. The series of secessions from it had a quasi-political basis and the Free Methodist churches were solidly Liberal. These other Methodist churches were based far more upon the humble, especially in the case of the Primitives. In Leigh their members were 'chiefly composed of the upper Artizan class',[4] and in Ashton-under-Lyne their Sunday School was 'a hot-bed of Radicalism'.[5] The Independent Methodists were concentrated in Lancashire, which provided the Presidents of their Conference in all but five years between 1880 and 1914.[6]

The Old Dissenters were, by and large, the sects of the well-to-do, and were, as a result, more subject to social pressures towards Anglicanism and Conservatism alike. In both Manchester and Liverpool the Unitarians were an exclusive group which comprised many of the leading families and which resisted erosion at least in part because of this; while in Ashton it was asserted

[1] See Tillyard, 'The distribution of the Free Churches in England', *Soc. Rev.*, January 1935.
[2] Davies, *North Country Bred*, p. 28; cf. Inglis, *Churches and the Working Classes in Victorian England*, pp. 10–11.
[3] Snowden, *An Autobiography*, I, 31.
[4] John Wood to C. P. Scott, 6 June 1902, MGP.
[5] R. Scholes to Max Aitken, 17 March 1912, Beaverbrook P.
[6] Vickers, *History of Independent Methodism*, pp. 209–10.

that 'the Members of the *local* Unitarian Church, are a very well-to-do Class'.[1] The Congregationalists, however, another wealthy denomination, were losing influential members to the Church in the late nineteenth century. With families like the Hopkinsons in Manchester this was a sort of religious corollary of Liberal Unionism. In St Helens some of the Pilkingtons had become Anglican in the 1830s while the rest remained pillars of Congregationalism; but all became Liberal Unionists.[2]

By the late nineteenth century the politics of Nonconformity were inherently and unabashedly Liberal. It was remarkable for a man to throw in his lot with the Tories and yet remain an active Nonconformist (though it seems to have happened more frequently after 1906). The Tory leadership clearly did not believe that it enjoyed any widespread support from Dissenters.[3] Nonconformist ministers had influential voices in local Liberalism. Men like Dr Aked in Liverpool or the Rev. Fred Hibbert in Blackburn were deeply committed in politics (both on the pro-Labour wing of Liberalism) and were regarded as potential parliamentary candidates. Partisan ministers had to satisfy partisan congregations. In Ashton, the Rev. Henry Parnaby was wary of mixing religion and politics too closely. 'I believe', commented the Conservative agent, 'his congregation desire he would be more pronounced in politics (Liberal of course) than he is, as the Albion Chapel the place where he holds forth is a place strongly opposed to us, especially in the past.'[4] Although the final phrase here may have been pregnant for the future, for the time being Nonconformity formed the backbone of Liberalism. A dominant version of this pattern can be seen at Rochdale in the mid-Victorian period, when a narrow group of Nonconformist businessmen were able to carry all before them.[5] But even in Liverpool, where Nonconformity and Liberalism were weak, a skeletal pattern existed, with Dissenters like the Holts and Rathbones propping up the local Liberal organisation. In mounting its attack upon the Liberals during the 1906 election the *Liverpool Courier* spent much of its time sneering at the 'Nonconformist conscience'. Many of the Liberal and Labour candidates of the generation before the

[1] A. Park to Aitken, 9 October 1912, Beaverbrook P.; cf. Sellers, 'Nonconformist attitudes in later nineteenth century Liverpool', *Trans. Hist. Soc. Lancs. & Ches.*, CXIV (1962), p. 218; Chorley, *Manchester Made Them*, p. 174.
[2] Chorley, *op. cit.*, p. 173; Barker, *Pilkington Brothers and the Glass Industry*, p. 116; St Helens Congregational Church, *Handbook*. At Crewe three railway officials, upon their election to the Council to represent the L.N.W.R.'s Conservative views, left the Congregationalists for the Church of England. See Chaloner, *Social and Economic Development of Crewe*, pp. 253–4. But the implications of this episode go rather beyond the point I am making here.
[3] 'I don't believe the Nonconformist Unionist Association carries much weight', wrote the Chief Whip, 'they are mostly a self-advertising lot.' Acland Hood to J. S. Sandars, 23 September (1905), BP 49771.
[4] J. C. Buckley to Aitken, 22 October 1912, Beaverbrook P.
[5] Vincent, *The Formation of the Liberal Party*, pp. 106–10.

War came from a background of Dissent. Augustine Birrell was the son of a Baptist minister and Spencer Leigh Hughes of a Wesleyan; Norval Helme and Edwin Hamer were Wesleyans of some local prominence, and David Shackleton was a Wesleyan Labour candidate; James Duckworth had been President of the United Methodist Free Church Assembly. Theodore Taylor did much active work for the Congregational Church; John Lea was active in Presbyterianism. John Haworth Whitworth, though brought up as a Congregationalist, was attracted to Quakerism; Alfred Emmott and J. Pease Fry were Quakers, as was Albert Bright who, working his passage back to Liberalism at Oldham in 1906, kept the fact to the forefront. Sir William Mather claimed to draw political inspiration from his own more nebulous religious beliefs. And Nonconformity was probably even more important in staffing the Liberal organisation. William Royle, who controlled the Liberal machine in Manchester, was a staunch Wesleyan. William Brimelow who was for twenty-five years secretary of Westhoughton Liberal Association was a prominent independent Methodist, as was Thomas Robinson, chairman of Stretford Liberal Association. John Wood, the Liberal chairman in Leigh, was active in Primitive Methodist affairs. None of these men was merely a formal adherent of either his church or his party, and the list could be multiplied.[1] These are isolated examples but the study of a particular town reveals a congruent pattern.

Information about the religion and politics of a number of the leading men in Warrington in the twenty years before the War is accessible. Many of these men were on the council, most were leading local employers, almost all were born between 1835 and 1855. Two-thirds of them were Conservatives, as against one-third Liberals. The religion of 21 is known. Of these, the twelve who were Anglicans were all Conservatives. Six of the Nonconformists were Liberals and one was a Conservative. (The exception was Alderman Arthur Bennett, a Wesleyan, who, as chairman of the Lancashire and Cheshire Conservative Working Men's Association, held 'advanced views on social reform'.) The remaining two were George Crosfield, a Congregationalist, who renounced his family's Liberalism in December 1910 because of the National Defence issue; and F. W. Monks, a Dissenter, who, after supporting the Conservatives in 1906 and January 1910, resumed his Liberal allegiance in December 1910 because of the House of Lords question.[2] Now this is by no means a perfect sample, but it does rather strikingly confirm the postulate

[1] The above is based chiefly upon well-attested statements in biographies.
[2] This survey is based upon the biographies of 45 'local worthies' in *Warrington Guardian Year Book*, 1896–1914. 26 were Conservatives and 13 Liberals, though one of these stood for the Council as an independent. There were two other independent councillors, two men of unknown politics, plus Crosfield and Monks. For Crosfield see below, p. 300 n.; for Monks see *M.G.*, 2, 3 December 1910.

that the active Conservatives were mainly Anglicans, the active Liberals mainly Nonconformists, and that those under cross pressures were most prone to defect.

The Roman Catholics were important not only in themselves but in the response their presence provoked in others. The overwhelmingly majority were Irish, and their working-class strength was almost wholly so since, despite a number of converts from the upper and middle classes, there was little conversion among the working class. At the beginning of the twentieth century there were about half as many Roman Catholics as Anglican priests in Lancashire, a far higher proportion than in any other English county. In the Salford and Liverpool dioceses alike the numbers of secular and regular priests increased between 1900 and 1914, as did the number of churches.[1] The Church of England was thus under some challenge on both flanks, and Lancashire was the only county where its clergy were outnumbered by ministers and priests of other denominations. It would be fallacious to infer from this that the Church was weak. On the contrary, the unique hold which it acquired over such a preponderantly working-class community demands further examination.

II

The diocese of Manchester was formed out of that of Chester in 1847 (Chester retaining what was to become the Liverpool diocese) and James Prince Lee was chosen as its first bishop. An autocratic Low Churchman, Lee purged his diocese of any 'popish' leanings. His episcopate was marked by a large amount of church-building; 163 new parishes and ecclesiastical districts were formed and it has been concluded 'that in this third quarter of the century the Church of England was at the least holding its own'.[2] The basis for an Anglican resurgence was laid. But Prince Lee himself was an unsympathetic character and in his later years, beset by ill health, he retreated to his palace of Mauldeth Hall near the Derbyshire border. In 1870, urged by Bright to appoint a known Liberal to succeed him, Gladstone persuaded James Fraser, a veteran of three Royal Commissions on education, to go to Manchester. 'As respects the particular see', Gladstone wrote, 'it is your interest in, and mastery of, the question of public education which has led me to believe that you might perform at Manchester, with reference to that

---

[1] *Census 1901*, General Report, p. 92; *Census 1911*, vol. x, pt. I, p. xix; *Catholic Directory*, 1900, 1914. The proportion of Roman Catholic priests to 100 Church of England clergymen was 48.0 per cent in 1901 and 46.5 per cent in 1911, as compared with figures for ministers of other denominations of 73.7 per cent and 82.6 per cent respectively.

[2] G. Kitson Clark, *The Making of Victorian England* (1962), p. 173 (calculated from the *Congregational Year Book 1881*); cf. *Edinburgh Review*, CLXIII (1886), p. 294; and for Lee see David Newsome, *Godliness and Good Learning* (1961) esp. pp. 135 ff.

question, a most important work for the Church and for the country. Manchester is the centre of the modern life of the country.'[1] Nor did Fraser fail this challenge. As well as continuing Prince Lee's church-building efforts – 105 new churches were consecrated in his fifteen years – he devoted himself to a work of school-building which gave Lancashire a lasting pre-eminence in the provision of Church day and Sunday Schools.

Fraser did far more than this. A conscientious and attractive exponent of muscular Christianity who might have come straight out of *Tom Brown*, he fully deserved to share the same biographer. In 1872 he managed to sell Mauldeth Hall to W. R. Callendar, and bought a more modest house in North Salford, within easy reach of the centre of Manchester. 'As you may suppose', the Registrar of the diocese had informed him at the outset, 'rich Dissenters abound, but, as a rule, *they* are tolerant and more than tolerant when they are not abused.'[2] Fraser consciously pursued better relations with Nonconformity, showing a wide tolerance in his diocesan work and promoting many schemes on a determinedly non-denominational basis. He threw himself into the public life of the diocese, taking part in all manner of movements for civic improvement. 'Without relaxing my hold on what I believe to be the great truths of Christianity', he declared, 'I still feel that the great function of Christianity is to elevate man in his *social* condition.'[3] So little sectarian spirit was there in his work that a Nonconformist mayor was led to describe him as 'the Bishop of all the Denominations', and Fraser's ingenuous goodwill once found him declaring in a sermon: 'If I could I would make every Roman Catholic and Nonconformist a full member of the Church of England to-morrow.'[4]

Fraser saw political differences as underlying any lack of cordiality between Church and Chapel, and he contested the idea that the lines of political and religious division were identical. Although he formally professed no politics, he was a milk-and-water Liberal who was capable, when aroused, of taking a leading role in the early stages of the Bulgarian agitation in 1876: thus revealing a political commitment which forced many Liberals to reconsider their opinion of Anglicanism.[5] Fraser reacted sharply against the unquestioning identification of the Church with the Tory party which was normal, especially in north east Lancashire. 'In Blackburn', he noted, 'the alliance between Conservatism and the Church – *religion* not having much

[1] Diggle, *The Lancashire Life of Bishop Fraser*, p. 41. For Bright's intervention see Vincent, *The Formation of the Liberal Party*, p. 207.
[2] Diggle, *op. cit.* pp. 45–6.
[3] *Ibid.* p. 22.
[4] Hughes, *James Fraser*, pp. 231, 352.
[5] See R. T. Shannon, *Gladstone and the Bulgarian Agitation, 1876* (1963), pp. 38, 46, 49–61; Mills, *The Manchester Reform Club*, p. 28.

to do with the compact – is closer than in almost any other Lancashire town.' But Fraser was resented in Blackburn when he ventured to admonish, and the alliance remained strong. During the 1900 Election, for instance, a sermon in the parish church on the miracle of the loaves and the fishes was spiced with the vicar's reflection that he 'hoped they would vote for the Conservative candidates, and thus support the Church'.[1] And it is plain that the traditional alliance was powerful right up to the Great War in Ashton where the Tory agent confidently assured Max Aitken of the loyalty of the several parishes, and the vicar of Christ Church pleaded as an excuse for troubling him, 'that I feel deeply – first for Religion & then for its hand-maid – the Unionist Party'.[2]

Fraser's worry had been that if the Church acted merely as the handmaid of the Tory party all religious harmony would be destroyed. In the section of his diocese where relations between the Church and Nonconformists were reported as 'hostile' he considered that 'the hostility seems to arise from political differences rather than religious, every Churchman being *ex hypothesi* a Conservative and every Nonconformist a Liberal'.[3] Ecclesiastical questions, however, were at the heart of party politics for much of Fraser's time. The 1860s had seen the lines of battle drawn in the Church of England with the foundation of the High-Church English Church Union in 1860 and the Low-Church Church Association in 1865. As the issue of Ritualism emerged, so did the politics of Protestantism revive. Parliament dealt with measure upon measure designed to remedy – or aggravate – the situation. And in the debates upon the redrafted Public Worship Regulation Bill of 1874 Disraeli spoke of 'putting down Ritualism' and stated his objection to 'mass in masquerade'. So a dispute in which Protestantism was the issue – reverberating on the Irish question at that – enmeshed two General Elections: that of 1868, in which, Engels noted, 'The *parson* has shown unexpected power', and that of 1874, in which the Conservatives confirmed their startlingly good results in the north west. The Church was no mere by-stander. When Jacob Bright was defeated at Manchester in 1875 the bells of Manchester Cathedral and of the parish church at Blackburn pealed out to celebrate a Tory triumph.[4]

Ritualism even trapped Fraser. With the Public Worship Regulation Act

---

[1] Diggle, *Bishop Fraser*, p. 454; 'The Tatler', *Blackburn Wkly Telegraph*, 6 October 1900.

[2] The Rev. F. H. Burrows to Aitken, 23 December 1912; cf. letters from J. C. Buckley to Aitken, 1911–12, Beaverbrook P, e.g. St John's Cricket Club 'a Church young mens Club, all of them likely to be your supporters'; St James's – 'The congregation are a good Tory lot'; 'Mr. Bird is the vicar of Christ Church, Stalybridge – he is a good Conservative and Churchman'.

[3] Fraser's Charge of 1880, Diggle, *Bishop Fraser*, p. 287.

[4] *Marx and Engels on Britain*, p. 546; Hughes, *James Fraser*, p. 240; Mills, *The Manchester Reform Club*, p. 31n. For the measures on Ritualism see F. Warre Cornish, *The English Church in the Nineteenth Century*, Pt. II (1910).

of 1874 in force he became embroiled in a *cause célèbre*, the Miles Platting Case, in the course of which the Rev. S. F. Green, one of his clergy, was imprisoned. The Bishop was represented as a persecutor. One outcome of the case was that in his admonition of 1881 Fraser laid down a maximum standard of ritual for the diocese – no vestments, no candles, no mixed chalice, no incense. Almost all the clergy accepted this limitation; indeed Fraser thought that its main effect was to help clergymen 'to raise their services from the level of baldness, if not of slovenliness, to something more akin to decency and order'.[1] Thus was the Protestant integrity of Lancashire Anglicanism maintained.

Fraser's very tolerance highlights the strength of those elements of Evangelical Churchmanship which were naturally exploited by an opportunistic Conservative party. The détente with Nonconformity so distinctive of Fraser's episcopate proved to be a personal appurtenance rather than a legacy to the diocese. 'The breadth of his Christianity', commented one Lancashire newspaper as Fraser prepared to retire, 'has not found the echo he might have hoped in this north country.'[2] And his second biographer has noted that, unlike Selwyn or Wilberforce, he left neither men nor institutions behind to perpetuate his work. In 1886 Bishop Moorhouse was appointed by Salisbury to succeed him. Like Fraser, Moorhouse belonged to no party in the Church, and, with the spectre of Miles Platting before him, determined to avoid litigation. Nor had he any wish to see bad relations between the Church and Dissent, though he was eventually to take a leading part in the Education Bill debates in 1902 and offend Nonconformist ideas of justice by carrying the amendment making the state liable for wear and tear in the voluntary schools. But Moorhouse's gifts did not match up to the demands of his diocese and he seems to have recognised the fact; he lacked the spontaneous warmth that enabled Fraser to establish rapport with Lancashire at large.[3]

The Liverpool diocese was formed in 1880, again out of the diocese of Chester. The Liverpool Tories who had endowed it were most anxious that the bishopric should be filled by Beaconsfield before he left office, and he made a stark Evangelical choice in John Charles Ryle, who had a great following in the city.[4] Ryle had joined his father's bank after Oxford and was groomed to enter Parliament, often appearing on political platforms as a Conservative and at religious gatherings as an Evangelical. But the bank

[1] Diggle, *Bishop Fraser*, pp. 177–8.
[2] Hughes, *James Fraser*, p. 257.
[3] See Rickards, *Bishop Moorhouse*, esp. p. 143; cf. Dean Oakley's comments, Russell, *That Reminds Me*, p. 306.
[4] See Disraeli to the Queen 10 April 1880, *Letters of Queen Victoria* (ed. G. E. Buckle, 1928), 2nd ser., III, 78.

crashed. Ryle had to settle for another career. He became ordained. During a period of nearly forty years in two Suffolk livings, Ryle produced two or three hundred 'Ipswich Tracts' to confound the Tractarians at their own game. More august than Dean Inge, he was both a pillar of the Church and twenty-six columns in the British Museum catalogue. He went to Liverpool as the most trusted and honoured of Evangelical leaders. 'You know what are my opinions', he told his new diocese. 'I am a committed man...I have nothing to withdraw or retract from the opinions I have expressed again and again. I come among you a Protestant and Evangelical Bishop of the Church of England.'[1] Ryle's uncompromising policy – his charge of 1893 was entitled *Stand Firm*! – must be seen in the context of his diocese's large Irish and Roman Catholic population. It led all too easily to that complete identification of Evangelical Churchmanship with Conservative politics which Fraser had deplored. In Liverpool more than anywhere else the intellectual gulf between combating Ritualism in the Church of England and making war on Roman Catholics was bridged by the ancient Lancashire tradition of 'No Popery'. Ryle lamented in 1897 that 'aversion to papistry', part of the nation's heritage, had disappeared,[2] but he needed have few fears for his own diocese.

In both the Liverpool and Manchester dioceses a massive uniformity in the character of Churchmanship prevailed. Fraser once asserted in Convocation that of 476 churches in his care vestments were worn only in seven, and that the Bishop of Liverpool had told him that there was only one such case in his diocese; in 1876 he wrote that in only four churches was confession taught by the clergy. Ryle reaffirmed his opposition to High Church practices in one of his last articles. 'If they continue to increase, and they are not checked', he wrote, 'the end will be disestablishment, disendowment, and disruption.' His successor, Chavasse, had no less apocalyptic a view: 'A lawless church will soon lead to a lawless state; and the swift Nemesis of lawlessness is ruin.' According to Bishop Knox, 'a remarkable prevalence of uniformity' continued in Manchester and so few were the 'ritual excesses' that the diocese needed no elasticity of worship; and Chavasse spoke warmly of the loyalty of his diocese in the evidence to the Royal Commission on Ritual, citing only two exceptional cases.[3]

The High Church party was by no means as insignificant as these statements imply, but it had little popular following; indeed Protestant agitation had quite a dash of anti-clericalism in it. When the Rev. S. F. Green had tried to enrich his 'dismal uninviting church' in Miles Platting ('where even common grass will not grow') he declared that he had sought 'to press into

[1] Loane, *John Charles Ryle*, pp. 47–8.
[2] Quoted in Inglis, *Churches and the Working Classes*, pp. 141–2.
[3] Diggle, *Bishop Fraser*, p. 185; Hughes, *James Fraser*, p. 262; Loane, *Ryle*, p. 54; Lancelot, *Francis James Chavasse*, pp. 149, 174; Knox, *Reminiscences of an Octogenarian*, p. 254.

the service of the Church everything which adds cheerfulness and beauty to it. My design has been to give the people something to love.'[1] But such innovations were received with suspicion in Lancashire. A broadside protesting at 'Romish' tendencies in Manchester cathedral probably expressed the general opinion when it made the Spirit of the Law declaim:

> The common people to me bent the knee,
> But now these priests have willed that I shall die. . .
> They own no law – unless 'tis made for them
> To make themselves, the masters of men's souls.[2]

And in the 1890s one of its representatives was brazenly claiming that the Church Association 'which represents the people' was doing all it could 'to take the power out of the Bishops and Clergy's hands and place it in the hands of the people'.[3] It was by tapping this vein that Archibald Salvidge was able to rally his democratic Tory supporters: and in the process he raised the hackles of those older families who were, as their Bishop delicately put it, 'loyal rather to the old Anglican tradition than to the prevailing type of Liverpool Churchmanship'.[4] Conversely, a High Churchman like A. F. Warr, the Conservative M.P. for East Toxteth, was *ipso facto* unpopular and fell foul of Salvidge. The High Churchmen attempted to hit back at 'the Salvidge clique' and in the 1900 election two Liverpool clergymen, the Revs C. C. Elcum and John Wakeford, openly opposed him, but their following among the workingmen could not match his.[5]

At the turn of the century, then, Lancashire Anglicanism was set in its mould. It had to rely, as the Conservative party had to rely, on the working class to a greater extent than in other parts of the country. Democratic Churchmanship, built up in the Church schools, had a rabidly Evangelical tone which made for a solid Conservatism. ('The *Evans.* are politically even more retrograde than the Sacerdotalists', noted Campbell-Bannerman.)[6] In the Liverpool diocese it was open in its hostility to Romanism; in the Manchester diocese, where Roman Catholicism was less strong, its ancient feud with Dissent was perhaps slightly less bitter than in the past. In both there were political benefits which the Conservative party enjoyed in being able to appeal to a particular temperament which the Established Church had moulded.

[1] Green to Fraser, 17 May 1877, Diggle, *op. cit.* p. 400.
[2] Manchester Broadsheet f/1885/1.
[3] E. Bromiley to C. P. Scott, 12 July 1895, MGP.
[4] Lancelot, *Francis James Chavasse*, p. 150.
[5] Gladstone's diary, 6 April 1900. HGP 46483 f. 65. See report of Elcum's sermon and Wakeford's article, *Liverpool D.P.*, 1 October 1900; cf. Salvidge, *Salvidge of Liverpool*, pp. 30–1, 35.
[6] Campbell-Bannerman to Birrell, 14 January 1907, secret, Birrell P. MS 10–2.

III

Spurred on by Fraser's efforts, Lancashire had taken full advantage of the provisions which Forster's Education Act made for the building of Church schools, and the voluntary schools dominated the educational system of the region. Indeed in many places – and not country districts but densely populated towns at that – no School Board was ever established. In England and Wales as a whole at the end of the School Board era the all-voluntary areas had a population of 43 per cent of those which came under School Boards. In an urbanised region like the West Riding, the proportion was only 21 per cent. But in Lancashire and Cheshire the population in the voluntary areas was 71 per cent of that covered by the School Boards. There were only eight County Boroughs in the country without a School Board; six of these were in the north west.[1] This state of affairs largely though not entirely reflected Anglican strength. 'It is idle to talk of universal School Boards', observed C. P. Scott. 'Radicals all over the place have been subscribing to voluntary schools & even to Church schools to keep them out and it isn't the Tories & clericals alone by a long way who are opposed to their extension.'[2] In Preston, for example, which, with a population of over 100,000, was the only really big town without a School Board, great sacrifices had been made, not only by the Church of England and the Roman Catholics, but also by Wesleyans, Baptists and Congregationalists, to prevent the town from becoming 'degraded' by provided schools. It was often as a second best to the establishment of a School Board that Nonconformists kept up their own schools, in face of mounting difficulties. 'Our Church', wrote a Primitive Methodist, 'possess a large number of village chapels, & our Scholars are compelled to go to Church of England Day Schools, but in spite of all that we flourish... We have but few Day Schools mostly in Lancashire, but in none do we teach dogmas. We are giving up our Day Schools in Leigh, because we refuse to burden the working men of our Church with an expense that should be borne by the ratepayers at large.'[3]

Even in towns which had established School Boards the voluntary schools were ascendant. In Manchester, where the School Board had an Anglican and Roman Catholic majority for the entire period of its existence, its chairman for twenty years was Herbert Birley, a member of the Tory and Anglican family whose liberality had been largely responsible for the burgeoning of Church schools in the city. Although Birley was no narrow partisan the Board naturally operated in a manner favourable to the voluntary

[1] *List of School Boards and School Attendance Committees in England and Wales.* P.P. 1902, Cd. 1038, lxxix, 559.
[2] Scott to L. T. Hobhouse, 27 May 1902, MGP.
[3] John Wood to Scott, 6 June 1902, MGP.

64

schools, and the efforts which the Manchester Liberal Union inspired in the 1890s to try to change its complexion had little effect. Such was the attachment to the Church schools in Lancashire that they had been able to charge more than the 2*d.* a week fees customary in the South. One Liberal recalled the contrast between a pair of fee-paying voluntary schools in Manchester which were legally overcrowded and a nearby Board School with free places for 1,200 which had only 400 children.[1] The enactment of free education in 1891, by undermining the finances of the voluntary schools, introduced that 'intolerable strain' for the Church which was one reason for the agitation in favour of a new educational settlement.

Churchmen were determined to fight for their schools on the grounds that they were essential to foster Church membership. There was a special Lancashire bent to this argument owing to the close-knit relations between the Church, the day schools and the Sunday Schools. The Lancashire Sunday schools had long been uniquely strong, a great 'feeder' of the Church in which scholars remained to an adult age. The tenacious loyalties which these institutions imbued were transferred, especially after 1870, to the day schools as well. Bishop Knox put the case at its highest:

There was, in fact, in Lancashire, a love of elementary schools something analagous to the patriotism of Public Schools, the force of which only residence in Lancashire could reveal...Church and School were two sisters there, and of the two sisters, school was often the more favoured...It was the weekday branch, so to speak, of the Sunday-school, and the Sunday-school, by its adult classes, was the Church in a democratic form. It was the parish on the Church side. It criticised the parson and the Church services. It was a weekly parochial Church meeting – very formidable if it fell out with the parson – a tower of strength if the two pulled together... In many instances the day-school teachers, with the Sunday-school, kept the parish going during the reign of an unsatisfactory incumbent. The school felt itself to be in a very real sense 'the Church'.[2]

Now this picture is no doubt idealised. A report on Lancashire schools in this period deplored the lack of exactly this pride in school and was able to quote the recollections of a voluntary school by one former pupil who concluded his chronicle of wanton punishment with the dismissive remark: 'And so the time eventually came for us to leave school and we gladly left.'[3] But the Knox version had a good deal of truth in it, and it was moreover the position to which the defenders of the Church schools were committed. If it

[1] Interview with T. C. Horsfall, recorded in C. F. G. Masterman's diary, 1900, Masterman, *C. F. G. Masterman*, p. 31; cf. Simon, *A Century of City Government*, pp. 229–30, 240–57; speech by James M'Farlane, M.L.U. Annual Meeting, 30 April 1895.
Knox, *Reminiscences of an Octogenarian*, p. 239; cf. *Edinburgh Review*, CLXIII (1886), p. 309; Hulbert, *Sir Francis Sharp Powell*, p. 34; Hall Caine, introduction to *Lancashire Biographies*, p. xlvii.
[3] *Report on the School Training and Early Employment of Lancashire Children*, P.P. 1904, Cd. 1867, 2–3, 14–16.

was the Nonconformist view that the Church of England had only itself to blame for the intolerable strain of providing schools, this might strike a Lancashire Churchman as precious near to calling the Church's whole work a waste of time. Part of the difficulty was that 'Cowper-Templeism' – the bare bones of a Bible-reading Christianity – seemed to many Nonconformists a fair compromise. (It was indeed not far removed from the full canon of much Free-Church religion.) To the Anglicans it was but a step on the slippery slope to secularism. The Nonconformists, having virtually let their own schools go, wanted public money to go only to publicly-controlled schools; the Anglicans, by and large, wanted to keep their own schools intact.

'Voluntary schools *are* "efficient"', admitted one militant Nonconformist minister, 'for the purpose for which nearly all of them were started, namely for attaching children to a church.'[1] The effectiveness of the Church in achieving its avowed objects can be assessed too in terms of its natural political effects. When the veteran Liberal editor Henry Dunckley tried to explain why the extension of the franchise had not led to Liberal successes in Lancashire, he called the Nonconformists 'the backbone of the old Liberal party' and declared that they had formed a larger proportion of the ten-pound voters than they did of the householders. 'Last, but by no means least', he continued, 'we have to reckon with the influence of the Church as exerted through its schools...A great part of the population has passed through its schools, and it is to a generation enlisted on its side by early associations that the Church appeals in any emergency, and not without success.'[2] The ramifications of Church influence in politics spread in many directions. There are of course numerous Liberal 'atrocity stories' which may possess a symbolic rather than a literal truth. In 1906 the Labour candidate at Preston, that Mecca of voluntaryism, contributed to this genre: 'He had heard of a teacher in a school in Preston who said to the children of her class: "Now, children, you like to hear me speak of Jesus Christ." "Yes, teacher," was the reply. "Well, if your father does not vote for Tomlinson and Kerr I shall not be able to speak to you about Jesus Christ any longer." (Cries of "Shame".)'[3] It is not necessary to postulate either that such crude propaganda was widespread or that it was, on this level, effective, in order to suggest that Church schools may be regarded both as a cause and as an index of the Toryism of many Lancashire towns.

There are really two relationships to distinguish. In the first place the Church of England schools were the rivals of the Board Schools (together with the odd Nonconformist schools). In political terms this kind of rivalry

[1] The Rev. J. Hirst Hollowell to C. P. Scott, 26 January 1896, MGP. He added a second objective, that of boycotting young Nonconformists from the teaching profession.
[2] 'Verax', *M.G.*, 23 July 1895.
[3] Speech by J. T. Macpherson, Preston, *Lancs. D.P.*, 12 January 1906.

reflects the Tory response to Liberal Nonconformity. But, as has been noticed, in the Liverpool area and to some extent in other places with a large Irish element in the population, democratic Toryism was identified in terms of Protestantism. In the second place, therefore, where Roman Catholic schools were in a strong position it may be more illuminating to see the Board Schools as primarily the Protestant schools.

There are 24 constituencies which may be regarded as adequately represented by the one or more borough School Boards or School Attendance Committees within them. Table 1 shows the proportion of children in Church of England and Roman Catholic schools in 1902, and groups the constituencies according to the number of victories which the Conservatives gained in the five General Elections 1885–1900. The two Liverpool constituencies have been grouped separately.

In the seats which the Conservatives won four or five times the average proportion of children in Church schools was 49 per cent; in the seats which they won three times or less this proportion was 30 per cent. In Bootle and Widnes, on the other hand, there was no such association; but these two constituencies, like all but one of those in which the Roman Catholic schools accounted for over 15 per cent of all children, were won on every occasion by the Tories. There can be no exact correlations here; discrepancies of almost every kind abound. In particular, no causal attribution can be made since even if the religious affiliations were representative they would represent the choice of a generation of parents whose own education is not known. Nonetheless this table tends to confirm the anecdotal evidence that the religious temper of a town was of crucial importance to its politics. 'Religious matters have seldom been dragged into politics in Burnley', noted a local newspaper in 1900, 'and there are at the present time no great religious difficulties agitating the community.' The Nonconformists, it said, were greatly in the majority, the Roman Catholics were not strong, and although the Church supported the Conservatives it had a High Church character.[1] Add to this the information that 50 per cent of the children went to Board Schools, 22 per cent to Church of England, 12 per cent to Roman Catholic, 10 per cent to Wesleyan and 7 per cent to other schools; and that Burnley only once elected a Tory but had a Liberal Unionist M.P. in 1886. Fragmentary though all the evidence is, the fragments can be assembled within a pattern. Politics could hardly avoid an admixture of religion when the social communities which were the mainstay of party were defined in religious terms.

The big cities are a special case. It is impossible to produce representative figures for each division, but the aggregation of results in Table 2 conceals important differences.

Lancs. D.P., 13 September 1900.

TABLE 1

No. of times won by Cons. 1885–1900	Constituency	Percentage in C. of E. schools	Percentage in R.C. schools
4 or 5 times			
5	Wigan	56	29
5	Birkenhead	55	16
5	Stalybridge	53	7
5	*Warrington	50	17
5	Blackburn	50	22
5	*Preston	48	33
5	*St Helens	44	35
5	Ashton	43	10
4	*Chester	60	11
4	Macclesfield	58	5
4	*Hyde	41	7
4	*Stockport	40	13
4	Bolton	39	11
	Average	49	17
3 times or less			
3	*Bury	49	12
3	Oldham	16	9
3	Barrow	15	10
2	Rochdale	26	8
1	*Accrington	40	9
1	Burnley	22	12
0	*Leigh	43	21
0	Rossendale	35	9
0	Clitheroe	25	9
	Average	30	11
5	Bootle	29	21
5	Widnes	16	30

* No borough School Board in constituency.

NOTES

Constituencies correspond to School Boards of the same name with the exceptions of Macclesfield (Congleton + Macclesfield); Rossendale (Haslingden + Bacup + Rawtenstall); Stalybridge (Stalybridge + Dukinfield); and Clitheroe (Clitheroe + Nelson + Colne). School Boards with a school population of less than 5,000 and those in large rural divisions were excluded as unrepresentative.

Liberal Unionists are counted as Conservatives except for 1886.

Figures calculated from Board of Education, *List of Schools under the Administration of the Board 1901–2*. P.P. 1902, Cd. 1277, lxxix.

TABLE 2

	Percentage in C. of E. schools	Percentage in R.C. schools	Cons. victories 1885–1900
Manchester	32	14	21 out of 30
Salford	40	15	12 out of 15
Liverpool	31	25	38 out of 45

It should be remembered that five of the seven gaps in the Conservative representation of Liverpool are accounted for by T. P. O'Connor in the Scotland division. The strength of the Church schools, especially in Salford, is considerable for such conurbations, and, taken in conjunction with Liverpool's high Roman Catholic figure, shows what a sure foundation the Tory party was building upon.

The general strength of the voluntary schools in Lancashire meant that the Liberals found difficulty in striking the right chord over the Education Bill in 1902. In Bolton, indeed, with nearly forty per cent of children in Church schools, its Anglican M.P. George Harwood boasted of having been the only Liberal Member to decline to vote against its introduction. At Leigh, where there was no School Board, C. P. Scott came under considerable pressure from his constituents, especially the Roman Catholics, to support the Bill. And although some Nonconformists resorted to passive resistance, in many areas they only exposed Nonconformist weakness thereby. The Passive Resistance League in Liverpool was a hopeless failure, and in the nearby Wirral division, where the Manchester Liberal Edwyn Holt had undertaken the candidature, his activities as a passive resister seem to have led to his subsequent withdrawal. Even in Nonconformist Oldham the Conservatives did not regard opposition to the Education Act as a widespread threat.[1] And it is noticeable, for instance, that when the Nonconformist leader Dr Clifford spoke in Manchester in 1906 he was using a language out of key with Lancashire Liberalism. When he insisted that 'the question of questions before us at the present is the education question',[2] he was playing into the hands of the Conservatives. Whatever may have been the case elsewhere, in Lancashire it was the Conservative party which was able to turn the education question to advantage.

IV

In 1900 Francis James Chavasse became Bishop of Liverpool and in 1903 Edmund Arbuthnott Knox became Bishop of Manchester. Together they were to rule over the Church in Lancashire until the War. Knox and Chavasse first met as undergraduates at Corpus Christi College, Oxford. 'We were both of us', Knox was to recall, 'rather "not at home" in a society consisting almost entirely of public school men, and both of us had given offence by not turning to the East in the recital of the Creed.'[3] They remained lifelong

---

[1] See Harwood's speech, Bolton, *Bolton Chron.*, 5 January 1906; constituency correspondence, April–June 1902, MGP; Sellers, 'Nonconformist attitudes', pp. 215-17; for Wirral see *M. Courier*, 18 December 1905; for Oldham see Churchill to Balfour, 6 October 1902, BP 49694.
[2] *M.G.*, 9 January 1906.
[3] *Francis James Chavasse. Impressions by five of his friends*, p. 10.

friends – and Evangelical allies. Knox stayed on at Oxford as a Fellow of Merton, seeking to raise the academic level of the college through Evangelical influences. Chavasse began his career in Preston but in 1877 returned to Oxford, as vicar of St Peter-le-Bailey which he remained until 1889 when he became Principal of Wycliffe Hall, the University's Evangelical theological college. Knox later explained his leaving Merton in 1884 as being 'partly because the advent of Chavasse to Oxford as Principal of Wycliffe Hall made it less incumbent on me to represent Evangelicalism there'.[1] So Knox and Chavasse, in succession and together, had helped keep the Evangelical flag flying at Oxford long before they were called to higher things in the more characteristically Protestant pastures of Lancashire.

In 1891 Knox heard that he was going to be offered the Deanery of Manchester by Balfour. The Low Churchmen thought that they had secured this through Sir William Houldsworth; but at the last minute Knox's expectations were dashed and the appointment of the brother of Sir John William Maclure, a yet more august Manchester Tory, let in a High Churchman. So Knox spent the next twelve years, not in Manchester, but in or near Birmingham, where he learnt to fight Dissenters and Liberals on the schools issue and to respect the Grand Panjandrum of Birmingham politics, Joseph Chamberlain. He later admitted that he was attached to Birmingham 'with no slender cords'. Then in 1903 Knox received from Balfour the offer of the Bishopric of Manchester. He could not help but be mindful of 1891 and explained later that 'Mr Balfour's position at the moment was extremely hazardous... The King, at Marienbad, was already coquetting with Campbell-Bannerman.'[2] Knox accepted by return of post. It was a sound Conservative appointment.

In their episcopates Chavasse and Knox were confronted by all the old Lancashire problems. Chavasse was inevitably involved with the Merseyside movement for Church discipline which Salvidge exploited at the turn of the century. When Chavasse had been instituted to the living of St Peter-le-Bailey the Bishop had said to him: 'Mr Chavasse, be a man of peace.' Chavasse had replied: 'My Lord, I cannot work with Tractarians.' But neither would he condone Protestant intolerance, and told one Liverpool gathering: 'You make the good name of Protestantism to stink in the land.'[3] His instincts were in fact towards peace. He had been ordained by Bishop Fraser and obviously emulated him, even down to carrying his own robes in his bag, a habit about which both bishops encountered criticism from those over-solicitous for their dignity. Among Chavasse's Liverpool friends was

---

[1] Knox, *Reminiscences of an Octogenarian*, p. 101. Knox has somewhat contracted the series of events here; in 1884 Chavasse was still at St Peter's.
[2] *Ibid.* pp. 129, 205, 207–8; cf. Evelyn Waugh, *Ronald Knox* (1959), p 37.
[3] Lancelot, *Francis James Chavasse*, pp. 70–1, 162.

John Lea, a Liberal Presbyterian, and during Lea's Lord Mayoralty relations were close between the Town Hall and the Bishop's palace. It was all very well for Chavasse to work towards a détente on the Fraser model, but the Liverpool Conservatives relied on narrower Church loyalties. Nor could Chavasse, a total abstainer, give his full approbation to the other pillar of Liverpool Toryism, beer, and his support for temperance proposals led him to clash with the trade. He told his diocesan conference in 1909 that the spiritual life of the Church in Liverpool had been 'crippled and weakened' by sectarianism, political partisanship and parochialism. 'There has been a tendency in this diocese as in others', he said, 'to identify the Church of England with one of the great parties in the state, forgetful of the fact that she is the Church of the nation.'[1]

In the Manchester area the main ecclesiastical backwash in the 1900 Election had centred on Nonconformist anger at the Clerical Tithes Commutation Act. These 'doles' seem to have found little support anywhere in the north west. George Whiteley, one of the Conservative M.P.s for Stockport, crossed the floor on this issue at the time of the Oldham by-election, during which Churchill repudiated the Bill in somewhat ignominious fashion. In Stockport itself the local Tories agreed to allow Whiteley to serve for the rest of the Parliament rather than face a by-election.[2] It was an issue over which the Liberals could make hay – 'The late Government had been one of doleful woes and woeful doles', pronounced Charles Schwann, Manchester's only Liberal M.P.[3] – but it was somewhat marginal and perhaps its main effect was to make the Church wary of exposing itself.

Indeed the most prominent ecclesiastic to participate in the General Election of 1900 was working not with the Tories but with the Liberals. This was Edward Lee Hicks, who had been in Manchester since 1886, becoming a Canon in 1892; he was to be offered the Deanery by Campbell-Bannerman on terms which he would not accept and, as a committed Liberal, felt that his claims had been rather overlooked until, in 1910, Asquith made him Bishop of Lincoln. Hicks was well aware of 'the awful difficulty of being a Bishop & a Liberal' but felt that neither of the existing Liberal Bishops had 'the backing which I have, & *hope to* retain, in the sympathy & convictions & approval of a vast industrial population such as Lancashire'.[4] Not that Hicks's views had been universally popular in Lancashire. During the South African war he had been active as a 'pro-Boer' and this and his interest in temperance work combined to bring him into open support of Leif Jones

---

[1] Speech to the Liverpool Diocesan Conference, *L. Courier*, 24 November 1909.
[2] See Gladstone's diary, 29 June 1899, HGP 46483 ff. 24–5; *Companion*, I, 1034, 1036.
[3] Speech at Manchester North, *M.G.*, 28 September 1900.
[4] E. L. Hicks to C. P. Scott, 11 April 1910, MGP. For Hicks see Fowler, *The Life and Letters of Edward Lee Hicks*.

71

of the United Kingdom Alliance, whose misfortune it was to champion the pro-Boer case in the Manchester South by-election in May 1900. If he had not been earlier, this episode made Hicks a controversial figure, taunted by the Tories as 'the pro-Boer Radical parson'.[1] After 1903 Hicks found in his Bishop an equally committed politician and although there were many personal ties between the two men they were constantly and publicly at odds over politics.

In the Manchester diocese the schools question reactivated the animosity between Church and Chapel and Knox was plunged into the controversy from the beginning of his episcopate. Although Chavasse too defended the Church's position as clear, simple and just, Liverpool was more concerned to exploit other issues of Church and State which could provide an anti-Catholic weapon – whereas over education Anglicans and Romans had a common interest. It was Manchester, therefore, which played a leading part in rallying the Church forces; the Manchester Church Day Schools' Emergency League was founded in November 1903 and in July 1904 it assumed national form. The energetic management of the League by Canon Cleworth did not escape a taint of personal advertisement and it was Morant's opinion (hardly disinterested itself) that it was 'a matter of great regret that Knox, with all his ability and great knowledge of the Education question, should identify himself with such a hot-headed irreconcilable as Cleworth'.[2] In the 1906 election, in response to an invitation by the Ruridecanal conference of Prestwich and Middleton, Knox issued a pastoral letter in strong defence of the schools. Salford, of which Canon Hicks was Rural Dean, made no move, for Hicks resolutely refused to follow the Bishop's lead, arguing that the more Churchmen who were known to be on the Liberal side, the more favourable to the Church would the new compromise be. At the height of the campaign a demonstration of Churchmen was held in the Free Trade Hall, attended by Knox and addressed by leading Tories like Sir William Houldsworth, Balfour, C. A. Cripps and Joynson Hicks. 'It must be said to the Bishop of Manchester's credit', commented the *Manchester Guardian*, 'that he is no mere fair-weather friend of Protectionism...' Now that Protection was sinking, it suggested, Knox had asked for 'a stalwart crew of foundation managers' in order to take off Balfour, Cripps and Joynson Hicks, at least, in the lifeboat of Religious Education.[3] In Liverpool Chavasse's restraint had led some to pine for full-blooded episcopal Toryism in the Knox manner. 'Is there not some danger', wondered the *Courier*, 'of the

---

[1] Comment on Hicks, *M. Courier*, 1 October 1900. For the Manchester South election, see pp. 182–3.
[2] Sandars to Balfour, 19 January 1905, private, BP 49763. For the Church Schools' Emergency League see Sacks, *The Religious Issue in the State Schools*, p. 55.
[3] *M.G.*, 12 January 1906; cf. 13 January 1906 for a report of the meeting and a letter of dissent from Hicks. For Knox's pastoral see *M.G.*, 20 December 1905, 8 January 1906.

earnestness of the laity being chilled by the apparent indifference of their Diocesan?'[1]

When Birrell's Bill was before Parliament Chavasse showed himself a keen opponent and one of the most successful demonstrations of his episcopate was held against it in the Philharmonic Hall. This was not enough for Knox. There had been a great Nonconformist demonstration in London itself and this, he was sure, had made a big impression upon the legislators. Plans were therefore laid for ten thousand Lancashire men to march on the Albert Hall during the Whit Wakes. A nice blend of religion and politics was planned; first the Lord's Prayer, Collects and Creed, then Cripps, Joynson Hicks and F. E. Smith. The effort was prodigious. 'No fewer than thirty-three excursion trains are to be run from the North', it was announced. '. . . The procession will walk, weather fair or foul. It will be led by the Bishops of London and Manchester, who will be supported by many Lancashire ecclesiastics, Lord Mayors, mayors, Aldermen, Councillors and magistrates.'[2] And so it went off – the greatest Whit Walk of all. Knox had reason to be pleased. 'Looking back, as I write, to the Lancashire march in London', he recalled, 'I cannot doubt that it contributed greatly to the preservation of the Balfour Education Act on the Statute Book.'[3]

The Lancashire March was a token of the widespread loyalty in Lancashire to the institutional position of the Church. There was a recognition in both parties that if Religious Education were to be an election issue it would help the Conservatives. Hence the persistent Liberal attempts to achieve some kind of concordat with the Church; hence too the frequent claims by Conservatives that Churchmen should vote on the strength of Religious Education, and the pleas by Churchmen that the demotion of the fiscal issue was the necessary price of such support. When Joynson Hicks was fighting the Manchester North West by-election in 1908 Canon Cleworth and Bishop Knox both appealed to Lord Robert Cecil to come and support him, on the grounds that education, not Tariff Reform, was the issue. When Cecil himself fought Blackburn at the next General Election he drew the protest of the Bishop of Hereford at his partisan use of his position as Secretary of the National Society; and Cecil's own appeal for help in exploiting the schools issue was met with Balfour's languid opinion that 'the subject is so well understood in Lancashire, and there is so much unanimity among the Tory working-men there on the subject, that I should have thought that our candidates would have had an easy time as regards that aspect of our con-

[1] *L. Courier*, 2 January 1906.
[2] *Souvenir of the Great Demonstration at the Albert Hall against the Education Bill*, 8 June 1906, Manchester Broadsheet f/1906/2; cf. Knox, *Reminiscences*, p. 242; Taylor, *Jix*, p. 74.
[3] Knox, *op. cit.*, p. 245.

troversy.'[1] Many Tory churchmen sought salvation in 1910 by resuscitating the cry of the Church in danger. Chavasse had already been led into fierce denunciation of Welsh Disestablishment – 'it was robbing God' – and though his annual letter to his diocese disavowed any intention of urging partisan votes, its tone was such as to earn the plaudits of his erstwhile critics in the Tory press.[2] Again it was Knox who was to the fore with a forthright endorsement of the Unionist Party. His grounds, moreover, were unashamedly political. Although religious education was naturally prominent, and in his manifesto he invoked the memory of the Lancashire March, he was also prepared to counter the criticism of Lord Stanley of Alderley by allusions to Home Rule and the threat to the navy.[3] Debate among Churchmen continued in the correspondence columns of the *Manchester Guardian*, with Canon Hicks as the leading exponent of Liberalism. Since Knox was openly working for the Conservatives and Hicks was busy trying to put a Liberal spoke in the wheel, it was left for Bishop Welldon, the Dean of Manchester, to affirm that electioneering was no essential part of ecclesiastical duties. One outcome was that Liberal fire was turned directly upon the Bishop. After the Liberal victories, Sir Charles Schwann delighted his audience by bidding them 'think of that chamber in the bishop's house where an old gentleman is wiping his streaming eyes with his episcopal petticoats'.[4]

Possibly chastised, the Church leaders made no direct intervention of this kind in the election of December 1910, but the Church did not cease *ipso facto* to be a political agency. There remained an alliance of wealthy Churchmen with the Evangelical masses which paralleled with extraordinary felicity the alliance of the Tory élite with the Conservative working men. Indeed they were usually the same people, at both levels. Democratic Churchmanship, like democratic Toryism, needed and accepted the leadership of the wealthy. Knox found, on going to Manchester, that it had 'a far richer store of wealthy Churchmen' than Birmingham and that 'there were still left some ten churchmen to whom I could appeal at any time for a donation of £1,000 and be sure of a favourable reply'.[5] Chavasse found the same at Liverpool, though there, in religion as in politics, the old families and the workingmen had their mutual suspicions. In Lancashire the working class was characterised by Conservative politics and aggressive Churchmanship; by a certain

---

[1] Telegrams to Cecil from Cleworth and Knox, 14 April 1908, CP 51158; open letter from the Bishop of Hereford, *N.D.T.*, 21 December 1909; Balfour to Cecil, 16 December 1909, copy, BP 49737.

[2] See Chavasse's speech on the Welsh Church to Liverpool Diocesan Conference, *Liverpool D.P.*, 25 November 1909; for his letter and leader comments see *L. Courier*, 1 January 1910.

[3] Knox's reply to the *Church Family Newspaper*, Stanley's letter and Knox's reply, *M.G.*, 22, 23, 27 December 1909; Knox's manifesto, *M. Courier*, 8 January 1910.

[4] Speech after the Poll at the Reform Club, *M.G.*, 17 January 1910.

[5] Knox, *Reminiscences*, p. 220.

racial and religious intolerance; by acceptance of good Tory principles of hierarchy, loyalty, and a solid unquestioning patriotism which could slide into jingoism. It is surely no accident that the Earl of Derby, that lynchpin of Lancashire Toryism, proved to be the great recruiting sergeant during the Great War. A syndrome of loyalties which may have gone back to early conditioning in the Church schools was implicitly recognised by Knox in a comment on the Lancashire March. 'That religious earnestness', he wrote, 'had been fostered in their Sunday-schools. When the War came, this earnestness was evidenced by the attendances of Lancashire regiments at *voluntary* services...They were the first to volunteer for service, and few, alas! far too few, found their way home.'[1]

[1] *Ibid.* p. 245.

4 Cotton

I cannot too strongly emphasise the fact that the cotton trade is the mainstay of all who make their living within a radius of 40 miles from Manchester, no matter what their occupation may be.

Charles Macara, 1906

I

The localisation of the cotton industry remained extraordinarily static. Although it was totally dependent upon imported raw materials, it was not pulled towards its major port; instead, with the completion of the Manchester Ship Canal in 1894, the port moved to the industry which kept to the grits and coal-measure sandstones of Rossendale and the Pennines. Despite favourable humidity, cotton mills were of minimal importance in the area around Liverpool bounded by Southport, St Helens and Warrington.[1] Like mining, the industry was concentrated in definite centres which it dominated. Only two large towns were shared by coal and cotton – Burnley was a cotton town with coal, Wigan a coal town with cotton. And in Wigan few men were employed in textiles; not only was the industry carried on there almost exclusively by women but, unlike a cotton town proper, almost exclusively by single women. The miners sent their daughters but not their wives to the mill. The extent of female employment was, indeed, a good index of the extent to which a town depended upon cotton. In 1901 and 1911 alike around three-quarters of unmarried women in the spinning and weaving towns were at work. For those under the age of twenty-five the figure was around ninety per cent, the token of a virtually universal working-class practice. But it was not just the younger women who were involved; by 1911, in the weaving towns over half of all married women up to the age of forty-five were employed. In response to the industry's growing needs the older women had been 'called up as a veteran reserve'.[2] One effect of the widespread employment of women was that the dependence of the cotton towns upon their staple industry, heavy as it was in terms of the number of men involved, was further accentuated by the presence in the mills of the wives and daughters of the male workers. Further, the whole family was often involved in the work-situation directly, not vicariously through the head of the household. Family

[1] Ogden, 'The geographical base of the Lancashire cotton industry', *Jnl. Textile Inst.*, XVIII (1927).

[2] *Census 1911*, vol. X, pt. I, p. xcvi. All figures for employment have been calculated from the Census figures.

pressures and a common experience combined to form a consistent and set outlook throughout the community.

Originally cotton spinning and weaving (or manufacturing) had increasingly come together, but by the 1880s over three-quarters of the spindles were in the area to the south of Rochdale and over three-fifths of the looms in the area to the north. This tendency towards polarisation continued, and the number of combined spinning and weaving mills showed a commensurate decline; virtually none were built after 1900.[1] By the late nineteenth century, then, spinning was concentrated in an arc of towns to the immediate north and east of Manchester, especially in Bolton and Oldham; and weaving in another arc farther to the north, in Blackburn, Burnley and a number of smaller centres. The weaving towns depended upon female employment. The vast numbers of women employed in the weaving processes in Blackburn and Burnley reinforced the pre-existing degree of specialisation among the men. In Preston, where male spinners actually outnumbered male weavers, they made clear the town's bias towards the weaving rather than the spinning side of the industry. Well-defined though these divisions were in 1901, by 1911 they had been further reinforced. The weaving towns concentrated more on weaving and the spinning towns more on spinning. There was a further distinction between the fine counts spun around Bolton and the coarser counts around Oldham; likewise between the finer and lighter cloth produced around Preston and the Indian goods manufactured in Blackburn and north east Lancashire.

The high degree of specialisation meant that cotton towns were homogeneous to an extent unrivalled except by coal villages. Often the only other industry of at all major proportions was engineering, the presence of which reflected the industry's reliance upon a high degree of mechanisation. Textile engineering was a necessary subsidiary which, as in Bury or Rochdale, might employ large numbers. It was always to a considerable extent dependent upon the fortunes of the cotton industry. It is possible to assess the limits of the direct electoral power of the cotton workers in those towns in which the boundaries of the parliamentary and county boroughs were broadly the same. In 1911 the proportion of occupied males employed in textiles and in the general engineering associated with textiles was just under one half in Blackburn, Burnley and Rochdale; just under two-fifths in Bury and Stockport; and about one-third in Preston.[2] But despite this

---

[1] Chapman and Ashton, 'The sizes of businesses, mainly in the textile industries', *Jnl. Roy. Stat. Soc.*, LXXVII (1913–14), p. 491–2.

[2] Blackburn 47.2 per cent; Burnley 46.8 per cent; Bury 38.0 per cent; Preston 33.1 per cent; Rochdale 48.7 per cent; Stockport 37.1 per cent. The Stockport figure includes hatting. These are proportions of *occupied*, not total, males. Calculated from *Census 1911*, Summary Tables, Table 60.

concentration the cotton workers could not have exercised absolute political control as Table 1 shows.

TABLE 1

	(1) Adult males employed in cotton industry	(2) Total adult males	(3) Electorate 1911
Blackburn	10,780	35,576	22,616
Burnley	9,487	29,591	17,368
Bury	2,550	17,223	10,041
Preston	5,991	30,258	19,729
Rochdale	5,209	25,679	15,229

(1) Adult males in each industry calculated from *Census 1911*, vol. X, pt. II, table 13. Numbers aged 20–1 were taken as identical with those aged 19–20.
(2) Total adult males calculated from *Census 1911*, vol. VII, table 8.

NOTE

Cols (1) and (2) relate to the county borough. There are gross discrepancies between county and parliamentary borough populations of up to 3 per cent in the case of Blackburn, Burnley and Bury; 5.6 per cent in Preston; and 10.1 per cent in Rochdale.

In towns that were as emphatically committed to the cotton industry as were Blackburn and Burnley, cotton workers accounted for less than one-third of all adult males. Even on the most favourable assumptions it is clear that the cotton workers, unlike the miners, could not have relied upon unilateral political action – as indeed their unions always insisted.

The size of firm in the industry seems typically to have been determined by the factors determining the most efficient size of factory. Each mill tended therefore to be an autonomous concern, and only a small proportion of firms were established in more than one district. In the 1880s the most common type of spinning firms had been small private companies but by 1911 joint-stock companies dominated the industry at every size of firm above 20,000 spindles. In cotton manufacturing the joint-stock company had been very much of a rarity in the 1880s and the subsequent fall in the number of private companies was not as great as in spinning. In weaving, unlike spinning, there was virtually no technical lower limit to size, and men with little capital were able to hire 'room and power' in a mill. In Burnley, for instance, this system was common and family businesses survived until relatively late as a normal form of organisation. This was a difference between towns as much as between sections. In Preston, where cotton spinning was important and was the preserve of the Limiteds, forty per cent of the manufacturing firms were joint stock in 1901 and sixty per cent by 1913. Moreover there was a marked trend in this direction in the early twentieth century. Between 1900 and the

War the proportion of public companies among those engaged in weaving in Blackburn increased from one quarter to three-fifths, and in Burnley from one-fifth to one half.[1] There was, then, a slight tendency – if only a slight tendency – for weaving firms to remain family businesses longer than spinning firms. And whatever the position around 1900, there was a far greater uniformity in this respect between the two branches of the industry in 1914.

The cotton industry continued to expand until the Great War. There were, however, few major innovations and it has been argued that cotton output per operative suffered a check at about the turn of the century. Overall employment in the industry showed a small decline at the same time, though at ages fifteen and up it continued to increase marginally. In the early twentieth century it expanded once more (there was an increase in numbers of 14.4 per cent between 1901 and 1911). In the fifty years before the Great War the annual growth of production still averaged $1\frac{1}{4}$ per cent, but there was a tendency for development to become irregular. Booms like that of 1905–7 alternated with depressions like those of 1903–5 and 1909–11. Similarly, exports continued to expand, though with some fluctuations. In 1913 Lancashire wove 8,000 million yards of cloth, of which 7,000 millions were exported – 3,000 millions to India.[2]

In the late nineteenth century India had occupied an even more prominent position in Lancashire's trade, accounting for two-fifths of cloth exports by bulk, at a time when the buoyancy seemed to have left the export market. India was therefore regarded with a particular concern. During times of famine in India, in 1897 and again in 1900, large sums were raised in Lancashire, and the *Manchester Guardian* led the way in making conditions there known in England. Indian fiscal policy attracted the closest interest. It was a principle of Indian taxation that no tariffs should be protective. The financial needs of the Indian Government, however, led it to look upon a textiles duty as a fruitful source of revenue. The Manchester Chamber of Commerce led a campaign against the Indian import duties in 1874, during which it based its foremost argument not on the self-interest of Lancashire but on the welfare of India – 'an unsound commerce is being fostered in that country which will, sooner or later, cause embarrassment and distress to the

[1] See Chapman and Ashton, 'The size of businesses', pp. 470–8, 485–8, for a comparison of the position in 1884 and 1911. The conclusions about developments 1900–14 are based mainly on Barrett's *Directories* of Burnley, Blackburn and Preston, 1899–1915.
[2] For generally optimistic accounts of the cotton industry see Chapman, *The Lancashire Cotton Industry*; Robson, *The Cotton Industry in Britain*; Smith, 'A history of the Lancashire cotton industry', Birmingham Ph.D. thesis; R. E. Tyson, 'The cotton industry', in D. H. Aldcroft, (ed.) *The Development of British Industry and Foreign Competition, 1875–1914* (1968), pp. 100–27; cf. Phelps Brown and Handfield Jones, 'The climacteric of the 1890s', *Oxford Econ. Papers*, n.s., IV (1952), 275.

native capitalists and workmen.'[1] The repeal of the duties in 1882 was therefore a triumph for the pure doctrine of Free Trade, the rigours of which,
in so far as they fell upon the Indian, Lancashire businessmen were prepared
to bear with fortitude.

II

By the end of the nineteenth century, labour relations in cotton had set into
what was to be their final pattern. The origins of associations of operative
cotton workers stretch back to the mid-eighteenth century. Even in the early
nineteenth century the spinners and the weavers showed a divergent
strategy – the spinners essentially self-reliant and opportunistic, the weavers'
strikes in effect general movements of protest – in which it may not be
entirely fanciful to see the symptoms of later political divergence. From the
1840s there was a great development of trade unionism on a more stable and
reliable basis, comprising a northern phase of growth, mainly among the
weavers, from 1840 to 1870, and a southern phase, mainly among the
spinners, from 1870 to the 1890s. The emphasis which both spinners and
weavers put upon piecework meant that skilled permanent officials were
needed to enforce the 'lists' from which the rate for each job was calculated.
In this the Weavers led the way and in 1878 had twenty to thirty paid
officials as against perhaps half a dozen in the Spinners' unions.[2] By 1887
there were nine spinning lists in operation, the two basic ones being the
Oldham and Bolton Lists.

In terms of membership the cotton unions were enormously successful.
In 1889 the overall density of trade-union strength in cotton was about
25 per cent, ranging from about 90 per cent among male spinners to less than
20 per cent among female cardroom operatives. The spinners were the most
fully organised major group of British labour. If the weavers had a lesser
union density, their organisation was nonetheless remarkable considering the
number of women involved, and it has been persuasively argued that their
achievement casts doubt upon the theory of a labour aristocracy as a precondition for mass unionism. For the Spinners were organised as a craft
union, controlling the supply of labour, whereas the Weavers were precursors
of the New Unionism.[3] The Spinners used their opportunities to entrench
their position, largely at the expense of their assistants, the piecers. Piecework rates were paid for the 'mule' as a whole and the spinners took the
lion's share of this. In 1906 the weekly earnings of big piecers were between

[1] Memorial to the Prime Minister, 29 January 1874. See Redford, *Manchester Merchants and Foreign Trade*, II, 26–31; cf. Dey, *The Indian Tariff Problem*, pp. 45–8.
[2] Turner, *Trade Union Growth, Structure and Policy*, pp. 50 ff., 76, 120, 137.
[3] *Ibid.* pp. 110, 138, 157–9, 167.

one third and one half of the spinners', and those of the little piecers between one sixth and one third. Now the little piecer was normally only a youngster, but the big piecer was a grown man only debatably less skilled than the spinner himself. The position *vis-à-vis* trade unionism was peculiarly difficult. On the one hand the piecers' lack of organisation did much to account for their exploitation, yet attempts to form a piecers' union stumbled on the fear, ambition and poverty that were inherent in their position.[1] There were other disparities within the cotton unions. The well-paid sections like the spinners, tapesizers, beamers, twisters, drawers and over-lookers, could afford high weekly contributions which were quite beyond the means of the cardroom operatives and the weavers. It was inevitable then that the attempt of the Cardroom Amalgamation to unite with the Spinners in 1890 should fail.[2] The two unions always had to act together in disputes but their resources were too unequal for fusion.

There was a long tradition of associations of employers as well as of operatives, possibly going back to the days when the two classes were not separate. The revival of trade unionism among the spinners from the 1860s stimulated the formation of employers' organisations, at first local groupings which were jealous of any encroachments, but later more comprehensive bodies, which took final shape in the early 1890s. Around 1890 there were a number of incidents over the question of 'bad spinning'. Early in 1891 a dispute at Stalybridge came to a head and the opportunity was taken of forming the Federation of Master Cotton Spinners' Associations under the leadership of three men who saw the need to extend the employers' system of organisation, Arthur Reyner, J. B. Tattersall and Charles Macara. In May 1892 some sort of settlement was reached in the Stalybridge dispute, but in September the new federation decided to impose a five per cent wage cut and in November 1892 a lockout began. James Mawdsley, who was leading the Spinners, was bitter about the employers' action, but the illness of both Tattersall and Reyner during the final stages meant that there was room for a meeting of minds between him and the more flexible Macara. In March 1893, after an all-night session at the Brooklands Hotel on the outskirts of Manchester, agreement was reached. As well as providing for a compromise settlement on the immediate issue, the Brooklands Agreement set up a com-prehensive negotiating and conciliation system with an appeals machinery.[3]

[1] Chapman, 'Some policies of the cotton spinners' trade unions', *Econ. Jnl.*, x (1900), esp. pp. 469–70; Jewkes and Gray, *Wages and Labour in the Lancashire Cotton Spinning Industry*, Table VI, p. 32; cf. pp. 14, 155.
[2] Webbs, *Industrial Democracy*, p. 105; Clegg, Fox and Thompson, *British Trade Unions*, I, p. 113.
[3] For this episode see Smith, 'A history of the Lancashire cotton industry', pp. 459–515; Macara, *Recollections*, pp. 17–26; Porter, 'Industrial peace in the cotton trade, 1875–1913', *Yorks. Bull.*, XIX (1967), pp. 49–53.

Formative influences

Charles Macara was to occupy a unique position in the Lancashire cotton industry. He was a strong man. In 1884 he had ruthlessly smashed a strike in Ancoats by bringing in blackleg piecers, and had refused to take back the strikers. 'In my long connection with the cotton trade', he placidly recalled later, 'I have always kept constantly before me the rights of labour.' Yet this was not mere humbug, for what Macara really believed in was comprehensive reciprocal organisation. In cotton, he claimed in 1918, 'we are so thoroughly organised as practically to be free from industrial troubles'.[1] It was back to the Brooklands Agreement that Macara looked, for it inaugurated the classical period of labour relations; it was for him the 'reign of law'. The Agreement lasted in effect until the War. Macara remained in office for the employers for twenty years and was unanimously voted into the chair at every conference between masters and men in the 'final court'. Apparently he once said 'that if the people of Lancashire knew and valued Mr James Maudesley as he did they would put up a statue to his memory. The employers in Lancashire had no doubt as to the value of organisation on both sides and of collective bargaining.'[2] Although in its early days there had been some unfavourable appraisals of the Brooklands Agreement and in 1912 it threatened to break down altogether, its very survival made it venerable. Doubtful as it may be whether it conferred any material benefits upon the operatives, yet it acquired an aura which was not dispelled by its practical imperfections. (It would not be the first time that the Lancashire workingmen had been institutionalised within a structure that offered them no obvious advantages.) In 1903, for instance, the *Cotton Factory Times* was applauding Macara as an architect of the Brooklands Agreement, 'The Magna Charta of the Cotton Trade', and calling him a man in whom the operatives could 'place implicit confidence, who is absolutely fair in all his dealings, takes a broad and liberal view of the trade, and is always anxious to consult the welfare of both employers and employed'.[3]

It was the ethos of the unions no less than that of the employers to avoid class hostility. The *Cotton Factory Times* once laid down the dictum: 'Operatives lose nothing by conciliatory actions.'[4] Labour relations in cotton were normally calmer and less embittered than in other heavily unionised industries. There still seems to have been a considerable degree of mobility within the industry, especially on the weaving side; the 'room and power'

[1] Macara, *Social and Industrial Reform*, pp. 29, 31; cf. *Recollections*, pp. 11–15; Mills, *Sir Charles W. Macara*, p. 69.
[2] Quoted by G. H. Wood in the discussion on his paper, Wood, *The History of Wages in the Cotton Trade*, p. 162.
[3] *C.F.T.*, 23, 30 January 1903. For an unfavourable assessment of the effects of the Agreement upon wages see Porter, 'Industrial peace in the cotton trade', pp. 57–9.
[4] *C.F.T.*, 2 June 1905.

system had an attendant instability which was the converse of the opportunity it offered to ambitious operatives. A survey just before the War showed that three-quarters of the employers called themselves self-made men at any rate; and, more reliably, personal inquiry in 'a well-known cotton manufacturing town with 100,000 inhabitants' (surely Burnley?) showed that 63 per cent of the bosses were first generation.[1] One route to the top was through the trade unions. Because of the intricacies of the list system union officials were selected for their technical virtuosity rather than their militancy. Their expertise was as useful to the bosses as to the operatives, and many poachers turned gamekeeper. J. B. Tattersall himself had been an operative and trade union leader. Moreover, this process does not seem to have provoked any necessary sense of betrayal in the unions they left.

The exercise of Mr Howarth's skills [ran the bland report of one such case], are henceforward to be devoted to the interests of the employers in the fine spinning branch...But that does not mean, we take it, that he will by any means stand to oppose the interests he has hitherto espoused...Far from being rare, examples of this kind are happening more or less every day...Good men in the long run get to the top, and it were futile to quarrel with a well-established law of nature.[2]

The dominant mood of the operatives at the end of the nineteenth century was to accept the world as it was. The very process of organisation by which they asserted their class demands served to integrate them into an established industrial structure. The unions were active enough. The number of days lost in cotton disputes is evidence of their militancy. But strikes remained in a sense domestic matters. They were rare, but usually prolonged; they made no immediate impact upon the general public; and picketing was not normally required since in a general stoppage – and most stoppages were general after Brooklands – the employers knew that they must eventually take back the same body of operatives.[3] It was a firmly ordered world, and when the operatives became angry it was often because they considered that their employers' sharp practice had breached an established code; most disputes were about 'bad spinning', 'time-cribbing' and the like. It might have been the Lancashire workingman, that paragon of joiners, of whom Baernreither observed in the late 1880s 'that his world of thought is filled with things clearly practicable and attainable, and that no Utopias find place in it'.[4]

---

[1] Chapman and Marquis, 'The recruiting of the employing classes', *Jnl. Roy. Stat. Soc.*, LXXV (1912), esp. pp. 296–7.
[2] *C.F.T.*, 27 May 1904; cf. 20 October 1905 for another example.
[3] K. G. J. C. Knowles, *Strikes, a study in industrial conflict* (Oxford, 1952), pp. 198, 203, 293; Webbs, *Industrial Democracy*, p. 719 n.
[4] Baernreither, *English Associations of Working Men*, p. 21.

III

Ever since the dalliance of the early unions with Chartism the cotton unions had sought to avoid involvement in party politics. The United Textile Factory Workers' Association (UTFWA) had been set up to deal with Parliamentary matters but even this was not the permanent institution that some modern historians have implied. Chapman, who was a well-informed contemporary observer, explained that the UTFWA 'is constituted when questions of legislation affecting factory life become pressing'.[1] It was, then, only an *ad hoc* forum and could not have been other, for it represented no settled and united political convictions. Even in industrial terms local autonomy and sectional differences fragmented the cotton unions, and politically their divisions reflected also those of the Lancashire working class as a whole. The split between Liberals and Conservatives showed itself most simply as one between weavers and spinners, but it manifested the complexities of many different lines of cleavage. The division may suggest also a distinction between northern Lancashire and south east Lancashire; between weaving villages and conurbations; between small family firms and large joint-stock spinning mills; between quasi-patriarchal labour relations and the depersonalised conflict of capital and labour; between the religious unity of all classes in Nonconformity and the alienation of an Anglican proletariat from Dissenting bosses. It was a palimpsest, with one line of division etched on top of another, sometimes to modify it but often to score it more heavily.

The Webbs calculated that in 1895 three-quarters of the 132,000 members represented by the UTFWA lived in ten constituencies within twenty miles of Bolton. This is, of course, to imply that the electoral position of the unions was stronger than it was; as the *Cotton Factory Times* said, 'textile workers having votes are not sufficiently numerous in any place to enable them to return a member'.[2] The Webbs attributed to the Association the fact that legislation in the cotton trade had been taken further than in any other industry. Under the guise of protecting women and children, the 60-hour week had been enacted in 1850 and was reduced to 56½ hours by Cross's Factory Act of 1875. In 1892 slackening demand set in train another agitation for shorter hours, this time 'in its true colours' and not behind demands for women only. The UTFWA lobbied M.P.s of both parties, who agreed to handle a Bill. But a ballot of the membership in 1894 showed only a small majority in favour of the change – trade had revived – and the measure was dropped.[3]

[1] Chapman, *The Lancashire Cotton Industry*, p. 236.
[2] Webbs, *Industrial Democracy*, p. 258; cf. *C.F.T.*, 12 December 1902.
[3] *Ibid.* p. 338; Clegg, Fox and Thompson, *History of British Trade Unions*, pp. 243 ff.

Although the lobbying methods of the UTFWA had considerable advantages there was some pressure for a scheme of direct Parliamentary representation. Since the Weavers were predominantly Liberal but the Spinners were, at least to a large degree, Conservative, a scheme more subtle than that of the Miners was called for. In 1894 a representative meeting of the UTFWA would probably have taken some action but for the caution of some officials. A ballot that autumn produced a stalemate (which was put down to the influence of the women members) but at a further representative meeting a firm decision to go ahead was made. The choice of two candidates could not be other than Mawdsley of the Spinners and David Holmes, whose word was law at that time among the Weavers. Mawdsley, of course, was a Tory: Holmes a Liberal who had several times been considered as a Lib-Lab candidate. It was proposed, therefore, to approach each of the parties about one candidature. But Mawdsley's refusal to stand apparently led a section of the Spinners to shy away from the prospect of approaching the Liberals alone, and the proposals were rescinded. 'It is evident from what has taken place', commented the *Cotton Factory Times*, 'that the mill workers in Lancashire are still strong adherents to party, and that the time is far distant when the bulk of the operatives will give up their political principles.'[1] The Weavers, it seems, were far more united upon a Lib-Lab solution than were the Spinners upon any alternative to it. When Mawdsley stood at Oldham in 1899 it was not as a Textile Workers' candidate.

On the one occasion that the UTFWA took effective and united political action it was not directed against the employers but was in concert with them. When in 1894 the Government of India was forced to reimpose customs duties it was deterred from including cotton by the hostility to this proposal in Lancashire. In order to meet the objections, a scheme was devised for countervailing duties on Indian production, and in December 1894 a five per cent import duty was imposed on all cotton piece goods and on all yarns above 20s counts. This was balanced by five per cent excise duty on Indian yarns of 20s and above. Lancashire spoke with one voice in denouncing these duties. 'It is deplorable', wrote the *Manchester Guardian*, 'that a Liberal Government should have been brought to such a pass.' And even at such a loyalist gathering as the Annual Meeting of the Manchester Liberal Union the proposer of the resolution of confidence in the Government openly regretted its action on the Indian import duties.[2] The Conservatives naturally

---

[1] *C.F.T.*, 10 April 1895; cf. 8 February 1895, 28 February 1902. For Holmes see obit., *Lancs. D.P.*, 15 January 1906.

[2] Leader, *M.G.*, 18 December 1894; speech by T. C. Abbott, M.L.U. Annual Meeting, 30 April 1895. For the Indian side of this affair see Harnetty, 'The Indian cotton duties controversy, 1894–1896', *Eng. Hist. Rev.*, LXXVII (1962), pp. 684–702; cf. Dey, *The Indian Tariff Problem*, pp. 49–51.

ran the issue hard. R. G. C. Mowbray, the Conservative M.P. for Prestwich, was one of the few in his party who sought to put the Indian Government's case. After a confrontation with a joint deputation of cotton employers and operatives he told the Viceroy that 'for two hours I felt like Mary Queen of Scots being thundered at by John Knox. In fact there is no doubt that, if one does not vote with one's constituents, one may as well save oneself the trouble of standing again by resigning one's seat at once.'[1]

There were really two intellectually respectable arguments which could be mounted against the duties. One was that their necessity stemmed from the workings of the gold standard and that the true remedy lay in bimetallism. The other was that in any case the duties were protective in their incidence, not only upon piece goods (since the excise duty was levied upon the yarn alone) but also upon yarn (since yarn under 20s counts, which escaped duty altogether, did in fact compete with finer counts). The Free Trade campaign therefore comprised a two-pronged attack. When the *Cotton Factory Times* delivered an election homily about the issues affecting the workers it expatiated first upon the currency system, secondly upon the Indian import duties, and only thirdly upon 'working class questions'.[2] The list of supporters of the Bimetallic League reads like a roll-call of cotton union officials. Similarly, the unions and employers were able to form a joint Indian Imports Duties Committee. This body took as its chairman the widely respected cotton manufacturer Tom Garnett, and acted as the trustee of Lancashire's Free Trade conscience. During the General Election of 1895 it enjoyed spectacular success as a pressure group. It extracted an unconditional repudiation of the duties from almost every serious candidate standing for a cotton seat. Three contests attracted particular interest. In Heywood not only had the unfortunate Liberal M.P. voted for the duties but the excuse he offered, that he had done so by mistake, brought him into further disrepute. The return of his opponent, George Kemp, was taken as an emphatic reaffirmation of the sanctity of Free Trade. In Prestwich alone did the issue redound to the advantage of the Liberals, and Mowbray lost his seat. In Oldham there was considerable controversy as to whether the action of Sir John Hibbert, a junior minister in the Liberal Government, in abstaining on the crucial division adequately fulfilled a pledge that he would be found 'on the side of his constituents'. Hibbert lost. His opponents had represented the duties as an impost upon Oldham: 'Look to your bread and butter; vote for Oswald and Ascroft and the repeal of the £100 weekly tax on cotton mills.'[3] This is the argument from self-interest. It is clearly

---

[1] Mowbray to Elgin, 14 February 1895, Harnetty, *loc. cit.*, p. 691.   [2] *C.F.T.*, 28 June 1895.
[3] Conservative poster, *M. Courier*, 15 July 1895. The replies to the Indian Import Duties Committee questions are listed in *C.F.T.*, 12 July 1895. Copies of this circular and those of the UTFWA and the Bimetallic League are in MGP.

consistent with later Tariff Reform propaganda about 'taxing the foreigner'. Now it may be contended that this is merely the honest avowal of the universal intent that India should be sacrificed to Lancashire. But the fact is that when the Lancashire operatives and employers (not squeamish men but men who prided themselves upon being unsentimental, hardheaded and plain-speaking) agreed upon denouncing the duties they did so by espousing a Free Trade doctrine of singular purity. The Manchester Chamber of Commerce succinctly expressed the tenet that 'the duties are bad in principle and are injurious alike to the interest of the Indian people and to the British manufacturing industry'.[1] This was a proposition and a fiscal theory to which not only Liberals, and not only labour representatives, but also Unionists, like Tom Garnett and George Kemp, were to hold when Free Trade came under more general attack.

As far as the immediate question was concerned, in January 1896 the duties were lowered to 3½ per cent and readjusted so as to bear directly upon cloth; and with the return alike of prosperity and rising prices the problems of trade with India slipped out of politics until the War. The Textile Workers seemed, at the time, happy enough with the upshot of this controversy. They counted it a great score that so many M.P.s were pledged to press for the abolition of the Indian duties, and viewed the results of the General Election as 'a surprising justification' for the scotching of their own plan for parliamentary representation. 'If a workman votes for a man with a carriage and pair', read the complacent comment of the *Cotton Factory Times*, 'it is because he believes that his views will be more adequately and efficiently represented by him than by his opponent, who may have to do his business on foot.'[2]

Even when legislation designed to improve conditions in the industry was under consideration the unions and the bosses did not necessarily part company. The UTFWA washed its hands of any attempt to deal with the anomalous 'half-timers', whose position was persistently attacked by those concerned with the education of children torn between school and mill. 'I am convinced from observation of the children', wrote one parson, 'that the present system is very deleterious to them both mentally and physically. They get taken away from their school work, and "broken in" to worse things at the age of 11. How can we cultivate in them a love of reading, after this?' And a Board of Education report confirmed that the system 'goes very far to undo the good effects of school life'.[3] But since, as Hyndman testified, 'the parents themselves strongly supported this ruinous sweating of their

[1] Annual Report for 1896, Redford, *Manchester Merchants and Foreign Trade*, II, 41.
[2] *C.F.T.*, 26 July 1895.
[3] The Rev. J. K. Watkins to C. P. Scott, 17 February 1899, MGP; *Report on the School Training and Early Employment of Lancashire Children*, P.P. 1904, Cd. 1867, p. 22.

own flesh and blood',[1] the UTFWA had to be wary of succumbing before the admitted weight of humanitarian sentiment. 'The Trades Councils and Unions of all kinds ought to oppose this at once', ran the comment on the reform proposal, 'or the schoolmasters will jump on them.'[2] In 1898 James Kenyon, the Conservative M.P. for Bury, initiated a measure which would have taken a modest step towards the abolition of the system and in the following year a Bill proposed the raising of the age limit from 11 to 12 years. In the 1900 General Election Kenyon was forced to protect his flank on this issue; and at Middleton where the Liberal James Duckworth had been one of his supporters the half time question quite overshadowed that of the War. In the latter part of the campaign Duckworth had to devote all his efforts to defending his actions and he and his wife were spat upon by the women of one village. The Liberal press not unnaturally attributed his defeat to the issue, but this would not appear to be the case.[3] The Tory candidates in Burnley and Darwen had no qualms about making political capital out of their vigorous defence of the peculiar institution. In this narrow attitude they were abetted by the unions. While leaders like David Shackleton had no desire to preserve the system, they were the prisoners of their membership. In 1901 they opposed the restrictions on child labour when the Factory Bill was in committee. Nor, on this point, did change come quickly. When, in 1908, the Legislative Committee of the UTFWA boldly voted in favour of excluding twelve-year olds there was a ballot; the vote went against raising the age limit by five to one.[4] Although the leadership recognised that the position was indefensible they deferred for the time being to the brute prejudice of their members.

The instinct of the cotton unions had always been to fear the disruptive effects that the intrusion of party politics into their affairs would cause. They knew that the interests which kept their unions together were not those around which political parties were constituted. They had remained, therefore, on the side-lines, applying pressure *ad hoc* to both parties alike. And few of the political issues of the 1890s, even insofar as they were economic in character, were such as to divide masters and men. The character of

---

[1] Hyndman, *Further Reminiscences*, pp. 61–2.
[2] *C.F.T.*, 30 March 1900.
[3] *M.G.* and *Lancs. D.P.*, 10 October 1900; Hirst, *Alexander Gordon Cummins Harvey*, p. 35; J. A. Bright to C. P. Scott 10 October 1900, MGP; cf. Kenyon's apologia, 'The Half Time Question', 29 September 1900, leaflet in Bury local collection. But Middleton had only been won by the Liberals at a by-election in 1897 and there was a pro-Liberal swing over 1895 similar to that in neighbouring divisions.
[4] Out of 184,691 votes there were 150,723 against and 33,968 in favour. Every section of the industry showed a large majority. *C.F.T.*, 26 February 1909. For their equivocal position on this issue see leader, *C.F.T.*, 6 August 1909; Shackleton's speeches at Haggate, *Lancs. D.P.*, 14 December 1909; and at the Oldham Weavers' Jubilee, and at Clitheroe, *M.G.*, 20 December 1909, 20 January 1910.

politics in the next decade, however, was to be transformed and with it the political orientation of the cotton unions. Although the old methods were used in one last campaign, for a further hour off the working week, it was with a diminished conviction in their efficacy.

In 1899 the Cotton Employers Federation set up a Parliamentary Committee. Partly as a result, the UTFWA, which had not met since 1896, was reconvened to take control of the agitation for the 'twelve o'clock Saturday'. The unions were dissatisfied with the Home Secretary for taking no notice of their views in preparing his Factory Bill of 1900; and the Home Secretary was Sir Matthew White Ridley, one of the most venerable Lancashire Tory M.P.s. 'It is evident that the claims of the workers for better labour surroundings are now receiving less consideration at the hands of the Government and members of Parliament than was the case some years ago', commented the *Cotton Factory Times* sourly, not a year after Mawdsley had dilated to the electors of Oldham on their ability to 'squeeze' the Tories.[1] At the General Election the unions acted to impress their views, and at least one M.P. promptly bent the knee; Rutherford, the notoriously malleable Tory M.P. for Darwen, publicly and unashamedly changed his mind on the 'twelve o'clock Saturday'.[2] A ballot of the UTFWA in the spring of 1901 showed a majority of 95 per cent in favour of the provision, and the Factory Bill of the new Home Secretary, Ritchie, was welcomed. Indeed at one stage he was thought 'likely to make one of the best Home Secretaries we have had since Mr, now Lord, Cross held the position'. But this invocation of the great days of Tory Democracy could not be sustained. Not two months later Ritchie was attempting to jettison the twelve o'clock provision. 'Of late years', read the animadversion on this tergiversation, 'it looks as if our statesmen have been assuming that no attention need be paid to Lancashire operatives.' And the next week it had become clear that the employers 'had nobbled the Home Secretary, and there can be no question about his being a tower of strength to their side'.[3] The old lobbying methods nonetheless took the strain and the Bill was passed with the 'twelve o'clock' provision intact. On the division on that clause thirty-six M.P.s from the north west took part. Although sixteen Conservatives (only two of them holding cotton seats) voted against it, not only did seven Liberals support it but thirteen Conservatives broke ranks and joined them. But since Lancashire Toryism was accustomed to advance the claim that Factory Acts were peculiarly its forte, this was not perhaps a very impressive showing.

[1] *C.F.T.*, 9 March 1900.
[2] *N.D.T.*, 2, 3 October 1900.
[3] *C.F.T.*, 14 June, 9, 16 August 1901.

IV

Although by the turn of the century there was growing dissatisfaction with the existing pressure-group methods of intervention in politics, this did not lead the cotton unions to support the foundation of the L.R.C. This was written off as 'an attempt to saddle another national organisation on the shoulders of that patient carrier of burthens – the British workman'.[1] Not that they were opposed to labour representation as such, though they were resigned to its failure to be implemented in the cotton industry. It was admitted during the General Election that if the workers would vote for labour representation they could 'command that consideration of fair treatment in labour questions which they cannot get under the present system', and David Holmes gave his best wishes to the Labour candidates in Preston and Blackburn.[2] But the traditional methods of lobbying Liberal and Conservative candidates were all that were available in most cases. 'So far as the textile trades are concerned', wrote the *Cotton Factory Times* briskly, 'those employed in them have not yet got to the point where they are willing to sink their differences and to concentrate on labour.' The paper wasted no time in crying for the moon but it was far from happy with the course politics were taking. 'In the last Parliament', it reflected after the elections, 'labour had not too many friends, and in this they will be fewer still, measured by what is termed direct labour representation', and concluded that 'one may be excused for despairing of ever bringing it about'.[3]

It is clear what was desired – trade unionists in Parliament to represent textile interests. The aim itself and the process by which within a few years it was achieved both illustrate the essentially limited ambitions of the unions. Action on Lib-Lab lines would in many ways have suited them well, but such an accommodation had been ruled out by the loyalty of a considerable section to the Conservative party. First, then, the Conservatives were to forfeit the credit which they had painstakingly built up with the cotton operatives over a couple of generations. Disillusionment in matters concerning the cotton industry or trade unionism grew into wholehearted opposition to all the main lines of policy of the Balfour government. This removed a negative check. As far as positive action was concerned, the Weavers were better equipped and more eager to promote an electoral challenge since they did not have the Spinners' workingmen-conservative tradition to overturn; and the influence of socialism in north east Lancashire was the final spur to action. By this stage probably all but a section of the Spinners were prepared

---

[1] *C.F.T.*, 12 January 1900.

[2] *Ibid.* 7 September 1900; David Holmes in *Preston Guardian*, 29 September 1900. Keir Hardie and Philip Snowden were fighting for Labour in the absence of Liberal opposition. See p. 312.

[3] *C.F.T.*, 21 September, 12 October 1900.

to respond to the sympathetic overtures towards labour which the Liberals were now making. And all these tentative readjustments came to a head in the Clitheroe by-election in 1902.

The progress of conversion can be traced in the columns of the *Cotton Factory Times*. In September 1900 it complained that the law on labour disputes was 'twisted to suit the objects of the employers', yet when the Railway Servants had been badly hit by the Taff Vale judgement it commented, 'The worst of it is that the men who get into these legal difficulties at once send round the hat for help to get out. Perhaps it will be all the better for them in the future if they are allowed to get out themselves.' Far from being reconciled to the L.R.C., a fortnight later it again attacked it as being superfluous.[1] Nor did the vials of wrath pour forth when the House of Lords gave the final Taff Vale decision in July 1901. Indeed the tautologous bromide, 'that if pickets can manage to keep on the right side of the law, the Taff Vale decision need have no terrors', was elevated into an expression of policy. The cotton unions did not have to rely upon picketing, and when the Spinners resolved to abandon the practice altogether this example was commended to other trade unions: 'We consider the law is very clear as it now stands, and if members of trade unions will act up to the same when on picket duty there will be no need for filling the pockets of lawyers with fees out of the contributions of the workers.'[2] This proposition, however, was to prove untenable. The Blackburn Weavers' case, which brought Taff Vale very near home, showed that even when no question of intimidation arose picketing could make trade unions liable for civil damages.[3]

Although, then, the editorial line was broadly unsympathetic to the T.U.C. position over picketing, gradually concern over the unions' liability for damages became more apparent. The paper insisted that these were two quite separate issues, and for non-picketing, but rich, unions they were. When the case for damages – 'Taff Vale Number Two' – was eventually decided against the unions in December 1902 the *Cotton Factory Times* no longer doubted where it stood. 'The law as it stands simply cannot be tolerated', it wrote and went on to explain: 'Taff Vale Number One was a breach of the understanding arrived at in 1871, but badly set down in the Act of that year. Taff Vale Number Two is a flagrant wrong.'[4] By this time, however, the former policy of the UTFWA had been overtaken by events with David Shackleton's sudden election as a Labour M.P.

Early in 1902 it was noted that the Weavers had again taken up the question of Parliamentary representation. The attitude of the UTFWA as a

---

[1] *Ibid.* 7 September, 16, 30 November 1900.
[2] *Ibid.* 30 August, 13 September 1901.
[3] See Bealey and Pelling, *Labour and Politics*, pp. 78 ff.
[4] *C.F.T.*, 26 December 1902.

whole was more cautious; everyone recalled the fiasco of 1895. How far it was a desire for sectional rather than pure 'labour' representation may be judged from the *Cotton Factory Times*'s comment that 'it would certainly be advantageous for the cotton operatives to have representatives in the House of Commons who thoroughly understand the technicalities of their work, and who have worked at the trade themselves'.[1] Little wonder then that when in June 1902 a vacancy in the Clitheroe division offered the opening for a Labour candidate, the Weavers were uninterested alike in a socialist propagandist or a Lib-Lab from another union: they wanted their own man, David Shackleton. There was a strong socialist following in the Clitheroe division but Shackleton was not of their number; he had indeed been ready to come forward as a Liberal candidate and had spoken from Liberal platforms at the previous election.[2] The Socialist element in fact would take no active part in running Shackleton. Philip Stanhope who, as the possible Liberal candidate, was attempting to avoid an open clash, found that 'the real trouble is that the labour movement springs from the Weavers' Unions and they have funds and a wonderful organisation. The whole thing is a great surprise to everyone, but there it is.'[3] The Labour leaders were, as he said, 'hopelessly intractable', and that because only one man fitted their bill. Had they wanted a socialist no doubt they could have settled for Stanhope; but since they wanted a weaver it had to be Shackleton. Once it was clear that Shackleton's candidature was serious, Campbell-Bannerman and Herbert Gladstone used their influence with the local Liberals to ensure him a clear run; although this was ill received in Clitheroe itself all the Lancashire Liberal M.P.s agreed that Shackleton could not be opposed.[4] On 1 August 1902 he was returned unopposed as Labour M.P. In its issue of that date the *Cotton Factory Times* declared that the UTFWA's endorsement of him 'indicated a change in the opinions of the textile operatives in regard to labour representation in Parliament'. And from this point onward all doubts as to the wisdom of mixing trade unionism and politics disappeared.

Thereafter the *Cotton Factory Times* made constant propaganda for the L.R.C., which only two years previously it had deprecated. Now it wrote of 'The Labour Representation Crusade'. During the ballot that was subsequently held it urged members to vote in favour of affiliation to the L.R.C.

[1] *Ibid.* 28 February 1902.

[2] Gladstone's diary, 19 July 1900, HGP 46483 f. 74; meeting at Oswaldtwistle, *N.D.T.*, 5 October 1900. There is an excellent account of the Clitheroe by-election in Bealey and Pelling, *Labour and Politics*, ch. 5, pp. 98–124.

[3] Stanhope to Gladstone, n.d. (July 1903), HGP 46059 f. 249.

[4] Gladstone's diary, 10 July 1902, HGP 46484 f. 17. This source was not available to Bealey and Pelling. The record of this crucially important interview is the main respect in which it supplements their account.

and disparaged the 'twelve o'clock Saturday' agitation – the last success of the old methods – claiming that it had been lucky in being pressed near a General Election and when a Factory Bill was already in the pipeline. In the ballot there were heavy majorities both for Parliamentary representation and for a levy, even without the votes of the Clitheroe, Colne and Padiham Weavers who were already paying a levy to support Shackleton. The Weavers voted nearly five-to-one in favour of affiliation; more surprisingly, the supposedly Conservative Spinners voted by more than three to one in favour.[1] It was decided to put up two further candidates and the necessity of doing so in places heavily unionised by different trades was stressed. Not surprisingly Bolton and Oldham were selected. Oldham, it was said, had never been tested by labour – Mawdsley being renounced as 'distinctly a party man' – and Bolton had shown encouraging municipal results. By May 1903 two candidates were in the field, A. H. Gill at Bolton and Thomas Ashton at Oldham, both of them Spinners' officials.

Opposition to the legal attack on the trade unions continued to provide the main impetus behind these candidatures. Shackleton's prominent part in pressing the Trades Disputes Bills in Parliament dramatised the issue and warnings were solemnly given that Lancashire M.P.s who opposed the Bill would not be forgiven. (The paying off of these scores at the 1906 Election was to be duly celebrated.) The attitude of the UTFWA towards party politics had been defined at the meeting which decided to affiliate to the L.R.C. It was agreed that 'their policy should be a broad one and embrace all the practical items in the general Labour policy'.[2] This formula of concurrence, with its proviso about 'practical items', was in fact that increasingly being employed by those Liberals who looked in the new phase of party politics towards a progressive alliance.

The cotton unions were swiftly emerging from their customary neutral corner. Labour victories in Parliamentary and municipal elections were welcomed, whether or not there was any connexion with cotton. At the time of the Preston by-election in May 1903, however, the cotton workers took a more sectional view. The UTFWA had decided to contest the seat and felt that their own man would have been a more appropriate candidate than

---

[1] *C.F.T.*, 6 February 1903. The figures were:

	In favour	Against
Cardroom Workers	14,173	4,573
Spinners	9,978	3,057
Beamers, Twisters and Drawers	2,509	377
Weavers	54,637	11,352
Overlookers	1,210	170
Bleachers and Dyers	1,647	327
TOTALS	84,154	19,856

[2] *C.F.T.*, 6 February 1903.

Formative influences

John Hodge of the Steel Smelters whom the L.R.C. settled upon. But Hodge was endorsed by the UTFWA and the example of the secretary of the Preston Spinners resigning from the committee of the Conservative Working Men's Club in order to support him was followed by others.[1] Apart from such specialised issues as Shackleton's attack upon 'time-cribbing', and such safe ones as old age pensions, the *Cotton Factory Times* also came out against 'slavery in the Transvaal' and in favour of the taxation of land values. And with Tariff Reform too bringing them into a strongly anti-Conservative position, the cotton unions were strong partisans in the 1906 Election. Their hopes of contesting three seats were dashed by Ashton's retirement at Oldham, and the vacancy in this obvious cotton seat was left to the Liberals in 1910 also. The UTFWA intervened in all cotton constituencies to ensure that its members' votes did not go astray, and Shackleton and Gill fought successful campaigns as Labour candidates. This was a political revolution. The union report to the Tory Spinners in Tory Preston was an attack upon Tory policies.[2] And there were difficulties, as had always been forecast should the unions engage in politics. At Burnley criticisms were levelled at the L.R.C. and it had to be denied that the Weavers' Association was being broken up through contact with it.[3] It was unfortunate, too, that by mistake the initial UTFWA circular asked support for the Trades Disputes Bill as amended by its Conservative opponents instead of in the original draft.[4]

The importance of the cotton unions' new political strategy should be related not so much to their own parliamentary representatives as to the general shift in Lancashire from Toryism to the acceptance of progressive M.P.s. Of the UTFWA's own M.P.s, Gill continued to represent Bolton, but Shackleton resigned in 1910 upon his appointment as Senior Labour Adviser at the Home Office. There had been rumours of such an appointment the previous year and while his loss was a considerable blow to the Labour movement in Lancashire, the ethic of the cotton unions accepted such defections without bitterness. The choice of a successor lay between the Weavers' secretaries of Nelson, Colne and Burnley, while both the Socialists and the Liberals also threatened to intervene. Eventually Albert Smith of the Nelson Overlookers was chosen. He was Chairman of the Labour Executive and though he came from a Tory family had never been associated with any party but Labour. Smith was elected in a straight fight with the

[1] *M.G.*, 2, 9, 13 May 1903; *C.F.T.*, 8 May 1903. For the Preston by-election see below, p. 319.
[2] *Lancs. D.P.*, 29 December 1905.
[3] *N.D.T.*, 5 December 1905.
[4] Interview with J. Cross, *Lancs. D.P.*, 10 January 1906. The Conservative candidates at Blackburn and Preston made much of the fact that they had replied favourably to the UTFWA's question, only for its terms to be changed in order to make them reply negatively.

94

Conservatives.[1] There were several attempts to see that the Card Room workers should have their own M.P. so that the three largest sections of the industry should each be represented. In October 1909, therefore, the candidature of W. H. Carr was promoted at Stalybridge, and his name was also mentioned in connexion with Accrington, though the UTFWA's endorsement of this idea seems to have been based upon confusion of the two. This betokens a lack of coordinated activity which events in Stalybridge confirm; Carr was withdrawn owing to other unions proving unenthusiastic.[2] And though he contested Preston in December 1910 he did not win. On this occasion Carr fought in double harness with a Liberal, as Gill did all along, and the cotton workers at large were fairly clearly committed to the Liberal candidates in other seats. This alliance was cemented in 1910 by the Osborne Judgement, after which writs were taken out against all sections of the UTFWA.[3] For the cotton unions political neutrality was not only dead but damned.

V

The pattern of booms and slumps gave a certain instability to the industry's basic prosperity. The causes of bad trade were least contentious when it could be put down to difficulties in the supply of raw material. The most notorious example of this kind occurred in 1903–4 when Daniel Sully, an American speculator, managed to corner the new crop. Short-time working had to be organised in Lancashire and it was asserted that the distress was as acute in many districts as during the American Civil War. Restriction of output continued for seventeen weeks. This episode highlighted the need for organisation to avoid such risks. An international organisation of cotton manufacturers was formed and the British Cotton Growing Association, which had been founded in 1902, came into its own.[4] The Association's aim of promoting cotton-growing within the British Empire was universally regarded as a worthy objective, although its activities made no serious impact upon the industry before the War. Both Balfour and Churchill took pains to stress their respective parties' warm interest in the scheme but when the matter was pressed neither party had the face to claim exclusive credit. At Oldham, for instance, the Conservative cotton spinner Stott admitted that he had issued placards saying, 'Vote for Hilton and Stott and Support

---

[1] For previous rumours see *Lancs. D.P.*, 23 December 1909. For the reception of Shackleton's appointment see *C.F.T.*, 18 November 1910; cf. I.L.P. meeting at Nelson, *Lancs. D.P.*, 21 November 1910. For Smith's politics see his speech, *Lancs. D.P.*, 1 December 1910. For the S.D.P. and Liberal roles, see below, pp. 325 n., 331.

[2] *N.D.T.*, 17, 18 November 1909; *C.F.T.*, 10 December 1909.

[3] *C.F.T.*, 4 November 1910.

[4] *C.F.T.*, 18 September, 16 October 1903, 11 November 1904; Macara, *Recollections*, pp. 34–42.

and help British Cotton growing', but added that he had no objection to his opponents issuing similar bills since all were agreed that it was an absolute necessity for Lancashire.[1] Although tempted, then, the Conservatives did not claim Empire Cotton as an adjunct to Tariff Reform.

Once fiscal policy had become a central electoral issue the economic fluctuations of the cotton industry took on fairly direct political overtones. When Tariff Reform was launched in 1903 there was indeed some evidence that cotton might go. In their end-of-year surveys the employers' paper compared the industry to 'a ship without compass and without rudder, driven hither and thither by every wind and current', and the operatives' paper called the previous year 'one of the worst that the cotton trade of Lancashire has ever experienced'.[2] Though both sides of the industry agreed that trade was bad, both sides also agreed that Tariff Reform was no answer. On 21 July 1903 a joint conference of fifteen employers' representatives and nine trade union officials was held in Manchester in order to consider Chamberlain's proposals. Macara, who took the chair, made a speech in favour of Free Trade, as did Tom Garnett, the former chairman of the Indian Import Duties Committee, and Thomas Ashton, the secretary of the Oldham Spinners'. A resolution was then put:

This Conference of the Cotton Employers' Parliamentary Association and the United Textile Factory Workers' Association (representing the whole cotton trade as employers and operatives), firmly convinced that the great cotton industry of the United Kingdom owes its pre-eminence to and can only be maintained by the policy of Free Trade, pledges itself to oppose to the utmost of its power any proposals which, by imposing taxes on food or raw materials and so raising the cost of production and living, will cripple it in its already severe struggle to uphold its position in foreign markets, by which 80 per cent of its productions are absorbed.

Albert Simpson, one of the employers, sought to amend this but was supported by only one of his colleagues. The resolution was therefore passed with two dissentients, though two other employers seem to have abstained.[3]

The action of this gathering was to be the subject of controversy for many years. In the authorised version it was the considered verdict of the cotton industry upon Tariff Reform. The *Cotton Factory Times*, for instance, declared at once that 'no doubt can now remain as to the attitude of the cotton trade in regard to Mr Chamberlain's proposals... This is no question

---

[1] Stott at Oldham, *Oldham Chron.*, 1 January 1910; cf. letter from Balfour to Gerald Arbuthnot, *L. Courier*, 1 December 1910; Sandars to Balfour, 11 October 1905, BP 49764; Ronald Hyam, *Elgin and Churchill at the Colonial Office. The Watershed of the Empire-Commonwealth* (1968), pp. 451–6.

[2] *Textile Mercury*, 26 December 1903; *C.F.T.*, 1 January 1904.

[3] This account is based on *M.G.*, 22 July 1903; *Textile Mercury*, 25 July 1903; letter from Albert Simpson, *The Times*, 4 January 1910.

of ordinary politics. So far as the cotton trade is concerned, it involves our very existence.'[1] But four main charges were subsequently levelled by the Tariff Reformers, with the object of destroying the credentials of this highly damaging resolution. First, it was said that the employers were not properly represented since some of those present were only officials. But it is not disputed that ten or eleven were actually in business and it must be remembered that this was the body which was accustomed to speak for the employers whether in wage negotiations or in lobbying M.P.s. Secondly, it was held that, even so, the conference had no mandate to pronounce on the question insofar as it related to a tax not on cotton but on food. This is quite true. Thirdly, it was later implied that the resolution had hurriedly been sprung upon a routine meeting of the Parliamentary Committee. But the contemporary evidence plainly shows that this was a specially convened joint conference. Fourthly, it was asserted that the resolution had been passed under the mistaken impression that a tax upon raw cotton was proposed. Whether the conference seriously believed this is unclear but it is true that the *Textile Mercury* soon afterwards got Chamberlain to repudiate the suggestion.[2]

There is really no doubt about the operatives' attachment to Free Trade. But while it seems fairly certain that a large number of the employers also preferred it on business grounds, they had more difficulty in reconciling this with their politics. In 1906 events conspired to allay their doubts. Not only was the Liberal policy reassuringly undefined but the upswing in trade made its main principle of preserving Free Trade particularly attractive. In the years 1905–7 profits in the cotton spinning industry were running at invigoratingly high levels. There was indeed a large increase in the number of spindles owing to the 'mill-building mania' which was a manifestation of the boom mentality.[3] In 1906 very few cotton bosses were disposed to challenge the assumption that, whatever the attractions of Tariff Reform for other industries, the prosperity of cotton depended upon the maintenance of Free Trade. In the cotton towns the Tariff Reform argument failed by default. Macara was allowed to pontificate on behalf of the industry in advocating votes for Free Traders, and the resolution of 21 July 1903 was frequently invoked. Of the cotton manufacturers who stood for Parliament on this occasion only Thomas Stuttard at Eccles seems to have come into open

[1] *C.F.T.*, 24 July 1903.
[2] *Textile Mercury*, 1 August 1903. The main attacks upon the credentials of the conference are developed in the letters from J. H. Butterworth, *M.G.*, 22 July 1903, from William Thompson and from Simpson, *The Times*, 28 December 1909, 4 January 1910.
'Campion, 'Pre-war fluctuations of profits in the cotton spinning industry', *Jnl. Roy. Stat. Soc.*, XCVIII (1934), pp. 627, 631; Chapman and Ashton, 'The sizes of businesses', pp. 551, 555; *C.F.T.*, 26 May 1905.

collision with Macara and to have tried to make out the Tariff Reform case for cotton, though Albert Simpson, now in retirement, protested at Macara's use of his position for political ends.[1]

The operatives stood by Free Trade not only in 1906 but in 1910. It was generally held that cotton workers were fairly prosperous in the early twentieth century.[2] It is true that in no other industry had wages shown such a great proportional advance since 1850, but while it seems that cotton workers were better off in real terms in 1900 than they had been ten years previously, they were less well off ten years later. The list prices were the most obvious factor (though not necessarily the most important) in determining earnings. The Weavers agreed on an increase of $7\frac{1}{2}$ per cent in 1905, to be implemented over the following two years. In 1905 too the Spinners negotiated a 5 per cent interim increase which was granted outright in 1906. 'No one who understood the situation at all', commented the *Cotton Factory Times*, 'could believe that the employers would deny their workpeople such a modest participation in the abnormal profits which the trade was known to be reaping.'[3] At the time of the 1906 Election, then, Free Trade was filling the pockets of both capitalist and worker, the latter, naturally, with more restraint. And in 1907 the Spinners climbed another five per cent to put them ten per cent above the net list. But the good times were coming to an end. After a lockout in 1908 the Spinners lost five per cent, and at that level the lists remained until the War. This, however, was not the difficulty – they were still five per cent above the net list – but the extensive short-time working of 1909–10 made nonsense of the high list prices. Temporarily in 1908, and for a prolonged period in 1909–11, earnings per head plunged to levels ten and sometimes twenty per cent below those of 1907, before recovering to a relative stability. The employers too felt a cold wind and made heavy losses in 1909 and 1910.

Clearly 1910 was not such an easy year as 1906 in which to defend the *status quo*, and Free Trade could no longer be represented as the non-partisan policy of the whole industry. Macara again entered the battle, notably by sending two open letters which were widely publicised. One he sent to Tom Garnett, the chairman of the Free Trade League, recalling Garnett's part in the conference of 21 July 1903 and referring back to the arguments

[1] See letters from Macara, *M.G.*, 3 January 1906, *The Times*, 12 January 1906; letter from Simpson, *M. Courier*, 6 January 1906.

[2] See Smith, *Parsons and Weavers*, pp. 55–7; Bowker, *Lancashire under the Hammer*, pp. 92–3; Rowley, *Fifty Years of Work without Wages*, p. 4.

[3] *C.F.T.*, 27 April 1906. On the changes in wage rates and earnings see Wood, *The History of Wages in the Cotton Trade*, pp. 3–4, 147–8; Jewkes and Gray, *Wages and Labour in the Lancashire Cotton Spinning Industry*, pp. 19, 198; Smith, 'A history of the Lancashire cotton industry', pp. 694–711; cf. table of profits and losses per £1,000 of paid-up share capital, Campion, 'Pre-war fluctuations of profit', p. 627.

then advanced. The other he sent to Arnold Morley, President of the Free Trade Union, and in this he emphasised that the present depression in cotton was worldwide. Unlike 1906, Macara was now challenged on virtually every point, from the substance of his arguments, to the credentials of the 1903 conference, and his own right to speak for the industry. He was writing letters, said Bonar Law, 'which led one to suppose that he not only represented the cotton trade, but that he was the incarnation of the cotton trade'.[1] The Manchester millowner William Thompson took the lead in coordinating the Conservative counter-offensive, though this never quite managed to live up to the promises that it would scotch Macara's claims. Macara did not lack support. A manifesto signed by all the cotton union leaders was put out by the Free Trade League and a cotton trade manifesto specifically endorsing his position was launched in Manchester. In December 1910 there was another battle of manifestoes. After a Free Trade meeting in Manchester at which Macara said that he hoped that no-one would be gulled by Balfour's pledge not to implement Tariff Reform without holding a referendum first, a manifesto was prepared on the lines of that in January, and by polling day it had collected 1,200 signatures. None of these documents seems to have been very rigorously compiled and it is difficult to estimate the balance of feeling. The important point is that there now was a balance: that Conservative employers would no longer let the Free Traders have it all their own way.

All the signs, then, are that *most* of the cotton bosses would have preferred Free Trade to Tariff Reform; but *many* of them were not prepared to take this preference as far as supporting the Liberals. The claims of the Conservative party had an increasingly strong pull upon them. Their paper, the *Textile Mercury*, had preached a cautious policy of retaliation for twenty years, and it was its editor, Edward Marsden, who was one of the moving spirits behind Balfour's pledge.[2] 'For the most part, cotton employers are sound', wrote a Free Trader in 1908; 'but blind and ignorant partisanship appears here and there to be loosening the bonds.'[3] In 1910 a Cotton Trade Tariff Reform Association was formed. Moreover, cotton employers were again emerging as Conservative candidates. In 1900 many of the cotton towns were represented in Parliament by local employers of a Conservative persuasion: men like William Tomlinson at Preston, Sir Harry Hornby and Sir William Coddington at Blackburn, William Mitchell at Burnley, George Kemp at Heywood, and James Kenyon at Bury. In 1906 only Hornby was

---

[1] Bonar Law in Manchester South West, *M.G.*, 14 January 1910. Macara disingenuously claimed that he was acting as a private individual; see his letter, *The Times*, 12 January 1910. Macara's main interventions were a statement published 8 December 1909; the open letters, 10, 23 December 1909; and 'a final word', 14 January 1910.

[2] Gollin, *The 'Observer' and J. L. Garvin*, pp. 258–9; cf. *Textile Mercury*, e.g. 13 January 1906.

[3] Letter from William Tattersall, *The Spectator*, 4 April 1908.

re-elected – as a Unionist Free Trader. Coddington was defeated, Kemp had crossed the floor, the rest retired. Apart from Thomas Stuttard at Eccles, no cotton employer of any standing came forward as a Tariff Reformer in 1906. By 1910, however, the Conservatives were able to bring out John Wood in Stalybridge, Colonel J. Craven Hoyle in Rossendale, P. S. Stott and A. E. Wrigley in Oldham, and Colonel G. Hesketh in Bolton, while (the next best thing) the cotton spinner Walter Pilling was chairman of the Rochdale Conservative party. Pilling loudly asserted that hundreds of cotton manufacturers were as strongly in favour of Tariff Reform as he was himself. 'That might be so', an opponent admitted revealingly, 'but he thought that they had simply taken that course in following their leaders.'[1] It is usually implied that the cotton employers were Liberal because they were Free Traders. By 1910 many of them were Tariff Reformers because they were Conservatives.

[1] Speeches by Walter Pilling and Harold Shawcross at Rochdale, *M.G.*, 30, 31 December 1909. Shawcross was also a cotton spinner. It is true that Hesketh stood as a Free Trader – the only Unionist to do so. All the examples quoted above are of *bona fide* local employers and do not include candidates who had more tenuous connexions with the industry, like Micholls (Accrington, 1900), Hartley (Oldham, 1906), or Blayney (Clitheroe, 1910).

PART THREE
THE TERMS OF THE CONTEST

Electoral style was related to the electoral system. This was far from democratic, and as the Liberals became increasingly dependent on working-class votes they were increasingly penalised. In order to function efficiently, the system relied on the efforts of the parties; the franchise was therefore largely reserved for known party men, and the apathetic fringe was very small. The Liberals recognised that they ought to reform the system but lacked the will to break through the complications, notably woman suffrage, which bedevilled the question. As it was, popular interest in elections, whether measured by turnout or palpable enthusiasm, ran at a high level. The whole community participated in the campaign and the public reception of the candidates provided a surprisingly accurate guide to the mood of the electorate.

5 The pale of the Constitution

We have got now a democratic suffrage, but not so democratic as it ought to be – a suffrage which will not be truly democratic until we have not only abolished plural voting but we have got rid of many of the restrictions and technicalities which prevent access to the register from being as easy as it ought to be.

Asquith, December 1910

I

After 1885 the checks upon democracy were more real than apparent. They were, however, effective enough to invalidate the imputation of a constituency's political representation to its general composition. For example, in 1911 Oldham elected a Conservative M.P. in a three-cornered by-election. Those who voted for him amounted to no more than 5.8 per cent of the population, and 21.5 per cent of the adult males. Although precise figures are only obtainable in Census years, it seems plain that in a three-cornered contest, like that at Manchester South West in January 1910, the winner had the support of about 17 per cent of the adult males; and even in a straight fight, like that at Walton in December 1910, F. E. Smith was elected by the votes of less than a quarter of the adult men in his division. In practice, then, household suffrage meant that the effective political decisions lay in the hands of the few rather than the many. Not that there was any shortage of franchises. In the counties there were three main ways of becoming enfranchised by reason of ownership, plus one through lease-holding; in both counties and boroughs there were franchises for ten-pound occupiers, inhabitant householders and lodgers; and in the boroughs there were certain reserved rights, the most important being those of freemen. Since under certain conditions an ownership vote in the county could be established on behalf of borough property, the existence of a class of 'outvoters' was perhaps the major anomaly resulting from the retention of the obsolescent distinction between counties and boroughs. Otherwise the composition of the electorate in both types of seat was broadly similar.

Most adult men who failed to become voters had been prevented from doing so by one of five obstacles: outright debarment, the qualifying period, the procedure for registration, the difficulties of the lodger franchise, or the ordeal of the revision courts. Each of these provisions separately had the effect of keeping poor men off the register, and in conjunction they weighted the whole electoral system heavily in favour of the wealthy. The simplest obstacle was the disqualification of various classes of person, notably paupers. Those disqualified in this way have been estimated at five per cent of the adult male population in 1908.[1] The period of qualification for the franchise was a more complex problem because it had differential effects. The qualifying day was 15 July, but while in the case of the ownership vote only six months tenure (or in certain circumstances none at all) was required, in the case of occupiers and lodgers twelve months occupation was necessary. Then there was registration itself, which was undertaken annually by the Poor Law overseers. Ownership electors had to claim initially but once on the register were entitled to remain there indefinitely unless struck off by the revising barrister. Lodgers, however, had to claim annually. In theory, occupiers had the easiest part since they were put on the roll by the overseers and had to claim only if they had been left off the occupation list; but in practice the overseers' lists were far from perfect and initial exclusion made subsequent entry more difficult. This system gave the overseers considerable power to decide, usually on the basis of liability for rates, whether a man was or was not an occupier. On this point there was no consistent practice. It is pretty clear that, as Sir Charles Dilke insisted, there were different assumptions about 'houses' and 'heads of households' in different parts of the country, and while the various 'latch-key' cases had considerable effect in London they do not seem to have done so in Lancashire.[2]

The position of the lodger was even less clear. While his right to the franchise was admitted, he was not encouraged by the system of registration. There was no generally accepted definition of a lodger, and since this franchise was intended to be kept separate from that of an occupying tenant, a man had to be sure that he claimed under the right qualification.[3] The

---

[1] Rosenbaum, 'The General Election of 1910 and the bearing of the results on some problems of representation', *Jnl. Roy. Stat. Soc.*, LXXIII (1910), p. 476. For electoral law my account relies upon *Rogers on Elections*, vol. I (17th edn 1909). For an excellent survey of several problems raised in this chapter see Blewett, 'The franchise in the United Kingdom, 1885–1918', *Past & Present*, 32 (December 1965).

[2] Dilke in discussion, Rosenbaum, *loc. cit.*, p. 521. 'The Latch Key decision will not trouble us here I am glad to say', reported the Conservative agent for Ashton. J. C. Buckley to Max Aitken, 14 September 1911, Beaverbrook P.; and see discussion in *M.G.*, 1 August 1911; cf. Thompson, *Socialists, Liberals and Labour*, pp. 71–2. At Devonport a new revising barrister with a different conception of a 'householder' caused the electorate to grow from 9,000 to 15,000 between 1902 and 1904. Sir Joseph Leese to Gladstone, 24 January 1904, HGP 46017 ff. 173–4.

[3] For instance, if a man did not qualify as a lodger because his landlord did not have the requisite control over the premises, he might often *ipso facto* qualify as a rateable tenant – but would nonetheless remain disfranchised for the current year through making the wrong claim. The revising barrister's summing up in the case of John Umpleby at Blackburn in 1900 illustrates both the importance and the impossibility of holding to nice distinctions. 'You are not your daughter's tenant', Umpleby was told, 'because you did not agree to pay rent...And you are not her lodger, because you furnish the whole of the money for the establishment. If anything

lodgings had to be of ten pounds annual value, reckoned, it seems, as 5*s*. or 6*s*. a week furnished.[1] New claims had to be fully established and although in subsequent years the onus of proof was shifted on to any objector, the claim remained an essential preliminary to appearance on the old lodgers' list.

All these difficulties were compounded by the operation of the revision courts which sat in the autumn. By this stage the parties were committed to the hilt; indeed the work of the revising barrister was largely to adjudicate between the party agents who claimed votes for known supporters and objected to the rest. Many claimants were objected to by both sides, presumably because their politics were unknown to either. Such men were unlikely to surmount an objection since they had no friend at court. There was a premium, then, on party affiliation. Furthermore, since an objection could best be countered by the production of a declaration witnessed before a magistrate, the resources of party were also extremely useful in bringing defendants and J.P.s together. When both parties were well organised, as at Blackburn in 1900, the proceedings became a dreary ritual:

> Liberals object to the claims of so many hundred Conservatives, and Conservatives challenge the qualifications of so many hundred Liberals...The process is intolerably tedious. Try eight or ten hours of it, and the dry disputations and contradictory wranglings will convince you that what is urgently needed is a bill for the suppression of party agents and such a simplification of the Registration Laws as will abolish their occupation for ever and for ever.[2]

Clearly neither side was gaining any net advantage from the expenditure of a lot of money. But what when one party was much better organised than its opponents? In the Liverpool area the Liberals' weakness was as much a weakness in the revision courts as anywhere else. 'Their opponents had decided not to contest the seat', declared the Chairman of Bootle Conservative Association in 1900, 'on the ground that the register looked rather bleak. In his opinion, a great many elections were won in the revision courts, and at the last revision of the voters' lists they had made a gain of over 700.'[3] Success on this scale could only be achieved in a division that was not hotly contested; in turn it made an election unlikely. But in marginal seats the prizes were even more valuable and the efforts to persuade and

---

you are a lodger, and yet I don't think you are a lodger. I don't know what you are (laughter)... Your case will no doubt be considered by the Legislature at some time or other, but at present I have no power to give you a vote. I am very sorry.' *Blackburn Wkly Telegraph*, 15 September 1900.

[1] See the leaflet, 'Are you a Labour Voter', Gorton local collection.

[2] 'The Idler', *Blackburn Wkly Telegraph*, 15 September 1900. There is a good description of the parties' role in registration in Ostrogorski, *Democracy and the Organisation of Political Parties*, I, 375–82.

[3] T. Stanley Rogerson, Bootle, *Liverpool D.P.*, 26 September 1900. It was the same story at Ormskirk, *L. Courier*, 28 December 1905; but cf. *Liverpool D.P.*, 30 December 1905 for Liberal efforts in Southport.

cajole the revising barrister were one of the high points of a party agent's year. 'I did exceptionally well with the new Barrister', wrote one in 1912, 'and got all my Lodgers through without difficulty. I had of these a clear gain of 34. The question I feared he would spring upon us, was unfounded, and at a little dinner I gave him I explained our position satisfactory.'[1]

The records of the Manchester Liberal Federation clearly illustrate the parties' role in registration through the figures they contain for twelve of the years in the period 1886–1913. In 1886 the new system had hardly had time to settle down, as the incomplete figures for five of the six divisions show.

TABLE 1. *Results of revision, 1886**

		Number	Proportion sustained (%)	Net effect on Liberal strength
Objections	by Liberals	2,552	74	+1,892
	by Conservatives	3,861	76	−2,919
Claims	by Liberals	5,116	16	+ 794
	by Conservatives	4,795	10	− 470

* Full returns for all divisions except South, M.L.U. Minutes, 25 October 1886. The other years' registration for which the M.L.U. and later M.L.F. Minutes give figures, more or less useful, are 1895–1900, 1904–5, 1907, 1911 and 1913. These are the dates of revision and were the basis of the following years' registers.

Both parties, but especially the Liberals, concentrated more on claiming than on objecting. Although the Liberals made not only more claims but better claims (judged by the number upheld) the balance of success favoured the negative approach. The Tories can hardly have been oblivious to the fact that to gain a relative advantage of 3 votes they must make 30 claims – or 4 objections. Whatever the reason, by the 1890s the parties were relying more upon objections to do their work. At this time it was normal for the parties to object to over ten per cent of those on the overseers' lists and to make claims on behalf of at least as many again. Their justification for doing this was that 'large numbers of persons were left off the lists or were mis-described in such a way as to be liable to be objected to, and therefore to require the assistance of the party agents in making claims & declarations'.[2] This was the means of effecting a considerable alteration in the composition of the electorate. Neither side could afford to let a possible advantage slip, with the result that, as the Chairman of the Liberal Union put it, 'when they came to practical work they saw the two parties doing all they could to

[1] J. C. Buckley to Max Aitken, 20 September 1912, Beaverbrook P.
[2] M.L.U. Annual Report, 24 March 1896.

expunge from the register people who ought certainly to be on that register. As long as the registration system remained as it was at present both parties, through their agents, would continue to behave in this extraordinary way.'[1]

Manchester provides a good indication of the extent to which the incompetence of the overseers rather than the factiousness of the parties was the root of the registration difficulty. The parliamentary borough spread over three separate Poor Law Unions, one of which, the Manchester Township, was the object of frequent criticism. The number of claims and objections arising from the overseers' lists is far more closely related to which Union a division was in than to its social composition.

TABLE 2. *Claims and objections by both parties, 1895*

Division	Poor Law Union(s)	Claims	Objections
		(as per cent of total on overseers' lists)	
North West	Manchester and Prestwich	10.0	13.0
North	Manchester and Prestwich	7.5	17.0
North East	Manchester and Prestwich	10.5	15.5
East	Prestwich and Chorlton	6.4	11.0
South	Chorlton	4.0	3.0
South West	Chorlton	4.0	2.8

The northern divisions, then, suffered from bad administration, but whether this was abnormal is another matter. In the 1890s each party was making between two and three thousand claims and between four and five thousand objections annually. The less complete figures for 1904–13 suggest that the balance tipped back once more in later years towards an increasing number of claims – three or four thousand by each party. The number of objections, on the other hand, fell as a result of the overseers' lists becoming better, and this in turn may have been related to the City Council's acquiring the right to appoint the Manchester overseers from 1898 in the course of its campaign to rationalise poor relief.[2]

The workings of the registration system may be assessed from the very full figures available for 1897, which seems to be a not unrepresentative year.[3] It is surprising to find the Liberals doing so well. They seem both to have had

[1] Edwin Guthrie, M.L.U. Annual Meeting, 11 April 1899.
[2] Redford, *History of Local Government in Manchester*, III, 193. The table is taken from M.L.U. Annual Meeting, 24 March 1896. The composition of the Poor Law Unions is summarised in Redford, *op. cit.*, II, table facing p. 128; cf. the map of townships, *ibid.* I, frontispiece; and map showing housing conditions in Marr, *Housing Conditions in Manchester and Salford.*
[3] Registration report, M.L.U. Minutes, 23 May 1898.

TABLE 3. *Claims at revision court, 1897*

Division	Claims by Liberals		Claims by Conservatives	
	Number made	Proportion sustained (%)	Number made	Proportion sustained (%)
North West	538	19	372	17
North	465	50	468	42
North East	372	27	350	18
East	211	56	477	42
South	321	33	254	13
South West	300	43	305	19
Overall	2,207	40	2,226	28
Net Lib. advantage (in votes)	+782		−625	

TABLE 4. *Objections at revision court, 1897*

Division	Objections by Conservatives		Objections by Liberals	
	Number made	Proportion sustained (%)	Number made	Proportion sustained (%)
North West	729	81	747	83
North	1,318	81	1,102	88
North East	942	84	1,112	88
East	687	80	1,074	77
South	171	73	202	82
South West	256	50	272	86
Overall	4,103	80	4,509	85
Net Lib. advantage (in votes)	−3,259		+3,817	

more of their opponents struck off and to have registered more initially-excluded supporters than the Tories. In the North division, however, the only one held by the Liberals, the Conservatives seized an advantage; 1,067 Liberals were struck off, as against 978 Conservatives; while 224 Liberals and 200 Conservatives were added. When these figures are seen in relation to an electorate of a little over 10,000, and a Liberal majority at the next election of 19 votes, they illustrate the critical importance of the revision court.

It might be expected that the lodger franchise would account for much of this furious activity. This does not seem to have been the case. It is not known how many of the parties' 10,000 claims in 1886 were for lodgers, but only about a hundred were registered as a result. If the claims which the Liberals made are separated into their respective franchises, it does not seem that those on behalf of new lodgers comprised a very large part.[1]

	Liberal claims		Conservative claims (Lodgers only)
	Divs 1, 2 and 3	Lodgers	
1896	2,434	122	
1904	2,215	487	278
1905	2,236	394	
1913	3,118	419	628 (includes Labour)

It seems that there was more eagerness to exploit this franchise in later years but wider divergences remained in its extent. In 1910 there were only 68 lodgers on the register in Manchester North East. The Conservative agent was content to put this down to the division's social characteristics,[2] but the contrast between here and Manchester South, where there were over 1,000, still seems strange. (Were the overseers in some way responsible?) The party balance of the lodger vote is difficult to assess. Several clues combine to suggest that on the 1906 register Manchester's 1,265 lodgers (two-thirds of them in South) may have contained about 650 Liberals and 575 Conservatives.[3] The Liberals certainly had no built-in majority. In 1911 they made efforts to strengthen their lodger voters in South, making reclaims for 431 and new claims for 260;[4] since there were 1,332 lodgers on the 1912 register, even the most favourable assumptions would give the Liberals barely half, and about 600 is a likelier figure.

II

It is possible to estimate with a fair degree of certainty what proportion of adult males were enfranchised in each constituency.[5] These estimates reveal a wide variation: from 84 per cent in Stretford in 1901 to 38 per cent in Everton in 1911. By and large the smallest electorates were in the large cities and the largest in the county divisions, with undivided boroughs somewhere in between. To some extent these differences reflect the distorting element of

[1] Lodger claims are listed separately only for these years. Registration reports, M.L.U. Minutes, 4 December 1896; M.L.F. Minutes, 7 September 1904, 24 August 1905, 10 September 1913.
[2] Interview with C. E. Smith, *M. Courier*, 24 November 1910.
[3] During registration in 1905 the Liberals sent in 460 claims for old lodgers and 394 new claims. M.L.F. Minutes, 27 July, 24 August 1905. It is likely that almost all the old and at least half of the new lodgers would have got on to the register. The Conservative registration agent claimed that revision reduced the Liberal majority on the lodgers' list from 197 to 72. Interview with G. N. Carter, *M. Courier*, 5 December 1905.
[4] M.L.F. Minutes, 31 August 1911.
[5] See Appendix B, Table 1.

the plural vote; since this was concentrated in a number of county divisions, these will appear to have a higher proportion of men possessing the vote.

This, is however, less important than it seems. The most extreme case was Stretford which had outvoters from Manchester, Salford and part of Stockport, to the number of about 4,500 in 1911. In part this accounts for the very high enfranchised proportion of 77 per cent, yet even if the outvoters are excluded completely that proportion still stands at about 65 per cent. In most cases the outvoters from a single borough did not distort the county electorate to this extent. Some of the county divisions which showed the highest proportions enfranchised – the High Peak, for instance – did not include a borough at all. Moreover, though all outvoters were ownership voters, many ownership voters were really occupiers. There was a return of non-resident county voters in 1888 but the Liberals abstained from pressing the issue subsequently for fear that, because of the defective nature of registration, a fallacious return showing too few non-residents would be produced.[1] The 1888 return clearly cannot be taken at face value. The number of non-residents given for those Lancashire divisions which did not contain a parliamentary borough is uniformly low; only in Lancaster was it over one hundred and in most of the rest it was around five per cent of the total ownership vote. Yet in the three comparable divisions of Cheshire – Macclesfield, Crewe and Northwich – all of which were in part industrial, between 30 and 40 per cent of the ownership vote was put down as non-resident, and in addition the figures for non-resident occupiers bulk ten times as large as the negligible Lancashire totals. The main difference here seems to be one of assiduity in finding out. The return makes no attempt to count the borough freeholders but the divisions in which they voted in several cases had high totals for non-resident ownership voters; there were 600 in Stretford, 700 in Bootle. This suggests rather that large numbers of city freeholders were non-resident than that these divisions happened, improbably, also to contain the highest numbers of other kinds of non-resident voters. In 1910 Stretford had over six thousand ownership voters but no other division approached this number. Stretford apart, the presence or absence of outvoters bore no very obvious relationship to the size of the ownership vote. For example, three of the four north Lancashire divisions included boroughs; yet in Lancaster, which had no such body of borough freeholders, the ownership vote was not lower than in the other three. And there were consistently less ownership voters in Clitheroe, which took Burnley's outvoters, than in Accrington, which contained no borough. While the plural vote cannot wholly be discounted, then, its presence does not vitiate the estimates. Where

---

[1] P.P., 1888, LXXIX, 919; cf. Dilke's arguments against a similar return, Dilke to Alexander W. Black, 14 July 1905, HGP 46063, f. 29.

these show a high figure there were almost certainly a large number of adult men on the register.

Just as there were disparities in the franchise as a whole between constituencies, so there were disparities in the lodger franchise in particular, but the one does not explain the other. The northern county divisions, with almost no lodgers in 1900, had a high proportion of men on the register; yet in Birkenhead, with the high number of 900 lodgers in 1900, only 53 per cent of adult men were registered. By 1910 there were in general more lodgers on the register. Two thousand lodgers in Stretford help explain the figure of 77 per cent (or 65 per cent without outvoters) but in Darwen the figure was 78 per cent (or 69 per cent without outvoters) – with only eight lodger voters. The case of Darwen, a hyper-marginal seat for a generation, also shows that to see the lodger vote as 'a mere agent's franchise'[1] is far too simple. Dilke strongly contested the assumption 'that the lodger was a person who could put himself on the register if he chose to take the trouble', and cited in support the numbers of lodgers in Darwen (8), Clitheroe (20), Accrington (2) and Rossendale (4). 'That was not apathy', he concluded; 'that was a different habit of life.'[2] The activity of the party agents must be set against the idiosyncrasies of the overseers or the revising barristers, for the lodger qualification must obviously have been subject to widely different interpretations; in some places it was still strictly defined in 1910, though the evidence that the floodgates were opening is quite strong.

The period of qualification seems to have been the aspect of electoral law which most affected the extent of enfranchisement. Where mobility was greatest the voters were fewest. In the city divisions of Manchester, Salford and Liverpool only about half the adult males were on the register, and those divisions associated with the migratory Irish had the smallest proportions of all. The suburban seats, which were subject to a lesser extent to the same influences, have lower proportions than other county seats. Outside the cities there were three categories of constituency. First, the mining seats, whether boroughs or counties. The five Lancashire seats with the largest number of miners all had a low proportion enfranchised – around 55 per cent for the most part. Second may be grouped the rest of the boroughs, with the exceptions of Warrington, Barrow and Birkenhead; they show a proportion of around 60 per cent, with one or two well over this mark. In contrast to the coal divisions, then, a substantial proportion of men was on the register in the cotton towns. The third category consists of the remaining county divisions. With the exception of Ormskirk, all had over 60 per cent on the register; the general level was over 65 per cent; and not a few were about 70 per cent.

[1] Blewett, 'The franchise in the United Kingdom, 1885–1918', p. 41.
[2] Sir Charles Dilke in discussion on Rosenbaum's paper, *Jnl. Roy Stat. Soc.*, LXXIII, p. 521.

There is no direct and simple correlation between how many men had the vote and how those who had it used it. The more popular party, however, ought to have benefited disproportionately from greater enfranchisement; that is, by 1910, the Liberals ought to have done better in those constituencies with a larger working-class element in the electorate. In testing this hypothesis it must be assumed that a marginal increase in the level of enfranchisement represents an increment of (preponderantly) working-class votes. Clearly, then, the divided cities, with their socially separated populations, must be excluded. For the rest, those boroughs with over 60 per cent of adult males on the register, and those counties with over 65 per cent, will be taken as showing a 'high' level of enfranchisement, and those with less a 'low' level. The General Election results (including unopposed returns) will be compared, for 1895 and 1900 with the 1901 estimates, for January and December 1910 with the 1911 estimates, and for 1906 with the averages of the two.

In the General Elections of 1895 and 1900 the Conservatives were predominant in both categories of constituency, and although the Liberals did better relatively in 'high' than 'low' divisions this difference is so slight that no weight can be put upon it.

General Election of 1895

Level of enfranchisement	M.P.s returned	
	Liberal	Conservative
High	8	19
Low	5	21

General Election of 1900

Level of enfranchisement	M.P.s returned	
	Liberal	Conservative
High	8	19
Low	6	20

In 1906 this tendency is rather more marked; the Conservatives managed to save one quarter of the 'low' seats but only one tenth of the 'high' seats.

General Election of 1906

Level of enfranchisement	M.P.s returned	
	Liberal	Conservative
High	25	3
Low	19	6

It is only in 1910, however, that a definite relationship (though not necessarily a causal one) can be established. Broadly, the more democratic seats were more often Liberal. This was clearest in December, when the Liberals won two-thirds of the seats with large electorates, whereas the Conservatives won three-fifths of those with small electorates. It is 95 per cent certain that this did not happen by chance.[1]

General Election of January 1910

Level of enfranchisement	M.P.s returned	
	Liberal	Conservative
High	24	7
Low	14	8

General Election of December 1910

Level of enfranchisement	M.P.s returned	
	Liberal	Conservative
High	21	10
Low	9	13

One indication of the development of this dichotomy can be gained by comparing *seriatim* the sums of the diagonally opposite cells in these tables.

	1895	29:24
	1900	28:25
	1906	31:22
January	1910	32:21
December	1910	34:19

Too much should not be made of this trend. The factors accounting for a large or small electorate are themselves too complicated to admit of ready inferences being drawn from this kind of evidence. But that the evidence, such as it is, points in one direction can hardly be denied.

III

It is true that the plural vote did not reward property alone but scattered property; it was a rich man's prerogative for all that. *Plural voters* were of all kinds and conditions. *Duplicate voters*, properly called, were men who had more than one qualification as electors but were entitled to only one franchise. *Outvoters* were non-residents, the great majority of them borough freeholders.

---

[1] Taking counties and boroughs together, the relationship between a high level of enfranchisement and a Liberal result is statistically significant using the chi-square test at a 5 per cent level ($\chi^2 = 2.75$). I am indebted to Mr R. C. Floud for his help on this point.

A borough freeholder was not entitled to a vote in the county on behalf of property which would entitle him to a vote in the borough. The qualifying property, then, could not be his residence since this entitled him to a borough vote as an inhabitant householder. If a man resided outside but within seven miles of a borough, however, ownership of business premises of ten pounds annual value within it would probably give him a second vote on one of two grounds. If he occupied, he got a borough vote as a ten pounder; if he did not occupy, he got a county vote as a forty-shilling freeholder. (There was also the more remote possibility of an occupier becoming an outvoter on behalf of property worth less than ten pounds.) In Lancashire the business quarters of the large towns produced many of the plural votes but whether they were exercised in the boroughs or in the counties was largely a matter of chance. The 1888 return of non-resident borough voters is just as dubious an egg as that for the counties; but parts of it are excellent.[1] It shows that in the business divisions the non-residents were on the register in force. In Manchester North West they amounted to 35 per cent of the electorate. In Liverpool they were split between Exchange and Abercromby, comprising 18 per cent of the electorate in each. These are the best figures available; but impressionistic evidence suggests that in later years the non-resident vote in Manchester North West did not bulk quite so large as this, and that in Liverpool, Exchange rather than Abercromby came to possess most of the business vote.

The outvoters were not only the most important element in the plural vote but the easiest to identify due to the manner in which their qualification was acquired.[2] Technically their qualifications lay within the constituency in which they were outvoters – but quite apart from this legal fiction there were real reasons why they should be in a position to act as full participants in its affairs. They certainly held property, probably worked, and possibly lived, near it. Moreover, the outvoters were a definite body of men who met face to face; the parties held special meetings for them; on polling day things were made easy for them by the provision of polling stations in the boroughs.

[1] P.P. 1888, LXXIX, 907. In the county return, outvoters resident in the borough were not counted as non-residents because, in the technical sense, the borough was a part of the county. Similarly, in the case of borough voters, residence within seven miles of a borough was held to be equivalent to residence within it. Lowell, whose information was usually extremely soundly based, states that the borough return excluded persons in this position. (*The Government of England*, I, 215.) This is cited by Blewett, 'The franchise in the United Kingdom, 1885–1918', p. 46; but neither he nor Lowell appears to see that there is here a serious anomaly which has a considerable bearing on estimating the total plural vote. For in that case, since such residence was *a necessary condition* of the occupier franchise, how could the return show any 'non-residents' at all? And indeed it showed none for 8 out of the 19 boroughs in the north west; this is, if not very helpful, at least logical. The inconsistent boroughs, on the other hand, fortunately included Liverpool and Manchester, for which there seems to be a real return of non-residents.
[2] See Appendix B, Table 2.

There is every reason to suppose that they polled quite heavily. But it must be emphasised that their numbers were not as great as is often supposed. Stretford is a special case, but even there it can be seen that between 1900 and 1910 the importance of the outvoters declined both absolutely and relative to the electorate as a whole. The rest of the plural voters were in a much less favourable position. For men who were isolated and remote there was at once less incentive to vote and a great deal more trouble involved in doing so. It is true that many of them had ample means and leisure for making the journey and that there are notable and prodigious cases. In 1910 men came to Southport to cast their votes from as far as Penzance, Dumfries, Surrey and Gloucester.[1] In 1900 at Leigh the veteran Liberal J. P. Thomasson was sparing no efforts to round up individual non-resident voters.

Besides sending my brougham [he reported], I drove over myself in a Victoria & took an old man of 84 to poll, who had been at the nomination of Dr Bowring for Bolton in 1841. Then finding a voter was to be at the corner of a street in Bolton at 1.30 I undertook to fetch him & drove back; put up the horse for $1\frac{1}{4}$ hour at a Liberal Public & then my groom took the voter to the Poll.[2]

But these are stories of difficulties being overcome at a disproportionate cost. The plural vote had an inbuilt check: the more flagrant the non-residence the less likely the appearance on polling day.

The politics of the outvoters were the politics of business. They were believed to be a valuable, even an invaluable, help to the Conservatives. The *Manchester Guardian* was stating it as a matter of common knowledge in 1900 that at Stretford 'the Tory successes in this division have been gained entirely by the votes of non-resident property-owners, who, thanks to our ridiculous franchise laws, were thus enabled to convert a minority of the real electorate into a majority'.[3] But this is probably to claim too much. At Northwich at this time there were only 299 outvoters, of whom (so the Liberals believed) 136 were Liberals, 141 Conservatives and 22 doubtful.[4] This indicates, if accurate, a state of affairs far from a Conservative hegemony. The contemporary evidence from Manchester bears this out; in the 1890s the Liberals reckoned that they had over half the plural vote.[5]

It seems unlikely that the Liberals had more to fear from the plural vote than from many other sections of the electorate in 1900. In 1906 the outvoters were even felt to be an advantage to the Liberals on occasion, as at Stretford where Free Trade was expected to bring over the Manchester businessmen.[6]

---

[1] *M. Courier*, 13 December 1910.
[2] J. P. Thomasson to C. P. Scott, 17 October 1900, MGP.
[3] *M.G.*, 26 September 1900.
[4] Report prepared for Sir John Brunner, 1900, in the Brunner Papers.
[5] See Appendix B, Table 2.
[6] *M.G.*, 17, 19 January 1906; but cf. *Stockport Advertiser*, 19 January 1906.

In 1910, however, the plural vote undoubtedly worked in favour of the Conservatives. Not only did the Liberal press make vociferous complaints (for instance that at North Lonsdale the outvoters came 'to swamp the Liberal vote')[1] but the Conservative press obviously wrote on exactly the same assumptions. Thus it was said that the Rochdale outvoters were 'practically solid' for the Conservative candidate and that it was well known that the great majority of the Chester outvoters were Conservatives.[2] The *Liverpool Courier* went to great pains in January 1910 to give guidance to outvoters over the exercise of their rights. When the chairman of the Conservative party undertook an inquiry into the probable effects of the removal of those rights, he quailed at the prospect.[3] In January 1910 the Manchester Liberal Federation was responsible for polling those Liberal outvoters who lived in the city. Admittedly, many of the freeholders lived farther afield, but since there were over 4,000 Stretford outvoters all told, whereas the M.L.F. only canvassed 500, it does not seem that very many were recognised Liberals. And in December 1910 a Stretford election worker reckoned that instead of a Liberal majority of one thousand, 'counting the residents only the majority would have been over 3,000',[4] suggesting that the outvoters split at least 3 to 1 in favour of the Conservatives. It would be very odd if the best informed men in both parties consistently made, and allowed to go unchallenged, statements of this kind both in public and in private unless they were well founded. It is almost certainly erroneous to claim (as does the best modern study of this question) 'that the plural vote was distinctly less partisan than is often alleged'.[5] Indeed, its estimate that in 1910 the plural

[1] *M.G.*, 10 December 1910.
[2] *M. Courier*, 6 December 1910; *L. Courier*, 13 December 1910.
[3] Sir A. Steel-Maitland to Bonar Law, 27 January 1913, BLP 28/2/86.
[4] M.L.F. Minutes, 3 February 1910; *M.G.*, 13 December 1910. Since the outvoters had separate polling stations and boxes this estimate is likely to have been well-founded; cf. above, p. 23.
[5] Blewett, 'The franchise in the United Kingdom, 1885–1918', p. 50; but cf. Jones, 'Further thoughts on the franchise, 1885–1918', *Past & Present*, **34** (1966), pp. 136–7. Insofar as this conclusion is based upon the election results of January 1910 it is an inference from the fact that the Conservative poll seems to have been inflated by about 3 per cent in constituencies with a large plural vote as compared with neighbouring divisions. The crucial question is, how large is the plural vote which is presumed to account for this 3 per cent advantage? *viz.*, what is the *difference* between the proportion of plural voters in constituencies where they are admittedly numerous and the proportion in those nearby with which these are being compared? The claim that the plural vote was Conservative by about 3:2 can only be justified on the assumption that this difference is of the order of 20 per cent (comprising 11½ Conservatives to every 8½ Liberals). If, on the other hand, the difference is, say, 5 per cent, the plural vote would need to be Conservative by 4:1 to produce a 3 per cent advantage. And in fact the assumption of a 20 per cent difference is not valid for those constituencies in the north west which it purports to cover. This is to overestimate the strength and the degree of concentration of the plural vote, and consequently to underestimate its partisanship. In Lancashire no division apart from Manchester North West had a plural vote of 20 per cent (12 per cent was a high figure for outvoters) and since the divisions with a large number of outvoters were unlikely to have many plural voters of other kinds, the plural voters as a whole were not spread in a grossly uneven fashion. Furthermore, it cannot be

vote was Conservative by 2 to 1 ought to be regarded not as an upper but a lower limit; a more typical split would probably be 3 to 1, and it could easily have approached 4 to 1.

IV

The electoral system worked in favour of the wealthy; the Conservatives were the party of the wealthy; yet the Liberals did not change the system when they were in power. This was a failure of will rather than perception. 'All the force of the electoral system was cast against the poor man', asserted J. F. L. Brunner, and it was a *cri de cœur* that came as readily to the lips of Irish Nationalist and Labour speakers as Liberals. 'The truth was', said the Liberal Charles Russell, 'that the people of England were not governing the land. Only one in every two had a vote and every seventh man was a plural voter.'[1] The battle with the House of Lords sharpened the democratic rhetoric which the progressives employed, and raised the expectations of change. 'The next Government', proclaimed a Labour candidate confidently, 'would proceed to pass electoral reform, giving one man one vote – votes not for bricks but for brains, votes for men not for mortar, votes for souls and not for sods – and with this reform the working men of England would come into their own. – (Cheers.)'[2]

In the 1890s the main thrust of Liberal criticism had been against the registration procedure and there were frequent proposals for a shorter qualifying period, three months meeting with considerable favour. The removal of the Poor Law disqualification was also often advocated, though, as in most thinking about the Poor Law, the notion lingered on that it might be possible to discriminate against 'habitual' (and presumably undeserving) paupers. The deserving poor, on the other hand, were seen as the victims of a double assault on their political as well as their economic rights. 'Many decent folk have become disqualified through accepting Poor Law relief', said Sutton, the Labour candidate for Manchester East, in January 1910. 'It is one of the saddest things.'[3] Most Liberals agreed that this was inequitable but in their eyes the system's most inequitable feature was plural voting. Fabulous cases of men with twenty or so votes were cited as proof of its injustice. In 1910 the Lords' defeat of the Government's Plural Voting Bill was often recalled. C. P. Scott, for instance, confessed that he was a bloated pluralist in Salford North. 'The House of Lords', he said, 'would not allow

assumed that they would poll as heavily as residents. The effective difference between the plural vote in seats where it was large and that in contiguous divisions was probably around 5–7 per cent of the electorate (splitting, presumably, in a ratio between 4:1 and 5:2).
[1] J. F. L. Brunner at Northwich, Charles Russell in Salford South, *M.G.*, 30 November 1910.
[2] Henry Twist at Ince, *M.G.*, 12 December 1910.
[3] Interview with J. E. Sutton, *M.G.*, 11 January 1910.

him to be deprived of his vote, and he was going to reward the Lords by voting for Mr Byles. (Cheers.)'[1] Strong as was Liberal feeling against the Lords on other grounds, their belief that the undemocratic pillars of the constitution were propping each other up gave them both an immediate sense of frustration and a faith in their ultimate triumph. 'We have always recognised that in normal times this was a tolerably safe Tory seat', mused the ejected Liberal M.P. for Darwen in December 1910; but the Liberal Government would, he was confident, 'destroy or modify the veto of the House of Lords. (Cheers.) After that we shall have "one man one vote" – (Cheers) – and this ought then to be a tolerably safe Liberal constituency. (Cheers.)'[2] And when Asquith went to speak in the High Peak at the very end of this election he laid bare the Liberal grievance.

There is not an intelligent man [he stated deliberately], to whatever political party he may belong, who does not know that I am speaking the truth when I say that if the plural voter had been wiped off the register – as he would have been but for the House of Lords, – not ten, not twenty, but thirty or forty of the county constituencies which have voted Tory would have been sending representatives to the House of Commons in support of the Liberal party. – (Cheers.)[3]

Yet the Reform Bill which Asquith's Government presented failed, and with it the longstanding Liberal hopes of achieving one man, one vote, as well as any chance for the more recent proposals from Liberal organisations in favour of the alternative ballot.

Many of the difficulties in the way of electoral reform came from the Conservatives, whose tangible advantages from the existing system were not lightly to be renounced. Conservative candidates were to be found saying flatly that they did not believe men in receipt of public money ought to have the vote, or that they would oppose the abolition of plural voting. The distaste with which they regarded such proposals found perhaps its best expression in Curzon's famous defence of the House of Lords at Oldham, when, casting around for iniquities which might be visited upon a country deprived of its protecting arm, he conjured up, side by side with Home Rule and Disestablishment, 'even manhood suffrage'.[4] Such were the difficulties of electoral reform, however, that it was possible to combine an ostensible willingness in principle to create a more democratic system with a determined conservation in practice of the *status quo*. The more sophisticated Conservative opposition came, therefore, from those who insisted on a redistribution of seats – by which they meant Irish seats – as the price of Reform. And

[1] Scott at Salford North, *M.G.*, 2 December 1910.
[2] F. G. Hindle at Darwen, *Lancs. D.P.*, 9 December 1910.
[3] Asquith at Glossop, *M.G.*, 15 December 1910.
[4] Curzon at Oldham, *M.G.*, 16 December 1909.

Balfour himself introduced another condition when in 1906 he stated that he could not consider the extension of the suffrage without women.

More than anything else, the question of woman suffrage prevented electoral reform of other kinds. Some Liberals like Hilaire Belloc and George Harwood wanted an extension of male suffrage while continuing to exclude women. Harwood attempted an ingenious justification of this distinction, claiming that the basis for the vote was the liability to be shot, or, alternatively, that the position of the British Empire as the largest Mahometan power in the world was a barrier – 'If they gave women the vote did they suppose they would have the confidence of all these Mahometans?'[1] But these are eccentricities. It is true that not every Liberal candidate was able, like Sir John Gorst, to claim, more than forty years on, that he had voted for Mill's amendment to the 1867 Reform Bill,[2] but most were nonetheless sympathetic to woman suffrage. The Liberal party as such never committed itself to the cause, but the more hopeful spirits clearly hoped that it would do so. When, in private and intemperately, Mrs Pankhurst accused so firm a friend as C. P. Scott of 'making it quite clear to us that you prefer the smallest party advantage to human freedom for women',[3] she showed characteristically little understanding of how to achieve her goal.

Experience showed [declared Scott when he was President of the Manchester Liberal Federation], that no great cause was carried to success unless it had behind it, at all events at some period, the support of party interest and party feeling. Women were perfectly right in taking up at present a non-party attitude, but he looked forward to the day when the suffrage question should cease to be a non-party question – when one or other of the great parties should have made it its own. He hoped that party would be the one to which he himself belonged.[4]

In 1900 it had still been possible for candidates to deflect questions on the suffrage with the opinion that, 'The greatest obstacle to granting it was the fact that so many women were apathetic on the question.'[5] Whilst the subsequent suffragist agitation was successful in dispatching this objection, increasingly it provoked a different kind of antagonism. In 1906 Christabel Pankhurst held that Campbell-Bannerman's refusal to pledge his Government on the question justified the tactics of disrupting meetings held by Winston Churchill who was at that time a supporter of the women.[6] Thereafter, the meetings of many prominent Liberals were disturbed by the militants and Churchill's meetings in Lancashire in 1909 were surrounded by

[1] Harwood at Bolton, *M.G.*, 6 January 1910.
[2] Gorst at Preston, *Lancs. D.P.*, 18 December 1909.
[3] Mrs E. Pankhurst to Scott, 21 July 1909, MGP.
[4] Scott at a meeting organised by the North of England Society for Women's Suffrage in support of George Kemp, Liberal candidate for Manchester North West, *M.G.*, 14 January 1910.
[5] W. H. Lever, Wirral, *L. Courier*, 26 September 1900.
[6] Letter from Miss C. H. Pankhurst, *M. Courier*, 11 January 1906.

elaborate precautions against such trouble, either by refusing women admission altogether or by exacting pledges of good conduct. The Pankhursts had a particular animus against Churchill. His successor in Manchester North West, Sir George Kemp, was an unequivocal supporter of the women's cause and encountered no trouble. In general, however, Liberal candidates, whether sympathetic or not, were vigorously opposed by the W.S.P.U. in January 1910 even though less extreme groups of suffragists often rallied round a friendly Liberal. In December 1910, in the more reasonable 'Conciliation' phase of the controversy, the W.S.P.U. was rather more selective in its targets. In Liverpool, for instance, where the only Liberal M.P. was a member of the Conciliation Committee, the W.S.P.U. was neutral and reserved its fire for the unregenerate anti-suffragist Vivian in Birkenhead.[1]

Independent political action for woman suffrage went further: there were two candidates who stood under the auspices of the Lancashire and Cheshire Women's Textile and Other Workers' Representation Committee, and a third suffragist candidate was seriously threatened. Thorley Smith fought at Wigan in 1906 with help from Mrs Pankhurst and others, and although he did not, as he had hoped, get Labour endorsement, Nonconformists and the Temperance Party published manifestoes on his behalf and his poll was respectable. And in January 1910 a candidature was promoted at Rossendale, on the grounds of the large number of women workers in the constituency and the antipathetic attitude of Lewis Harcourt, the sitting M.P. A. K. Bulley, a Liverpool cotton broker, was the eventual standard bearer here. Rossendale Labour Council decided to stay neutral but Bulley appealed for Labour support on general grounds and managed to poll six hundred. In Salford South, where Hilaire Belloc had gone so far as to call woman suffrage immoral, he met with opposition from suffragists in January 1910; and in December it was threatened that H. N. Brailsford would stand against him as a suffrage candidate. It was not, however, as a direct result that Belloc withdrew, although when he had done so the woman suffrage candidature was, as the Conservatives put it, 'merged into' that of his Liberal successor.[2]

Until the first 1910 election the suffragist agitation was on a rising curve, and the probability seemed to be that, willy-nilly, the Government would accept the principle as embodied in the Conciliation Committee's proposals. The idea of a limited enfranchisement, however, based as it was upon a democratic claim, was itself open to democratic objections. The founders of the People's Suffrage Federation felt that it would lead to 'two serious

[1] *L. Courier*, 26 November 1910.
[2] See communication from Brailsford's election committee, *M.G.*, 24 November 1910; speech by J. G. Groves, *M. Courier*, 26 November 1910; letters from Belloc, *M.G.*, 22 November 1910, *The Times*, 30 November 1910.

results: (1) that the women voters would not represent the needs of the great body of workingwomen (trade-unionist & married) & (2) that the present men's electorate – already unfair to the workers – would be still further weighted against them.'[1] This was the reasonable fear that preyed upon the minds of realistic Liberal suffragists, yet Christabel Pankhurst chose to regard an Adult Suffrage Bill as 'simply a wicked move on the part of Mr Lloyd George & Mr Churchill'.[2] The W.S.P.U. could only see the prospective new voters in terms of their sex, the Government only in terms of their class. The idea of a Conciliation Bill was agreeable enough, but to support it demanded considerable magnanimity from Liberals who felt that the nature of the franchise already discriminated against them. 'The Conciliation Bill', wrote Lloyd George, 'would on balance add hundreds of thousands of votes throughout the country to the strength of the Tory Party.' And, declaring that the Liberal party had 'never really faced the situation manfully and courageously', he urged that it must choose between 'an extended franchise which would put the working-men's wives onto the register as well as spinsters and widows' and 'no female franchise at all'.[3] This was the dilemma. The Government might have resolved it by bold steps which would at once have settled the woman suffrage question and cleared the decks for other electoral reforms; as it was, the W.S.P.U. leaders sought to resolve it in the only way they knew how. The outcome was that their militant tactics alienated the very margin of support which they needed for success. 'The action of the Militants is ruinous', Lloyd George told Scott.[4] And ruinous, too, it proved for all contingent measures of electoral reform.

V

Whatever the inadequacies of the electoral roll at the time of its compilation, these were magnified by the passage of time. Even when the register came into force in January it was six months out of date, and, especially in the large towns, there would already have been many removals: probably between ten

[1] Margaret Llewelyn Davies to C. P. Scott, 4 September (1909), MGP.
[2] Christabel Pankhurst to Scott, 14 July 1910, MGP.
[3] Lloyd George to the Master of Elibank, 5 September 1911, EP 8802 ff. 308-11. The extreme difficulty of the Government's position is not properly appreciated in Rover, *Women's Suffrage and Party Politics*, pp. 130-4, 182-4, which accepts at face value the highly contentious estimates put out by the Conciliation Committee as to whom their Bill would enfranchise.
[4] Lloyd George to Scott, 30 November 1911, copy, LGP C/8/1/1. This effect can clearly be seen in the case of Max Aitken, M.P. for Ashton, who was induced to support the Conciliation Bill under the influence of G. H. Coop, the President of Ashton Conservative Association. Yet by October 1912 Coop was telling Aitken that 'the events that have recently transpired in connection with militant suffragists have caused me to seriously reflect', and that 'public opinion here has not improved for the reason above'. And Aitken was now refusing to pledge himself on woman suffrage, saying that he was 'quite indifferent'. Coop to Aitken, 23 October 1912; Aitken to R. S. Oldham, 25 October 1912, Beaverbrook P.

and fifteen per cent of the electorate. As the year wore on, the number of removals increased and the register became increasingly unrepresentative, particularly of those who had to move in search of work. Although the party agents might hope to keep abreast of the changes for some months, there came a point when they had to cut their losses on the old register. From mid-summer, of course, the next year's registration work was in full spate and it was only natural to look forward to the new register. But though the summer was a natural break and it was tempting to write off the old register at that point, the hazards of doing so should there be an election late in the year were considerable. In Manchester North, for instance, most of the two thousand removals up to June 1910 had been traced but between then and the second General Election there were at least as many again.[1] Tracing removals was onerous but, in Liverpool at least, it was 'rendered important by the fact that working men voters never go to the poll unless they have received a voting card. They have a firm belief that the card is a sort of authority to exercise the franchise, and unless their present address is discovered it is, of course, impossible to communicate with them.'[2] The parties, moreover, had to adopt guerrilla tactics in hostile terrain.

The difficulty of tracing these removals [explained a Conservative agent], is enhanced by the disinclination of neighbours to assist in giving information – from reasons of delicacy, maybe. To surmount these difficulties a strong band of ladies has been formed, the reason being that the wives of the working men are more open in dealing with their own sex, among whom there are, as yet, no bailiffs.[3]

An old register militated against the popular party, and there are abundant indications that the timing of every General Election was influenced by the Liberals' desire to fight early in the year and the Conservatives' to fight late. In 1895 Robert Hudson, the Secretary of the Liberal Central Association, had unsuccessfully pressed the Government to 'go on' in order to be able to fight on a new register.[4] The dissolution that July was felt by the Liberals to be uncomfortably late in the year. In August 1900, with the Unionists in power, Herbert Gladstone was apprehensively wondering whether 'the Govt. seriously intend so dirty a trick as to go khaki on the old register'.[5] And when these indeed proved to be the terms of the Government's appeal to the country there were bitter complaints about the stale register from Liberals and socialists. 'The war was begun', said Philip Snowden, 'ostensibly for the enfranchisement of 100,000 Britishers in South Africa, who

---

[1] *M.G.*, 30 November 1910.
[2] *Liverpool D.P.*, 28 September 1900.
[3] Interview with C. E. Smith, Conservative agent in Manchester North East, *M. Courier*, 24 November 1910.
[4] Stansky, *Ambitions and Strategies*, p. 170.
[5] Gladstone to Campbell-Bannerman, 9 August 1900, CBP 41215 ff. 288–9.

preferred not to be enfranchised, and it ended by disfranchising at the approaching general election nearly 1,000,000 British subjects.'[1] The Irish vote was, not unnaturally, generally supposed to be hardest hit (though a writer in *The Clarion* claimed that the disfranchised were 'all Socialists, I feel convinced').[2] On the whole the city divisions were most affected and the rural divisions least. Removals accounted for one in three of those on the register in Oldham and Liverpool, one in four in Manchester, and one in four or five in cotton divisions like Heywood and Accrington. The Conservatives were mostly rather defensive about the age of the register. Balfour, however, was firm enough in denouncing as absurd and dangerous the doctrine that Parliament should be dissolved only in the first four months of the register, and the Home Secretary, Sir Matthew White Ridley, was more hardfaced altogether: 'He did not think any political party was bound to dissolve at the moment most agreeable to its adversaries.'[3]

When the possibility arose of a dissolution in the autumn of 1905 considerations of this kind were not absent from the minds of the party leaders. 'I frankly recognize', wrote the Conservative Chief Whip, 'the advantage which, according to our tradition, accrues to us from taking an election upon an old register.'[4] Since Balfour eventually preferred to end his Government by resignation, it was Campbell-Bannerman who fixed the date of the dissolution and there was never any question but that the election would be taken as soon as the new register was in force. Similarly, under Asquith, the appeal to the country over the Budget should in the natural course of things have come in November 1909 but it was felt necessary so to engineer the situation as to await the new register; although the possibility of accelerating it seems to have been explored the risk of holding on until January 1910 had to be taken.[5]

It is, therefore, all the more surprising that the Liberals fought next time in, of all months, December. Derby had written with great suspicion as early as May that with the Government 'knowing that an election in the summer is always more favourable to us than to them they wish to postpone the General Election till a time that suits them, namely the beginning of the year'.[6] So powerful was the assumption that the Liberals would only fight on a fresh

---

[1] Philip Snowden, Blackburn, *Lancs. D.P.*, 21 September 1900.

[2] 'The Whatnot', *Clarion*, 29 September 1900.

[3] Balfour at Manchester East, *M.G.*, 27 September 1900; White Ridley at Blackpool, *Lancs. D.P.*, 28 September 1900. The numbers of removals are taken from *M.G.*, 27 September 1900; *M. Courier*, 22 September, 2 October 1900; *L. Courier*, 20 September 1900; *Liverpool D.P.*, 28 September 1900; *N.D.T.*, 20 September 1900; *Lancs. D.P.*, 26 September 1900.

[4] Memorandum, 'The General Election', 10 August 1905, over Acland Hood's name but in fact written by J. S. Sandars, BP 49771.

[5] See Chamberlain, *Politics from Inside*, pp. 182–4; Hewins, *Apologia of an Imperialist*, I, 247.

[6] Derby to Garvin, 9 May 1910, Gollin, *The 'Observer' and J. L. Garvin*, p. 189.

register that, for instance, when Earl Winterton was given the news of the Constitutional Conference's breakdown in the middle of a speech, he went on without hesitation to talk of doing 'everything we can between now and next January'.[1] The decision to override the conventional wisdom of every party manager and to hold the election immediately was effectively that of the Chief Whip himself, the Master of Elibank, who believed that the Liberals would gain between 25 and 30 seats.[2]

The number of removals to be traced was enormous. In the more typical county divisions between one sixth and one eighth of the electors had moved house; in most towns the proportion was a third or a quarter; and in the big cities it was between a third and a half.[3] Reports from the constituencies showed Liberal and Labour organisations putting a good front on things. Vigorous efforts were certainly made in the way of personal canvassing and advertisements in the press. There were optimistic estimates of how many removals had been traced, and the damage expected to progressive chances was minimised. The report from Bolton that it was thought that 'the Liberals will not suffer much more than the Conservatives from the staleness of the register' catches the mood here.[4] But if the Liberals seldom enlarged upon the matter, the Conservatives were clearly in no doubt but that the old register was an advantage to them, and this seems particularly to have been the case in the mining constituencies of Leigh, Newton, Wigan and Ince. Frederick Cawley at Prestwich was one of the few Liberals to say plainly during the campaign that, 'It was always against the Liberal party to fight an election on an old register...'.[5] It was, after all, a Liberal Prime Minister who had fixed the date of the poll.

It is, then, the more significant that Tory protests about the timing of the election should have been so muted. Only in Liverpool did both parties have equal cause to regret that the election would not be on the new register, though there the Conservatives' expertise in tracing removals gave them little cause for concern either way. Even F. E. Smith could only find it to criticise a December election as 'inconvenient'.[6] H. E. Howell, whose democratic Tory movement failed to take him to victory in Manchester North, claimed that a large number of his supporters would have been enfranchised by the

---

[1] Speech at Rusholme, *M.G.*, 11 November 1910.
[2] See Masterman, *C. F. G. Masterman*, pp. 175–6; Murray, *Master and Brother*, p. 59; Jesse Herbert to Elibank, 9 November 1910, confidential, EP. 8802, ff. 129–30.
[3] See Appendix B, Table 3.
[4] *M.G.*, 21 November 1910.
[5] Cawley at Crumpsall, *M.G.*, 8 December 1910. For the acknowledged advantage of the register to the Conservatives in the coal seats see *L. Courier*, 2 December 1910; *M.G.*, 5, 7 December 1910; *M. Courier*, 7, 12 December 1910.
[6] *The Times*, 25 November 1910; for Liverpool cf. *L. Courier*, 9, 21 November 1910; *Liverpool D.P.*, 19 November 1910.

new register:[1] but this was something of a curiosity. Elsewhere, Conservative candidates were content to cavil at the timing of the election on such grounds as the interference caused to the Christmas trade, and they were obviously well pleased to campaign at the tail-end of the year. Moreover, after the polls, when Liberal candidates could vent the grievance with less constraint they were more ready to seize upon the stale register to explain why they had not done better. While it is improbable that the effect of the new register would have been enough, as was claimed, to have turned defeat into victory at Preston, or to have given Snowden 4,000 more votes at Blackburn, there is little reason to doubt the more modest statements of the Liberal M.P.s for Radcliffe, Leigh and Lancaster, that the timing of the election worked to their disadvantage.[2]

VI

In some elections, then, a considerable number of men whose names were on the register were not really potential voters. The relationship which has been suggested[3] between low turnout and a high Conservative share of the poll may thus reflect the staleness of the register rather than voluntary abstentions. Turnout is always important in elections, and before 1918, when the electorate was smaller and party allegiance stronger, it was even more important than now. It is not a simple matter, however, to elucidate the meaning of apparent levels of turnout. Nationally, turnout was 74.6 per cent in 1900, 82.6 per cent in 1906, 86.6 per cent in January 1910, and 81.1 per cent in December 1910. It is fair to conclude that in December 1910 political participation was greater than it had been in September/October 1900; despite a register several weeks older, turnout was up by over six per cent. It follows, too, that abstentions played a lesser part in January 1910 than in January 1906. But while it is easy enough to compare like with like, it is more difficult to assess the comparative levels of voluntary abstention in January and December 1910, a point with considerable bearing upon the turnover of seats in the north west between the two elections.

No-one expected that it would be possible to repeat the extraordinary poll of January 1910 in December; but Lord Crewe for one thought it was 'curious' that 'the polls in many places are smaller than can be accounted for by the fact of the old register'.[4] If this is true at all it is so in only a small degree. A comparison of the English results with those in Scotland, where a

[1] Interview with Howell and speech at Conservative Club, *M. Courier*, 5 December 1910.
[2] Speeches after the poll by Carr at Preston and Snowden at Blackburn, *Lancs. D.P.*, 6 December 1910; Taylor at Radcliffe and Raffan at Leigh, *M.G.*, 12, 14 December 1910; Helme at Lancaster, *Lancs. D.P.*, 8 December 1910.
[3] Cornford, 'The transformation of Victorian Conservatism', *Vict. Studies*, VII (1963), pp. 54 ff.
[4] Pope-Hennessy, *Lord Crewe*, p. 123.

new register was in force, suggests that a drop in the turnout of up to four per cent may be regarded as involuntary.[1] Now in the north west the average turnout fell by rather over four per cent between January and December. Considering the urban character of most of the constituencies, this does not seem an excessive measure of the toll of ten months' wastage. The December polls were regarded as being heavy and the discrepancy was happily put down to deaths and removals.

It certainly seems improbable that differential abstentions accounted for the swing to the Conservatives. Of the seats which had an above-average drop in the poll (those in which there presumably *was* deliberate non-voting) several also show a swing *against* the Conservatives. In at least four cases a heavy fall in turnout benefited the Conservatives little or at all. For the rest, larger than average falls were often associated with the disappearance of third candidates as compared with January 1910; where these had been Labour men this resulted in a relative (though not always absolute) improvement in the Liberal vote. These exceptional cases apart, there was a general pattern of consistent but small falls in the level of turnout, coupled with consistent but small swings to the Conservatives. It is not unreasonable to conclude that the two were related.

Perhaps this is a case in which the actual voting figures are a more reliable guide than the percentages since the same electoral roll was used in both elections. It is noticeable that the improvement in the Conservative position was seldom effected by a higher actual Conservative vote in December than in January. In divisions where it did increase – this happened mainly in the coal area – there had been a self-evident turnover of votes and a real change of allegiance. But elsewhere it was probably the decision to hold the election in December which hurt the progressives; the Master of Elibank had less reason than he supposed to be 'very triumphant over his results'.[2]

The age of the register was not the only reason why turnout figures cannot be taken at face value. The state of the register might never have been good in the first place. Dependent as it was upon the cut and thrust of the party agents to prune its anomalies, it soon went to seed in the absence of party rivalry. At the Chorley by-election in 1903, for instance, the register was in a shocking state and some names were on it as many as four times.[3] The turnout figure there of 86 per cent should therefore be regarded as extremely high. There is a third reason why things may not have been what they seemed – personation.

[1] See Table 15:6, Blewett, 'The British General Elections of 1910' (Oxford D.Phil. thesis 1967), p. 700.
[2] Masterman, *C. F. G. Masterman*, pp. 186–7.
[3] *Liverpool D.P.*, 2 January 1906.

Personation, of course, inflated rather than deflated the number of votes cast; it was a form of direct action to remedy the deficiencies occasioned by deaths and removals. The Irish were particularly adept practitioners. James Sexton, the Labour candidate for West Toxteth in 1906, later recalled how Jim Larkin, acting as his agent on that occasion, had 'competed with our opponents in the risky game of impersonation then played at almost every election in Liverpool'.[1] The Conservative candidates in the Exchange division regularly took precautions against it by obtaining lists of dead voters and those at sea (two cases were brought to court there in January 1910). When, in December 1910, with the standing temptation of a decrepit register, rumours of wholesale personation in the Scotland division were rife, the Conservatives undertook their first full canvass there in many years as a prophylactic.[2] The publicity these measures received may have been their main point. It is true, for what it is worth, that on this occasion turnout in Scotland fell by ten per cent as compared with January 1910, but in divisions of this character there were other reasons why it should have fallen heavily late in the year. In Liverpool turnout was always relatively low; but there are indications that the towns which had the highest levels of turnout may also have engaged in dubious practices. H. M. Hyndman recorded that, after his defeat at Burnley in 1895, 'we began to look seriously into the voting, and we discovered that 93 per cent of the total electorate had gone to the poll on a three-years-old register in the very middle of the annual holiday'. He was confident that 'the graveyards of Burnley were brought to the poll with assiduity and success on a scale never before heard of', and recalled meeting a Radical caucus man who claimed to have polled 47 'dead 'uns' himself at one election.[3] In the same vein, the Labour candidate at Preston in 1906 claimed to know of a man who had voted 16 times in the previous election, and alleged that the Conservatives trained men to 'vote early and vote often'.[4] At Accrington in 1900 the Liberals issued similar warnings; the poll there, at 91.5 per cent, was the highest in the north west and, allowing for the 500 electors who were dead or abroad, was 95 per cent of the available electorate.[5] Turnout figures like these are almost too good to be true, even without clear evidence of skullduggery. In Lees, a part of Oldham, about 97 per cent of the votes were recorded in January 1910; two men who waited until evening to go to the poll found that they had been personated earlier in the day. And in Darwen, which was not only highly marginal but usually had a higher

---

[1] Sexton, *Sir James Sexton*, p. 204.
[2] See *L. Courier*, 3 October 1900, 15 January 1906, 19–20 January, 3 December 1910.
[3] Hyndman, *Further Reminiscences*, pp. 69–70. The '*three*-years old register' is, of course, rather hyperbolic, as is the 93 per cent poll; turnout was 90.5 per cent.
[4] J. T. Macpherson, Preston, *Lancs. D.P.*, 12 January 1906.
[5] *Lancs. D.P.*, 10, 11 October 1900.

turnout than any other county division, a former Labour Councillor was sent for trial in December 1910 on a personation charge.[1] It is difficult to escape the conclusion that in some places the dead were called to the help of the living.

This is not, however, a very considerable factor and it is safe enough to assume that turnout can usually be explained in less nefarious terms. High levels of participation in elections can be seen as either a social phenomenon or an organisational achievement. It seems generally to be true that the people who can be most relied upon to vote are those who are most fully integrated into the community. The close-knit social structure of the cotton towns provided a context within which it was peculiarly easy to acquire the habit of voting. The north west region as a whole produced consistently high levels of turnout not only in this period but later too, with the weaving towns outstanding.[2] The numbers voting there in January 1910 – around 95 per cent in Burnley, Blackburn, Darwen, Accrington and Rossendale – must have represented virtually the entire electorate. No doubt such prodigies were only possible because of the character of these towns, but it was organisation which finally brought them forth.

In Liverpool, where voting levels were substantially lower, it was held in 1900 to be 'notorious that but for the exertions of the political organisations not 25 per cent of the electors would ever see the inside of the polling booth'.[3] Even if it may be suspected that this would not have been true in the weaving area, no chances were taken and the party machines there were famous for their high state of efficiency. In Darwen, for instance, organisation was said to be 'as near perfection as is possible' in 1900, and on that occasion the Liberals were later said to have 'polled their last man'. And while Darwen remained pre-eminent alike for its turnout and its party machinery, the 'capital electioneering organisation' in Accrington, another high-voting division, was of like order.[4] The machine's greatest triumph came with the record poll of January 1910 which was achieved despite heavy rainfall over most of Lancashire. In some districts of Rochdale and Blackburn every voter was polled and the party workers were able to close their committee rooms early in the evening, one hundred per cent successful.[5]

The voters, then, proved readier than in a later age to come to the aid of

[1] *Oldham Chron.*, 22 January 1910; *Lancs. D.P.*, 14 December 1910.
[2] On all these points see A. H. Birch, 'The habit of voting', *Manc. School*, XVIII (1950); cf. John Cotton Brown, 'Local party efficiency as a factor in the outcome of British elections', *Political Studies*, VI (1958).
[3] *Liverpool D.P.*, 28 September 1900; cf. Ostrogorski's estimate of 35–40 per cent, *Democracy and the Organisation of Political Parties*, I, 454.
[4] For Darwen see *M.G.*, 5 October 1900, 20 January 1906; cf. *M. Courier*, 7 December 1910; for Accrington see *Lancs. D.P.*, 19 September 1900.
[5] *M.G.*, 17 January 1910; *Blackburn Times*, 22 January 1910.

the party. From first to last, indeed, the franchise was very much a party affair. It was the party which put men on to the register, the party which prevented them from being struck off, the party which sought them out when they moved house, and the party which shepherded them to the poll. Moreover, the operation of the franchise was so anomalous that the parties had a keen, though often confused, interest in reforming or preserving it. The advocates of each piecemeal reform encountered not only the open hostility of avowed preservationists but also the covert opposition of those who (whether as a matter of conviction or as a tactical ploy) were advocating alternative piecemeal reforms. Paradoxically, wholesale change would have been easier for the Liberals to implement and more difficult for the Conservatives to oppose. With the advent of class politics, the Liberals could no longer afford to perpetuate a system which over-represented their natural opponents and excluded many of their potential supporters. Yet the logical strategy – a fourth Reform Bill – was confounded by the Government's irresolution. In obstructing the claim for woman suffrage the Liberal party risked being hoist with its own petard.

6 The politics of the street

Whatever one may think about democratic government, it is just as well to have practical experience of its rough and slatternly foundations. No part of the education of a politician is more indispensable than the fighting of elections. Here you come in contact with all sorts of persons and every current of national life. You feel the constitution at work in its primary processes. Dignity may suffer, the superfine gloss is soon worn away; nice particularisms and special private policies are scraped off; much has to be accepted with a shrug, a sigh or a smile; but at any rate in the end one knows a good deal about what happens and why.

Churchill, *Great Contemporaries*

I

Election campaigns were entered upon with zest and lived out their phrenetic course in a blaze of histrionics. Their importance did not rest in their capacity to effect dramatic conversions (they were the road to Westminster not Damascus) but their effect upon voting, although imponderable, cannot be ignored. The Edwardians acted out their politics in public, in a style more reminiscent of their fathers' forthrightness than of their descendants' reticence. An election campaign was perhaps a time to articulate inherent social attitudes politically, or perhaps a time for a preconceived political role to be cast off: a period for the crystallisation or disintegration of previous loyalties: a time for affirmation, or denial, or withdrawal. The electorate was systematically induced into a state of heightened political consciousness and it was this rather than ordinary life that voting reflected.

Election news took the lion's share of newspaper space. The serious papers took the campaign most seriously; on a typical day in December 1910 *The Times* carried four pages of reports and the *Manchester Guardian* seven. The weekly local papers heroically recapitulated the week's speeches *in extenso*. The more specialised journals, like the *Cotton Factory Times* or the various editions of the *Catholic Herald*, took some share, mainly by allowing election addresses to be printed in their columns. But the brunt was borne by the daily papers, which both recorded and participated in events as they crowded upon one another. There were rather over a dozen evening papers in the north west, of which three were particularly influential. All three professed Liberalism, though of slightly different shades. The *Lancashire Daily Post* in Preston was owned by George Toulmin, M.P. for Bury from 1902, and preached a rather staid Liberalism of a distinctly Imperialist hue.

The Tillotson family's *Bolton Evening News* took a line nearer the middle of the road, and its influence permeated too through the local *Weekly Journals* which it spawned over much of central Lancashire. The most radical of the three was the *Northern Daily Telegraph* in Blackburn which, under the influence of A. G. Gardiner, who was on its staff for fifteen years, and its proprietor, T. P. Ritzema, was an early champion of a progressive policy.

The battle for Lancashire's soul, however, was most earnestly contested in the region's four great morning newspapers. The *Liverpool Courier* was owned by Sir John Willox, who was for many years Conservative M.P. for Everton. Its rival was the *Liverpool Daily Post* which, under Sir Edward Russell, its editor from 1869 until after the Great War, took cognisance of the prevailing political temper of its native city by cleaving to a rather Whiggish Liberalism. In Manchester too there was a Tory *Courier*, but just as in Conservative Liverpool the Conservatives probably had the better paper, Manchester's faded Liberal tradition was at least given fresh lustre by the *Manchester Guardian*. As in C. E. Montague's 'Halland', the spirit of close rivalry between these journals in both cities was sustained by a running battle of innuendo between them, and 'when these salutes were shot, unaddressed, into the ambient ether, Halland knew well enough at whose receivers they were aimed'.[1] Indeed, at Manchester in January 1910 even these decencies almost disappeared. The *Guardian* carried every day an inset column containing a Liberal view of 'The Alternatives', which was virtually a political advertisement; within three days of its first appearance, the *Courier* was carrying every day an inset column, 'The Alternatives Refuted'. Just as the *Guardian*'s role in inspiriting the Liberal effort in Lancashire was fully recognised, so the Conservative candidates for Manchester paid tribute to the loyal support of the *Courier*.

The press was not used for large-scale political advertising until 1910. In January 1910 a full-page advertisement in the *Liverpool Courier* was using letters 2.6 inches high to denounce Lloyd George, and in December a series issued by the Unionist Publicity Association was prominently displayed not only in the Conservative press but, among other papers, in the *Manchester Guardian*. The *Manchester Courier* on the other hand, claimed to have refused rival advertisements, stating that it could not 'on any terms publish statements which, from its point of view, are wholly erroneous and antagonistic to the policy it has consistently advocated'.[2] The campaign in the press, however, was hardly a thing of itself: it was the chronicle of what happened out of doors.

In the constituencies the parties employed both new and traditional

---

[1] C. E. Montague, *A Hind Let Loose* (Penguin edn, 1936), p. 16.
[2] *M. Courier*, 30 November 1910.

methods of contacting the voters. Each candidate issued an address, which was circulated to the electors and usually appeared also in the press, either as news or as an advertisement. Election addresses, though, were somewhat stereotyped documents (it seems that from 1900 the Liberal Publication Department offered candidates guidance on their composition).[1] They vary from the comprehensive to the exiguous, and in neither case offer a very good indication of what an election was *about*. Other forms of election literature were perhaps more eagerly perused in a less sophisticated age. The Liberal Publication Department sent out catalogues to all candidates and agents, and was probably the biggest supplier on their side; its efforts were supplemented by the publications of friendly pressure groups. In Preston in January 1910 it seems that Gorst, the Liberal candidate, was responsible for issuing some seventy leaflets altogether.[2] A large number of these had been obtained from the L.P.D., but there were also leaflets published by the Land Values Publication Department, the Budget League, the United Committee for the Taxation of Land Values, the Free Trade Union and the Free Trade League, as well as those issued by the local newspaper offices and the day-to-day bills printed locally. Most of these leaflets sought to make a particular case to a general audience, but some made a general case to a particular audience, for instance the series issued by the Free Trade organisations, running from 'Are You a Grocer?' and its fellows to the several appeals to cotton workers. There is no record of how many copies were distributed in Preston but in the same election the Manchester Liberal Federation sent out half a million leaflets and handbills, an average of more than seven for every elector.[3]

Wall posters were obtained in much the same way, the L.P.D. being responsible for getting the cartoons of Carruthers Gould on to the walls of towns like Preston in 1906. In 1910 the Conservatives appear to have had a clear advantage in this respect in many places: they were in the field earlier and had more posters. Not that the Liberals were inactive. The Manchester Liberal Federation gratefully took up offers such as that of the Globe Metal Polish Co. to place at its disposal 55 positions on the hoardings for the duration of the campaign, and booked other sites on its own account. In all the Federation provided 1,100 posters in January 1910; this compares with over 2,000 posted by the Tariff Reform League on the Manchester hoardings that December.[4] The Conservative *pièce de resistance* was T. B. Kennington's genre picture of a destitute family which, under the title 'Free Trade', was

[1] See Gladstone's diary, 23 July 1900, HGP 46483 f. 75.
[2] These were collected by H. W. Clemesha, the historian of Preston and one of Gorst's supporters, and are preserved in the Preston local collection.
[3] M.L.F. Minutes, 3 February 1910.
[4] M.L.F. Minutes, 30 December 1909, 3 February 1910; T. W. A. Bagley to Edward Goulding, 10 December 1910, copy enc. in Goulding to Bonar Law, 13 December 1910, BLP 18/6/144.

reproduced, frame and all, not only as a poster but also in the Conservative press. 'Its simple story', *The Standard* noted with satisfaction, 'will be told at this election from the hoardings of practically every town in England.'[1] But stories like this were too simple for some. In Stockport there were complaints in 1906 about the 'lying Radical posters' which showed Chinamen chained together, and in several constituencies there were party agreements not to use pictorial posters in 1910 on the principle that: 'Often enough they were pictorial lies, which neither side would use from the platform.'[2] Oldham joined Knutsford and Northwich in banning them in 1911, and in April 1914 a draft agreement between the parties was drawn up to do the same in Manchester.[3]

Both parties employed sandwichmen to bear appeals through the streets. For the Conservatives, who used them extensively in January 1910, when there were plenty of unemployed men available, the medium was the message. The 'dump shops' were another favourite device of the Tariff Reformers; in December 1910 every division of Manchester and Salford had one. And there were other forms of propaganda which had some effect. The Manchester Liberal Union was experimenting with lantern slides at the turn of the century, and, on the model of the *Clarion* Van, a Liberal Van run by the Lancashire and Cheshire Liberal Federation was in use in the elections of 1910.

Although canvassing was an integral part of registration work, the house-to-house canvass was a relatively minor aspect of the campaign. W. H. Lever was one who held the scrupulous belief that it was 'highly improper for an employer of labour to canvass his workmen',[4] but the feeling against the practice went beyond this delicacy. The *Lancashire Daily Post*, for example, published a sententious leading article on 'The Ethics of Canvassing', which it wished to see abolished, and the Dean of Manchester denounced from the pulpit 'the humiliating and unnecessary art of canvassing, humiliating because it was a frequent source of inveracity, and unnecessary because if a man was fit to give a vote at all he was fit to give it without being worried by electioneering'.[5] Yet canvassing of one sort or another went on unabashed. At Blackburn in 1900 the Conservative canvassers were said to number a thousand; in 1906 the Conservative candidate in Manchester South West made a personal house-to-house canvass of the constituency.

---

[1] *Standard*, 4 January 1910; cf. the story of its procurement by Percival Hughes, the Conservative Chief Agent, *M. Courier*, 30 December 1909.
[2] Speech by A. J. Sykes, Knutsford, *M.G.*, 28 November 1910; cf. *Stockport Advertiser*, 5 January 1906.
[3] *Oldham D. Standard*, 25 October 1911; M.L.F. Minutes, 2, 22 April 1914.
[4] Leverhulme, *Viscount Leverhulme*, p. 110.
[5] *Lancs. D.P.*, 28 September 1900; Bishop Welldon at Manchester Cathedral, *M. Courier*, 17 January 1910.

The terms of the contest

Women workers were especially useful, like Mrs Holt, wife of the Liberal candidate for Liverpool West Derby, who had interviewed 1,100 voters before New Year in 1906; though in the dense industrial districts of Salford it was reported that the married women did not like women canvassers chasing after their husbands.[1] And even those candidates, like J. E. B. Seely, who made it a rigid rule never to ask for a vote were forced to unbend a little; Seely was made by his chairman to shake hands at least with two-thirds of the electorate.[2]

Although the candidate sometimes did not ask the electors for their support, they invariably asked him for his. C. P. Scott's papers show that when he stood as Liberal candidate for Leigh in 1895 he was approached by at least a score of pressure groups of one sort or another. There were manifestoes from trade unions, like the UTFWA, the Shop Assistants and the Railway Servants, asking if he would support their legislative demands; and from bodies like the National Union of Teachers and the Poor Law Officers' Association raising matters of professional concern. Temperance bodies like the Church of England Temperance Society, the Direct Veto League, the Leigh Temperance Association and the United Kingdom Alliance asked support for their respective policies. The Church Association and the Protestants wanted pledges on religious questions, as did the Bimetallic League and the Indian Import Duties Committee on economic policy. Some organisations, moreover, fearful of the written word, insisted on sending deputations to see the candidate. On one day in 1906 Balfour received deputations from the Manchester Box Manufacturers, the Protestant League, the Licensed Victuallers' Association, the Butchers' Association, and the Women's Social and Political Guild.[3] On the basis of assurances they received, organised groups like these usually branded candidates as favourable or unfavourable. Even though there can usually have been little surprise over who supported whom, the more representative of these organisations clearly played a considerable part in the outcome of elections.

This was the golden age of the platform. The development which was begun by Gladstone was brought to its culmination by Balfour when he virtually excluded the fiscal question from discussion in Parliament from 1903 to 1905, and thus gave a final fillip to the dominance of public meetings. 'In those days', Augustine Birrell recalled, 'elections were merely speaking-matches.'[4] Increasingly, vast numbers of meetings were being arranged. In 1900 the Conservative candidate in Lancaster was thought to be energetic in

---

[1] *Lancs. D.P.*, 24 September 1900; *M. Courier*, 10 January 1906; *Liverpool D.P.*, 28 December 1905; cf. *M. Courier*, 4 January 1906.
[2] Seely, *Adventure*, p. 110.
[3] *M. Courier*, 9 January 1906.
[4] Birrell, *Things Past Redress*, p. 179.

134

holding 38 meetings by polling day; his successor in January 1910 had already addressed 40 meetings with seventeen days to go, while in North Lonsdale Bliss, the Liberal candidate, had been holding three or four meetings a week for the previous eighteen months.[1] And though the election campaign in December 1910 was short, meetings were desperately crammed into the available days. At Radcliffe the Conservative candidate addressed 40 meetings in ten days, in Blackburn 30 in five working days.[2] At the height of the campaign three a night was quite normal.

The attendance at these meetings, moreover, was commensurate with the oratorical efforts. Naturally the biggest crowds were drawn by the visits of 'star' speakers, and then the only problem was to find somewhere large enough to accommodate all those who wished to attend. When Campbell-Bannerman went to Liverpool in 1906 there were over 3,000 at his meeting in the Sun Hall and 1,500 in an overflow; when Redmond visited Manchester in January 1910 he spoke to between seven and eight thousand people in the Free Trade Hall and the Grand Theatre; and there were 7,000 present when Asquith spoke at the skating rink in Burnley in December 1910, plus 3,000 at an overflow meeting in the Gaiety Theatre. The roller-skating rinks which had sprung up all over the country were a new resource in 1910 and made possible meetings twice as big as previously. They were pressed into service not only at Burnley but Preston, Darwen, Chester and Manchester South. The more orthodox accommodation offered by the Free Trade Hall in Manchester, the Sun Hall in Liverpool and the Pavilion in Wigan regularly saw crowds of five or six thousand. In the open air the throngs were on occasion larger still. On Philip Snowden's return to Blackburn from America in the middle of the election of December 1910 he was met by a torchlight procession for which it was estimated that forty to fifty thousand people turned out. At the declaration of the poll in 1906 there were ten to fifteen thousand at Preston, fifteen thousand at St Helens, twenty thousand at Newton. The announcement of the Manchester results, when Albert Square was always packed, was one of the great events of every General Election.

It was not only at such climactic moments that numbers were great. Even without a visiting celebrity there was in 1906 a Conservative meeting of 8,000 at Southport and in 1910 Liberal meetings of 6,000 at both Wigan and Birkenhead; meetings totalling, with overflows, up to eight thousand were recorded at Blackpool and the Wirral. At Preston in January 1910 three meetings of six or seven thousand were held within a few days of each other. When a popular candidate like F. E. Smith filled the Sun Hall one night in January 1910 so many had to be turned away that another mass meeting for

[1] *Lancs. D.P.*, 9 October 1900; *L. Courier*, 3 January 1910; *M.G.*, 24 January 1910.
[2] *M. Courier*, 8 December 1910; article by Lindon Riley, *L. Courier*, 7 December 1910.

later in the week was quickly arranged. In Churchill's contest at Manchester North West in 1906 his afternoon meetings regularly overflowed, and even with a couple of evening meetings, each with an overflow hall, some were still excluded. The personality of the candidate, however, was not the whole story; when the stolid Sir George Kemp succeeded Churchill in Manchester North West his meetings too were notably crowded. In Manchester, certainly from 1906 onwards, the crowds were always there, and the same seems to have been true elsewhere.

It is a remarkable thing that in Churchill's campaign men would stand in a Manchester street on a January night and join in the cheers which were all they could hear of the meeting going on indoors. When Churchill first tasted the experience in Oldham he had written of 'the succession of great halls packed with excited people until there was not room for one single person more – speech after speech – meeting after meeting – three even four in one night – intermittent flashes of Heat & Light & enthusiasm – with cold air and the rattle of a carriage in between.'[1] In such circumstances the demand for admission meant that the audience arrived early, and the packed schedule meant that they often sat for several hours waiting for the candidate. And what should they do to wile away the time but sing election songs? For sheer mindlessness it is hard to beat a good election song. The Liberals had several highbrow efforts of a Gladstonian vintage, like 'The Good Old Pilot' and 'God Bless the Grand Old Man' (with which this book began). Later, of course, they had the Land Song. But what the people wanted to sing were crude and repetitive parodies to well-known tunes, by far the most popular being 'Tramp, the Boys are Marching', to which they sang either:

Vote, vote, vote for Mr. Hindle

or

Barlow's the man for us in Salford

or

Cast your vote again for Labour.[2]

The level of public interest in elections had not always been as high as it was in 1910. In 1900 the reports from such contrasting places as Lancaster and Liverpool suggest that indifference was widespread. In Lancaster it proved extremely difficult to get meetings together at all in the country districts, while in the Scotland division, 'The depression was such that an Irishman, who had been accustomed to more stirring times, remarked in

[1] Churchill to Pamela Plowden, 2 July 1899, *Companion*, I, 1036.
[2] There is a Labour Song Sheet among the Gorton election leaflets, Manchester local collection; cf. *M. Courier*, 3 December 1910, and the songs printed in Ostrogorski, *Democracy and the Organisation of Political Parties*, I, 392 ff.

disgust, "Be jabers, if the candidates don't put more life into it they will both lose!"[1] By 1910 there was a perceptible quickening of the pulse. 'The largest available halls for meetings – and there are many – are crowded', wrote the *Northern Daily Telegraph*, 'whereas a few years ago the members' appearances were few and far between, and the attendance betokened no deep or abiding interest in politics.'[2] Churchill's visit to Burnley at this juncture aroused so much interest that it was decided to suspend traffic in the area of his meeting. Now it is true that there were occasional reports of lack of interest in the election of December 1910; on one day the *Manchester Guardian* wrote that Eddisbury 'does not seem to be outwardly excited by the election', that in Southport it 'does not appear to arouse intense interest', and that at Crewe the public were 'taking only a languid interest in the contest'.[3] This was not a widespread reaction but undoubtedly some constituencies took the election quietly. A previous General Election, with its unprecedentedly long and gruelling campaign, was only a few months behind them; in the case of Crewe, owing to a by-election in July, this was the third election that year. Perhaps the lack of demonstrativeness just meant that they had heard it all before – twice over in the case of Crewe. Judged by the turnout figures public interest was running very high.

II

The democratic model was predicated upon free will and free speech but in practice these principles were often vitiated. It was still worth noting in 1899, of a candidate seeking a Lancashire borough seat, that he was 'particular about a place free from bribery'[4] and a certain laxness, albeit more venial than venal, persisted in some towns. In Macclesfield, which had been disfranchised for corruption in the 1880s, the Conservatives were supposed to have considered attempting to unseat the Liberal M.P. on those grounds in January 1910.[5] In Balfour's constituency of Manchester East the Liberals brought a petition after the 1892 election with the object of exposing 'practices that were demoralising to constituencies especially to one like East Manchester where the voters are mainly working men'.[6] 140 charges were brought, mainly relating to treating, but despite stories of pints of beer changing hands for insufficient money and men in blue ribbons being treated, the evidence was thin and only one case, that of a man who admitted 'promiscuous

[1] *Lancs. D.P.*, *Liverpool D.P.*, 5 October 1900.
[2] *N.D.T.*, 14 December 1909.
[3] *M.G.*, 10 December 1910.
[4] Interview with J. M. Astbury, Gladstone's diary, 12 December 1899, HGP 46483 f. 53.
[5] *M. Courier*, 8 December 1910; cf. Hanham, *Elections and Party Management*, pp. 267–70.
[6] Circular of appeal to defray the expenses incurred by the Liberal candidate, J. E. C. Munro (December 1893), MGP; cf. shorthand writers notes, P.P. 1893–4, LXX, 805.

treating', was sustained. The Manchester North West by-election of 1908, however, revived Liberal zeal and a Vigilance Committee was formed to watch over the Manchester polling in January 1910, drawing workers from all over Lancashire. 'All of them are not teetotallers', it was noted, 'and consequently there will be opportunities for observation both inside and outside the public houses.'[1]

In two of the areas where corruption was most general, however, the Liberals were themselves deeply implicated. At Burnley in 1906 the Socialists alleged that the Liberals were not only buying votes but laughing it off by saying it was 'only a pint', and on polling day, according to Hyndman, 'at the last moment the "resources of civilisation" in a very tangible shape were brought into play. Of this we have sworn evidence of the most respectable character.'[2] Elections in the Ashton and Stalybridge area took place under similar conditions. 'I know Stalybridge', Jesse Herbert told the Chief Whip. 'Our people there have ways dark & peculiar. They compete with the Tories in half-crowns and free beer.'[3] When Max Aitken contested Ashton at short notice in December 1910 he was inevitably drawn into the prevailing system. Three days before the poll he and Mrs Aitken held an At Home for three thousand women (had they been men this would have constituted treating) and when the time for an election petition to be presented expired everyone breathed a sigh of relief.[4] Aitken, however, was far from happy with this state of affairs and decided as a first step to take his stand on an agreement to refrain from corruption in municipal elections which had been made with the Liberals at a conference in Manchester. Unfortunately, when an election took place at Hurst, a northern part of the borough, in April 1911 the Liberals held that the Manchester agreement did not apply to it, and the election was exceedingly corrupt, several public houses being run as 'free beer houses' during polling and for some days previously. Aitken was itching to take action but when it transpired not only that the Conservative agent agreed with the Liberals that Hurst was outside the scope of the agreement but that the Conservatives had been guilty too, he was forced to back down for the time being. 'There is every reason why we should fight a clean election this November', he told his lieutenant Morison later in the year. 'If we do not then the difficulties of a parliamentary election are going to be tremendous.' Aitken's prodding probably had some effect and inter-party cooperation was

[1] *M.G.*, 14 January 1910.
[2] Hyndman's article, *Clarion*, 26 January 1906; cf. speech by Dan Irving, *N.D.T.*, 13 January 1906; Hyndman, *Further Reminiscences*, pp. 71–2.
[3] Herbert to Gladstone, 30 November 1904, HGP 46026 ff. 77–9; and see Lee, *Social Leaders and Public Persons*, p. 54.
[4] *M. Courier*, 1 December 1910. Correspondence in the Beaverbrook Papers, especially between Aitken and Dr J. M. Woodburn Morison, the head of the working men's Unionist organisation, is the basis of this account.

secured for electoral rectitude. In 1912 it was the Conservatives who were accused of a breach of faith. 'Our party have not perfectly clean hands', Morison conceded, 'but it is generally admitted that this has been the purest election ever fought in Ashton-u-Lyne.'[1]

There were stronger inducements than free beer for men to adjust their opinions. In 1910 the *Manchester Courier* wrote of 'overwhelming evidence of a system of what can only be called terrorism exercised on behalf of the late Radical member' for an unnamed Lancashire division, where

under the shadow of our Radical 'big-wig's' mill chimney, no man dare call his soul his own. 'Yo' see, I mun think o' my bread and butter', the free and independent electors say with bated breath: 'it'd be as much as my shop was worth if I went agin' him'. Even the ballot, they think, cannot be trusted. 'He's spies all about,' they say, 'he might find out.' Men dare not be seen at Conservative meetings; among their workmates suspicion and fear put a guard on their speech. Their Radical 'representative's' foremen badger them on their own doorsteps; at Radical meetings they must never show the dissent they feel.[2]

This story, though perhaps overdrawn, has the ring of truth about it and it seems not improbable that one of the half-dozen Liberal M.P.s to whom it might have referred was unfairly exploiting his position. Intimidation was a live fear especially where a single industry predominated. At Crewe in the 1880s the Railway Company had kept hold of the town by this means. At Wigan in December 1910 it was alleged that the Coalowners' Association had put pressure on the colliers by threatening their employment (it was suggested that this explained Conservative successes in four other seats where the Association could make its influence felt). And the Conservatives were accused of intimidating tradesmen not only in Wigan but also in Southport and Birkenhead.[3]

Intimidation was not essentially plutocratic; it had given a foothold for democracy in the mid-nineteenth century and even when the object of influencing votes was less clear, force of numbers made failure to conform hazardous. Brute force was uncommon but the moral intimidation of a hostile crowd was not. The American Lowell noted that 'Englishmen regard an ordinary political meeting as a demonstration, rather than a place for serious discussion, and as such they think it fair game for counter demonstration'.[4] Heckling (in the sense of informal interjections) was an accepted convention. In some towns, like Oldham and Blackburn, visiting

---

[1] Aitken to Morison, 10 September 1911; Morison to Aitken, 11 November 1912, Beaverbrook P.
[2] *M. Courier*, 18 January 1910.
[3] For Wigan see speeches by Henry Twist, *M.G.*, 26 November 1910, *L. Courier*, 5 December 1910, and letter from 'South Lancastrian', *M.G.*, 9 December 1910; for Southport see letter issued by the Liberal agent, *M.G.*, 17 January 1910; for Birkenhead see speech by Henry Vivian, *L. Courier*, 1 December 1910; cf. Chaloner, *Social and Economic Development of Crewe*, pp. 153–66.
[4] Lowell, *The Government of England*, II, 65.

candidates were impressed by the 'courtesy and good taste' which meant that there was 'no attempt to break up political meetings or prevent any candidate from presenting his case'.[1] But in the larger towns of south Lancashire there was no such tradition.

Some candidates were better equipped than others to ride out the storm and heckling was a great leveller. When Balfour faced critical audiences, as he did in 1906, he proved surprisingly vulnerable, largely owing to his frequent use of the rhetorical question to initiate a line of argument; the more he was interrupted, the more rhetorical questions would he pose in attempting to resume his train of thought, and in an uneasy dialogue deliver himself again to the mercies of 'the voice'. Thus at Manchester:

Now what is the point in debate? (Cries of 'Free Trade' and 'Protection') What is the point in debate between us? (Cries of 'Free Trade' and cheers) I will come to free trade a little later...What is a Radical? (A voice – 'Joe Chamberlain')... I ask, what great changes are desired by the school of thinkers of whom Sir Edward Grey is the leader? (a voice – 'The abolition of Chinese labour')...But there is another. (A voice – 'We do not want a shilling income tax') I quite agree. (A voice – 'Then why don't you take it off?' cheers, and laughter.) I do not think you are listening very well, some of the gentlemen at the back. (A voice – 'Buck up, we'll soon be dead')...What is dumping? (A voice – 'Dumping them down', and laughter.) Well, what is dumping them down, as the gentleman prefers to say? (Interruption). Gentlemen, are you not even going to listen to me on free trade?[2]

To say that 'the ex-Premier's urbanity prevailed'[3] sounds like wishful thinking; it is hard to escape the suspicion that a less courteous and academic manner could better have withstood this brutal treatment. But no amount of skill on a speaker's part could quell determined interruption by a hostile audience. For example, in 1906 the Conservative candidate for St Helens, Sir Henry Seton-Karr, was interrupted at one of his meetings and a fight broke out in the hall. 'During the scene which followed', it was reported, 'the chairman appealed for order and Lady Seton-Karr made a brave attempt to sing "Home, sweet home", which led someone to shout out, "wouldn't you be better in a home", which provoked roars of laughter.'[4] When T. O. Ockleston contested Liverpool Scotland for the Conservatives in December 1910 he met with sustained opposition from the Irish (largely, it seems, in retaliation for what went on in the other Liverpool divisions) which made his campaign virtually impossible. In praising his 'ingenuity and resource', the *Courier* commended his latest stratagem of advertising his

[1] Churchill, *Companion*, I, 1034; Cecil, *All The Way*, p. 113.
[2] Balfour at Manchester East, *The Times*, 6 January 1906.
[3] *M. Courier*, 6 January 1906. It seems equally odd to call Balfour's efforts on this occasion 'the best platform speeches of his life'. Dugdale, *Arthur James Balfour*, I, 432.
[4] *St Helens News*, 16 January 1906.

meetings for one place and making his speeches at another:[1] just about as desperate an expedient as can be imagined. Incidents like these were not random examples of rowdyism; they had a distinct political significance.

In 1900 the Liberals suffered manifest unpopularity not only in places like Widnes, where their committee rooms were attacked, but in many other constituencies where they had difficulty in getting a hearing. Birrell remembered it as 'a beastly election'. In Manchester North East he and his wife were followed on polling day by a mob who spat on them and threw mud; and in St Helens Mrs Conybeare, the wife of the Liberal candidate, was struck by a piece of macadam while driving round the polling stations.[2] Much the same happened to the family of J. E. Lawton, the Liberal candidate in Salford North, which is a particularly interesting case. At that time it was Lawton who maintained that his supporters never interrupted the meetings of the Conservative Platt-Higgins, who was to poll over 55 per cent of the vote. By 1906, however, when there was a swing to the Liberals of over 12 per cent, the boot was on the other foot. Now it was Platt-Higgins who was constantly interrupted, and the *Guardian* self-righteously concluded that this was 'unofficial' retaliation for the 'authorised' Conservative doings of 1900.[3] In January 1910 the Conservatives again found difficulty in getting a hearing there and they threatened to have Liberal meetings broken up unless things improved.

In 1906 the Conservatives met with openly hostile audiences not only in Manchester but in such places as Preston, Darwen, Chester, Stockport, Birkenhead, Newton and Altrincham. Mention of 'Chinese Labour' was often the flashpoint for noisy disturbances. In the Manchester seats opposition elements were often so powerful that the 'fit and proper' resolution was lost. This seems to have happened several times to the sitting Members, Balfour in East, Fergusson in North East, and Galloway in South West (as well as to Sowler, the Conservative candidate in North); it also happened to Lord Stanley at Westhoughton and the Conservative M.P.s at Preston. In all these seats big Conservative majorities were overturned. Although in Manchester North East things were no better four years later, elsewhere Conservatives were spared this indignity in January 1910, although they frequently faced interruptions. It is an odd thing that the Liverpool Conservative candidates, who had virtually escaped in 1906, met with far more trouble of this kind in January 1910, and that in several of the Liverpool divisions there was an anti-Conservative swing.

[1] *L. Courier*, 3 December 1910.
[2] Birrell, *Things Past Redress*, p. 151; *Liverpool D.P.*, 5 October 1900. The only example I have found of a Conservative having serious difficulties is that of Colonel Foster in Lancaster. See *Lancs. D.P.*, 5 October 1900. The Liberals gained his seat.
[3] *M.G.*, 5 January 1906; cf. speeches by Lawton, *M.G.*, 28, 29 September 1900.

The Liberals, on the other hand, seem to have had a quiet time after 1900. In 1906 a spate of heckling at Chorley and the breaking up of a meeting at Widnes were exceptional (both were Tory strongholds which held firm). Indeed when an objector tried to challenge some figures at a Labour meeting in Manchester South West it was upon himself that the gathering turned.[1] In January 1910 there were a handful of minor incidents, and in December 1910, the Scotland division apart, the Conservatives too received a much better hearing.

It is virtually impossible to disentangle the rights and wrongs of such incidents from the skein of allegations and counter-allegations which provide most of the evidence about them. In 1906 the Conservatives often alleged or implied that the interruptions were organised. This was vigorously denied, and in many cases Liberal candidates went out of their way to appeal for fair play for their opponents. In particular the Labour party was several times accused of planning the disruption of their opponents' meetings, but this seems to have been just one aspect of the general vilification of Labour candidates. Even as Liberal and Labour candidates dissociated themselves from disturbances, they made it clear that they did not allow that their opponents were spotless martyrs. J. R. Clynes said that 'just as we discountenance [rowdyism], I would remind you that it was the sort of thing that was fostered and encouraged by the Tories themselves in the days of the Boer War'.[2] Now it is quite true that the parties were not above arranging for the harassment of their opponents. The Conservative agent at Preston seems to have laid on a very rough session for the visit of the Lord Advocate in the autumn of 1909, and three-fifths of his speech was spent answering interruptions.[3] But this is not a sufficient explanation of the changing party fortunes. The unhappy experience of so adroit a performer as Balfour in 1906 was quite a jolt. The Labour candidate G. D. Kelley said that: 'His own theory of the disturbances was that the late Government had held on to office so shamelessly that the public was unable to restrain its anger and disgust'; and the *Liverpool Daily Post* breezily commented that 'the moral is that the Home Rule bogey has not caught on'. The Conservative press, on the other hand, purported to see the disturbances as 'the last resource of a discomfited and discredited party' and 'further illustrations of that decline in the Liberal "morale" which was so marked throughout the last session of Parliament'.[4] This was whistling in the dark. No one had any real doubt but that disturbances occurred because of a party's unpopularity. By December

---

[1] Meeting held by G. D. Kelley, *M. Courier*, 10 January 1906.
[2] J. R. Clynes at Manchester North East, *M.G.*, 8 January 1910.
[3] See John Sanderson to Bonar Law, 24 September 1909, private & confidential, BLP 18/5/104.
[4] G. D. Kelley at Manchester South West, *M.G.*, 6 January 1906; *Liverpool D.P.*, 6 January 1906; *M. Courier*, 5, 8 January 1906.

1910 the *Manchester Courier* was writing that, 'casting our recollections back to 1906, the feature of this campaign as compared with that of four years ago, is that no longer are Unionist meetings considered to be fair game for stupid, irrelevant, and rude interruptions', and concluded that 'the proletariat, who have been so much appealed to by the "philanthropic party", have apparently begun to have their doubts. One now experiences the spectacle of what would have been almost sacrilege in 1906 – the spectacle of a Liberal candidate being actually heckled at one of his public meetings.'[1] It may seem remarkable that behaviour at public meetings should be so sensitive a barometer of the mood of the electorate, but this is what the evidence suggests. When Sir William Vaudrey accused the Liberals of organising interruptions in January 1910, the *Guardian* for once brutally spelt out that: 'It is not usually a winning side that makes such a charge.'[2] Intolerance at elections was the contempt of the strong for the weak, and pleas for fair play and free speech were advertisements of weakness.

III

Most elections were fought out according to a code of fair practice which, though often infringed, was seldom upset. Many candidates took pride in their cordial personal relationships with their political opponents. Indeed the more gladiatorial the contest, the more the candidates seem to have been drawn together (two men from a more sophisticated political world, living in hotels in the middle of towns to which they did not really belong, had much in common). J. E. B. Seely first found the friendship of F. E. Smith during the 1906 campaign. 'We would denounce each other's policy in unmeasured terms every night from different platforms in the great city of Liverpool', he recalled, 'and afterwards we would continue the denunciation over the supper-table in the Adelphi Hotel.'[3] Despite the great set-piece battles in Manchester North West, Joynson Hicks was on friendly terms with Churchill and later Kemp. When Kemp fought Bonar Law there this tradition was maintained, and Kemp was to be found scrupulously investigating the publication of an unofficial handbill attacking Law.[4] It was, indeed, common form for candidates to pay tribute to their opponents after the poll and to affirm their lack of personal animosity; but when this understanding broke down the breach was complete. The contests in Manchester in January 1910 epitomise this. In four of the six divisions there was mutual cordiality despite the hard-fought campaign. But in South West the three-cornered contest

[1] *M. Courier*, 26 November 1910.
[2] *M.G.*, 8 January 1910.
[3] Seely, *Adventure*, pp. 112–13.
[4] Taylor, *Jix*, pp. 58–9, 110; Kemp to Law, 7 December 1910, BLP 18/6/140.

became a bitter wrangle, and in North Charles Schwann was shaken by the in-fighting of the democratic Tory candidate, H. E. Howell. 'Four years ago we had a thoroughly honourable opponent', he said. 'The other man is quite a different character.'[1] The Conservative candidates for the neighbouring divisions of Gorton and Hyde in December 1910 both reproached their opponents in classically disdainful terms: Smith 'would rather lose Hyde a thousand times' – White 'would ten thousand times sooner be defeated' – fighting a clean and honourable fight than fight as their opponents had done.[2]

Unfair tactics really came down to misrepresentation of various kinds. 'It is not the lie that passeth through the mind, but the lie that sinketh in, and settleth in it, that doth the hurt.' Misrepresentation aroused such strong feelings because it was felt to be impossible to overtake a falsehood. Un-identifiable rumours were the most insidious influence. It was an old trick to suggest that a candidate would not go to the poll, as was done about Dan Irving when he stood as S.D.F. candidate for Accrington in 1906.[3] A similar rumour was used in January 1910 against the Liberal in the fight at Man-chester South West, where its plausibility presumably inhered in the fact that in the other three-cornered fight in Manchester the Liberal had withdrawn some time earlier.[4] In the same way, the idea that eminent candidates whose constituencies polled early had contingency plans to stand elsewhere should they be defeated, as was rumoured of Balfour in 1906 and Joynson Hicks in 1910, had a shred of plausibility which made it damaging to both sets of candidatures.[5] The report that Sir John Brunner, who was then contesting Northwich, was about to be raised to the peerage in 1906 was also unsettling, though none of these can have been so frankly discouraging as the rumour at Rochdale in 1895 that the Liberal candidate had died.[6]

Another manoeuvre was to issue posters in the opponents' colours. Where Liberals stood down in favour of Labour, as in Manchester North East in 1906 and Manchester East in 1910, it was worth the Tories' while appealing for votes in red (Liberal) ink in the hope that this would be taken as official advice; and in Manchester North in 1910 the Tory Democrat Howell was optimistically putting out yellow (Labour) posters in a straight fight with the Liberals.[7] The indomitable Archibald Salvidge found an ingenious twist to this tactic in December 1910 when he sent sandwichmen through the com-mercial quarter only of Liverpool Exchange with a message printed on a

[1] Schwann after the poll, *M.G.*, 17 January 1910.
[2] Henry White at Gorton, Tom Smith at Hyde, *M.G.*, 13, 16 December 1910.
[3] *N.D.T.*, 6 January 1906.
[4] *M.G.*, 17 January 1910.
[5] *Times*, 16 January 1906; speech by Hicks, *M.G.*, 12 January 1910.
[6] *M.G.*, 8 December 1905, 13 January 1906; *Rochdale Reform Association*, p. 31.
[7] *M.G.*, 15 January 1906, 2, 3 December 1910.

green background: 'To all good Irishmen! Vote for Muspratt – the Home Rule candidate.'[1] The method was versatile. If it was hopeless to try to win votes the enemy might at least be divided in two-member boroughs by giving false instructions to plump. Thus at Preston in 1910 placards were issued in Labour and Liberal colours urging adherents to vote only for their own candidates. The Conservatives denied issuing them.[2] Again it was Salvidge who essayed a more ambitious attempt to split the Liberal vote when he apparently stiffened the resolve of E. G. Jellicoe, F. E. Smith's Liberal opponent of 1906, to stand again as a third candidate in January 1910 by laying on a welcoming crowd at the critical juncture.[3] And at Accrington in 1900 the socialist candidate appears to have been financed by Tory gold.[4]

Calumny was a useful weapon, provided it did not backfire. 1900 was a dirty election, conducted, thought Chamberlain, 'with the greatest malignity by the baser sort on the other side'.[5] But as far as individual candidates were concerned it was the Liberals who had more to complain of. Cawley, the Liberal M.P. for Prestwich, was accused of contributing to Kruger's war chest on the strength of a subscription to the Manchester Transvaal Committee, and at St Helens it was being alleged ('in a jocular spirit', said the Conservative candidate) that the Liberal Conybeare was being financed by Kruger. Both candidates made preparations for legal action.[6] At Liverpool Exchange a letter was used against Richard Cherry alleging, on the basis of a shipboard acquaintance, that he was a Boer partisan.[7] In 1906 there were further incidents at both Exchange and St Helens, suggesting that the political style of a constituency was more immutable than the issues. In Liverpool, too, a Liberal attack on the Tory Watson Rutherford, saying that he did not come before them with clean hands, had to be withdrawn under threat of legal proceedings.[8] Balfour himself was the victim of a smear campaign in 1906, when a leaflet appeared reviving allegations about the financial probity of a distant forebear. 'Does Breed Tell?' it asked. 'If it does, every vote given to a Conservative is a vote given to the "Imperial Thieves' Kitchen".' The Liberal candidate's repudiation of this leaflet – 'I am fighting with the sword

[1] Salvidge, *Salvidge of Liverpool*, p. 100.
[2] Statements by C. Peach, E. Hilton Young, and Labour agent, *Lancs. D.P.*, 17 January, 3 December 1910.
[3] Salvidge, *Salvidge of Liverpool*, pp. 87–90; letter from Francis Joseph, *Liverpool D.P.*, 19 March 1934; obit. of Jellicoe, *ibid.* 7 August 1935; leader, *ibid.* 23 November 1909.
[4] See *Lancs. D.P.*, 9 October 1900, *N.D.T.*, 10 October 1900. On nomination day the Conservative and socialist candidates arrived together and both paid in gold.
[5] Garvin, *Chamberlain*, III, 603.
[6] For St Helens see *St Helens News*, 29 September 1900; *Liverpool D.P.*, 29 September 1900; *L. Courier*, 3–4 October 1900; for Prestwich see *M.G.*, 10, 12 October 1900.
[7] *L. Courier*, 4 October 1900.
[8] Letter from John Moir unreservedly withdrawing his previous remarks, *Liverpool D.P.*, 6 January 1906; cf. *L. Courier*, 9 January 1906.

of the gladiator, not with the dagger of the assassin' – did not prevent suggestions that he should retire from the contest forthwith on a point of honour; but it is difficult to believe that Balfour can have been harmed by the incident after his dignified retort that the scandal was a hundred years old while he, on his own account, had been in public life for thirty-one years.[1] The same is probably true of all the more gross attacks.

The rough and tumble was a part of every election (the only question being how rough) and the fastidious had to steel themselves for what Churchill, in one of his more jaundiced moments, called 'this wearing clatter'.[2] The archetypal election, at least in its outward manifestations, was that described in *The Ragged Trousered Philanthropists*. 'The Liberal and Tory parties waged a determined little war on the hoardings. As one party posted placards, the other placed bills on each side bearing the words "False", "Another Tory dodge", etc.' Not Mugsborough but Accrington in 1900.[3] The mechanics of such operations, of course, were outside the hands of the candidates and the format of controversy was adaptable to any substantive issue. Thus:

Dear Mr Scott,
I see our Opponents are publishing the statement of Sir James Furgusson: that you opposed the Passage of the Ship Canal Bill: which is Calculated to do you much harm. it is advisable to at once give this Lie A blank Denial in something like the following terms
Who supported the Ship Canal
Scott
Who told Lies for Party Purposes
Furgusson.[4]

There were fixed points in party mythology which affected the whole style of campaigning. The Conservatives, as the patriotic party, nearly always paraded the Union Jack (and sometimes the Royal Standard too) on election cards. When Sir George Kemp, a former Unionist standing as a Liberal candidate, did likewise, it was greeted as 'Radical Presumption' in the Tory press, and Kemp was firmly told that 'he is not now of the party of the Union Jack'.[5] As a corollary, the Conservatives were normally ready to decry 'foreigners' when they stood as candidates. In Salford South Alfred Mond had trouble on this score in 1900, and Hilaire Belloc succeeded to this

[1] The leaflet, 'War Supplies' Scandals...Past and Present', is in the Manchester local collection; statement by Horridge (Liberal) and speech by Balfour, *M.G.*, 11 January 1906; cf. 'Concilio et Labore', *M. Courier*, 12–13 January 1906.
[2] Churchill, *My Early Life*, p. 227.
[3] *N.D.T.*, 10 October 1900; cf. Robert Tressell, *The Ragged Trousered Philanthropists*, p. 537.
[4] Geo. Beresford to C. P. Scott, 1 July 1886, MGP. Scott was the Liberal and Fergusson the Conservative candidate for Manchester North East.
[5] *M. Courier*, 7 January 1910.

legacy of xenophobia in 1906. Although Charles Schwann had been Liberal M.P. for Manchester North since 1886 he was still meeting in 1910 taunts from his Conservative opponent that he was 'not too much of an Englishman'. Schwann attempted to turn the King-and-Country argument upon him by saying that the King too had German blood in his veins.[1] In view of their tradition the Conservatives in the High Peak were therefore peculiarly embarrassed with a candidate called Profumo, and George Wyndham privately denounced 'the absurdity of fighting with candidates called "Profumo" or "Bellilios"'.[2] It was an outgrowth of this sentiment that inspired the ferocious attacks on the 'anti-British behaviour' imputed to some Liberal candidates in 1900.

Some Conservatives believed that they had a prescriptive right not only to Country but to God. It was a classic charge to level against a socialist that he was an atheist. The barrister Fred Brocklehurst, when standing as I.L.P. candidate in Manchester South West, threatened legal action against anyone repeating the statement about him but most Labour candidates had to fight back with such weapons as came to hand. J. R. Clynes seized on the real point when he told a questioner, 'you are not behaving fair to Labour candidates. You have public men, some of them in this city now seeking the views of the people, leading statesmen in both parties, who have been in high office, who are pronounced Agnostics. You never think of insulting any of these men by asking them what their religion is.'[3] But when Philip Snowden hit back even more specifically by saying that Balfour was no Christian and had 'written monumental works in defence of philosophic doubt and the right of agnosticism', Balfour called this 'a stupid lie'.[4] Some Liberals got caught in the crossfire. The Blackburn progressive, the Rev. Fred Hibbert, who worked for Snowden, was criticised for supporting socialism which was opposed to religion.[5] At Southport Marshall Hall, standing as Conservative candidate, declared that they were fighting 'methods of Atheism' on the part of the Liberals, and at Darwen the Tory John Rutherford, trying in 1906 to revamp a slogan that had served well in 1900, came up with: 'Every vote given to a Radical is a vote for Atheism.'[6]

There were some constituencies, Southport and Darwen among them, which seemed to thrive on this level of electioneering – in 1910 Rutherford's

---

[1] Speeches by H. E. Howell and Charles Schwann, *M.G.*, 12, 13 January 1910.

[2] Wyndham to his father, 16 January 1910, Mackail and Wyndham, *Life and Letters of George Wyndham*, II, 649.

[3] J. R. Clynes at Manchester North East, *M.G.*, 12 January 1906; cf. letter from Brocklehurst, *M.G.*, 29 September 1900.

[4] *The Times*, 17 January 1906.

[5] *M. Courier*, 5 January 1910.

[6] Speech by Hall at Southport, *L. Courier*, 13 January 1906; leader on Rutherford's booklet, *N.D.T.*, 19 January 1906.

opponent was branded as 'the man who wants to vote himself £300 a year and a free railway pass'[1] – and to ignite new controversies almost by spontaneous combustion. Labour and socialist candidatures seem to have been especially incendiary. Nearly every one ran into trouble of a kind that Liberals encountered much more rarely. Thomas Glover in St Helens took legal action against a local newspaper after a furious campaign in December 1910 and obtained an apology in open court.[2] At Rochdale in 1906 S. G. Hobson resorted to the law when he had been accused of running a bucket-shop to speculate in cotton, which, two years after the activities of Sully, was an extremely damaging charge.[3] There was always the consolation that Keir Hardie had been subjected to worse slanders, and Labour candidates became resigned to the welter of misrepresentation. Stephen Walsh was led to the reflection that: 'He supposed no stick was too dirty to beat a Labour man's back with.'[4]

Opponents were usually equally incensed. Gorton, as a Labour constituency, regularly witnessed fierce disputes of the less exalted kind. In one speech in 1906 the Labour candidate John Hodge asserted that his opponents were resorting to personalities because fighting a lost cause, asked his audience to beware of any Conservative circulars, denied statements that the Labour party had been tearing down Tory placards, rebutted the statement that he did not want Liberal votes, and denied charges that he was a protectionist.[5] The timbre of the contest in January 1910 can be judged from one of Hodge's leaflets, 'A Tory Lie Killed', which was a copy of a letter to his opponent, Henry White:

So long as you confined your statements to the platform 'that I was spreading broadcast a statement that your name was not White', I contented myself by appealing to my audiences if at previous meetings they had heard me do such a thing, and in every instance they affirmed I had not...

This ought to have given you pause before circulating the libellous lie contained in your leaflet headed 'A Coward's Lie'.

Your Party have never, in my experience fought a clean fight. I don't think they could.

In December when, with Hodge absent, the Free Trade League came to the assistance of Labour, White called this 'a contravention of all the written or unwritten canons which should govern the conduct of gentlemen'. In retaliation the Conservatives booked up all the halls in the division and attempted

---

[1] Rutherford leaflet, *M.G.*, 7 December 1910.
[2] Fay, *The Life of Mr Justice Swift*, pp. 24–5.
[3] Report of the hearing, *M.G.*, 13 January 1906; cf. article by S. G. Hobson, *Clarion*, 2 February 1906; Hirst, *Alexander Gordon Cummins Harvey*, pp. 61–2.
[4] Walsh at Ince, *M.G.*, 30 November 1910.
[5] Hodge at Gorton, *M.G.*, 16 January 1906.

to impose conditions on their opponents as to their use.[1] The leaflet campaign was in the same vein. Labour's effort, 'Workers! Do not be Deceived and Bluffed by Mr White', was answered by 'Workers! Do not be Deceived and Bluffed by the Last LIE of the Socialist Party'; the Conservatives' charge, 'How the Labour Members Bleed the Workers', confuted by 'Biting the Hand that fed them'. Through a cumulative process of interaction White's personality and reputation had become an obstacle to political debate. An interested Conservative reported a few months later that White 'will not contest again & it is much better so'.[2]

Even in the best conducted constituencies the campaign could become distracted if disputes which admitted no conclusion were left to founder day after day. The fiscal question, when it descended from high theory to practical examples, threw up any number of these endless controversies. It was never demonstrably clear just why factories had closed down: whether they were in fact equipped with foreign machinery: or precisely what was the origin or the price of goods in Tariff Reform shops. Charges and rebuttals usually failed to resolve these points. It was doubtless an impatience with inconclusive exchanges which produced the frequent formal challenges to opponents. At its simplest a challenge meant staking money in the hope of gaining a definite answer: but most challenges petered out in a plethora of unacceptable conditions, inadmissible evidence – and counter-challenges. The swashbuckling John Rutherford at Darwen was a great challenger; in 1900 he was staking £100 in a counter-challenge and in 1906 £500 on his credentials as a Free Trader. Similarly, at Rochdale in 1900, Blackburn in 1906 and Gorton in December 1910, there were Conservative challenges of between £100 and £500 on particular points in dispute. Liberal challenges were often more modest, like Alfred Emmott's £20 in 1900 or P. S. Raffan's offer to pay for the printing of a Conservative poster in 1910. But some of the richer Liberals were less inhibited. At Chester, where the Tory R. A. Yerburgh had offered to back up his contention that white labour was impossible in the South African mines by sending out six men at his own expense, his opponent, Alfred Mond, did send out five men, whose progress and working conditions became the subject of considerable controversy.[3] And so sure was W. H. Lever that Tariff Reform would bode no good for the soap industry that he challenged the *Liverpool Courier* £1,000 to show that tariffs helped Germany or the U.S.A. to sell soap.[4] It was a Liberal, too, Baron de Forest, who raised

[1] Labour leaflet, 'Square Tactics', Manchester local collection; cf. *M. Courier*, 6 December 1910; *M.G.*, 10 December 1910.
[2] J. M. W. Morison to Max Aitken, 7 May 1911, Beaverbrook P.
[3] *L. Courier*, 27 December 1905; speech by H. Andrews at Chester, *Liverpool D.P.*, 9 January 1906; Bolitho, *Alfred Mond*, pp. 120–2.
[4] *L. Courier*, 20–1 December 1909, 22 January 1910.

the stakes highest. Arguing about the valuation of land at Southport, the Conservatives put its value at £585,000 and said that the landlords would sell like a shot at that price – whereupon de Forest, the heir to one of Europe's great fortunes, promptly made an offer: on the strength of which F. E. Smith accused him of trying to buy the constituency.[1] But what was perhaps the most dramatic challenge put more at hazard than money. In November 1910 Bonar Law challenged Churchill to return to Manchester North West and fight him, the loser to stay out of the next Parliament. Even Sir George Kemp's riposte that Austen Chamberlain or Balfour should take Law's place against himself could not save from anti-climax the failure of this beguiling idea to develop further.[2] This was, however, the way with challenges. No-one was surprised that much of the sound and fury should signify nothing, but electioneering was not without significance. Popular politics by definition had a certain vulgarity; it was the cost of making elections important events not just in the life of the nation but in people's lives too.

[1] *The Times*, 22 January 1910; speech by F. E. Smith at Southport, *L. Courier*, 22 January 1910.
[2] Speeches by Law and Kemp, *M.G.*, 29, 30 November 1910.

PART FOUR

THE RECONSTITUTION OF LIBERAL LANCASHIRE

The Liberal revival gave evidence of its scale in 1906 and of its durability in 1910. In one sense this represented the triumph of the progressive idea. The basis of progressive policy, as elaborated after 1906, was formulated in the 1890s, and the career of C. P. Scott is of particular significance here. Scott's efforts in Manchester politics did not bear fruit in the short term; but he and L. T. Hobhouse were educating their party. The Boer War had the effect of reconciling Gladstonians, collectivists and organised labour – three elements in the progressive coalition which ruled Britain from 1905. In the era of Liberal success Scott found, first in Churchill, then in Lloyd George, sympathetic exponents of his kind of views. Policy was one indispensable condition of Liberal revival: organisation was another. Here the Liberals were less happily placed, principally because they lacked a ready source of funds. But they made the best of what they had through a process of centralisation, which was one reflection of the growing importance of national as against local influences in politics. This tendency can be seen too in the matter of candidates. In 'Tory Lancashire' local candidates and local issues had been the norm. But most of the progressive M.P.s who took over from them were professional politicians deployed on a national basis.

7 C. P. Scott and Progressivism

> When in 1897 Scott invited this writer to join his staff the reason he gave was his belief that the relations of Liberalism and Labour must govern the future of politics, and that the problem was to find the lines on which Liberals could be brought to see that the old tradition must be expanded to yield a fuller measure of social justice, a more real equality, an industrial as well as a political liberty.
>
> L. T. Hobhouse

I

When C. P. Scott retired in 1929 after fifty-seven years as Editor of the *Manchester Guardian* he was universally acclaimed as one of the world's great journalists. It was only after 1914, however, that he had taken to writing a large share of leading articles himself, and during half of the twenty years before the War the daily production of the paper in Manchester was carried on by others while he attended to his Parliamentary duties at Westminster. It would be a mistake, therefore, to imagine that Scott's own pen was exclusively responsible for his importance or for that of the *Manchester Guardian* in this period. Important he certainly was, though; Ensor, who had served under him from 1902 to 1904, described him as, in 1914, 'probably the most influential liberal in the country outside the cabinet'.[1] Much of this chapter will be concerned with Scott as a politician in his own right and with his role, through the paper he controlled, as the propagandist of a strain of progressive politics which was at the core of the Liberal revival in the north west.

The emergence of the *Manchester Guardian* in the vanguard of radicalism in the late nineteenth century was in many ways a surprising development. Its origins had been in the events of Peterloo but under the successive editorship of its founders, John Edward Taylor and Jeremiah Garnett, it remained for the first forty years of its life the local Whig organ. It was Archibald Prentice's *Manchester Times* (later *Examiner and Times*) which was associated with the Leaguers and indeed the *Guardian* not only opposed Bright's selection as candidate for Manchester in 1847 but played a large part in defeating him in 1857. In 1855 the *Guardian* became Manchester's first daily paper and in 1857 its price was reduced to a penny; already sixty per cent of its sales were outside Manchester itself.[2] From this time dates the

---

[1] Ensor, *England 1870–1914*, p. 489 n.
[2] Wadsworth, 'Newspaper circulations, 1800–1954', *Trans. Manc. Stat. Soc.* (1954–5), p. 21; cf. Read, *Cobden and Bright*, pp. 99–102, 128, 136–7.

active connexion with the paper of John Edward Taylor the second who was to remain proprietor until his death in 1905. Having no wish to stay in Manchester himself, being concerned with improving the access of the provincial press to London and world news, he brought into the Cross Street offices his cousin C. P. Scott and in 1872 made him Editor. Scott was only twenty-five and Taylor still supervised the management of the paper from London; indeed, throughout his life the senior partner expected and, in his later years at least, sometimes rather touchily demanded, to be treated as an active collaborator on all matters of policy. The new Editor came from a Unitarian family which in an earlier generation of Scotts and Taylors had attended dissenting Academies. Charles Prestwich Scott, however, not without some difficulties, went up to Corpus Christi College Oxford as an undergraduate.[1] There, in the 1860s, he encountered several men whose dissimilar religious views or similar political views were oddly to keep them among those Scott would have dealings with in Lancashire: Knox and Chavasse, the future Bishops; Hicks the future Liberal Canon of Manchester; A. G. Symonds the future secretary of the National Reform Union.

Scott was far from being out of sympathy with the *Guardian*'s political ethos and it was left to the *Examiner*, under its Editor Henry Dunckley, with its sister paper, the *Weekly Times*, to make the pace for Manchester Liberalism. The Home Rule crisis, however, caught the *Examiner* unprepared, it 'found salvation' too late, and within a few years became Unionist and died. For the *Guardian*, on the other hand, Home Rule precipitated a move to the left, and in securing a weekly article from Dunckley it secured also most of its rival's goodwill.[2]

As a result of becoming the single distinctive Liberal organ in Manchester, the *Guardian*'s longstanding rivalry with the Tory *Manchester Courier* became intensified. The *Courier* had been founded in 1825 by Thomas Sowler, and Harry Sowler, a grandson, remained connected with the paper in its difficult later years. John Edward Taylor described it as 'a non paying concern' in 1902 and the Tory businessman W. J. Galloway, who at one stage offered to take it over for £60,000, was relieved in November 1904 that Harmsworth rather than he stepped into the breach.[3] Not that Harmsworth

[1] Hammond, *C. P. Scott*, chs 1 and 2. This is an excellent study of the Editor and national figure whom Hammond knew in later years. This chapter, concerned mainly with an earlier Scott, the politician and the Mancunian, will not dwell at any length on those aspects of Scott's career with which Hammond has made us familiar.

[2] One workingman wrote in 1889: 'I have taken the Manchester Weekly Times regularly for the Last 15 years but as it has become a Liberal Unionist Paper Sailing under false colours Tory like and pretending to be the genuine old Liberal paper permanently Enlarged I shall no longer support it'; D. J. Brown to the Editor, 8 November 1889, MGP; cf. Mills, *The Manchester Reform Club*, pp. 115–18.

[3] Taylor to Scott, 11 January 1902, MGP; Sandars to Balfour, 30 November 1904, BP 49762.

regarded it in any more favourable light, for he put up only £5,000 of his own money at that stage and then probably only because he wanted a peerage. Balfour himself invested a considerable sum. Nicol Dunn was brought from the *Morning Post* to edit it, but his chief innovation, to imitate the *Guardian* as closely as possible, did not seriously worry even the apprehensive Taylor. Northcliffe was annoyed at the failure of the local Conservatives to support his new property, the condition of which remained critical, and he was prevented from starting an evening paper by Lord Derby's loyalty to Edward Hulton, the publisher of the *Daily Dispatch* and the *Evening Chronicle*, neither of which was reliable from the Tory point of view. In 1911 the *Courier* lost its seat in the Reporters' Gallery, and early in 1912 North-cliffe wrote to Bonar Law that it was 'in extremis' and that there was 'no possibility of its ever paying'.[1] No amount of subsidy for political reasons could save it and it collapsed during the War, leaving Northcliffe to wipe out a deficit of £35,000.

The inability of the Manchester Conservatives to sustain a penny morning paper of their own is quite revealing in its way about the position which the *Manchester Guardian* had carved out. Many Conservatives did not forebear to express their admiration of the *Guardian*. In the midst of an election campaign one Manchester Tory referred to it as 'his favourite newspaper' and called it 'a paper of great traditions, and a paper which is fair to its opponents'.[2] As a strong partisan, bitterly as it was reviled for its opinions – 'Some years ago', said another Conservative candidate in 1910, 'great attention would have been paid to that paper, but he thought that the Boer War settled its reputation to a great extent'[3] – it was seldom attacked for alleged suppression or distortion of news. Its Editor not only professed, but his fellow townsmen believed, that in the *Manchester Guardian* comment was free but facts were sacred.

As has been seen, the demise of the *Examiner* to some extent broadened the social composition of the *Guardian's* readership; but penny papers were hardly the normal working-class diet. Any fancy that they were is effectively dispelled by the first-hand impressions which one A. Yates, very probably a printer on the paper, retailed to Scott in 1912: 'Among cultured and earnest people, on the one hand, and mere commercial men, on the other, the "M.G." is undoubtedly a great force', he admitted. 'But the majority of the electors belong to the working class, and working men do not read the "M.G."'[4] The mass electorate did not come under the *Guardian's* influence

1 Northcliffe to Law, 13 February 1912, BLP 25/2/16; cf. Sandars to Balfour, 22 December 1909, BP 49766; Reginald Pound and Geoffrey Harmsworth, *Northcliffe* (1959), pp. 291, 296.
2 Elvy Robb, Manchester East, *M.G.*, 23 December 1909.
3 Ketby Fletcher, Altrincham, *M.G.*, 8 December 1910.
4 A. Yates to Scott, 10 August 1912, MGP.

face-to-face; that influence was exerted, rather, upon men who were them-selves opinion-formers. The men who made speeches at Liberal meetings, big and small, throughout Lancashire were themselves briefed by the *Manchester Guardian*. Lloyd George was not just flattering Scott when he told him how important it was that they 'should have the support of a paper like the "Manchester Guardian", which appeals so strongly to the "intel-lectuals" of our Party...No Paper carries such weight with this class as yours.'[1]

The paper's success provoked emulation. Just as Northcliffe had tried to provide a Tory *Guardian*, so the Liberals at times wished they could have a halfpenny *Guardian*, or a Yorkshire *Guardian*, or a London *Guardian*. Thus in the winter of 1901–2, when the *Daily News*, recently 'captured' by the Pro-Boers, ran into complications of ownership, George Cadbury approached Scott for advice about the suggestion that he should become sole proprietor. But while Scott was willing to advise on the selection of an Editor, and to be open to consultation by him, he would not agree to Cadbury's idea that Scott should control this Editor by laying down lines of policy. The outcome was satisfactory to all, however, in that A. G. Gardiner, a man whose views were close to Scott's, moved with Ritzema from Blackburn to be Editor and the work of both met with Cadbury's approval.[2] In response to pressure from the Manchester Liberal Federation, Cadbury agreed in 1908 to institute a Northern Edition of the *Daily News*. In promoting it his company was careful to stress that this was being done 'in no spirit of rivalry to that great national champion of all good causes, the "Manchester Guardian". We desire to supplement, not to rival its efforts. We know, and we believe our contemporary fully realises, that a penny Liberal paper cannot adequately counteract the influence of its halfpenny Tory rivals.'[3]

In 1904 L. T. Hobhouse informed Scott that two of the leading Yorkshire Liberal newspapers, the *Leeds Mercury* and the *Bradford Observer*, were in a position to be acquired and a proposal seems to have been put before Taylor, without result. In March 1905 the proprietors brought the matter before Herbert Gladstone who agreed in an interview with Hobhouse that the best solution was for the *Guardian* to take over.[4] Gladstone therefore pressed the suit with Scott, stressing the need for his expertise and the importance of the project to Yorkshire Liberalism; but Taylor reacted to the proposal by

[1] Lloyd George to Scott, 4 September 1913, copy, LGP C/8/1/9.
[2] Cadbury to Scott, 3 January, 18 February 1902; Scott to Cadbury, 12 January 1902 (copy), MGP; Cadbury to Herbert Gladstone, 9 June 1902, HGP 46059 f. 218. For this episode, cf. Spender, *The Fire of Life*, pp. 107–13, 123–4: a graphic but surely inaccurate account.
[3] Circular enc. in G. G. Armstrong to Scott, 22 December 1908, MGP; cf. M.L.F. Minutes, 15, 22 May, 3 December 1908.
[4] A. R. Byles to Gladstone, 23 March 1905, HGP 46062 ff. 171–2; diary, 24 March 1902, HGP 46485 f. 28.

maintaining that the £65,000 which was being asked for the *Bradford Observer* was excessive.[1] Since Taylor remained opposed to taking on any outside responsibilities Gladstone eventually had to look elsewhere but Scott continued to be available to advise on the affairs of the paper, as he did at the Whips' behest in 1910.

The most beguiling dream, though, was of a London *Guardian*. The expense, however, was a great barrier. In 1905 Franklin Thomasson undertook to launch a penny Liberal London paper which Hobhouse hoped would be like the *Manchester Guardian*. Somewhat to his surprise Thomasson did not consider him too socialistic and he became chief leader writer with independence of the managing editor. Relations on the *Tribune*, however, were from the first subject to some tension and when Hobhouse's discretion was removed in January 1907 he resigned, not long before the paper itself collapsed. 'To create a new Guardian in London I wd. give up my books', he still maintained.[2] Although, early in 1908, it was made easier to obtain the *Guardian* in London there was still pressure on Scott to provide a real London edition. In January 1914 Lloyd George brought Scott into contact with Sir Charles Henry, the part proprietor of the *Westminster Gazette*, on the grounds that Henry might provide the capital for a London edition; but this proposal too proved unacceptable to the Scotts.[3] For all its expanding influence, then, the *Guardian* remained the *Manchester Guardian*. 'The public has its rights', said Scott on his eightieth birthday. 'The paper which has grown up in a great community, nourished by its resources, reflecting in a thousand ways its spirit and its interests, in a real sense belongs to it.'[4]

II

Although he had often been active in School Board elections, Scott took no direct part in Parliamentary elections in Manchester until after the city had been divided into six constituencies in 1885. In June 1886, however, with Home Rule before the country, he accepted the invitation to contest the North East division. This division was in many ways considered, at least by himself, to be the natural preserve of Alexander Forrest, a self-made businessman, philanthropist and support of trade unions; but the excuse that he had had to decline the nomination for business reasons in 1885 and

[1] Gladstone to Scott, 3 April 1905, MGP; Scott to Gladstone, 9 April 1905, HGP 46062 ff. 192–3; Taylor to Scott, 4 April 1905, MGP. Taylor's remark that, 'I never thought the M.G. worth so much', is piquant in view of later developments; after Taylor's death Scott was allowed under the terms of his will to buy the *Guardian* for £242,000.
[2] Hobhouse to Scott, 19 April 1907, MGP; cf. Hobson and Ginsberg, *L. T. Hobhouse*, pp. 44–6.
[3] Interview notes, 15, 16 January 1914, SP 50901 ff. 90–3; Scott to Hobhouse, 28 January 1914, MGP.
[4] Hammond, *C. P. Scott*, p. 300.

1886 (and again in 1889 and 1891) almost certainly concealed his Executive's reluctance to persevere with one whom they considered a weak candidate.[1] In view of the *Guardian*'s Whiggish past it is interesting to see that Scott campaigned on a full democratic programme addressed to workingmen, objecting 'to an Hereditary Chamber overruling the People's House', wishing 'to make those most able bear the greater share of taxation', coming out for shorter Parliaments and payment of Members, and proposing taxation of the land. His defeat might well have ended his connexion with the division, for he wrote to Forrest in 1888 making his prospective candidature conditional, and in 1889 evidently withdrew altogether. Scott represented the North East on the Committee of the Manchester Liberal Union, a body which the division had initially viewed with great suspicion. Either because his division only reluctantly acquiesced in the exercise of its somewhat limited powers, or because he himself was uninterested, Scott was an infrequent attender in the years 1887-9. Scott's emergence as a public figure in 1886 was thus followed by a withdrawal almost as definite in the late 1880s.

In September 1891, however, Sir James Fergusson, the Conservative M.P. for North East Manchester, had to face a by-election as a result of his appointment as Postmaster-General, and Scott came forward to challenge him. In questioning Scott during the campaign, the secretary of the North East Manchester Fabians assured him that 'your admirable address is sufficient stimulus for our support and we are busy canvassing in your interest'; and in his reply Scott reaffirmed his principles of equalising the burdens, first of taxation, secondly of the conditions of life and opportunity, by the use of state and municipal machinery.[2] Although Scott was again defeated his candidature was warmly applauded by all sections of Liberal opinion. Jacob Bright spoke of the contest's 'great educational value to the whole city', and James Bryce, while regretting that Scott would be absent from Westminster, said, 'I am not sure but what you will find the direction of the best organ of Liberalism more interesting than a session in a languid and expiring House would have been.' Undoubtedly the by-election brought Scott's name and his policy before a wider audience and helped to consolidate the influence which the *Guardian* was acquiring. Perhaps most important, though, it pulled Scott back into public life; his friend William Mather told him late in 1891: 'You are now in the political stream & you must go on.'[3]

Although it was not without striking vicissitudes, Scott's public life for

---

[1] W. H. Johnson to Scott, 21 July 1890; *Men of the Period*, p. 107.

[2] J. W. Scott to C. P. Scott, 28 September 1891 and draft reply, 4 October 1891, MGP.

[3] Jacob Bright to Scott, 9 October 1891; James Bryce to Scott, 7 October 1891; W. Mather to Scott, 17 November 1891, MGP.

the next twenty years was really all of a piece. Moreover, the objectives towards which he was working were already apparent, though for several years they were perhaps imperfectly apprehended and certainly imperfectly realised. Scott wanted three things. He wanted the Liberals to commit themselves to a progressive policy in the form of bold measures of social reform. As a corollary he hoped for the creation of a progressive party on the basis of a rapprochement between Liberalism and Labour. Thirdly, he wanted a charismatic leader to establish himself in Manchester and lead Lancashire into these progressive paths. From this time onward, then, Scott became much more active politically, especially in the affairs of the Manchester Liberal Union. In contrast to the attitude of suspicion towards the caucus which he seems earlier to have shared, now, with another General Election in the offing, he emerged as the champion of centralisation in order to secure efficient surveys of removals.[1] In August 1892 Professor J. E. C. Munro resigned as Vice-President of the Union and Chairman of the Executive Committee; Alderman Edwin Guthrie was unable to take over and thereupon Scott was elected. In consenting to serve, Scott was assuming the organisation's heaviest executive responsibility at a time when the affairs of the Union were in a state of such uncertainty that the same meeting which unanimously elected Scott also unanimously gave notice to its Secretary on those grounds. In the period up to the next General Election Scott was extremely active in his attendance at all committees and in addition had thrust upon him the most delicate problem of all, that of arbitrating between the divisions over duplicate votes.

In the General Election of 1892 Scott had once more been defeated in North East Manchester. If he wished to enter Parliament he must clearly move. There are indications that at the end of 1892 he was seriously considering a seat elsewhere, much to the real or affected surprise of Taylor who took up the high ground in disapproval. 'I confess', he reproved Scott, 'my feeling does not tend much to favour the notion that a newspaper Editor should go into Parlt.'[2] To encounter this sentiment at this stage, after Scott had already three times gone to the hustings, seems odd only if one overlooks the unpromising nature of his previous contests; it was but recently that Scott's political ambitions had become keener. But for the time being he remained prospective candidate for North East.

Partly in consequence of his position as Vice-President of the M.L.U. and partly as an independent development, these years saw him playing a much larger role in the affairs of the Liberal party not only in Manchester but also elsewhere. In 1893 he was elected President of the Gladstone Liberal Club

[1] M.L.U. Minutes, 22 December 1891, 24 March, 18 July 1892.
[2] Taylor to Scott, 17 December 1892, MGP.

in Manchester. In October 1894 he became a member of the General Purposes Committee of the National Liberal Federation, effectively as the representative of Manchester. Taylor was eager that Scott should keep up this connexion and before it was terminated the next year by Scott's return to Parliament, it had entailed at least one notable event; at the N.L.F. meeting in Cardiff in January 1895 Scott moved and Lloyd George seconded a motion supporting Home Rule and attacking the House of Lords. Scott was also acquiring a less formal position of personal influence, being asked to recommend candidates not just for northern seats like Rossendale but for constituencies in the Home Counties too.

But although he was asked by others to send Manchester candidates elsewhere, Scott had difficulties enough in trying to secure strong Liberal candidates for Manchester itself. The search for a leader of some prominence who would be an effective proponent of *Guardian*-like views was to be a standing pre-occupation with Scott. In 1888 he evidently tried to persuade John Morley to leave Newcastle and fight a Manchester seat, probably his own North East division; but Morley was characteristically pusillanimous and, while admitting that 'some great effort to put fresh heart into the county' was necessary, concluded that 'it is easier said than done'.[1] It was the prestigious North West division, geographically and commercially the central division of Manchester, which now, as later, absorbed most of Scott's attention. The division had been represented since its creation by the widely respected Conservative businessmen and landowner, Sir W. H. Houldsworth, and had been left uncontested in the General Election of 1892. In the late summer and autumn of that year Scott evidently wrote round to influential Liberals in search of a strong candidate. Several names emerged, notably those of W. S. Robson (suggested by Sir Edward Grey), C. P. Trevelyan, and Leif Jones of the United Kingdom Alliance. The sort of candidate Scott had in mind, however, was hard come by in the mid-1890s and Joshua Rowntree in Yorkshire told him that 'in the matter of a candidate we are the last people to turn to' and that they scarcely knew 'even where to look in this transition time between the old liberalism of the middle classes and the new of all'.[2] No inspirational champion was forthcoming and in 1895 North West was contested largely to maintain the organisation.

Scott's friendship with James Bryce gave him an influential voice in the selection of J.P.s when Bryce became Chancellor of the Duchy of Lancaster in 1892. Bryce was acutely aware of the need for more workingmen on the Bench and turned to Scott for advice not only upon Manchester but upon whom to consult elsewhere. Professor Munro, Balfour's tireless opponent in

---

[1] Morley to Scott, 26 February 1888, MGP.
[2] Rowntree to Scott, 8 November 1892, MGP.

Manchester East, joined Scott in urging the claims of Matthew Arrandale
and G. D. Kelley, the Chairman and Secretary of the Manchester Trades
Council, and they were among Bryce's first batch of J.P.s.[1] Bryce was
broadening the social composition of the magistracy in all the Lancashire
boroughs.

The most difficult thing [he wrote to Scott on 28 October], has been to get good
working men; sometimes because there are scarce any who can give the time,
sometimes because the local middle class Liberals who boss the Associations don't
like having working men, especially where the latter have begun to take a semi-
independent line; and it is hard to convince them that conciliation is the best way
of preventing further alienation and the setting up of an Indept. Labour Party.

Bryce made it clear that he had no objection to appointing a Tory working
man of whom Scott thought highly. Scott also made great efforts to clear the
obstacles to his becoming a magistrate which a railway man of his choice
found placed by the company: for which he was thanked by the A.S.R.S.
It was not only the middle-class but also the Protestant character of the
Bench that the Liberals sought to remedy. This too was far from straightforward since the Irish and English Roman Catholics had their own mutual
jealousies. One nominee of the Catholic Registration Association was
appointed without difficulty, and Scott was instrumental in introducing its
secretary to Bryce at the Manchester Reform Club in order that further
representations might be made. Clearly Bryce wished to find suitable
Irishmen (of whose Liberal loyalty they persistently reminded him) if only
he could, rather than take Cardinal Vaughan's nominees. Bryce's successor,
Tweedmouth, also turned to Scott for the names of working men and, more
remarkably, when Lord James of Hereford became Chancellor of the Duchy
in the Unionist Government he also corresponded with Scott about J.P.s.

III

Scott's consent to become President of the newly formed Manchester
Corporation Workmen's General Labour Union in 1891 was an example of
his practical sympathy with the industrial aims of organised labour; labour's
political aims met with no less approval. For years he was associated through
the M.L.U. with Dr R. M. Pankhurst who until his death in 1898 was active
in Liberal and socialist politics in Manchester.[2] Scott was aware that the
National Reform Union, of which his friend A. G. Symonds was secretary,

[1] J. E. C. Munro to Scott, 16 September 1892; Bryce to Scott, 13 October 1892, MGP.
[2] When Pankhurst died the M.L.U. Committee passed a resolution expressing its deep sense of
loss and 'its appreciation of his invaluable gifts devoted throughout a lifetime of continuous
effort to promote the political, social, & intellectual progress of this district and of the nation'.
M.L.U. Minutes, 8 July 1898.

had earlier had contacts with the Labour Electoral Association, but it was the emergence of the I.L.P. that really thrust the issue of labour representation forward. The circular summoning the M.L.U. Committee meeting after the municipal elections in 1893 warned that a proposal might be made to communicate with the Labour party with a view to avoiding further Liberal-Labour opposition. All types of reactions to the question were expressed at the meeting. One of the delegates from the South West said that after several attempts he was satisfied that there could be no understanding; while another delegate from the same division declared that he had joined the I.L.P. and no longer desired to be connected with the Liberal party there, active members of which had supported Conservative candidates. A similar charge was made about the Gorton Liberals. Although Scott, as Chairman, expressed no views, his hand can surely be seen in the two resolutions which were put. The first, that steps should be taken to draw up an advanced Municipal Programme for Manchester, was carried. The other urged the adoption of 'representatives of labour as candidates at the next Municipal vacancies', and was defeated.[1]

Scott's tactics were evidently to work for a Liberal-Labour understanding by interpreting the terms of the resolution on policy so broadly that they would encompass those of the defeated resolution on candidates. The Municipal Programme was drawn up by an *ad hoc* sub-committee of five meeting under Scott's chairmanship. He took the London programme of 1891 as his model, though it was to be much amended by the sub-committee, the full committee, the Liberal members of the Council and finally the '1200'. At the same time meetings were held in five of the six divisions to discuss labour and social questions and there is no doubt that the programme aimed at enabling the Liberals, as one of those who drafted it said, to 'take the wind out of the sails of the Labour people' by 'doing on their own account a great many of the things that the Labour party went in for'. The Progressive Programme as adopted at a meeting of the 1200 in September 1894, with Scott in the chair, consisted of thirteen municipal points plus five further measures which required legislative action. Among the things it advocated were fair wages and the eight-hour day for Corporation workmen, the provision of work for the unemployed, the eventual municipalisation of the Tramways, the demolition of slums and provision of workmen's dwellings – in short, London-style municipal socialism. Further, Parliament was urged to adopt the betterment principle in rating, to institute the Second Ballot and to abolish the offices of Alderman and Overseer. A proposal modestly tucked away as point 5 of the programme was underlined by the meeting's carrying a resolution, proposed by Scott, 'That every effort be made to

[1] M.L.U. Minutes, 17 November 1893; cf. 21 December 1893.

place a considerable number of working-men in the City Council and on other local public bodies.'[1]

The Progressive Programme put Manchester Liberalism on a better footing all round. 'It has been very well received', Scott told Rosebery at the end of 1894, '& has already done us good service.'[2] During the year Scott had taken a personal and more direct step towards an entente with Labour. In March 1894, after Leonard Hall of the I.L.P. had emerged as a third candidate in North East, Scott withdrew, much to the annoyance of his committee. His 'signal act of magnanimity', as Dr Pankhurst called it, was not welcomed in that spirit by Hall himself, though the secretary of the Levenshulme branch of the I.L.P. wrote to say that Scott's expressed hope that the constituency could still be won for Home Rule was shared by all his party.[3] Taylor regretted Scott's decision and thought it very hard for him 'to have to retire, after so much labour & so many hard contests, just when success seemed attainable'.[4] Now there can be no doubt as to Scott's sincerity in the matter, nor as to the real sense of sacrifice which he felt; but in the circumstances of the 1890s success was far from being attainable in North East, and his withdrawal in fact brought his return to Parliament much nearer. Almost immediately he was offered two winnable seats, Leigh and Prestwich, and Symonds, the secretary of the N.R.U., held out other possibilities. The difficulty about Leigh was that it had been intended by the Liberals there to offer it to a Labour candidate when Caleb Wright, the present M.P., retired. Scott was naturally anxious to avoid further trouble with the I.L.P., as perhaps were they with him, and it seems clear that the invitation which he received was sent with the concurrence of Labour: Taylor's goodwill assured, he was now ready to accept.

Until the General Election Scott was as active as ever in Manchester. The Municipal Programme was all very well, but there was a wider field which Scott's kind of progressivism needed to conquer, and in this sense the I.L.P. challenge in Manchester was only a symptom of the general crisis facing the Liberal party. In March 1894 Scott complimented Rosebery on making a good first speech as Prime Minister, which he thought would give great satisfaction in Lancashire, and early in May Rosebery attended a demonstration in Manchester which was, according to a later report, the biggest and most enthusiastic since a meeting of John Bright's in 1884[5]. It is difficult

[1] M.L.U. Minutes, 25 September 1894.
[2] Scott to Rosebery, 8 December 1894, Rosebery P.
[3] Pankhurst to Scott, 24 March 1894; A. F. Winks to Scott, 3 April 1894, MGP; cf. Scott's letter to the *Clarion*, 3 April 1894.
[4] Taylor to Scott, 26 March 1894, MGP.
[5] Scott to Rosebery, 30 March 1894, Rosebery P; Theodore Gregory (Hon.Sec.) at M.L.U. Annual Meeting, 30 April 1895.

either to recapture or to exaggerate the high hopes which Liberals of all shades put upon the prospects of Rosebery's premiership. These Scott shared, and perhaps Rosebery's position as the white hope of Liberalism was thrown into contrast by the black events of the summer of 1894.

Perhaps his experiences had left Scott somewhat disenchanted with the I.L.P. He certainly seems to have been more prepared to listen to the tougher talk of his colleague on the M.L.U. committee, Edwin Guthrie. 'The I.L.P. are hopeless enemies to Liberal principles', Guthrie would reiterate, 'and we should fight them by putting up Working Men Liberal Candidates in every suitable place.'[1] In June 1894 the Municipal Programme sub-committee amended its previous advocacy of 'Labour Representatives' to that of 'working men'.[2] If this was one straw in the wind, Scott's overtures to the Labour Electoral Association were a more positive indication of his modified attitude. His main qualm seems to have been that the 'independence' of the L.E.A. was rather suspect. He warmed to it only after it had suffered a reverse, for when, just at this time, the Liberal caucus at Attercliffe (Sheffield) spurned one of its most prominent members, this made Scott readier to support the L.E.A. because at least its independence had now been vindicated.[3] He contributed to its funds himself and persuaded Taylor too to give £25.

In mid-July the M.L.U. Committee received a letter from Guthrie summarising his views. He admitted that the result of the next election was dependent upon the Liberal party's relations with Labour but argued that there were two Labour parties.

One of them; – the I.L.P. is small in numbers and has pronounced itself at enmity with the Liberal Party [he wrote]. It is moreover founded upon the old false principle of *class representation*, the very principle which it has been the aim of the Liberal Party to break down in favour of Liberty, Equality and Fraternity. The other party comprises the great mass of working men...I think therefore, that, the Liberal Party should confer with the Labour Electoral Assn. with a view to the selection of a considerable number of working men as candidates at the next General Election.

He urged the M.L.U. to approach Rosebery and the Whips in order to promote allied action. At a meeting later in the month Guthrie warned 'that the Liberal Party will suffer disintegration unless steps are taken to forestall & undermine the action of the I.L.P.'[4] Since Scott had received a discouraging letter on the subject from Schnadhorst, it was decided to send a deputation to the N.L.F. to press the matter.

[1] Guthrie to Scott, 25 May 1894, MGP.
[2] M.L.U. Minutes, 13 June 1894.
[3] Scott to T. R. Threlfall, 18, 30 June 1894 (drafts), MGP.
[4] Guthrie to Scott, 15 July 1894, M.L.U. Minutes, 16 July 1894; M.L.U. Minutes, 26 July 1894.

Scott had earlier been given the N.R.U.'s opinion by Symonds. This was that although Rosebery himself, the former Chairman of the L.C.C., was in advance of the party as a whole on the Labour question, Schnadhorst was the only man at headquarters who understood such matters.

But he [continued Symonds] is enamoured of the caucus & the Federation, & cannot see that they are leaving the working men outside the organisations. It may be that the working men are themselves to blame; for they could, if they liked, capture the organisations, man them with their own class, & so force the choice of candidates according to their pleasure. But in the first place those of us who have ever taken any active part in politics know that the working men won't come to Ward meetings to elect representatives; and secondly, they appreciate fully the fact that the money is in the hands of a few men who wd. refuse to subscribe for the election expenses of a working man. Ergo, they will have nothing to do with the caucuses.[1]

Now Symonds had his own axe to grind, but his plan of 'going to the working men if they will not come to us', was probably the only serviceable principle for the Liberals to adopt. It was, however, one on which the N.L.F. committee, confronted by the Manchester deputation in October, refused to take any practical step.

The M.L.U. made efforts itself on these lines in regard to the Council and School Board elections, coopting three members of the Trades Council on to a sub-committee dealing with the question; but although deputations from it visited all six divisional executives, the secretary had to give the somewhat lame report that: 'The recommendations of the Committee were favourably received but had not resulted in the selection of any Working-man Candidate for the reason that the local Committees had entered into engagements which would prevent it this year.'[2] Within the year, however, trade unionists were elected as Progressives, among them Matthew Arrandale, chairman of the Trades Council and now a J.P. Although the L.E.A., too, did establish itself in Manchester – it offered help to Mrs Scott in the next School Board elections – progress was slow.

Little wonder, then, that when Rosebery asked his opinion Scott replied that the political situation was critical.

There is undoubtedly among Liberals in Manchester a growing sense of discouragement [he wrote]. In part no doubt this is due to the attacks of the Independent Labour Party. Everywhere they are hampering us and losing seats at the local elections and they are likely to do the same at the General Election. These things, however, wd. be of comparatively little consequence if our own party were in good heart and saw its way clearly. But the reverse is the case. I can remember no time in which people were so entirely at sea on the greatest political issues of the day.

---

[1] Symonds to Scott, 28 June 1894, MGP.
[2] M.L.U. Minutes, 26 July, 1, 14 August, 19 December 1894.

The helplessness of the party, especially in the face of the House of Lords, was 'inducing among many a sense almost of despair. It is this which makes us powerless to cope with the flank attack of guerrilla enemies like the I.L.P. and which, if steps are not speedily taken to rouse and animate the party, will prepare the way for what may prove a crushing defeat at the polls.'[1] Scott urged that the Liberals must fight the House of Lords. Rosebery disarmingly professed full agreement and both in conversation and in correspondence Scott continued to press upon him the view that in the long run an attack on the Lords could not fail.

Nothing materialised, however, to fulfil the bright promise of Rosebery's leadership, and, unlike Sir Edward Russell, Scott grew increasingly out of sympathy with him. It is probable, though, that before he left office Rosebery offered Scott a peerage and certain that he (subsequently) offered Taylor a baronetcy; with their high notions of journalistic independence both declined as a matter of course.[2] Scott was by no means alone in his disillusionment with Rosebery. John Trevor of the Labour Church, who told Scott that he had seen in Rosebery 'another Gladstone', found it 'a great mystery' that he had become so uninspiring a leader.[3]

The General Election of 1895 was as a result an impossibly uphill battle for the Liberals, especially in Lancashire. There was no progressive alliance, nor a progressive policy before the country on which to base it. The *Manchester Guardian*'s leader on the first day of polling put forward the theory that in voting Liberal, electors would 'vote primarily to vindicate the authority of the representative House against the intolerable usurpations of the House of Lords', and a handbill put out by Sir Henry Roscoe, one of Manchester's three existing Liberal M.P.s, gamely concluded: 'The Issue now is Are the People or the Peers to Prevail?'[4] This was to fight the election that they would have liked it to have been. In similar vein, Dr Pankhurst, who stood as I.L.P. candidate for Gorton against a Tory, 'challenged Liberals to discover in the I.L.P. faith one iota in which they differed from the Liberal progressive programme'.[5] The elections went

---

[1] Scott to Rosebery, 30 September 1894, Rosebery P. His criticism of flaccid leadership and his advocacy of an offensive posture were strikingly echoed in another letter to Rosebery written at the same time by a far more loyal Roseberyite, Sir Edward Russell, Editor of the *Liverpool Daily Post*. Russell to Rosebery, 20 September 1894, Rosebery P. It was at this time that Scott's friends the Pankhursts joined the I.L.P. and that Jacob Bright's wife Ursula offered to; see Pankhurst, *The Suffragette Movement*, p. 119.

[2] See Hammond, *C. P. Scott*, p. 58; J. Wood to Scott, 24 March 1902; *Daily Dispatch*, 24 March 1902 (enc.), MGP.

[3] Trevor to Scott, 14 August 1895, MGP.

[4] *M.G.*, 13 July 1895; South Manchester election leaflet, 1895, in Manchester Local History Library.

[5] Speech at Gorton, *M.G.*, 16 July 1895. There were even milk-and-water Liberals capable of taking these brave words seriously enough to defect! 'I *did vote Tory* this time', wrote one of

disastrously for the Liberals all over Lancashire; in Manchester they lost two seats including Roscoe's. The official explanation made much of 'the combination of privilege and self-interest arrayed against the Liberal party' and of the socialists' attacks. There was also an alleged 'want of appreciation by those masses whose lot the legislation and administration of the late Government were to a large extent designed to ameliorate'.[1] But had the Liberals deserved to do better? Measured against Scott's vision of a broadly-based progressive party their limitations were only too obvious. He himself saw clearly how far there was to go, and deprecated precipitate action in regard to leadership, programme or organisation, despite his recognition of their shortcomings. Harcourt would lead in the Commons, and, he told Robert Hudson, in opposition nothing else much mattered. 'It will be time enough presently', he added, 'to think about what we shall do in office. We shall be older – perhaps wiser. Perhaps the whole conditions of the problem will have changed.'[2]

IV

The General Election saw Scott elected to Parliament as Member for Leigh, a position he was to hold for the next ten years. He made no very great mark in the House and his attendance was far from assiduous. But he could hardly be expected to continue all his work in the M.L.U. where, as the Secretary said, he had been 'practically the official head of the party'. In 1896, though, he succeeded Jacob Bright as its President and, complimented on his continued services in 1897, declared that 'he would always feel his home was in Manchester – his political home as well as his home in every other sense'.[3] Only in 1899, by which time his wife's deteriorating health was making long visits abroad necessary, did Scott sever his formal connexion with the M.L.U.

During Scott's absences the nightly work of getting the *Manchester Guardian* out devolved initially upon the chief leader-writer, W. T. Arnold. His successor, C. E. Montague, shared this task first with L. T. Hobhouse and after 1902 with Herbert Sidebotham who came to the fore during the Boer War. Scott was always reluctant, however, to make a clear delegation of his authority and Taylor was far from satisfied. 'The Editorial organisation is, I fear', he complained, 'so far as suggestion direction & initiative go, nonexistent for ⅔ds of the year.' Firmly as Scott might deny this and offer to

Scott's correspondents, 'after much thought and indecision but I felt that the democracy of labour was becoming too tyrannical, and the liberal party as represented by the government were legislating, not for the liberals as a whole, but for what they were told was the party by the labour leaders'. R. H. Edmundson to Scott, Thursday (1895), MGP.

[1] Secretary s report, M.L.U. Annual Meeting, 24 March 1896.
[2] Scott to Hudson, 30 August 1895 (copy), MGP.
[3] M.L.U. Annual Report, 24 March 1896; M.L.U. Annual Meeting, 9 April 1897.

resign the day Taylor wished it,[1] the previously unclouded confidence between Proprietor and Editor seems to have become increasingly overcast. Had the *Guardian* been a one-man band Taylor's forebodings would no doubt have been fulfilled. It was largely because of the exceptionally gifted team of men which Scott gathered around him that these years, far from seeing the decline of the paper's influence, saw its real emergence as a national force. J. A. Hobson, F. W. Hirst, John Masefield, R. C. K. Ensor, H. N. Brailsford, R. H. Gretton and H. W. Nevinson were all at various times employed by the paper; and Harold Spender and H. W. Massingham were for a time on the staff after the *Daily Chronicle* had changed hands during the Boer War; Graham Wallas, Augustine Birrell and Hilaire Belloc were but three among many contributors of similar distinction. Many of these 'new Liberals' were introduced to the paper by L. T. Hobhouse, whose own contribution, and that made by the two men, Arnold and Montague, who acted as 'assistant editor' to Scott, merit rather closer attention.

W. T. Arnold, a nephew of Matthew Arnold, and a considerable classical scholar, had had an influential voice in the *Guardian*'s decision on Home Rule in 1886, but by the late 1890s failing health made him a less central figure. Haslam Mills put him 'with Scott and Montague as one of the chief modern makers of the paper' and claimed that he was 'the true founder of the *genre* school of *Guardian* writers, a body as defined and distinguishable in its way as the Glasgow school of art'.[2] It was C. E. Montague, however, who was this school's most distinguished exponent. He had joined the *Guardian* from Jowett's Balliol in 1890 and in 1898 married Scott's daughter. Montague's stylistic finesse could sometimes suggest a measure of condescension, not only towards London – a 'slight disdain' of which Mills thought the spiritual secret of the *Guardian* men – but also towards a public less perceptive than himself of the nuances of Liberalism. J. B. Atkins, who worked with both Arnold and Montague in the 1890s, conceded to Arnold the broader political grasp at that time, but admitted: 'It was *Montague*'s qualities I was after, though I must add that Montague's model of writing was a snare to many... Imitation Montague was a disaster.'[3] Montague's unswerving commitment to the aims of the paper made him an ideal lieutenant to Scott and it was he who gave the *Guardian*'s views their most felicitous expression.

The strengthening of the editorial staff was achieved at a financial cost which disturbed Taylor. Editorial salaries rose by fifty per cent between 1895 and 1898 (or so Taylor said), and while Taylor, in his letters to Scott from the watering places of Europe, pressed for increases for individuals he was

[1] Taylor to Scott, 22 December 1899; Scott to Taylor, 9 January 1900, MGP.
[2] Mills, *The Manchester Guardian*, pp. 118–21; cf. Hammond, *C. P. Scott*, pp. 54 ff.
[3] Elton, *C. E. Montague*, p. 39.

appalled at the natural consequences when they had been granted. He increasingly exhibited an old man's fears that uncontrolled expenditure was making the paper less profitable than it should have been. At one point, while admitting that the staff was strong and that good work was being done, he came very near to the ultimate heresy in confessing himself 'doubtful whether the four to five columns of rather lengthy & heavy leading articles fully justifies the cost of their production or the space they occupy'. Yet his pride in the growing position of the paper could also lead him to express his gratification 'especially that its reputation has been won by the employment of great literary ability inspired by high & noble aims'.[1] The crisis for the paper's fortunes represented by the Boer War was faced by Scott with buoyant fortitude. He admitted that some old readers had been alienated.

But the talk about the paper being seriously weakened is all moonshine [he told Hobhouse]. The war will cost us a lot of money & we don't gain the full compensating advantages of increased circulation common in wartime, but that is all. On the other hand the future will justify us, the character of the paper is raised & the deserters will mostly come back.

He took comfort too from the large increase in postal subscribers after the *Daily Chronicle*'s change of ownership.[2] Taylor, on the other hand, was more worried by the cost of covering the War and this did nothing to restore his equanimity about the paper's future. At the end of 1900, for instance, a tiny incident was enough to trigger off exchanges between him and Scott. 'Will you kindly remember that I am not dead yet', wrote Taylor, '& that a certain decent respect to my position is due?' Scott replied (overdoing it a little): 'I have never allowed myself to look upon myself as other than your servant like any other man on the staff.' Unmoved, Taylor responded: 'I have never treated you as such, have never wished you to hold such a degrading position nor have I ever seen any such attitude on your part.'[3]

Part, at least, of the dissatisfaction with Scott's direction of the *Guardian* which Taylor came to feel must have stemmed from his sense of betrayal over policy: that the new Liberalism had too little time for the Nonconformist shibboleths which he held dear. It was Taylor's outlook which would have justified Margot Asquith's retrospective characterisation of the *Manchester Guardian* as the mouthpiece of 'the non-Conformist Conscience'.[4] Taylor's own belief in Local Veto had led him in 1895 to suppose that it was an electoral trump card and he had assured Scott that 'the Dissenters & the

[1] Taylor to Scott, 28 November 1897, 17 January 1899, MGP.
[2] Scott to Hobhouse, 30 November 1899, 4 January 1900, MGP. The circulation of the *Guardian* fell steadily from 48.8 thousand in 1898 to 36.8 thousand in 1905. Wadsworth, *Trans. Manc. Stat. Soc.* (1954–5), p. 25.
[3] Taylor to Scott, 31 December 1900, 5 January 1901; Scott to Taylor, 2 January 1901, MGP.
[4] *The Autobiography of Margot Asquith*, II (1922), 168.

Temperance men are both in good heart and if they are full of enthusiasm they can wield a mighty power'. The *Guardian* did not, he believed, attach proper weight to the question and this he deplored, declaring in 1898: 'If the Liberal Party be not true to its Temperance Programme let it pine for ever in the cold shades of Opposition!'[1] And again in 1904 the Liberal fight over the Licensing Bill disappointed him. Taylor also shared the Nonconformist suspicion of Roman Catholicism, while the *Guardian* under Scott refused to indulge in this form of bigotry. There were persistent allegations by Non-conformists that there were 'Catholics in high places on the *M.G.*'. It was just after the Nonconformist M.P., R. W. Perks, never much of a Home Ruler, had approached him in this regard that Taylor told Scott that he must not commit the *Guardian* to the policy of an independent Parliament for Ireland.[2] Scott had not only just voted for this in Parliament, but almost immediately refused to yield to Nonconformist pressure from his constituency on the Irish University question. Nor had Scott's great interest in the education question led him into sectarian paths, and in 1902 Taylor 'was rather astonished at the comparatively favourable reception given to the new Educatn. Bill by the *M.G.*'; while Scott's own policy, of constructive amendment within the framework of a measure he saw as capable of achieving much, was argued at length in a letter to Hobhouse.[3]

Hobhouse – here is the crux. If Taylor tried to draw Scott back to an older Liberalism, Hobhouse would lead him on to a more rigorously formulated progressive policy. (Not that Taylor was personally unappreciative of Hobhouse, for he much admired his work.) Hobhouse, then a Fellow of Corpus Christi College Oxford, had been recommended to Scott by his Oxford friend Arthur Sidgwick as 'a strong Liberal & progressive of the best type'.[4] Hobhouse had envisaged doing part-time work from London, but after a trial period at Manchester Scott's admiration for his work and his own sympathy with the *Guardian* led to his taking a house there in 1897. Scott's high expectations of Hobhouse were more than fulfilled and he was soon writing to him that 'none of us could have known what a big reinforcement you wd. bring to everything that is best in the paper or how much you wd. help us all round'.[5] When Scott was in London, and Hobhouse and Montague were bearing the brunt of the leader-writing, he and Hobhouse were in constant communication. Hobhouse later wrote of his Manchester period: 'I was in my right milieu there as I have never been before or since.'

[1] Taylor to Scott, 29 June 1895, 22 January 1898, MGP; cf. Hammond, *C. P. Scott*, pp. 82–3.
[2] Taylor to Scott, 17 February 1898, MGP.
[3] Taylor to Scott, 2 April 1902; cf. Scott to Hobhouse, 27 May 1902, MGP; and leader, *M.G.*, 9 May 1902.
[4] Sidgwick to Scott, 20 November 1896, MGP.
[5] Scott to Hobhouse, 1 February 1898, MGP.

And after his death Scott recalled the 'delightful companionship of five years'.[1] It laster no longer than that because ultimately Hobhouse's academic ambitions were incompatible with full-time journalism. Between February and June 1901 Scott and he tried to thrash out the difficulties of his position, which were complicated by Scott's absences. Scott told him: 'You have given us a great deal and much of it will I think remain as part of the life of the paper. It wd. be absurd to complain if it cannot be more.' And, while he would not contest the claims of philosophy, he went on to admit: 'My absences are I know a pretty heavy drawback because the arrangements I have to make are of necessity provisional and I sometimes doubt – and more than doubt – whether I am justified in thus dividing myself. It is your problem in another form.' Hobhouse wished to leave that autumn since no better arrangements seemed feasible: Scott was troubled lest any sense of grievance should mar his going. 'Personally too I shall miss you dreadfully', he told him, 'but probably it is my own fault.'[2] In the event Hobhouse was persuaded to stay until the autumn of 1902, and he remained a confidant of Scott and a contributor to the *Guardian* (in later years a director too) for the rest of his life.

Scott's basic political attitudes, of course, were formed long before he ever met Hobhouse, as his public life up to 1895 shows. One of his correspondents had recalled in 1893: 'Many years ago I heard you say, when we were discussing Socialism, that you would gladly give all you possessed to the people if only they could use it.'[3] He was on cordial terms with many socialists, Hyndman and Blatchford for instance. At Oxford, Hobhouse, in his homespun and red tie, explaining the cause of the unskilled unions, might have been taken for a socialist; but he was never a socialist *pur sang*. Though an avowed collectivist, he had written in 1890: 'I don't go as far in Socialism as Webb does'; and neither he nor Scott had much rapport with the Webbs – 'They have been raking among statistics too long', said Scott.[4] Hobhouse's essential aim in his *Guardian* period was the intellectual reconciliation of Socialism with Liberalism and hence of the Liberal party with the Labour movement.

In his earlier book *The Labour Movement* Hobhouse had dealt sympathetically with trade unions, Co-operation, and municipal and state socialism. 'What really unites these movements', he had written, 'is the general character of the means they adopt for the furtherance of their ends. In one form or another all three alike are introducing the principle of the collective

---

[1] Hobhouse to Scott, 19 April 1907, MGP; Scott's Introduction to Hobson and Ginsberg, *L. T. Hobhouse*, p. 7.
[2] Scott to Hobhouse, 21 February 1901; 4 June 1901, MGP.
[3] T. C. Horsfall to Scott, 29 August 1893, MGP.
[4] Hobson and Ginsberg, *L. T. Hobhouse*, p. 30; Scott to Hobhouse, 3 June 1899, MGP.

control of industry by the community in the interests of all its members.' After the payments made for services rendered in industry there remained a surplus which it was the state's duty to redistribute. 'We cannot afford to pay £500,000,000 a year to a number of individuals for wealth that is due partly to nature and partly to efforts of their fathers.' Thus Rent, Interest and Profits formed a natural reservoir which should be tapped for public purposes through a graduated income tax, death duties and the taxation of ground rents. If Hobhouse did not claim that the bourgeoisie would produce its own grave-diggers he did state: 'In this way we should make Rent and Interest pay for their own extinction.'[1]

The four aspects of the 'Labour movement' which Hobhouse applauded had all received Scott's support and encouragement. And the *Guardian*'s support for the Engineers in their disastrous strike in 1897, for example, brought accusations that it had helped prolong a fruitless struggle. Hobhouse would airily talk to Scott about what 'we collectivists hold' in regard to industrial developments.[2] Perhaps his warmest advocacy in the legislative field was reserved for the series of leaders in 1899 on old age pensions, which he fondly recalled to Scott when the subject had become practical politics in 1908. It was the relationship between this question and land taxation that he and Scott were particularly concerned to explore. 'With this financial weapon', Hobhouse wrote, 'it wd. be possible to give local authorities – parish councils as well as municipalities – more power in direction of building & also to deal with Old Age Pensions. Practically this union of measures is what I beg to propound to you as the social programme of the party!'[3]

He believed, of course, that the Liberal party had been too slow in taking up such a programme, and, when unhappy, as in February 1901, he could write to Scott that 'unless some great & unforeseen change occurs the Liberal party seems to me destined to futility & I find some difficulty now in writing from any point of view but that of an avowed independent. Of course one wants to work with them but – you know what I feel.'[4] His earlier enthusiasm for collectivism had become not blunted but tempered. His Oxford friend Francis Hirst, on meeting him in 1899, thought that his views had changed a great deal in the previous three years. 'He speaks and thinks very differently now of Cobden and Bright', Hirst noted.[5] This was just as well in view of his new audience. It was one thing for political iconoclasts to toy with the philosophical maxims of T. H. Green in the common rooms of Oxford; it

---

[1] *The Labour Movement*, with an introduction by R. B. Haldane (1893), pp. 45–6, 78.
[2] Hobhouse to Scott, 14 March (1899), MGP. He was arguing that they should support the move for a combination of cotton employers.
[3] Hobhouse to Scott, 25 February 1899, MGP.
[4] Hobhouse to Scott, 14 February 1900 (1901), MGP.
[5] Diary 21 August 1899, Hirst, *In the Golden Days*, p. 174.

was quite another to explain to Lancashire Liberals, the sons and grandsons of the followers of Bright and Cobden, that they must treat Labour not as a rival but as a partner, and an equal partner at that. 'There is no more important political truth', Hobhouse was proclaiming to them at this time, 'than that social reform as conceived by the best reformers of our time is a legitimate outgrowth and development of the older Liberal principles. To throw over these principles in the name of Socialism is to turn towards reaction in the search for progress.'[1] The antithesis of Liberalism *or* Socialism was false. Progress – 'or what is the same thing, social justice'[2] – must spring from a union of Liberalism *and* Socialism. Hence, in practical terms, the progressives might move from this ideological synthesis towards electoral unity.

It is not surprising that when Hobhouse returned to the themes of *The Labour Movement* in two later books, there was a significant shift of emphasis. In *Democracy and Reaction*, published in 1904, his view of the problem of social progress was inevitably coloured by the experience of the Boer War. 'Militarism, based on Imperialism', he stated, 'has eaten up the national resources which should have gone to improve the condition of the people.' And in a footnote he alluded to the truncated pensions campaign of 1899, stalled for the lack of funds only half as great as the increase in the military budget.[3] Both this book and *Liberalism*, published after the elections of 1910, were much more conciliatory towards traditional Liberal thinking, and he recalled previous attitudes in the tones of a sadder and a wiser man.

The old Liberalism, we thought, had done its work. It had been all very well in its time, but political democracy and the rest were now well-established facts. What was needed was to build a social democracy on the basis so prepared, and for that we needed new formulas, new inspirations. The old individualism was standing in our way and we were for cutting it down.[4]

Even in *The Labour Movement* Hobhouse had spared attention to justify the new Liberalism as a development of the old; but there was a more sustained attempt in the final chapters of the two later books to demonstrate, in the first place, the essential continuity of Liberalism from Cobden onwards, and in the second, the mutual dependence of Liberalism and socialism.[5] The Boer War had helped vindicate an older strain of Liberalism, and the subsequent working arrangement between Liberal and Labour was depicted as a natural outcome of this.

[1] Leader, *M.G.*, 7 July 1899. It cannot, of course, be *proved* that this was written by Hobhouse.
[2] *Democracy and Reaction* (1904), p. 226.
[3] *Ibid.* p. 31 and n.
[4] *Ibid.* pp. 209–10.
[5] *Ibid.* pp. 209–37; *Liberalism* (1911), pp. 214–26; cf. *The Labour Movement*, pp. 88–98.

V

Even before the stormclouds of war in South Africa had given vent, the translation of the *Guardian*'s ideas into Liberal policy was posing considerable difficulties. The social policy did not, of course, stand in isolation, and Scott and Hobhouse were much exercised about the issue of Imperialism as manifested not only in South Africa but in the Soudan and elsewhere. Primarily on these grounds they saw John Morley as the surest exponent of their views, and sought to bolster up his position in order to keep Campbell-Bannerman up to the mark. Indeed at the end of June 1899 matters went further; Morley was invited to contest Rochdale and Scott thought that he would probably stand 'if we urged him and it comported a general movement to assert our view of things, which is pretty much his view, at the Election'. After an interview with him Scott reported that he 'felt fairly satisfied that he wd. be right on both sides of our policy' but wished Hobhouse also to see him. 'If he finally decides to throw in his lot with us in Lancashire', Scott added, 'we shall have to make a big push and possibly form an independent organization for the county.'[1] Working on the basis of Hobhouse's fuller elaboration of the progressive policy, did Scott now hope to fulfil his other two ambitions by building a progressive party in Lancashire around the person of Morley? This *démarche* could hardly have been imminent since Scott's faith in Campbell-Bannerman, though jaundiced, had not quite disappeared. Moreover, the Liberal leadership – Herbert Gladstone and Asquith at least – approved the idea of Morley moving, though doubtless they were ignorant of all the implications.[2] When Hobhouse saw Morley he found him on the point of refusing Rochdale. 'One of his main motives', Hobhouse reported, 'was the fear of complications with Labour. I satisfied him however that on the lines we are going upon there wd. be little difficulty from this cause, & incidentally satisfied myself that he will go with us in our "social programme".'[3] If Morley had taken on, not a good chance like Rochdale, but a really uphill battle, his Montrose Association was apparently ready to keep his seat open; he may have hankered after challenging Balfour in Manchester East, although there a Liberal candidate was already in the field.

Official Liberalism had its own plans for concerting the challenge to the Tories in Manchester which this unfruitful independent initiative did not affect. When Scott had welcomed W. C. Steadman, M.P., to the M.L.U. Annual Meeting in 1898 as a 'direct representative of labour', he was taken

[1] Scott to Hobhouse, 25 June 1899, 14 July 1899, MGP.
[2] Gladstone's diary, 14 July 1899, HGP 46483 f. 30.
[3] Hobhouse to Scott, 21 July 1899, MGP.

up by Guthrie who made his usual plea for the use of the term 'working man'. Nonetheless, when in the summer it was agreed to summon a conference of all the divisions, the delegate from North West, S. Norbury Williams, urged that in selecting six candidates they ought to admit the Labour party's claim to one seat.[1] At this conference, in October 1898, Williams pressed his case and a resolution was put advocating one 'Labour Candidate'. Guthrie's motion to insert 'Working Man' instead failed by 27 votes to 18. Scott concluded the meeting with a pregnant speech from the chair in which he declared his opposition to treaties or bargains but dropped the broad hint 'that the Divisions should have regard not only for their own interests but also for the interests of the Liberal Party generally throughout the City'.[2] In South West the I.L.P. duly selected Fred Brocklehurst as candidate and Tom Ellis, the Liberal Chief Whip, in writing to Scott in March 1899, hoped that he would get Liberal support. He also made a plea for A. H. Scott's candidature in East, and pointed to the absence of Liberal candidates in the three other Tory-held divisions.[3] Why there should have been doubt over Liberal support in A. H. Scott's case is not clear – he had always been an active Liberal – and it was presumably he whom Guthrie had in mind when he made his familiar speech in support of workingmen candidatures at the M.L.U. meeting that April.[4]

The need for a 'star' candidate remained. In November 1898 the M.L.U. resolved to support North West in their effort to enlist the help of the Leadership in securing a candidate of Cabinet rank 'on the grounds that the presence of such a candidate is, not only necessary because of the commercial & high character of the NW Div, but also on a/c of the effect it would have in the constituencies of Lancashire, Cheshire, & Derbyshire'. When the deputation put this point to Herbert Gladstone the next spring, his diary recorded mixed reactions: 'I asked why select this divn., wh. can hardly be won, while admitting desirability of the proposal. We discussed this & at end I remained doubtful whether if a leader cd. be found, he shd. fight this divn.'[5] Gladstone's view that on strategic grounds the prestige of North West was outweighed by its hopelessness from a Liberal point of view led him to urge them to find a local candidate, since he was sure that they could.

The cryptic references in Gladstone's diary, however, chart the emergence of a grand design to put Liberalism back on the map in industrial England.

[1] M.L.U. Annual Meeting, 15 April 1898; Minutes, 8 July 1898.
[2] M.L.U. Minutes, 6 October 1898.
[3] Ellis to Scott, 24 March 1899, MGP.
[4] M.L.U. Annual Meeting, 11 April 1899. Fred Maddison, another Lib-Lab M.P., was chief speaker. He made a self-congratulatory speech applauding the principles of the Manchester School and attacking Socialists; fortunately for his own composure Scott was absent.
[5] M.L.U. Minutes, 18 November 1898; Gladstone's diary, 25 April 1899, HGP 46483 f. 3.

Asquith should fight a Birmingham seat and either Birrell or Bryce be drafted, not to opulent Manchester North West, but to Manchester North East, Scott's old territory. By late June 1899 it appeared that if Herbert Paul, a rather lesser luminary, would take on Birmingham, Gladstone could implement his alternative plan of sending Asquith into Manchester. Asquith's name, however, was soon lost sight of altogether, and with Paul on offer to Birmingham, the Manchester arrangement crystallised around Birrell. Birrell himself was not unwilling when Gladstone broached the plan to him at the end of July, and when the Secretary of the M.L.U. heard of it a few days later he told Gladstone that 'he felt sure that N E M'ter wd. joyfully accept Birrell'.[1] As part of the two-pronged attack, Campbell-Bannerman delivered his only major policy speeches until the General Election at Manchester and Birmingham respectively, both in November 1899. The Manchester meeting fulfilled all the hopes pinned upon it – 'an unqualified success', the Secretary of the M.L.U. rejoiced; 'an enormous success', admitted the honoured visitor. It also gave Campbell-Bannerman a chance to test feeling and he was much impressed by the earnest entreaties of the North East deputation for Birrell.[2]

Early in December 1899 Birrell met the North East officers himself and came to a provisional arrangement with them. 'I wish you had left me alone', he concluded his report to Gladstone. Campbell-Bannerman too was beginning to rue a plan which, conceived as a fair-weather enterprise, seemed foolhardy in heavy seas; 'in my opinion', he confided to Gladstone, 'B. had better be left where he is at present. We had not calculated on this war imbroglio; and I confess I would not have believed that my countrymen wd. have been so carried away.' But by this stage it was too late to draw back; money could easily be found, and the danger to Birrell's Fife seat if he left had to be weighed against the compensating advantages to Manchester. 'The proposal that B. shd. fight Fergusson has been received in Lancashire with *enthusiasm*', Gladstone wrote to Campbell-Bannerman, and urged him to make a personal appeal.[3] And so Birrell was persuaded to forsake a secure constituency for an unpromising one, with the satisfaction that he was doing as his Leader wished.

I saw enough when I was in Manchester in November [Campbell-Bannerman told him], to convince me that the effect of your candidature would be very great. What the honest folk there want is warmth & encouragement. Now you are very

---

[1] Diary, 4 August 1899, HGP 46483 f. 41.

[2] T. Gregory to Gladstone, 16 November 1899, HGP 46057 ff. 212–13; Campbell-Bannerman to Gladstone, 17 November 1899, HGP 45987 ff. 39–42.

[3] Birrell to Gladstone, 10 December 1899, HGP 46057 ff. 228–9; Campbell-Bannerman to Gladstone, 9 December 1899, HGP 45987 f. 52; Gladstone to Campbell-Bannerman, 16 December 1899, CBP 41215 f. 180.

warming & very encouraging. I am sure it will be a great comfort to you to be told that you are permeating Lancashire, even if you don't win a seat for yourself: but I have little doubt that the seat will be all right, and at the same time you will help the victory of others.[1]

Such was the hope; and indeed the extent to which Manchester Liberalism had come to terms with 'Labour', both in regard to policy and candidatures, while it now had the prospect of a first-class leader in its midst, made it more formidably equipped to face an election than at any time since the Third Reform Act. When the election came, however, all this was over-shadowed by the War.

VI

Scott had been berating the foreign policy of the Salisbury Government for being jingoist long before War broke out in South Africa. In his presidential address to the M.L.U. in 1897 he claimed that the Tories' greatest failure had been over events in Armenia, Crete, the Soudan, the Transvaal. 'He alleged against the Government's foreign policy that it had been weak, that it had been aggressive, and that it had been bullying.' He deplored 'continuity' in foreign policy, and asserted that there was 'practical unanimity' between Tory workingmen and Liberals in this matter.

They needed to test their policy [he concluded], by the simple principles of morality and right dealing between man and man, and they needed to curb the gross and wanton spirit of aggrandisement and of commercial and territorial greed which was eating like a canker into the heart of the people. – (Applause.) The mass of the people were far more free from these influences than the rich and powerful.[2]

There are here, of course, echoes of a Gladstonian preference for the judgement of the masses rather than the classes. But for Scott a 'democratic foreign policy' was never a substitute but a precondition for a vigorous social policy. 'More and more', he was soon writing, 'one feels that foreign policy is the touchstone of all policy.'[3]

It was because of a common concern with combating Imperialism, then, that in Scott's and Hobhouse's eyes Morley improbably emerged – how improbably later became clearer – as the prospective leader of their progressive movement. The attempt in 1898 to induce Morley and Leonard Courtney to speak out in Manchester under the auspices of the Manchester

---

[1] Campbell-Bannerman to Birrell, 5 January 1900, private, Birrell P. '*Moriturus sum*', Birrell began his reply. Birrell to Campbell-Bannerman, 6 January 1900, CBP 41235 ff. 177–8.

[2] M.L.U. Annual Meeting, 9 April 1897.

[3] Scott to Courtney, n.d. (September 1899), Gooch, *Life of Lord Courtney*, p. 372. The anti-Imperialist side of the progressive case is ably examined in Bernard Porter, *Critics of Empire, British radical attitudes to colonialism in Africa, 1895–1914* (1968), esp. chs 3 and 6.

Society for the Protection of Native Races, which kept a watching brief on the Soudan, foreshadowed the alignments of the pro-Boer agitation. In making Morley the President of this small society Hobhouse hoped that 'by asking him we shd. encourage him a bit in the direction of coming forward more'. The lack of Liberal leadership on these 'Imperialist' questions distressed Hobhouse who repeatedly dismissed Campbell-Bannerman's efforts as 'feeble'. He complimented Scott in April 1899 on achieving 'an influential, if not leading, position among the peace Liberals', and admitted that Morley 'is inclined to look upon you as a hen on the duckling that takes to the water'.[1]

As the South African situation worsened in the late summer of 1899 it became more urgent to get Morley to take to the water himself. Scott and Hobhouse hoped to lure him to Manchester for a big demonstration and, receiving a qualified assent, had the M.L.U. Committee specially convened on 29 August. Scott implied to them that Morley had taken the initiative, and it was resolved to hold a meeting, the arrangements being left with Scott and the officers. At Scott's behest, however, a nominally separate Transvaal Committee was set up instead at a meeting in Manchester on 5 September, with himself, Guthrie, and other leading members of the M.L.U. as founders, to whose number the names of seven ministers of religion were added.[2] The formation of this committee was welcomed by old and new Liberals alike. Taylor was delighted, and rejoiced that his temperance ally, Leif Jones, who had been present at its inception, met with Scott's approval. Similar support – warm and financial, that is – came from Gladstonians like William Mather and J. P. Thomasson; and Albert Bright, who had followed his illustrious father into Unionism, was persuaded to take the chair. Leonard Courtney was without difficulty induced to attend as an earnest of the non-party character of the meeting.[3] The real problem was to stir up Morley himself who, mistrusting Scott and Hobhouse as 'unpractical and too fanatical',[4] and fearful of splitting the party, considered that he had done his duty by addressing a meeting in his constituency. Manchester was a gamble. It represented the call for a fervent moral crusade in the Gladstonian tradition; but Morley, then writing the Gladstone biography, would have preferred chronicling his hero to emulating him. After sending F. W. Hirst to spy out the ground in Manchester, where he found Hobhouse annoyed at the effect of so many vacillations, Morley finally consented. 'The

[1] Hobhouse to Scott, 19 October 1898, 7 April 1899, MGP.
[2] M.L.U. Minutes, 29 August, 12 October 1899; papers relating to the formation of the Manchester Transvaal Committee, 31 August 1899, MGP; *M.G.*, 6 September 1899. F. W. Hirst's diary of this period, printed in *In the Golden Days*, pp. 174–84 gives Morley's side of the episode.
[3] Gooch, *Life of Lord Courtney*, pp. 369–70.
[4] Hirst, *In the Golden Days*, p. 179.

demonstration', wrote the *Guardian*, able to announce it at last, 'comes in the nick of time, a moment of great danger but still of hope.'[1]

The Free Trade Hall had been unobtainable; in order to get the St James's Hall Scott had to buy out a Grocers' Exhibition and 'even drank champagne with the principal grocer in the middle of the day to keep him good-humoured'.[2] The hall was packed on the night, not entirely with sympathisers. Albert Bright was unable to make himself heard and the beginning of Morley's speech was subjected to the same treatment. But Scott had apparently made prior arrangements with the Chief Constable and interrupters were run out of the hall as they revealed themselves. So Morley was able to launch into his resounding peroration, telling his audience that war would bring no profit, but loss of human life: 'It will be wrong.' They might add a province to the Empire: 'It will still be wrong.' And in a final thrust – 'you may send the price of Mr Rhodes's Chartered up to a point beyond the dreams of avarice; yet even then it will be wrong, – (Loud and prolonged cheers, the audience rising and waving handkerchiefs and hats.)'[3] The undemonstrative Hobhouse declared that 'Morley's one hour speech was worth months of ordinary life'.[4] As Morley wrote: 'The grand potent monosyllable with which I wound up was not to be resisted.' Or, as Scott later recalled, with his grimmer appreciation of the temper of Manchester's jingoists: 'You could have heard a pin drop. He was awfully pleased. He thought his eloquence had convinced them, but it wasn't that. They'd all gone.'[5]

The impression created by the meeting was considerable. Scott received fulsome congratulations from all the principals for instigating it. There were, however, serious obstacles to clear if the peace movement were to maintain its momentum. The exchange of telegrams between Scott and Campbell-Bannerman, then in Marienbad, had elicited only tepid expressions of good-will.[6] The movement attempted, too, to go beyond party, and Courtney was staunch enough. 'He himself alas', his wife admitted, 'can't be said to be an embodiment of many Unionists.'[7] Again, it was all very well for Scott to receive the impression of one sympathiser, 'that yr. association like the Cornlaw League – will be stronger as a local than as a London one',[8] but to a somewhat awesome extent the anti-War Liberals could now only look for a

[1] *M.G.*, 12 September 1899.
[2] Scott's recollections in 1923, recorded in Masterman, *C. F. G. Masterman*, pp. 328–30.
[3] *M.G.*, 15 September 1899.
[4] Hirst, *In the Golden Days*, p. 184.
[5] Morley, *Recollections*, II, 85–7; Masterman, *C. F. G. Masterman*, p. 330.
[6] See Scott draft to Campbell-Bannerman, n.d., and Campbell-Bannerman's telegram, 19 September 1899, MGP; cf. Spender, *Campbell-Bannerman*, I, 242–3; *M.G.*, 20 September 1899.
[7] Kate Courtney to Scott, 20 September 1899, MGP.
[8] Lord Farrer to Scott, 23 September 1899, MGP.

firm lead to Manchester. Morley's failure to kindle anti-War feeling into a national movement – a paralysis of will all too typical of him – left the Manchester Transvaal Committee doing what it could within its own area.

With the outbreak of War in South Africa and his disillusionment with Morley, Scott came to modify his opinion of Campbell-Bannerman, and from this point onwards his attitude, though not yet admiring, and still not wholly set, was broadly sympathetic. Campbell-Bannerman's visit to Manchester in November 1899 did much to rally and unite the Manchester Liberals, whom he found 'in a rather subdued & *funky* state of mind: even among themselves, divided, – Aldn. Southern, anti-Boer; Aldn. Guthrie, Chairman of the Transvaal Committee'.[1] The M.L.U. managed to remain substantially united over the War, though the framing of the resolution for the Annual Meeting in 1900 occupied three committee meetings; Guthrie finally had it amended so that it combined stiff criticism of the War's pursuance with deprecation of the neglect of domestic legislation which it had caused. Scott's hopes in the winter of 1899–1900 were pinned upon the attempt to rally the Liberal organisation in this way and to get the leaders to stand firm. Campbell-Bannerman's speeches now impressed him. 'It looks as though he had more in him both of courage & statesmanship than we had known', he told Hobhouse, '& if this proves to be the case his caution & canniness are all to the good.'[2]

In these months of decision the choice was becoming starker between Campbell-Bannerman's leadership and – what Taylor feared – 'a Liberal party led by Rosebery, Grey, Fowler & that lot'.[3] The rift between the Imperialist and pro-Boer sections of the party was becoming more conspicuous. While the *Manchester Guardian* with one mind rallied to the existing leadership, the *Liverpool Daily Post* hankered after just the sort of Liberal party which Taylor described. To some extent, throughout the War period, Lancashire Liberalism was to be torn between the two and the contrast at each critical juncture in Liberal fortunes between Scott's Manchester and Russell's Liverpool is instructive. Sir Edward Russell, the *Daily Post*'s Editor, had throughout the 1890s acted as a channel of provincial opinion for Rosebery, and he would not accept Rosebery's retirement from the Liberal leadership as at all final. 'No one can do for Britain what you can do', he had implored. 'My dear Lord, pray do it, sooner or later. Give us all a lead.' All Rosebery's disclaimers could not damp Russell's ardour. But Russell was too ingratiating to be factious. ('Let me too worship the risen sun', he wrote to Campbell-Bannerman, all too revealingly, in February

[1] Campbell-Bannerman to Gladstone, 17 November 1899, HGP 45987 ff. 39–42.
[2] M.L.U. Minutes, 9 March, 4, 10 May 1900; Scott to Hobhouse, 4 January 1900, MGP.
[3] Taylor to Scott, 2 April 1900, MGP.

1899.) Perhaps his long and discouraging experience as a Liverpool Liberal taught him to bend before the wind – any wind. So, late in 1899, he was simultaneously assuring Campbell-Bannerman that he was quite of his opinions over the Transvaal, admitting to Asquith that the *Post* did not speak as he wrote, and telling Rosebery: 'Your return to official power is just a question of time.' Again Rosebery refused to be drawn, but even in describing this prospect as 'if not impossible, (which nothing is), in the last degree improbable',[1] he left the door open that chink through which the hopeful Liberal Imperialists who wrote the *Daily Post* could always discern some light.

Scott, on the other hand, became a committee member of the League of Liberals against Aggression and Militarism, along with men in the *Guardian* circle like G. W. E. Russell, Harold Spender, F. W. Hirst, J. A. Hobson, H. N. Brailsford and J. L. Hammond, aided by other pro-Boers like Sir John Brunner and Lloyd George. This body, which took effective shape in February 1900, was formed to provide support for Campbell-Bannerman's policy – against Rosebery's, it was not necessary to add. Such alignments did much to reconcile the Gladstonians with Labour which, with few exceptions, stood by them.[2] Scott felt, too, that while financial assistance to the I.L.P. might be open to objection on the grounds that it would be promoting opposition to Liberal candidates, it ought to be possible to work with the I.L.P. locally on the basis of a peace policy.

In February 1900 Scott's friend William Mather had won a by-election in the Rossendale division easily enough despite his association with the Transvaal Committee. A sterner test was to come. In Manchester South a time bomb had been ticking away for years, since the Duke of Argyll, whose son and heir held the seat, was in failing health. In 1896, and again in each of the next two years, the South Manchester Liberals beseeched the M.L.U. Committee to allocate all duplicate votes to them, on the grounds that the Unionists were doing the same; but to no avail. The Committee's faith in the old Duke's longevity must have suffered a considerable blow when, early in April 1900, it was reported that he appeared to be dying. Leif Jones, the prospective Liberal candidate, promptly informed his Chief Whip that the

---

[1] Russell to Rosebery, 13 July 1898, 6 December 1899, Rosebery P; Rosebery to Russell, 10 December 1899, Rosebery–Russell corrce; cf. Russell to Campbell-Bannerman, 7 February, 3 November 1899; and 4 December 1899 enc. Russell to Asquith, 29 November 1899 copy, CBP 41234 f. 159, 41235 ff. 95–7, 122–8.

[2] The possibility that Brocklehurst, the I.L.P. candidate for South West Manchester, might be 'wrong' on the War set Scott wondering about 'getting rid of him' in March 1900. See Scott to Hobhouse, 7 March 1900, MGP. Scott no doubt felt that while it was fit and proper to support Labour men who were 'right' on the War, and it might be impolitic to oppose Liberals who were 'wrong', it was out of the question for progressives to go out on a limb for Labour Imperialists. In the event, as will be seen, Brocklehurst redeemed himself.

division would be contested. 'The Liberals ought', he maintained, 'to have a better chance of doing well in Manchester than in some other places, as the Guardian has done a great educational work in the city, & the Manchester Transvaal Committee, of which I have been a member since its foundation has done something to stem the war fever throughout Lancashire.' Gladstone, on the other hand, contented himself with hoping that the Duke of Argyll would not die since there could hardly have been a worse time for a by-election, and added that since Jones's view of the War was not held by the party generally, 'the contest will have to be fought in a sense independent of the party'. Jones, angry at the rebuff from headquarters, enlisted the aid of Scott, and of Guthrie, who was his divisional chairman. 'Unfortunately it is true', Guthrie admitted to Gladstone, 'that a great number of the members of the party are in favour of the war, but I think it is, at all events in the North here, the minority.' They were ready to fight, he reaffirmed, and must fight on the War, 'for it is quite clear, whether we will or not, the contest will have to be on the subject of the war. The other side would see to that if we did not.'[1] How true! With the by-election upon them in May, the Conservatives issued a leaflet which stated that: 'In choosing as a candidate a member of the *Manchester Transvaal Committee* the Radicals have thrown down to you the challenge to fight the election on the question of the war in South Africa.'[2]

The Manchester South by-election was the paradigm of khaki electioneering. It was bad enough for Jones at the start of the campaign in the second week of May; on the defensive, he was forced into tendering elaborate assurances that he had no sympathy for 'the Tory Government of President Kruger', and that he was not a 'Pro-Boer' but a 'Pro-Briton'. Whether Jones was helped by Scott's commendation that 'he had got the root of the matter in him' is doubtful. On the same night that it was given a leading Unionist, while calling Leif Jones a bird of passage, continued:

But he had committed himself to the principles of the 'Manchester Guardian' which they had with them always, and were they going to support a man who was capable of holding – and they would give him credit for holding honestly – such abominable opinions as they read in the 'Guardian' every day? As long as the 'Guardian' continued always on the side of the enemies of England there would be plenty of Unionists in Manchester.[3]

If all this were not bad enough, on May 18 the news was received in Manchester that Mafeking had been relieved. The enthusiasm was enormous. Electioneering was temporarily abandoned. One poster now urged the

---

[1] Leif Jones to Gladstone, 3 April 1900; Gladstone to Jones, 5 April 1900; Guthrie to Gladstone, 14 April 1900 – all copies by Jones enc. in Jones to Scott, 17 April 1900, MGP.
[2] Leaflet in Manchester Local History Library.
[3] Speeches by C. P. Scott and Dr Sinclair, *M.G.*, 10 May 1900.

electors to 'let their first message to gallant Mafeking' be that of a Liberal defeat. Leif Jones had acquired considerable Labour backing, and Fred Brocklehurst of the I.L.P. sought to rally his party to the decision they had made to give him open support. It was all as dust in the balance. Scott deplored the 'Mafeking mania' to Hobhouse and admitted: 'Anything short of an utter rout wd. satisfy me now.'[1] But a rout it was; the Unionist majority which had been under a hundred in 1895 was now over two thousand, a pro-Government swing of eleven per cent. Peel, the new M.P., asked his supporters, as well he might, that in their dreams they would 'remember Mafeking'.

VII

The Manchester South by-election showed how lonely was the position of the *Guardian* even in its native city. During the War its offices were often threatened with violence and were sometimes under police protection, as was Scott's house. Scott received, both personally and as Editor, many letters from subscribers of up to thirty and forty years' standing who were giving up the *Guardian*. Now it is true, as Haslam Mills pointed out, 'that many people, after "giving up the *Guardian*" for one offence, were found to be in a position to "give it up" again somewhat later...'. T. C. Horsfall, who now told Scott that he was forced 'to believe that either political life has partly deprived you of your reason or that you have preferred the supposed advantage of a political party to the good of the country', was certainly one of these.[2] The letters which survive in Scott's papers savage the *Guardian* for its 'insane drivel, in condemnation of one's country, & the support of the enemies of one's country', for its 'grossly partisan tone', for the impression it gave 'that its sympathies were with England's enemies rather than with England itself', and urged Scott to 'insist that the writer of your leading articles shall pull himself together, and cease to write such puerile stuff'.[3]

Naturally the *Manchester Courier* was not backward in attacking the *Guardian* and Scott himself, and with the General Election approaching stepped up its pro-War campaign. The by-election had not encouraged Liberal efforts; in July, for instance, the Altrincham Liberals were refusing to fight in an autumn dissolution, even though they had a good candidate. There was an attempt to bring in Courtney to take on Manchester South as a Liberal but he wisely refused to consider a seat that was 'assuredly hopeless'. In the end, a local man, Edwyn Holt, did contest the division for the Liberals; he was another member of the Transvaal Committee, 'the body which',

[1] Scott to Hobhouse, n.d. (May 1900), MGP.
[2] Horsfall to Scott, 2 July 1900, MGP; Mills, *The Manchester Guardian*, p. 130.
[3] See the bundle of letters to Scott at the time of the War, MGP. All those quoted are dated between October 1899 and August 1900.

according to Peel's address, 'by its support of the Boers, is largely responsible for the War'.[1] Birrell's candidature in the North East division remained as a reminder of a more confident Liberal mood. Gamely as he put his hopes for the advancement of Labour before the Manchester electorate – 'They ought by this time to have representatives in the Cabinet', he claimed – the War had, as he fully realised, not only scotched his chances but reduced the point of the whole exercise.[2] The *Courier* several times printed its 'Pro-Boer Pillory' in which Scott figured high on 'The Black List', as did quotations from the *Guardian* among its 'Pro-Boer Tit-Bits'. Indeed it even affected the distinction in its tabulated lists of candidates of not only (C.) and (R.) for Conservative and Radical but also – (Pro-Boer).

Conversely, Taylor was critical of the distinctions the *Guardian* drew between the policies of different sections of the Liberal party on annexation. The *Guardian* did offer some degree of support to all shades of Liberals. The same is true of the similarly pro-Boer *Northern Daily Telegraph* in Blackburn and also of the Liberal Imperialist *Lancashire Daily Post* in Preston. The *Liverpool Daily Post*'s version of Liberal Imperialism consisted of saying very little, and that little as non-controversially as possible and it deplored Liberal factionalism. The *Guardian*'s responsibility for the dismal showing of the Manchester Liberal candidates is difficult to assess. 'It is a fitting conclusion', wrote one correspondent, 'that our party should be finally ruined & broken in the City by a journal which has befriended every interest hostile to our country for years past'; and the Liberal Imperialist press in Lancashire was no less slow to assert – perhaps more in sorrow than in anger – that the Manchester Liberals had 'paid the penalty of the "Manchester Guardian's" policy on South African affairs'.[3]

Scott's own candidature at Leigh made him an exposed figure. He held a strong position in the loyalties of the workingmen in the division and his early anti-Imperialist speeches in the Commons seem to have pleased the local party. In August 1900, however, his agent resigned over Scott's views on the War, just after the local press had viciously attacked Scott for aiming at the discomfiture of his own country – 'he will only be content when any power gets the better of the United Kingdom' – and had further insinuated that Kruger had paid the *Guardian* £26,000 to advocate his views.[4] Scott, in short, had to face both before and during the Khaki Election a barrage of calumny, and it is little wonder that Herbert Gladstone privately singled him

[1] Gladstone's diary, 16 July 1900, HGP 46483 f. 74; Courtney to Scott, 13 September (1900), MGP; Peel's Election Address, September 1900, Manchester Local History Library.
[2] Speech in Manchester North East, *M. Courier*, 27 September 1900; Birrell, *Things Past Redress*, pp. 148–51.
[3] J. J. Bisgood to the Editor, 3 October 1900, MGP; *Lancs. D.P.*, 3 October 1900.
[4] *Leigh Observer*, 11 August 1899; John Wood to Scott, 7 September 1899, MGP.

out, together with Lloyd George, among five Liberal M.P.s whom he expected to lose their seats. The relief and rejoicings at Scott's safe election were therefore correspondingly the greater. It is probably no accident that the letters of congratulation – forty or more – are preserved among Scott's papers on this but no similar occasion. The result so encouraged his friends because, as one of them put it, 'your enemies and traducers are as numerous as they are persistent and unscrupulous'. Not only pro-Boers felt this, for Haldane wrote a warm letter in which he claimed that there was 'no real difference of *principle* between the two sections of the Liberal party', and stressed the need now for 'a strong, resolute *lead*'.[1]

The difficulties over the leadership remained acute as long as the War lasted, and the War was to last unexpectedly long. The *Guardian*'s policy remained highly controversial – according to Scott, most of the paper's own sub-editors disagreed with it – but the War's lack of striking successes gave its critics some sense of practical justification; in November 1901 Lloyd George paid Scott a notably generous tribute at Leigh which was already phrased somewhat retrospectively.[2] The M.L.U. too remained steadfast, and applauded the characterisation of the measures taken against the Boers as 'methods of barbarism' in July 1901 which, as Hobhouse later noted, marked the real emergence of Campbell-Bannerman as a leader; in August Alderman Southern, who had earlier been the leader of the pro-War faction, went out of his way to affirm his loyalty to the Leader. A proposal for an anti-War meeting, to be addressed by Lloyd George and John Burns, however, split the Committtee that October and, had it materialised, would have caused the resignation of its Honorary Secretary, Theodore Gregory.[3]

Scott's own relations with the leadership were warmer now and he seems to have accepted that the Whips were not responsible for promoting those Liberal Imperialist candidatures, of which he disapproved in any case, but more strongly when they were in opposition to Labour. 'I have risked more for the Labour party than any of my predecessors', Gladstone truthfully assured him.[4] Scott was even prepared to envisage cooperation with Rosebery at the time of his Chesterfield speech in December 1901, though he looked to Campbell-Bannerman to keep the party from being put 'in any way in his hands'.[5] In Liverpool, where the Liberal Imperialists continued to have the

[1] Whip's memorandum book, 1900, HGP 46108 f. 122; Henry Harwood to Scott, 10 October 1900, Haldane to Scott, 17 October 1900, MGP.
[2] *Leigh Journal*, 8 November 1901, transcript in LGP A/10/1/32.
[3] M.L.U. Minutes, 1 July, 17 October, 27 November 1901; Annual Meeting 14 August 1901; cf. Hobhouse, *Liberalism*, p. 222. The voting in October 1902 was 11–5 in favour of holding the anti-War meeting under official auspices.
[4] Gladstone to Scott, 30 October 1901, MGP; Scott to Gladstone, 31 October 1901, HGP 46059 ff. 84–5.
[5] Scott to Campbell-Bannerman, 29 December 1901, CBP 41236 ff. 259–60.

upper hand, Edward Evans, the local leader, proudly told Gladstone of how he had drummed up all the pro-Boers for a meeting addressed by Grey[1] and when a meeting of the Liverpool Reform Club was summoned to welcome the Chesterfield speech they were drummed up once more. But at it Sir Edward Russell raised their hackles by exceeding his brief in seconding the motion before the gathering. He had described Rosebery's claims as being those of a statesman of a traditional type, which democracy had been putting aside, 'not of the new type that people thought of when they used such catch-phrases as "the new diplomacy", "the new Liberalism", and the other new things'. These claims, he firmly implied, now entitled Rosebery to the leadership of the party.[2] In gratitude for this demonstration Rosebery himself held a dinner at the Club and Evans and Russell continued to pursue him well into 1902, though Evans was always careful not to compromise his official position in the National Liberal Federation.[3]

After 'methods of barbarism', even when Scott criticised Campbell-Bannerman for lack of 'backbone', it was in no hostile mood – 'His good nature and simplicity make him an easy prey'. And he was loth to see Asquith shut out, regarding him as 'a great Parlry. force, possible yet to be utilized'.[4] It is difficult to imagine, however, that Scott could have had much sympathy with the Manchester Liberal Federation (which replaced the M.L.U. in 1903) when the new body made overtures for a Rosebery meeting in Manchester. But just as the organisation was new, so there were new issues and new men to confront them. Alderman Guthrie's death in 1904 removed one stern opponent of independent Labour representation. The new Executive Committee found itself effecting between the Liberal and Labour parties adjustments which would have been impracticable ten years previously, in the interests of a progressivism now seen primarily in Parliamentary terms. L. W. Zimmerman, representing East Manchester on the M.L.F., emerged as the central figure in these matters. In municipal affairs the problem was more difficult. Although this was not primarily the province of the M.L.F. some efforts were made. In 1904, for instance, the Liberals of Bradford Ward were determined to keep a council seat which they had always held and resisted the efforts of the M.L.F. Executive 'to avoid the opposition of two Progressive candidates', and when, after an election in which the M.L.F.

[1] Evans to Gladstone, 18 November 1901, HGP 46059 ff. 87–8.
[2] *Liverpool D.P.*, 21 December 1901. Russell naturally put a more equivocal gloss on his position when he wrote to Campbell-Bannerman. Russell to Campbell-Bannerman, 21 December 1901, CBP 41241 ff. 236–7.
[3] The correspondence is in the Rosebery Papers. It is a case study in Churchill's apothegm: 'At first they said "He will come". Then for years "If only he would come." And finally, long after he had renounced politics for ever, "If only he would come back."' *Great Contemporaries*, p. 18.
[4] Scott to Hobhouse, 23 January, 23 June 1902, MGP.

C. P. Scott and Progressivism

had thereupon decided to take no part, the Bradford Liberals sent a deputation to express their annoyance, the Executive unyieldingly restated its view 'that in a Ward where ninety per cent of the population were of the working class it was not desirable to oppose a Labour Candidate for the Council who conformed to the Progressive Programme'.[1] The lack of any fundamental ideological conflict between the Progressives and Labour may be judged from two leaflets used in these same 1904 elections. Electors were asked to support James Archer of the I.L.P. on account of 'the far-reaching and constructive policy of Social and Temperance Reform which the Independent Labour Party exists to advance'; while George Jennison, a Progressive, propounded as his leading tenet: 'We must look after the poor – the rich will look after themselves.'[2]

With the approach of the 1906 General Election, then, the Liberal party seemed far more promising as an instrument of Scott's kind of progressivism, and he felt happier within it. His own position too had been strikingly vindicated. In 1904 Hobhouse sent a message to be read at the dinner of the '95 Club which, founded on the morrow of a Liberal debacle in Lancashire, now faced happier times ahead. No man deserved better of the club than Scott, wrote Hobhouse, in a tribute which throws considerable light on Hobhouse's own attitudes as well:

His services to Liberalism have not been those of the ordinary party man. They have been much greater. Through years of reaction & dissolving political faith he has laboured unceasingly &, in the end I believe successfully, to keep the party true to its best principles. Month by month Liberals, & not Liberals alone, are coming more & more to see how vital those principles are to the welfare of our country, the order & contentment of society, the smoother working of the institutions of the modern state. It was his staunch adherence to these principles wh. inspired Mr Scott's determined opposition to the policy of territorial aggression wh. a short while ago was so popular.

I have never heard of anyone who supported Mr Scott's view at that time & has since regretted that he did so, but I have heard of many who were not convinced by him then, but who have seen in the subsequent course of events ample proof that Mr Scott's action was as well-grounded as it was undoubtedly patriotic.[3]

But just as Scott was leaving his troubles behind him in his public life, in his private life they were mounting. The *Guardian* faced severe difficulties, not so much through the War as the competition of the halfpenny press. Taylor had become a crabbed old man. Worst of all, Scott's wife was now very sick. With these increasing burdens, Scott's Parliamentary work became a distraction. His constituency of Leigh had stood by him well in difficult times; he in turn had been 'an ideal member for this industrial division of the

---

[1] M.L.F. Minutes, 3, 10, 17, 22 February, 9 March 1904.
[2] Broadsheets f. 1904/1/H,S, Manchester Local History Library.
[3] Hobhouse to F. Willets, 12 October 1904, MGP.

187

County'.[1] In April 1903 he warned his supporters that he might not be able to stand again and in September made his resignation definite, hoping at the time that he might be preparing the way for a Labour candidate. He was doubtless as sorry as his supporters that he was leaving just when he was 'now more appreciated than ever' and the next election promised 'a triumphant return'.[2] Lloyd George told him that the pro-Boers in Parliament would miss him sorely. Scott's successor was not a Labour man but the son of Sir John Brunner, for whom he made way at the General Election, having decided in March 1905 that he would prefer to see the Parliament out rather than force a by-election.

At the end of 1905, however, there came the great crisis of Scott's life. In October Taylor died and under the terms of his will as understood by the trustees it seemed that Scott's connexion with the *Guardian* must cease. Moreover, Mrs Scott's condition was giving rise to great anxiety. Montague, who for years had wished Scott out of Parliament, now hoped that he could be persuaded to seek election again. 'Just think how it would be', Montague wrote to Hobhouse, 'if he gave up politics now, and if then his wife were to die before him & he were left with not one of the three things he has been absorbed in.'[3] At the end of November Rachel Scott died. Taylor's trustees took a view of the will highly unfavourable to Scott, and it looked as though Scott's *Guardian* – 'the M.G. as we have known it', he called it when he wrote to Hobhouse[4] – would expire and his team be dispersed. 'All the gods be thanked that we got right through the war before this came', Montague confided, '& that C-B is safely in, & the "Tribune" starting, & things looking decent generally.'[5] And then, with the General Election almost upon them, and the reversion to Reid's old seat at Dumfries offering Scott himself a political lifeboat, the trustees relented; Scott was to be enabled to buy the paper – at a price; his family rallied round; the enterprise was mortgaged to the hilt. But, for all the awkwardness, it could only be regarded as a triumphant resolution of the difficulties which saw not the *Guardian* destroyed but the *Guardian* preserved.

VIII

When Scott left Parliament, to use Haslam Mills's words, he 'entered with a definite renewal of the spirit upon his editorship. He came home.'[6] It was, moreover, a Liberal Lancashire that he came home to; and from this time

[1] Resolution passed by Executive of Leigh Liberal Association, 28 September 1903, MGP.
[2] William Karfoot to Scott, 2 October 1903, MGP.
[3] Montague to Hobhouse, 14 November 1905, MGP. The full story of the crisis is set out in Hammond, *C. P. Scott*, pp. 89–95.
[4] Scott to Hobhouse, 2 November 1905, MGP.
[5] Montague to Hobhouse, 8 December 1905, MGP.
[6] *The Manchester Guardian*, p. 145.

until the Great War Scott found himself in the mainstream of events, since the form of progressive politics on behalf of which he had so long proselytised now took practical shape before his eyes; if he wished to see his work he had only to look around him. Precisely because his policies became assimilated into the common stock of Liberalism there is less need to distinguish his individual efforts in this period from those of the party as a whole.

The old problem of providing first-rate leadership for Manchester itself remained. When Arthur Haworth, an active officer of the M.L.U. and later of the M.L.F., visited Herbert Gladstone in 1902, they discussed the general situation in the city. 'They want a local *leader* & have not got one', noted Gladstone. The Whips were to provide solid help in this respect, but insisted that the local men also work to a plan of campaign. George Agnew, a scion of Salford's leading Liberal family, confirmed the next year that, 'Manchester has indeed been frightfully slack in recent years. We have no big men at the head of our party there.'[1] Salvation in this respect came not through self-help so much as outside intervention. Winston Churchill's candidature for North West Manchester in 1906 gave the city and its political hinterland the charismatic leadership which it had sought for so long. At the time that the candidature was fixed, Churchill reflected that 'when you consider that there is no Free Trade politician of the smallest eminence in Lancashire you will see for yourself the possibilities which it offers'; and he rightly told Gladstone before the elections that his efforts would be most effective if concentrated on Manchester itself.[2]

Churchill's association with Scott's Manchester was part of his education as a Liberal, and he emerged as not only an eloquent but also an effectual exponent of Scott's kind of progressivism. Of this development in Churchill's political thinking one example – but a crucial one – may be cited here. Hobhouse had discussed in 1904 the apparent conflicts between Liberals and Socialists. He wrote that

the Liberal is for the unimpeded development of human faculty as the mainspring of progress. The Socialist, or if the vaguer term be preferred, the Collectivist, is for the solidarity of society. He emphasises mutual responsibility, the duty of the strong to the weak. His watchwords are co-operation and organisation. The two ideals as ideals are not conflicting, but complementary.

As early as October 1906, in the speech in which Churchill defined the Liberal cause as 'the cause of the left-out millions', he too went on to consider the relation between Socialism and Liberalism.

[1] Diary, 1 July 1902, HGP 46484 f. 15; G. W. Agnew to Gladstone, 23 August 1903, HGP 46061 ff. 14–15.
[2] Churchill to Hugh Cecil, 26 March 1904, *Companion*, II, 320–3; Churchill to Gladstone, 19 January 1905, HGP 45986 f. 124.

It is not possible [he said] to draw a hard-and-fast line between individualism and collectivism. You cannot draw it either in theory or in practice...No man can be a collectivist alone or an individualist alone...For some purposes he must be a collectivist, for others he is, and he will for all time remain, an individualist...The whole tendency of civilisation is, however, towards the multiplication of the collective function of society.[1]

No longer could it be said that Churchill was a Liberal only because he had shown the courage of his Free Trade convictions.

From his Manchester base Churchill became, almost at a bound, a Radical leader. Before 1906 was out, Campbell-Bannerman was weighing with Birrell the arguments for his taking over the Board of Education, conceding that 'he had done brilliantly where he is, and is full of go and ebullient ambition. But he is only a Liberal of yesterday, his tomorrow being a little doubtful.' The Prime Minister felt that for the reward of the Cabinet to be offered so soon was to put the parable of the eleventh-hour workman under too tenuous a construction, and he characterised Churchill in a final and dubious phrase: 'Further, anxious at all hazards to make a splash.' True enough, no doubt; but the service that Churchill could give to the Liberal cause justified allowances being made. When Masterman saw him one evening in February 1908, finding him 'full of the poor whom he had just discovered', Masterman challenged him with enjoying the power and prestige which his speeches brought. 'Of course I do', was Churchill's reply. 'Thou shalt not muzzle the ox when he treadeth out the corn. That shall be my plea at the day of judgment.'[2]

When Churchill was beaten in the Manchester North West by-election, the *Guardian* mourned the party loss as less than the 'irreparable' personal loss of 'a rising and formative political force which we would gladly have kept for our special help and service'.[3] But for a while Churchill's special relationship with Lancashire survived. Around this time Churchill and Scott enjoyed a blossoming cooperation and mutual confidence. When Margot Asquith took it into her head to try to influence Scott's editorial line, it was to Churchill she turned – 'You told me in Scotland and indeed several times that the *Manchester Guardian* was a *most* important Liberal paper', she remonstrated;[4] but was soon persuaded that such an approach would be injudicious. Churchill showed himself formidably equipped to fulfil a role which Scott had always known he could not himself: that of inspirational

---

[1] Hobhouse, *Democracy and Reaction*, pp. 226–7; speech at Glasgow, 11 October 1906, Churchill, *Liberalism and the Social Problem*, pp. 79–80; cf. Hobhouse, *The Labour Movement*, p. 94.
[2] Campbell-Bannerman to Birrell, 25 December 1906, Birrell P; Masterman, *C. F. G. Masterman*, pp. 97–8.
[3] Leader, *M.G.*, 25 April 1908.
[4] Mrs Asquith to Churchill, 11 December (1908), *Companion*, 11, 849–50.

leader, leading, moreover, in the direction which Scott had mapped out. At its zenith their relationship represented the fusing of such complementary elements as made progressive achievements possible. Nothing could have pleased Scott more than that in May 1909 the fate of the Budget should impel Churchill to come to Manchester to tread out the corn in his best fashion. Here was the right issue and the right man to rally Lancashire to it; and here was Scott, proud to play host to him – surely their finest hour? And throughout 1909 Scott gave what help he could in ensuring that Churchill's important speeches received full-dress treatment in the *Guardian*. When Churchill decided to publish them in book form – the volume that was to be *Liberalism and the Social Problem* – he naturally turned to Scott for help; but Taylor Garnett's lack of a general printing department meant that the work had to be done elsewhere. Such an edition, Scott told him, 'ought to succeed very well now & there can be no part of the country in wh. you are more closely followed than in Lancashire'.[1] Churchill's decision to capitalise on this and undertake his Lancashire 'pilgrimage' in December 1909 brought the *Guardian*'s fullest support; night after night, Haslam Mills, the leading reporter, covered his meetings with three, four, six – in Manchester itself, eight – reporters assisting him. It was, complained Curzon, impossible to elude Churchill: 'Every day there are four or five columns in the "Manchester Guardian" consecrated to his honour.'[2]

By the time that Campbell-Bannerman became Prime Minister Scott had become one of his admirers. His fears, like those of one of his correspondents, Corrie Grant, M.P., had always been that Campbell-Bannerman might be just 'a gentle, rather over-good-natured, over-fed man', and Scott would now concur in Grant's view of him as 'the first Radical premier we have ever had'.[3] A complimentary dinner to Campbell-Bannerman in May 1907 was attended by four hundred Manchester Liberals. While the Prime Minister lay dying in 1908 Hobhouse wrote several times to Scott with suggestions as to how the *Guardian* might make a protest against Asquith's taking over: a delicate undertaking. 'I am clear now', Hobhouse eventually concluded, 'that we cannot directly oppose Asquith for the present.' Many of those who had been closely identified with the later phase of Campbell-Bannerman's leadership had similar doubts at this juncture – Morley confessed that his 'violent inclination was to *bolt*' and was 'much haunted by the feeling of "turpe senex miles"' – but Asquith in fact soon allayed any doubts that he was a sectarian Liberal Imperialist. Harold Spender, no Asquithite, presenting Lloyd George's views in 1909, assured Scott that Asquith 'has

[1] Scott to Churchill, 10 August 1909 (copy), MGP.
[2] Curzon speech at Oldham, *M.G.*, 22 December 1909; cf. Reporters Diary, 1909, MGP.
[3] Corrie Grant to Scott, 21 October 1906, MGP.

always treated him very well', and was to write in his memoirs: 'Those were Mr Asquith's great days.'[1]

The constitutional crisis of 1909–11 tested Asquith and his Cabinet to the full. Although the issues involved were grave they were at most of the crucial phases straightforward, with the major exception of a period at the end of February 1910 while the Cabinet was making up its mind about the form of action to take; it was then that relations with the party outside were put under their severest strain. Scott was kept fully informed of the arguments within the Cabinet by almost daily letters from Hobhouse in London, who saw the principals on his behalf – Morley, Lloyd George, Churchill, Masterman, Arthur Ponsonby, and journalists like Massingham and Gardiner. Grey had seen Scott early in the month to try to persuade him of the advantages of Reform of the House of Lords as against merely curbing its Veto, but Scott was 'convinced that such a change of policy wd. mean disaster'.[2] Asquith's statement (of which Scott was given advance warning) that his Albert Hall declaration before the election of January 1910 concerning the Lords' powers did not, as most Liberals had assumed, mean that the King had guaranteed to create Liberal peers if that should be necessary, put the whole question into the melting-pot. Both Churchill and Lloyd George toyed with the idea of a democratic Reform but in his conversations Hobhouse pressed for the retention of the Veto policy, while Scott urged the same thing in the *Guardian*. Churchill went further in urging that Reform be implemented by use of the referendum, for which he knew Scott had a weakness. But Scott told him firmly of the bad effects that the Government's wobbling had already caused. 'Men go about', he wrote, 'declaring broadly that they have been betrayed and that seats have been won on false pretences.' The Veto policy was simple and it was well understood. 'The fighting spirit of the party is still strong', he added, 'but if they are not strongly led and speedily, it will evaporate, and we may whistle for our North of England majorities.' The Cabinet eventually decided to stick to the Veto, and Churchill, unabashable, told Scott, 'what you have to do is to make the very best of the cards we have replaced in your hand'.[3]

In April 1910 the Master of Elibank, the Chief Whip, spoke to the Lancashire and Cheshire Liberal Federation in Manchester and, in words that had been carefully vetted by Asquith, insisted that 'you must trust us – (hear, hear) – to choose under conditions of exceptional and even unprecedented difficulty the best means for giving prompt and adequate effect to

---

[1] Hobhouse to Scott, 3 March 1908, MGP; Morley to Birrell, 23 April 1908, Birrell P; Spender to Scott, 29 January 1909, MGP; Spender, *The Fire of Life*, p. 135.

[2] Scott to Grey, 8 February 1910 (draft), MGP.

[3] Scott to Churchill, 24 February 1910, *Companion*, II, 977; Churchill to Scott, 2 March 1910, MGP. William Royle had written in the same sense as Scott.

our declared policy. – (Cheers.)' The *Guardian* welcomed this as far as it went, but stressed that at a further election the issue should be not the principle but the implementation of the Veto policy.[1] Scott was approached by the Whips later in the month for his opinion as to whether a referendum on the question would be an adequate substitute for a General Election. He replied:

I find only one opinion – that the attempt to substitute a special referendum for a general election would be disastrous. That I am confident would be the almost universal (opinion) of the party here and personally, though I am an advocate of the Referendum as part of the ordinary machinery of Government, I share it. The almost universal feeling would be that it was a pure evasion and confidence, shaken before & only now recovering, would be destroyed.[2]

As soon as the Cabinet resolved to fight on the Veto policy and by using established procedures, the *Guardian* gave unfaltering support to its stated views and, indeed, Scott rejected an article by Ponsonby in September on the grounds that the *Guardian* was in favour of a Second Chamber, thus honouring even the preamble to the Parliament Bill.

IX

Since 1899 Scott had held no official position in Manchester Liberalism. In 1909 he was elected President of the Manchester Liberal Federation and took a fairly active part in its work. In February 1912 he made an attempt to give up the post but was persuaded to stay on until 1913 when he handed over to Arthur Haworth. Scott was also President of the divisional Association in North West, and was associated with the League of Young Liberals in that and the South West divisions. He was approached by his old constituency of Leigh and also by Darwen with a view to his becoming a candidate in the first 1910 Election, but after considering the matter decided he should not stand again. He kept himself free for political work, however, by declining Herbert Samuel's proposal that he should become High Sheriff of Lancashire. Increasingly, though, his role was now that of the Editor of the *Manchester Guardian* and the confidant of Ministers, dividing his time between the corridors of power and the Old Corridor in Cross Street.

The results of the two General Elections of 1910 in Manchester, and in Lancashire generally, brought many tributes to Scott's work. 'There can be no doubt', wrote William Mather in January, 'that the splendid results in Manchr. & Salford are largely due to you & your staff…you may indeed be happy in the response made on every side to your great leadership.' After the December election the Master of Elibank sent Scott his 'thanks for the splendid work which the "Manchester Guardian" has done and is doing for

---

[1] *M.G.*, 9 April 1910; cf. notes for the speech in EP, MS. 8802 ff. 49–50.
[2] Scott to Jesse Herbert, 9 May 1910, copy, MGP.

the party. Your cooperation has been of the greatest possible help to me in my work.'[1] And in January 1911 the Liberal Members for Lancashire presented Scott with a cup as a mark of recognition. In July of that year Scott recorded of one of his visits to London: 'Churchill said to Ll:G. that I ought to be kept constantly informed as to all important matters. Ll:G. said that was just what he tried to do & rather reproached me for not coming to him sooner now. Ll:G. rather laid it on about "M.G." – it wd. smash party if we & Govmt. were at odds.'[2] To conclude that it was good policy for Ministers to flatter a powerful Editor only raises the question, why was the Editor powerful? And why else but that it was the case should a retiring Chief Whip write: 'I feel I cannot bring my official connection with politics to a close without telling you how deeply I have appreciated all the personal kindness which I have invariably received at your hands and how great is my sense of the value of the services you render to Liberalism'?[3]

A large amount of Scott's time was devoted to the cause of women's suffrage, of which he was a strong supporter. Hammond has given a full account of Scott's activities over this question and the story will not be retold here. The family of the late Dr Pankhurst were not unnaturally among his frequent correspondents. He had little time, however, for 'the distinctive methods of the N.W.S. & P.U.',[4] though he was always prepared to plead the cause of the women who found themselves imprisoned as a result of those methods. After he became President of the Manchester Liberal Federation that body became much more receptive towards suffragist views. Its Secretary told a deputation in July 1909 that 'on the Suffrage question the Committee were practically unanimous in their feeling of sympathy towards the claims of women', and in June 1910 a sparsely attended meeting of the 1200 passed a resolution asking the Government to give time to the Conciliation Bill.[5] As the issue became more pressing there was increasing need for someone like Scott to mediate between the various shades of suffragists and the Cabinet. Mrs Pankhurst told him of her belief that 'you perhaps more than any single man outside the Cabinet have the power to bring this dreadful struggle to an end'. But the struggle had gone beyond the stage when it could be settled, as Scott wished, on its merits, and, in Hammond's phrase, 'he lived with his usual composure in a world of bitter recriminations'.[6] Resignations were threatened if the M.L.F. took any further

---

[1] Mather to Scott, 17 January 1910, Elibank to Scott, 17 December 1910, MGP; cf. interview with Sir George Kemp, *M.G.*, 17 January 1910.

[2] Scott's interview notes, 22 July 1911, SP 50901 ff. 23–30.

[3] Elibank to Scott, 7 August 1912, MGP.

[4] Scott to Sylvia Pankhurst, 13 December 1908, copy, MGP.

[5] M.L.F. Minutes, 29 July 1909, 22 June 1910.

[6] Mrs E. Pankhurst to Scott, 27 December 1910, private, MGP; Hammond, *C. P. Scott*, p. 117.

part in the controversy, for or against, and the actions of the militants made previously sympathetic Ministers less inclined to spend their energies on such an intractable problem. In May 1912 the Lancashire and Cheshire Liberal Federation by a narrow majority refused to allow a woman suffrage resolution to be put to its Annual Meeting. Still Scott kept up his pressure on Ministers, despite all the setbacks. He set great store by Grey's steadfastness among the women's supporters, and well on into 1913 one of Lloyd George's correspondents mentioned that Scott 'still has a lingering hope that you may even yet come out of your tent and lead the Women's Suffrage cause to victory'.[1]

It was into Lloyd George's orbit that Scott was increasingly drawn. As long as Churchill was prepared to work on progressive lines and to act virtually as Minister for Lancashire, Scott conceded him admiration and support. It is noteworthy that Lloyd George attended scarcely any major political meetings in Lancashire in these years, though the mounting pressure from Liberal organisations in 1913 and 1914 would doubtless have drawn him more actively into the region soon; in the phase of politics encompassing the 1910 Elections Churchill carried almost alone the burden of presenting the Radical case in the north west, and with striking success. Scott and Lloyd George, of course, were old pro-Boer allies. When the naval estimates provoked discussion in the Cabinet in 1908 the new Chancellor kept Scott briefed and to this extent he was again brought into close cooperation with Lloyd George – and Churchill, of course, for they fought the same battle.

Forced to choose between the two leaders, though, as he was to be after 1910, Scott found Lloyd George the more dependable ally and the weightier political figure. Churchill's combination of impatient ambition, egotism, and almost pathological instability of purpose, made him a difficult colleague in a peacetime Liberal Cabinet. In the autumn of 1910 Churchill had unsuccessfully tried to persuade Scott of the utility of a naval loan, and in February 1911 Scott found Lloyd George practically isolated in his stand against the new estimates.[2] Thereafter, while Scott did not lose his affection for Churchill, he evidently found it difficult to take him entirely seriously. 'Every question with him becomes a personal question', he observed in July. Scott also seems to have found credible, or at least illuminating, the anecdote 'of his comment that he had left the Tory party as otherwise he wd. now be its leader & his indignation at being told that he couldn't change

[1] Miss C. E. Marshall to Lloyd George, 26 July 1913, LGP C/9/4/85.
[2] Scott to Churchill, 3 November 1910, *Companion*, II, 1204–5; and Scott's memorandum of Churchill's letter of 22 October 1910, burnt at Churchill's request, MGP; Scott's interview notes, 16 February 1911, SP 50901 ff. 7–8.

twice'. And when Scott next saw Churchill he privately dismissed him as 'a queer emotional creature'.[1]

On the other hand, recurrent crises saw Scott in almost daily attendance on Lloyd George and he undoubtedly bolstered the Chancellor's resolve to cut armaments expenditure. Lloyd George's last words as they parted on one occasion were, 'I think your journey is worth 4 millions to the nation – and a half' – the amount of the reduction which had been imposed.[2] In the Cabinet fight over the naval estimates in January 1914 Churchill himself was the obstacle, and in his advice to Lloyd George Scott showed that while he sought an acceptable way out, he insisted that there must be real concessions to Radical feeling.[3] For Scott, militarism had always represented the anti-thesis of social reform; to combat the one was to clear the ground for the other. 'Curious', thought a less visionary Manchester progressive, as he saw Scott leave for London on this occasion, that he 'should feel more deeply about the wrongs of the tortured Albanians or Armenians than of the starving slum-dwellers of Manchester! And prefer Home Rule to a minimum wage.'[4] Scott's support for Lloyd George, however, implied no such preference.

It was Lloyd George's willingness, and above all his ability, to act over the whole range of the *Guardian*'s concerns that commanded Scott's allegiance, and made him tolerant for the time being of certain shortcomings. At the beginning of 1913 Lloyd George outlined to Scott the main aims of his projected land reforms, under the heads of a minimum wage for agricultural workers, an assault on the housing problem, and the use of land in the public interest.[5] The Land Campaign proposed action on lines which Scott and Hobhouse had explored in previous years. It promised to provide the basis of the next phase of Liberal social policy, especially insofar as it would for the first time make housing a national issue and raise also the question of a minimum wage for the towns as well. Hobhouse was brought in by Lloyd George to help formulate the programme and in the autumn of 1913 wrote a series of articles for the *Guardian* in conjunction with it. Scott's only reservation was that the campaign should not be hurried since the issues it raised were so fundamental that they must be fought right through.[6] Alas, the parallel with the *Guardian*'s earlier initiative on these lines, when war had precluded the policy's development, was all too close.

On 3 August 1914, having been summoned to London that morning by

[1] Interview notes, 22 July 1911, 7, 24 January 1912, SP 50901 ff. 23–30, 56–9, 60–5.
[2] Interview notes, 17 February 1911, SP 50901 ff. 9–10.
[3] See esp. interview notes, (22 January 1914), SP 50901 ff. 100–1; Scott to Lloyd George, 25 January 1914, LGP C/8/1/16.
[4] Ernest Simon's diary, Stocks, *Ernest Simon of Manchester*, p. 54.
[5] Interview notes, 6 January 1913, SP 50901 ff. 77–9.
[6] Scott to Lloyd George, 7 June 1913, LGP C/8/1/4; and see Hobhouse's articles, *M.G.*, 2–10 October 1910.

Lloyd George, Scott continued to press the case for non-intervention in the War to John Simon over lunch. 'Previously', Scott recorded, 'he had asked me Did I think it wd. be possible if we engaged in this war to carry on the kind of agitation against it in the country which had been carried on during the Boer War and I said I thought not; the stakes were too great.'[1] Scott was unable to see Lloyd George again that day and returned to Manchester. Despite all the Radical protests the Liberal Cabinet took steps which led Britain into the War. But on the last day of August Scott once more resumed his correspondence with Lloyd George. 'Everything has changed', he wrote, 'since the day when last I saw you for those few minutes – Now it is not a question of going or not going into the war but of what is to come after it.'[2]

[1] Interview notes, 3 August 1914, SP 50901 ff. 148–57.
[2] Scott to Lloyd George, 31 August 1914, LGP C/8/1/20.

8 The sinews of war

They could not go back to the idea that every single constituency could act entirely by itself...Given a programme and given the organisation agreed on by the Chief Whip and agents of the party, all that was necessary in each Division was for them to carry out that policy and to act up to that organisation.

George Wyndham, 1908

I

In order to fight, a party needed organisation and money; and it was money, to a considerable extent, which dictated the form that organisation took. Politics were not cheap. There are Parliamentary returns showing the cost of each election to each candidate which tell part of the story. Their statements are somewhat notional. 'You will see I have put down your personal expenses as £85-10-0', Bonar Law's chairman told him after his contest in Manchester North West. 'The actual sum spent does not really matter.'[1] But there is no reason to doubt their general import, that it cost between £500 and £1,000 to fight a borough and between £1,000 and £2,000 to fight a county division. The tradition was for the candidate to be a beast of burden, if not a milch cow. When Sir Ughtred Kay-Shuttleworth was preparing to leave Clitheroe he reported to Herbert Gladstone: 'The Chairman thinks that there is still a strong feeling – as there always has been – among the leading men in the council that a candidate shd. pay his own way.'[2] In Leigh, however, the Liberal chairman was prepared to assert to Scott that: 'It is contrary to Liberal principles (as I understand them) to call upon a few rich men to pay all the expenses, besides which it makes it next to impossible for any but the very wealthy men to be M.P.s.'[3] But what he was talking about was the annual registration cost, and the election expenses Scott had to shoulder alone. Symonds of the National Reform Union had told him that when Liberal Associations came to him in search of talent, 'they sift the candidates submitted to them, never failing to put strongly forward the money test'[4] – one which, however it was applied, could not fail to exclude many from a Parliamentary career. Sir William Byles, the Liberal M.P. for

[1] Percy Woodhouse to Law, 30 December 1910, BLP 21/3/20. This topic is treated on the basis of the official returns in Gwyn, *Democracy and the Cost of Politics*, pp. 55–60.
[2] Kay-Shuttleworth to Gladstone, 13 June 1902, HGP 46060 ff. 202–3 (bound with 1903 correspondence).
[3] John Wood to Scott, 1 June 1896, MGP.
[4] Symonds to Scott, 28 June 1894, MGP.

Salford North, claimed that many of his friends had had to retire at the end of the 1906 Parliament because they could not afford to carry on, and that in his own long search for a constituency he had been denied selection many times through poverty.[1]

The basic expenses of a constituency were usually expressed as a share of any election expenses plus so much a year payable to the Association for registration. These expenses were largest in the county divisions. A Liberal candidate would have to expect to pay over £1,000 for an election in Clitheroe, 'a cool thousand' in Eddisbury, probably about the same in Knutsford, and £900 in Leigh. In the Wirral he could get away with £300 but when Gorton found a candidate who was prepared to give that amount, the shortfall of £1,000 or £1,200 could only partially be made up by the 'some hundreds' which the constituency could find.[2] A working-class constituency like Gorton could not hope to be self-sufficient. The Conservative agent, J. W. D. Barron, was to be found pointing out in 1911 'that we were only a poor district and could expect practically nothing financially from within hence applying for help outside as we had none but working class members.'[3] Henry White, who stood there twice in 1910, claimed to have spent over two thousand pounds, and when he was deposed Max Aitken had no difficulty in persuading the Conservative Executive of the merits of his rich but absent friend Otto Kahn. Indeed its members started to behave as though they had been waiting all their lives for such a one as Kahn. 'We had a very enjoyable evening yesterday', Barron reported to Aitken, '& my chairman ordered a case of champagne at Mr Kahn's expense.' At which Aitken had to restrain them – 'I advise you to go slowly with Mr Kahn' – lest their innocent spirit of plunder wreck all.[4]

There were some divisions which cost much less. In Southport the Conservatives seem to have been prepared to meet all the election expenses of a candidate whom they desired; they did so for Curzon in 1886 and offered the same terms to Churchill if he would become their candidate in 1900.[5] At Darwen in 1900 there was the remarkable spectacle of a candidate who could not afford the expenses being too proud to accept help from the division.[6] But it was to the boroughs that the more impecunious candidates normally gravitated. Churchill stuck by his existing arrangement with

---

[1] 5 *Hansard*, XXIX, 1616 (14 August 1911).
[2] All these figures come from the Whips papers – HGP 46060 ff. 202–3 (Clitheroe); 46026 ff. 7–10 (Eddisbury); 46025 ff. 161–3 (Knutsford); 46483 f. 59 (Wirral); 46483 f. 56 (Gorton).
[3] J. W. D. Barron to Max Aitken, 8 December 1911, private, Beaverbrook P.
[4] Barron to Aitken, 28 March 1912; Aitken to Barron, 3 April 1912, Beaverbrook P; cf. Henry White to Law, 22 November 1912, BLP 27/4/48.
[5] Even Curzon had to contribute annually to registration. See Gwyn, *Democracy and the Cost of Politics*, p. 106; Marjoribanks, *The Life of Sir Edward Marshall Hall*, p. 138; *Companion*, I, 1148.
[6] *Viz.*, Charles Russell; Gladstone's diary, 25 January 1900, HGP 46483 f. 58.

Oldham in 1900 and the Duke of Marlborough paid on his behalf four hundred pounds election expenses and a hundred pounds a year for registration.[1] In the boroughs five hundred pounds went a long way in such matters, Herbert Gladstone advising a candidate going to Wigan in 1905, for instance, to put down £500 and make the constituency find the rest.[2] There were not many Liberal Associations like that at Ashton which made no difficulty over expenses; most had to drive a hard bargain even with a candidate whom they very much wanted. When Birrell went to see the Executive at Manchester North East in 1899 he found them 'solid well set-up fellows & very business-like, as Manchester men ought to be. Our talk was satisfactory enough on all points except *expenses*. There they are afraid it would cost me *£150* a year *at least* & it might well be in subscriptions &c £200 a year.'[3] This sort of annual demand upon an M.P. seems to have been typical. Ostrogorski's suggestion of an average expenditure of £250 per annum is the best informed estimate. When Bonar Law was offered Manchester North West in 1910 it was understood that the seat would cost £450 a year, but when he became M.P. for Bootle he ended up paying an annual subscription of £250, the same as Max Aitken was then paying in Ashton and John Wood in Staly-bridge.[4] But a subscription was not all. Aitken, for instance, was paying out sums like £324 for arrears and £200 for propaganda in 1911. And there were the costs of nursing a constituency, too, which might be greatest of all.

The Labour candidates escaped many of these problems. They never set up as anything other than representative men and the question of finance and organisation was one to which the resources of the trade-union movement were applied. But money was still a difficulty, especially for an M.P. like Philip Snowden who had no trade-union base. His campaigns at Blackburn were financed by selling threepenny stamps to workingmen, and with only £200 a year from the I.L.P. his very maintenance in Parliament required careful management. As he demonstrated to the House of Commons in the debate on the payment of Members, his expenses for travel, living in London, business at the House, and postage, took the whole of the two hundred pounds. 'I visit my constituency from twelve to twenty times a year', he explained, 'and I cannot go down without incurring railway expenses and hotel expenses for each different visit amounting to a sum of about £4, and to use a homely expression, an expenditure of £4 makes a very big hole in a

[1] *Companion*, I, 1214.
[2] Diary, 10 October 1905, HGP 46485 ff. 37.
[3] Augustine Birrell to Herbert Gladstone, 16 December 1899, HGP 46057 ff. 228–9.
[4] Ostrogorski, *Democracy and the Organisation of Political Parties*, I, 450 n.; for Manchester see Edward Goulding to Law, 4 August 1910, BLP 21/3/10; Law's and Aitken's subscriptions are evident from their papers; for Wood see G. H. Coop to Aitken, 20 May 1912, Beaverbrook P.

weekly allowance of something like £4.'[1] The question of whether a man was so poor that he could not support himself in Parliament is, however, a different one from whether a man who was not by politicians' standards rich could afford to support not only himself but his constituency organisation too. Since the Home Rule split at least, party finance had been an acute problem for the Liberal party. A new generation of Liberal candidates were often unable to shoulder such burdens. '*Good* Liberal candidates who can pay their own way are remarkably scarce', lamented one constituency chairman.[2] Yet the constituency parties were more in need than ever before. In the cities organisation could be rationalised in order to let them work out their own salvation, but for many no answer could be found within the ambit of local politics. The age of self-help was over.

II

The salient feature of the development of Liberal organisation between the Home Rule crisis and the Great War was the growth of centralisation. The process came partly through choice but mainly through necessity. In Manchester the question was whether the effective unit of organisation should be a single central body or six constituency organisations. When Manchester was divided in 1885 there had been little doubt about the answer: all power went to the divisions. 'Within the district of each Parliamentary Division', it was laid down, 'the authority of the Divisional Association is absolute, and no control or interference can be exercised by any other association *or by any central organisation.*' A central organisation was created only under sufferance. 'For the purpose of preserving the political unity of Manchester, the Six Liberal Associations decided to federate and form the Manchester Liberal Union.'[3] It was constituted as a talking-shop; its Committee had over sixty members and was to meet only every three months. This structure, however, soon proved itself ill-adapted to the new phase of politics. It was founded upon the proposition that each division was independently equipped to fight for the Liberal cause, but the leaders upon whom Manchester Liberalism relied were hardly numerous enough to man six organisations effectively, nor was the wealth of the city equally spread between the divisions. Only North West and South had adequate financial resources. When C. P. Scott approached Charles Schwann, who

---

[1] *5 Hansard*, XXIX, 1622–4 (14 August 1911); cf. *Blackburn Wkly Telegraph*, 15 January 1910.

[2] S. Compston (Rossendale) to Scott, 1 July 1890, MGP.

[3] Constitution of the Manchester Liberal Union. The words italicised were specially added, M.L.U. Minutes, 31 March 1886. A useful history of the M.L.U. was written by Philip Whitaker in 'The growth of Liberal organisation in Manchester from the 1860s to 1903' (Manchester Ph.D. thesis); unfortunately, Manchester University Library inform me that this has been lost. My conclusions about the role of the central organisation are the opposite to Whitaker's.

bore the brunt of the expense in the poor North division, about an alternative scheme, Schwann told him, 'I am, of course, anxious to see the expenses of the M. Liberal Union cut down & a larger grant made to the 4 poorer Divisions, but I think the remedy is to cut down the exps. of N.W. & allow a large percentage of the subscriptions from the Central (N.W.) Division to go into the Liberal Union coffers.'[1] It seems that Schwann had an exaggerated notion of the wealth available, for the North West officers had earlier pleaded their difficulties to Scott on account of the drop in subscriptions owing to defections. The fact remained that the M.L.U. was an inefficient means of using existing resources.

The original constitution of the M.L.U. had given it only one practical function, that of exercising 'a general supervision' over registration. Since registration absorbed two-thirds of the expenses of organisation the combination of this responsibility with financial problems gave the M.L.U. Committee a bigger role than had originally been envisaged for it. Only the M.L.U. could adjudicate on the allocation of duplicate votes between competing divisions. This was a matter which had most effect in the two richer divisions of North West and South, which in other respects had least to gain from participation in the Union's work; but the battle between them in the early 1890s for the M.L.U.'s favour on this point, and the subsequent arrangement whereby duplicates were advised to choose South, gave South a vested interest in the running of the Union which it would not otherwise have had. The need for proper registration was the spur for the next stage of the M.L.U.'s growth. In 1891–2, proposals for the establishment of a joint organisation with Salford were shelved as too visionary, but the practical benefits of a simultaneous registration survey, not only in Manchester but in the surrounding divisions, were considerable. And though it proved impossible fully to coordinate such an enterprise, at least the idea of standardising registration in Manchester itself gained ground. In May 1892 a plan for amalgamating North West, North, North East and East for registration and general political purposes was laid before the Committee. It was decided to postpone the matter until after the General Election, but meanwhile the urgent problem of attending to North West, where the Executive refused to stir themselves, was entrusted to a small sub-committee under Scott's chairmanship. Change was in the air. A Committee on Registration and Future Arrangements, again under Scott, met in November 1892; at this there was a 'long conversation' on 'the future arrangements for conducting the official work of the Union &c &c', and before the end of the year it had been agreed to set up a common registration scheme. The North West, North East, South and South West divisions were prepared to

---

[1] Schwann to Scott, 7 July 1888, MGP.

cooperate. The new post of Registration Superintendent and Secretary of the M.L.U. was to be filled by either J. Wigley, the agent for North West, or A. D. Jackson, agent for South. Since Wigley was appointed, South continued independently with Jackson, while Wigley coordinated registration for all divisions and was directly responsible for it in three.[1] The M.L.U. thus assumed responsibility for laying down the conditions under which registration was performed, and by telling the divisions to incur certain charges it inevitably assumed a greater responsibility for finding the money. When North East asked for its grant from the Union in 1893 its treasurer stressed that the survey had been undertaken 'in accordance with the request of the Liberal Union Committee'. And the treasurer of South West wrote that, owing to the withdrawal of two large subscriptions, 'we are worse off than we have been since our existence as an independent (well, that hardly looks the right word to use in an appeal for assistance – I will say since the division of the City) constituency'.[2]

Well might the divisions speak diffidently of their autonomy: they were in all important respects dependent upon the M.L.U. But the Union was in no position to help. When four of the divisions said that they could make no special surveys in 1894 unless special grants were made from the Union, no special surveys were made. The M.L.U.'s income never rose much above seven hundred pounds a year, and with the annual grants to North, North East and East of £150, to South West of £50, and a contribution of £100 to Wigley's salary, this left precious little leeway. In 1895 the possibility of setting up an election fund for the poorer divisions was explored and the officers made considerable efforts in semi-private capacities. Subscriptions fell if anything; yet with South West appealing to be put on the same basis as the other poor divisions claims upon the M.L.U. were increasing.

In 1898, therefore, a sub-committee on finance and organisation was set up under Edwin Guthrie's chairmanship. At its first meeting the Honorary Secretary 'expressed the opinion that the time had come when it should be considered whether a better administration of the funds could be effected by a greater degree of centralised organisation'.[3] The pressures for centralisation took several forms and not everyone had the same reasons for favouring it. The argument from money was the most telling. For the progressive section one attraction of a central organisation was that it could look to the interests of the city as a whole; it would make it easier to offer one of the divisions to Labour. Guthrie, who would have no truck with this position,

---

[1] M.L.U. Minutes, 28 November, 2, 8 December 1892.
[2] W. Birkbeck (N.E.) to W. H. Watts, 25 July 1893; Sam Woodcock (S.W.) to Watts, 24 July 1893, M.L.U. Minutes, 27 July 1893.
Theodore Gregory, M.L.U. Minutes, 17 June 1898.

was attracted towards a centralised scheme as a better means of allocating duplicates.[1] The process, once started, gained its own momentum and could only result in the sacrifice of particularism to conformity. Manchester had once sneered at 'the caucus' and had had nothing to do with the Birmingham innovations of the National Liberal Federation. Now Manchester was humbly asking (among other cities) Birmingham how Liberalism was organised there.

At a meeting of the M.L.U. Committee in February 1901 Guthrie declared that he was a convert to the view that centralisation was necessary for the party in Manchester, and he submitted a memorandum which, with only minor amendments, became the constitution of the Manchester Liberal Federation two years later. Its rationale was to replace the divisions by a central executive which should have control of money and all other matters except the selection of parliamentary candidates. At first North declined to come into this scheme on the grounds that it must retain its own offices, but accommodations were made. There was no-one who supported the existing system as such, one member declaring bluntly 'that divisional management had been the ruin of the Liberal party in M/C'.[2] Guthrie held fast to his main objective of creating 'a small & powerful Executive Committee who shall control & be responsible for the fortunes of the Liberal party throughout the City'.[3] The continuing doubts of North and North West caused the scheme to be shelved for over a year, but in March 1903 a deputation met the M.L.U. Committee to press for action. By this time East and North East in particular were in a state of virtual bankruptcy. When East asked the Committee to bail it out in May 1903 the representative of North East impatiently cut through to the real issue, asking, 'does not all this hang upon the question of reorganisation. "We assent to the scheme in order that we may share the plunder".'[4] Although North still had doubts, East and North East were by this time prepared to go on without it; some intensive bargaining on minor matters in June 1903 produced a settlement; and the Manchester Liberal Union was thereupon replaced by the Manchester Liberal Federation.

Whereas the M.L.U. Committee had been large and had met quarterly, the M.L.F. had an Executive of thirteen which usually met weekly. This body, with a new chairman, William Royle, was the main centre of Liberal activity. It controlled all the finances and employed all the staff; was responsible for organisation and registration; intervened in elections;

[1] Guthrie's speech at the conference of the six divisions, M.L.U. Minutes, 6 October 1898.
[2] Alexander Porter (N.E.), M.L.U. Minutes, 11 February 1901. Guthrie's memorandum was presented to this meeting of the committee and was subsequently amended, most notably at a meeting on 7 June 1901.
[3] Guthrie, Reorganisation sub-committee, M.L.U. Minutes, 22 May 1901.
[4] J. N. Walker, M.L.U. Minutes, 8 May 1903.

distributed literature; organised Liberal Weeks and cooperated with organisations like the '95 Club for propaganda purposes. Furthermore, because it
represented the interests of the city as a whole, it was in a much better
position than the divisions to adjust the claims of Labour and Liberalism in
areas where the progressive strategy demanded this. By 1910 there was
pressure for a Greater Manchester organisation on the same lines.[1]

It was not only in Manchester that localism was being overridden. In 1890
the Lancashire Liberal Federal Council was formed in order to remedy the
difficulties which many constituencies were facing. It employed an agent to
help constituency organisations in such matters as raising subscriptions,
arranging meetings, and, where necessary, selecting candidates; and the
Cheshire Liberal Federation undertook the same tasks in that county.[2] In
some of these respects the Councils were duplicating the work of the National
Reform Union. The N.R.U. had had its origin in the 1860s but in its late-
nineteenth-century form dated from 1876, at which time it had taken as its
Secretary Scott's friend A. G. Symonds. After 1880 the N.R.U. came into
fairly direct competition with the National Liberal Federation, and although
in the country as a whole the N.L.F. was far the more successful, in Lancashire the N.R.U. remained a considerable force, aided by the strong
Manchester aversion from treating with a Birmingham organisation. Relations
between the N.R.U. and the N.L.F. were minimal but glacial; as the N.L.F.
moved more into the ambit of official Liberalism Symonds became increasingly contemptuous of the position of his more successful rival. His
animosity grew the keener during the Boer War since he attributed the
N.R.U.'s reverses to the unequivocal anti-War position which it adopted.

If we had taken up the compromising & *fainéant* policy of the Nat. Liberal
Federation & the Liberal Central Assocn. [he told Scott], & had played for the
support of Rosebery & the Liberal Imperialists, the cause wd. have suffered greatly,
for we shd. have been educating the electorate on their lines. Thank God! we had
no inclination to do this, & Stanhope[3] & I were prepared to break up the Union
had my Committee & our members & Branches gone in that direction.[4]

The official leaders in Parliament Street fully reciprocated the distaste –
Herbert Gladstone called it 'that dirty body the NRU'.[5] After Schnadhorst's

[1] See leader, *M.G.*, 10 December 1910.
[2] For the work of the Lancashire Liberal Federal Council see its circular of 14 November 1891 in
MGP; for the Cheshire Federation, the Brunner Papers contain evidence of the work undertaken.
[3] Philip Stanhope (later Lord Weardale), President of the N.R.U., and the recently defeated
Liberal M.P. for Burnley.
[4] Symonds to Scott, 22 October 1900, MGP. For the early history of the N.R.U. see Ostrogorski,
Democracy and the Organisation of Political Parties, I, 217–21 and Cowling, *1867. Disraeli,
Gladstone and Revolution*, pp. 242 ff.
[5] Gladstone to Robert Hudson, 24 July 1903, HGP 46021 ff. 11–12. The N.R.U. had, as Gladstone
saw it, been soliciting subscriptions under false pretences; see below p. 215.

retirement from the N.L.F. in 1893 the M.L.U. seems to have buried its old suspicions and increasingly during the 1890s it participated in the Federation's affairs, and in June 1899 even invited it to Manchester for its annual conference. And when, a few months later, the N.L.F. divided the country up into organisational districts, Wigley of the M.L.U. became the district agent for south east Lancashire. Conversely, Symonds would admit in 1900 that 'in Manchester I count for nothing, & have long been systematically snubbed by the men who are supposed to be the leaders of the party there – a very inferior, third-rate set of politicians, who will never pull the party together or inspire it to victory'.[1]

To the extent that Lancashire Liberalism came under the influence of the N.L.F. rather than the N.R.U. it was not only the substitution of a national for a regional influence but of an official for an independent one. By the turn of the century the N.L.F. was to all intents and purposes under the control of the Liberal Whips. Its offices were at 42 Parliament Street and those of the Liberal Central Association at No. 41; the two houses were turned into one.[2] The Liberal Central Association was an association in the sense that the Board of Trade was a board: it was the vehicle of the Chief Whip. During Herbert Gladstone's period as Chief Whip from 1899 to 1906 he controlled the party organisation personally, working in close harmony with Robert Hudson, who was secretary both of the N.L.F. and of the L.C.A. Gladstone was assiduous in his duties, interviewing and corresponding with local leaders about candidates, money, and organisation alike. In May 1899, for instance, there was a two-hour meeting of the organisation committee on Lancashire. Assisted by his political secretary Jesse Herbert and his private secretary R. H. Davies, Gladstone would collect information about the constituencies and offer help, advice and encouragement to those in need of attention. 'In the election of 1906', he wrote later, 'Headquarters knew the condition of every constituency in England.'[3]

In 1908 the Liberal organisation was recast through the establishment of regional Liberal Federations. As far as the Chief Whip was concerned this represented a delegation of power in some matters; but as far as the constituency parties were concerned it was a concentration. As J. A. Pease, the Chief Whip, told the Lancashire and Cheshire Liberal Federation on its inauguration, its chief roles were those of improving intelligence between

[1] Symonds to Scott, 22 October 1900, MGP.
[2] Herbert Gladstone in Spender, *Sir Robert Hudson*, pp. 193–4. This account of the Liberal organisation at headquarters is based mainly on Spender, pp. 38–46, 192–9; Mallet, *Herbert Gladstone*, pp. 188–96; Gladstone's autobiography, HGP 46118 ff. 60–76; and his memoranda of 8 December 1922, 7 April 1923, 28 July 1924 and 18 November 1924, HGP 46480 ff. 35–44, 52–5, 93–102, 129–37.
[3] HGP 46480 f. 41.

the Whips and the localities and of providing effective help at the regional level. The Federation had no connexion with the National Liberal Federation: rather it was the creature of the Whips. Jesse Herbert became chief organiser in the country in charge of the Federations, and regional Whips were detailed to attend their meetings. It was Herbert Gladstone's view later that although the secretaries of these bodies were paid by the Liberal Central Association, they were 'the servants and are wholly at the disposal of the Divisional Federation Councils'. It would appear, however, that, until the War at any rate, the Chief Whip exercised a firm control; in 1912 the Master of Elibank referred unequivocally to 'Mr Burn, the Liberal Federation Secretary responsible to me for Lancashire and Cheshire'.[1] By the end of its first year 40 out of 57 Associations had affiliated, and in 1910 it became still larger when it amalgamated with the North West Liberal Federation which had covered some of the north Lancashire divisions as well as Cumberland and Westmorland. Under its chairman, Sir Ben Johnson, a Liverpool man, the Federation led a fairly active existence, organising thirty or forty meetings a month throughout the region in addition to tours by the two vans it bought. It gave assistance at by-elections and generally, in the optimistic words of Johnson, 'encouraged Liberals in the hopeless and feeble divisions and it strengthened and confirmed those who belonged to the zealous places which returned Liberals to the House of Commons'.[2] One of the main aims of the Federation was to enable the strong to help the weak. It took over from the Chief Whip the task of making grants to divisions which were not self-supporting. 'There were', said Johnson in 1911, 'at least a dozen derelict divisions which might be won for progress if only they preached to the people the gospel of Liberalism.'[3] A particular problem lay in sustaining organised Liberalism in the Labour seats, and in several of these the L.C.L.F. took over registration work directly. In short, it acted to coordinate the efforts of a party that was no longer working to a local strategy and to succour those Liberal Associations which no longer contained enough rich men to support them.

III

Those boroughs which could finance themselves were firmly expected to do so. Gladstone records that when in 1899 Alfred Emmott came to ask for a subsidy on behalf of such an historic centre of Liberalism as Oldham he

---

[1] HGP 46480 f. 40; Elibank's memorandum for the Prime Minister, 2 February 1912, confidential, EP 8803 ff. 16–18. Burn's career well illustrates the rising status of the party bureaucracy. The M.L.U. had employed Wigley at £250 p.a. When the M.L.F. was formed it wanted 'a superior man' who could relieve the Honorary Secretaries, and the post of Secretary was advertised at £500 p.a. Burn filled this position until he moved to the new L.C.L.F. at a salary of £600 p.a.
[2] L.C.L.F. Annual Meeting, *M.G.*, 8 March 1913.
[3] L.C.L.F. Annual Meeting, *M.G.*, 8 April 1911.

'politely intimated that Oldham shd. not come on the p[arty] f[und]'.
Likewise in 1904 when the Chief Whip was asked to pay the expenses in
two of the Liverpool divisions – 'Said emphat. I thought Liv. ought to find
the money'.[1] In Liverpool and Manchester the richer divisions could be
expected to help the poorer: this was, after all, the main reason for the
existence of the Manchester Liberal Federation. From 1903 to 1914 the
M.L.F. had an annual income of two or three thousand pounds a year. The
cost of running the central office was about £2,000 a year and once wages
and registration expenses had been paid there was nothing to spare; by 1914
the Federation was about £800 overdrawn. In 1909 a special fund was raised
which put the Federation temporarily into the black and enabled it to meet
the expenses of the General Elections. The only candidature to benefit
directly from this fund seems to have been that in South West, the poorest
of the divisions, which received a grant of £250. The treasurer of South,
however, was firmly told to expect no help.[2]

Manchester managed, then, not without considerable difficulty, to pay its
own way. Gladstone's papers reveal, however, that the Whips were besieged
with pleas for help from other parts of Lancashire, from candidates and
constituencies alike. In 1900 he spent £4,409 on registration and organisation
in the constituencies, chiefly doled out in amounts of £25 and £50, though
Knutsford benefited in all to the extent of £130 and Stretford of £70.[3] The
case of Knutsford illustrates the methods by which constituencies were
helped. After seeing the Secretary of its Liberal Association in 1903 Jesse
Herbert told Gladstone that a campaign costing £600 was being mounted of
which the local Liberals could find £400, and suggested that the funds of the
N.L.F. and the L.C.A. should each contribute £100.[4] But in the main
Gladstone preferred to leave a candidate responsible for making financial
arrangements with a constituency, and to help him directly when necessary.
Two of the good resolutions he made on his appointment as Chief Whip
guided him here: 'If c. doesn't pay all exs: extract as much as possible or
prudent from const.' 'Be flinty with men who get themselves adopted as
cands. & then ask for money.'[5] These principles seem to have been observed.
Thus Gladstone's note of an interview with the prospective candidate for
St Helens: 'Can I contribute? I said no, cd. only pay when money was not
forthcoming from constituency & candidate.' Or Herbert's report of an

---

[1] Gladstone's diary, interviews with Emmott, 7 June 1899, HGP 46484 f. 16; and with B. Furniss,
29 January 1904, HGP 46484 f. 63.
[2] M.L.F. Balance Book, 1903–14; M.L.F. Minutes, 30 December 1909, 20 January 1910.
[3] List of expenses for 1900, HGP 46105 ff. 143–4.
[4] Herbert to Gladstone, 14 September 1903, HGP 46025 ff. 161–3.
[5] Undated notes (1899), HGP 46105 f. 9. On the finance of candidates from the central funds cf.
Gwyn, *Democracy and the Cost of Politics*, pp. 107–21, and H. J. Hanham, 'British party finance,
1868–1880', *Bull. Inst. Hist. Research*, XXVII (1954), pp. 69–90.

approach for help by an agent: 'I closed that question by saying such a request must go from the candidate to you direct & privately.'[1] Given the Edwardian gentleman's delicacy in talking about money – and politics was still a gentleman's profession – making the candidate ask for help himself was a fairly effective test of need, and balked the more shameless attempts of the constituencies to siphon off funds. In 1905, for instance, Gladstone was confronted by a deputation from Warrington, where the extremely wealthy soapmaker A. H. Crosfield was candidate. 'Said the candidate ought to ask if he cant find the money', Gladstone noted drily, 'but he or the const. must find the money.'[2] This was a mere try-on. But a large number of otherwise willing candidates who could neither run to paying full expenses themselves nor induce their constituency to make up the difference were discreetly guaranteed a few hundred pounds.

The case of Sir Joseph Leese, M.P. for Accrington, is fully documented because he was a close friend of Gladstone (though the friendship seems to have become distinctly less close by the time all the negotiations were over). In June 1899 Leese wrote to Gladstone telling him that he did not intend to seek re-election at Accrington:

I have fought 4 elections there. In 1886 I lost, & my election exs. were nearly £900. In 1892 the expenses were I think 1200£, in '93 – £1350 & in 1895 rather more vy nearly 1400£. The contributions to registratn. & many party matters have also been serious. I desire therefore a cheaper seat & if possible a safer one. I cannot afford more than 200£ for an election now as my family obligations have much increased of late years...

P.S. I received a present from the Accn. Libs in 1886 when I was beaten of £600. I then became candidate & nursed the constituency till 1892. I paid all the 1892 & 1893 expenses but Ellis[3] assisted me with about 700£ in 1895. I mentioned to you a figure representing my total expenditure at Accn. wh. is not very far from the mark.[4]

As a result of this letter Gladstone came to Leese's aid and when he saw him in October 1899 he noted: 'Told him he must stand for Accrington & wd. see him through. Suggested he shd. get £500 from constituency.'[5] At the time of the General Election Gladstone sent at least one cheque for £500 and probably two. Leese, however, continued to find his burdens heavy and in 1902 was seeking a cheaper seat again. When the Accrington Liberals went to see Herbert Gladstone they asked whether Leese's resignation ought to

[1] Interview with J. Harrop, Gladstone's diary, 13 July 1899, HGP 46483 f. 29; Herbert's talk with Wigley (Cheetham's agent at Stalybridge), Herbert to Gladstone, 30 November 1904, HGP 46026 ff. 77–9.
[2] Diary, 25 May 1905, HGP 46485 f. 33.
[3] Tom Ellis, Liberal Chief Whip.
[4] *Viz.*, £10,000. Leese to Gladstone, 19 June 1899, HGP 46017 ff. 155–6.
[5] Diary, 10 October 1899, HGP 46483 f. 43.

be made effective. 'I thought yes from their his & my points of view', Gladstone wrote.[1] But they failed to find another candidate or Leese to find another seat. Consequently it was no surprise when Macalpine, the Accrington chairman, approached Leese in September 1904 about standing again. Macalpine's offer to relieve Leese of the registration expenses was not a sufficient emollient.

I left him [Leese told Gladstone] with the understanding that I was to write to him saying what I could do & he *then* said – 'If we (i.e. the Accrington Libs) can do anything towards the cost of the election, it must be in the way of a contribution of a fixed sum payable to you so that the final responsibility wd. rest with you & not with us.'

You were good enough to say that you could promise me £1000. I want you to increase that to £1250. I would then write to McAlpine, offering to find £1250 if the constituency wd. find £350 or £400 – wh. monies together wd. be sufficient to meet all the necessary expenses of the Election.[2]

But Gladstone would not be lured beyond his offer of £1,000 and Leese was left to make what bargain he could. 'I have not intimated to Macalpine that my offer to them depends in any way on you', he cautioned Gladstone. 'I think, if I did, that my position at Accrington wd. not be as strong as it wd. be otherwise.'[3] He refused to believe, however, that Gladstone's offer was final and arranged to meet him, evidently with the intention of squeezing out another £250. Of this interview Gladstone recorded: 'Said cd. not exceed £1. for Gen. El., but that I thought he shd. accept Accr. on definite promise of const. to find £400 for Gen. He agreed.'[4] Leese thereupon made his terms with the constituency. He managed to push its contribution up to £450 but in exchange agreed to take on £50 per annum of the registration expenses. And when he set out the agreement for Gladstone he plainly still had hopes of further help:

I hope you will consider, that *as things are*, I have made a fairly good bargain.

I will try to make the £1000 from you & the £400 from the constituency cover the whole cost of the election, but as the last two elections cost £1700 each I may be something short at the end. I put however security in the fact, that with these facts before you, you bade me 'go in' & that you intimated that I might rely on further assistance from you if the occasion arose.[5]

Gladstone's assumption of the responsibility for election expenses on a large scale was a new departure and it imposed considerable burdens upon the central party funds. His autobiography states that he received £17,000

---

[1] Diary, 18 November 1902, HGP 46484 f. 25.
[2] Leese to Gladstone, 21 September 1904, HGP 46017 ff. 179–82.
[3] Leese to Gladstone, 11 October 1904, private & confidential, HGP 46017 ff. 186–8.
[4] Diary, 14 October 1904, HGP 46485 f. 19.
[5] Leese to Gladstone, 18 November 1904, HGP 46017 f. 189.

from his predecessor in 1899 and handed over £24,000 to his successor in 1906. The annual charges of the party including by-elections averaged £16,000; the General Election of 1900 cost £60,000 and that of 1906 £100,000.[1] These are considerable sums. The Conservative party was not unaware of the obligations which the Liberal Whips had incurred in the build-up to the General Election of 1906.

Certain of our defeat [wrote the Tory Chief Whip in the autumn of 1905], they manned the constituencies with a tribe of 'carpet-baggers'. These men who accepted service were promised their election expenses, but the delay of more than a year and a half finds them quartered on Herbert Gladstone's exchequer in respect of maintenance, in addition to the capital outlay on their election expenses. It is well that this drain on the financial resources of our opponents should continue.[2]

After 1908 the Lancashire and Cheshire Liberal Federation took over the Chief Whip's role in organisation and with it the disbursements to Liberal Associations which he had been accustomed to make. Grants of up to £50 a year were made by the L.C.L.F. in aid of registration. Some of these were a continuation of a previous subsidy but some were new. In 1913 the Federation laid down that Associations seeking grants for registration should send a copy of the last balance sheet and a list of subscribers. Most applications were passed, but when an Association like the Wirral applied it was turned down; perhaps the presence there of a potential subscriber like W. H. Lever was sufficient reason.[3] These grants had formally to be passed by the Whips but there was never any difficulty from that quarter. By 1912 eight divisions were regularly drawing grants at a cost of some three hundred pounds a year. In addition the Federation was spending half that amount in conducting registration in four or five Labour seats. Both these sums were refunded by the Chief Whip. The biggest item of expenditure was for speakers. In 1912 the L.C.L.F. spent over £400 on speakers' fees and expenses, plus more than fifty pounds on the upkeep of the Liberal vans. The standard payment seems to have been a guinea a meeting. Over twenty speakers were employed that year, of whom six bore the brunt of the work, earning between forty and seventy pounds in the course of the year. These items, together with Burn's salary of £600 and the expenses of the office, accounted for virtually all of the Federation's expenditure of some two thousand pounds. Whatever else the reorganisation of 1908 did, it did not relieve the Chief Whip of any financial responsibility: on the contrary, the

---

[1] HGP 46118 f. 69. Variants of some of these figures are pencilled in the margin, i.e. that he received £15,000 and handed on £20,000.

[2] Acland Hood's memorandum, 'The General Election', 10 August 1905, BP 49771.

[3] For the conditions on which grants were given see L.C.L.F. Minutes, 11 February 1913; for Wirral see *ibid*. 22 April 1910. The rest of this section is based upon the accounts of the Federation, especially for 1912.

expenses of the central party organisation were increasing all the time as local deficiencies were remedied. Herbert Gladstone later asserted that the annual cost of party organisation in these years reached 'the astonishing figure of £100,000 a year'.[1] The Liberal organisation as a whole was becoming increasingly dependent upon the resources of the party fund.

IV

The cost of fighting elections was a problem for the Liberals for most of the late nineteenth century. There was a persistent feeling that, as the circular appealing for a National Liberal Election Fund in 1902 put it, 'a fund to promote the interests of democracy should be raised by democratic means'. But although a sceptical Chief Whip gave his approval to this appeal it produced only a derisory fraction of the sum that had been envisaged.[2] In 1886 the appeal for funds by the Manchester North East Liberal Association, of which Scott was treasurer, had been in the same vein. 'The bulk of the Party', it read, 'if they are to exercise the full control which rightfully belongs to them, and which a healthy condition of our politics requires that they should maintain, must be independent in financial as in other matters.'[3] But the divisional Liberal Associations in Manchester never achieved this independence. Of the £90 then subscribed in North East, Scott himself gave £25 and five other men £45 between them. It was the same story in East in 1890. Subscriptions were only £90 out of an expenditure of £300, the rest being made up by the M.L.U.[4] South was the most self-sufficient of the Manchester divisions but it did not prove possible to raise much more than £150 a year through subscriptions. In 1896 325 subscribers gave £153 15s. 4d. between them: in 1913 345 gave £162 6s. 6d. But while these sums helped to keep the division ticking over they could not support the electoral activities undertaken. South was not, it is true, quite so well placed to attract subscriptions as it seemed since after 1906 it allowed North West to take all its duplicate voters and in such cases its treasurer was, as he complained in 1910, 'met with the reply that the subscription is being given to the division in which the vote is'.[5]

The larger subscriptions went to the central body. Not that the M.L.U. was without severe difficulties. In 1887 a motion that the large subscribers who had seceded be invited back on conciliatory terms was defeated; instead

---

[1] HGP 46480 f. 42.
[2] There is a copy of this circular, assigned to 1922, in HGP 46110 ff. 188–90; the copy in MGP has a covering letter dated 30 September 1902; cf. Gladstone's comments, HGP 46118 f. 64.
[3] Circular from Manchester N.E. Liberal Assn, December 1886, MGP.
[4] Manchester E. Liberal Association Report for 1890, MGP.
[5] M.L.F. Minutes, 20 January 1910. Subscription lists for Manchester South in 1896, 1898, 1900 and 1913 are in the Manchester local collection.

several of the leading members of the old-guard Gladstonians agreed to double their subscriptions for that year.[1] This heroic measure epitomised the response of the small remnant of rich men in the Liberal party who shouldered such a disproportionate burden. The M.L.U. was supported by a small number of large subscriptions. The pattern in the early 1890s was that Thomas Ashton headed the list with £100. John Edward Taylor also gave £100, Scott gave £50, and the firm (Taylor, Garnett & Co.) £30 – so that the *Guardian*'s contribution was between a quarter and a third of the total. Charles Schwann, the M.P. for North, gave either £100 or £50; Jacob Bright, M.P. for South West, gave £50; as did those other pillars of Manchester Liberalism, Edward Donner and Arthur Haworth; and three or four other men each gave twenty pounds or more.[2] This small and fairly tight-knit group was the mainstay of the M.L.U., and even individual defections were a serious matter. 'I may say', reported the treasurer in 1895, 'that it is more & more difficult to maintain our list of large subscribers, £25 & upwards.' And it was the report of his successor in 1898 which led to the reorganisation of 1903: Thomas Ashton had just died, Jacob Bright was failing, John Edward Taylor was not regarded as robust – and together they accounted for nearly half the subscriptions.[3]

The M.L.U., moreover, did not stand alone. Whenever any Liberal cause needed subscriptions in Manchester the same men were appealed to. The reply Scott once received from the veteran Salford Liberal William Agnew, of the firm of art dealers, illustrates their position:

I think I gave you last year a fair cheque towards the Register Expenses in East Manchester.

Already this year I have given many hundreds. Bazaars, Liberal Clubs &c have absorbed a lot.

I have practically the party charges of the big Prestwich division on my back. Symonds is asking for more. A. Morley[4] driving at me too!

...I must have breathing time.[5]

When Scott appealed for funds for a new Liberal club in 1893 it was the same round. John Edward Taylor gave £100, Thomas Ashton £50, Edward Donner £50, Arthur Haworth £30. Charles Schwann declined on account of his heavy responsibility in North. The wealthy Salford engineering employer William Mather, who was at that time M.P. for Gorton, also refused

[1] M.L.U. Minutes, 27 June, 19 September 1887.
[2] The subscriptions for 1886–91 were tabulated for the meeting of the finance sub-committee, 13 May 1892; those for 1892 are given in Edward Donner to Scott, 18 April 1893, MGP.
[3] M.L.U. Minutes, 6 February 1895, 23 May 1898.
[4] Arnold Morley, Liberal Chief Whip.
[5] Agnew to Scott, 27 March 1889, MGP. For Agnew (1825–1910) see obit., *M.G.*, 1 November 1910.

owing to the enormous expense (comparatively) of my political work. Gorton is always in want & undoubtedly far away the most costly constituency in the County. I am now engaged on 2 Clubs there. I never ask anyone for a penny for anything. The burden is heavy & prevents me from helping much elsewhere altho' in the aggregate for our County work I have to do a good deal.[1]

The Bolton cotton spinner J. P. Thomasson was another willing donor. When the Native Races Society found itself badly off in 1899 it was to Thomasson that Hobhouse turned; he wondered whether Taylor might not contribute as well. And when Symonds asked Scott for a subscription to the N.R.U. he revealed that Thomasson had contributed and clearly felt most magnanimous about not having pressed Taylor.[2] In Cheshire Sir John Brunner, the head of Brunner Mond, fulfilled the same role and was, for instance, ready to pay election expenses in those divisions where it was needful.[3]

At the national level there were three main funds, those of the Liberal Central Association and the National Liberal Federation, and, most important, the party fund under the Chief Whip's personal control. The fact that each was used in a slightly different way is not very important: all came out of the same pockets. When the N.L.F. made a big appeal for funds in 1903 Sir John Brunner, W. H. Lever and J. P. Thomasson each subscribed £2,500.[4] When, not long afterwards, Gladstone too asked him for a subscription, Thomasson reminded him of this contribution and asked why there were two funds; but he was soon giving another £1,000 to the party fund. Thomasson indeed seems to have been one of the first businessmen to be regularly approached by the Whips; as early as 1880 he had given £1,000, but in 1900 he cut this down to £500, hedged about with the condition that it was not to go to jingo candidates.[5] Other Lancashire men did not make such limiting stipulations at that time. William Mather gave £500 and promised to double it if Lancashire local claims were not too heavy; Sir Ughtred Kay-Shuttleworth and William Agnew both paid up; Sir John Brunner gave £5,000, Lord Crewe gave £1,250, and Lord Ashton, the leading Liberal in Lancaster, probably gave £1,000.[6] Hudson's first effort with W. H. Lever, the head of Lever Brothers, produced £1,000. 'Why not ask him to become

[1] Mather to Scott, 20 July 1893, MGP.
[2] Hobhouse to Scott, 17 June 1899; Symonds to Scott, 20 March 1901, MGP.
[3] Brunner to William Handley, 4 February 1904, Brunner's letterbook.
[4] *M.G.*, 14 May 1903.
[5] Thomasson's contributions to the N.L.F. fund and the 'p.f.' are referred to in his letters to Gladstone of 11 and 21 January 1904, HGP 46061 ff. 115–16, 131–2; the arrangement in 1900 is set out in the letters between them of 15 and 16 March 1900, HGP 46057 ff. 283–5; for 1880 see Hanham, 'British party finance', p. 84.
[6] See Gladstone's correspondence with all of them, September 1900 (HGP 46058 between ff. 46–90, apart from Crewe to Gladstone, 19 September 1900, HGP 45986 f. 7).

a guarantor of £5,000 letting this £1,000 already sent form part of the £5,000?' Hudson suggested to Gladstone. 'He can afford *anything*, but I don't seem to have caught him at the right moment.'[1] Gladstone duly tried himself, got the full amount, and thereafter Lever became a reliable supporter of the work at Parliament Street. It was to this group of men whom Gladstone turned again in 1905. J. P. Thomasson was dead and his son Franklin was fully committed in financing the *Tribune*; William Agnew, his son George standing for Salford West, saved his resources for Manchester, as did William Mather who only sent a token £200. But Lever sent £10,000 and Brunner, who told Gladstone that he had taken advantage of his for-bearance to send 'a good deal of money' to the Free Trade Union, now promised the party fund £5,000 'and if later on you tell me that you are in dire straits, I will with pleasure go further'.[2]

The N.L.F. fund was not primarily for election purposes. It seems to have been used mainly for assisting Lib–Lab M.P.s, though in 1906 Hudson was able to make election grants totalling £7,000, and contributed £250 or £300 to three Liberal candidates in Lancashire seats.[3] The L.C.A. fund was run on an annual rather than an *ad hoc* basis, and it called upon subscribers like Lord Crewe and Lever. When the N.R.U., the activities of which were naturally quite independent of Parliament Street, attempted to poach subscriptions, feelings ran very high; the Whips not unreasonably held to a variant of the wages fund theory and considered that when the N.R.U. claimed subscriptions 'for the *party*' it was taking the bread out of their mouths.[4] Later, they evidently regarded the resources consumed by the Budget League in much the same light.[5]

The formation of the L.C.L.F. did not really provide another source of funds but only a channel. About a third of its annual expenditure of two thousand pounds was raised by subscription; the Chief Whip met certain expenses and also made a basic grant of £500 a year which was often supple-mented; from 1912 the N.L.F. paid an annual grant of £112 10s. About £700 a year came from subscribers. Sir Ben Johnson, the chairman, gave £100, and so did Sir John Brunner and W. H. Lever, who held honorary posts. There were about half-a-dozen subscriptions of between twenty and a hundred pounds, and two dozen or so between five and twenty pounds. The whole amount, then, was subscribed by about sixty men, among whom names like Sir George Agnew, A. H. Crosfield, Lord Shuttleworth and Neville Clegg,

[1] Hudson to Gladstone, 19 September 1900, HGP 46020 f. 68.
[2] J. T. Brunner to Gladstone, 19 December 1905, HGP 46063 ff. 222–3; cf. notes on cheques received 1906, HGP 46107 ff. 93–6.
[3] Hudson to Gladstone, 26 January 1906, HGP 46021 ff. 115–17.
[4] See Gladstone's memorandum, 22 July 1903, HGP 46060 ff. 254–5.
[5] J. A. Pease to Churchill, 25 November 1909, *Companion*, II, 923.

were, like those of Brunner and Lever, not new to Liberal subscription lists. Johnson largely devoted himself to the Federation; he was always ready to ease its work by laying on luncheons for large numbers of people, and when the finances were shaky in 1911 he stepped up his subscription to £200. He, Brunner, Lever, and Sir William Bowring, the Liverpool shipowner, accounted for half the subscriptions.[1] The rich men left in the Liberal party may have been few but they were generous. *O rare Ben Johnson.*

The main task of fund-raising, then, fell to the Chief Whip. 'In round figures', Gladstone wrote later, 'altogether I raised £275,000. How did I get it? I wrote in my own hand at least twice – in 1900 and 1905 – to every single person who might possibly be a subscriber.'[2] In 1900 he encountered some difficulties – 'I have had some disgusting rebuffs', he told Campbell-Bannerman – but a number of large contributions late in the day left him 'quite safe'.[3] The expenses for 1906 seem to have been met more easily, and more was disbursed. The Master of Elibank evidently used the same methods in 1910 and although the expenses of the party had increased by that time he was able to meet them. Geake of the Liberal Publication Department reported that Elibank 'apparently had plenty of money' and even Herbert Gladstone, who regarded the 1908 scheme of reorganisation as inaugurating a period of 'decadence', admitted that it 'may have worked effectively under the initial effort, with a Liberal Government in power supported by an unprecedented majority and a big bank balance'.[4] There is no great mystery as to why the Government Chief Whip should have had little difficulty in raising large sums of money. After Lloyd George's more blatant exploitation of the system, it is true, those, like Herbert Gladstone, who had been responsible for party finance before the War became highly sensitive to charges that they too had 'sold' honours. But although crude bargains may not have been the rule, the power of patronage clearly gave the Chief Whip a degree of leverage which he would not otherwise have had. Although the Conservatives were not backward in employing this, for the Liberals it was absolutely necessary. 'What would be the state of the Liberal party chest if it depended on the voluntary subscriptions of the rank and file?' the *Guardian* asked rhetorically.[5] Loreburn's opinion in 1914 that the central organisation was 'kept going solely by the sale of honours' cannot be far short of the truth, and since the Liberal party as a whole was now dependent upon this

---

[1] Subscriptions were listed as they came in the L.C.L.F. Minutes.

[2] Autobiography, HGP 46118 f. 69. There is a pencil note in the margin giving the total as £260,000.

[3] Gladstone to Campbell-Bannerman, 16 September 1900, CBP 41216 ff. 7–9; Gladstone to Hudson, 30 September 1900, HGP 46020 ff. 83–4.

[4] Charles Geake to Gladstone, 11 January 1911, HGP 46042 ff. 198–201; memorandum of 8 December 1922, HGP 46480 f. 38.

[5] Leader, *M.G.*, 18 November 1910. It was arguing the case against the Osborne judgement.

source of funds it was well that successive Chief Whips did not, as Gladstone put it, 'share the views of the purists who, far and away from the rough and tumble of work-a-day politics, refuse to weigh the facts and necessities of life and speak from the pinnacles of their own private virtues and practices'.[1]

v

It is extremely difficult to gauge the relative success of the parties in the matter of organisation, to which defeat and (if more rarely) victory were attributed, irrespective of its specific contribution. Moreover, although the idea of a professional and coordinated party organisation was less novel in Lancashire than in most other parts of the country, at the turn of the century important constituencies were still left to go their own way. When Churchill was Conservative candidate at Oldham in 1900 he thought that 'in this constituency the organization is still far from perfect as they will insist on managing it themselves, not allowing an expert or paid agent to do the work properly, the consequence is that you get an inefficient organization'.[2] But within a few years the party leaders were making it their business to see that the party should be well organised everywhere. In Liverpool, where Salvidge's organisation dominated the city's politics, Edward Evans made considerable efforts as Liberal leader to get the party on to an efficient footing and it was well known in the city that he relied upon the assistance of the Chief Whip. And although when Gladstone and Evans met in 1903 they agreed that Liverpool was still 'in wretched case', between them they managed to fill all the candidatures and the Liberals were at least able to put up a decent fight in later General Elections.[3]

The state of affairs at the Conservative Central Office was clearly unsatisfactory in the period before the General Election of 1906, but the attempts to reform it were so mixed up with intra-party warfare over policy and the leadership that the question was rarely treated on its merits. Acland Hood was not a bad Chief Whip as far as raising money was concerned; in 1905 he hoped to have £200,000 invested. This would, he claimed, 'put our

---

[1] Loreburn, Scott's interview notes, 30 June 1914, SP 50901 ff. 138–43; Gladstone's autobiography, HGP 46118 f. 74. There is some very odd correspondence among Gladstone's Whips' papers; and a revealing letter from Joseph Pease, Liberal Chief Whip at the time of the General Election of January 1910, to Elibank, 18 November 1910, EP 8802 ff. 146–7. The correspondence between Acland Hood, the Conservative Chief Whip, and J. S. Sandars, Balfour's private secretary, in September and October 1905, is even more open; and the report Steel Maitland made to Law in 1911 (Blake, *The Unknown Prime Minister*, p. 100) is also open to only one construction. Cf. Halevy, *History of the English People*, VI, 312–14, 334.

[2] *Companion*, I, 1201–2. For party organisation in Lancashire see Jones, 'Further thoughts on the franchise', *Past & Present*, **34** (1966), pp. 134–5.

[3] See interviews with Evans, Gladstone's diary, 6 February 1900, 30 September 1903, 23 March 1904, HGP 46483 f. 59, 46484 f. 53, 46485 f. 6; *Liverpool D.P.*, 21, 25 September 1900.

The reconstitution of Liberal Lancashire

Party Funds on a better basis than they have ever been', which was just as well since the calls on Headquarters were heavier than they had previously been.[1] After 1906 the position of the Central Office in relation to the organisation as a whole was appreciably stronger; it tightened its hold over the party and was the instrument for enforcing a far greater uniformity upon it.[2] Its efficiency, however, was more questionable; despite the energetic efforts of the Principal Agent, Percival Hughes, it was felt, even before the General Election of January 1910, that the office did not 'develop the actual indicated horse power, even under forced draught' owing to 'defective construction'.[3] It was, however, the Unionists' defeat in 1910, especially their failure to loosen the progressive hold upon Manchester, which caused them most heartsearching. In Manchester the Liberal Federation had played a very active part in the elections and although some suggestions for improvement seem to have been conveyed to Parliament Street, there was room for considerable satisfaction. The Conservatives, on the other hand, were prepared to attribute their poor performance in this area to poor organisation. William Vaudrey, the Conservative leader in Manchester, who had been regarded earlier as 'a most competent man', was now written off as 'a real obstruction' and his decision to contest a seat himself condemned as 'a fatal policy'.[4] As far as Lancashire, Yorkshire and Scotland were concerned, wrote Acland Hood, 'it is precisely because these Districts *will* run their own show, and will brook no interference from the Central Office that we did so badly there. Leaders and organizations are hopelessly out of date, and must be altered whether they like it or not.'[5] But Hood nonetheless did not meet the Manchester leaders for two months and then declared that the time available before the next General Election was too short for action; meanwhile Lancashire was left largely to the activities of the Tariff Reform League, which did great service in the Manchester area that December.[6]

It was generally felt that the second 1910 election would turn more than usually upon organisation. 'A dead lift effort such as this must come in the main from the machine', Churchill told the Master of Elibank,[7] and the

[1] Hood to Sandars, 8 September (1905), BP 49771; cf. memorandum, n.d. (December 1905) (by Sandars?), BP 49764.
[2] See McKenzie, *British Political Parties*, pp. 265 ff.; Jones, 'Balfour's reform of party organisation', *Bull. Inst. Hist. Research*, XXXVIII (1965), pp. 94–101. The implications for policy are explored in Blewett, 'Free Fooders, Balfourites, Whole Hoggers', *Hist. Jnl.*, XI (1968), pp. 95–124; and Clarke, 'British politics and Blackburn politics', *ibid.* XII (1969), pp. 302–27.
[3] Sandars to Balfour, 18 December 1909, BP 49766.
[4] Balfour to Chamberlain, 2 November 1905, Garvin and Amery, *Life of Joseph Chamberlain*, VI, 737–40; Sandars to Balfour, 21 January 1910, BP 49766. Vaudrey's candidature was a premeditated move; he had been in the field for two years.
[5] Hood to Sandars, 8 February 1910, BP 49771.
[6] Sandars to Balfour, 18 March 1910, BP 49766; Edward Goulding to Law, 13 December 1910, and encs., BLP 18/6/144. [7] Churchill to Elibank, 26 May 1910, EP 8802 ff. 63–4.

218

Liberal victory was felt to be peculiarly Elibank's triumph. Conversely, it sounded Acland Hood's death-knell. Although there were complaints from Manchester about the Central Office, the fault there seems to have lain nearer home. Lord Derby had made the gesture of taking command of the Conservative effort in order to emphasise the determination with which the city was being assailed. But comedy not competence was the keynote of nomination day. Nominations for the six seats closed at noon. At 12.06 p.m. the candidate for South turned up at the Town Hall to find that he had inadvertently given the Liberal Haworth a walkover. The returning officer's expenses had to be paid by 1.00 p.m. A few minutes before the deadline the Lord Mayor sent a messenger to the Conservative Club to find out why nothing had been paid by the candidate for East. The chief agent rushed to the bank. At 12.58 he threw a pile of banknotes in front of the Lord Mayor and collapsed into an armchair. When, a few minutes later, the far from athletic figure of Derby appeared, breathless, he found that the nomination had narrowly survived. 'One man saves the Empire by two minutes and another loses it by six', was Haworth's sardonic comment. This fiasco, moreover, provoked allegations that the entire Conservative campaign in South had been marked by laxness.[1] With Manchester totally discredited and the Central Office under a cloud, the Conservative achievements in Liverpool, where (it was said) 'Salvidge & Thompson have practically established Home Rule',[2] shone forth all the more clearly. It was to Salvidge that the party leaders turned for advice, and he was brought in to serve on the committee that was set up to report on reorganisation.

The fact was that the central party organisations had taken on tasks for which their machinery had never been designed. 'Personally', wrote Balfour, 'I find it hard to believe that any single person can do the work demanded of a modern head Whip.'[3] This was the same line of thought as had led the Liberals to make Jesse Herbert chief of the organisation in the country, and it now led the Conservatives to create the new position of Chairman of the Party to act as the head of the Central Office. It is no coincidence that just as the Liberals, first under Gladstone and then under Pease, had to adapt their organisation to a new role, so the Conservatives in 1906 and 1911 had to do likewise. When a new chief Conservative agent for Lancashire was appointed in 1912, Steel-Maitland, the Chairman of the Party, did not even consult the local men and chose an outsider.[4] Local autonomy in matters like these had become little more than a name.

[1] The incident was widely reported. Haworth at the Reform Club, *M.G.*, 5 December 1910; cf. letters from C. H. Croasdale, *M. Courier*, 5, 7, December 1910.
[2] Sandars to Balfour, 25 December 1910, BP 49767.
[3] Balfour to Akers Douglas, 17 January 1911, Chilston, *Chief Whip*, pp. 347–8.
[4] J. C. Buckley to Max Aitken, 25 November 1912, Beaverbrook P.

9 Men of light and leading

Many of us have to do with electioneering, and we know what happens constantly when a constituency has to find a candidate. The party looks round first of all for the man whom it knows, the local man whose character it knows, whose position it knows, because he has taken a considerable part in local politics, and very often it happens that it is unable to get a single man out of the constituency or even in the neighbourhood. They have to go to some rich outsider. What happens then is that the constituency has to choose without knowing the man. They have to take his character from the party Whip.   C. P. Trevelyan, 1911

I

One day in 1899 Herbert Gladstone had a discussion about candidates with one of the foremost Manchester Liberals, William Holland. 'Hugh Fullerton deficient in position', was their conclusion about one.[1] The kind of notions which underlay this comment were more clearly exposed by the Conservative M.P. for Gorton when he explained that a Member 'had other duties to perform than in the House of Commons', and that if his Lib–Lab opponent were returned, 'he would not be able to do anything to encourage the social life and institutions of the division'.[2] In the conventional view the candidate was still expected to be a social leader rather than a mere public person.[3] He was expected to give generously in the constituency, not only for political objects, but for a wide range of good and not so good causes. It was not uncommon to find posters advertising the candidate's generosity and even where these were not used word was expected to get around. It was not a universal practice but it was not one that could quietly be abrogated. 'What has our opponent done?' asked the Conservative chairman in Salford South about Hilaire Belloc. 'The only subscription of his I know of is the subscription of his name in taking the oath of allegiance as a British subject.'[4]

The papers of C. P. Scott as Liberal M.P. for Leigh and of Max Aitken as Conservative M.P. for Ashton both tell the same story: of a constant stream of demands according to a pattern which the individual Member could do

[1] Gladstone's diary, 17 July 1899, HGP 46483 f. 32. Fullerton was at that time candidate for Ashton-under-Lyne.
[2] Ernest Hatch at Gorton, *M.G.*, 8 October 1900.
[3] For these distinctions see Lee, *Social Leaders and Public Persons*, esp. pp. 5–6. See also Lowell, *The Government of England*, I, 234.
[4] Councillor Mather in Salford South, *M.G.*, 19 January 1906.

little to alter. It was a great anxiety to a Member's leading supporters that he should not be thought mean. Thus it was natural for Scott's chairman to write on one occasion that 'I fear we have let you in for a rather large gift', and not very effective for Scott to remonstrate: 'I shd. hardly think that people wd. expect the member who is present as it were officially to contribute on the same scale as those who are leading members of the church and have a duty as such towards it.'[1] If a Member contributed at all it must be in fitting style, for this was a public not a private act. 'I beg to ask if you would be so kind as to head my list with a substantial donation', Aitken was asked by one, 'I am desirous to get a subscription list in the local paper and your name at the head would be a considerable help.'[2] Acting on the advice of his agent, Aitken doled out annual subscriptions of a guinea or two to any number of cricket, football and other similar clubs, donations of five or ten pounds to church activities, and financed larger charities like a series of hot-pot suppers during the coal strike of 1912. Both he and Scott made more substantial contributions to local hospitals. And both of them on occasion made loans of several hundred pounds to leading supporters who were financially embarrassed, which (if this is at all representative rather than an extra-ordinary coincidence) illustrates the lengths to which the obligations of nursing a constituency were carried.

The role which an M.P. was expected to fill arose from the assumption that he would be a pillar of society. A local man of substance was the traditional stereotype of a parliamentary candidate. In the Ormskirk division, where the Earls of Derby had large estates, the sitting Member, the Hon. Arthur Stanley, comfortably conceded in 1906 that his opponent 'was an estimable man and a lawyer, but he [the speaker] failed to see any earthly connection between him and that constituency'.[3] In terms of the representation of a community by its natural leaders he was quite right; such challenges to the established pattern of deference could only be justified by a different conception of politics. In Lancashire the patriarchal political leaders of the old style were more often industrialists than landowners. When it could no longer plausibly be maintained that the political interests of employers and employed were identical, prominent businessmen were likely to find their position a disadvantage in appealing for working-class votes. 'The electors of Preston', maintained their Labour candidate, 'could not reasonably expect their two members to argue and debate and vote against their own personal interests. It was not human. If a man was wealthy he looked through different spectacles.'[4]

---

[1] John Wood to Scott, 6 June 1902; Scott to Wood, 8 June 1902, draft, MGP.
[2] John Andrews (Salvation Army) to Aitken, 16 August 1911, Beaverbrook P.
[3] Stanley at Ormskirk, *Liverpool D.P.*, 4 January 1906.
[4] J. T. Macpherson at Preston, *Lancs. D.P.*, 19 December 1905.

The reconstitution of Liberal Lancashire

Whenever an employer stood for Parliament he ran the risk of his business activities (real or alleged) being held against him. The firm of Brunner Mond, although it had introduced the eight-hour day in 1889 and had become an example of enlightened company welfare, was the victim of attack in a widely circulated book, *The White Slaves of England*.[1] Stories of the 'white-slave' genre dogged the political footsteps of Sir John Brunner in Northwich, his son in the three constituencies he contested, and his partner Alfred Mond in the two seats in the north west for which he stood. All three, however, were able to deploy the classic counter of a resolution refuting the charges passed by a mass meeting at the works. The story that W. H. Lever did not employ any men over the age of forty at Port Sunlight cropped up both in 1900 and 1906 and was denied in the same way. It was natural that such stories as these should proliferate, but, if untrue, they could be checked, and they were unlikely to harm an innocent employer with a good reputation. But there were other hazards than mere falsehoods. Richard Pilkington ran into trouble in 1906 over the employment of Poles in his collieries near Newton, and at the same election Colonel W. B. Blundell was generally reckoned to have been heavily handicapped by the strike then proceeding at his pits in the Ince division. It was when an employer's actions pointed a political moral that the lesson could most directly be drawn. In 1906, when Churchill was fighting a thorough-going Free Trade campaign in Manchester North West, his chairman, Samuel Lamb, was castigated for having established a weaving mill in Roumania, behind the tariff wall. 'Here', it was said, 'is a distinct case in which the Unionist policy would serve to benefit Lancashire.'[2]

The object of most of these attacks was plainly to alienate working-class electors from the bosses. It might seem that the Liberals, with their greater dependence upon working-class votes, stood to suffer more in this respect. But whereas it was fairly easy to link Conservative candidates with, for instance, the anti-trade-union policy of their party, rich Liberals found it possible to play off their own economic interest against the policies they advocated. Brunner and Lever were particularly adept at taking the bull by the horns in this way. Brunner maintained that he would make money 'beyond the dreams of avarice' if Tariff Reform were introduced. 'Rich as he was', said he, 'he would become infinitely richer by a Protective system, but the poor would become poorer.'[3] And with the 1909 Budget to fight on, Lever went even further in the delicate exercise of rousing class feeling against himself – in favour of himself. 'If they voted against him', he told the electors of Ormskirk, 'they did not hit him. The Budget hit him hard. If

[1] By Robert Harborough Sherard (Widnes 1897).
[2] Leader, *M. Courier*, 12 January 1906.
[3] Brunner speeches at Chester and Northwich, *M.G.*, 6, 12 January 1906.

222

they voted against him they were saying, "Mr Lever, we would rather see you richer – (applause) – and ourselves poorer." If they wanted to hit him hard vote for the Budget; if they wanted to hit themselves hard vote for Stanley.'[1] This candid recognition that the economic interests of rich and poor necessarily diverged did not vitiate the claim of enlightened employers to offer political leadership. Speaking in Warrington, Brunner declared that 'he was there in the capacity of a capitalist, standing in favour of a brother capitalist, Mr Arthur Crosfield, and he would advise the democrats of Warrington when they got a capitalist tamed to be sure to keep him (hear, hear).'[2]

Now it cannot be claimed that those Nonconformist millowners who still lent the Liberal party their support were progressives in the mould of such as L. T. Hobhouse. But, as time went on, the philosophy of John Bright was reconciled with the policies of Lloyd George. It was Jesse Herbert's opinion that most employers who remained after the Home Rule split were prepared to come to terms with Labour. 'The severe Individualists of the party who are wholly out of sympathy with the principles of the L.R.C. are very few', he wrote.[3] Old men, like J. P. Thomasson of Bolton, it is true, were still flatly opposed to 'socialistic nursing of the working classes' by means of such things as old age pensions.[4] But Thomasson's son Franklin was a man of a new generation. Hobhouse wrote of him that '(knowing the Lancashire type) I fancy I understand & can get on with him. But', he added, 'people who do not know the type wd. I think be put off by him.'[5] Franklin Thomasson did not in the end sit for a Lancashire constituency (though he contested two) but the 'type' is well represented by a Yorkshireman who did, Theodore Cooke Taylor. Taylor was a wool manufacturer from Batley, a Congregationalist, something of an autocrat in his business, yet an apostle of profit-sharing. His background was in some respects similar to that of Asquith but, choosing not to go to Oxford or Cambridge, Taylor remained more firmly rooted in it. Herbert Gladstone summed him up in 1900: 'Interesting, earnest, academic & rather visionary in politics but a man to be laid hold of. Not very rich, & much occupied. Wd. not feel "called" unless there was a good opportunity.'[6] And an old acquaintance recalled him later as 'a very strong Free Trader, anti-smoking, anti-drinking, and anti *most* things!'[7]

[1] Lever at Ormskirk, *L. Courier*, 5 January 1910.   [2] *Liverpool D.P.*, 15 January 1906.
[3] Herbert's memorandum of 6 March 1903, HGP 46025 ff. 127–36.
[4] J. P. Thomasson to George Cadbury, 19 December 1901, Scott's copy from original enc. in Cadbury to Scott, 20 December 1901, MGP.
[5] Hobhouse to Scott, 24 August 1905, MGP. It can, of course, be argued that Hobhouse's unhappy spell on Thomasson's *Tribune* vitiates this comment; but for Hobhouse, full-time journalism in a subordinate capacity had inherent difficulties.
[6] Gladstone's diary, 15 March 1900, HGP 46483 f. 64; cf. Taylor's remark that if he were to succeed 'that would appear to be a Providential call', in his memoirs quoted in Greenwood, *Taylor of Batley*, p. 53.
[7] Greenwood, *op. cit.*, p. 152.

Gladstone sent him into the Radcliffe-cum-Farnworth division, which comprised two small cotton towns with a strong Nonconformist tradition. He won the seat from the Tories at the Khaki Election, finding the fact that he was not a 'Lancashire lad' only a minor drawback, and told Gladstone, not unjustly, 'I think I may say that the constituency & I are fairly suited for each other'.[1]

II

At least until 1906 many constituencies in the north west enjoyed political leadership of the traditional kind: from local men with a stake in the town. Churchill once wrote of Chamberlain's achievement in carrying 'into the crowded streets, clacking factories and slums of Birmingham those same loyalties which had heretofore thrived only in the Highland glens'.[2] But though notable this was not unique. Throughout industrial England smaller men in smaller towns were establishing a comparable position. In Blackburn the Hornby family had represented the borough at Westminster for most of the nineteenth century and, so Philip Snowden put it, 'Toryism has become Hornbyism'.[3] Sir Harry Hornby, like his father before him, was popularly known as the 'owd gam' cock' and the cries of 'Hornby for ever' and 'Vote for t'owd gam' cock' were enough to carry him to victory in every election in which he stood, including that of 1906. Hornby was no politician. In twenty-four years in the House he never attempted to make a speech. But, proud of his family's tradition, he was prepared to yield to the pressures of the party managers, who would have been sorely pressed without his influence. He was a good employer, a strong Churchman, and, as emerged later, an unrepentant Free Trader. He used to walk around the town with his pockets filled with sweets for the children he met. In 1900 he and his fellow Member, Sir William Coddington, claimed to have subscribed to over nine hundred causes in the town within the previous twelve months. The personality of Sir Harry was above criticism even from opponents. One Liberal argued in 1906 that since Hornby did not care for Parliamentary life and election could give him no added honour, there was no reason to return him: 'He would be just as much our most respected townsman did he never leave the town except for his holidays.'[4]

Sir Harry Hornby was remarkable because of the degree to which he

---

[1] Taylor to Gladstone, 19 October 1900, HGP 46958 ff. 143-4.
[2] Churchill, *Great Contemporaries*, p. 56.
[3] On Hornbyism see Clarke, 'British politics and Blackburn politics', *Hist. Jnl.*, XII (1969), esp. pp. 303-14.
[4] Letter from H.W., *N.D.T.*, 13 January 1906. This is a good illustration of the point that, unlike a public person, a social leader 'can surrender public office and still retain his social standing'. Lee, *Social Leaders and Public Persons*, p. 5.

relied upon patriarchal claims rather than political activity. But there were many others in the same mould. In the county division of Darwen, which surrounded Blackburn, the political style of John Rutherford did not clash with that of Hornbyism. Like Hornby, Rutherford was no speaker; but since Darwen was a single-member constituency he could not, like Hornby, rely upon a running-mate to make speeches for him. Rutherford was a wealthy Blackburn brewer with a taste for the turf, and, known as 'Eawr Jack', enjoyed a good deal of easygoing popularity in which his philanthropy played an important part. The Liberal George Harwood, himself a rather erratic politician, sought to lift the veil in 1900. Rutherford was

a very pleasant man [he conceded] and we are very good chums, and dine frequently together. But what I should say about Mr Rutherford is this. What, in the name of heaven, has Rutherford to do with politics? It strikes me he is the last man in the world to know anything about them. As a matter of fact, I will say this that Mr Rutherford in social life does not pretend to know anything about politics.[1]

But Rutherford and Hornby – like Sir Francis Sharp Powell, 'Wigan's Grand Old Man' – kept their seats in 1906 when the 'politicians' among the Lancashire Tories were being toppled.

The borough and county divisions formed a single political unit too in St Helens and Newton, where the Pilkington family had interests not only in the glass works in the town but in outlying collieries too. The head of one branch of the family, William 'Roby' Pilkington, was a keen Conservative and had been chairman of the local association since its beginnings in 1868. He refused to stand himself when the borough seat was created in 1885 but supported the candidature of his son-in-law, Henry Seton-Karr, who was to hold the seat until 1906. 'Peerages', Seton-Karr told Salisbury, 'have often been given for smaller services than his.'[2] The other branch of the family, under William Windle Pilkington and his brother Richard, only became Unionist in 1886, but thereafter combined with Sir David Gamble, the most influential local landowner, in giving strong Liberal Unionist leadership to the town (though when Richard became M.P. for Newton in 1899 it was as a Conservative). The district was effectively controlled in every way by a tight-knit group of men centred round the Pilkingtons and the Gambles. They were the borough aldermen, they were the magistrates for the St Helens Petty Sessional Division, they provided both local M.P.s, they were the main support of the local schools; and as employers the Pilkingtons ruled with a rod of iron. But in 1906 both Seton-Karr and Richard Pilkington were defeated, and although when Pilkington died in 1908 his son was asked to

[1] Harwood at Darwen, *Lancs. D.P.*, 9 October 1900; for Rutherford see esp. *Lancs. D.P.*, 20 September 1900, *M. Courier*, 22 January 1906.
[2] Barker, *Pilkington Brothers and the Glass Industry*, p. 199.

succeed him as candidate for Newton, neither of the Conservative candidates in 1910 had any connexion with the family.¹

In Warrington there was a pattern of rivalry between dynasties. The leading Conservative family were the Greenalls, landowners who were connected with a local brewery; and the Crosfields, a family of soapmakers, were the leading Liberals. It was as natural for a Greenall to be president of the Conservative Association as for a Crosfield to be president of the Liberal. In both 1885 and 1886 Sir Gilbert Greenall had defeated a Crosfield, and the town's representation remained Conservative, Greenall being succeeded in 1892 by another local man of substance, Robert Pierpoint. The Crosfields felt a deep responsibility for maintaining the local Liberal party. When George Crosfield was apprised of its financial difficulties in 1886 he told his brother John that 'it wont do to give up the club – it would be considered tantamount to throwing up the sponge & giving the Tories the Borough & that we will *not* do'.² It was, however, George's ill health in 1899 which prevented his brother Arthur from committing himself at that time to fighting the borough, for the business still depended largely upon their efforts. But Gladstone assured Arthur that 'he was the man to win the seat & it wd. pay the constituency to wait'.³ This crisis overcome, Arthur became the champion of the Warrington Liberals while his two brothers George and John increasingly took over the affairs of the business. In 1900 Arthur Crosfield returned from abroad 'to represent the good old cause of Liberalism, which nearly a century ago his grandfather, Joseph Crosfield, was fighting for, and which for the last sixty years his dear old father had fought for (applause)'.⁴ His three contests with Pierpoint, for whom the new Sir Gilbert Greenall acted as chairman, were conducted with friendly rivalry. Pierpoint won in 1900, Crosfield in 1906 and January 1910. Although during 1910 both his brothers seceded to the Conservatives, his defeat in December 1910 should probably not be seen primarily in terms of local considerations, for his opponent, Harold Smith, was a complete stranger to the town, and the first outsider to be elected for it. Smith declared that he had had

as an opponent a man whose personality all Warrington respected; a man who was intimately connected with a great Warrington works employing hundreds of

¹ This account is based upon Harris and Barker, *A Merseyside Town in the Industrial Revolution*, pp. 467 ff.; the booklet *Now Thus – Now Thus* privately printed by Pilkington Brothers (1926); *St Helens Reporter*, 21 September 1900; *M. Courier*, 20 January 1906; *St Helens Newspaper*, 28 April 1908; and St Helens *Year Book*, 1900–14.
² George Crosfield to John (Crosfield), 12 January 1886, letter among correspondence of Henry Roberts in Warrington local collection. The *Warrington Guardian Year Book* contains material on Pierpoint (1901), the second Sir Gilbert Greenall (1903) and Arthur Crosfield (1901 and 1911).
³ Gladstone's diary, 21 and 22 June 1899, HGP 46483 f. 21.
⁴ Crosfield at Warrington, *Liverpool D.P.*, 3 October 1900.

Warrington people, and in spite of that, in spite of his family traditions, in spite of his personality, he (the speaker) – charged with being a 'carpet bagger' – beat him in a fight which only lasted three weeks. (Applause.)[1]

There was something of the same spirit at Oldham and at Bolton. George Harwood was a highly idiosyncratic Liberal who shared the representation of Bolton with a Conservative on an unopposed basis in 1900, and with Labour thereafter. His father, a Unitarian, had been mayor of both Salford and Bolton, but George Harwood not only became a Churchman but had to be dissuaded by Bishop Fraser himself from taking orders. Although remaining a cotton spinner, he was actively involved in the work of the Church Reform Union, Toynbee Hall and the Ancoats Brotherhood. When he was prevailed upon to become Liberal candidate for Bolton in 1895 he showed his individual approach from the first. 'When he gave them his views', he reasoned, 'they said, "But this is not the Newcastle programme"; and he replied, "No; but we can make as good a programme in Bolton." – (Laughter and cheers.)'[2] Harwood's breezy style inevitably gave offence in some quarters. He had publicly warned his followers in 1895 of the harm which 'the almost idolatrous regard' in which Mr Gladstone was held did the party, and in 1899 was maintaining that Gladstone was 'a second-rate man'. ('Proportionately what wd. be Harwood's rate?' wondered Hobhouse.)[3] But his hold upon the town was firm. 'George Harwood will be a Liberal member for Bolton as long as he likes to be, and there is no argument about that', said a Conservative in 1910.[4] Indeed he remained M.P. until his death in 1912: whereupon the Liberals plumped for a man who was, as far as possible, from the same stable. Thomas Taylor too was a cotton employer, a Churchman and something of a local institution – but hardly much of a politician. 'If he went to Parliament', he admitted, 'he would not go to take up political life. He was not young enough to start a new job, and his voice might never be heard in this Parliament.'[5] But he was, as the Conservatives found, held in great esteem locally, even being called in to settle domestic quarrels which might otherwise have gone to court – 'It is for instance quite a common occurrence for working people who have a dispute to say "Let's go and see Daddy Taylor" & they abide by his decision.'[6]

[1] Smith at Newton, *M. Courier*, 7 December 1910; on Smith's contest cf. Birkenhead, *Contemporary Personalities*, pp. 314–15 and Salvidge, *Salvidge of Liverpool*, pp. 100–1.

[2] Harwood at Prestwich, *M.G.*, 20 July 1895. For Harwood see obits., *Bolton Evg News*, 7 November 1912, *Bolton Chron.*, 9 November 1912; cf. Rowley, *Fifty Years of Work Without Wages*, pp. 13–14, 27.

[3] Hobhouse to Scott, 17 June 1899, MGP.

[4] *M.G.*, 6 January 1910.

[5] Speech by Taylor, *Bolton Evg News*, 15 November 1912; cf. biography, *Bolton Chron.*, 16 November 1912.

[6] J. M. W. Morison to Aitken, 26 November 1912, Beaverbrook P. Morison had made a special inquiry into the result of the by-election.

In the more industrialised county divisions the possibilities of political leadership were much the same. The Northwich division of Cheshire was the fief of Sir John Brunner. 'I have lived here in Cheshire for 27 years', he declared in 1900, 'during which time I have held every office to which you could elect me, from overseer of the poor to a member of Parliament. I have not received a penny for any of these services, and I have been perfectly content with the love and friendship with which you have accredited me.'[1] His manifest claim was to be the father of his people. Proofs of his generosity littered the division. The Brunner Mond works at Winnington, employing six to seven thousand men, were another influence – one Conservative candidate complained of having to fight 'against a solid phalanx of Winnington men'.[2] Brunner was eager for his son also to find a seat. J. F. L. Brunner sat for Leigh in the 1906 Parliament and, on his father's retirement, took over Northwich in 1910. He held Northwich without difficulty, though in December 1910 his majority was hauled down. The *Manchester Courier* maintained that 'Brunnerism has sustained a blow from which it is doubtful whether it will ever recover'.[3] This is, of course, a wild exaggeration; but the remarkable fact has already been noticed[4] that Northwich, which should by all traditional criteria have been one of the seedbeds of Liberalism in the north west, was the one constituency in which Liberal strength had declined since the 1880s.

The High Peak division of Derbyshire, centred on Glossop, was another industrialised county division. There the Partingtons, who were Non-conformist papermakers, confronted the Sidebottoms and the Woods, an interrelated family of Anglican millowners. Captain Edward Partington was at one time urged to become Liberal candidate for Bury, and T. H. Side-bottom was for many years Conservative M.P. for Stalybridge, a position which John Wood later occupied; but it was Glossop that the families really fought over. The Partingtons employed about twelve hundred men in the town and were great benefactors; indeed, their gift of £30,000 for the endowment of a nursing home came only a month before the 1906 election. Colonel W. Sidebottom, brother of the M.P. for Stalybridge, had represented High Peak from 1885 until his retirement in 1900, whereupon Edward Partington's son Oswald came forward for the Liberals and captured the seat. The Conservatives had no luck with outside candidates, but in January 1910 they were given a great fillip when Samuel Hill-Wood (of the Wood family) agreed to stand. He was not only popular as a benevolent employer but could

---

[1] Brunner at Northwich, *M.G.*, 12 October 1900; cf. Lee, *Social Leaders and Public Persons*, pp. 37–8.
[2] C. L. Samson after the poll, *M.G.*, 16 October 1900.
[3] *M. Courier*, 9 December 1910.
[4] See above, p. 13.

appeal to local patriotism on sporting grounds; he was a pillar of Derbyshire County Cricket Club and had poured money into Glossop Football Club, taking this small-town team into the First Division. It was not possible to gainsay Hill-Wood's appeal as a 'sportsman' by the retort that 'one would imagine this election was for the Turf Club'.[1] There was, it was said, 'more than a suspicion of a contest of clans' about the 1910 elections in the division.[2] Although Partington won the first round, in December 1910 he was defeated.

There was a rather different twist to the elections in Lancaster, where the opposition of town and country interests was more marked. Colonel W. H. Foster of Hornby Castle was a substantial landowner who had represented the division for the Conservatives since 1895. His interests lay in such pursuits as horse-breeding and, the complete country gentleman, he had given 'that full share of time to philanthropic work and social amenities which is expected from a Parliamentary representative'.[3] His opponent in 1900, on the other hand, was Norval Helme, a linoleum manufacturer from the town of Lancaster. There is no reason to doubt the claim that from the Liberal point of view Helme was 'by far, the best local man'.[4] He had been Mayor, County Councillor, chairman of the Liberal Association and of the Free Church Council, and President of the Chamber of Commerce. Helme and Foster went out of their way to maintain cordial relations; if they were canvassing in the same place they would have lunch together, and the spirit of the contest was described as one of 'old-world courtliness and chivalry'.[5] It was, said the Conservative chairman at one meeting, against the grain to vote against a friend and neighbour like Helme. When Helme addressed the farmers he said openly that he was 'not conversant with matters relating to agriculture', and after the poll Foster admitted that Lancaster itself 'had gone very solidly for Mr Helme'.[6] Helme defeated Foster both in 1900 and in 1906, but thereafter the Conservatives had to rely upon carpetbaggers.

This sort of tension between urban and rural forces was not uncommon, but in the more agricultural divisions the Liberals were unlikely to be able to challenge the landed interest on its own terms. The landowners of Cheshire provided most of the Conservative M.P.s there, like H. J. Tollemache of Eddisbury, 'whose boast it is that he never made a speech in the House of Commons'.[7] The Liberal country gentleman was rather a contra-

[1] Captain Arthur Murray, *M.G.*, 14 December 1910. For the position of the old families see Birch, *Small Town Politics*, esp. pp. 18–28.
[2] *M. Courier*, 13 December 1910.
[3] *Lancs. D.P.*, 18 September 1900.
[4] Lord Ashton to Gladstone, 20 September 1900, HGP 46058 f. 73. For Helme see *Lancs. D.P.*, 18 September 1900.
[5] *Preston Guardian*, 29 September 1900.
[6] Helme at Garstang, Foster at the Conservative Club, *Lancs. D.P.*, 4, 10 October 1900.
[7] *Liverpool D.P.*, 5 January 1906.

diction in terms. James Tomkinson, a Gladstonian who had once told his leader that he was the only member of the landed interest in Cheshire not to go Unionist,[1] and who sat for Crewe, was almost the last of the breed. With his death in the Parliamentary Steeplechase in 1910 an era passed.

III

Men of this type were not important because they became parliamentary candidates: they were important already. Since their personal influence was considerable their support was eagerly sought at elections, whether or not they stood themselves. The Pilkingtons were the real power on the Conservative side in St Helens whoever the actual candidate was, and the same is true of Sir Gilbert Greenall in Warrington. When former Conservative M.P.s like Sir Harry Hornby in Blackburn or Sir William Tomlinson in Preston were to be found working for their successors, it was because their help was still valuable; their parliamentary careers had been built upon a bedrock of constituency support. Members for other constituencies were often leaders of the local party in their own homes. Sir James Duckworth was President of the Rochdale Reform Association while he was M.P. for Middleton, at the same time as Gordon Harvey, who was President of the Middleton Liberal Association, became candidate in Rochdale (an arrangement about which Herbert Gladstone had his doubts). The activities of W. H. Lever spanned several divisions, and Sir John Brunner's interests were even more widespread; as well as overseeing affairs in most of the Cheshire seats he was at various times president of the Liberal Associations in the Everton division of Liverpool and in Wigan.

Henry Gladstone, Herbert's elder brother, was several times approached to stand for the Wirral or Chester after he had become established at Burton Manor near Chester. While admitting in 1905 that 'it ought to be Wirral or nothing',[2] he would not in the end come forward himself, though he was an active supporter of the Liberal cause in that part of Cheshire. Another Liberal who could have become a candidate in any time he wished was Frank Hollins, a cotton spinner who was president of Preston Liberal Association. It was part of the Whips' job to cultivate such men, and in 1904 Gladstone was making arrangements for Hollins to be elected to the Reform Club. Another man of the same kind was Edward Donner of Manchester. When Campbell-Bannerman was visiting Manchester in 1899 he was assured 'that Edward Donner is the best man to act as your host. He is an Oxford man & a very nice fellow, also quite one of the leading M'ter Liberals.'[3] And

---

[1] Lee, *Social Leaders and Public Persons*, p. 37.
[2] H. N. Gladstone to Gladstone, 4 August 1905, HGP 46045 ff. 226–7.
[3] Gladstone to Campbell-Bannerman, 26 October 1899, CBP 41215 f. 118.

although the Leader on that occasion stayed in an hotel it was Donner who entertained him on his visit in 1907. It was Donner too who was pressed into service as Churchill's chairman in the Manchester North West by-election of 1908, when it was imperative to put up a respectable front to the business-men. The calls on his support were numerous. On one evening in November 1910 Donner spoke for Schwann in Manchester North, Haworth in South, and was appointed to Kemp's election committee in North West.

When the Lancashire and Cheshire Liberal Federation was formed in 1908 its Executive Committee became the Liberal senate for the north west. Sir John Brunner was made president, though the active work devolved upon the chairman, Sir Ben Johnson. Johnson was happier in committee than on the platform; indeed his lack of activity during the elections of December 1910 provoked the Conservative press to ask, 'Why is the Radical leader so persistently silent?'[1] Among those initially elected to the Executive were Allan Bright, who had taken over from Sir Edwards Evans as Liberal leader in Liverpool; Norval Helme of Lancaster; Sir Frank Hollins of Preston; Joseph Bliss of North Lonsdale, for which he was an indefatigable parlia-mentary candidate; Sir George Macalpine, the Chairman of Accrington Liberal Association; Colonel Jesse Pilcher, a pillar of all the Liberal organisa-tions in Stretford and Old Trafford; William Brimelow, a prominent Independent Methodist who was connected with the Tillotson newspapers and did much to keep the Liberal organisation alive in Westhoughton; and Dr William Hodgson, who had been largely responsible for breaking the hold of the L.N.W.R. and the Conservative party over the politics of Crewe.

There exists a fairly precise guide to those Liberals of considerable social standing who were not M.P.s, for the Chief Whip on one occasion drew up a list of them. The list of possible peers which the Master of Elibank compiled in July 1911 is not an authoritative document. Its main purpose may well have been 'to bluff the Tories',[2] and Asquith thought that none of the 'gentlemen hypothetically concerned' had been 'sounded as to their possible intentions'.[3] The main list runs to 245 names, of whom about thirty were connected with the north west. (Its preliminary nature can be judged from the fact that two men on it, Colonels Henry Platt and William Windle Pilkington, were Conservatives.) The main list includes the names of a number of ex-M.P.s, including Sir William Mather, Sir John Brunner, Sir Henry Roscoe, Sir W. H. Lever, Albert Bright, Sir Edward Holden, Oswald Partington, Austin Taylor, Lord Richard Cavendish and Sir Joseph Leese.

[1] *L. Courier*, 2 December 1910.
[2] Note in R. H. Davies's writing with Elibank's list, EP 8802 f. 251.
[3] Asquith, *Memories and Reflections*, I, 191. The main list is in EP ff. 252–65 and is identical with the list in the Asquith Papers printed in Jenkins, *Asquith*, pp. 539–42. There are other notes and lists at ff. 266–70 and a list of Manchester names at f. 271.

Also named are Alfred Emmott, who was at that time still M.P. for Oldham, Franklin Thomasson, the former M.P. for Leicester, and three younger Liberal candidates who were heirs to peerages: the Hons. L. U. Kay-Shuttleworth, A. L. Stanley and C. C. Bigham.[1] The list also includes the landowners Henry Gladstone and Sir T. T. Scarisbrick; Sir Frank Hollins of Preston; and the Liverpool Liberals Sir Ben Johnson, Sir Edward Evans, Sir Edward Russell, E. K. Muspratt and Sir William Bowring.[2] In addition, three names appeared also on the separate Manchester list: Sir William Crossley, head of the engineering firm of Crossley Brothers and a great benefactor in the Altrincham division, which he represented in Parliament between 1906–10; and the Manchester Liberals Sir Edward Donner and F. H. Smith. Among thirteen other names on this list were those of Samuel Lamb, Churchill's chairman of 1906; Sir William Stephens, a former mayor of Salford; C. H. Scott, a member of the Executive of Manchester Liberal Federation; and C. P. Scott. These peerages, of course, were never bestowed. But Lancashire Liberals claimed a fair share of titles in the years after 1906. Five textile manufacturers became peers – George Whiteley (Lord Marchamley, 1908), William Holland (Lord Rotherham, 1910), Thomas Gair Ashton (Lord Ashton of Hyde, 1911), Alfred Emmott (Lord Emmott, 1911) and George Kemp (Lord Rochdale, 1913). And as to knighthoods, the anonymous conclaves of wirepullers were transformed into a Liberal Camelot.

IV

The representation of the city divisions was a rather special case. In the Parliament of 1895 the Conservatives held eight of the nine Liverpool divisions, and eight of the nine divisions of Manchester and Salford. When Herbert Gladstone made a survey of candidates in January 1900 he found that no Liberal candidate was in sight in any of these sixteen seats. On seeing Robert Holt some months before he had noted: 'Pitched into him about L'pool & found him very feeble & goodnatured over it. He said we took away their young men to other constituencies! I urged that at least they shd. get ready in Exchange & Toxteth (where he said the best chance was) & suggested that if L'pool Libs. could not fight they might at least give me money.'[3] It was quite true that Liverpool Liberals were reluctant to contest their own city – ten fought in other parts of the country in 1900 – and it was commensurately difficult to persuade outsiders to come in. Attempts to

[1] Bigham had learnt in January 1911 that his name was on a list then being compiled of 'the eldest sons of peers to be called up with others to the House of Lords if necessary'. Mersey, *A Picture of Life*, p. 232.

[2] The last two are given only by their surnames; it is possible, though unlikely, that the references are to Max Muspratt and F. C. Bowring.

[3] Gladstone's diary, 4 July 1899, HGP 46483 f. 26.

mount candidatures in the two picked divisions failed, and at the outset of the General Election the only opposition to the Conservatives came from the Irish Nationalist T. P. O'Connor in the Scotland division. 'Where is the Liberal party?' its leaders were being asked.[1] But after a visit to London by Edward Evans, two carpetbaggers were hustled into Kirkdale and Exchange, where, of course, they were soundly beaten.

The Conservative M.P.s for Liverpool were an odd bunch. One of them wrote later that he was struck by their 'apparent political mediocrity' and asked what it was about Salvidge that accounted for this.[2] Only F. E. Smith in Walton and, later, Leslie Scott in Exchange were of ministerial calibre. The rest were genial nonentities who were prepared to knuckle under to Salvidge. The millionaire shipowner R. P. Houston, who sat for West Toxteth, was a striking figure with his ever-brilliant red beard – F. E. Smith once called him 'the original dye-hard'[3] – and his political style was equally extravagant. It is no surprise to find him in 1912 vaingloriously confiding to Bonar Law that 'I think I have pretty well killed Lloyd George in Liverpool with ridicule'.[4] It was, however, the Member for West Derby, Watson Rutherford, who attracted most notice. Rutherford made the most extreme claims of any of those who called themselves Tory Democrats. 'For his own part', he once said, 'he was fain to admit that he claimed to be a progressive Tory, and not merely a Unionist, but a Democrat, and perhaps even a Social Democrat (applause).'[5] In 1907 he propounded a democratic Tory programme, advocating such measures as nationalisation of the railways, state employment of the unemployed, old age pensions, payment of M.P.s, and universal franchise.[6] Rutherford had a great hold upon his constituency and in November 1910 a manifesto in his support was signed by nearly three thousand voters.

The Conservatives who represented Manchester until 1906 were less flamboyant if more able than their Liverpool counterparts; but they were like them in possessing strong claims of a certain kind. The three safest Conservative seats in Manchester were held from their creation by men of some eminence. Sir W. H. Houldsworth was the perfect candidate in the business division of North West and had the strongest local claims of the

---

[1] *L. Courier*, 19 September 1900.

[2] Letter from J. B. Brunel Cohen (M.P. for Liverpool Fairfield from 1918), *Liverpool D.P.*, 21 March 1934.

[3] Lord Beaverbrook, *The Decline and Fall of Lloyd George* (1963), p. 223.

[4] Houston to Law, 22 March 1912, BLP 26/1/51.

[5] Speech by Rutherford at the Conservative Club dinner, *L. Courier*, 30 November 1905.

[6] Lord Robert Cecil, who as an M.P. was a recipient of this programme, thought that Rutherford's views were 'much more nearly in agreement with those of the Independent Labour Party' than of the average Conservative. Letter, *The Times*, 30 October 1907. Rutherford stood by all points except nationalisation in 1910. See his speech at West Derby, *L. Courier*, 11 January 1910.

three; Balfour sat for East, having come to Manchester in 1885 as the rising hope of the party in order to raise the Tory standard there; and Sir James Fergusson, a veteran of the Crimean War and of many Parliaments, represented North East (and held office briefly although Balfour considered he had 'not the ability...for a big department').[1] The other seats were held by influential local employers. W. J. Galloway was a member of a family engineering firm in South West. 'My family', he proclaimed in 1906, 'has been connected with Hulme for over one hundred and twenty years – (cheers) – and so far as I know there has never been until now any suggestion that these interests were not the interests of the people of Hulme.'[2] The real power in Salford South lay with the Conservative chairman, J. Grimble Groves, who in 1900 became candidate himself. Groves was also chairman of Groves, Whitnall, the Salford brewery, and his whole interests were identified with the borough, in the public life of which he played a leading part. 'Vote for our Jim, the Salford lad', read his posters, and his local connexions, reinforced by an openhanded support of constituency charities, made him a popular figure.

Against such men the Liberals had at one time been able to field strong local candidates of their own: men like Benjamin Armitage, William Holland, Jacob Bright, Sir Henry Roscoe, Professor J. E. C. Munro and C. P. Scott. But by 1895 Liberal opposition was much weaker, and in 1900, when Augustine Birrell came to Manchester, he was described as 'the only Radical big-wig numbered among the Manchester candidates'.[3] In 1906, however, a generation of Conservative M.P.s was scythed down in completely undiscriminating fashion. 'Two old members of great personal popularity were dismissed by enormous majorities, after twenty years' service, as sternly as if they were unknown "carpet-baggers"', wrote the *Guardian* of Balfour and Fergusson.

In one of the Salford divisions [it continued], a former member who owns nearly all the public-houses was easily routed by an almost complete stranger to the borough...A candidate had only to be a Free-trader to get in, whether he was known or unknown, semi-Unionist or thorough Home Ruler, Protestant or Catholic, entertaining or dull. He had only to be a Protectionist to lose all chance of getting in, though he spoke with the tongues of men and of angels, though he was a good employer to many electors, or had led the House of Commons, or fought in the Crimea.[4]

It was a clean sweep.

[1] For Fergusson's appointment as Postmaster-General in 1891 see J. P. Cornford, 'The parliamentary foundations of the Hotel Cecil', in Robson (ed.), *Ideas and Institutions of Victorian Britain*, pp. 295–8.
[2] Galloway in South West, *M. Courier*, 21 December 1905.
[3] *M. Courier*, 25 September 1900.   [4] Leader, *M.G.*, 15 January 1906.

The Liberal candidates, it is true, were much better now. Churchill took over the crucially important candidature in Manchester North West, and he and Hilaire Belloc, who fought Salford South, provided the rhetoric (at this time Belloc more in the progressive vein than Churchill). George Agnew, son of Sir William Agnew, was a strong local candidate in Salford West; Arthur Haworth, another scion of a famous Liberal family, now came forward in Manchester South. And two seats were fought by good Labour candidates, G. D. Kelley of the Manchester Trades Council and J. R. Clynes. After Churchill left Manchester in 1908 he was replaced by Sir George Kemp, who was in most respects an even better candidate for the businessmen. From 1906 onward it was the Conservatives in Manchester who had difficulty in finding candidates, for the old guard were not easily replaced. Kemp's chairman proudly pointed out in January 1910 that Manchester was contested on the progressive side by four men closely connected with business and two working men: on the Conservative side by four lawyers, a journalist and an ex-soldier.[1] This in itself, perhaps, was no great condemnation. But the Conservatives themselves were conscious of the defects. 'It must not be forgotten', wrote their organ of the Manchester results, 'that many of the Unionist candidates were new to the constituencies and previously unknown to the electors.'[2] It was much the same that December. The fact that the candidate was changed in six of the nine Manchester and Salford divisions was itself a bad sign. There was, it is true, the odd man rising in the party (like Arthur Colefax in Manchester South West) or the philanthropic local businessmen (like Arthur Taylor in North East) but the rest were a weak lot, and Bonar Law's last-minute intervention in Manchester North West was all too fleeting. The Conservatives were determined not to be so outgunned again. In 1912 Steel-Maitland was wondering whether they could not 'really besiege Manchester' by getting better candidates in three or four of the seats. Thinking on the same lines, Percy Woodhouse, one of the Manchester leaders, took up Law's offer to help them and asked if he could send them 'some man at present in the House, who could present the arguments of our party in North Manchester', to replace the present candidate.[3] It is a measure of how seriously Law took the problem that he was evidently prepared to ask F. E. Smith to move there; but this was to outrun Woodhouse's ambitions for such a doubtful prospect.

In Liverpool 1906 was not a political watershed and the old order was undisturbed. Edward Evans, the Conservatives pointed out, had had to

[1] Speech by Tom Stott, Manchester North West, *M.G.*, 13 January 1910.
[2] *M. Courier*, 17 January 1910.
[3] Steel-Maitland to Law, 4 February 1912, BLP 25/2/4; Woodhouse to Law, 16 August 1912, BLP 27/1/42; cf. letter from 'Conservative', *M. Courier*, 7 December 1910.

import three of his five candidates, whom they characterised as one Liverpool man, one localised barrister, one ex-M.P., one Irish lawyer, and one colonial barrister. 'On the other hand', they concluded, 'the Unionist phalanx embodies the inspiring sentiment – Liverpool men for Liverpool constituencies.'[1] The 'ex-M.P.' was a great catch for the Liverpool Liberals – J. E. B. Seely, who had crossed the floor on Free Trade and now led a vigorous and successful assault on the business division of Abercromby. But 1910 found the Liberals hanging on by their fingernails. Seely was defeated in January, and Max Muspratt, who took over the other business division, Exchange, only just got home. The leaders of Liverpool Liberalism could no longer be accused of refusing to fight; indeed, there were misgivings because so many of the active leaders were candidates. Sir Edward Evans had to be called out of retirement to run the organisation while his successor Allan Bright went off to fight in Stalybridge, and, among other officials, Muspratt stood for Exchange, Dr Permewan for Bootle, Francis Joseph for Walton, and John Lea for East Toxteth. In December 1910 the Liberals shuffled their men around somewhat and in place of Seely managed to get the shipowner F. C. Bowring to stand for Abercromby. But their hopes were plainly pitched low and Sir Charles Petrie, the Conservative leader, alleged that Liverpool Liberalism had 'scarcely a kick left'.[2] Whereas there was great difficulty in filling the candidatures in the city itself, four Liverpool Liberals, including Bright, went off to fight elsewhere, joining the four who were already Liberal M.P.s for other constituencies. 'The contrast', it was explained, 'does not necessarily, however, reflect on the local organisations. The past histories of such divisions as Everton and West Derby cannot be kept out of consideration.'[3] It was impossible to make bricks without straw. In many ways the Liberal 'merchant princes' who met with so much criticism had done as much as could reasonably be expected. Herbert Reynolds Rathbone stood for East Toxteth in 1902; Richard Durning Holt fought West Derby in 1903 and 1906 before seeking a seat elsewhere; Max Muspratt was M.P. for Exchange until he was thrown over in December 1910, and stood again at Bootle against Bonar Law in 1911. It was not because of the quality of the candidates on either side that Liverpool remained rooted in Toryism. But – in contrast to Manchester – because the colour of its politics never underwent a violent reversal the style of its leadership was not transformed either.

[1] *L. Courier*, 8 January 1906.
[2] *L. Courier*, 23 November 1910.
[3] *Liverpool D.P.*, 22 November 1910.

V

The choice of candidate did much to set the political tone of a constituency. 'Both in theory and in practice', wrote Balfour, in a classic exposition of the traditional view, 'we endeavour to have a representative Association in each Division, and on them – and them only – lies the responsibility of selecting their Candidate. With that choice the Headquarters of the Party never interfere.'[1] Balfour here displayed a firmer grasp on the theory than on the practice, for in both parties the central party organisation was acquiring much greater influence in this process.

A good local man was preferable to a good outsider, but even when the obvious man was before them, living in their midst, the constituency leaders quite often had to seek the Whips' help in persuading him to stand. What could smack less of central manipulation than that a Holt should stand for a Liverpool seat at a by-election in 1903? Yet even this could not remain a local transaction, and Jesse Herbert told Gladstone that the Liverpool Liberals 'recognise fully that they owe his consent to you & are very grateful'.[2]

Party activists from one part of the region often fought constituencies in another. On the Liberal side the connexions established by the Manchester Reform Club probably helped here. A. G. Symonds of the National Reform Union was actively engaged in placing candidates in the north west, at least in the 1890s; and prominent individuals like C. P. Scott were asked for help by constituency parties. The Conservatives worked in much the same way. Lord Derby, that prince of middlemen, could call upon Salvidge's aid in finding Liverpool lawyers to farm out; in December 1910 Liverpool men were Conservative candidates in St Helens, Ince, Altrincham,[3] West-houghton, Leigh, Warrington, Preston, North Lonsdale and Blackburn. Derby resented any infringement on his position.

The other day you asked me to try and secure you a candidate [he wrote to the Gorton Conservatives in 1911]. I at once set to work and I think I might have been able to get one for you, but I heard that you had privately consulted Sir Max Aitken and asked him to find you one. Under the circumstances I naturally decline to take any further interest in your constituency and must ask you to allow me to withdraw from any participation in your political affairs.[4]

Aitken in fact looked after Gorton to the extent of introducing to it the rich American Otto Kahn, and was also approached by the Hyde division with a view to his finding them a candidate.

[1] Balfour to Selborne, 6 March 1908, BP 49708.
[2] Herbert to Gladstone, 10 January 1903, HGP 46025 ff. 122–3.
[3] Though here it was more a case of J. R. Ketby Fletcher fleeing the influence of Salvidge, with whom he had quarrelled some years before; he had previously fought Rossendale.
[4] Derby to J. W. D. Barron, 10 September 1911, copy enc. in Barron to Aitken, 9 November 1911, Beaverbrook P.

The reconstitution of Liberal Lancashire

It was a characteristic mixture of official and unofficial approaches that brought Harold Cox to Preston as Liberal candidate in 1906.

The first time I ever heard of the borough of Preston in a political sense [he recalled] was under somewhat curious circumstances. I had been speaking at a Free Trade meeting in one of the suburbs of London, and as I was going back in the train, very tired, a gentleman opposite to me, whom I did not know in the least, suddenly addressed me by name, and said: 'Why don't you stand for Preston?' I said: 'Why do you ask? Why should I?' 'Well,' he said, 'I know all about Preston, and I think I know a good deal about you, and I am convinced your opinions are exactly the opinions of a large majority of the people of Preston.' And I heard no more about Preston, and, to be quite frank, I thought no more, because I was very busy, spending every moment earning my living and fighting day and night for the cause of Free Trade. But a year later, quite unexpectedly, I received an express letter from Mr Herbert Gladstone, then the Chief Liberal Whip, stating that four gentlemen had come to him from Preston to look for a candidate, and he had recommended them to see me. I went to meet these four gentlemen, and I explained my opinions, and I remember I was very much impressed with their powers as cross-examiners (laughter).[1]

Sometimes the Whips were not involved at all, even in the bringing in of an outsider. At Rossendale, for instance, when Sir William Mather retired in 1904 he suggested to his old friend Sir William Harcourt that his son 'Loulou' should succeed him and Herbert Gladstone was only informed of this arrangement later.[2] But the Whips were involved more often than is at first apparent, and it is well to beware of those rather over-simplified and over-drawn recollections which suggest otherwise. Churchill's account of how, after Ascroft's death in 1899, the Oldham Conservatives 'immediately pitched on me', and how he 'received straight away without ever suing, or asking, or appearing before any committee, a formal invitation to contest the seat'[3] is not inaccurate; but its bravura ring can easily cause the fact that in his search for a constituency Churchill punctiliously deferred to the suggestions of the Central Office to be forgotten.

'It fell to me, or course', wrote Herbert Gladstone of his time as Chief Whip, 'to interview many hundreds of candidates and *pari passu* to be in consultation with all Liberal Associations. It was necessary to know what political question weighed most with each constituency and then to suggest the candidates most competent to suit local requirements.'[4] His Whips' papers show how he went about this extensive business of brokerage. On the basis of his correspondence and round of interviews, endless lists were drawn up and worked over: lists of 'names for consideration', 'good chance Seats

---

[1] Cox at Preston, *Lancs. D.P.*, 25 November 1909.
[2] See Mather, *Sir William Mather*, pp. 157–8.
[3] Churchill, *My Early Life*, pp. 226–7.
[4] Gladstone's autobiography, HGP 46118 ff. 101–2.

vacant', 'candidates introduced but not yet adopted', 'candidates allocated who have not yet accepted allocation'. Prospective candidates were classified. There were lists of 'young men without money' and of '"A" selection of most competent' and (the *pis aller*) '"B" men with money'. The hard-headed local leaders with whom Gladstone dealt knew as well as he that a constituency would get a candidate only as good as its electoral prospects. 'Also', wrote Alfred Emmott, relaying to him the *desiderata* of the Oldham Liberals, 'they want a Non-con if possible. However they may not be able to get all they want.'[1] J. P. Thomasson was altogether more impatient with his Liberal friends in Westhoughton: 'And after all the constituency must not be particular: ought not a barrister with the gift of the gab from Manchr. or indeed anywhere to satisfy them?'[2]

Gladstone's activities were most noticeable when a stranger was introduced, perhaps at the last moment. In 1900 Liverpool provided an example of unadulterated carpetbagging. The General Election was already under way when Edward Evans travelled to London to see the Whips about a candidate for Exchange. Gladstone had at his disposal one F. W. Verney, whom he had failed to place for a London borough earlier in the year. On the morning of 25 September, nine days before the poll, Evans met Verney in London; afterwards he sent a telegram to Liverpool; this was read to a committee meeting there held at noon; Verney caught the 2.30 p.m. express and arrived in Liverpool at 6.15 p.m.; less than two hours later he had been adopted by the Liberal Association.[3] Such haste was indecent; a better match could be arranged when time allowed. In Chorley, for instance, Gladstone learned that there was a vacancy on 10 March 1904 and for some months this was left unfilled. Then on 23 June Gladstone had an interview with Eliot Crawshay Williams, the son of a former Liberal M.P., noting of him: 'Travelled. Well read. Q. rich. Keen. Might be very useful. Wd. like to fight a constituency.'[4] He was soon beginning an active campaign in Chorley, where his enthusiasm did much to stir up Liberalism in an admittedly safe Tory seat.

But the Whips' work was not confined to cases like these; Gladstone helped introduce to vacant constituencies men whom one might suppose would have needed no introduction. Sir William Mather is a case in point. The wealthy and philanthropic owner of a Salford engineering works, Mather was a pillar of Lancashire Liberalism and had represented two Lancashire constituencies in Parliament. When Rochdale fell vacant in 1899 the Liberal

[1] Emmott to Gladstone, 19 November 1905, HGP 46063 f. 116.
[2] Thomasson to Gladstone, 11 January 1904, HGP 46061 ff. 115–16.
[3] *Liverpool D.P.*, 26 September 1900.
[4] Gladstone's diary, 23 June 1904, HGP 46485 f. 15; cf. Crawshay Williams, *Simple Story*, pp. 50 ff.

chairman conferred with Gladstone and they agreed that Mather was the best man. Mather, however, was reluctant, and despite the hope that his family would make him stand nothing came of this idea. At the end of 1899 it became known that a by-election was imminent in Rossendale. The Liberals proposed to invite their president, Trickett, in the first place although it was not expected that he would stand. W. H. Lever had declined, and the other names Gladstone suggested were those of Albert Bright, son of John Bright, and the Hon. C. N. Lawrence, son of Lord Lawrence. On 4 January 1900 Gladstone's diary records: 'Trickett. Rossendale. Cannot stand. Eager for Mather. Lever declined. Lawrence they dont know, J. A. Bright they dont fancy.' The only minor snag was that Mather was in Switzerland at the time. Sir Joseph Leese, M.P. for Accrington, who preferred the claims of George Whiteley, the renegade Tory M.P. for Stockport, wrote to Gladstone that

I cannot see what claim Albert Bright has got, who proved himself one of the most bitter & vicious Unionists of Lancashire & who is a very second class performer at the best. Who on earth is C. N. Lawrence?

I shd. rejoice in Whiteley as a neighbour, but the others are - - - - - s:

Mather I know very well & failing his very splendid opinion of his own mediocrity he is not a bad chap. But you will find that he thinks himself a much greater wirepuller than you, whose special function, for the moment, it is. However Mather would be far the best of the three. But he has lost two seats, Salford & Gorton, & *neither ought to have been lost*.[1]

It was Mather who was chosen and elected: not, of course, *because* of Gladstone, for he was an obvious choice, but hardly independently of him either. Of Gladstone's other suggestions, Lever was to fight the Wirral, Bright later became Liberal M.P. for Oldham (they got their 'Non-con' after all), and only Lawrence was never heard of again. And although Gladstone considered Whiteley ineligible for this vacancy, the two were soon discussing the merits of several constituencies with a view to finding a mutually acceptable solution, for he was a notable recruit. Moreover, when Whiteley conceded to Gladstone that, for all his own preferences, 'as a good soldier I must fight where I am told',[2] he was displaying a grasp of the realities of modern electoral politics worthy of a future Chief Whip.

[1] Leese to Gladstone, 7 January 1900, HGP 46017 ff. 161–2; this account is based on Gladstone's diary, HGP 46483 ff. 5, 15, 32, 55–6, and his correspondence with Hudson of 26 and 27 December 1899, HGP 46020 ff. 25–9.

[2] Whiteley to Gladstone, 15 January 1900, HGP 46057 ff. 260–1.

VI

To ask what part the personality of the candidate played in a particular election is perhaps to ask the wrong question. The choice of candidate was important where it was expected or allowed to be important. There was a premium upon local men insofar as there was a premium upon local issues and local loyalties. Once the patriarchal structure of politics had broken down within a community, however, no individual candidate would ever have the same influence and independence again. The personal influence of Sir Harry Hornby was still crucially important in Blackburn in 1906 when he was elected to Parliament alongside Philip Snowden, whereas his running-mate polled over 1,300 fewer votes. Hornby had an independent power base which had not yet been eroded and as a Free Trader he was independent of the Conservative party in policy too. But such independence was coming to be regarded as heresy and candidates were finding that heterodoxy weakened rather than strengthened their position. Sir George Pilkington, for instance, whose Liberal Imperialism was of such an extreme cast as to lead the Southport Conservatives to offer to support him as Unionist candidate, did not thereby save his seat in 1900. His opponent asked, 'would they send back Sir George Pilkington to sit with Labouchere, Dr Clark and those men on that side?'[1] The Liberal Imperialists and the Unionist Free Traders both found that they were tarred with the same brush as the remainder of their parties.

This is not to say that within the right sort of context the personality of the candidate might not be extremely important. When Churchill squeezed in as Junior Member for Oldham in 1900, two hundred votes ahead of Walter Runciman, he wrote that 'nothing but personal popularity arising out of the late South African War, carried me in' and that 'without the personal, probably non-political vote, I should have been behind Mr Runciman'.[2] Oldham at that time was a town where such things had considerable effect; so was Stalybridge. In 1905 J. S. Sandars interviewed the Conservative agent for Stalybridge about the by-election there in which the Conservatives had been defeated.

In a word [he wrote to Balfour], he told me that the defeat was due to the sympathy at the last moment which was extended to the old man, as he called [J. F.] Cheetham, now the Radical member for the Borough. Cheetham had stood some 7 or 8 times since 1885 (3 I think for Stalybridge), and had only once been successful, and then at the close of a Parliament. He has lately given to the Borough a fountain and a free library, and he is a local employer of labour. Under these circumstances, at the last moment the Agent told me that many of their men, known Conservatives

[1] Marshall Hall at Southport, *L. Courier*, 2 October 1900.
[2] Churchill to Salisbury, 2 October 1900, *Companion*, I, 1204.

241

who had declared their Conservative opinions without doubt on the present occasion, and who had been canvassed and treated as admitted Conservatives, voted for Cheetham.[1]

While this account should not perhaps be taken at face value (it conveniently absolved both the organisation and Tariff Reform from blame) nonetheless it is consistent with the persistent style of Stalybridge elections. When Allan Bright lost there to the Tory John Wood for the second time in 1910 he attributed the result to local factors; Wood was popular as a large employer and a good fellow, and he thought the electors had put these considerations before his politics.[2]

It was when candidates could be identified with local interests, institutions, factions and followings, that they gained a strong personal hold. By the side of this, the factors that were conventionally thought to harm a candidate were of little weight. A bad division record, for instance, was a charge that was almost always entered against a delinquent M.P. Similarly, if a man's political opinions had undergone some change his inconsistencies were dredged up and his position as a 'turncoat' was used against him. John Rutherford of Darwen was guilty on both these counts yet his hold on the constituency was such as to get him elected even in 1906. Most of the candidates who had changed party, like the former Liberals Lindon Riley and Carlyon Bellairs, and the former Unionists Winston Churchill, George Kemp, Baron de Forest, J. E. B. Seely, and Sir John Gorst, seem to have encountered little difficulty over it. But Fred Brocklehurst, who had been one of the leaders of the Manchester I.L.P., was rather defensive on the subject when he fought as Conservative candidate for Prestwich in December 1910, and his poll must have been slightly disappointing since the Liberals improved their position compared with the previous January. And in North Lonsdale, Richard Cavendish, fighting as a Liberal in 1906, could not retain the seat which he had held unopposed as a Conservative, which was something of an upset.

A candidate who was absent or ill during a campaign lost the benefit of his personal exertions, but how much else he lost depended on whether he was already known in the constituency. The case of those candidates – all of them Conservatives – who were away in South Africa at the time of the 1900 election might be thought rather special. Colonel W. Bromley Davenport was not opposed at Macclesfield;[3] nor was Sir Elliot Lees at Birkenhead,

---

[1] Sandars to Balfour, 11 January 1905, BP 49763. In view of the district's reputation 'treated' was an unfortunate word to use; cf. above, p. 138. Cheetham had been a Liberal candidate five times previously (once in Stalybridge) and had sat for North Derbyshire 1880–5.

[2] Bright after the poll, *M. Courier*, 5 December 1910.

[3] 'Member's position strengthened by being at the war', the Cheshire Liberal Federal Council had been told in May 1900 (Brunner papers).

though after he had issued an inflammatory address the Liberals seriously considered running a candidate after all. It is hard to believe that Lord Stanley, who was well entrenched at Westhoughton, suffered at all. Captain H. H. Houldsworth, however, who was contesting Prestwich, was new to the constituency and the Liberal share of the poll increased slightly; but so it did in neighbouring divisions, which admittedly included Heywood where George Kemp was also absent. Similarly, in Manchester South, Peel had a less impressive victory than in the by-election earlier that year, but the movement since 1895 was comparable with that in other Manchester seats. It seems unlikely that the candidates' war service had much effect one way or the other.

Absence through ill health was less romantic. Weaknesses in the position of even a well-known absentee were illustrated in the High Peak, where Oswald Partington had had a breakdown after the by-election there in 1909. In January 1910 family and supporters managed to fill the breach, although they had to deny stories that his illness was a 'dodge'. In the next election, however, things were tougher. Partington, still convalescent, offered to stand down but was of course adopted regardless. The Conservatives this time made his health an issue – 'Sympathy cannot last for ever...'[1] – and put the Liberals in a dilemma. How to insist at the same time that Partington was still unfit to campaign and that he had made a full recovery? Partington was defeated. In two other constituencies, Ormskirk and Liverpool West Toxteth, the absence of the Conservative M.P.s in January 1910 was associated with low turnout and a poor Conservative poll. All these results are consistent with an explanation in terms of the candidate's failure to appear. Yet there are contrary indications. In December 1910 when E. L. Hartley, a local man, was too ill to participate at Bury the Conservative poll did not suffer. And the Labour vote actually went up at Gorton when John Hodge was absent on a sea voyage; the Conservatives had argued during the campaign that because of his tactlessness his absence would be an advantage to Labour.[2] There are a number of examples of candidates being out of the campaign for varying lengths of time, but in no case did this have an appreciable effect upon voting. In short, the candidate's presence during an election, especially if he were well known anyway, seems to have made no difference to the result.

The candidate was becoming a less important figure altogether in affecting voting. It is true that constituencies continued to hanker after social leaders of the traditional type. Carpetbaggers were neither emotive nor memorable. At Accrington in 1900 the candidature of 'Mr Empsall of Manchester' turned out to be that of John Hempsall (clearly not a household word) and

---

[1] Conservative handbill, 'Sympathy', *M.G.*, 9 December 1910.
[2] *M. Courier*, 6 December 1910.

poor Verney who had rushed to Liverpool at such short notice in 1900 was being recalled five years later as 'F. W. Fernie'. Candidates did all they could to remove the impression that they were mere birds of passage. At Accrington, a Conservative deputation went to London in December 1909 to ask the Carlton Club for a candidate and within twenty-four hours had secured the services of A. H. Jessel. 'Mr Jessel was not a carpet-bagger', insisted the chairman at his adoption three days later, 'and he had decided to pay the whole of his expenses, and not to have them shared from party funds or anywhere else (applause). That showed he meant business.'[1] Even so, Jessel was not to be candidate at the next election. For the fact was that the professional politician was fast taking over.

The General Election of 1906 precipitated a change in political style as well as political colour by ruthlessly deposing a generation of Conservative M.P.s of the patriarchal kind. Most of the progressives who replaced them as M.P.s were men of a different sort. Moreover, the men who replaced them as Conservative candidates were not cast in the old mould either. They were younger, they were Tariff Reformers, they were more often professional men, they were less often local notables. For example, in the three neighbouring boroughs, St Helens, Warrington and Wigan, there were Conservative M.P.s both in 1900 and December 1910. In 1900 they had been represented by Sir Henry Seton-Karr, Robert Pierpoint and Sir Francis Sharp Powell, all of them connected with local families with substantial industrial interests. In December 1910 the seats were won by Rigby Swift, Harold Smith and R. J. N. Neville – two Liverpool lawyers and a London lawyer.

The change, then, was independent of, though associated with, the party change. Some of the Liberal candidates who gained seats from the Conservatives in 1906 were men of the old school, like Sir William Crossley in Altrincham, Harry Nuttall in Stretford, or Sir George Agnew in Salford. But most were not. 'I am sure Mr Cox will not misunderstand me', said Sir Frank Hollins as chairman of Preston Liberal Association, 'when I say that I cannot [but] express a transient regret that among the capable and deservedly popular young men I see around me to-night there was not to be found one who was willing to place himself for Parliamentary purposes at the disposal of his Liberal fellow-townsmen.'[2] Almost all the Liberal M.P.s of the type which Hollins evidently found congenial (he might well have become one himself) had entered Parliament before 1906 and the new vintage did not add greatly to their number. Moreover, one change triggered off another. The 1906 Parliament was very different from its predecessors; it was less agreeable for old Members; just as old-fashioned Conservatives who had

---

[1] Speech by John Whittaker, *N.D.T.*, 14 December 1909.
[2] Hollins at Preston, *Lancs. D.P.*, 29 December 1905.

been elected in 1906 (like Sir Harry Hornby and Sir Francis Sharp Powell) retired at the end of it, so several Liberal war-horses went out to grass as well. Sir John Brunner, Sir W. H. Lever, Sir James Duckworth, J. F. Cheetham, J. A. Bright, Sir Joseph Leese and Sir E. H. Holden all decided not to seek re-election. James Tomkinson and George Harwood died; Alfred Emmott became a peer. A further dilution of this element was caused by the election of Labour M.P.s. In one sense these belonged more to the old regime, for nearly all were local trade union leaders and highly respected figures in their constituencies, like Thomas Glover in St Helens, A. H. Gill in Bolton, David Shackleton in Clitheroe, and G. D. Kelley in Manchester. But men with a career, if not in Labour politics then in the Labour movement as a whole, they were from necessity. And, most certainly, they were 'deficient in position'.[1]

The structure of politics in 'Tory Lancashire' had been a house of many mansions. It was destroyed in 1906. The patriarchs who were removed at that election were not replaced on the old terms. This is not to say that the traditional patterns of local leadership necessarily disappeared overnight. In many constituencies, especially the county divisions of which Darwen, Chorley, High Peak, Ormskirk, Macclesfield, Northwich and Eddisbury are examples, the reign of the old families and the old habits went on until the War. But in most of the towns, like Preston and Blackburn, an old conception of community representation had yielded to the modern imperatives of the national parties;[2] and the same was true of Burnley, Stockport, Clitheroe, Heywood, Middleton, Westhoughton, Ince, St Helens, Wigan and Warrington. This process was almost certainly under way in other divisions. Liverpool, admittedly, did not undergo any comparable change, but in Manchester and Salford, which had once so closely resembled it, developments were similar to those in most of the boroughs. Before 1906 the Liberals had been at a grave disadvantage in challenging the old guard of Conservative M.P.s; but by 1910 they were finding that they often had a ballistic superiority in the battle of the professional politicians.

[1] Which implied to some that they were deficient too in the qualifications of an M.P. 'Nobody expects a Socialist like Mr Sutton in East Manchester', ran one Tory comment, 'to rise any higher in national or world politics than thick twist and halfpenny car fares.' *M. Courier*, 2 December 1910.

[2] In 1900 three of the four Tory M.P.s in Blackburn and Preston owned cotton mills in the district; in 1910 none did. The demise of the cottonocracy was also apparent in the town councils. In Preston the 12 aldermen included 3 master cotton spinners in 1900, along with 4 professional men and 3 other manufacturers. Even by 1906 the millowners had gone; and by 1913, 7 of the bench were tradesmen. In Blackburn 8 of the 14 aldermen were cotton spinners or manufacturers in 1899 and 3 described themselves as 'gentlemen'. Of these aldermen only one remained in 1914 (William Thompson, the borough's veteran Conservative leader), and only one new cotton employer had been elected in that time. So in 1914 there were 2 cotton bosses and 2 gentlemen; the other 10 were shopkeepers and professional men. The bench had become *déclassé*. (Based on Barrett, *Directory of Preston*, and on *Blackburn Year Book*.)

PART FIVE
FIELDS OF RECRUITMENT

Where did the parties gain and lose ground in the early twentieth century? The indications given by organised electoral activity are incomplete but illuminating. The Liberals made little headway among the cultural groups of the old politics. But the importance of these was anyway in decline – a decline which seriously weakened working-class Conservatism. Free Trade helped the Liberals, especially in 1906. The work of the Asquith Government, however, frightened the economic liberals, and there was a steady drift of rich men into the Conservative ranks. Organised labour, on the other hand, which had once been cool towards Liberalism, increasingly settled for the progressive coalition rather than strict independence. Between 1900 and 1910 Liberalism and Labour drew closer together; and their conjunction was the most important single factor in the new politics.

10 Communal politics

I bewilder so many people by not being 'party'; I directly offend so many more by refusing to have anything to do with teetotalism, vegetarianism, suffragism, Buddhism, and Scientific Monism, that whole belts of people who voted for me last time will vote against me this time.   Hilaire Belloc, 1909

I

The activities of pressure groups were necessarily influenced by calculations as to ends and means; the behaviour of the communities for whom they spoke, on the other hand, was governed by subjective feelings of affinity. It was the function of a pressure group to articulate this common outlook in political terms. The social relationships arising from the structure of landed society are clearly of a distinct character, in which the role of authority can hardly be ignored. Yet, certainly after 1885, the political power of the landed interest, like that of the quasi-religious groups, was essentially dependent upon a community of sentiment, however induced. 'As things are in the Knutsford division', admitted the *Guardian*, 'it is difficult for any Liberal to persuade the electors that their interests do not necessarily coincide with those of the landowner whose tenants they happen to be, or those of the farmers in whose employment they are.'[1] This was more a matter of the labourer's consciousness than of the landowner's sanctions.

In Lancashire itself old landowning families were most important in the belt of county divisions running from North Lonsdale through Blackpool and Chorley to Ormskirk; this influence shaded off in the surrounding mining divisions of Westhoughton, Newton and Ince. The more important magnates were the Duke of Devonshire in North Lonsdale; the Earl of Derby in Blackpool, Westhoughton and Ormskirk (and also as ground landlord in the boroughs of Preston and Bury); the Earl of Crawford and Balcarres on the borders of Ince and Chorley; the Earl of Ellesmere in Ince; and the Earl of Selborne and Lord Newton, both in the Newton division. The Duke of Devonshire was also a force in the High Peak division of Derbyshire, especially at the Buxton end. In Cheshire a group of landed families controlled the politics of what were after 1885 the rural divisions

---

[1] *M.G.*, 13 December 1910; on this question see Thompson, *English Landed Society in the Nineteenth Century*, esp. pp. 199–204; and Howarth, 'The Liberal revival in Northamptonshire', *Hist. Jnl.*, XII (1969), pp. 85 ff.

for most of the nineteenth century. Eddisbury and Knutsford were their particular stronghold. The most important landowning peers were the Duke of Westminster, the Marquess of Cholmondeley, the Earl of Stamford, the Earl of Crewe, Earl Egerton of Tatton, and Lords Legh of Lyme, Tollemache, and Sheffield (Stanley of Alderley).[1] The peerage, while they formed only a part of the landowning group, were the most important part and gave political leadership to the rest. That leadership, of course, was overwhelmingly Conservative. In 1905 when Colonel E. T. Cotton-Jodrell began his campaign in Eddisbury, for which his first cousin H. J. Tollemache had sat previously, Tollemache acted as chairman of the Conservative Association, and by mid-December platform support had already been received from Sir Delves Broughton on the Nantwich side, Sir Philip Egerton on the Oulton side, George Barbour on the Bolesworth side and Harry Barnston on the Farndon side – leading landowners all. Only Lords Sheffield and Crewe gave practical help to the Liberals. Crewe was very conscious of his obligation to back up James Tomkinson for the Crewe division, and although Sheffield had been estranged from the Liberal party for twenty years after 1886 he gave active support to his son, who was candidate for Eddisbury three times between 1906 and 1910. In 1906 the Cavendish influence both in High Peak and North Lonsdale was on the Liberal side and in North Lonsdale Richard Cavendish continued to support the Liberals thereafter; and in Knutsford there were one or two defections from the Conservatives on Free Trade grounds in 1906. But these are a small number of exceptions to a very well established rule.

The landed interest was surprisingly successful in influencing voting. The degree of pressure exerted varied. In the Ormskirk division, for which the Hon. Arthur Stanley sat, the farmers were prosperous and, as the Conservatives believed, solidly with them; it was the fact that they were 'given more to thought than speech', it was held, that had led to the Liberals' impression that 'they have nowt in them but prejudice'.[2] Lord Derby would make no attempt to use his power as landlord to influence them; the Liberals were even allowed to use the Knowsley village hall free of charge for their meetings. In 1910 Derby denounced as 'absolutely untrue' the story that he had attempted to enforce upon his tenants which way to vote. 'I should be ashamed of myself if I ever tried to do such a thing', he said, 'as I should be ashamed of them if they were influenced by any attempt that I made.'[3] But there were landowners who went rather beyond this. For instance, in those

---

[1] Lord Egerton is given as the 'patron' of the Knutsford division in the period 1885–1900 by Hanham, *Elections and Party Management*, p. 405; and see Lee, *Social Leaders and Public Persons*, pp. 18–23.

[2] *L. Courier*, 28 December 1905.

[3] Speech at Bickerstaffe, *L. Courier*, 10 January 1910.

parts of the Knutsford division where landed influence was strong, not only did landowners get their agents to canvass tenants but it was usual for the Conservatives to send out stamped addressed envelopes asking for written pledges. And it was, said the Liberals, monstrous for Lord Cholmondeley to let his agent make a speech in Eddisbury in 1910 saying that because he had to pay £450 supertax he must discharge ten men.[1] But there were changes in even the most monolithic divisions. The Chorley by-election of 1903, the first contested election for eighteen years, was a turning point in that division. In 1906 the Liberal held an open-air meeting in the village of Hoghton on the assumption that Sir James de Hoghton would not let them use the school; but it was learnt 'that on this occasion Sir James had decided not to refuse the request for the school had it been made, but on account of previous refusals this had not been expected'.[2] At the other end of the division,

the deeps were breaking up in Rufford. It was found possible to have a Liberal meeting there and it was found possible to fill it full. There were not, to be sure, any hands held up for the resolution, and there was no hand-clapping, for there are watchful eyes to see in such places; but in the safer obscurity the audience shuffled their feet on the floor when the speakers made a point.[3]

Urbanisation changed the character of some divisions. Altrincham, Wirral and Southport, which had once been rural, became predominantly commercial and residential, and the same was true to a lesser extent of Blackpool and Chorley. Territorial influence diminished here. But in those divisions, mainly in Cheshire, where the traditional patterns remained relatively undisturbed, the Liberals found nearly as much difficulty as ever in gaining support, especially open support. They admitted that in Cheshire 'the influence of rural landlords is, for reasons largely creditable to them, unusually strong', and asserted knowingly too that 'there are peasants in the agricultural districts who don the blue even if they vote the other way'.[4] Doubts about the secrecy of the ballot fostered such attitudes. At Knutsford in 1906 the Conservatives erected a blackboard which purported to give the state of the poll at various polling stations throughout the day. In Blackpool there were widespread stories that voting papers could be identified at Somerset House on payment of a shilling. And in the Eddisbury division, A. L. Stanley, the Liberal candidate, made a big show of assuring the electors that the ballot was secret in December 1910 and arranged with the High Sheriff that party representatives should not be allowed to watch the

[1] Speech by A. L. Stanley, Tarvin, *M.G.*, 22 November 1910.
[2] *N.D.T.*, 8 January 1906.
[3] *M.G.*, 6 December 1910.
[4] *M.G.*, 29 January 1906, 13 December 1910.

emptying of ballot boxes, and that papers should be mixed before counting. Eddisbury was really the last bastion of traditional county politics. An account by a Liberal worker there illustrates the kind of moral intimidation which could still be applied, ten years into the twentieth century, when a landlord chose to go just about as far as he openly dared:

I am in the Eddisbury division of Cheshire, and when I visited the polling station at Bridgemere I found that Sir Delves Broughton, the greatest landlord in our district – I might say the only landlord, – was present in the school yard.

I carried voters to the poll some five times at different hours of the day, and Sir Delves was in the yard each time. He was accompanied by his agent, Mr Loring, and several big farmers who were his tenants. One of the checkers at the door was a carpenter employed on the estate, and seated at the table in the booth was Sir D. Broughton's chief clerk, Mr Cope.[1]

The writer admitted that Broughton was 'a very good landlord, and one who found his estate in a dilapidated condition and promptly took steps to put it in order and make his tenants comfortable', but that, no doubt, made it more rather than less difficult to run the gauntlet and vote Liberal.

II

At the time of the 1901 census there were over 160,000 persons in the north west who had been born in Ireland. This is not a full measurement of the size of the population which regarded itself as Irish but does provide a lower limit. 'Lancashire has spoken', said Gladstone during the 1885 elections. 'But if you listen to her accents, you will find that they are strongly tinged with the Irish brogue.'[2] And some years later his son was to draw up (with a proper scepticism) a list of seats 'dominated' by the Irish vote, among which he put 32 of the 66 constituencies in the north west.[3]

The Irish vote was organised by the United Irish League of which T. P. O'Connor was President; at election times the headquarters of the League were moved from London to Liverpool. O'Connor held the Scotland division as an Irish Nationalist with full Liberal support. The only threat of a three-cornered fight was in 1900 when the recently healed breach in the Nationalist party opened once more. Austin Harford, a local councillor, was adopted as an Independent Nationalist on the grounds that he would be more of 'a true Catholic and true Nationalist' than O'Connor.[4] But O'Connor had the support of the League's branches and of the priests; after an appeal from

---

[1] Letter from 'Bridgemere', *M.G.*, 27 January 1910. 'I can prove all I have said in this letter', he added.
[2] Quoted in O'Connor, *Memoirs of an Old Parliamentarian*, II, 14.
[3] See Appendix C.
[4] Speech by John O'Shea at his adoption, *Liverpool D.P.*, 24 September 1900.

Communal politics

Redmond Harford withdrew and supported O'Connor in that and subsequent elections. One of the grievances of Harford's supporters was that 'the constituency had been dragged in the mire, and Home Rule had been left in the background through association with the Liberal party'. O'Connor was happy to work closely with the Liberals and Labour (he promised he would remain an English M.P. after Home Rule) and in Liverpool the Nationalists and the Liberals were hand in glove. It was the Conservatives' broader strategy in Liverpool which led them to put up Watson Rutherford against O'Connor in 1900. 'Whether he won or not', Salvidge declared, 'he would have rendered a signal service to his party by keeping the Nationalist workers, who, in fact, were the only workers the Liberal party had got, in Scotland Division (applause).'[1] The working arrangement with the Nationalists was the lodestone of Liverpool Liberalism under Edward Evans, 'whose business & practice it has been for years', Sir Edward Russell assured Campbell-Bannerman, 'to cultivate and coincide with the Irish'.[2]

It was impressed upon local branches of the U.I.L. that they must wait for instructions from headquarters before committing themselves but the only real doubt as to what these would be arose in constituencies where there were both Labour and Liberal candidates. At Burnley, for instance, the League was evidently in two minds as to whether to support Hyndman and the Irish meeting which had been called there became noisy when a postponement was asked on the grounds that final instructions had not been received.[3] Hyndman's Liberal opponent was in fact endorsed. Although the League was formally committed to supporting Labour candidates in 1906 this was a mere form of words; the proviso that it would not do so if this put the seat at risk governed its practical action. Many of the Irish Catholics were in fact suspicious of the socialists,[4] but this reservation did not, of course, apply to those Labour candidates, like J. R. Clynes, James Sexton and James Conley who were of Irish extraction themselves. They in turn made the most of it. Local branches of the U.I.L. held meetings of Irishmen and these were often addressed by Liberal or Labour candidates. T. P. O'Connor sent out telegrams of support and sometimes came to speak himself. Those other Irish speakers who toured the constituencies often emphasised the common interests of the Irish and English working class. In the Nationalist constituencies, said Michael Davitt, 'no follower of Mr Chamberlain, no foeman

[1] Speech by Salvidge, *Liverpool D.P.*, 1 October 1900.
[2] Russell to Campbell-Bannerman, 3 November 1899, CBP 41235 ff. 95-7.
[3] See report of the meeting, *N.D.T.*, 8 January 1906.
[4] See, e.g., the comments on Keir Hardie, *Liverpool Catholic Herald*, 5 January 1906. 'We have no confidence in Mr Keir Hardie. We do not believe in his political honesty or integrity. We do not believe in his good faith. We believe that he is quite capable of being a Tory cats-paw, but he is something better than a mere Tory candidate.'

of labour, dare intrude his political nose. That was because years ago they ceased sending landlords and capitalists to represent them.'[1]

The cases of difficulty between the Irish and the progressive candidates were very few. In two cases the Irish would plainly have preferred a Liberal instead of a Labour candidate in 1906; at Manchester North East it was suggested that the Manchester Irish leader Councillor D. Boyle would have been a better candidate than J. R. Clynes, and at Ince it was threatened that Councillor James O'Donahue would intervene, but in neither case was opposition carried further. Once the U.I.L. manifesto had been issued a sympathetic gloss was put upon the attitude towards Home Rule of such lukewarm friends as Churchill was at that time.[2] In Liverpool the Liberal candidates had the problem of conciliating the Irish without appearing to be their clients. This was most acute in the Exchange division where, so it was reckoned, four-fifths of the Liberal vote came from the Roman Catholics and Nationalists. In December 1910 the Tories tried desperately (and perhaps successfully) to drive a wedge between the Liberal Muspratt and his businessmen supporters by piling on references to 'Pat' Muspratt, 'the Nationalist champion', whom the *Courier* inaccurately reported as attending a torchlight procession organised by the Irish. 'The assertion', it innocently apologised, 'that Mr Muspratt had attended meetings, called in support of his candidature by those with whom he is politically associated, seemed neither inherently improbable nor deeply reproachful.'[3] No one doubted that Muspratt would get the Irish vote at any rate.

Looking back on the Manchester North West by-election of 1908 the Liberal chairman attributed Churchill's defeat (almost certainly correctly) to the defection of 'the Irish'; but it should be observed that the U.I.L. had issued a manifesto *in favour* of Churchill. On this occasion, however, the Irish had not been persuaded to put 'their duty as Irishmen' first. Instead the Bishop of Salford had induced them to see 'their duty as Catholics', which led them to the Conservative side. As Joynson Hicks again told them in 1910, the Irish Catholics would have to choose between a candidate pledged to support their voluntary schools and one pledged to Home Rule.[4] This tension between ethnic and religious loyalties was the essence of their politics. Because of the Irish most of the towns contained very large numbers of Roman Catholic voters, even if they were not normally thought of as such

[1] Davitt at St Helens, *M.G.*, 6 January 1906.
[2] See *Manchester Catholic Herald*, 5 January 1906.
[3] *L. Courier*, 6 December 1910; cf. 6 December 1909 for the composition of the Liberal vote, quoting 'one of the most astute Radical electioneers in the city'.
[4] Samuel Lamb in Manchester North West, *M. Courier*, 21 December 1909; Joynson Hicks, *M.G.*, 8 January 1910; cf. report of meeting of Catholic Federation and manifesto of U.I.L., *M. Courier*, 21, 22 April 1908, and *Companion*, II, 787–8.

(at Bury, for instance, the Irish were 'not included in the body locally spoken of as "the Roman Catholic voters"').[1]

There was little doubt about the attitude of the hierarchy, of whose politics *The Tablet* was a loyal mouthpiece. *The Tablet* had an unmistakable Conservative bias and, representing the English Catholics, favoured the more hard-and-fast sort of tests for candidates. The numerous editions of the *Catholic Herald*, on the other hand, circulating mainly among the Irish, directed their efforts towards squaring religious education with Home Rule. In 1900 the Bishop of Salford ordered the circulation of the resolutions of the English Bishops on education, the drift of which was favourable to the Conservatives, and use was also made in the elections of the more open advice of Bishop Bagshawe of Nottingham. In Manchester and Salford the Catholic Registration Association, on the strength of its successes in School Board elections, took on the business of questioning the candidates; but although it was claimed that it had contributed to the defeat of the Liberal Alfred Mond in Salford South by catching him out in sharp practice, it was felt afterwards that without a mandate to direct the vote it could have little influence.[2] In 1906 a letter from Archbishop Bourne and the Bishops of the Province of Westminster was read in the churches without comment and, while questions were put to candidates on the lines it suggested, even the Toryism of *The Tablet* was muted. In January 1910, however, a much more militant policy was adopted. A joint Pastoral from the Bishops insisted that only the schools question should be put to candidates. In Manchester affairs were entrusted to the Catholic Federation, which produced a list classifying as satisfactory all the Conservative candidates for the thirteen seats in the area (plus Belloc and Clynes) and as unsatisfactory the rest of the Liberals. One of those who applauded the Federation's work 'in stripping evasions, verbiage and platitudes from the replies to the Pastoral question', estimated that while the 'Irish political vote' would go to the Liberals, the 'Irish Catholic vote' and the 'English Catholic vote' would be cast against the Government.[3] The clergy were told to post the replies outside their churches and to offer no other advice. This provoked a notable attack upon the Salford Catholic Federation by Canon Patrick Lynch who was closely associated with the United Irish League in Manchester. He accused the Federation of 'taking all power out of our hands, humiliating and degrading us before our own people and the outside public, as if we were not able to safeguard Catholic faith and Catholic interests without their control and advice'. He

[1] *M.G.*, 6 May 1902.
[2] On the Bishop of Salford's action see *Tablet*, 6 October 1900, p. 527; on the Registration Association, *Manchester Catholic Herald*, 5, 12 October 1900.
[3] Letter from 'Federationist', *Tablet*, 15 January 1910; for the Pastoral see *The Times*, 27 December 1909; and see the statement from the Federation, *M. Courier*, 7 January 1910.

claimed that in his own constituency of Manchester South West the reply of the Liberal Needham had not been dealt with satisfactorily.

There are [he wrote], between ten and eleven hundred Catholic voters in Hulme. I know the men well. They know me and trust me, and it is in common council that we decide how we are to vote. The action of the Federation might have serious consequences for Mr Needham. How we are to vote will be known on Saturday evening next.[1]

This letter released much pent-up resentment against the Federation. Another priest wrote that it had been 'a ghastly failure', with a small membership which misrepresented 'the national aspirations and political views of Irish Catholics, and of such to a degree, say, of 80 per cent is the Catholic Church in Lancashire composed'.[2] In Liverpool too, where there had been very little pulpit politics, there was adverse comment upon 'this very discreditable episode, which certainly means the end of the Catholic Federation in Manchester and perhaps elsewhere'.[3] This forecast proved to be substantially correct, for in December 1910 the Bishops issued no questions and the Catholic Federation resolved upon an attitude of absolute neutrality.

The attempt to make religious education the decisive issue in January 1910, just when Home Rule seemed so close, was badly conceived: far from asserting the Catholic Federation's power it undermined its reputation. When an Irishman was asked, one wrote, 'to prove a traitor to his country by voting for its avowed enemies, no wonder he mistrusts a Federation which would take from him his liberty of speech, action, and the right to vote, as our revered bishops have put it, according to his conscience'.[4] For all the efforts of the Federation on this occasion, Redmond was able to tell O'Connor that, 'By the admission of everyone, friend and foe alike, the Irish vote in Great Britain was never so united and so powerful as in the recent elections'.[5] Part of the difficulty was that the Bishops did not adopt acceptable criteria. They tended to consider which of the parties would in office deal most sympathetically with the denominational schools; but the parish priest and his flock (like Lynch and his workingmen in Hulme) with their Irish outlook were more concerned to extract a satisfactory minimum of concessions from the local Home Rule candidate. It was in the parishes that the issue had always been decided, and throughout this period the Liberals had always done far better among the Roman Catholics than the attitude of the hierarchy would suggest.

[1] Letter from Patrick Lynch, *M.G.*, 12 January 1910; also printed, with reply, *Manchester Catholic Times*, 14 January 1910.
[2] Letter from 'A Priest of the People', *M.G.*, 13 January 1910; cf. defence of Federation by Canon Lionel O'Kelly, *ibid.*
[3] *Liverpool Catholic Herald*, 15 January 1910.
[4] Letter from 'A Catholic', *M.G.*, 14 January 1910.
[5] Quoted in Jackson, *The Irish in Britain*, p. 122.

For the Liberals the major stumbling block lay in reconciling Roman Catholic and Nonconformist views on religious education. The prime illustration of the dangers involved in failure was the virtual destruction of the party in Wigan. The Liberal leader, Colonel William Woods, tried to rally that combination of Miners and Roman Catholics which could alone carry the borough, but his candidature was ill-fated. In 1903 Jesse Herbert reported that Woods had retired: 'The Catholic Liberals there have resolved to vote against anyone who will amend the Education Act, (they are 2,000 strong) and the Non-cons have resolved they will vote against anyone who will not amend it.'[1] When Gladstone met the leaders of the two sections he found them 'friendly but irreconcilable',[2] and all the bright ideas that he and Herbert spawned for a Roman Catholic candidate (like Hilaire Belloc), or a Free Churchman who would make an exception for the Catholics, came to nothing. Woods stood himself in 1906 with Roman Catholic support but could not win over the Nonconformists; he finished third on the poll, and the Wigan Liberal Association never recovered.[3] The name of Belloc, which cropped up for Wigan, came to mind also when Salford South, another constituency with a large Catholic element, was discussed by the Whips, and to Salford South he went, assuring Herbert Gladstone that he could capture the whole of the Catholic vote. This he seems to have done, and on his retirement in 1910 he was succeeded by another Roman Catholic, Charles Russell. The Labour candidates, J. R. Clynes in Manchester North East, and James Sexton and James Conley in Liverpool, also seem to have gained support as Catholics. But when Baron de Forest stood as Liberal candidate for Southport where the large Roman Catholic vote was English not Irish, he was opposed steadfastly by the local Catholic squirearchy.

In those constituencies where the Roman Catholic population was mainly Irish the Liberal candidates did not normally lack Catholic supporters, many of them men who were active in the United Irish League. It is true that the local priests sometimes gave open help to the Conservatives but those who were identified with the Irish cause did much to counteract the Conservative influence of the Bishops. At St Helens in 1906, for instance, the Labour candidate Glover was declared acceptable by the local priests. 'As regards the future of our schools', stated the Rector, 'I have no fear...My hope, however, lies not with the Tory or Liberal, but with the solid Irish party.'[4] This was one of the arguments that the Irish Nationalists used in reassuring Roman Catholics, and they sought too to depict the Tories' hostility to Home

---

[1] Herbert to Gladstone, 19 September 1903, HGP 46025 ff. 170–1.
[2] Interview with W. Johnson and Dr Benson, diary, 25 April 1904, HGP 46485 f. 9.
[3] See below, p. 323.
[4] Statement by Rector of St Helens, *St Helens Newspaper*, 16 January 1906; cf. *M.G.*, 11, 17 January 1910 for Eccles and Manchester North.

Rule as essentially an anti-Catholic policy. One leaflet circulated in Gorton went back to the Great Famine to show that the Conservative party was the Catholics' 'hereditary enemy', holding in its ranks 'all the intolerable bigots in politics from Colonel Craig, Sir R. Carson, F. E. Smith, to Pastor Wise'.[1]

It was especially important in Liverpool that the Liberal candidates should be acceptable to the Roman Catholics, but the events of the election of January 1910 illustrate the peculiar hazards in that city. At a meeting at the Reform Club (hardly the clandestine gathering as which it was later depicted) the Liberal candidates had agreed to answer the question of the Catholic Bishops in the affirmative. On learning of this the Tories seized upon 'this discrimination against the Protestant schools', which, on 11 January, the *Courier* dubbed 'The Great Betrayal'. The theme of the great betrayal was at once taken up by the Conservative candidates and became the leading catchphrase of the campaign.[2]

Throughout that part of Lancashire where there was a strong English element among the Roman Catholics the contest for their votes was on a rather different basis. There was a large Catholic population in Chorley whose support the Conservatives firmly enlisted in the by-election of 1903 and kept thereafter.[3] The Lancaster division was a traditional recusant stronghold; but the Liberal Norval Helme had represented the most Catholic ward in Lancaster on the town council and despite a running dispute with one of the Catholic leaders during the 1900 Election he seems to have been *persona grata*. The English Catholics were even stronger in Preston (one-third of the electorate was Catholic) and all candidates found it prudent to defer to them. In January 1910 they and the Conservatives were equally determined to make the Bishops' question the main issue even though all five candidates had answered it in the affirmative. 'What', asked the Labour candidate, 'was the real issue of this fight? (A voice, "Religion".) Religion was not the real issue. (Cheers.)... I do not know of one man in this contest but what has pledged himself to safeguard religious instruction. (Cheers.) In face of that fact, why is religion dragged into the arena?'[4] It was agreed on all sides that Catholic support had helped put the Tories in and one Catholic declared at the second election that: 'If they knew as much as he did about the angling which took place at the last election for the Catholic vote, they

---

[1] An open letter to Catholic electors (1910), Gorton local collection.
[2] Indeed, the *Courier* was so swept away by its own rhetoric that it quite forgot *who* had been betrayed (it was presumably either the Government or the Church of England) and by polling day was writing of 'the great betrayal of the Roman Catholics by the Liberal candidates in Liverpool'. 19 December 1910; cf. esp. 10–12 January 1910; and *Catholic Times*, 7, 14 January 1910.
[3] See John Whitworth (Liberal agent) to Jesse Herbert, 5 November 1903, HGP 46026 ff. 19–20; letter from Father Crank at Conservative meeting, *Lancs. D.P.*, 18 January 1906.
[4] J. T. Macpherson at Preston, *Lancs. D.P.*, 13 January 1910.

would sooner burn the ballot paper than vote Tory.'[1] The Preston Irish, meanwhile, were naturally supporting the progressive candidates, and the same pronounced split between the two groups can be seen at Rossendale and the Wirral in 1906 and at Darwen, Blackburn and Warrington in January 1910, in all of which the 'Roman Catholic vote' was a house divided against itself.

III

The Jewish community in Manchester, estimated at twenty to thirty thousand in 1910, was concentrated almost entirely in Cheetham and comprised the main part of the residential vote in the otherwise commercial North West division. Attitudes towards Jews in general became more controversial around the turn of the century. There was a distinct anti-semitic flavour to the denunciations by opponents of the Boer War, like Hyndman, of 'the Jews' War in the Transvaal'. Supporters of Micholls, the Conservative candidate for Accrington, who was Jewish, claimed that 'they had only to look at the Radical Press to find that there was a sort of Jewish persecution going on which was quite worthy of the treatment of the Jews in Poland by the Russians (cheers)'.[2] In the same vein, in 1906 several Liberal candidates (Hilaire Belloc, for instance) were to be found denouncing Chinese labour which 'Jews with unpronounceable names' had imported into South Africa.

But along with this animus against rich Jews the Liberals harboured a sympathy for poor Jews, against whom the aliens legislation of the Conservative Government was directed. Churchill was closely identified with the opposition to the restrictions on immigration and was thereby brought into cooperation with the leaders of the Manchester community, notably Dr J. Dulberg and Nathan Laski. Laski, indeed, was to be one of Churchill's staunchest supporters throughout his association with Manchester (when he died Churchill wrote that 'all my memories of Manchester and Cheetham are veiled in mourning')[3] and in 1906 did much to organise the Jewish vote on his behalf. The Manchester Liberal Federation had for some time adopted the principle of not objecting to alien voters. It is true that Zionists like Weizmann found Balfour more sympathetic, but by 1908 Churchill too had become converted to Zionism. During the by-election that year Churchill was able to satisfy the Jewish leaders on the question of the naturalisation fee and Laski took the chair at a great meeting in his support. A section of Conservative

[1] P. W. Williams at Preston, *Lancs. D.P.*, 30 November 1910; cf. letter from Thomas Gardner, *Lancs. D.P.*, 20 January 1910.
[2] Conservative chairman at Accrington, *Lancs. D.P.*, 27 September 1900; cf. Silberner, 'The anti-semitic tradition in modern socialism', *Scripta Hiersolymitana*, III (1956), pp. 386 ff.
[3] Quoted in Kingsley Martin, *Harold Laski* (1953), p. 6. For the Aliens Bills see Rabinowicz, *Winston Churchill on Jewish Problems*, pp. 46–80.

Jews objected to this on the grounds that there was 'no need to create a Jewish vote' but there is little doubt that such a vote effectively existed.[1] Although Joynson Hicks was elected he later admitted that both in 1906 and 1908 'the Jewish community were almost entirely my desperate and unforgiving enemies'.[2]

In 1910 the Jews were not organised in the old way. Laski was in India in January and the message of support he sent to the Liberal Kemp kept to the Free Trade issue, though Dulberg gave platform support to Kemp from a Jewish standpoint. And in December 1910 both candidates refused to make any special plea to the Jews (though after the Rothschilds had come to the aid of the Conservatives Dulberg replied in kind) and Sir Rufus Isaacs protested 'emphatically against the notion that there is a Jewish vote'.[3] Kemp's return was nonetheless put down to the Jewish influence. At the by-election in 1912, however, Laski remained neutral on the grounds that the Government had not fulfilled their promises on the naturalisation question, and although Dulberg supported the Liberals over Free Trade it was reckoned that instead of the Conservatives getting ten per cent of the Jewish votes as in the past this time they would get fifty per cent. It may be significant that a manifesto issued by about thirty members of the community, declaring that they had recently voted Liberal but were now supporting the Conservatives, made out its case on general political grounds; they were evidently voting as businessmen rather than Jews.[4]

Apart from the Irish and the Jews the only other group distinguished from the native population by any national characteristics were the Welsh. The Welsh, however, were as a rule more quickly and completely assimilated. Only on the coalfield does the Welsh language seem to have been turned to political use; in 1906 the Liberal address was translated into Welsh at Leigh, and in Newton a Liberal meeting was held with speeches in both English and Welsh. There was a considerable Welsh element too in St Helens where the Liberals brought up 'Mabon' to speak in 1900. Liverpool was probably the biggest Welsh centre and the Liverpool Welsh Free Church Council added its voice on the Liberal side in 1906. Most towns of any size had a Welsh chapel but perhaps these should be regarded primarily as a sub-division of Liberal Nonconformity.

[1] See letter from S. Rosenthal and reply by Dr Dulberg, *M.G.*, 23, 24 April 1908; and E. Marsh to Herbert Gladstone, 15 April 1908, HGP 45986 f. 131.
[2] Speech at Cheetham, *M.G.*, 13 January 1910; cf. Taylor, *Jix*, p. 101. Dulberg thought that Churchill had polled over 95 per cent of the Jewish vote; Dulberg to Churchill, 25 April 1908, *Companion*, II, 785.
[3] Letter from Isaacs to Liberal meeting, *M.G.*, 1 December 1910.
[4] See interview with Laski and letter from Dulberg, *M.G.*, 31 July, 3 August 1912; remarks of a Jewish solicitor and manifesto issued by 30 Jews, *M. Courier*, 2, 7 August 1912.

IV

The influence of the Church of England was thrown behind the Conservative party not just in a general sense, nor (as happened with the Roman Catholics) formally but not effectually. Following its historic tradition and the political bent of its Bishops, the Established Church in the parishes worked for particular Tory victories. The most obvious indication of this was the support which the local clergy gave to Conservative candidates. Some parsons appeared on Conservative platforms and there are many instances of meetings, especially in the smaller centres, with the local vicar in the chair; some organised special meetings of their own for Churchpeople, at which speeches of a partisan nature were made; and others issued advice either on the basis of questions to candidates, or in special manifestoes, or from the pulpit, or in such places as parish magazines.[1]

It was in 1906 and January 1910 that the Church's influence was most fully committed. The old Tory Sir James Fergusson felt it worth spending a day at the height of the 1906 campaign making calls at the clergy houses in Manchester North East. In Liverpool the Diocesan branch of the Church Committee for Church Defence and Church Instruction put questions on religious education and disestablishment to all the candidates in the area and tidily pronounced all the Conservatives satisfactory, all the Liberals unsatisfactory, and the two Labour candidates satisfactory on the first only.[2] In Lancaster the attitude of the clergy was communicated in a bill signed by the Archdeacon of the Lancaster, the circular having the name of the Conservative agent upon it.[3] At a meeting of the Eccles Rural Deanery one priest (Canon Cremer) met with protest when he expressed doubts about the justifiability of Establishment in Wales and left the room 'remarking that he was evidently in a minority of one, and had another engagement to attend to'.[4] The Vicar of St George's, Stockport, made a forthright attack on the Liberal candidate's policy of 'Free Trade in our markets, but no God in our schools'.[5]

There were similar incidents in January 1910, with Bishop Knox again in a leading role. Knox made personal interventions in all three Salford divi-

---

[1] Without compiling an exhaustive list, examples of this kind of open support from the clergy can be found in Newton, Hyde and Blackburn in 1900; in Manchester North, Gorton, St Helens, Darwen, Lancaster, Eccles and Stretford in 1906; in Warrington, Southport, Middleton, Northwich, Blackburn, Stockport, Preston and Chorley both in 1906 and in January 1910; in Ashton, Radcliffe, Bolton and Accrington in January 1910; and in Northwich, Manchester South and Darwen in December 1910.
[2] *L. Courier*, 13 January 1906.
[3] See speech by Helme at Lancaster, *Lancs. D.P.*, 18 January 1906.
[4] *M. Courier*, 1 January 1906.
[5] *Stockport Advertiser*, 5 January 1906.

sions, at Bolton and at Stretford on behalf of the Conservative candidates. Just how good a Tory the Bishop was can be inferred from the case of Knox and Cox. At Preston the Bishop's general advice to vote Conservative was being used against the independent Free Trader Harold Cox, whose leading supporter was the Churchman Frank Calvert. Calvert thereupon wrote to Knox, a family friend, asking him to declare that Cox was 'not objectionable'. Knox exceeded his brief and sent a public letter, declaring that Cox's record in Parliament was all that Churchmen could desire, which read as a warm endorsement. This, of course, was slighting to the two Conservative candidates and the Bishop was induced to write a second letter affirming that, Cox's merits notwithstanding, 'Churchmen who value the security of the Church on all important issues...will naturally throw their whole and undivided strength into the support of the two excellent Unionist candidates who are before the constituency.'[1] The Preston Church Defence Committee also backed the Conservatives rather than Cox on the grounds that only the Unionist *party* supported its aims.[2] The retiring Vicar of Blackburn, Bishop Thornton, whose claim it was to have remained conspicuously aloof from party politics, did his best to atone for his previous inaction. In Blackburn he led as many as fifteen of the local clergy on to the Conservative platform and also went to Chorley to address a large meeting of Churchpeople held in support of Lord Balcarres. The Liberal candidates in Liverpool would give no reply to the Diocesan Church Schools Association in January 1910 ('The Great Betrayal') on account of their agreement to give no assurances that might make a settlement more difficult; the candidates classified as satisfactory were therefore all Conservative apart from James Sexton, the Labour candidate for West Toxteth.[3]

As with the Roman Catholic Church, January 1910 was the high point in the Church's effort to make religious education the test question, and the noticeable withdrawal in December 1910 was a prudent abstention. This did not, of course, prevent local clergy from voicing their fears that the Liberals wished to 'tear up the Ten Commandments' and to 'banish religion from the schools',[4] but by and large the Church's influence was not systematically exerted. Many Liberal candidates, especially those who were Churchmen themselves, had deplored the Church's close association with the Conservative party, and some saw signs of change by 1910. 'There was a new spirit growing in the Church of England', said Alfred Emmott. 'The clergy were

---

[1] Letter from Knox read by Sir W. Tomlinson, *Lancs. D.P.*, 6 January 1910; cf. correspondence between Knox and Calvert in Calvert's speech, *Lancs. D.P.*, 7 January 1910.
[2] See their front-page advertisement, e.g. *Preston Herald*, 12 January 1910; cf. exchanges between Cox and W. H. Cockshutt (sec.), *Lancs. D.P.*, 12, 13 January 1910.
[3] See *L. Courier*, 11, 14 January 1910.
[4] Parish magazines in circulation in Manchester South, *M.G.*, 3 December 1910.

more in touch with their congregations; they knew what the people were thinking, and many of them felt, though few cared to say so publicly, that this was not a time in which they could afford to desert the people.'[1] There is probably some truth in this. While they were rare exceptions, there was now quite a handful of clergymen who were prepared to support Labour candidates. In 1906 the vicars of Preston and Ribbleton and one other clergyman went on to the Labour platform at Preston, and at least one of them spoke for the Socialist Dan Irving in Accrington; at the next elections the Vicar of Briercliffe took the chair for David Shackleton at Clitheroe, a curate from Halton went to speak for Hyndman at Burnley and the Rector of St Philips', Gorton, supported John Hodge; and in Blackburn there was considerable comment in October 1910 when the new vicar agreed to take the chair at an I.L.P. meeting.

Previously the main question dividing the Anglican clergy had been that of Church discipline. The militant Protestants identified with the Church Discipline Bill of 1900 were organised in the National Protestant (or Laymen's) League which was affiliated with the evangelical Church Association. In the Wirral where the Conservative Joseph Hoult accepted the League's policy, a manifesto against him was issued by the Deeside English Church Union of which five Wallasey vicars were the leading lights.[2] The centre of the League's operations was Liverpool and since it was closely allied with Salvidge's Workingmen's Conservative Association it was in a strong position to enforce its demands upon the Conservative candidates. Walter Long had gone already; all the remaining Liverpool candidates had to give favourable replies to its questions as the price of their political survival. At a meeting of the Liverpool Church Association one clergyman 'expressed gratitude that such men had been raised up as Austin Taylor and Alderman Salvidge'.[3] The Church Union was naturally less grateful; in the Exchange division, where it was believed to have a voting strength of 250, the Salvidge policy was denounced from the pulpit and at least one clergyman promised to support the Liberals.[4] The real power in the area, however, lay with the League. In Widnes the Conservative J. S. Gilliat would not support the League's Bill and after one of his district Conservative Committees had thrown him over and there had been threats of a League candidate he withdrew on health grounds.[5] In the fifteen seats in and around Liverpool the only Conservative candidate who resisted the League's

[1] Speech by Emmott at Hollinwood, *M.G.*, 31 December 1909.
[2] *Liverpool D.P.*, 2 October 1900; cf. letters from T. R. Lee and Leadley Brown, *L. Courier*, 1, 2 October 1900.
[3] Speech by Canon Hobson, *Liverpool D.P.*, 20 September 1900.
[4] See *Liverpool D.P.*, 2, 3 October 1900; and speech by Salvidge, *L. Courier*, 3 October 1900.
[5] See *Liverpool D.P.*, 20, 22 September 1900.

pressure was the Hon. Arthur Stanley, whose position in Ormskirk was impregnable. In Southport, where Salvidge was held to have turned the by-election on this issue, both candidates were favourable.

Farther afield, the Protestants had a considerable but not a decisive influence. In Hyde, it is true, the otherwise popular Conservative Member J. W. Sidebotham retired because, with his strong Ritualist views, he did not feel confident of satisfying the Protestant party.[1] In Manchester Balfour withstood attempts to make him give definite assurances but most of his Conservative colleagues capitulated. Few candidates of any party were as openly insouciant towards the Protestants as the Socialist Allen Clarke at Rochdale who accused them of 'trying to raise sectarian dissensions over bigoted nonsense'.[2] Most, like Churchill at Oldham, treated them with a wary respect, and though he managed to pacify both sections over Church discipline he was prepared to admit that: 'Luckily the question is not so acute here as in adjoining constituencies.'[3]

While in 1900 the Protestant League's influence had worked broadly to the Conservatives' advantage, by 1906 that section which was interested primarily in church discipline had become disillusioned with the Conservative Government. At a meeting of Protestant electors in Balfour's own constituency it was held that 'the time had come when their Protestantism should be placed before party politics – (cheers)...They should vote for Protestant candidates, whatever might be their views on Home Rule, Disestablishment, or the fiscal question.'[4] In its determination to brook no compromise the League broke with the Church Association, thereby losing the sympathy of its orthodox Tory supporters. In Manchester it made no recommendation in North East where the High Churchman Fergusson fought the Roman Catholic Clynes; it opposed Belloc, another Roman Catholic, and Schwann who, no doubt mindful of his Irish battalions, would make no reply. But the remaining eleven Liberals in the Manchester area were all approved, four of them being given a straight recommendation over their opponents. This advice considerably dismayed the rank and file who would not accept that, for instance, Churchill was preferable to Joynson Hicks, 'a man who has devoted his whole life and his splendid abilities to the cause of evangelical Protestantism'.[5] Moreover, Church discipline had always been understood as a euphemism for 'no popery'; to support a Home Ruler was a contradiction in terms. The Manchester Protestants were now assidu-

---

[1] See *M.G.*, 4 October 1900.
[2] Clarke's answer to the Protestant Alliance, *M.G.*, 21 September 1900.
[3] Churchill to Salisbury, 2 October 1900, *Companion*, I, 1204.
[4] Herbert Birch at Manchester East, *M.G.*, 9 December 1905.
[5] Letter from Rev. Charles Fenwick Ward, *M. Courier*, 12 January 1906; and see Protestant League recommendations, *M.G.*, 10, 20 January 1906.

ously reminded that 'Home Rule for Ireland means Rome Rule', and the Orangemen at least gave official blessing to the Conservatives.[1]

At Bolton the Protestants threatened to put up an independent candidate and only backed down after the Conservative candidate made certain concessions to them; and J. A. Kensit did stand as Protestant candidate for Birkenhead. His father, John Kensit, the founder of the Protestant Truth Society, had been killed at a meeting in Birkenhead in 1902. 'Kensit is a name to conjure with there', it was admitted,[2] and his campaign aroused great enthusiasm from crowds of up to ten thousand people. When Colonel T. M. Sandys, the Grand Master of the Loyal Orange Institution and Conservative M.P. for Bootle, announced his support for Kensit's Conservative opponent his action in supporting 'party politics in preference to a brother Orangeman' was condemned by the Derry Walls Lodge; attempting to speak in Birkenhead he was shouted down with the cries of 'Traitor' and 'Betrayer'.[3] There were threats of reprisals by Orangemen against Conservative candidates in Liverpool but these went no further than condemnations of Sandys's action. In Liverpool the Laymen's League supported all the Conservative candidates, as did Pastor George Wise, but the emphasis was shifted from Church discipline to opposition to 'Rome Rule'. In West Toxteth where the Roman Catholic James Sexton was Labour candidate his Tory opponent asked: 'Is Tory Toxteth, tried and true, going to accept any other member than a Conservative and Protestant?' And Salvidge confidently predicted that Liverpool would remain 'the metropolis of Protestant and Conservative principles (cheers)'.[4] These cries were enough to conciliate any disaffected Orangemen; a manifesto supporting the Conservatives was issued and all over the city the Lodges came to the aid of the Conservative candidates.

The story of Protestantism after 1906 is largely that of Liverpool. Charles M'Arthur, now M.P. for Kirkdale, gave Pastor Wise untiring support throughout 1909 and it was Kirkdale which set the tone for the elections of January 1910. M'Arthur assured his constituents that 'so long as I am in the House of Commons, or out of it, I shall always fight hard for the Protestant cause (cheers)'.[5] He held meetings in Wise's church schoolroom and the Pride of Kirkdale Orange Lodge gave him warm support. The climax of the Liverpool campaign was an anti-Home Rule demonstration outside St

[1] See e.g. letter from 'Observer', *M. Courier*, 11 January 1906 and Rev. W. Walmsley at Openshaw, *ibid.* 20 January 1906; meeting of Affability L.O.L., *ibid.* 8 January 1906.
[2] Leader, *Liverpool D.P.*, 12 January 1906.
[3] Orange resolution, *Liverpool D.P.*, 10 January 1906; Sandys's meeting, *L. Courier*, 12 January 1906.
[4] R. P. Houston at West Toxteth, *Liverpool D.P.*, 16 January 1906; Salvidge at the Sun Hall, *L. Courier*, 12 January 1906.
[5] Adoption speech, *Liverpool D.P.*, 15 December 1909.

George's Hall, in which the Orange bands played and between one and two hundred thousand people participated (or so the Tories claimed; the police estimate was 10–15,000). From five platforms speakers denounced Home Rule, all of them appealing to the Protestants of Liverpool to back up the Conservative candidates. 'Whatever other issues may arise in Liverpool at this election', said F. E. Smith, 'the one great issue for Protestant workingmen is that of Home Rule (cheers).'[1] In December 1910 the Conservative campaign was on the same lines: Home Rule to the fore in an appeal to the Protestants and support from Wise and the Orange Lodges. Colonel Hall Walker candidly explained at Widnes that he could not meet the views of Roman Catholics on the Coronation oath

because he, like the other Conservative representatives of Liverpool and district, was more or less pledged to the wishes of the Orange party in these matters. That, he thought, had been the platform of the Liverpool Conservative members in every case. He could not please both the Orangemen and the Roman Catholics, and the former were, and always would be, the stronger supporters of the Conservative party.[2]

In Bootle two thousand of the electors were Orangemen and they formed the bedrock of Sandys's support; when Bonar Law had succeeded him as Conservative M.P. he found difficulty in dissuading them from appearing at his meetings in full regalia.[3]

The only conspicuous Protestant agitation outside the Liverpool ambit in 1910 was fairly directly inspired by Alderman J. W. D. Barron of Hyde who (perhaps emulating Salvidge's rise to power?) was active in the democratic Tory and Protestant movements in east Lancashire. When Lord Robert Cecil was adopted as Conservative candidate for Blackburn he was attacked by Barron as a High Churchman and although the local Orangemen repudiated Barron the threats that the Protestants would mobilise two thousand votes against Cecil continued until, at a late stage in the election, a reconciliation was effected. After their defeat some Conservatives nonetheless blamed themselves for having 'allowed an outsider from Hyde to create dissension' in their ranks.[4] And the defeat of the Labour candidate at St Helens in December 1910 was put down by some to the defection of a section of Orangemen among the miners.[5] But throughout most of the region the politics of Protestantism seemed rather *passé* by 1910.

[1] See reports of the demonstration, *L. Courier, Liverpool D.P.*, 17 January 1910.
[2] Hall Walker at Widnes, *Liverpool D.P.*, 22 November 1910; cf. the resolutions of the St Paul's, No. 663, Star of the East, and Beaconsfield Orange Lodges and the Wallasey meeting of Orangemen, *L. Courier*, 2, 3 December 1910.
[3] See *The Times*, 21 January 1910; resolution of L.O.L. No. 724, *L. Courier*, 14 January 1910; Law to W. H. Clemmey, 6 December 1911, copy, BLP 33/3/28.
[4] Letter from 'Blackburn Elector', *Blackburn Gazette*, 22 January 1910; cf. report from Orange deputation, *N.D.T.*, 18 November 1909; letters esp. from 'Watchman', *ibid.* 30 November–7 December 1909; Barron at Blackburn, *ibid.* 10 December 1909.
[5] London letter, *M.G.*, 8 December 1910.

V

Since Dissent had often been the backbone of local Liberalism it is not surprising that Free Church Councils were often to the fore in mobilising the Nonconformist vote for the Liberal candidate or that Nonconformist ministers appeared on Liberal platforms. Such was the case at Gorton, Chester, Rochdale and Middleton in 1900. Yet even at Rochdale some defections, especially among Wesleyans, were reported.[1] At Widnes, the Liberal candidate believed that 1,500 Wesleyans had voted against him in 1900, but by 1906 they seem to have been back in the Liberal fold because of the Education Act.[2] 1906 was the peak of Nonconformist activity. Free Church Councils came out in open support of Liberal or Labour candidates at Hyde, Gorton, Blackpool, Preston, Blackburn, Accrington, Burnley and Birkenhead as well as in Liverpool and Manchester. The Salford South and West Free Church Council urged support as strongly for the Roman Catholic Belloc as for the Churchman Agnew.[3] In Manchester North West Churchill went out of his way to conciliate the Nonconformists. 'But I am told now', he said, 'that I described passive resisters as pantomime martyrs. I admit I said so. It was a stupid thing to say (laughter). I said a lot of stupid things when I worked with the Conservative party, and I left it because I did not want to go on saying stupid things (cheers and laughter).'[4] At Warrington the Liberal candidate attributed his victory in part to the Nonconformists.[5]

This pattern was repeated in an attenuated form in 1910. There was the added difficulty in one or two cases of a three-cornered fight. In January 1910 at Leigh, with one exception all the Nonconformist ministers who took part in the election did so on the Liberal side; the one Wesleyan minister (Rev. W. J. Bull) who supported Labour urged the claims of the Liberal in the straight fight that December. At Eccles the Free Church council found the claims of the Liberal and Labour candidates equally satisfactory in January 1910 and deplored the division in the progressive forces.[6] The *Liverpool Daily Post* somewhat gloomily wrote that the Liberals were 'sure of nothing – not even of the Dissenters', but had been able to print quite a list of local Nonconformist leaders who had spoken out in a Liberal sense.[7] At Bolton seventeen Free Church ministers put their services at the disposal

[1] *M. Courier*, 2 October 1900.
[2] Interview with Macinerney, Gladstone's diary, 15 July 1903, HGP 46484 ff. 48–9; *L. Courier*, 26 December 1905.
[3] *M.G.*, 8 January 1906.
[4] Speech at Manchester North West, *M.G.*, 11 January 1906.
[5] Interview with A. H. Crosfield, *Liverpool D.P.*, 16 January 1906.
[6] *M.G.*, 12 January 1910.
[7] Leader, *Liverpool D.P.*, 10 January 1910; cf. 17 December 1909.

of the progressive candidates, but there was the odd case, like that at Rochdale, of a Nonconformist minister going on to a Conservative platform.[1]

It was axiomatic that Nonconformity and 'the temperance party' were normally one. When Ernest Hatch, the Conservative M.P. for Gorton, had crossed the floor during the 1900 Parliament he at first proposed to stand as a Free Trader at the next election. It was put out that this plan collapsed because his connexion with the wine trade was regarded as a stumbling block by many Nonconformists. This was not, in fact, the true reason, but it made a plausible story.[2] Temperance feeling was not, of course, confined to Nonconformists. The Church of England Temperance Society, of which Canon Hicks and Joynson Hicks were active members, was strong in Lancashire. And since the Conservatives regarded the United Kingdom Alliance as 'a political association' they had their own Conservative and Unionist Temperance Association which, they maintained, 'was an honest association; it stated its name'. On the other hand, the secretary of the U.K.A. had an undeniable point when he said that it was 'the business of that remarkable Association to prefer the opinions on the temperance question of the Unionist candidate, whatever these may be, to those of the Liberal candidate'.[3] The temperance societies were most active politically in 1900, when acceptance of the Minority Report of the Royal Commission on Temperance (Lord Peel's Report) was used as the touchstone of commitment. An appeal on behalf of the Report was signed by the Archbishop of Canterbury and twenty bishops, including Liverpool but not Manchester. Nine of the Liberal candidates in the Manchester area were declared to be 'Peelites', but no Conservatives. The omission of Joynson Hicks (who had not replied) occasioned protests from the Conservative and Unionist Temperance Association which had earlier commended the Government's record on the question.[4] It would, perhaps, have been unwise for a candidate like Joynson Hicks to parade his unorthodoxy. (He was, however, one of three Conservatives to be supported, along with many Liberals, by the Band of Hope Union in 1906.) The normal pattern was, as in Southport, Burnley or Oldham, for temperance opinion to be favourable to the Liberals. In north east Lancashire, where Nonconformist attitudes were ingrained, temperance was part of a common tradition of radicalism on which Labour and Liberal candidates drew. In 1900 temperance played a large part in Philip Snowden's campaign at Blackburn, and at Preston Keir Hardie's chairman at one meeting

[1] See *M.G.*, 28 December 1909; *M. Courier*, 12 January 1910.
[2] See *M.G.*, 6 December 1905. It is quite clear that Hatch's business played only a minor part in his decision not to stand.
[3] Letter from James Whyte, sec., U.K.A., *M.G.*, 21 May 1900; cf. speech by W. Sandeman at Accrington, *Lancs. D.P.*, 9 October 1900.
[4] See list of 'Peelites', *M.G.*, 1 October 1900; letters from C. J. Gulland, *ibid.* 2, 6 October 1900.

declared that he was not a socialist but that temperance had brought him there. Even in 1910 the progressive candidates in that area were still standing up to be counted in favour of local option.[1]

In 1900 special efforts were made by the United Kingdom Alliance against the Conservative candidate in Salford South, J. G. Groves, who was a brewer. In such cases temperance activity was at least in part a reflex against the power of 'the Trade'. In Liberal martyrology electoral politics were often accused of being under the influence of drink. The Census shows that the numbers of men involved in the making and purveying of alcoholic drink were not of themselves very great. Even in such a recognised brewing town as Warrington only some three hundred were employed in the brewing industry in 1911. In Preston, Blackburn and Salford there were, in addition to those employed at breweries, large numbers of men retailing drink, mainly publicans. It must be remembered that these would be almost to a man registered electors, highly organised in their trade associations, and normally very politically conscious. If, for instance, in Blackburn there were about three hundred publicans on the electoral roll in 1901, even in an electorate of twenty thousand this was not small beer. And this is to take no account of brewery workers and other workers engaged in supplying drink (in both Preston and Blackburn between six and seven hundred men were directly employed in the drink trade).[2] Above all, it ignores the political influence of the Trade upon the consuming public. 'It is an axiom of political warfare', wrote A. G. Gardiner, 'that every public-house is worth five votes to the Tory party, and I do not think the axiom errs on the side of extravagance when applied to Blackburn, where every bar parlour is practically a Tory committee-room, exercising the subtle and corrupting influence that must always be associated with the drink traffic.'[3] John Rutherford, Conservative M.P. for Darwen, owned the Blackburn brewery of Shaw's. 'Every public-house – and Mr Rutherford himself owns a hundred – was a centre of influence in his favour', it was said in 1900.[4] In Blackburn, complained a member of the Conservative party in 1912, 'both the present president and the present chairman of the local Conservative party are pecuniarily interested in the drink trade, and are popularly known as brewers.'[5]

In Warrington there were three breweries: Bolton's, Walker's, and

[1] See list of candidates supported by U.K.A., *M.G.*, 14 January 1910; cf. Hardie's chairman, *Lancs. D.P.*, 28 September 1900.
[2] See *Census 1901*, County Reports, Table 35; *Census 1911*, vol. x, pt II, Table 13. Publicans are given as occupational category xx, 4b, and the (very small) number aged under 25 is distinguished.
[3] 'The Tatler', *Blackburn Wkly Telegraph*, 6 October 1900.
[4] Leader, *Blackburn Wkly Telegraph*, 13 October 1900.
[5] Thomas Marsden to Alfred Nuttall (chairman, Blackburn Cons. Assn), 12 December 1912, enc. in W. B. Boyd-Carpenter to Law, 14 December 1912, BLP 28/1/40.

Greenall, Whitley. William Bolton was a Conservative alderman, Sir Gilbert Greenall was president of the Conservative Association. J. Fulton Smith, the manager of Walker's, was the secretary of the Conservative Association, and Colonel W. Hall Walker, a director, was a Conservative M.P. and the leader of the Trade in the House of Commons. (In his constituency of Widnes the Liberals quailed before 'such a tremendous influence as Walker's Brewery'.)[1] Bolton's was only a small firm but the other two breweries had great influence in Warrington elections, and this they exploited in January 1910. Wherever two tied houses were opposite, slung across the road were strings of lights and big blue letters with Conservative slogans, and a special appeal was made to trade unionists on the grounds that 'the publican was the first to help you'.[2] J. G. Groves of the firm of Groves and Whitnall was chairman of Salford South Conservative Association and M.P. for the division in the 1900 Parliament. 'The streets of South Salford had run with beer before to-day', was the Liberals' lurid warning in 1900.[3] In the 1906 election the firm issued a circular to the Trade; the Liberal candidate, Belloc, also wrote to all licence-holders, espousing their interests against the brewers, and it seems that he captured the votes of many Irish publicans. Groves and Whitnall was again active in January 1910 and issued a confidential circular in Manchester North; while Belloc's personal criticisms of the licensing clauses of the Budget could not apparently outweigh his party's unpopularity with the publicans.[4] It was very rare to find a man like Councillor Jackson, of the Lancaster brewers Yates and Jackson, supporting the Liberals. At Preston the Labour party solemnly 'warned publicans that if free drinks were allowed on polling day their licences would be opposed at the next licensing sessions'.[5]

The Liberals sometimes tried to win the sympathy of the brewers' tenants. 'When Mr Balfour says we are attacking the licensed victuallers', said the Liberal Horridge in 1906, 'I throw it back in his face. We are not attacking them, but the great brewing interest which has returned him to Parliament for East Manchester for the last twenty years.'[6] Those Liberals who were not temperance extremists seized upon the tied-house system as a means of dislodging the tenants from the brewers. The Manchester Licensed Victuallers' Association asserted in 1906 that the interests of the wholesale and retail branches were identical and predicted that Liberal efforts to split

[1] Bernacchi (Lib. cand.) at Liverpool Junior Reform Club, *L. Courier*, 14 January 1910.
[2] See *M.G.*, 15 January 1910.
[3] Alfred Mond in Salford South, *M. Courier*, 21 September 1900.
[4] See speech by Belloc, *M.G.*, 6 January 1906; and circulars issued by the brewery, *ibid.* 9 January 1906, 11 January 1910; cf. Speaight, *Life of Hilaire Belloc*, pp. 280–3.
[5] Cllr Woolley at Preston, *Lancs. D.P.*, 15 December 1905; cf. Cllr Jackson at Skerton, *ibid.* 12 January 1906.
[6] Horridge at Manchester East, *M.G.*, 6 January 1906.

them would fail. In 1910, however, John Hodge was able to use the story of one licensed victualler's exploitation by the brewery as an argument for the Licensing Bill.[1] The licensed victuallers – many of whom were really grocers, a notably Liberal body of tradesmen – were almost certainly less Conservative than the brewers. In Stockport fifteen town councillors in the years 1901–13 were in the drink trade. Only two were brewers, both Conservatives, serving 8 and 11 years respectively. Of the rest – licensed victuallers and beersellers – there were nine Conservatives who served 36 years between them, and four Liberals who served 30 years.[2] But it was a licensed victualler in the Altrincham division who was reported as saying in 1910: 'we have worked very hard to throw Crossley [Liberal] out, very hard indeed. I know six of my own customers who voted for him last time but who voted against him this election.'[3]

In both Manchester and Liverpool the Conservative party was associated with the brewers. The chairman of the Liquor Trades Confederation and the Brewers' Central Association from 1901–6 was Alderman W. T. Rothwell, later chairman of the Conservative Association in Manchester North East and deputy chairman of the Manchester Conservative Association. It was he who offered to succour the ailing *Manchester Courier* in the party's interest in 1912, provoking Northcliffe's reflection that: 'An unobtrusive gentleman like alderman Rothwell, who ladles out money by the hatful on very slight security, without asking for anything, is a rarity in a democracy.'[4] Rothwell had been succeeded as chairman of the Trade organisations by Alderman Edward Holt, one of the leaders of Prestwich Conservative Association and also later deputy chairman of the Manchester Association. It was, no doubt, Holt and Rothwell who were referred to when Lord Cromer was told in 1908 that 'on the Conservative Association there are some important brewers and that they are very anxious to avoid anything in the nature of a split on fiscal questions'.[5] In Manchester the pubs took little ostensible part in the elections of January 1910 until two days before polling, when nearly every one became 'a bill-posting station without and a Committee-room within'.[6] In Liverpool Salvidge himself was managing director of Bent's Brewery. Allegations in the *Daily Post* that the Conservative party was unduly influenced by the brewers over licensing led to a libel action

[1] See the Licensed Victuallers' manifesto, *M. Courier*, 5 January 1906; 'Mr Hodge and the Licensing Trade', leaflet in Gorton collection.
[2] Stockport municipal elections by party and occupation are given in *Cheshire Year Book* and *Stockport Express Annual*.
[3] Letter from 'Old Resident', *M.G.*, 13 December 1910.
[4] Northcliffe to Law, n.d. (1912), BLP 25/2/20.
[5] Tootal Broadhurst's remarks reported in Cromer to Robert Cecil, 19 March 1908, CP 51072. Clearly this was no time to weaken the opposition to the Licensing Bill.
[6] *M.G.*, 15 January 1910 (Manchester East).

against Sir Edward Russell in December 1905, and on his acquittal he was given a congratulatory dinner at the Reform Club. The Licensed Victuallers' Association worked against the Liberals in 1910 although there were attempts to mobilise the barmen in their favour. Sir Edward Evans made much of 'the meeting which Mr Smith recently addressed, and which was attended by 1,400 publicans with the chief publican [i.e. Salvidge] sitting beside him (laughter and hear, hear)'.[1] And in December 1910 Evans was again making sarcastic references to the fact that it was Salvidge himself who organised the licensed victuallers. At their meeting Colonel Hall Walker denied the Liberal charge 'that every public-house was a committee room for the Conservative or Unionist party', and claimed that 'instructions had been given for many years in his firm, and he believed in other firms, that licencees should forbid so far as possible all discussions in their houses on political or religious matters (applause)'.[2] The Colonel's facts were doubtless correct, but the comment of one Labour candidate that, 'Booze and Conservatism go generally together',[3] is probably a better summary of the relationship.

It is significant that it should have been the Liberals of Liverpool who were still capable of seeing the influence of the drink trade as their main enemy in 1910. The fossilised politics of Merseyside still rested upon antagonisms between the Trade and Temperance, between the Irish and the Orangemen, between Catholics and Protestants. But elsewhere the old groupings had become noticeably less important. In 1906 the Liberals had made a clean sweep of the Cheshire seats from under the noses of the landed interest: a gain that was not permanent but which fatally disrupted the old patterns of political life. By 1910 landed influence was important only in three or four divisions in the north west. The Roman Catholic attempt to bring out the vote in January 1910 failed miserably (except in one or two places like Preston) and this cannot be put down entirely to the contrary pull of Irish nationalist loyalties, for the Church of England met with an almost identical rebuff at the same time. For both churches 1910 showed the limits of their power. The votes of the Irishmen, it is true, were still largely motivated on the old basis, but it is important to notice here that their class interests were also pulling in the same direction. In the two smaller communities, the Welsh shared the fate of the Nonconformists, and some of the richer Jews were forsaking the loyalties of the ghetto. Protestantism, which had once been a force throughout Lancashire, became, in Salvidge's hands, merely a means of holding the Liverpool Conservative party together. Nonconformity rallied to Liberalism with impressive solidarity in 1906 but in 1910 was

[1] Evans at the Junior Reform Club, *Liverpool D.P.*, 19 January 1910.
[2] Hall Walker at meeting of licencees, *L. Courier*, 3 December 1910.
[3] G. D. Kelley at Manchester South West, *M.G.*, 11 January 1906.

clearly no longer the dominant element in the party. Similarly with Temperance, a dying cause even in 1906 and a dead one in 1910. The fact that the Trade had been hammered not in a Licensing Act but in the Budget gave it respectable allies among the Tariff Reformers; it also made it just another plutocratic interest with cause to complain. Of course, the old loyalties, values and prejudices still had a certain pull, and there were many for whom they were still the central political preoccupation. In some places, notably in Preston and in the Liverpool area, they were still dominant; but in the politics of most of the towns the communities were perceptibly disintegrating.

11 The rise and fall of the Free Traders

We Unionist Free Traders must fight on as best we can and at any rate go down with our flag flying. One thing I will not do, however, and that is either by word or deed admit that those are true free traders who confine their observation of free trade principles to exports and imports and violate those principles in the most cynical way in all the other departments of public activity.

St Loe Strachey, 1909

I

It is usually asserted that the Liberals did well in Lancashire from 1906 because of Free Trade: with the implication that *laissez-faire* Liberalism enjoyed a freak revival. On this reading, the Liberal party remained essentially a bourgeois instrument and the millowners rallied to it in defence of the precepts of the Manchester School. Now this chapter will not seek to deny that for many Lancashire men Free Trade was the most fundamental of political truths, nor that Lancashire as a whole was unenthusiastic about Tariff Reform. But, whatever was the case in 1906, it is grossly misleading to attribute the Liberal victories of 1910 in any significant degree to the businessmen's preference for Free Trade. Far from fiscal attitudes dictating party allegiance, it would be truer to say that party allegiance dictated fiscal attitudes.

This chapter will examine the behaviour of two sorts of men, those who were nominally Liberal and those who were nominally Conservative. In practice they were much of a muchness. As far as the Unionist Free Traders are concerned two points can be demonstrated. First, that by 1910 the Lancashire Conservatives accepted the policy of Tariff Reform – or ceased to be Conservatives. Second, that notwithstanding this acceptance they did not believe in Tariff Reform. It is surely clear, then, that conviction about the 'first constructive policy of the party' was not in fact a necessary condition of Conservatism: the corollary is that belief in Free Trade was not a sufficient condition of Liberalism. To find economic liberals within the historic Liberal party should come as no surprise, but such men were clearly *in* rather than *of* a progressive party. By 1910 they too had either made the necessary adjustments in their political philosophy or had decided that *laissez faire* was better represented by the Conservative party. 'I have never accepted the view', wrote Lord Cromer, who was in many ways their leader, 'that a Free Trade policy means merely an absence of taxes imposed for protective purposes. It means a great deal more than this. It means the support of individualism against collectivism.'[1] Many of these men, of course, had long felt out of sympathy with the trend of progressive thought. An archetypal figure here is Edward Hopkinson who, his daughter has written, 'carried his practical acceptance and his theoretical dislike of Conservatism to quite comic lengths', and

had usually voted Liberal except during the Home Rule crises. Since all of these fell within his manhood it could hardly be said that his support of the Liberal Party was very continuous, nor was it ever very enthusiastic except when Free Trade was directly threatened. It ended for good when Lloyd George produced his Radical Budget of 1909...[2]

II

Free Trade became a political issue once more in 1902 with the imposition of a registration duty on corn. In the by-election at Bury that May this duty became the central issue, and the unexpected Conservative defeat therefore gave a fillip all the greater to the somewhat jaded prospects of Liberalism. The protectionists, while admitting that the result was 'a serious reverse in an unfortunate quarter and at an unfortunate hour',[3] refused to see it as one for Free Trade as such. However that may be, the old Free Trade cries, once raised, would not be stilled, and the Government's hope that Lancashire's resentment would be shortlived was not borne out. 'The Corn Tax is vy. unpopular', reported the Conservative M.P. for Oldham six months later.[4]

When the corn duty was repealed in 1903, however, Lancashire Conservatives were reported to be unimpressed, even those who had been against it feeling that it was a great mistake to reopen the question. Chamberlain's Birmingham speech of 15 May 1903, in which he launched the idea of Tariff Reform, was seen by the *Manchester Guardian* as an exercise in 'separating himself from the action of the Cabinet in abolishing the Bread Tax', and those Free Trade susceptibilities which had been shocked by that episode were now ready to be affronted by the larger policy. There was a large number of Conservatives who could not accept Chamberlain's proposals, and in the autumn of 1903 the obvious possibilities of their working with the Liberals were explored. The Duke of Devonshire was said to be 'prepared

[1] Cromer to Bernard Mallet, 23 February 1910, Zetland, *Lord Cromer*, p. 323.
[2] Chorley, *Manchester Made Them*, pp. 236–7.
[3] Farrer Ecroyd to Joseph Chamberlain, 16 May 1902, Garvin and Amery, *Life of Joseph Chamberlain*, v, 216–17.
[4] Churchill to Balfour, 6 October 1902, BP 49694. But Churchill loyally defended the tax to his constituents.

for almost any degree of cooperation'[1] and other Unionist Free Traders, less eminent but more active, were of similar disposition.

In the summer of 1903 Lord Hugh Cecil collaborated with Herbert Gladstone over the foundation of the Free Trade Union, of which L. T. Hobhouse became secretary. This was primarily a central propaganda body though it maintained relations with spontaneously formed local Free Trade organisations. The most important of these was the Free Trade League of Manchester, which was established under the chairmanship of Tom Garnett, the former chairman of the Indian Import Duties Committee. One of the treasurers was Frank Calvert, a cotton manufacturer and a former president of Preston Conservative Club, and one of the secretaries instrumental in founding the League was F. R. B. Lindsell, who had 'created the Unionist party in the Altrincham Division'.[2] When the Free Trade Union decided in January 1904 to stimulate the formation of local organisations it took the Free Trade League as its model. The Free Trade Union carried on the work of the Liberal Whips by other means; the Free Trade League, on the other hand, was genuinely independent of the Liberals, and the central organisation to which many of its members looked was not so much the Free Trade Union as the Unionist Free Food League and its successor the Unionist Free Trade Club. The Club was founded at the end of 1904.[3] The Duke of Devonshire was naturally elected president and was supported by several M.P.s from the north west, including Ernest Hatch, R. A. Yerburgh, Richard Cavendish and Austin Taylor. Among its provincial members was Edward Tootal Broadhurst, the leader of the Free Trade League in Manchester North West, and such stalwarts as Frank and Henry Calvert; and the venerable St Helens Liberal Unionist Sir David Gamble was with them in spirit. This Club was important too as a nexus between Lancashire and the Cecils – Lord Hugh and Lord Robert – who were among its most active members.

For those Unionist Free Traders who were sitting Members it was plainly rather important to know how far the Liberals would support them in their revolt against their party. By the end of 1903 enough soundings had been made to indicate that the Liberals, regarding opposition to protectionist Conservatives as the first priority, might on occasion leave room for a local entente with the Unionist Free Traders. 'But it wd. not do', wrote Campbell-Bannerman, 'to set up a general rule that these are to be undisturbed.' And the attempt at a more general concordat on the '1886 model' foundered

---

[1] Lord Crewe to Gladstone, 21 November 1903, from Chatsworth, HGP 45996 ff. 11–12.

[2] T. W. Killick to Churchill, 3 December 1904, *Companion*, II, 381–2.

[3] For the formation of the Unionist Free Trade Club see Elliot, *Life of Goschen*, II, Appendix V, pp. 285–7. Herbert Gladstone's papers illuminate the close working arrangements between the Liberal Whips and the Free Trade Union.

early in 1904.[1] At about this time, Herbert Gladstone, working with the Free Trade organisations, drew up a list of the Free Fooders which included the following M.P.s from the north west:[2]

W. S. Churchill	Oldham
R. F. Cavendish	North Lonsdale
E. F. G. Hatch	Gorton
Col. G. Kemp	Heywood
Sir Lees Knowles	Salford West
Charles M'Arthur	Liverpool Exchange
Hon. W. Peel	Manchester South
Austin Taylor	Liverpool East Toxteth
Herbert Whiteley	Ashton-under-Lyne
R. A. Yerburgh	Chester

It can be taken that all of them disliked intensely the policy of taxing food, but some – Knowles, M'Arthur, Peel, Whiteley and Yerburgh – nonetheless found it possible to square their convictions with loyalty to Balfour. This left five rebels. Austin Taylor, the Protestant champion, shared none of the enthusiasm for Chamberlain which his former comrade Salvidge was then displaying and emerged somewhat improbably as a staunch Free Trader. 'He seems to carry his theological narrowness into his political economy, – and with equally unfortunate results', was Balfour's mordant comment.[3] Salvidge, however, was in no mood to oppose him and deterred F. E. Smith from coming out against him as a Tariff Reformer on the grounds that 'it would never be understood by the Protestant masses'.[4] Cavendish too remained a candidate in his own constituency though he had to change parties more openly. The cases of Churchill, Kemp and Hatch all created more difficulty.

Already out of sympathy with Toryism, Churchill was ready to respond quickly and decisively to Chamberlain's proposals. 'The one real difficulty I have to encounter is the suspicion that I am moved by mere restless ambition', he had written some months previously: '& if some definite issue – such as Tariff – were to arise – that difficulty would disappear.'[5] Within ten days of the Birmingham speech he wrote to Balfour saying that if the Prime Minister were committed to Chamberlain's policy, 'I must reconsider my position in politics'.[6] Although as late as September 1903

---

[1] Campbell-Bannerman to Gladstone, 9 November 1903, HGP 45988 ff. 59–61; and see McCready, 'The revolt of the Unionist Free Traders', *Parlty Affairs*, XVI (1963), 188–206.

[2] Unionist Free Food League M.P.s, HGP 46106 ff. 119–22; cf. list for 1904, *ibid.* ff. 147–50; and list in Churchill to Hugh Cecil, 30 May (1903), *Companion*, II, 190–2.

[3] Balfour to Sandars, 15 October 1903, BP 49761.

[4] Salvidge to F. E. Smith, 13 January 1905, Salvidge, *Salvidge of Liverpool*, p. 63.

[5] Churchill to Rosebery, 10 October 1902, *Companion*, II, 167–8.

[6] Churchill to Balfour, 25 May 1903, most private, BP 49694. In an earlier form only lightly excised he had written, 'I must resign my seat'.

Churchill sought to give the impression that he was supported by a Free Trade majority in the Oldham Conservative Association, his position there was being steadily undermined. In mid-October his chairman (a Free Trader himself) told him that 'unless you agree blindly to follow Mr Balfour the party in Oldham will repudiate you'; and within a matter of days Churchill was committing to paper his intention of joining the Liberals.[1] The rest was a matter of manœuvre. Churchill was acting at this time as broker between the Liberal Whips and the Unionist Free Traders and even before he crossed the floor Herbert Gladstone was trying to fix him up with another seat. What was wanted was a prestigious commercial seat like the Central divisions of Sheffield or Birmingham, both of which were considered. Then, at the end of February 1904, the Liberal candidate for Manchester North West died. It was a heaven-sent opportunity. Negotiations were opened with Churchill and he was soon Liberal and Free Trade candidate, under the auspices of the Free Trade League, for the greatest commercial seat in the north of England. Sir William Houldsworth, who had committed himself to preference, decided to stand down; and the erstwhile Tory free-lance groomed himself not only to fight the Liberal fight but (rather less plausibly) to step into Houldsworth's shoes. It was as much of an implied warning as a compliment when the secretary of the Free Trade League told Churchill that 'Lancashire is disposed to take you very seriously'. And when Campbell-Bannerman visited Manchester at the end of the year he heard 'doubts expressed whether our friend Winston, with all the cleverness & variety of his speeches, is quite the sort of man to capture the quiet non-party voter who went for Houldsworth because of his solidity, and stolidity, and eminent respectability'.[2]

George Kemp, the Unionist M.P. for Heywood, though his position was in some respects similar to that of Churchill, was a man of a very different type. He was a pocket-sized Sir Edward Grey who could allay the fears of the timid; and like Grey, his use to the party was such that his genuine disinclination to continue in politics had to be overcome by those who needed him. For the time being, however, he was allowed to return to his mill and was not a candidate in 1906. Ernest Hatch was not a great catch. The fact that he too was not a candidate in 1906 was not due to any backwardness on his part, but the pressures brought to bear upon him were such that he withdrew from his candidature at Gorton.

---

[1] See Churchill's letter to the Duke of Devonshire, 1 September 1903, Holland, *Life of the Duke of Devonshire*, II, 319–21; J. T. Travis-Clegg (chairman, Oldham Conservative Assn) to Churchill, 15 October 1903, and Churchill to Hugh Cecil, 24 October 1903, not sent, *Companion*, II, 238, 242–4. Churchill's position is fully documented by correspondence in BP, HGP and *Companion*, II, esp. 232–47, 261–71, 275–8, 283–312, 322–4, 335–40, on which the whole of this paragraph draws.
[2] T. W. Killick to Churchill, *Companion*, II, 349; Campbell-Bannerman to Gladstone, 5 December 1904, HGP 45988 f. 132.

Of the four Conservative M.P.s who had made a clean break with their party, then, Churchill and Cavendish were to fight again in 1906 and Kemp and Hatch retired. J. E. B. Seely was another Member who had crossed the floor and although he had previously sat for the Isle of Wight the Whips now looked out for a Lancashire seat for him. The candidatures at Hyde and at Middleton (for which Kemp had briefly been canditate) were both discussed before, early in 1905, he accepted the invitation to fight as Liberal candidate at Liverpool Abercromby. The Liberal Whips drafted one other candidate who was primarily a Free Trader into Lancashire. The idea of Churchill fighting Preston in harness with the local Free Trader Frank Calvert had been mooted at one stage but the more distinctively Liberal names Gladstone suggested in lieu were not seized upon. There then appeared upon the scene Harold Cox, a former secretary of the Cobden Club and a Liberal of rigorous *laissez-faire* views. 'I think he is a *bad egg*', Gladstone had written earlier,[1] but now he introduced him to Preston and it was arranged that Cox and Calvert should be the Free Trade candidates. The only difficulty – 'the *hat* question'[2] – was resolved by the decision that the Liberals should run Cox. The following year, however, Calvert's candidature was abandoned in favour of that of a Labour man.

III

It is difficult to arrive at a definitive list of Unionist Free Trade candidates in 1906. Of those M.P.s who had been members of the Free Trade League M'Arthur, Member for Liverpool Exchange, could no longer be regarded as a supporter of Free Trade, which he now declared to be 'unsound'. Yerburgh stood at Chester as a Balfourite with strong Free Trade leanings, committing himself only to 'the exercise of negotiations with the power of retaliation behind it'.[3] Sir Lees Knowles at Salford West, while affirming his loyalty to Balfour, emphasised his consistency in calling himself a Unionist Free Trader and was not opposed by the Free Trade League. All these three lost their seats and their fiscal views were not put to the test in the new Parliament. The position of Austin Taylor in East Toxteth was most curious. The *Liverpool Courier* began by taunting the Liberals for not having the courage to oppose him but later in the contest admitted that it was the Unionists who were allowing him a walkover. He was nominated by a number of Conservatives in their private capacity as well as by Liberals. The *Daily Post*'s view that he went to Westminster 'as a Liberal quite as much as a Conservative' was confirmed by events since he crossed the floor early in the new Parlia-

---

[1] Gladstone to Campbell-Bannerman, 16 November 1903, CBP 41217 ff. 35–6.
[2] Interview with Cox, Gladstone's diary, 8 March 1904, HGP 46485 f. 2; cf. the account by Calvert in a speech at Preston, *Lancs. D.P.*, 25 November 1909.
[3] Yerburgh at Chester, *L. Courier*, 9 January 1906.

ment.[1] Two Unionist Free Trade M.P.s from other parts of the country fled to Lancashire to fight as Conservative candidates. The Hon. George Goschen, son of Viscount Goschen, moved from East Grinstead to Bolton where he urged the importance of returning 'some Unionist Free Traders to the House of Commons at the next election to support Mr Balfour', being prepared himself to experiment with retaliation if it caused no injury.[2] And at Bury R. J. Lucas explained that he had left his seat at Portsmouth because his supporters had become Chamberlainites. It was alleged, however, that 'with the exception of one or two official persons the Unionist party in Bury are ardent Tariff Reformers',[3] and threats were made to withhold support unless Lucas explicitly declared his support for Balfour, which he promptly did. Some of the same tensions appeared at Blackburn where the sitting M.P., Sir Harry Hornby, though he belonged to none of the recognised Free Trade organisations, was an unrepentant Free Trader and brought in the likeminded former M.P. for Derby, Geoffrey Drage, as his running mate. In the neighbouring division of Darwen the position of John Rutherford, M.P., was less well understood and indeed much of the campaign was spent in trying to discover whether or not he was a Free Trader. He had never been counted among the rebels on the set-piece fiscal motions in the House of Commons, but then neither had Hornby. Rutherford's belief in Free Trade, in fact, seems to have grown upon him during the election, especially after the earlier results had indicated its popularity. He was prepared to call himself a Balfourite but preferred bluff evasions – 'for ten years they had known John Rutherford, and did they think it possible that he would do anything to increase the cost of living to the workers?'[4] And with polling only a few days away he offered a £500 challenge if the Liberals could show that he had in any way departed from the spirit of Free Trade, proposing John Morley and the Duke of Devonshire as judges. Both ruled against him; though Rutherford claimed that they had been 'nobbled'. Sir Francis Sharp Powell at Wigan was in much the same position; an old and loyal Tory M.P., he made no issue of his Free Trade views. Hornby, Rutherford and Powell all kept their seats and were among the small band of Unionist Free Trade M.P.s who sat in the 1906 Parliament.

Richard Cavendish, who stood again in North Lonsdale, is often, though incorrectly, described as a Unionist Free Trader, an error that can be traced to the Duke of Devonshire's misapprehension of the position. The Duke

[1] *Liverpool D.P.*, 13 January 1906; cf. *L. Courier*, 5 December 1905, 8 January 1906.

[2] Speech by Goschen, *M. Courier*, 13 December 1905; answers to questions, *Bolton Chron.*, 5 January 1906.

[3] Letter from 'Fairplay', *M. Courier*, 2 January 1906.

[4] Rutherford at Darwen, *N.D.T.*, 4 January 1906. For the Blackburn contest see Clarke, 'British Politics and Blackburn Politics', *Hist. Jnl.*, XII (1969), pp. 310–11.

knew that Cavendish had Liberal support – he sent a cheque for £20 to the Ulverston Liberal Club in recognition – but persisted in describing his nephew as an independent Free Trade Unionist. Cavendish was a Unionist only in the sense that he did not accept Home Rule. He declared himself a supporter of Campbell-Bannerman's Albert Hall statement of policy and was adopted by the North Lonsdale Liberal Association, drawing a clear distinction between his former independent position and the party fight that 'we Liberals' were now engaged in.[1] Nonetheless, he was inevitably regarded as first and foremost a Free Trade candidate, and the same is true of Harold Cox in Preston nearby. Cox warned the Liberal Association from the outset that, although he claimed to be a keen Liberal, he would not be 'a mere party man' and had seen too much of the House of Commons 'to wish to become one of those walking automata on two legs, who come in when the division bell rings and vote as they are told'.[2] If any of the Preston Liberals dismissed these sentiments as conventional platitudes they were soon to be disillusioned when Cox, unlike Cavendish, was returned to Parliament to give evidence of his convictions.

The two ex-Unionists, Seely and Churchill, who fought in the business divisions of Liverpool and Manchester respectively, clearly grounded their appeal more than most upon Free Trade. The contest in Manchester North West would in any case have been the crucial test case for Tariff Reform; and, wherever he had fought, Churchill's campaign could not but have turned largely upon Free Trade; for Churchill to fight in North West was therefore not only a logical matching of predilections but made this contest beyond any dispute the cockpit of the fiscal controversy. As Joynson Hicks, the Conservative candidate, said, North West was 'the blue riband of the Conservative Party in Manchester, perhaps in Lancashire'.[3] Churchill was adopted not just as a Liberal but as Free Trade candidate too and the Free Trade League played a vital part in his campaign, at least among the important business section of the electorate. The moving spirit here was Edward Tootal Broadhurst, himself a cotton manufacturer and formerly president of Prestwich Conservative Association. James Arthur Hutton exemplifies the tradition that these men represented. The son of a respected member of the Chamber of Commerce who had for a short time been Conservative M.P. for North Manchester, he had succeeded him as head of a firm of cotton merchants in the export trade, and had himself, like many

[1] For the Duke's donation see *M. Courier*, 11 December 1905; cf. Holland, *Life of the Duke of Devonshire*, II, 392–3. For Cavendish's adoption and the unequivocal speeches he then made see *Lancs. D.P.*, 8, 9 January 1906. The Conservative Chief Whip had no hesitation in putting him down as a Liberal; Acland Hood's memorandum, *c.* 15 June 1906, BP 49771.
[2] Cox at Preston, *Lancs. D.P.*, 29 December 1905.
[3] Joynson Hicks in Manchester, *M. Courier*, 8 January 1906.

another of the Free Traders, been involved in the work of the Bimetallic League.

Plainly the Free Trade vote was the great prize. 'Apart from a large number of Unionist Free-traders', it was once explained, 'there are in North-west Manchester many men who have attached themselves to no party but who are still proud to call themselves Liberals of the old school – staunch Free-traders, of course, but men who distrust what they call the New Liberalism.'[1] Tootal Broadhurst declared that 'personally he believed that the constituency was Unionist rather than Liberal, and it was only by the absolute vote of Free Trade Unionists being given for Free Trade that they could secure the return of Mr Churchill'.[2] Although Churchill was a member of the Government he was at this stage not yet fully in sympathy with his Liberal supporters. 'When he and they first met', the *Guardian* recalled later, 'it was on the common ground of Free Trade; around and about this firm surface there were topics on which it was well not to touch'.[3] But this, of course, was no disadvantage at all in the eyes of the men whom Broadhurst represented. 'Free Trade is not a party question', wrote Broadhurst in his final appeal; and he asked his 'fellow Conservative and Unionist Free-traders to sink personal feeling and party differences' and vote for Churchill.[4] Churchill's victory, then, was in large measure the work of men who were primarily Free Traders. 'We were fighting', said Joynson Hicks, 'what undoubtedly was the great Free Trade centre of Lancashire. – (Hear, hear)...It was saturated through and through with the old Free Trade doctrine.'[5] And it was later asserted that Churchill 'owed more than his large majority, from actual canvassing statistics, to the votes of Conservative and Unionist Free-traders'.[6]

Manchester North West was on this occasion but the apogee of a more general set of opinion. Both the Duke of Devonshire and Lord James of Hereford had in their time been Lancashire M.P.s, and both wrote open letters which the Liberals put to considerable use in Lancashire. The leaders of the Free Trade League threw their weight behind the Liberal candidates in their home constituencies. Frank Calvert was the undisputed leader of the Preston Free Trade League, the membership of which was said to be 340, and though it gave the Conservative candidates an ostensibly equal chance to show their adherence to Free Trade it was obvious all along that it would support Harold Cox and the Labour candidate, J. T. Macpherson. It was

[1] Letter from Barnard Ellinger, *M.G.*, 29 July 1912.
[2] Broadhurst at the F.T.L. meeting, *M. Courier*, 11 January 1906.
[3] *M.G.*, 26 November 1910.
[4] Free Trade League manifesto, *M.G.*, 12 January 1906.
[5] Joynson Hicks after the poll, *M.G.*, 15 January 1906.
[6] Letter from 'Conservative Free-Trader', *Spectator*, 11 April 1908. The votes given at successive elections by some of the Free Trade leaders are tabulated in Appendix D.

Calvert's belief that 'we Free Traders – we Tory Free Traders – are doing the best for our party in voting only for Free Trade candidates. (Cheers.)'[1] He was joined by two other prominent Conservatives associated with the cotton industry, Henry Bell and J. W. Pateson, and the movement they represented seems to have given a serious blow to the Conservatives. After their defeat one of the Tory leaders declared that 'we have been beaten by lies, chicanery, and secession from our immediate ranks ("Shame".)'.[2] It was much the same story in Darwen. A meeting organised by the Free Trade League saw Tom Garnett and Frank Calvert on the platform along with a number of other local manufacturers; and at a meeting at Walton-le-Dale Frank Calvert, Henry Calvert and Herbert Calvert all turned out, along with other Unionist Free Traders including the former Conservative agent. 'Since 1886', Frank Calvert reflected, 'there has never been a Tory meeting held in this room without a Calvert occupying the chair.'[3]

The same pattern was repeated in Lancaster, Accrington, Manchester South, St Helens, Newton, Chorley, Stretford, Gorton, Leigh and Knutsford. Even in the Liverpool area there were some defections from the Conservative ranks. At Birkenhead J. M. Laird, head of the shipbuilders Cammell Laird, declared that he was opposed to Tariff Reform although younger members of the family favoured it.[4] There was a branch of the Unionist Free Food League in Liverpool at this time. Two Birkenhead men with Liverpool interests – the shipowner J. H. Beazley and the former chairman of the Birkenhead Conservative Association, F. C. Danson – independently made clear their opposition to Chamberlainites (like Lees in Birkenhead) while not ruling out support for retaliationists (like M'Arthur in Exchange).[5] The Exchange and Abercromby divisions contained most of Liverpool's business vote, and there were Liberal victories in both. The Liberal *Post* believed that the defection of commercial men had been crucial in Exchange, though the Tory *Courier* attributed the result to the Irish strength. Salvidge, however, was prepared to admit to Chamberlain that there had been 'abstentions on the part of some of the commercial community' in both these divisions, with which he contrasted 'the democratic constituencies of Liverpool'.[6] If Free Trade was not the power there that it was in the Manchester area it still helped to woo the businessmen in 1906.

[1] Calvert at Annual Meeting of Preston F.T.L., *Lancs. D.P.*, 21 December 1905.
[2] Ald. Greenwood at the Conservative Club, *Lancs. D.P.*, 16 January 1906.
[3] Calvert at Walton-le-Dale, *N.D.T.*, 12 January 1906; cf. the meeting at Darwen, *N.D.T.*, 5 January 1906.
[4] Speech by J. M. Laird at Birkenhead, *L. Courier*, 15 January 1906.
[5] See letter from J. H. Beazley, *Liverpool D.P.*, 16 January 1906; and references to Danson, *ibid.* 8–9 January 1906.
[6] Salvidge to Chamberlain, 14 February 1906, Salvidge, *Salvidge of Liverpool*, pp. 70–1; cf. *L. Courier*, 17 January 1906 and *Liverpool D.P.*, 18 January 1906.

IV

In 1906 the Free Traders were able to dictate the terms of the fiscal controversy. Because they showed themselves unafraid to vote Liberal there was real competition for their votes; many Conservative candidates claimed that their policy of retaliation was a means to true Free Trade. After 1906, however, a full programme of Tariff Reform became the policy of the party; but at the same time the experience of a Liberal Government put the Free Trade alliance of 1906 under severe strain. In short, both parties became less attractive to the Unionist Free Traders. Their hopes of at least maintaining their influence in the Conservative party by some kind of gentleman's agreement foundered upon the Tariff Reformers' more realistic faith in majorities. Joseph Chamberlain had written in 1904 of his belief that 'the Unionist Party of the future will consist almost, if not absolutely, of fiscal reformers', and had said publicly in 1905 that: 'In parties, as in countries, after all, the minority must yield to the majority, or nothing can get on.'[1] Most reports agreed that the local leaders of the party, if not the rank and file, were convinced Tariff Reformers and the Tariff Reform League was clearly determined to have good value for the large sums of money it was spending after 1906. Balfour's policy still stopped short of the full programme but as long as the general belief persisted that this would prove merely a halfway house (so Lord Robert Cecil maintained) 'we should have no chance of recovering our position in Lancashire, nor, I think, in several of the agricultural counties'.[2] Balfour's Birmingham speech of November 1907, however, committed him to the full Tariff Reform policy and, this done, the party organisation was turned against Cecil and his Free Trade friends. As Acland Hood expostulated to one of them when he complained that headquarters were undermining his constituency association: 'Surely you do not suggest that where an Association might be loyal to the Member personally but unwilling to support the Policy advocated by the Leader and accepted by the Party in the Country, the Central Office should give support to that Association?'[3] This position was not taken up in public for another year or so but it was a clear enough indication that in the eyes of the leadership the Free Fooders no longer had a *locus standi*. 'I don't think there is much chance', explained Hood privately, 'of the Free Fooders running men in opposition to Tariff Reform Candidates. Their following is very small, and they have nothing to offer.'[4]

[1] Garvin and Amery, *Life of Joseph Chamberlain*, VI, 637–8, 710.
[2] Cecil to Balfour, 17 January 1907, BP 49737. Throughout this chapter references to 'Cecil' are to Lord Robert not Lord Hugh.
[3] Hood to George Bowles, 30 December 1907, Bowles's copy enc. in Bowles to Cecil, 28 December 1907, CP 51072.   [4] Hood to Sandars, 11 January (1908), BP 49771.

It was, then, the contemptuous attitude of the Conservative leadership – made clear enough when Cromer attempted to negotiate with Lansdowne – which led the Unionist Free Traders to try to strengthen their organisation early in 1908. A fund was collected and the Unionist Free Trade Club set up a committee to see what action might be taken. Feelers were put out towards the Liberals and the possibility of forming a joint organisation with the Free Trade Union was discussed. But the difficulty was 'that joint action in the localities always came in the end to the support of the Liberal candidate'; whereas, far from supporting Liberal policy, the Free Traders' main ambition was by now to 'make the Government realise that Free-trade is not to be undermined by lavish expenditure and bloated taxation'.[1] So that when a member of the Manchester Free Trade League pointed to the useful work it had done in returning Free Trade M.P.s, he had also to admit that since most were Liberal or Labour 'they are now nearly all supporting legislation which must in the end defeat Free-trade'.[2] It was the introduction of old age pensions which unmistakably marked the parting of the ways between economic liberalism and progressivism.

When the Unionist Free Traders came to consider what action they could take the only provincial leaders they found worth consulting with were those in Lancashire. Lord Cromer, the Unionist Free Traders' most distinguished recruit, had become President of the Free Trade League in succession to the Duke of Devonshire, and Tom Garnett insisted that it was most anxious to strengthen the Unionist element he represented. Tootal Broadhurst was brought on to the Unionist Free Trade Club's sub-committee considering the running of candidates. This body agreed to concentrate its efforts upon Lancashire and asked Broadhurst to take steps to form a strong Unionist Free Trade organisation based on Manchester. At this stage, however, matters were precipitated by a by-election in, of all seats, Manchester North West.

Such an election had not been unforeseen. There was a widespread expectation that Churchill would enter the Cabinet sooner or later. Joynson Hicks was again the Conservative candidate and would personally have chosen to conciliate the Free Traders; but he was under heavy pressure from the Chief Whip to fight as a full supporter of Balfour's programme. The Free Traders were more than ready to come to terms with him if he were allowed to fight on the lines he preferred. 'I begin to doubt if we could persuade Unionist Free Traders *not* to vote for J. H. on his address as proposed, even if we wished', commented Broadhurst at one point.[3] And the question of

---

[1] Strachey to Cecil, 26 March 1908, confidential, CP 51158; editorial note on letter from 'Conservative Free-Trader', *Spectator*, 11 April 1908.
[2] Letter from 'Mancunian', *Spectator*, 4 April 1908.
[3] Broadhurst to Strachey, 3 February 1908, Strachey P.

tactics was not far from their minds. From their point of view the best outcome would be for Hicks to show himself amenable and win with their
support. The second best, if Hicks proved obdurate, was for Churchill to
win with their support. But if they could not be on the winning side, then it
was a lesser evil that they should support Hicks even in defeat. The worst
possible outcome would be if they supported Churchill and Joynson Hicks
won without them. This, however, was what happened. Acland Hood still
refused to allow Joynson Hicks any latitude on fiscal policy, and his address,
published on 13 April, committed him to the Birmingham programme,
which he promised to advocate at length at the next General Election. This
was too much for Broadhurst – 'he has failed me', he told Cecil, 'and although
for tactical reasons he will try not to fight on tariff reform, he has made it *an*
issue of the election'.[1] Moreover, since the Tariff Reform League found
Hicks's address sufficient reason to support him the Free Trade League too
applied a fiscal test, asking both candidates the stereotyped question, whether
they favoured a tariff for other than revenue purposes. This could cut only
one way. Broadhurst, as Chairman of the Manchester Free Trade Unionist
Association, organised a Free Trade meeting on the lines of 1906, while
Churchill tried desperately to resurrect the rest of the coalition which had
carried him to victory on that occasion.

Rightly or wrongly, the Unionist Free Traders were considered to hold
the balance. Some of those who had supported Churchill in 1906 now
prepared to vote against him; Broadhurst was accused of playing into the
Tariff Reformers' hands by ensuring that Hicks's election would be claimed
as a Tariff Reform victory. Similarly, E. L. Oliver, a devotee of a centre
party, was prepared to vote against the Government on this occasion although
he hoped that there would be a Unionist Free Trade candidate in every
Lancashire and Cheshire seat at the General Election unless Balfour would
promise to appoint a Royal Commission on Tariff Reform. The great mass
of organised Unionist Free Traders, however, acted up to the Tory description of them as 'the hired assassins of the Radical party'.[2] F. R. B. Lindsell
indicated the nature of their support for Churchill: 'Let there be no doubt
with regard to the relations of Unionist Free-traders with the Liberal party.
We do not love them, they do not care for us. – (Laughter and "Hear,
hear.")'[3]

Churchill's defeat – by four hundred votes – was not an unexpected blow

---

[1] Broadhurst to Cecil, 14 April 1908, CP 51158; and see Hood to Stanley (9 April 1908), *Companion*,
   II, 770–1.
[2] Speech by H. E. Howell, *M.G.*, 20 April 1908. Their dilemma was explored in correspondence in
   both Manchester papers; see esp. letters from Charles Hughes and E. L. Oliver, *M. Courier*,
   21, 23 April 1908.
[3] *M.G.*, 23 April 1908.

to the Free Traders. It is indeed doubtful whether it had much to do with Free Trade. 'The real difficulty of the problem', concluded Sandars, who investigated the outcome for Balfour, 'is that Winston's performance moved the ordinary currents so curiously out of their true course.' The Central Office view was more simple. But for Joynson Hicks's hedging on the Birmingham policy, Hood believed, 'the majority would have been four figures, and his manœuvres really spoilt the enthusiasm which a straightforward policy would have engendered'.[1] Not only, then, did this become the received opinion in official quarters, but the action of the Manchester Free Traders had 'roused the bitterest feelings'[2] among Conservatives generally. In 1906 they had not been loved but they had been feared; now, fighting on their own ground, they had shown themselves not only disloyal but impotent.

For the rest of that year the Unionist Free Traders did what they could to secure their position. Frank Calvert was now ready to stand for Preston and the Hornby influence was relied upon to keep Blackburn in line; although Broadhurst refused to stand himself, his associates in Manchester North West hoped to run a candidate at the General Election, and the possibility of St Loe Strachey, the editor of the *Spectator*, fighting another Manchester seat was explored. By Christmas 1908, however, the progressive bent of the Government's policy was giving them solid reasons for making their peace with official Conservatism, Tariff Reform and all. Cromer prognosticated that 'the next Budget will not only constitute a turning point in our fiscal policy, but will also rather tend to crystallise party lines'.[3] And Strachey, believing it to be certain that the Government would be defeated at the next General Election, thought it was 'also certain whether our leader advises it or not, that the bulk of the Unionist Free Traders will vote against the government, socialism and a single Chamber. Tactically, therefore, it is of very great importance that we should have the right to claim a share in that victory.'[4] Conversely, Cecil looked for an opportunity to warn the Government

that they cannot expect the support of moderate men if they go in for wild cat finance. To me it seems that both Liberals & Tariff Reformers imagine that provided taxes are imposed for the purposes of social reform they are no longer a burden on the taxpayer or that the burden can be shifted on to the foreigner or the millionaire.[5]

Hitherto, for men in Cecil's position, it had been the quasi-religious issues which divided them from Liberalism, whereas they had broadly accepted

[1] Sandars to Balfour, 1 May 1908, BP 49765.
[2] Walter Long to Cecil, 24 April 1908, CP 51072.
[3] Cromer to Cecil, Christmas Day 1908, CP 51072.
[4] Memorandum by Strachey, 29 December 1908, CP 51158.
[5] Cecil to Cromer, 5 January 1909, copy, CP 51072.

287

the Liberals' economics; now that economic issues were coming to the forefront their disagreements with the Government became more fundamental
than ever.

But just at the point when a rapprochement with Unionism seemed
imminent, the Free Traders found that the terms demanded of them were
made stiffer. In January 1909 it was announced that the Central Office would
deny official support to candidates who could not accept the Birmingham
programme and a blacklist of those M.P.s who fell under this ban was
published. As amended, this list named ten Members who hoped to stand
again, including George Bowles and Robert Cecil, and five retiring members,
including Sir Harry Hornby (though not Sir Francis Powell); and among a
further five described as doubtful was John Rutherford. This step, Bonar Law
told Salvidge, 'will inevitably have the effect, without making any fuss
about it, of bringing candidates into line on this question'.[1] For the Unionist
Free Traders it was a singular blow. The Liberals were sounded out again
but the terms they offered were hardly likely to have improved. Once more
the only practicable course of action was to strengthen their own organisation. As for running Unionist Free Trade candidates, Cecil was well aware
that all they could hope for was 'a dozen or more forlorn hopes', since even
this required 'a fairly strong local backing and this seems to exist hardly
anywhere'.[2] This was realistic if not encouraging. Hornby, whom the
Guardian once referred to as 'the most unmistakable Unionist Free-trader
in public life',[3] was an old man who had lost the will to control events even
in his native Blackburn. The only other provincial Unionist Free Trade
leader of any standing, Tootal Broadhurst, was not the man to galvanise
Hornby or anybody else. Not only was he 'plainly funking the prospect of
any fighting', but he was 'very doubtful if his Manchester U.F.T. friends
would rise to it'.[4] The membership of Broadhurst's Unionist Free Trade
Association was only about seventy and he could not believe that the limited
action to which the Free Traders' strategy was restricted could be effective.
He told Cecil: 'You say that the vital thing is that we should organize. Yes,
but what puzzles me so much now is, – to what end is such organization to
be used?'[5] Short of threatening to bring out a candidate in every Lancashire
seat he did not expect the Unionist Free Traders to be taken seriously. In
the spring of 1909 moves were nonetheless made investigating the possibility
of an arrangement with the Manchester Conservatives, whereby the two

[1] Law to Salvidge, 28 January 1909, Salvidge, *Salvidge of Liverpool*, p. 83. The list was published
in the *Morning Post* of 18 January 1909; on 20 January 1909 two names were withdrawn.
[2] Cecil to Strachey, 4 February 1909, Strachey P.; memorandum, n.d., CP 51075.
[3] *M.G.*, 8 October 1909.
[4] E. G. Brunker to Cecil, 23 February 1909, CP 51072.
[5] Broadhurst to Cecil, 22 March 1909, CP 51159.

divisions (Manchester South and Salford South) where there was no Conservative candidate should adopt Free Traders who in return would support the Tariff Reform candidates in the other divisions. But this was an unrealistic bargain, and the threat that otherwise the Unionist Free Traders would run three or four candidates including one in Manchester North West was unlikely to be carried out. As Cromer had predicted, the Budget tended 'to crystallise party lines'. Broadhurst told Cecil:

That the more I think of, and the more I discuss with friends, the Budget proposals, the more do I realize the difficulties it has raised for Unionist Free Traders. It will make it more difficult than ever to oppose the Unionist Party on what are practically Budget proposals.

If, as is the case, we don't approve of their Budget and its ruinous proposals, we must be confronted with the question, as indeed I have already been, 'Then what are your methods of raising the necessary monies?' and it will be awfully difficult to return candidates who are avowedly going to oppose the Unionist Budget (whenever it may be produced) as that will imply some approval of their so called 'Free Trade Budget'.[1]

V

It was clear by the autumn of 1909 that the Unionist Free Traders would be in no position to offer an independent challenge at the coming General Election. The Unionist Free Trade Club was on its last legs. For a small remnant, Free Trade still outweighed other considerations. Arthur Elliot, for instance, found that the Lords' rejection of the Budget plus the Conservative leaders' protectionism 'form together too big a *bolus* for me to swallow'. But the larger body was that which now prepared to retreat back to Conservatism. 'Nothing will ever persuade me', wrote Strachey, 'that predatory Socialism plus demagoguey of the most reckless and unscrupulous description are not worse than tariff reform.'[2] The Free Traders were everywhere drawing in their horns. In Manchester North West the Cecils helped heal the rift between the Free Traders and Joynson Hicks – 'we have been coming to it gradually during the past 12 months', Broadhurst admitted, 'and the recent speeches of certain Ministers have put on the finishing touch – at the same time it is all rather hateful, and I cannot say that I feel like taking any active part in the coming election, but rather to quietly record my votes.'[3] In Blackburn as well the Free Traders were trying to patch up the succession to Hornby. John Rutherford, sitting for the neighbouring division of Darwen, helped to persuade the Blackburn Con-

---

[1] Broadhurst to Cecil, 8 May 1909, CP 51159; cf. memorandum of his interviews with Percy Woodhouse and Sir William Vaudrey, copy, 4 May 1909, CP 51071.
[2] Elliot to Cromer, 29 September 1909; Strachey to H. Cecil, 30 October 1909, Strachey P.
[3] Broadhurst to Cecil, 15 October 1909, CP 51159.

289

servative Association to take George Bowles as one candidate with the aid of the good offices of Cecil. R. A. Yerburgh too used his influence there to smooth things over. Yerburgh, indeed, who was once more candidate for Chester, was a notable trimmer; a Unionist Free Trader of sorts at the previous election, Lord Hugh Cecil had considered that he deserved the epithet 'Mr Pliable' in 1907; and his response to the test of orthodoxy laid down in January 1909 was to affirm: 'I am now, as I have always been, a supporter of Mr Balfour's policy...Mr Balfour is a Free-trader.'[1] Little trouble, then, for Yerburgh at Chester; and his hope of securing Lord Robert Cecil himself for Blackburn was unexpectedly realised before October was out. Although the Blackburn Conservative Association was committed to Tariff Reform, the Hornby faction, represented by the old-fashioned Free Traders Henry Lewis and J. H. Hartley, was conciliated by the adoption of Cecil and Bowles as official candidates, probably because at this late stage they were by far the most able men available to take on a far from hopeful contest.[2]

In November 1909 the Conference of the National Union was held at Manchester and its new President, Lord Derby, whose reluctance to accept Tariff Reform was well known, affirmed now that he had always been ready to follow Balfour 'with blind devotion', and added in an important passage:

What I did ask the Chairman of the Lancashire branch was that great latitude should be given to those who at the first outset could not see eye to eye with us... To-day, thousands of men who might have been driven out of the party are now running breast high for fiscal reform, and I think I may state with confidence that there will not be a single seat in Lancashire uncontested at the general election by men who will support that principle. If they do not support it they will not get in. – (Applause.) But let me say that while I did plead for latitude I plead for it no longer.[3]

Derby's insistence that candidates should accept the principle of Tariff Reform somewhat embarrassed those who like Cecil and Bowles could only go as far as retaliation. A further indication of the way the wind was blowing came with the annual meeting of the Free Trade League in December. The Budget, explained T. W. Killick, had put the League in a new position and one of the objects in its rules, 'to persuade the electors to vote only for Free-trade candidates for Parliament', now no longer expressed the priorities of many members. 'The League, therefore', Killick proceeded, 'is faced with this dilemma, either it must expect the resignation of many Unionist

---

[1] Hugh Cecil to Balfour, 4–6 May 1907, BP 49759; letter from Yerburgh to Blackburn Conservative party, *M.G.*, 23 January 1909.
[2] For the contest at Blackburn in January 1910 see Clarke, 'British Politics and Blackburn Politics', pp. 320–3.
[3] *M.G.*, 18 November 1909.

members or it must alter the rules.'[1] By altering the rules and confining itself thereafter to educational work the League bowed to necessity and voted itself into obscurity. The Free Trade Union had hitherto kept out of Lancashire. By this time, however, it had enlisted those Unionist Free Traders like Arthur Elliot and Lords Balfour of Burleigh and James of Hereford, who were prepared to work with the Liberals. Its Lancashire branch took over the political work which the League had performed previously, though what with Garnett's own sympathies and the Presidency passing from Cromer to James, the League still did as much as it dared. Less inhibited, the Union determined to take an active part in the elections in north and east Lancashire and established its headquarters at Preston. Its denials that it was a Liberal organisation, though technically true, had a rather hollow ring.

Preston was the scene of the only independent Free Trade candidature. Harold Cox had lost sympathy with the Government over old age pensions and from the beginning of 1909 at least had been working with the Unionist Free Traders. Indeed, Strachey was privately raising subscriptions for his election fund. This must have left Frank Calvert looking for a *casus belli* with the Liberal Association, and when, at the end of October 1909 they selected as their candidate in his place the former Unionist Free Trader Sir John Gorst, he seized his chance. This action, wrote Calvert, 'appears to me to treat with open contempt the consistency of those who, like myself, have remained Unionist as well as Free Traders when that particular quality has been of the greatest service to the cause we support in common.'[2] Calvert explained that although Cox could not, as Lord Cromer and others wished, be run as the candidate of the Free Trade League, he would support his independent candidature, and added that 'if Mr Cox had not come out under these circumstances, I would have done so myself (Cheers)'.[3] The hopes that had at one stage been pinned upon Calvert were now, therefore, transferred to Cox who, although he stood as an independent Liberal, was both acceptable to and accepted by the Unionist Free Traders. Cox could fairly point back to the warnings he had given in 1906. 'Everybody knows I stood primarily as a Free Trader', he said, 'and that I approached all the political questions from the Free Trade point of view.'[4] Cox received the support of old-fashioned Liberals like Alderman Ord and Lord Ribblesdale, unconventional Liberals like Hilaire Belloc and Richard Cavendish, prominent Unionist Free Traders like Cromer, Balfour of Burleigh and Hugh

[1] *M.G.*, 17 December 1909.
[2] Calvert's letter to the Liberal Association of 30 October 1909, *Lancs. D.P.*, 29 November 1909. Strachey's role is clear from his papers.
[3] Speech by Calvert, *Lancs. D.P.*, 25 November 1909.
[4] Cox at his adoption meeting, *Lancs. D.P.*, 25 November 1909.

Cecil, and local Free Traders who had supported the Liberals in 1906 like H. H. Owtram and Henry Bell. Cox in fact represented the policy that the Free Traders would have liked to cleave to: *laissez faire* pure and simple, as unadulterated by social reform as by Tariff Reform. Like the *Spectator*, he sought to teach the electorate that 'wasteful public expenditure means private loss'.[1] Little wonder that a visiting Liberal speaker called him 'one of the most reactionary of reactionaries that ever sat upon the Liberal benches in the House of Commons'. Cox, on the other hand, justified his stand in terms of his belief that 'the large number of Free Traders of Preston were either Conservatives or moderate Liberals'.[2] But he finished well down on the poll: not a very impressive result for a candidate who had powerful local Unionist Free Trade backing and a claim on Liberal loyalties as well.

At Blackburn Cecil and Bowles preached a policy different only in emphasis from the Balfour policy; and although those local Conservatives who hankered after Free Trade, like Henry Lewis, J. H. Hartley and Sir Harry Hornby, gave them ready support, their campaign had more than a taint of Tariff Reform about it. Their differences with their party were a source of weakness rather than strength; they fought in almost complete isolation from their fellow candidates; only F. E. Smith would go to Blackburn to help them; and after their defeat they left immediately instead of staying to help in the county divisions as was the normal practice. Why were they not involved in the Darwen campaign? After all, meetings for the Darwen outvoters were held in Blackburn itself. Did not Rutherford share their fiscal views? The last thing Rutherford wanted was any discussion of his attitude to Tariff Reform; although it was 'understood' that he was a Free Fooder he had kept his position wrapped in obscurity for years now. On his adoption he let fall some generalities about supporting Balfour in any measure to enlarge British markets but would say no more and a few days later was parrying tricky questions with aplomb.

Questioner: 'How would you raise the money for old-age pensions?'
Rutherford: 'My answer to that is very obvious. I would have to ask the gentleman to put me in power before I begin to raise it.'[3]

Sandars described Rutherford to Balfour as 'perhaps one of the few men, if not the only man, who stood as a Unionist candidate with avowed leanings to Free Trade', and he found his defeat in a seat that had not gone Liberal in 1906 'interesting'.[4] Among other candidates who had at some time been Free

---

[1] 'An Alternative Budget', *Spectator*, 31 July 1909.
[2] E. G. Hemmerde at Preston, Cox's reply, *Lancs. D.P.*, 6, 7 January 1910.
[3] *N.D.T.*, 20 December 1909.
[4] Sandars to Balfour, 26 January 1910, BP 49766.

Fooders, Yerbergh's accession to the ranks of the Tariff Reformers was proclaimed by the *Manchester Courier* upon his adoption at Chester; and Gershom Stewart the candidate for the Wirral, who had once corresponded with Cecil about his difficulty in accepting Tariff Reform, was now happily taking his stand against the Budget.

Elsewhere, among the rank and file, the movement was the same. In Leigh, for instance, the President of the Atherton Conservative Club who had hitherto regarded himself as a Free Trader now said that Free Trade was not the good cause he had thought it was; at Preston the cotton manufacturer Arthur Smith declared that he had come to the conclusion that Free Trade was 'played out'; at Clitheroe William Garnett, a former Liberal leader and an uncle of Tom Garnett, announced his conversion to Tariff Reform; at Warrington John Crosfield, a brother of the Liberal candidate, seceded to the Conservatives. And there were other cases of prominent businessmen reconsidering their fiscal views in the light of the Budget; as was said in the Manchester Chamber of Commerce, it 'amounted to a revolt of income-tax payers'.[1] One of the most notable defections was that of James Watts, head of a big Manchester firm of warehousemen, who went away during the election rather than vote against the Budget.[2]

In Manchester there were cross currents. Although Tootal Broadhurst promised to vote for the Conservative candidate in Manchester South,[3] it is doubtful whether he took any part at all in the North West contest. North West was a case apart. Both sides set such store by its verdict that politics there had become frozen in the pattern of 1906 when Free Trade or Tariff Reform was the overriding question. Joynson Hicks was by now a straight-forward Tariff Reformer. 'I am not a Protectionist but I want fair dealing', he asseverated in a style altogether more robust than his previous evasions.[4] His opponent, however, was no firebrand but the eminently respectable George Kemp, now knighted, whom the Liberals had enticed back to public life in order to champion Free Trade. Kemp was a Unionist Free Trader in the strictest sense; for him neither the Union nor Free Trade was in any way negotiable. Just as over the Indian import duties in 1895 he had used

[1] Redford, *Manchester Merchants and Foreign Trade*, II, 105. For the above examples see speech by Capt. E. Fletcher at Atherton, *M. Courier*, 8 January 1910; letter from Arthur Smith, *Lancs. D.P.*, 13 January 1910; message from William Garnett to Conservative meeting at Low Moor, *Standard*, 13 January 1910. See also speeches by C. F. Critchley and John Whittaker in Accrington, *N.D.T.*, 21, 23 December 1909; reports of secession of John Garner and Henry Seddon at Northwich, *L. Courier*, 18 January 1910; announcement of conversion of C. J. Robinson and N. Clegg in speech by A. G. O'Neill at Middleton, *M. Courier*, 16 November 1909; letter from William Bolton of Widnes, announcing secession, *L. Courier*, 24 January 1910; list of Liberal seceders, *M. Courier*, 15 January 1910.
[2] Statement by Humphrey Watts, *M. Courier*, 13 January 1910.
[3] Announcement by Ward Jackson, Manchester South, *M. Courier*, 8 January 1910.
[4] Speech by Joynson Hicks, *M.G.*, 4 January 1910.

Free Trade against the Liberals, so now he was prepared to do battle on their side. But his principles had undergone no modification. 'He is', wrote Scott, 'exactly the type of the substantial, capable business man of high local standing and moderate views who attracts the confidence and disarms the opposition of the employing class and at the same time his great personal popularity gives him a strong hold on the mass of the constituency.'[1] He was, then, a formidable candidate of a certain kind, not least because he was a former Lancashire county cricketer. A comment of 1910 captures him perfectly: 'He was a rattling good free bat. As a democrat he is somewhat of a stonewaller.'[2] The choice of Kemp dictated the tenor of the campaign. When Leo Maxse came to speak for Hicks he called Kemp 'a milk-and-water moderate put up in that division to capture the milk-and-water vote'.[3] And the Liberals virtually admitted as much. At his adoption meeting they spoke in hushed tones of that 'very fine type of business man' Sir William Houldsworth, the division's previous Conservative M.P., to whom Kemp would provide so suitable a successor. Reassurance was all. The Liberal Chairman was Samuel Lamb, described by the *Courier* as 'an exceedingly conservative politician of the Mesopotamic brand', who acted as 'the self-constituted Manchester School henchman of the quite aristocratic and anything but proletarian Sir George Kemp'. And although there was no Broadhurst or Lindsell to organise the Unionist Free Traders, and Francis Ashworth (the new President of the Chamber of Commerce) also stood aside, some men like E. H. Langdon (his predecessor) were still prepared to come on to a Liberal platform, and the canvassers apparently found that many electors who had had no hesitation in declaring their intention to vote Conservative in the by-election were now 'doubtful'. As the poll drew near it was almost like old times to find J. A. Hutton moving a vote of confidence in Kemp. 'It is', he said, 'rather a strange resolution for a Conservative to move. (Loud cheers and cries of "Bravo".) There are some times when you must sink your party. – (Hear, hear.) I am a Free-trader first and other things afterwards. (Hear, hear.)'[4] The same could have been said of Kemp himself; and there were enough men of that ilk to reverse the verdict of the by-election and restore the seat, in name at least, to Liberalism.

VI

Because Free Trade had been overshadowed by the Budget in January 1910 many Free Traders had voted for a party now committed to Tariff Reform. But in the one seat, Manchester North West, which was generally held to

---

[1] Scott to Elibank, 20 July 1910, copy, MGP.
[2] Harry Beswick, *Clarion*, 2 December 1910.
[3] Speech by Leo Maxse, *M.G.*, 12 January 1910.   [4] *M.G.*, 14 January 1910.

have a unique influence over the results in Lancashire as a whole Free Trade had carried the day. Since the Tariff Reformers made no secret of their belief that if they could but capture Lancashire victory was near, the pivotal importance of Manchester North West more than ever impressed itself upon the party managers on both sides. Scott himself had been pressed to act as Kemp's chairman in the January election and had declined on account of other commitments; but from this time on he found himself increasingly drawn into the division's activities and was to be chairman there in the next two elections. In June 1910 he learnt that Kemp did not intend to stand again. Scott wrote to him immediately urging him to hold his hand. Kemp's retirement would, he said, 'be nothing less than disastrous', and he argued that the fact that Kemp was not 'altogether with the party that returns you on all points' did not preclude 'an honourable cooperation'.[1]

Kemp's disinclination to continue in public life on account of the heavy claims of his business was well understood, but Scott hoped that if the Whips could hold out some prospect of office Kemp might be persuaded to reconsider. 'Kemp is essential to us in Manchester,' he told the Master of Elibank.[2] Elibank fully realised the importance of what was at stake and, after the Prime Minister had been brought in, Kemp at least proposed no further action for the time being. 'We want him not for one election or for two elections but permanently', Scott had written. This, however, was to ask too much and the most that could he hoped for was a little time. It seems indeed that North West had another candidate in view should the worst come to the worst; but when that autumn it was revealed that the Conservative candidate would be none other than Bonar Law, Elibank made a final effort with Kemp, promising him a peerage the next year if he would fight once more.[3]

The Liberal candidature, then, was arranged by manœuvres in which the highest echelons of the party were closely implicated. No less was true of the Conservative candidature. In August 1910 Edward Goulding of the Tariff Reform League broached to Bonar Law the idea of his contesting North West. 'Unless we win Lancs', he wrote, 'we are not coming back and your candidature would win Manchester and enable Lancs constituencies to be

---

[1] Scott to Kemp, 18 June 1910, copy, MGP.
[2] Scott to Elibank, 20 July 1910, copy, MGP.
[3] Kemp's record of this meeting in the Whips' room deserves to be quoted in full:
  'I said I could not stand = successor chosen. M of E – If business prevents close connexion would you care to keep in touch with politics by being in H of L – *yes*, but I must leave during 1911 – because of business. M of E – I don't promise it at Coronation, but at any rate within year. G.K. – I could not promise to stay longer. M of E agreed – and said even if B.L. victorious promise holds good. M of E – One thing more – try and be sympathetic to Irish. G.K. – I will but you know my views.
  M of E – *Don't say word to anyone of this.* (Grey Haldane know of this.)'
  (Kemp's draft of a letter to the Prime Minister, n.d. (March–April 1912), MGP.)

won.'[1] Although Balfour had qualms when told of the plan, he assured Derby that he regarded Lancashire as 'the very key and centre of the next electoral battle-field'.[2] With Derby's promise that another seat could be found for Law should he fail, Balfour pressed the invitation upon him. Law was willing enough in principle but wished to have a realistic notion of his chances. He therefore arranged that the matter should stand over until after a meeting he was to address in Manchester on 8 November.

This meeting effectively represented the start of the campaign in North West, although at the time Law spoke only as an eminent visitor. Never before had any Tariff Reformer taken the war to the Manchester businessmen in this style.[3] 'There is – we all recognise it – a strong and widespread feeling', Law admitted, 'that whatever might be the case in regard to other industries Tariff Reform would ruin the cotton trade.' This he sought to dispel. Moreover, he refused to accept that the problems facing the industry could not be understood by outsiders (although in the process he can be held to have provided a demonstration of just this):

You know that these gentlemen who know all about the cotton trade – (laughter) – speak as if it were a sublime mystery known only to themselves about the fine counts which are spun in Lancashire. We all know that Lancashire has been driven more and more to spinning fine counts. But what advantage is that to the working men of Lancashire unless the employment in the trade as a whole has increased by that change in the nature of the goods?

Austen Chamberlain called this speech 'a splendid & convincing perform-ance',[4] but there was an answer to it and this Kemp gave two days later. Battle had been joined. Although Law was warned off by at least one prominent Conservative voter in the division, there was no going back. Law accepted the invitation to become the candidate and was adopted on 21 November. Having impressed himself upon the constituency as a Tariff Reformer, the rest of his campaign was spent in trying to broaden his appeal. In speech after speech he stressed his claims as a man who had spent the best years of his life in business and made a particular appeal to those voters 'who considered that the policy of the Unionist party, even with Tariff Reform which they dislike, is better than the policy represented by Lloyd-Georgeism, which they have reason to dislike much more – (Cheers.)'[5] These were just the kind of men whom Kemp had been put up to reassure, and he did his best. 'Our opponents', he said with *gravitas*, 'make the charge

---

[1] Goulding to Law, 4 August 1910, BLP 21/3/10.
[2] Balfour to Derby, 6 October 1910, copy, BP 49743.
[3] The only parallel is Joseph Chamberlain's Preston speech of 1905. Law's speech is taken from *M.G.*, 9 November 1910.
[4] A. Chamberlain to Law, 12 November 1910, BLP 18/6/131.
[5] Law at Cheetham, *M.G.*, 26 November 1910.

that we are trying to carry out a revolution. Well, I am not a revolutionary. – (Laughter.)' He claimed further that since Law was the chief champion of Tariff Reform, 'it would be the most disastrous blow to the Free Trade movement imaginable if the citadel were to fall at the coming election'.[1] The odd Unionist Free Trader was duly produced at his meetings, and Sir Ernest Hatch (whose commitment to Liberalism was surely of long enough standing by this time?) was also pressed into this role. But right from the start the more representative men were supporting Law.

Despite this, Edward Marsden, the editor of the *Textile Mercury*, was not satisfied with the progress that Law had made, and on 26 November telegraphed J. L. Garvin of the *Observer* asking him to advocate that any Tariff Reform proposals should be submitted to a referendum.[2] He told Law of what he had done and, somewhat unexpectedly, Law was prepared to ask Balfour to consider the idea. Yet this was not a panic move; Law declared that 'if anything, I am more hopeful than when I came'.[3] Was it rather that having altruistically embarked upon a forlorn hope – 'morally you could not lose', was how Garvin himself had urged him on[4] – he now sensed that the Free Trade businessmen were teetering on the brink? With one more push might they not fall into his arms? Within the next few days Balfour was due to speak at the Albert Hall in London and Rosebery at the Free Trade Hall in Manchester. What would be the effect in Manchester if Balfour agreed to submit Tariff Reform to a referendum and Rosebery were to endorse this, Law was asked by Sandars, who was working hand in glove with Garvin and desperately wanted the right sort of testimony to lay before his chief. Law replied by telegram on the morning of Balfour's speech. He had doubts about the practicability of such a scheme and it was an article of faith among Tariff Reformers that the working class was favourable to them. But the statement in his telegram that 'all wealthy unionists even strong tariff reformers would say such declaration would mean victory'[5] clearly reflected the opinion of his Manchester entourage. After Balfour had given his pledge Law set about eliminating Tariff Reform altogether from the contest. Sir Edward Donner told a Liberal meeting: 'It reminded him of the king of Israel who, before meeting the enemy, said to his allies, "I will disguise myself and enter into the battle." (Laughter.)'[6]

When the Unionist Free Trade Club had broken up those of its members who could not work with the Liberals had, with Cromer at their head,

[1] Kemp speech, *M.G.*, 24 November 1910.
[2] For this episode see Gollin, *The 'Observer' and J. L. Garvin*, pp. 257–66.
[3] Law to Balfour, 26 November 1910, copy, BLP 18/8/14.
[4] Garvin to Law, 10 August 1910, BLP 21/3/12.
[5] Law telegram to Sandars, 29 November 1910, BP 49693.
[6] *M.G.*, 2 December 1910.

founded the Constitutional Free Trade Association. Early in the General Election this body issued a manifesto calling upon all men of moderate views to vote Unionist; it was signed, as well as by Cromer and the Cecils, by men like Lord Balfour of Burleigh and Lord Avebury, whose position at the previous election had been, to say the least, equivocal. This caused more than a ripple in Manchester and a statement calling attention to it was signed by many of the leading Unionist Free Traders.[1] When Rosebery came to address a 'non-party' meeting in the Free Trade Hall on 30 November most of these men were on the platform. By this time, of course, the famous referendum pledge had been given and Rosebery duly proclaimed it satisfactory. It is interesting, in view of his refusal earlier in the election to speak for any candidates, to see that Sir Alfred Hopkinson, the Vice-Chancellor of Manchester University, took the chair,[2] and he was joined on the platform by his brothers John and Edward. That night, too, five of the six Conservative candidates in Manchester took their stand upon Balfour's pledge. Arthur Taylor, however, the candidate in the working-class North East division, repudiated it saying that 'he wanted to sail under no false colours', and believed Tariff Reform to be the solution to unemployment.[3]

Now it is true that much of the former hostility to Tariff Reform had already been broken down among men who were determined to stay with the Conservative party. The Conservative candidate at Oldham, A. E. Wrigley, confessed that four years previously he had believed that Free Trade was the best policy for the cotton industry but believed it no longer. At Darwen John Rutherford too admitted that he had 'made some advancement on the fiscal question'. The only Conservative candidate to stand out in any respect was Colonel Hesketh at Bolton who, while asking for 'a free hand' over Tariff Reform asked Tariff Reformers 'to support him as a general supporter of Mr Balfour, in the same way that he rendered loyal support to Tariff Reformers when they happened to be candidates (Hear, hear.)'.[4] And there were other indications that Tariff Reform was no longer an electoral liability. In Manchester North an employers' manifesto with 44 signatures showed that nearly all the leading employers in the division now accepted Tariff Reform; at Warrington two former Liberal leaders defected and embraced Tariff Reform.[5]

[1] *M. Courier*, 25 November, 2 December 1910.
[2] Cf. his letter, *M. Courier*, 26 November 1910.
[3] Comments by all Conservative candidates on the pledge, *M. Courier*, 1 December 1910.
[4] Speeches by A. E. Wrigley at Oldham, *M. Courier*, 29 November 1910; Rutherford at Darwen, *Lancs. D.P.*, 26 November 1910; Hesketh at Bolton, *Bolton Chron.*, 26 November 1910; cf. speech by R. A. Yerburgh at Blackburn, *Lancs. D.P.*, 10 November 1910; interview with Robert Clayton, *Blackburn Gazette*, 26 November 1910.
[5] Manchester manifesto, *M. Courier*, 2 December 1910; defection of W. Furniss and E. England, *L. Courier*, 2 December 1910.

The typical Conservative reaction was nonetheless to welcome the referendum pledge. Almost everywhere it had the effect, not of transforming the situation but of accelerating a pre-existing tendency for Free Traders to throw in their lot with the Conservatives. In Liverpool the Liberals had won both the business divisions in 1906. In January 1910, however, Seely lost his seat at Abercromby; and Muspratt, making the customary visit of a newly-elected Member to the Exchange newsroom, was howled down by the commercial men in an unprecedented demonstration of hostility. As he conceded later, 'he did not claim that the majority of the business men of Exchange Division voted for him at the last election'.[1] The Conservatives were determined this time to capture Exchange too, and they did their best to exploit Muspratt's difficulties in appealing to both the Irish and the businessmen. On 24 November, five days before Balfour's Albert Hall speech, Sir William Forwood, the most respected of the Liverpool Unionist Free Traders, wrote to Salvidge in the same vein as the Cromer manifesto, and as the days went by other Unionist Free Traders did likewise. A letter from Robert Gladstone – who was not only one of the Liverpool Gladstones himself but had married a niece of the Grand Old Man – affirmed that while he was still strongly in favour of Free Trade he supported Leslie Scott, the Conservative candidate. All the Conservatives were conciliatory and Colonel Chaloner in Abercromby went so far as to offer his own referendum pledge unofficially on the same night that Balfour spoke. The Liberals were badly shaken by Balfour's speech. 'I am afraid now', said one, 'that Bonar Law will win North West Manchester, and that Max Muspratt is an absolute goner.'[2] There were fears in the Liberal camp for those voters who had revolted over the land taxes in the Abercromby division at the previous election, and at a meeting at the Junior Reform Club they were warned of the perils of assisting the return of a Tory Government. As the *Courier* commented, not unjustly: 'It must have been humiliating to the party leaders that the Chairman should have to make a special appeal to Liverpool members of a Liberal club to "Vote Liberal this time".'[3] One leading Liberal had already declared that he had been 'compelled by stern conviction to part company with the party to which I had so long belonged', on account of its tendency towards socialism.[4] Exchange fell to the Conservatives by a small majority, and although the *Daily Post* concluded from this that the strength of the Unionist Free Traders had not been very great, in Abercromby, where the Liberals were again defeated, their candidate

---

[1] Report of the newsroom visit and speech by Muspratt, *L. Courier*, 20 January, 23 November 1910.
[2] *L. Courier*, 1 December 1910.
[3] Speech by R. T. Barnes and comment, *L. Courier*, 2, 3 December 1910.
[4] Letter from Thomas Utley, *L. Courier*, 30 November 1910.

asserted that he had received 'no support whatever from the business community of Liverpool'.[1]

Those Liberals who had come to the end of their patience with the Government were not likely to wait upon such flimsy inducements as the referendum pledge before seceding. A number of prominent men had already broken with the party on account of its socialistic tendency.[2] But the Albert Hall declaration was at least the occasion if not the cause of other changes of heart. In Blackburn the Tariff Reform candidates already had the support of Free Traders like Henry Lewis, but on 1 December Sir Harry Hornby himself appeared on their platform amidst scenes of great enthusiasm.[3] In Preston the pledge marked the reunion of the Conservative party since both Frank Calvert and Harold Cox were satisfied by it. 'In advising others', said Calvert, 'he had to speak as a sort of trustee, representing a great number of people; but he said that any Free Trader was perfectly safe in voting for the Conservative party. (Cheers.)'[4] And there were similar incidents in other constituencies. At Hyde, for instance, Oswald Carver ordered the removal of Liberal hoardings from his mill and, speaking from a Conservative platform, told his audience that his principles on Free Trade and religion were the same as they had always been, 'but the principles of the Liberal Party were not remaining the same (Applause)'.[5]

In the one contest upon which all eyes were fixed, however, the Conservatives were beaten. Sir George Kemp was again elected for Manchester North West. The supreme efforts of the Liberals were rewarded. 'Though I don't think we could have won with another candidate', wrote Kemp's agent to Scott, 'it is just as true to say we could not have won with another chairman or another paper than the Manchester Guardian.'[6] It had been a near run thing. Derby gave Law his opinion 'that large as was your majority in the banking & business part of the town – the majority in the foreign Jew quarter was too strong for us'.[7] There was no doubt but that Law had in-

[1] *Liverpool D.P.*, 6 December 1910; speech by F. C. Bowring after the poll, *L. Courier*, 6 December 1910.
[2] For R. H. Prestwich see letters from him and Sam Luke, *M.G.*, 2, 3, 5 December 1910; for E. W. Johnson see *M. Courier*, 30 November 1910; J. C. Cheetham's letter to Conservative meeting at Crompton, *M. Courier*, 30 November 1910 and comment by Alfred Emmott at Shaw, *Oldham Chron.*, 3 December 1910; letter from John Watson, M.L.F. Minutes, 13 December 1910; speech by George Crosfield at Warrington, *M.G.*, 28 November 1910.
[3] Lewis at Conservative adoption meeting, *Blackburn Gazette*, 26 November 1910; Hornby's reappearance, *N.D.T.*, 2 December 1910.
[4] Speech by Calvert, *Lancs. D.P.*, 2 December 1910.
[5] Speech by Carver at Marple, *M. Courier*, 6 December 1910; cf. speech by Bellhouse, *M. Courier*, 1 December 1910; letter from T. C. Horsfall, *M.G.*, 26 November 1910 and speech at Macclesfield, *M. Courier*, 9 December 1910; letter from Francis Ashworth to Sykes, *M. Courier*, 13 December 1910; leader on Altrincham and Darwen, *Lancs. D.P.*, 10 December 1910.
[6] E. C. Pearson to Scott, 5 December 1910, MGP.
[7] Derby to Law, 4 December 1910, BLP 21/3/18; cf. leader, *M. Courier*, 5 December 1910.

creased his stature by the contest. 'You didn't win your own constituency', F. E. Smith told him, 'but you nearly won all Manchester which would have been stupendous.'[1] And Scott told him (or so Law recalled) 'that he had lost our votes but won our respect, to which he answered he would have preferred the votes'.[2] Although Law had lost in North West, then, it was under circumstances which were hardly likely to be repeated. The Lancashire Conservatives owed him a huge debt of gratitude (on which the petulant Derby nonetheless tried to renege, not even providing the alternative constituency which he had promised). Law had played a notable part in reconciling to Conservatism those Free Traders for whom the golden days of Unionism had seemed to end in 1903. 'More than one of those who ordinarily hold aloof from politics', one of his supporters told him, 'has said that your visit has elevated the tone of M'chester Unionism & that a longer stay would win for you the complete confidence of Lancashire. No Unionist leaders save Lord Salisbury & Sir M. Hicks Beach have won such a place in the respect of the shrewd practical Manchester man.'[3] No doubt it said something about Law – but surely more about the Free Traders? – that by 1910 an unashamed Tariff Reformer could be greeted in the citadel of Free Trade as the new Hicks Beach.

VII

Ostensibly the Conservative party had re-established its unity (and gained a few recruits into the bargain) because of its conversion to Tariff Reform. But in reality cause and effect were reversed. The party had learnt the lesson of unity and so would loyally accept the Tariff Reform proposals – or indeed any alternative policy that the leadership from time to time put in their place. The unanimity with which the party acquiesced in the 'first constructive policy' in January 1910 was impressive, but no more impressive than the unanimity with which, at a moment's notice, it agreed virtually to eliminate this policy as an issue from the General Election of December 1910. The next few years were to illustrate how completely fiscal convictions were to be sacrificed to considerations of party loyalty: a loyalty, then, which was plainly founded upon other things. Derby, for all his affirmation in November 1909 that he asked for 'latitude' no longer, had never had much faith in either the practical or electoral merits of Tariff Reform. But when he threatened to rock the boat, so firm a Free Trader as Lord Hugh Cecil had to warn him that public dissension was 'a worse and more unpopular thing than even food taxes'. 'We must not get back to the situation of 1904 and

---

[1] Smith to Law, 3 January (1911), BLP 18/7/151.
[2] Scott's interview notes, 6 December 1922, quoted in Hammond, *C. P. Scott*, p. 291.
[3] H. W. Freston to Law, 7 December 1910, BLP 18/6/141.

1905', wrote Cecil. 'Signs of our divisions must surely be kept hidden if we are to have any hope of winning. And we MUST win. Everything fiscal must be subordinated to getting the Govt. out.'[1] This time, however, it was to be the Tariff Reformers who did the subordinating.

The Tariff Reformers eagerly maintained, both at the time and afterwards, that their cause was gaining ground in Lancashire. 'The Lancashire working men's branches of the Tariff Reform League were amongst the strongest we had in the country', W. A. S. Hewins was to write later.[2] But even their conspiracy of optimism betrayed a certain lack of conviction. One of the Tariff Reform leaders in Ashton told Aitken at the time of Bonar Law's accession as leader that although in Ashton they could preach Tariff Reform and gain by it he would not be surprised if Law reverted to the referendum policy.[3] Law had assured Derby at this time that, on the contrary, he intended to press straight on. This Derby felt to be a great mistake, and he exerted his influence in an attempt to stop the Shadow Cabinet from abandoning the referendum pledge. In March 1912 he wrote to Law: 'Please believe me whatever you hear to the contrary, there is still as great an opposition to the food taxes in Lancashire as there was when the proposal was first brought forward.'[4] Derby's opinion, moreover, was corroborated by that of Walter Long, who visited Manchester and Liverpool at this time to spy out the land. From Manchester Long reported that there was 'undoubtedly practically an unanimity of opinion that Tariff Reform had not made any headway since the last Election, and nearly everybody I spoke to on the subject was convinced that there is great hostility to the Food Taxes'.[5] Even Tom Smith, who had played an active part in the Tariff Reform movement and had stood twice as a Workingman Conservative candidate for Parliament, admitted to Long that food taxes 'would not go' in Lancashire. Smith also 'stated that the Tariff Reform League organisation in Lancashire was mainly a paper one and that the supposed great improvement which had taken place in the prospects of the Tariff Reform Party was entirely mythical.' The leaders of the Tariff Reform League in Liverpool had already complained to Law that relations with the Conservative party had been 'not very cordial', and that, although Law's leadership was being backed up, the local Tories were 'very cautious not to push Tariff Reform down the throats of certain Free-Trade Conservatives'.[6] This was understandable since, so Long was

---

[1] Hugh Cecil to Derby, 18 December 1912, Churchill, *Lord Derby*, pp. 165–6; cf. pp. 146–83 for much useful documentation of Derby's role in these years.
[2] Hewins, *Apologia of an Imperialist*, I, 237.
[3] H. S. Heap to Aitken, 16 December 1911, Beaverbrook P.
[4] Derby to Law, 14 March 1912, strictly confidential, BLP 25/3/32.
[5] Memoranda by Long, 29 February 1911 (1912) (Manchester) and 8 March 1912 (Liverpool), BLP 26/1/76.
[6] James Reynolds to Law, 14 February 1912, BLP 25/2/19.

assured, 'if elections in Liverpool were fought with this question as the main issue, we should certainly lose the Exchange Division, and it is very questionable if the Abercrombie Division could be held'.

The Conservatives must have felt especially anxious not to offend the businessmen since the National Insurance scheme was completing the work of the Budget in driving former Liberals into their arms.[1] The prospects of the Liberals holding Manchester North West at such time as Kemp should insist on retiring were plainly rather bleak. The month after the General Election Kemp had written to Scott saying, 'I have irrevocably made up my mind to devote myself in the future to my business.'[2] Since the seat was highly unlikely to be held by any Liberal except Kemp, the party managers thereupon fought a long rearguard action to try to postpone the by-election until a time when the Government might feel able to take a defeat in its stride. This time, of course, never arrived. Kemp did not wish to let the Liberals down, even though he could not stomach Home Rule; moreover, he wanted his peerage. Together, this meant that the Whips had a certain leverage over him. Elibank never gave up hope of buying time. 'Surely', he expostulated to Scott in March 1912, 'it would be possible for Kemp to let it be known that he intended to give up political life on the grounds of business & let him remain quietly at his mills in Rochdale?' Scott, who knew Kemp better, warned the Chief Whip not to presume too far. 'I think I ought to tell you that it is hopeless to keep him in suspense beyond June', Scott wrote; 'he would almost certainly chuck his peerage & go pretty definitely into opposition.' Scott now thought that 'the time has come to accept it & take our chance';[3] but what a slim chance it was the defeat of Sir Arthur Haworth that month at a ministerial by-election in Manchester South amply demonstrated.

On account of the coal strike Kemp agreed with Asquith to retain his seat until the beginning of June. In April, however, Scott himself seems to have asked Kemp if the by-election could not be delayed until the recess. But Kemp now threatened to go, willy-nilly. 'Hitherto', his secretary wrote, 'one delay has always meant another, and I do not wonder that he has lost both patience & faith!'[4] Kemp's decision was this time accepted by Asquith

---

[1] E.g. in June 1911 the Manchester Liberal Federation had a letter from Tom Shaw 'intimating that if Mr Lloyd George's Bill becomes law he will be obliged to withdraw from the Party'; and in the Oldham by-election that October the cotton spinner Thomas Wright confirmed that he had seceded from the Liberal party because he refused to be a party to taxing capital and through it labour. (Letter from Shaw, M.L.F. Minutes, 29 June 1911; statement by Wright, *Oldham D. Standard*, 13 November 1911.)

[2] Kemp to Scott, 27 January 1911, MGP.

[3] Elibank to Scott, 1 March 1912; Scott to Elibank, 2 March 1912, copy, MGP. The leaders of the M.L.F. were very pessimistic about their chance of holding the seat; see William Royle to Churchill, 18 December 1911, *Companion*, II, 1359–60.

[4] Eva Peate to Scott, 26 April 1912, MGP.

but since he had now taken an open stand against the Home Rule Bill it was felt that to announce his peerage that summer 'would in the circumstances give rise to a good deal of speculation and possible misunderstanding'.[1] So the peerage was again deferred. Even now that Kemp was resigning regardless, under pressure the date was pushed further and further forward. On 25 July he finally reaffirmed his resolve to go. 'I hope you will not think me abrupt', he wrote to Scott, 'when I ask you to take this decision as final.'[2]

So ended one of the most extraordinary and sustained campaigns to keep a man in Parliament against his will. It had been a great boon for the Liberals to have Kemp to hold North West for them; but now they had to pay the price, for Kemp was irreplaceable. His successor, the lawyer Gordon Hewart, was an able enough man but he lacked Kemp's special advantages with the business community. Sir John Randles, the Conservative candidate, on the other hand, could claim to have spent many years in business in Manchester. At one point in the campaign he referred to himself as 'an out-and-out Tariff Reformer', but his main effort was to counter the efforts of the Liberals to make Tariff Reform the main issue.

In their own interests [he said], and in the interests of their case I am doing them a great service by not making it the most important and prominent question at this by-election. If I laid it down that the one question that you in Manchester had to determine at this election was the question of Tariff Reform, then it would be clear after the election was over that Manchester had emphatically repudiated the present Free Trade System. – (Cheers.)[3]

The veteran Unionist Free Trader Thomas Gibson Bowles, father of George Bowles, was approached to stand as an independent candidate, but although Scott advised him that such an action would benefit the cause by putting Free Trade in the forefront, he and his supporters were content to hold their hand. When invited to speak for Randles, Bowles replied that it was the duty of all to oppose a revolutionary and predatory Government but that he could not actively help a food taxer. It seems that E. L. Oliver was Bowles's Manchester representative, and in a correspondence with the *Guardian* he urged all Unionist Free Traders to vote for Randles in the security that if Bonar Law repudiated the referendum pledge a Unionist Free Trade candidate would be put up at the General Election. The *Guardian* maintained that the pledge was no longer current and challenged Oliver, who insisted that it remained in force, to write to Law to find out.[4] The Liberal

---

[1] Asquith to Kemp, 14 May 1912, confidential, copy enc. in Kemp to Scott, 20 May 1912, MGP.
[2] Kemp to Scott, 25 July 1912, MGP.   [3] Speech by Randles, *M.G.*, 31 July 1912.
[4] Note of telephone message from Bowles and Scott's draft reply, n.d., MGP; Bowles's telegram as given by Percy Woodhouse, *M. Courier*, 2 August 1912; letter from Bowles complaining that it had been doctored, *M.G.*, 6 August 1912; letters from E. L. Oliver, *M.G.*, 6–8 August 1912, countering the claim in a leader of 2 August 1912 that, contrary to what Bowles imagined, the referendum pledge 'has long been withdrawn and its author with it'.

argument was that in North West, 'the most famous Free Trade seat in England', the issue could not help but be Free Trade versus Protection, and that the result could not but be so interpreted. But many Free Traders were saying that although they could be relied upon at a General Election, Free Trade was not the issue now and that they would support Randles; or quite simply: 'We have had too much "Lloyd-Georgeism".'[1] Lord Hugh and Lord Robert Cecil both supported Randles, and Sir Charles Macara, a notable opponent of the National Insurance Bill, made a gnomic intervention in which he avoided urging the claims of the Free Trade candidates. The only friction between Randles and those Free Traders who supported him, occurred at a meeting when Basil Peto, M.P., a Tariff Reformer from Wiltshire, came to support him in rather unrestrained fashion. Alfred Crewdson, who followed Peto, said that Randles had done very wisely to say little on Tariff Reform, and continued: 'I can assure him that the less he says on the fiscal policy the better – (Laughter). Free Trade is dear to the bulk of Manchester people, and I am very sorry Mr Peto has come down here to introduce the the question in such a prominent way.'[2]

The Liberals had expected to be defeated and they were. Randles assured Law that, as a result of the Conservative tactics, 'we got everyone into our camp who ever is likely to be', including 'a substantial body estimated by my friends in N.W.M. at 500/700 who are hostile to Tariff Reform.' And he added: 'We kept men like Sir C. Macara quiet, if such men will keep so Lancashire is won.'[3] The victory in Manchester North West, far from being (as the Tariff Reform League predictably claimed) 'a deadly blow' to Free Trade, stiffened the antipathy of Lancashire Conservatives to the full Tariff Reform programme. Percy Woodhouse, Randles's chairman, told Law that many good Tariff Reformers had said to him, 'if we could hang up Tariff Reform for a Parliament we could sweep the country'. And in an angry outburst to the Chief Whip, Derby wrote: 'I am coming out against the Food Taxes. I can't stand them any longer. If Tariff Reformers had had their way we shd. have lost N.W. Manchester. T.R. hasn't gained the least ground in Lancashire.'[4]

Derby knew what the general public did not know: that the referendum pledge, upon which many Free Traders had pinned their faith during the by-election, had been secretly repudiated by the Shadow Cabinet in April. When Lansdowne announced this in November 1912, the reaction from

[1] See e.g. letter from H. Allen, *M.G.*, 29 July 1912; and comment by a (Liberal) Manchester surgeon, *M. Courier*, 31 July 1912.
[2] Speech by Crewdson, *M.G.*, 1 August 1912.
[3] Randles to Law, 10 August 1912, BLP 27/1/33.
[4] Woodhouse to Law, 1 September 1912, BLP 27/2/1; Derby to Balcarres quoted in Balcarres to Law, 5 September 1912, BLP 27/2/7.

Lancashire was almost uniformly unfavourable, as Law's correspondence shows. 'The almost universal opinion of Unionists of every shade', Law was told, 'is that this policy, if persevered in, must issue in defeat here in Lancashire.'[1] The Tariff Reformer Boyd Carpenter, for example, sent Law two letters he had received which testified to the 'widespread alarm' which had been created. One, from the Chairman of the Blackburn Conservative Association, stated that dropping the referendum would do them 'a great deal of harm at the next general election'. The other, from Thomas Marsden, a local solicitor, announced that he was resigning from the party.[2] And from Ashton the Tariff Reformer J. M. W. Morison reported to Aitken 'a curious undercurrent of talk about Lancashire Conservative Candidates dropping Tariff Reform as a pledged part of their policy at the next general election', citing the loose talk of which Sir John Randles was held to have been guilty as an example.[3]

Then, on 12 December, with Law himself due to speak at Ashton four days later, the *Liverpool Courier* printed a long article, pleading for a restoration of the referendum pledge. James Thompson, the Conservative agent in Liverpool, wrote that it expressed 'what I hear *all round me*'.[4] Salvidge had had no part in this, but, as he told F. E. Smith: 'I have received protests from numbers of business men who have votes in both Exchange and Wirral and who intend to abstain at the next election unless the Referendum pledge is restored. That is the way the wind blows.[5] And Salvidge was more of a political weathercock than most. Even Morison in Ashton admitted that the *Courier* article would have 'an enormous effect in Lancashire'.[6] Ashton, though, remained loyal to Aitken, loyal to Tariff Reform, and loyal to Bonar Law when he spoke there in full support of Lansdowne's declaration on 16 December.

On 21 December the Lancashire division of the National Union was to meet under Derby's chairmanship and it was widely feared that he would (in the leadership's eyes) prove disloyal, or (as the Free Trader E. L. Oliver put it to him) 'that patriotism and duty will compel you to raise your

---

[1] Canon Edward Rees to Law, 12 December 1912, BLP 28/1/21.
[2] W. B. Boyd Carpenter to Law, 14 December 1912, BLP 28/1/40, enc. Alfred Nuttall to Boyd Carpenter, 11 December 1912, and Thomas Marsden to Boyd Carpenter, 12 December 1912. In a pamphlet published earlier that year (*An Exposure of Present-Day Radicalism*, Blackburn 1912) Marsden had castigated the Government for the uses to which it had put its majority after 1906. 'The majority', he had written, 'was a Free Trade majority, really a Conservative majority.' But now he saw the recent pronouncement as 'a direct challenge to all Free Traders; and if they are true to the cause which Cobden and Bright so gloriously championed, and have any faith in them, they are, I think, bound to accept the challenge'.
[3] Morison to Aitken, 2 December 1912, Beaverbrook P.
[4] Thompson to Law, 12 December 1912, BLP 28/1/22.
[5] Salvidge to Smith, 24 December 1912, Salvidge, *Salvidge of Liverpool*, pp. 125–6.
[6] Morison to Aitken, 12 December 1912, Beaverbrook P.

standard in favour of a moderate conservatism to which 60 to 70 per cent of the party will gladly devotedly and enthusiastically rally at once'.[1] No doubt Derby's loyalty was severely strained, but the suspicion and distrust with which he was regarded at this time by Law and his circle can only be put down to the chronic optimism of those Tariff Reformers who refused to acknowledge the unpopularity of their creed. As Balcarres was later to admit after seeing Derby: 'The evidence of disquiet is so substantial that there is (alas) no need to think he has stimulated it.'[2] Derby was if anything a moderating influence, though in order to retain control of the meeting at all he had to work with the grain. In his own account of it he took credit for having avoided a vote, but according to the secretary of the Lancashire branch of the Tariff Reform League the meeting voted by about 117 to 3 against the withdrawal of the referendum pledge, though many thought only the food taxes needed be ratified in this way. Derby had the meeting adjourned for three weeks to consider three leading questions as to the electoral effects of these proposals. The report of the meeting which Law received through Steel-Maitland was highly unreliable. By painting Derby as the villain of the piece it concealed the real seriousness of the position in Lancashire.

Within days rather than weeks, however, this was at last brought home to Law. The Chairman of the Birkenhead Conservative Association put the matter cogently:

If we are to be returned at the next General Election we must gain 80 seats nett. A large proportion of these 80 seats must be won in Lancashire and Yorkshire. There is no good shutting our eyes to the facts. With the present programme this cannot be done. On the contrary we shall probably lose ground rather than gain any. In my opinion we are going forward to disaster.[3]

There were not many to contradict him. Max Aitken urged his own Chairman to 'strike the first blow in the direction of loyalty to our Leaders' by writing to the press; but even he refused to take the initiative, saying, 'I am afraid people would say the letter was inspired coming from the source it did'.[4] Apart from Aitken himself none of the nominal Tariff Reformers in Lancashire was prepared to make a fight for the policy their leader had so recently laid

---

[1] Oliver to Derby, 18 December 1912, Churchill, *Lord Derby*, p. 168.
[2] Balcarres to Law, 28 December 1912, BLP 28/1/98. Derby's reports of the meeting to Law and Balfour, and Law's own information are set out in the correspondence printed in Churchill, *op. cit.*, pp. 171–6. The rest of the story can be pieced together from the accounts in Percy Woodhouse to Law, 22 December 1912, BLP 28/1/75; Harry Sowler to Law, 2 January 1913, BLP 28/2/11; E. Ashton Bagley to Law, 23 December 1912, BLP 28/1/81; Bagley to Aitken, 24 December 1912, Beaverbrook P.
[3] Cecil Holden to Law, 23 December 1912, BLP 28/1/79.
[4] Aitken to G. H. Coop, 30 December 1912, copy; Coop to Aitken, 31 December 1912, Beaverbrook P.

down. Yet this implied no hostility to Law himself. When, for instance, Bartley Denniss, the M.P. for Oldham, assured him that, 'you may count on my loyal support as my leader in your present policy' he was careful to add: 'and in any modification of that policy which as my leader you may determine on'.[1] And this of course showed the way out: a demonstration of confidence in the leaders combined with a remarkable *volte face* on their policy. Law and Lansdowne were to stay, food taxes were to go. 'It is, of course, as you know an unheard of thing for one Provincial Division of the National Union to formulate the policy of the Party', Law had coldly informed Derby before Christmas.[2] But effectively that is what had happened.

The Conservatives had not solved all their fiscal difficulties. There was, as Law had foreseen that there would be, pressure from Manchester for the disposal of the question of duties on manufactured articles as well as that of food taxes. And the Liberals were certainly not prepared to write off Manchester North West. Their new selection committee under Sir Arthur Haworth ought to have been able to find a strong candidate, but it exceeded all expectations by securing a Cabinet Minister, Sir John Simon. Simon was warned of the difficulties by Scott, but after consultation with the Prime Minister he agreed to fight, presumably having some guarantee of the alternative seat which Scott had hinted would be a wise precaution.[3] It was a considerable *coup*. 'Simon & Manchester is significant', Aitken at once told Law. 'You must put one of your lieutenants into Manchester. Unless you do so you will lose ground there. This is very important.' And Lord Hugh Cecil's reaction was the same. He called Simon's plan of fighting on Free Trade 'astute & menacing', and suggested as a remedy the replacement of Randles by his brother Lord Robert.[4]

The dropping of food taxes did not mean that a test of party orthodoxy was waived for prospective candidates. Derby wished to bring in Gibson Bowles as a candidate and Law acquiesced on condition that he was 'willing, sans phrase, to support the policy of the Party on the Fiscal question'.[5] Derby had it in mind to have him stand for Rochdale, but Bowles's stipulation that he would tell the electors that he would resign if an anti-Home Rule majority

---

[1] E. R. Bartley Denniss to Law, 30 December 1912, BLP 28/1/105.
[2] Law to Derby, 24 December 1912, copy enc. in Law to Balcarres, 24 December 1912, copy, BLP 33/4/81. The crisis from Law's point of view is described in Blake, *The Unknown Prime Minister*, pp. 108–16.
[3] M.L.F. Minutes, 1 April 1913; Minutes of the Executive of Manchester North West Liberal Association, 7 July, 14 August 1913; Scott to Simon, 7 August 1913, copy, MGP.
[4] Aitken to Law, 15 August 1913, BLP 30/1/20; H. Cecil to Law, 28 August 1913, BLP 30/1/28. The Conservatives had similar fears for the Exchange division of Liverpool, for which Leslie Scott sat; Law's papers show that in their efforts to avoid a by-election in 1913 they treated Scott almost as a Conservative Kemp.
[5] Law to Derby, 15 April 1913, copy, BLP 33/5/23.

were used to implement Tariff Reform was unacceptable to Law and Derby alike. Bowles told Derby: 'I especially regret that you, the leader of the Lancashire Free Traders should adopt that view, and should require its adoption by Unionist Free Trade candidates in your county, as a condition of your countenance and support.'[1] But Bowles evidently misunderstood the nature of the modification of the party policy; it had been made less extreme, not more elastic. It was expected that candidates should swallow their principles about tariffs in order to unite the party. Many men within the Conservative party made no secret of the fact that they hankered after Free Trade; concessions had been made to them; but only so that what was now regarded as a side issue would not impede the real work of the party.

Votes were no longer at stake. It was only while they were prepared to make fiscal policy the line of division between the parties that the Free Traders had an important pivotal position. But once they came to believe that progressivism, although it held to Free Trade, represented a more serious threat to *laissez faire* than did Tariff Reform, they no longer had the will to oppose the Conservative party. Thus many businessmen embraced Tariff Reform, not because they believed in it, but because it was the Conservative party's armour against what they called 'socialism' or 'Lloyd-Georgeism'. And if these were the businessmen's priorities, it cannot be generally true that the Liberal revival after 1906 gained much strength from economic liberals.

Economic liberalism and Tory Democracy are really two sides of the same coin; its currency is the result of three kinds of partisan myth-making. First, the Liberals naturally sought to foster the impression that the leaders of the cotton industry favoured Free Trade; second, it was part of the Chamberlain-ite creed that Tariff Reform appealed strongly to the workers and hence that 'cosmopolitan merchant princes' formed the hard core of the Liberal party; third, it has been the contention of the Labour party, in proving itself more democratic than the Liberal party, that Liberalism was the bourgeois ideology of *laissez faire*. All these presumptions were entertained by contemporaries and there was just enough truth, and just enough party advantage, in them to make determined refutation impolitic. All that the historians have done is to conflate them into a single model. But the truth is less tidy. Contrary to the Liberal hope, the commercial men did not cleave to Free Trade when this meant supporting progressivism; contrary to the Conservative expectation, Tariff Reform did not tap a vein of working-class resentment against the Cobdenite bosses; contrary to the socialist postulate, the Liberals did not march away from *laissez faire* at the pace of their slowest man. In weighing the speculative merits of Free Trade as against Tariff

[1] Bowles to Derby, 2 January 1914, copy enc. in Derby to Law, 4 January 1914, BLP 31/2/14.

Reform, many men who were predisposed to vote Conservative on other grounds allowed their politics to dominate their economic judgement. There is nothing psychologically implausible about this.[1] But it makes it necessary to abandon any interpretation of Lancashire Liberalism which leans heavily on the hard-faced men who looked as if they had done very well out of Free Trade.

[1] Asked about the balance of payments situation in March 1970, following the dramatic move from deficit into substantial surplus, 32 per cent of Conservatives persisted in believing that it had got *worse* over the previous few months. Opinion Research Centre, *Sunday Times*, 22 March 1970.

12 Labour

We realize that an accession of strength to Labour representn. in the H. of C. is not only required by this country in the interests of labour but that it would increase progressive forces generally and the Liberal party as the best available instrument of progress.   Herbert Gladstone, 1903

I

Organised labour was the most powerful of all the sectional groups. Labour and socialist candidates were the only ones who could offer a serious challenge to the dominion of the national parties. This chapter will show that during this period Labour attained its greatly enhanced electoral importance within the framework of an alliance with Liberalism. C. P. Scott's efforts in favour of this kind of 'progressive party' in the 1890s had, as has been seen, some measure of success in 1900. The candidature of Fred Brocklehurst of the I.L.P. in Manchester South West had been a matter of discussion between the Manchester Liberals and the Liberal Whips and they were ready enough to grant him a straight fight against the Tories. So although at the General Election the divisional Liberal Association was apparently too ruffled by the manner of his intervention to feel inclined to give him official backing, his own declarations in favour of the Liberal candidates in other divisions, along with their reciprocation, meant that he had substantial Liberal support.[1] In Gorton too the Liberals were all out to conciliate Labour, though there they hoped to do it on a Lib–Lab basis. W. P. Byles, a progressive from Bradford, had agreed to stand, but only on condition that the I.L.P. did not oppose him, no doubt hoping for some wider entente between Liberalism and Labour; failing the I.L.P.'s consent, however, he withdrew in January 1900. With some encouragement from Gladstone, C. A. V. Conybeare thereupon considered fighting the seat in the hope that his own close relations with the I.L.P. and trade union leaders would make him *persona grata* on all sides.[2] There is no doubt that some more general arrangement between 'Labour' (probably the new Labour Representation Committee) and the Liberal Whips was in the air at this time, and while nothing formal came of it,

[1] See *M.G.*, 1 October 1900 for a letter explaining why he had been denied official Liberal support and a leader urging his claims; cf. *M. Courier*, 26 September 1900; *Clarion*, 29 September 1900; *The Times*, 3 October 1900.
[2] Gladstone's diary, 2, 10 May 1899, 17 January 1900, HGP 46483 ff. 6, 8, 56; Conybeare to Scott, 17 March 1900, MGP.

friction was to a large extent avoided in the matter of candidatures. In Gorton itself the Trades Council put up a London journalist, William Ward, as a Labour candidate and he was subsequently endorsed by the local Liberal Association.[1]

The Liberal party's inability to contest more seats in the Khaki Election helps explain this amity, for by September 1900 they were often glad of socialist interventions. In the *Guardian*'s view, it 'remained for the Independent Labour party to step in and attempt to save the situation' at Blackburn, where only Philip Snowden opposed the two Conservatives, and Keir Hardie, fighting Preston on the same basis, was described as 'the actual, if not the nominal, champion of Liberalism'. The Liberal party there was, according to the Liberal Imperialist *Lancashire Daily Post*, 'in a state of childish impotence; it has not a candidate because it is in a hopeless minority and in a state of utter disorganisation'.[2] Hardie's tactics were to concede the merits of R. W. Hanbury, the able senior Member, and to attempt to get Conservative voters to desert Tomlinson, their mediocre second candidate; whilst all the time angling for Liberal support. Since Tomlinson had been 1,300 behind Hanbury in 1895 there seemed a reasonable chance. But many of the local Liberals, led by the *Post*, were hostile to Hardie, and Tomlinson unexpectedly improved his position.[3] In Blackburn, where the *Telegraph* newspapers supported Snowden, the Liberals were somewhat readier to vote Labour and, as at Preston, there was a sizeable amount of cross-voting between the Labour candidate and the more popular of the two Conservatives.

There was a considerable degree of cooperation between socialists and Liberals in many places – fullest where agreement over the War was itself fullest. At Hyde and Prestwich, for instance, the I.L.P. supported the Liberal candidates and at Salford North, Darwen and Burnley, the S.D.F. did so too.[4] The Manchester and Salford Trades Council supported, as well as Ward and Brocklehurst, three orthodox Liberals; three others were denied support.[5] The picture, then, is for the most part one of muted cordiality and desultory cooperation between Liberals and Labour under the somewhat cramping conditions of the War. Even this measure of accord was absent in three constituencies where there were three-cornered contests. James Johnston at Ashton-under-Lyne and John Hempsall at Accrington were I.L.P. candidates, and Allen Clarke at Rochdale was sponsored jointly

[1] *M.G.*, 4 October 1900.
[2] *M.G.*, 1 October 1900; *Lancs. D.P.*, 1 October 1900.
[3] See interviews with Hardie and his agent, *Lancs. D.P.*, 1, 2 October 1900; cf. *Preston Guardian*, 29 September, 6 October 1900 for a more favourable Liberal view of Hardie – a surprising divergence since this paper and the *Post* were both owned by George Toulmin, then Liberal candidate for Bury.
[4] *M.G.*, 2, 10, 11 October 1900; *N.D.T.*, 8, 10 October 1900.
[5] *M.G.*, 29 September, 2 October 1900.

by the S.D.F. and the I.L.P. Hempsall was the only I.L.P. candidate in the country who did not have the support of the L.R.C.; indeed his candidature was specifically repudiated by Snowden, Hardie and the general secretary of the I.L.P., John Penny; and the Accrington S.D.F. passed a resolution disavowing any connexion with him.[1] Herbert Gladstone, speaking in the constituency, claimed that 'the Liberals had dealt very fairly and very generously with those parties who, while not associated with the Liberal party, professed Progressive principles'. But, while they had allowed them many straight fights, the socialists had, he said, brought forward other candidates whose effect would be simply to keep the Liberal out.[2] It was the general opinion in Accrington, however, that the socialists would take as many votes from former Conservatives as from former Liberals, and indeed they seem to have done so. Nor can it be claimed that the socialists cost the Liberals their chance of victory at Ashton, where the Conservative polled an absolute majority. Even at Rochdale, where the Conservative majority was only nineteen and Allen Clarke of the S.D.F. polled 900, there was room for argument. Clarke maintained that in the absence of a candidate of their own the local socialists would, 'from reasons of policy', have voted Conservative, though he was subsequently forced to admit that this was only his own opinion.[3]

The vigour of the socialists in north east Lancashire contrasted oddly with Liberal lassitude and left Liberal minds in some confusion. 'By the time another General Election comes round', wrote the *Lancashire Daily Post*, 'it is to be hoped there will be a general understanding as to the position of the Socialist candidates. Are Liberals to regard them as friends or foes?'[4] The fine words about those who 'professed Progressive principles' had to be matched by deeds before the answer to this question became unambiguous.

II

By the time of the next election the whole situation had been transformed by the Gladstone–MacDonald entente, under the terms of which official Liberals and L.R.C. candidates were, as far as possible, to be allowed straight fights against the Conservatives. Herbert Gladstone's diary reveals that irrespective of any more general agreement, relations between Liberalism and Labour in Ashton had improved by 1903 and Johnston proposed to leave the field open to the Liberals, while the Manchester Liberals were being prodded by Gladstone into effecting a local rapprochement on the basis of

[1] *N.D.T.*, 26 September 1900; *Lancs. D.P.*, 28 September, 9 October 1900.
[2] Gladstone at Accrington, *M.G.*, 8 October 1900.
[3] See letter from Clarke and subsequent correspondence, *M.G.*, 5, 8, 10, 11 October 1900.
[4] *Lancs. D.P.*, 9 October 1900.

leaving Brocklehurst and Ward where they were and surrendering a Salford candidature as well to Labour.[1] The broader 'entente' was negotiated in 1903 on Ramsay MacDonald's initiative; on the Liberal side it was primarily the work and the responsibility of Herbert Gladstone, aided by his secretary Jesse Herbert, and it is unlikely that Campbell-Bannerman did more than approve its outcome.[2]

In order to understand why the pact provided such an appropriate instrument for Liberal–Labour cooperation it is important to observe its preconditions. The Liberal leadership had long wished to see more workingmen in Parliament but it was usually the case that in each local constituency there were peculiar difficulties on one side or the other. Now, as MacDonald impressed upon Herbert, 'The workingmen throughout the country and of all shades of opinion (except the Miners and the Social Democratic League and Federation) were uniting in support of the L.R.C.' There was thus scope for a national arrangement with a single representative body. Further, MacDonald could convey the assurance that 'The candidates of the L.R.C. will be found to be in almost every instance earnest Liberals, who will support a Liberal Government'. Thirdly, Herbert learnt that the L.R.C. would have a fighting fund of over £100,000. 'This', he wrote, 'is the most significant new fact in the situation. Labour candidates have had hitherto to beg for financial help, and have fought with paltry and wholly insufficient funds.'[3] Lastly, it may be noted that whereas it was extremely difficult for party headquarters to dictate to the constituency associations which candidate should be chosen, it was far easier to stop the local party from fighting at all (as the electoral pacts operative in 1886, 1918 and 1931 show). These factors in conjunction, then, meant that recalcitrant local caucuses could be bypassed. Gladstone publicly reaffirmed his wish to see 'a strong party representing all shades of progressive politics' and appealed to the constituencies to 'refrain from looking too much to adjectives and names'.[4]

It is clear from the Whips' papers that the L.R.C. was at once offered a clear run in a number of seats in the north west without much parley. The Liberals were prepared to concede Labour one candidature in each of the three seats – Clitheroe, Bolton and Oldham – which the cotton unions at that

[1] Diary, 4 February, 1 July 1902, 9 March 1903, HGP 46484 ff. 11, 15, 31.
[2] Many of the documents bearing on these negotiations are printed, with some inaccuracy, in Frank Bealey, 'Negotiations between the Liberal Party and the Labour Representation Committee before the General Election of 1906', *Bull. Inst. Hist. Research*, XXIX (1956), pp. 263–74. Professor Bealey overrates Campbell-Bannerman's role in concluding the arrangement, largely because he interprets Herbert's references to 'the Chief' as being to Campbell-Bannerman; in the Whips' office 'the Chief' meant the Chief Whip. The best account is in Poirier, *The Advent of the Labour Party*, ch. 10.
[3] All quotations from Herbert's memorandum, 6 March 1903, HGP 46025 ff. 127–36.
[4] Open letter, *M.G.*, 2 May 1903.

time proposed to contest, and also in Blackburn, Gorton, Manchester South West and Preston, where there had been Labour candidates in 1900. In addition, Salford South, which had been contested by the S.D.F. in 1892 and the I.L.P. in 1895, was given to the L.R.C., St Helens was put on offer, and Ince and Newton were earmarked for Miners' candidates. Since Ashton had already been abandoned by the local I.L.P., the only remaining seat which the L.R.C. had contested in 1900 to remain outstanding was Rochdale, which was 'unadjustable'. When Gladstone informed Campbell-Bannerman of the details of the scheme in August 1903 he listed six constituencies in the north west which had Labour candidates fixed and in which no difficulty was anticipated, and a further nine which were being left open for a candidate sponsored by the L.R.C., including, by this stage, Westhoughton, Manchester North East, one Stockport seat and two (unspecified) Liverpool divisions.[1]

The difficult cases were rapidly being adjusted. After Brocklehurst's withdrawal in Manchester South West, the Liberals there evidently threatened some trouble, but the selection of G. D. Kelley, a former Liberal, as his successor probably mollified them and nothing more was heard of the plan for a third Manchester Labour candidate in East. Nor in the end did a Labour candidate contest any of the Salford seats since John Harker (successively candidate for West and South) moved to Manchester North East. When, in June 1904, it was rumoured that he was about to retire, the local Liberals resolved to put up their own candidate, but when he actually did so in May 1905 the Manchester Liberal Federation urged the North East Association to give the Labour party the opportunity of putting another man in the field, which they did in the person of J. R. Clynes.[2]

The 'unadjustable' case of Rochdale, however, was not really solved. S. G. Hobson was the socialist candidate there and he resisted I.L.P. pressure on him to stand down. He recorded later: 'John Penny, the secretary of the Party, came to ask me to withdraw. I asked why. "Because," said he, "we want Rochdale to bargain with for somewhere else."'[3] The outcome was that Hobson stood in a three-cornered contest as an I.L.P. candidate without L.R.C. endorsement. Nor could MacDonald and Gladstone be of any real assistance at Barrow; but there the constituency was able to work out its own salvation. Although Gladstone advised the Liberal Conybeare to persist with his candidature in 1903, at a time when even MacDonald suspected that Duncan, of the Engineers, was 'being run in the Conservative interest with Conservative money', by late 1904 it was clear that he was making ground and the Liberals were ready to withdraw.[4]

[1] Gladstone to Campbell-Bannerman, 7 August 1903, CBP 41217 ff. 1–2.
[2] M.L.F. Minutes, 9 June 1904, 11 May 1905.   [3] Hobson, *Pilgrim to the Left*, p. 111.
[4] Gladstone's diary, 1 December 1903, 25 October 1904, HGP 46484 f. 58, 46485 f. 19. Herbert's memorandum, 7 September 1903, HGP 46106 ff. 2–5.

Paradoxically, some of the greatest bitterness in relations between the Liberals and the L.R.C. came in those constituencies which had earlier been most generous in their recognition of the claims of labour. This was the case in Gorton where, in 1900, Ward had stood as a Lib–Lab. Although John Hodge was now in the field for Labour the Liberal Association persisted in running its chairman, Wainwright, as candidate, despite Gladstone's repeated declaration that he 'did not wish to be mixed up in it'. When Wainwright saw Gladstone in June 1904, he 'said the Libs did not wish to be told to support the Labour cand.'.[1] The problem *vis-à-vis* Wainwright solved itself in that when Ernest Hatch M.P. crossed the floor over Free Trade Wainwright's own candidature slipped from view; but Hatch himself now wished to stand as a Liberal. Gladstone, however, mindful of his obligations to Hodge, was reluctant to guarantee him official recognition in Gorton, and when Hatch found that Churchill too, as well as A. H. Scott, the Liberal candidate for Ashton, would not support his candidature he saw the writing on the wall and soon withdrew.[2]

III

The rest of this chapter will examine Liberal–Labour relations in the post-entente era. The double-member boroughs were the arena for the most obvious sort of compromise, that of splitting the representation, for which the 'Derby policy' of independent cooperation was the model. Labour acquired rights to one seat in four of the five two-member boroughs in the north west from 1906 onwards. This accommodation was assisted by the fact that at Preston and Blackburn the Liberals had been extremely weak, that at Stockport they had only been strong enough to win one seat in 1900, and that at Bolton they were already sharing the borough's representation – with the Conservatives – and so merely had to swap partners.

It was for long assumed that Oldham would be contested by the cotton unions, and it is pretty clear that had either Thomas Ashton or James Crinion wished to stand as Labour candidate he could have done so with Liberal goodwill; the *Manchester Courier* explained their inaction by saying that they were 'best described as Lib–Lab trade unionists'.[3] Alfred Emmott, the sitting Liberal M.P., had declared that Labour's refusal to put a candidate in the field in the 1906 election 'ought not to stultify them in the future. The least the Liberals could say to them was that whenever there was a vacancy

---

[1] Gladstone's diary, 13 November 1903, 8 February, 14 June 1904, HGP 46484 ff. 57, 64, 46485 ff. 14.

[2] See Hatch to Gladstone, 19, 23, 27 November, 2 December 1905 and encs. HGP 46063 ff. 117, 123–4, 127–8, 138–42.

[3] *M. Courier*, 7 December 1909.

in the Liberal candidatures in Oldham again the position of the Labour party should not be prejudiced by the selection of a second Liberal candidate on this occasion.'[1] Probably the need for a Labour candidate of their own seemed less urgent because J. R. Clynes, an Oldham man, sat as Labour M.P. for the neighbouring North East division of Manchester. A large number of activists went to help 'our townsman' in 1906 and his return was greeted with such enthusiasm that one may regard him as a vicarious Labour M.P. for Oldham.

After 1910, however, W. C. Robinson, the secretary of the Beamers, Twisters and Drawers, was put forward as a Labour candidate. He was already in the field, therefore, when, in October 1911, Emmott provoked a by-election by joining the Ministry with a peerage. But there was no reason, Robinson maintained, why there should be a three-cornered contest.[2] It was recalled that when Ashton had been candidate the Liberals had promised not to oppose him, but, despite reported overtures to Labour, a Liberal candidate was nonetheless brought out in the person of A. Lyulph Stanley, the son and heir of Lord Sheffield, whose record as M.P. for Eddisbury in the 1906 Parliament was somewhat suspect in Labour eyes. Although there was some talk of Robinson's being an 'extreme socialist' he fought his campaign as a good trade unionist, claiming credit on behalf of the Labour party for the Government's social reforms. 'His Liberal opponents told him', he said, 'that they were surprised that the Labour men had come to split the Progressive vote, but he asserted it was the Liberals who had done the splitting. At least some of the Liberals could not be termed Progressives.'[3] Stanley was put firmly in this latter category. Although the Liberals grew more confident after their shaky start, in the event Robinson took a bigger share of the poll than anyone had expected – 25 per cent to Stanley's 35 per cent – thereby enabling the Conservative to win. It had been impolitic for the Liberals to oppose a candidate put up by the Textile Workers in a constituency to which they had commanding claims. At a future General Election they would have done well to defend the seat they still held and let Labour attack that now held by their opponents.

In Stockport there had been two Liberal candidates in 1900, of whom one was returned; the local I.L.P. had angrily denied supporting either.[4] In 1906 the Liberals had apparently wished to run their candidate in double-harness with G. J. Wardle, the Labour man. Although Wardle fought a nominally separate campaign, and afterwards wrote proudly of his nicely judged course in both preserving independence and collecting Liberal votes, Labour and

[1] *M.G.*, 9 December 1905.
[2] Interview, *Oldham D. Standard*, 24 October 1911.
[3] Speech, *M.G.*, 2 November 1911.
[4] Letter from W. Scott, *Stockport Advertiser*, 28 September 1900.

Liberals were in fact closely identified. The analysis of the poll[1] reveals that while six thousand voters voted for the progressives, over six hundred plumped for Wardle and another six hundred or so split between him and one of the Tories; that is, thirteen hundred of those who voted Labour were not prepared to vote for a Liberal as well. In 1910 the cooperation was closer, and whereas in 1906 Wardle had been 750 ahead of the Liberal, in January 1910 his lead was only forty (in December 1910 the difference was 75 in the other direction). In both elections cross-voting between Conservatives and progressives was minimal – less than in Oldham where there were two Liberal candidates. It is especially interesting that in December 1910, when the Conservatives put up a workingman candidate of their own, less than a hundred votes were split between the two 'labour' champions. The unreconciled socialists and the undefiled Liberals who continued to plump for their own men numbered about three hundred each. The Conservatives now pinned their hopes on breaking up this 'unholy alliance'. 'It is almost safe to say', commented their organ, 'that if the Radicals fought a straight fight they would have been beaten, and it is self-evident that Mr Wardle without the Radical support would be hopelessly out of it.'[2]

The pattern in Bolton was much the same. The old-fashioned Liberal J. P. Thomasson blithely confided in 1904 that the Labour party 'dont want us Liberals to adopt their candidate or apparently do anything but *vote* for him! Of course he is all right.'[3] This was A. H. Gill, the Spinners' parliamentary candidate. The situation in 1906 was less favourable to progressive politics since the Conservatives only put up one candidate. Their fears that nonetheless 'a deep game' was being played in order to 'bamboozle' the Conservative working men were to some extent borne out by the poll.[4] Nearly eight thousand votes were shared by the Liberal and Labour candidates. On the other hand, there were 2,300 Liberal and 1,800 Labour plumpers; and about 800 each of those who voted Liberal or Labour voted also for the Conservative. Although this manifested an imperfect degree of cooperation, it was a hazard of triangular contests, as the disparities in the polls of the two Conservatives at Preston and Blackburn in 1900 show.

Gill, however, was no firebrand. The *Manchester Courier* called him 'a very worthy Liberal–Labour member' who 'would not offend the mildest Liberal in his loyalty to Lloyd-George'.[5] In the orthodox four-handed contest of January 1910 the Liberal and Labour votes fully fused for the first time.

---

[1] The detailed breakdown of the voting totals was not given officially but was often published in the local press. Since these figures are not readily available they are printed in Appendix E.

[2] *Stockport Advertiser*, 9 December 1910.

[3] Thomasson to Gladstone, 21 January 1904, HGP 46061 ff. 131–2.

[4] *Bolton Chron.*, 9 January 1906.

[5] *M. Courier*, 8 December 1909.

While there were five hundred plumpers for each, cross-voting virtually disappeared, and neither Conservative came within four thousand of victory. Gill's chairman 'hoped that it was only the beginning of still greater achievements in the Progressive cause'.[1] Moreover, in December, when the Conservatives reverted to their former tactics of putting up a single candidate, the progressives stuck together and the poll, as George Harwood, the Liberal M.P., said, 'showed they had been loyal, and that their supporters had been loyal to them'.[2] Again there were about five hundred plumpers for each, and altogether there were eight hundred splits with the Conservative. The result indicates a complete transformation of Liberal–Labour relations, even as compared with 1906. Further, when George Harwood died in 1912 the Liberal right to the vacant seat was respected. The Conservative candidate, who had made great play of his democratic Toryism, complained in the hour of defeat that the Liberal and Labour parties had 'not forgotten the understanding by which they have hitherto secured a member of each in Bolton' and that he had 'failed to get the support of the normal labour vote which I might reasonably have expected'.[3]

In Blackburn and Preston the socialists had borne the heat of the battle in 1900 when the Liberals thought it unpropitious to fight, and had polled much of – though very far from all – the Liberal vote. Philip Snowden stood somewhat apart from the Liberal at Blackburn in 1906 and his large number of plumpers, together with the considerable cross-voting, returned him to Parliament with a Conservative colleague. In 1910, however, he fought closely with the Liberal candidate and the assimilated progressive vote came to dominate the situation.[4] Preston's democratic Conservative tradition had been even stronger; there was even talk at one stage of a 'local Tory Labour candidate'.[5] The Labour party there was acutely anxious not to become contaminated by Liberal embraces, and when John Hodge stood as their candidate in a by-election in 1903 his whole strategy was to conciliate Tory workingmen. He praised not the Liberals but the Conservatives for standing aside at Clitheroe, and made the apolitical claim of being 'a Labour man and trade unionist pure and simple'. When, therefore, the Preston Liberals decided to support him and Gladstone sent a telegram welcoming their action, this was promptly used by the Conservatives to impugn Hodge's independence and Labour attributed their relatively poor showing to this.[6]

[1] Cllr J. Parr at the Spinners' Hall, *Bolton Chron.*, 22 January 1910.
[2] Harwood after the poll, *Bolton Chron.*, 10 December 1910.
[3] Speech by Arthur Brooks, *Bolton Evg News*, 25 November 1912.
[4] See Clarke, 'British Politics and Blackburn Politics,1900–1910', *Hist. Jnl.*, XII (1969), pp. 321–6.
[5] Memorandum (March 1903?), HGP 46106 f. 35.
[6] See Herbert's memorandum, 7 September 1903, HGP 46106 ff. 3–4; *M.G.*, 9–15 May 1903. It was thought that 70 per cent of the Liberal vote would go to Hodge.

The situation there in 1906 closely resembled that in Blackburn in that, while the Liberals endorsed the Labour candidate, this action was not reciprocated. By 1910, however, Liberals and Labour were in open co-operation. 'The forces of progress', declared the defeated Liberal that December, 'had worked hand in hand throughout the contest, and had remained true to one another. (Cheers.)'[1] It is clear that the trend in Preston was similar to that in those boroughs for which the detailed voting figures are available, and that the Liberal–Labour alliance, which worked well in 1906, worked much better in 1910.

IV

In addition to these larger boroughs, the Labour party was also strong in another clearly defined group of seats, those dominated by coal. The overwhelming majority of miners lived in the seven constituencies of the coal area – sixty thousand out of ninety thousand in 1900, and over seventy thousand out of one hundred thousand in 1914.[2] In other places mining was at best only a subsidiary industry, albeit an important one in Burnley, Accrington, Radcliffe, Prestwich and three or four other constituencies; for instance, the fact that the three thousand miners in Burnley were on strike during the election of December 1910 may have had considerable bearing on the result. The industry was, of course, heavily unionised. The Lancashire and Cheshire Miners' Federation had 30–40,000 members in 1900 and 50–60,000 in 1910, having briefly touched a peak membership of over 70,000 in 1907–8.[3] Sam Woods of the L.C.M.F. was returned as a Lib–Lab for Ince in 1892, while his colleague Thomas Aspinwall was rejected at Wigan.[4] After Woods had lost Ince in 1895 he was looked after by the Liberal Whips to the extent of being found a London seat. But although as secretary of the T.U.C. he was an august figure in Lib–Lab circles, his ill health and increasingly tenuous links with Lancashire combined to rob him of much practical influence there in later years.

In Ince it was recognised in 1900 that the burden of opposing the Conservatives must again fall on the Miners. They selected Aspinwall, and his candidature was unanimously endorsed by the Liberal Association, but he himself withdrew on the grounds that time was too short.[5] The possibility of

---

[1] Hilton Young at the Reform Club after the poll, *Preston Guardian*, 10 December 1910.
[2] Eccles, with 7,500 miners in 1914, should in many ways be considered a part of this group. These figures are derived from the Home Office *List of Mines* by a method similar to that explained in Gregory, *The Miners and British Politics*, pp. 192–7, which gives (p. 96) a useful guide to the position in 1909.
[3] Arnot, *The Miners*, p. 393.
[4] It is incorrectly stated that Woods was M.P. for Wigan in Gregory, *The Miners and British Politics*, p. 82.
[5] *L. Courier*, 21–4 September 1900.

Sam Woods's contesting Newton had also been mooted earlier, and the Westhoughton Liberal Association had hoped to induce Thomas Greenall of the L.C.M.F. to fight there, with no results.[1] There were, then, no Miners' candidates, but such Liberal candidates as stood in the coal area – C. P. Scott, C. A. V. Conybeare, Franklin Thomasson and Col. W. Woods – were all advanced Liberals and acceptable to the union. In these constituencies, and others like Eccles and Salford West, the Liberal candidates worked hard for the Miners' vote on the basis of their support of the Eight Hours' Bill. In Radcliffe, where the Liberal Taylor obtained the Miners' support and pulled off a surprise Liberal gain, the Conservatives blamed his defeat on the mining vote which, he maintained, had been misled by the Union into thinking him hostile to the Miners' aims.[2]

Ince and St Helens became Miners' seats in 1906, and in Newton and Westhoughton other Labour candidates were supported by the Miners. In all these constituencies the Liberals had been weak and virtually leaderless; the miners had long held the effective power, and the device of joining the L.R.C. – an action they took at an early opportunity – allowed the L.C.M.F. to make its will effective. In St Helens, for example, the Liberal Association was admittedly 'in a feeble way' in 1903; the Trades Council, on the other hand, made rapid strides after its re-formation in 1902 and after consultation with the Whips the Liberals agreed to support Glover, the able Miners' agent, as Labour candidate.[3] In the same way, W. T. Wilson of the Carpenters was supported at Westhoughton by a more healthy Liberal Association which had long seen the need for some species of Labour candidate.[4] At Ince the local Liberals at first objected to the Miners' candidate – it was the familiar case, in a seat with a long Lib–Lab tradition, of resentment at what seemed a gratuitous and ungrateful affront to their *amour propre* – but the advent of the Labour party did not in practice change things very much; the Ince Liberal Registration Society (Registration Agent, Wm Shaw) ceased to exist and there subsequently appeared the Ince Division Labour Registration Association (Registration Agent, Wm Shaw).[5]

The L.C.M.F.'s affiliation to the Labour party posed the greatest threat of open conflict with the Liberals not in any of the mining seats proper but in Accrington where there were less than three thousand miners all told.

[1] Memorandum, January 1900, HGP 46105 ff. 14–19. Gladstone's diary, 2 May 1900, HGP 46483 f. 66.
[2] Letter from James C. Cross, *M.G.*, 10 October 1900.
[3] Gladstone's diary, 15, 23 July 1903, HGP 46484 ff. 48, 50. *Liverpool D.P.*, 1 January 1906; *St Helens News*, 16 January 1906. Over half the electorate were later said to be miners, but this seems exaggerated. See *M.G.*, 6 December 1910.
[4] *M.G.*, 8 December 1905, 31 December 1909.
[5] See Herbert to Gladstone, 19 September 1903, HGP 46025 ff. 170–1; officers listed in *Wigan Almanac*, 1900–14.

Thomas Greenall, the most militant of the L.C.M.F. leaders, wished to stand there – apparently in order to assure the substantial Conservative section among the miners that their Federation was unafraid to take on a Liberal.[1] But, as so often, a solution was expedited from headquarters and Greenall withdrew. In 1906, therefore, the candidates supported by the L.C.M.F. did not anywhere come into collision with the Liberals. However, when the L.C.M.F. decided to take over Leigh, which by 1914 contained more miners than any other division in the north west, conflict became inevitable. For in Leigh the Liberal party was strong, and while C.P. Scott was its M.P. its links with the local miners had been reinforced. When Scott decided to retire in 1903 he was anxious that the Leigh Liberals should take the initiative in selecting a Labour candidate as his successor. His concilia-tory influence seems to have had some effect for although neither of the names under consideration was thought to be 'acceptable to the Labour Party' the Liberal Chairman declared himself 'anxious not to have our Party committed to a candidate as I feel sure that a Labour man will be run in which case we could not withdraw if we have selected a man'.[2] This suggests that at this stage the Liberals were prepared to give Labour a clear run. In the event, though, it was the Liberal candidate, J. F. L. Brunner, who had a straight fight since this was not one of the Miners' chosen seats.

In January 1910, however, Brunner moved to Northwich and Greenall contested Leigh for Labour. The Liberals imported P. W. Raffan, a Welsh-man, to fight their battle. He was loud in his insistence that there was no item in the practical programme of the Labour party or the M.F.G.B. which he could not support. It was noticeable that Walsh and Glover, the two Miners' M.P.s, both of whom relied in large measure on Liberal goodwill, did not come to Greenall's aid. J. R. Clynes did so, on the grounds that 'we cannot hope to build up a great Labour party without at times clashing with the interests of the Liberals'. Alfred Emmott, on the other hand, in making out the progressive case, denied that it made 'any difference in the present state of political parties whether a Labour or Liberal member was returned, but he understood that Labour could not win in the Leigh division, and therefore he asked them to vote for the Liberal candidate'.[3] The result was a rather considerable triumph for the Liberals, for they showed that they could defeat the Conservatives in a division in which over half the electorate were miners – even when opposed by a nominee of the Miners' Federation. Greenall refused to stand again in December 1910 and plans for another Labour candidature fell through. The Miners nonetheless seemed determined

[1] See Shackleton's explanation that 'the Lancs. Miner's Fedn. having put out 3 cands v Tories say they must now fight a Liberal'. Gladstone's diary, 14 April 1904, HGP 46485 f. 8.
[2] Myles F. Burrows to Scott, 12 October 1903, MGP.
[3] Speeches by Clynes and Emmott, *M.G.*, 26 January 1910.

to capture Leigh and at the outbreak of war Greenall was the prospective Labour candidate, with the prospect of another three-cornered contest in view.[1]

The Miners put up two further candidates in January 1910, one of them in Manchester East, which was not a mining seat as such, and the other in Wigan, which most definitely was. In 1906 the Wigan Liberal party had been hopelessly split, largely on religious grounds, and the Woman Suffrage candidate, while he did not get Trade Council backing, collected considerable Labour support.[2] Under the circumstances it is not surprising that the Liberal Association expired shortly afterwards; nor was it disagreeable to most Liberals that the Miners stepped in with a properly backed Labour candidate, Harry Twist, before the next election. In the autumn of 1909 the Liberal Association was revived under the auspices of the L.C.L.F., with some lack of local enthusiasm. Lest this weakly body had thoughts of fighting in its own right, its newly elected President, Sir John Brunner, publicly reminded it that it was 'no longer the sole official exponent of progressive principles' and that Labour now championed their cause.[3] The reorganised Association's work for Twist gratified its creators and while there were reports that a section of Liberals were refusing to support Twist, it is likely that his defeat in December had more to do with the unpopular side-effects of the Eight Hours' Act on the Wigan coalfield.[4]

Indeed, in Wigan, as in St Helens and Newton, organised Liberalism, never very vigorous, could hardly sustain an active existence without help from outside. The Associations there played a muted part in the 1910 elections; in 1912 the Wigan Association was succoured by a grant from the Lancashire and Cheshire Liberal Federation; and by 1914 it had joined Gorton, Newton and St Helens among those 'constituencies where no fully constituted Association exists'.[5] It is remarkable, though, that not only did the Westhoughton Liberal Association continue to exist independent of the Federation but actually helped out the Federation in 1914 by lending its agent for two months. This was exceptional. In the coal area as a whole, and with the significant exception of Leigh, Labour rather than Liberalism had acquired the rights to the winnable seats.

---

[1] See Gregory, *The Miners and British Politics*, pp. 49–52, 87.
[2] See *Liverpool D.P.*, 8, 10 January 1906; *L. Courier*, 29 December 1905.
[3] Letter from Sir John Brunner to Wigan Liberal Association, *L. Courier*, 23 December 1909; cf. 30 December 1909; L.C.L.F. Minutes, 13 October 1909.
[4] L.C.L.F. Minutes, 8 April 1910; *M. Courier*, 6 January 1910; *L. Courier*, 2, 9, 10 December 1910.
[5] For St Helens see *L. Courier*, 27 December 1909; for Newton see *M. Courier*, 6 December 1910; L.C.L.F. Minutes, 12 November 1912, 14 October 1913, 9 June 1914. The Federation ceased its registration work in these constituencies in 1916.

V

It would be correct, if pedantic, to assert that nowhere in the north west did a Labour candidate appear in the field against a Liberal in 1906. At Eccles the Liberals had felt safe enough in selecting a candidate in 1903 since the Miners were not likely to fight the seat and the socialists there were in very small numbers.[1] Although in the event Ben Tillett was put up as an L.R.C. candidate he was absent throughout the campaign owing to ill health and did not prevent the Liberal from winning the seat. At Liverpool it was understood all along that Conley of the Boilermakers would have Liberal support in Kirkdale and the Conservative candidate there took pains to remind his supporters 'that Mr Conley came there with Mr Edward Evans' blessing, and that Mr Edward Evans was the leader of what was called the Liberal party in Liverpool'.[2] At West Toxteth, on the other hand, the Liberals had had a candidate of their own in mind; but when James Sexton of the Dockers was put forward by the Liverpool L.R.C. in December 1905, the Liberal, who was in any case in Argentina, cabled his withdrawal in terms which seem to have removed any bitterness, though in Tory Liverpool Sexton was scrupulously evenhanded in his references to both older parties.[3] In Manchester the Liberal Federation asked that the divisional associations in North East and South West, which were being fought by Labour, 'should take the needful steps to support the return of the Progressives', and they complied by coming to the aid of Clynes and Kelley with posters, circulars and handbills.[4] In Gorton, although one leading Progressive spoke out in favour of active support for Labour,[5] the Liberal Executive as a whole were conspicuously silent, but in Barrow the Liberal Association was active in support of Charles Duncan of the Engineers, who further calmed Liberal apprehensiveness by denying that he was a socialist.[6]

In addition to the thirteen Labour M.P.s elected in 1906, many other Labour candidatures were considered before the next election. In 1908, for instance, a survey of the north west, carried out by the Unionist Free Traders, indicated that Tillett was still candidate for Eccles, that a Labour man was in the field at Oldham, and that there was a similar prospect in view at Hyde, Crewe, Rochdale, and Salford West.[7] There was also a possibility of retaliation by the Liberals in seats which Labour held. The Clitheroe

[1] Gladstone's diary, 7 October 1903, HGP 46484 f. 54.
[2] Speech by David MacIver, *L. Courier*, 4 January 1906.
[3] See speeches, *L. Courier*, 20 December 1905, 6 January 1906.
[4] M.L.F. Minutes, 4, 11 January 1906.
[5] Speech by George Jennison, *M.G.*, 15 December 1905. For Jennison, see p. 187.
[6] See *Lancs. D.P.*, 30 December 1905, 5, 9 January 1906.
[7] Enc. in Brunker to Robert Cecil, 1 February 1908, CP 51072.

Liberals seem to have been particularly restive.[1] The fact that from 1909 onwards the Lancashire and Cheshire Liberal Federation was responsible for the organisational work in constituencies 'where, by reason of the non-contesting of seats held by Labour, the association had become moribund'[2] meant that these at least were directly amenable to instructions from head-quarters. The Federation asked the Chief Whip's advice in November 1909 about the three-cornered contests promised in the north west where, it said, 'the position is specially serious, in as much as several seats will certainly be lost unless an understanding can be arrived at in respect to the third candidate'.[3]

The problem was at its most acute in Manchester. In the East division, of which the progressive L. W. Zimmerman was Liberal chairman and un-disputed leader, the Liberals had beaten Balfour in 1906 on a very consciously 'Labour' platform, as Horridge, the new M.P., and Zimmerman testified.[4] In 1908, however, the Miners decided to run J. E. Sutton there, despite its not being a mining seat. This move destroyed the understanding that Labour should have two, and the Liberals four, of the Manchester divisions, and throughout 1909 the Manchester Liberal Federation was anxiously taking counsel with the Chief Whip and its constituent associations over what course to pursue. The outcome was that when G. D. Kelley decided not to fight South West again for Labour the Liberals put forward their own candidate, and Zimmerman himself emerged as Liberal candidate for East. It was suggested by *The Times* as early as 16 November that Zimmerman, whom it not unjustly called 'the moderator of Liberal and Labour politics', had stood because he was 'the only conspicuous Liberal in Manchester who would not mind being sacrificed at the last moment in order to bring about an under-standing between his own party and that of the Labour men, and it would appear that a "deal" between these two parties in Manchester is at least contemplated'. This came pretty near the truth. At the request of the M.L.F. the Chief Whip sent a representative to confer with it and in December a special committee was set up to consider the two cases of Liberal–Labour conflict. Overtures were made to the Miners to withdraw Sutton but these were not surprisingly rejected.[5] The Liberals' prime aim, however, was un-

---

[1] L.C.L.F. Minutes, 17 March, 16 June 1909. When a by-election threatened in November 1910 they were loud in their protestations that 'they had stood aside long enough' and that 'if the authorities in London would not let them have a candidate they must do all they could to find one for themselves'. Speeches by Cllrs D. Tattersall and C. Atkinson at Nelson, *Lancs. D.P.*, 19 November 1910. But what with pressures from headquarters and an impending General Election they eventually backed down.

[2] L.C.L.F. Minutes, 8 April 1910.   [3] *Ibid.*, 19 November 1909.

[4] See interviews, *M.G.*, 15 January 1906.

[5] Meeting of the M.F.G.B. Executive, *M. Courier*, 10 December 1909. The Minutes of the M.L.F. provide a full record of its part in the crisis. There was also some talk of a socialist or Labour candidate being run in Manchester North. See *M. Courier*, 27 November 1909.

doubtedly to secure the withdrawal of M'Lachlan, the Labour candidate in South West, whom they would support under no circumstances. There is no doubt either that the Labour leaders, whom the M.L.F. approached, were also making strenuous efforts behind the scenes to avoid three-cornered fights. But Sutton and M'Lachlan, Henderson told William Royle, the M.L.F. Secretary, could only be withdrawn by the Miners or by the I.L.P. respectively. 'I do not know if you are aware', he wrote, 'that already nearly twenty candidates...have been withdrawn, & I have yet to learn of any being withdrawn on the Liberal side.'[1]

The withdrawal of Labour candidates at this time was indeed so noticeable that Labour leaders were stung into protesting their freedom from any formal compact with the Liberals. While Snowden insisted that 'there never had been anything in the nature of negotiations or even proposals for negotiations', Clynes explained that it was the 'merely contemplated or tentative candidates' which were being abandoned.[2] It was in this context that, when the Labour leadership met in conference in Manchester, the M.L.F. Executive empowered C. P. Scott and William Royle to inform Henderson that if M'Lachlan were withdrawn they would recommend Zimmerman's retirement also. But it was too late in the day for such a solution. On 20 December the M.L.F. Executive nonetheless recommended the East Association to withdraw Zimmerman, which they refused to do. On the 22nd the Executive had an interview with a deputation from South West at which Scott and Royle 'made opening statements explaining to the deputation the desire of the Federation to avoid if possible a splitting of the Progressive vote in Manchester by three cornered contests'; it concluded with the M.L.F. reaffirming their support for the Liberal candidate.[3]

By this stage rumours that the Liberals would climb down in East were so current that it came as no great surprise when, at Christmas, Zimmerman wrote to his chairman resigning his candidature. 'This leaves the field free', he said, 'for the remaining Progressive candidate to receive the united support of the whole Progressive party...'.[4] This set the tone for the rest of the campaign. Sutton accepted the implications of Zimmerman's action and the Liberal machine set about working for him. The Liberals made a house-to-house delivery of leaflets, filled all the hoardings which had been previously booked, organised public meetings and sent every elector an 'autograph' letter from Zimmerman. That Sutton should have made, as the subsequent

[1] Arthur Henderson to William Royle, 11 December 1909, copy, MGP.
[2] Snowden speech at Middleton, interview with Clynes, *M.G.*, 13, 16 December 1909.
[3] M.L.F. Minutes, 22 December 1909.
[4] Open letter from Zimmerman to T. H. Kelly, *M.G.*, 27 December 1909.

I.L.P. Conference put it, 'better appeals for Liberalism than for Socialism' was inevitable.[1]

In South West, meanwhile, there was no reconciliation. 'I am defending the ground that Labour already holds', declared M'Lachlan, 'and I am going to defend it to the best of my ability.'[2] After Zimmerman's withdrawal he was under constant pressure to retire, but instead he struck back hard at the Liberals, describing them as the workers' real enemy, and anticipating his victory as 'the death knell of Liberalism in Manchester'. He attacked the *Guardian* for 'the insidious method' of describing Clynes as a Labour candidate but himself as an Independent Socialist, but there was some basis to the distinction, as *The Clarion* admitted when it suggested that M'Lachlan had been opposed because he was a militant socialist, unlike 'the indirect, crooked ways of Messrs Arthur Henderson, Ramsay MacDonald, and Company'.[3]

The same interaction can be observed in the three other constituencies where, like here and Leigh, there were triangular contests; because there was already a Liberal alternative to the Conservative candidate in the field, there could be little doubt that the Labour candidates stood for a distinctively socialist policy. These were bitter contests with no quarter given.[4] In Manchester South West, the first of these results known, the Conservative gained the seat on a minority poll. The Liberal candidates in the other three-cornered fights thereupon set up a rather shrill ululation to the effect that the lesson must be taken to heart. Perhaps it was, for all four held their seats. Moreover, in December 1910 there were no Liberal–Labour fights in the north west (and the Liberals were able to wrest Manchester South West from the Tories).

After 1910 the familiar inter-election problems over the allocation of Liberal and Labour candidatures re-emerged. When the Liberal M.P. for Crewe died in 1912 there was a three-cornered contest which, unlike that in January 1910, enabled the Conservatives to win the seat. This by-election

[1] Quoted in Reid, *The Origins of the British Labour Party*, p. 197.
[2] Reply to question, Labour meeting, *M.G.*, 3 January 1910.
[3] M'Lachlan speech, *M.G.*, 6 January 1910; *Clarion*, 21 January 1910.
[4] Though at Crewe, where F. H. Rose of the Engineers did not receive a cordial reception even from his own society, the grounds of dispute were rather different. Tomkinson, the Liberal candidate there, declared that he and Rose were completely agreed on practical politics; further, he alleged that three Labour M.P.s had told him that they would do all they could to prevent Rose's opposition though they now denied it. (Speech at Crewe, *M.G.*, 20 January 1910.) No doubt they had, in the insulated camaraderie of Westminster, made friendly noises of this sort; but it was rather gauche of Tomkinson to publicise the fact. In any case, the Liberals had only themselves to blame for the intransigence of the local Labour party – which was to cost them the seat in 1912 – for in the 1908 municipal elections they had concluded an arrangement with the Conservatives. It worked out disastrously for the Liberal party and the I.L.P. alike. See Chaloner, *Crewe*, pp. 167–8.

was inextricably entangled with that proceeding concurrently in the nearby mining seat of Hanley: an internecine fight between Labour and the Liberals for the reversion to an old Lib–Lab seat. Had there been no Liberal candidate at Hanley it is likely that there would have been no Labour candidate at Crewe.[1] As it was, James Holmes of the Railway Servants was put up, and although some members of his Society signed the Liberal's nomination papers he undoubtedly had fuller trade union support than Rose had had in 1910. It was a curious campaign. For two weeks all eyes were on Hanley; speakers dodged from one to the other; the same issues predominated at both. Although the Hanley result – it was won by the Liberals and the Labour poll was less than twelve per cent – was a blow to Holmes, since the election dragged on another fortnight Labour morale had time to recover. He polled 2,500; the Liberal vote dropped by the same amount. But if, as he maintained, Holmes had taken one vote from the Conservatives for every two from the Liberals, there must have been other Liberal defections.

Scott had earlier warned Elibank that he was afraid there would be a lot of three-cornered contests.[2] The pressures at work can clearly be seen in Manchester. The East Manchester Liberal Association in 1912 urged the M.L.F. to agitate for electoral reform 'so that when the time comes East Manchester may take its fair share of the fight', and in this they were joined by North, a Liberal division in which Labour intervention was anticipated.[3] Considerable pressure was put on the Whips in favour of the alternative vote through the M.L.F. and the L.C.L.F. Similarly, in 1913 North East's wish to adopt a Liberal candidate led to a further deputation seeing the Chief Whip. 'We said', read its report, 'how difficult it was to keep the Liberal organizations together in our Labour constituencies. With a prospect of "Second Ballot" or "Alternative Vote" in operation, local Liberals would be satisfied as they would then have the possibility of testing the strength of the Liberal party in the Divisions without any likelihood of the seat being lost to the Progressive party.'[4] Such a scheme of electoral reform, however, had no high place on the Government's agenda, and the next General Election would be fought under the same constraints as the previous three. The Labour party was threatening to increase its number of candidatures; no doubt if it brought out a man in Manchester North the seat might be lost to Liberalism. But Clynes held the neighbouring division for Labour by a majority only one third as large; in April 1914 the Liberals of North East, upon whom he depended for re-election, pointedly asked the M.L.F.'s advice as to what

[1] See interview with G. H. Roberts, M.P., *M.G.*, 5 July 1912; for Hanley see Gregory, *The Miners and British Politics*, pp. 171–3.
[2] Scott to Elibank, 5 December 1911, draft, MGP.
[3] M.L.F. Minutes, 11 April, 6 June 1912.
[4] M.L.F. Minutes, 23 July 1913; cf. 9 July 1913.

action they should take if official Labour candidates were nominated in seats held by Liberal M.P.s.[1] It is an unanswered question, how militant would Clynes and the other Labour leaders have been when the General Election of 1915 was upon them?

At the 1900 Election, when the Social Democratic Federation was affiliated to the L.R.C., the only Labour candidate whom it sponsored was Allen Clarke at Rochdale. For the S.D.F., many of whose supporters were former Conservatives, hostility towards Liberalism was never very effectively masked; after it had seceded from the L.R.C., and more particularly after the Gladstone–MacDonald entente, the distinction between the position of Labour candidates and Socialist candidates became all important. It is true that the Lancashire branches had not wished to cut themselves off from the Labour party and that in later years the Blackburn and Burnley branches took the initiative in attempting to reaffiliate,[2] but the S.D.F., unlike the I.L.P., had little basis for any kind of accommodation with the Liberals, as Hyndman's own attitudes show. From 1903 onwards it was clear that Hyndman would once more contest Burnley, but that the local Liberals had no intention of backing down. The result was that the old-fashioned Lib–Lab Fred Maddison, under a cloud in trade-union circles since his dismissal by the Railway Servants in unedifying circumstances, appeared as their candidate. Herbert Gladstone refused to interfere, hoping to avoid the bitterness that Maddison's candidature provoked, and after an interview with him reported to Campbell-Bannerman: 'He thinks he can win *if* Hyndman persists.'[3] Evidently the expectation was that Hyndman's candidature would take more Conservative votes than Liberal, or at least prevent the committed Socialists from voting Conservative on tactical grounds. When, therefore, the Socialists approached Campbell-Bannerman in the next year Gladstone agreed with him that they should 'keep the S.D.F. courteously at arms length'.[4]

In Burnley the Socialists were influential in the official labour organisations and the Trades Council passed a resolution supporting Hyndman with only one dissentient at the end of 1905. Apparently Maddison was not asked about his views and retorted sarcastically about the Council's 'perfect right to choose a Socialist capitalist, instead of a man who held his trade union

[1] M.L.F. Minutes, 8 April 1914.
[2] See Tsuzuki, *Hyndman and British Socialism*, pp. 163, 166; *idem.* 'The "Impossibilist Revolt" in Britain', *Internat. Rev. Soc. Hist.*, I (1956), pp. 380–96; Lee and Archbold, *Social Democracy*, pp. 161–2.
[3] Gladstone's diary, 7 October, 2 November 1903, HGP 46484 ff. 55–6. Gladstone to Campbell-Bannerman, 3 November 1903, CBP 41217 ff. 28–9.
[4] Gladstone to Campbell-Bannerman, 14 November 1904, CBP 41217 f. 134.

ticket'.[1] Dan Irving, Hyndman's leading supporter, had earlier dealt with the criticism that there were employers in the Socialist movement by saying, 'these men were like the plums in the sailors' pudding – there was a lot of pudding between the plums'. And Hyndman himself, while admitting that 'he belonged to the slave-driving class', insisted that 'his claim to their support was that he had used his position, his education, and his time to be a traitor to his own class'.[2] Maddison, on the other hand, was attacked as the man who had 'sold the railway men'. Whilst a speaker representing the Crewe railwaymen came to testify to their distrust, Maddison's only counter to this charge was a message of support from the secretary of the Waltham-stow branch of the Railway Servants, the as yet obscure W. V. Osborne.[3] Although Maddison was at the top and Hyndman at the bottom of the poll, only 350 votes separated them.

The same three candidates fought another round in January 1910, and although Maddison then received more substantial trade union support his feud with the Trades Council was by no means over. Hyndman believed that he would have won if he had accepted 'Mr Lloyd George's preposterous Budget', but made no concessions to progressive opinion, declaring at the outset 'that it was absolutely necessary under present conditions that men should go to the poll pledged to revolutionary socialism, and to nothing else'.[4] Although the Liberal vote held steady there was a sufficient swing away from the Socialists to give the seat to the Conservatives. This shift, although small, was decisive, and in December 1910 it must have seemed to many that, while Hyndman could not win himself, the three-cornered contest helped the Conservatives. With Maddison's departure, too, much personal bitterness with Labour was removed. Hyndman's poll fell by over one thousand and, since the defectors split two-to-one in favour of the Liberals, this enabled them to regain the seat. Irving confessed himself downhearted that after seventeen years' work their vote should recede to this extent, and Hyndman too found it 'a very great setback and a very great disappointment'.[5]

Elsewhere, the Socialists had never had any real chance of capturing a seat. At Accrington, however, Dan Irving was able to perform impressively in the absence of a Conservative candidate. Even allowing for Irving's fears that the well-to-do class would sink their differences and support the reactionary candidate, the result indicates that his own poll of five thousand must have come largely from ex-Conservatives. Given the division's polling record, it is

---

[1] *N.D.T.*, 28, 30 December 1905.
[2] *N.D.T.*, 5 December 1905, 8, 12 January 1906.
[3] *N.D.T.*, 6, 10 January 1906; *Lancs. D.P.*, 11 January 1906.
[4] *N.D.T.*, 14 December 1909; cf. Hyndman, *Further Reminiscences*, p. 72.
[5] *Lancs. D.P.*, 7 December 1910.

a fair estimate that ten per cent of the electorate – the obedient Conservatives – deliberately abstained. Indeed the Socialist and Conservative votes seem to have been interchangeable to much the same extent as the Liberal and I.L.P. votes in other places. So in January 1910, when a Conservative took Irving's place, there were virtually no abstentions. The Liberal vote increased by 1,700; allowing for the larger electorate, and on the assumption that fifteen hundred Conservatives had stayed at home in 1906, this suggests that the erstwhile Socialist vote now split about four to one in favour of the Conservative.

Despite the national agreement, in 1906 the Rochdale I.L.P. nonetheless cooperated with the S.D.F. in running S. G. Hobson, another bourgeois intellectual, whose candidature, the *Guardian* was quick to note, 'has nothing to do with the movement for the direct representation of working men by working men'.[1] There was also a strong Socialist challenge in another constituency from which the L.R.C. had withdrawn, Salford West. A. A. Purcell claimed to be the Labour candidate there in January 1910, saying that he did not sign the Labour party constitution because it would not let him run as a Socialist.[2] There was apparently an attempt to buy him off which the Liberals had to disclaim.[3] He was in the field again in December 1910, and talked also of bringing in Ben Tillett to contest Salford South, but, refusing to accept money from 'a tainted source', he had to retire on financial grounds.[4] Compared with the January poll, a Socialist withdrawal here did not help the Liberals; and at Ashton it may have harmed them.[5]

Despite the S.D.F.'s disparagement of the Labour party, only once does it seem to have threatened serious opposition to a Labour candidate. When David Shackleton retired from Clitheroe in November 1910 on his appointment as Senior Labour Adviser to the Home Office, Labour, Liberals, Conservatives and Socialists all talked of running candidates at the coming by-election. The secretary of the Nelson S.D.P. insisted that there was no Labour candidate whom they were not justified in opposing, and their national executive sanctioned the decision to fight. When it became apparent, however, that a General Election would supervene and that the local Liberals acquiesced in the choice of a Labour candidate, the S.D.P. abandoned their plans in order to concentrate upon helping Hyndman at Burnley.[6] Reluctant support, for Labour candidates at least, was usually given. The Openshaw

---

[1] *M.G.*, 8 January 1906.   [2] Speech at Salford West, *M.G.*, 10 January 1910.
[3] See statements by Agnew, Purcell and his agent, *M.G.*, 13, 14 January 1910.
[4] *M. Courier*, 22, 23, 26 November 1910; statement by Purcell, *M.G.*, 2 December 1910; article by Harry Beswick, *Clarion*, 9 December 1910. According to one report his supporters actually turned up at the Town Hall on nomination day with their share of the expenses but could not find their candidate in time. *L. Courier*, 3 December 1910.
[5] For the Ashton contest in December 1910 see Appendix F.
[6] See *Lancs. D.P.*, 15, 21, 28 November 1910.

Socialist Club, for instance, was a nuisance to John Hodge in Gorton, but gave him guarded support at election times.[1] In Manchester South West the S.D.F. supported the moderate Labour candidate Kelley in 1906, but in Manchester East the S.D.P. would not help Sutton in January 1910.[2] At Blackburn the S.D.P. supported not only Philip Snowden, but also the Liberal candidate, in January 1910, to the dismay of some of its members.[3] In the case of a Liberal–Conservative fight it was far more common for the Socialists to abstain, and they may have denied the Liberal victory by so doing at Darwen in 1906. At Hyde and at Eccles matters went further in December 1910 when some socialists were conspicuous in their opposition to the Liberal as a result of the ill-feeling caused by the three-cornered fights the previous January, and it is true that in both cases the Liberal benefited only marginally from the Labour withdrawal.[4]

VII

Clearly Lancashire Conservatism could be sustained only by a large measure of working-class support, but it does not follow that the Conservatives need therefore be conciliatory towards organised labour. They might represent their anti-trade union activities as friendship for unorganised labour. But while this sort of gloss was commonly put upon their support of the Taff Vale and Osborne judgements, they were for the most part loth to write off the labour vote. When the Conservative candidates at Preston in 1906 or at Gorton in 1910 were accused of complicity in the work of the Free Labour Association they indignantly repudiated what they evidently found a wounding charge.[5] Indeed at Gorton, where the Association had gratuitously intervened in the division, the Conservative candidate issued a handbill declaring that he would 'in the future, as he has always done in the past, stand for the protection of labour, and do everything he can to confirm and extend the position, the power, and the influence of Trade Unionism'.[6] It was not politic to fall foul of trade unionism in Lancashire. Lord Stanley, who as Postmaster-General had called the Postal Workers 'bloodsuckers', withdrew the remark when he came to face his constituents at Westhoughton.[7]

More positively, many Conservative candidates sought to affirm that their

[1] Hodge, *Workman's Cottage to Windsor Castle*, p. 156; Davies, *North Country Bred*, pp. 117–19.
[2] *M.G.*, 6 January 1906; *M. Courier*, 12 January 1910.
[3] See letter from Young Socialist, *Blackburn Times*, 25 December 1909.
[4] *M.G.*, 12, 14 December 1910 (Hyde); *M. Courier*, 5, 6 December 1910 (Eccles).
[5] See letters between Tomlinson and Macpherson at Preston, *Lancs. D.P.*, 3 January 1906; Labour leaflet, 'Mr. White's Statements Analysed', Gorton collection; speech by White, *M.G.*, 10 December 1910.
[6] Handbill issued on behalf of Henry White, n.d. (December 1910), Gorton collection.
[7] *Liverpool D.P.*, 19 December 1905.

party was the 'real' Labour party. Sir Charles Cayzer at Barrow pressed his claim to be considered 'a true labour member' and Seton-Karr at St Helens was another who indulged in this new rhetoric. 'They heard nothing more', wrote the L.R.C. Chairman, 'about the man of birth and breeding – they were all labouring men, every one of them, Sir Henry Seton-Karr included. (Laughter.)'[1] The Conservative campaign there relied heavily, too, on the newly formed Conservative Workingmen's Association which contained many trade unionists. At Hyde, where a similar organisation was active, the Conservative member had voted for such measures as the Miners' Eight Hours and the Trades Disputes Bills. Several Conservatives went out of their way to express sympathy for socialism and to imply that in other circumstances they might have been socialists themselves,[2] or at least maintain that the ultimate ends of the Conservative party and the Labour party were the same.

The existence of the Conservative Labour Party was a standing affirmation of this view. In Warrington it seems to have excited some attention at its foundation in 1905 but the signs are that it continued to exist thereafter in a formal rather than a vital sense.[3] The Blackburn Conservative Labour Party was founded after the 1906 election; it worried the local I.L.P. by its attempts to capture official positions in the Blackburn trade unions and took an active part in the contest there in January 1910.[4] The appearance of a United Trades Unionist League at Preston at this time had much the same objects.[5] At Gorton, however, although a Working Men's Liberal Unionist Association claimed twelve hundred members in 1905, and extracted expressions of regret from the Conservative agent for the fact that it had not been consulted over the choice of candidate, it was probably only the empty shell of a Chamberlainite pressure group – and the lack of consultation rather than the apology is the real point.[6]

With the arrival of the Labour Party in Parliament, and especially in view of its close identification with the Liberal Government, some Conservatives sought to reassert more sharply their party's claims to be representative of labour. On the Chief Whip's advice Balfour became President of the Conservative Labour Party early in 1909. 'Why', Milner had asked, 'should we not have Unionist Labour members as well as Radical Labour members?'[7]

[1] Speeches by Cayzer at Barrow, *Lancs. D.P.*, 1 January 1906; the Rev. R. P. Farley, St Helens, *St Helens News*, 2 January 1906.
[2] Speeches by Groves at Salford South, MacMaster at Leigh, Howell at Manchester North, *M.G.*, 26 September 1900, 20 January 1906, 2 December 1910.
[3] See A. H. Crosfield to Lloyd George, 14 February 1905; LGP A/1/2/2; *L. Courier*, 29 December 1905; *Warrington Guardian Year Book*, 1906–13.
[4] See *Blackburn Labour Journal*, February 1907; *Blackburn Wkly Telegraph*, 8 January 1910.
[5] See its meeting addressed by Tom Smith, *Lancs. D.P.*, 7 December 1909.
[6] See report of its meeting, *M. Courier*, 21 December 1905.
[7] Speech at Rugby, 19 November 1907, Gollin, *Proconsul in Politics*, p. 154.

The question was not new but the difficulties were persistent. The Chief Agent in the 1880s had insisted that, however desirable the object might be, 'it would be a farce and do more harm than good if a working man was elected by the Conservative Party and run with Conservative money'.[1] In short, no scheme for Con–Lab M.P.s would be satisfactory until representative working-class organisations could find their own finance – as the replacement of the Lib–Labs by the L.R.C. served to demonstrate. In order to overcome this difficulty, at least in part, *The Standard* launched a fund for three Conservative workingmen candidates in the autumn of 1909. They would, it explained, 'be in every respect an integral part of the Unionist party'.[2] Further, the paper's part in the matter would be over when the fund had been handed over to the local associations in the selected constituencies. The fund officially closed in mid-November, and when it was handed over to Central Office the next month it stood at over six thousand pounds, allegedly contributed by over ten thousand workingmen.

The general secretary of the Executive of the Conservative Labour Party, speaking at its annual meeting at this time, came out in favour of a large number of such candidates being run, and he was echoed by Leo Maxse a few days later at the Conservative Conference in Manchester. 'They would like', said Maxse, 'to have a powerful group of 50 or 60 working men members, who would neutralise the so-called Labour Party, the misrepresentatives of Labour – (hear, hear)...'[3] This kind of attack on the Labour party, for failing to fulfil its professed aim, was to be a recurrent theme in Conservative propaganda.[4] The first of the workingmen candidates to appear was Tom Smith, a Tariff Reform lecturer, and formerly a journeyman clogmaker in Burnley, who stood at Clitheroe. Another Tariff Reform League official, E. Ashton Bagley, the Lancashire secretary, stood as a workingman candidate at Leicester, and there was a third *Standard* man in the Orkneys. Smith fought a hard campaign against Shackleton, during the course of which he had to deny the innuendo that the bulk of his funds did not really come from workingmen, and even *The Standard*'s correspondent admitted that the spectacle of a Conservative Working Man candidate was regarded in the division as a huge joke.[5]

[1] Captain Middleton to Cropley, 25 June 1888, Chilston, *Chief Whip*, p. 177.
[2] *Standard*, 27 October 1909.
[3] Speech by Maxse, *M. Courier*, 19 November 1909; cf. *N.D.T.*, 15 November 1909 for the Conservative Labour Party.
[4] It was to be seen at its most simplistic, perhaps, at Gorton, where a leaflet cited the expenses claimed at one meeting by Will Crooks and John Hodge, and concluded: 'These are the charges for attending Meetings to tell us how they represent us. No wonder they don't want to lose their jobs, it BEATS WORKING'. 'How the Labour Member Bleed the Workers', Gorton collection.
[5] Speech by Smith at Colne, *N.D.T.*, 10 December 1909; *Standard*, 7 January 1910.

The Osborne judgement evoked warm sympathy among those who believed that the Labour Party had been captured by an unrepresentative clique. A meeting of the Trade Union Defence League in Manchester in November 1910 passed a resolution deploring its reversal and proclaimed its intention of founding a new British Labour party.[1] The Conservatives were now ready to put six workingmen candidates in the field, four of them for seats in the north west. The arrangements for these candidatures were made by the Tariff Reform League. Smith moved from Clitheroe to Hyde, where the Trades Council passed a resolution earnestly advising trade unionists not to vote for him.[2] Ashton Bagley moved from Leicester to fight at Radcliffe; he campaigned as the People's Man, replying favourably to Trades Council questions on municipal enterprise, the Right-to-Work Bill and the Minority Report of the Poor Law, and agreeing to be guided by the majority of trade unionists on the Osborne judgement.[3] In all cases they tackled not Labour but Liberal opposition. None of these candidates, however, seems to have polled any better or worse than other Conservatives. While the 'Tory–Labs' were an interesting experiment, therefore, their appeal does not seem to have been at all distinctive; and their lack of any resources independent of the Conservative party vitiated their claim to a special 'Labour' status. As Sandars wrote to Balfour, 'if these men had been elected who can doubt but that they wd. have become a charge upon our Party Exchequer?'[4]

There were other Conservative candidates who made a direct and explicit bid for the Labour vote. In North Manchester, for instance, H. E. Howell and his League of Democratic Conservatives were obviously after the Labour vote in a Liberal division. But at Ashton-under-Lyne matters went further. Probably because it had been the scene of a Socialist candidature in January 1910, Ashton had evidently been earmarked by the Conservatives for a workingman candidate. By November, however, the young Canadian Max Aitken had emerged as the favoured choice, though he at first declared himself humiliated at being 'offered a seat intended by the Central Office for a Labour candidate'.[5] But he duly stood; the Trades Council issued a manifesto recommending him; and he was elected. The defeated Liberal, A. H. Scott, was widely reported when he declared that this was 'a most discreditable trick, unworthy of a Labour party that has had so much loyal support from me in all my twenty years of public life', and implied that it had placed itself 'under the degrading influence of men who have little

[1] *M. Courier*, 21 November 1910.
[2] *M.G.*, 9 December 1910. The correspondence between Tom Smith and Max Aitken in the Beaverbrook Papers illustrates the role of the Tariff Reform League in these candidatures.
[3] Answers to Trades Council questions, *M. Courier*, 9 December 1910.
[4] Sandars to Balfour, 2 October 1910, BP 49767.
[5] Aitken to Bonar Law, n.d. (November 1910), BLP 18/6/134.

regard for any principle except that of direct opposition to a man fighting under the Liberal flag'.[1] Such charges may be thought common form in the circumstances: but they are (though *ex parte*) a not unfair summary of what had happened. Like much else in Aitken's political career, the episode was freakish and cannot support a more general moral.

VIII

Ashton was the only example of the recognised Labour organisation preferring a Conservative to a Liberal candidate. Because in the north west the Trades Councils were usually themselves the local Labour parties, their actions had to conform with the provisions in the party constitution forbidding co-operation with other parties. For this reason, even when Labour organisations were pretty clearly giving effective support to a Liberal candidate this had to be dissimulated. It is more common to find individual unions, like the Railway Servants or the Textile Workers, giving straightforward endorsement of Liberal candidates than Trades Councils or, *a fortiori*, local L.R.C.s.

It is interesting that some of the greatest bitterness between Liberalism and Labour occurred as a result of the presence of Lib–Lab candidates, and nothing could more clearly indicate the extent to which the advent of the L.R.C. made this style of Labour politics anachronistic. There is no denying that at Burnley Fred Maddison was a less effective candidate than an orthodox Liberal precisely because of his Lib–Lab position, which necessarily betokened his hostility to the new phase of the Labour movement. Another Liberal trade unionist, Henry Vivian, ran into trouble at Birkenhead on the same grounds. There is little doubt that he was brought into the constituency in 1903 as a Lib–Lab, and he devoted his early efforts to securing the local trade unionists' support. During the election campaign, however, largely, it would seem, in response to socialist taunts that he was sailing under false colours, he made it clear that he was not standing as a 'Labour candidate', because he would not consent to be a mere delegate of an organisation. This disavowal may be ambiguous, but before polling day he became specific. He was asked by an I.L.P. questioner: 'Why did you come to Birkenhead as a "Liberal and Labour" candidate, and, if you had a right to that title, why have you dropped the word "Labour" now?' Vivian replied: 'I never did come to Birkenhead as "Liberal and Labour" candidate. ("Oh".) I am either a liar, or I am not. I always objected to the word "Labour" being given against my name. ("Oh".)'[2] In view of this statement it seems hardly fair

---

[1] *Ashton Evening Reporter*, 5 December 1910. Since, if this case were at all representative, it would vitiate the argument of this chapter, it is subjected to investigation in Appendix F.

[2] *Liverpool D.P.*, 12 January 1906; cf. 30 December 1905; Gladstone's diary, 2 April, 1 October 1903, HGP 46484 ff. 35, 53.

to class him as a Lib–Lab. His attitude towards the trade unions after the Osborne judgement was notably unsympathetic and he continued to offend the socialists. Indeed, in December 1910 a manifesto was issued urging socialists, of whom there were said to be six hundred, to 'vote against Vivian, the workers' enemy', and it was considered that this played some part in his defeat.[1]

The moral is surely that whereas Lib–Lab candidates had once been a concession to Labour, now that the Lib–Labs were a mere rump they were a provocation. These cases apart, the general tendency was towards an acceptance of the progressive arguments in 1910 even where they had not carried conviction in 1906. Thus one member of the S.D.P. in Rochdale, where there had been some kind of socialist candidate at every election since 1895, argued in December 1909 against their running a candidate again. 'He travelled to Manchester every morning', he said, 'with nine other Socialists, all of whom voted for the Socialist candidate at the last election. This time every one of them would vote for the Liberal candidate.'[2] There was the same shift at Darwen where F. G. Hindle, the Liberal candidate, blamed his defeat in 1906 on concerted Labour abstentions. At the next election, however, the socialists on one occasion surrendered their prior booking of a room in order than Hindle might hold a meeting, at which he made an appeal to them in the shoulder-to-shoulder vein.[3] In December 1910 he was cheered when he said he believed they would have the Labour party with them and Philip Snowden intervened to say that he would have no hesitation in voting for Hindle.[4] And this, it should be noted, was in the socialist area of Lancashire.

The transformation which had overcome the attitudes of many Liberals towards Labour may be gauged to some extent from the press. The *Lancashire Daily Post* which had once preached a rather narrow Liberal Imperialism, in December 1909, following the speeches by Arthur Henderson and Stephen Walsh on triple candidatures, carried a most sympathetic leader entitled, 'Unity of the Progressive Forces'. 'We hope all Progressives will read these speeches', it said, 'for they indicate at once the imperative need for the consolidation of forces and the extreme difficulty of securing this end.' The paper had not in earlier years shown much recognition of even the desirability of this object, but now, far from treating Labour activities as a sort of insubordination, it went on to ask for understanding of the difficulties which the Labour party faced.[5] The Conservative press is even more revealing at

[1] *L. Courier*, 3 December 1910; *Liverpool D.P.*, 7 December 1910.
[2] Intervention by J. Sutcliffe, Rochdale S.D.P. meeting, *N.D.T.*, 6 December 1909.
[3] Hindle speech after the poll, *Lancs.D.P.*, 24 January 1906; meeting at Harwood, *N.D.T.*, 8 December 1909.
[4] *Lancs. D.P.*, 28 November, 6 December 1910.   [5] *Lancs. D.P.*, 15 December 1909.

this juncture. The Conservative attitude towards progressive politics was uncertain but adaptable. Comment varied between flesh-creeping tales of the unholy alliance and scornful exposures of its incipient ruptures; between sorrow for the good old Liberal Party now fallen into bad ways, and concern for independent Labour now ensnared by the wily Radicals. The *Manchester Courier* particularly resented the trick 'of trying to disguise Socialist candidates as "Labour" men', under which innocent label the overthrow of religion, family life and existing society was sought. 'Socialism', it concluded, 'is a branch – and the most important branch – of the heterogeneous agglomeration of political malcontents who desire to be known as the "Progressive" Party.'[1]

Whatever attitude tactics may have dictated during a campaign, after the poll Conservative candidates were normally fairly unequivocal in their tributes to the effectiveness of the combination. 'I have had to fight', said Sir William Vaudrey, 'against a combination of Radicalism, Liberalism and Socialism, and in a working-class constituency nowadays a Unionist has a great deal to do in trying to fight against a combination of that description.'[2] Similarly, although in Manchester South West in the second 1910 election the Conservative agent had vehemently maintained that those who had previously voted Labour there would not automatically support the Liberal in a straight fight, his defeated candidate put his failure down to just such a combination.[3] At Gorton, where John Hodge, the Labour M.P., had considerable Liberal support in the same election, his opponent made great play of asking, 'did they think that any man, going to the House of Commons, and going by the help of Liberal votes and support, would be independent in that House?' And the *Courier* positively frothed at the mouth in describing 'the Labour-cum-Liberal-cum-Socialist-cum-Hatch cause in Gorton', 'this mosaic of "progressive" effort', 'this agglomeration of nondescripts, this tatter-demalion army'.[4] Perhaps the most instructive of all these Conservative reactions to progressive politics was the speech H. E. Howell made to his North Manchester League of Democratic Conservatives in December 1910.

As regards home politics [he said], the most striking feature of the election is the disappearance of the Labour Party. There is no Labour Party. Mr Clynes, in North-East Manchester, was as much a Liberal candidate as he was a Labour candidate...The Labour Party can no longer claim to be an independent party. They have made their bed and they must lie on it; they have chosen their bedfellows and they must sleep with them. (Laughter and cheers.)[5]

[1] *M. Courier*, 29 December 1909.
[2] After the poll, Manchester North East, *M.G.*, 17 January 1910.
[3] Interview with Hesketh, *M. Courier*, 22 November 1910; Arthur Colefax after the poll, *M.G.*, 5 December 1910.
[4] Speech by Henry White, Gorton, *M. Courier*, 6 December 1910; leader, *ibid.*, 9 December 1910.
[5] *M. Courier*, 17 December 1910.

This was, in its own terms, a fair enough description of the position not only in Manchester but throughout the north west. The socialist strength in north east Lancashire had been compounded for Labour M.P.s; that is, in the only area where there was a prospect of socialist M.P.s, this had been sacrificed in favour of trade-union representation. In Blackburn and Preston, where Liberalism had appeared to be defunct in 1900, and had been clutching at Labour's coat-tails in 1906, the Liberal candidates were polling at least as well as Labour by 1910. Elsewhere, socialism was not a powerful force. It was as a trade-union organisation that Labour acquired possession of all but one of the winnable mining seats and was given a half share in all but one of the two-member boroughs.

The electoral importance of the Labour vote can be exaggerated; it was still an aristocracy of labour that was allowed to send its sectional representatives to Parliament with Liberal cooperation – albeit one rapidly being expanded. It was Labour's propensity to 'grow' which has led to the further inference that it would inevitably 'grow up' and 'grow out' of progressivism. But there were severe constraints upon a party based on trade unionism. In the progressive view, the legitimate grievances of labour were a special case of a more general maldistribution of resources in the community. On the other hand, it was more difficult to generalise particular trade-union interests into prescriptions for society as a whole. One way of doing so, of course, was to adopt a thoroughgoing socialist critique; but that was hardly the formulalation towards which the workingmen of Lancashire were groping. Labour, then, could form no more than a section of a party representative of the poor against the rich; it was not of itself the true church of the working class. It fulfilled itself after 1900, not through rivalry with Liberalism such as it had earlier displayed, but through a cooperation that grew increasingly close. 'I should like to say this', Churchill once said, taunted with the prospect of Labour's inexorable march. 'A great many men can jump four feet, but very few can jump six feet.'[1] Under these conditions, it was, of all the electoral pressure groups, labour which brought the new strength to the Edwardian Liberal revival. Despite all the obvious shortcomings of the arrangement, the national understanding between Liberalism and Labour was a considerable advantage on both sides: its rupture would have been a considerable disaster on both sides. Moreover, it was a more potent influence than difficulties with Liberal caucuses, or with local socialist groups, and rendered much of the bidding and counter-bidding for trade-union support at constituency level irrelevant. And it gave rise to a fruitful genre of progressive politics. Though Liberals might sometimes regard Labour independence as the grit in the machine it was really the sand in the oyster.

[1] Speech at Glasgow, 11 October 1906, *Liberalism and the Social Problem*, p. 76.

339

PART SIX
GOING TO THE COUNTRY

The live political topics changed in character between the General Elections of 1900 and those of 1910. The Conservatives' case had stressed the national interest and the unity of classes. The progressives increasingly brought other issues to the forefront. 'They are great class and they are great economic and social issues', said Churchill, their most notable propagandist in Lancashire. The Liberals asserted that it was because of these that the House of Lords rejected the 1909 Budget; and the Conservatives argued that a Government so tainted with socialism needed to be kept in check by a second Chamber. The results of the General Elections suggest that, following their marginal gains in 1900, the Liberals were supported indiscriminately in 1906; but that the most solid element in their support, both then and in 1910, was the working-class vote. Only in the Liverpool area did Tory Democracy survive. The signs, then, point to a long-term shift rather than the effect of snap issues or temporary bandwagons; and the fragmentary evidence of the by-elections between 1911 and 1914 does nothing to discredit this conclusion.

13 The core of the argument

As far as I can make out every argument used in attack and in defence has its separate and independent effect. They hardly ever meet, even if they are brought to bear upon the same mind.   Quoted by Graham Wallas, 1908

I

The rhetoric of election campaigns cannot be taken at face value but it was rather more than the hunt for a 'cry'. The argument was about power. To some extent the politicians were asking for support on their own terms: and to some extent they were seeking votes on any terms. The 'issues' of an election reflect this tension. Some were articulated by powerful sectional forces (albeit in terms of what was feasible under party government); and some were articulated by the politicians (albeit in terms of what was palatable to the electorate). Some issues were argued out in the country and others were merely referred to (by and large it was the sectional issues which were taken as read). At the turn of the century no-one spent much time in exploring the merits of Home Rule, or of temperance reform, or of religious education, which is not to say that they were unimportant in influencing votes. The politically creative argument, on the other hand, centred on other issues of government which were in a real sense taken to the people by the politicians. It was the running debate over these which defined the grounds upon which the parties asked for power. These issues, moreover, were more clearly associated with particular leaders; men as well as measures were to be weighed in the balance.

In its last phase of power the Unionist Government narrowed down its claim to rule to the single but sweeping assertion that it was the national party. Following Chamberlain's lead the Conservatives insisted that they represented not a party interest but the national interest. They 'appealed to all Englishmen to put party politics on one side, and stand shoulder to shoulder with the men who had been giving their lives, money and blood for the country'; they asked them, 'not as Conservatives, and not as politicians, but as Englishmen, to induce men to register their votes in favour of that policy for which our gallant soldiers had fought, and for which the hills and plains of South Africa had been dyed red with their blood.'[1] It was commonly asserted

---

[1] W. J. Galloway at Manchester South West, *M.G.*, 25 September 1900; W. Mitchell at Burnley, *Lancs. D.P.*, 12 September 1900. This theme is well illustrated in McKenzie and Silver, *Angels in Marble*, pp. 55 ff.

343

or implied that if the 200,000 soldiers were at home there would be 200,000 more Unionist votes. Against this the Liberals could only plead that it was not the soldiers but the policy which they criticised. 'Their Tommy Atkins would be able to tell them something of the management of the War when he came back', they hinted, and maintained that: 'The Liberals also wanted the war for one of the issues – the whole war with its miscalculations and bungling, its slow transport, inadequate guns, lack of horses, and hospital scandals (cheers).'[1] But even here the backbench Tories could distance themselves from the War Office ('whose proceedings appeared to be a series of consummate blunders') and rest on their appreciation of 'how the Lancashire lads had fought, bled, and died'.[2] A straightforward identification with the flag was to override all else. 'Patriotism, after all, was the main thing just now, and it was important that they should vote straight on the one great issue.'[3]

It was, then, the soldier's cause, not the management of the War, that was to be the issue. As to the broader question of imperialism, that too was held to be no matter of opinion but a proving ground for the obtuseness of the Liberals. 'They hate the word "Imperialists"', one Unionist explained.

They call it vulgar imperialism, but how anybody can help being an Imperialist when he belongs to the British Empire, which contains over four [hundred] millions of people, and which is ruled over by Queen Victoria, I don't know (applause). I believe she is the greatest Queen that has ever lived (loud applause). And do you think the Queen never thinks of her 400 millions of subjects? Do you think she never thinks of the colonials? The Queen must be an Imperialist, and I glory in the name of Imperialist, because I believe that the sovereign and everybody in the country worthy of the name is proud to be called an Imperialist (applause).[4]

This being so, the Conservative party naturally had to provide a home for all those of right mind since 'this was not so much of a party fight as some had been before', and consequently 'they might count with confidence upon the support of all the patriotic Liberals'.[5] For if a Liberal Government were returned, 'every enemy of England would rejoice', whereas if the Unionists were returned 'every enemy of England would hide his head'.[6] It was a choice 'between giving the government of affairs to Lord Salisbury or "Lord knows who"'.[7] The Liberal party was not wholly iniquitous but, fragmented as it was, it could not be entrusted with the future of South Africa. As Balfour put it, 'the mere fact that one party is united and the other party divided affords an adequate reason for sending us and not our

[1] Sir J. Leese at Accrington, G. Toulmin at Bury, *Lancs. D.P.*, 29 September, 3 October 1900.
[2] Sir F. S. Powell at Wigan, *Lancs. D.P.*, 27 September 1900.
[3] O. Leigh Clare at Eccles, *M.G.*, 8 October 1900.
[4] Richard Pilkington at St Helens, *St Helens Reporter*, 28 September 1900.
[5] R. W. Hanbury at Preston, *Lancs. D.P.*, 22 September 1900.
[6] R. A. Yerburgh at Chester, *L. Courier*, 25 September 1900.
[7] Marshall Hall at Southport, *Lancs. D.P.*, 3 October 1900.

rivals to manage your affairs at Westminster'.[1] Although it was recognised that some Liberals supported the War and stood apart from the notorious pro-Boers like Scott, Labouchere, Clark and Ellis, nonetheless they belonged to the same party; if returned to Parliament, said F. E. Smith, a Liberal like W. H. Lever 'would find himself as likely as not rubbing shoulders with Dr Clark, Mr Ellis and Mr Labouchere (applause and hisses)'.[2] While the pro-Boers were fundamentally misguided, the Liberal Imperialists seemed either ingenuous or disingenuous; their position was 'really becoming too complicated for men of average intelligence'.[3]

The Liberals, on the other hand, argued that, whatever the merits of past diplomacy, since their party now accepted annexation the War was not properly an issue at all. 'Once the War was declared the country's cause became our cause', stated Campbell-Bannerman at Rochdale.[4] Both pro-Boers and Liberal Imperialists could now unite upon Liberal principles, most mellifluously expressed, of course, as Peace, Retrenchment and Reform. The Gladstonian William Mather congratulated the Liberals of north east Lancashire on having 'preserved amid all vicissitudes their loyalty to the old watchwords, which were the device of the Manchester school, "Peace, Retrenchment, and Reform" (great cheering)'.[5] The slogan, however redolent of the old Liberalism, was elastic. Retrenchment and social reform were not obvious bedfellows; but if peace would allow military retrenchment the way to reform might be unblocked. Progressives of all shades of opinion on the War agreed that if the country could afford the large military expenditure it could afford old age pensions. 'Sir William Harcourt had, by readjusting the death duties', explained the pro-Boer Conybeare, 'provided large surpluses for the Tory party to deal with. In doing that, he had introduced the principle of gradation, and if that principle was applied to the income-tax, at least £5,000,000 a year could be secured for providing, as far as it would, old age pensions.' And Sir Edward Grey, speaking in Oldham, met the challenge as to how he could associate with Harcourt by the retort: 'You all remember Sir William Harcourt's Budget – (cheers); that is the sort of Liberalism I have been glad to support (cheers).'[6]

That the Unionist Government had promised old age pensions and had done nothing about them was a common Liberal taunt. Some Tories apologetically affirmed their conviction 'that the Government would during

[1] Balfour at Manchester East, *M.G.*, 28 September 1900.
[2] F. E. Smith in the Wirral, *L. Courier*, 26 September 1900. Smith was as yet unknown but his speech 'had the unique experience of being encored'.
[3] Leader, *M. Courier*, 24 September 1900.
[4] Campbell-Bannerman at Rochdale, *M.G.*, 29 September 1900.
[5] W. Mather at Accrington, *Lancs. D.P.*, 5 October 1900.
[6] C. A. V. Conybeare at St Helens, *Liverpool D.P.*, 21 September 1900; Grey at Oldham, *M.G.*, 1 October 1900. Grey was not on this occasion pledging himself to old age pensions.

345

their next lease of power deal with the matter satisfactorily'.[1] But if pensions were a casualty of the War they were one that went unmourned by those Conservatives who believed that 'if they were going to convert Parliament into a sort of wet-nurse for the people they were going to ruin the British Empire'.[2] And it was with the British Empire that the workingman's interests, as Briton and as Imperialist, were ineluctably bound up. In St Helens Seton-Karr noted that his opponent Conybeare 'very often talked about the classes and the masses, setting the working men and their employers at loggerheads', and set forth the Conservative creed 'that the interests of the men and of the employers were absolutely identical'.[3] For the Conservatives the War was a means of dramatising the essential political unity of the nation. They thought they were healing rifts; their opponents accused them of only papering over the cracks. 'Don't be misled', read a Liberal bill. 'Kruger's a Tory; Balfour's another.'[4]

II

The personal attacks upon Chamberlain illustrate both the Liberals' deep distrust of him and his own ascendancy. It had been Chamberlain's War; it was Chamberlain's Election. This was, it was said, 'practically the dictatorship on the part of one man',[5] and his personal motives and conduct were put under the most unfavourable construction. Chamberlain was accused by Philip Stanhope, Liberal M.P. for Burnley, of having whitewashed Rhodes under threat of blackmail. 'If Mr Chamberlain can be discredited', Stanhope's strategy was elucidated, 'then the Government's house of cards is irretrievably demolished.'[6] Stanhope's was an extreme example of a political vendetta but there were personal vendettas too, which accused the Chamberlain family of war-profiteering. 'It was a blessed thought to remember', said a Liberal M.P., delivering his prepared sallies,

that as the Empire expanded the Chamberlain family 'contracted' (applause). Let not the people forget, whatever they thought of Mr Chamberlain politically, that he had always proved himself to be an excellent 'family man' (applause). To his relatives he was always a firm friend, and the friend of their firms (hear, hear)... Mr Chamberlain had said that the war was a feather in his cap; it was a feather in his nest (applause).[7]

[1] J. W. Maclure at South Reddish, *M. Courier*, 2 October 1900.
[2] W. J. Galloway in Manchester South West, *M.G.*, 29 September 1900.
[3] Seton-Karr at St Helens, *L. Courier*, 1 October 1900.
[4] Bill in Manchester East, *M.G.*, 3 October 1900.
[5] W. Mather at Burnley, *Lancs. D.P.*, 3 October 1900.
[6] Leader, *Lancs. D.P.*, 3 October 1900. On the 'missing telegrams' on which Stanhope's case rested cf. Garvin and Amery, *Life of Joseph Chamberlain*, III, 108–25.
[7] Ellis Griffith at Southport, *Lancs. D.P.*, 11 October 1900.

346

Moreover, the mistrust upon which this kind of invective fed was widespread. It was not a Whig who contrasted 'this Brummagem upstart, who had no thought beyond his own personal ambition, had neither sense of responsibility nor sense of honour', with 'the old leaders of the Conservative party': it was Keir Hardie.[1] The future drift of his policy was anticipated with deep misgivings. Imperialism might well bring protection in its wake. 'Mr Chamberlain', it was recalled, 'had already had some little philanderings with protection and the people of England must beware lest protection stole upon them like a thief in the night.'[2]

When it came, therefore, the reaction against Chamberlain and his policies tapped a fund of latent hostility and suspicion. 'What had a Blackburn weaver with £1 a week or on short time got to do with an Empire and glory?', Philip Snowden had asked.[3] After the War, progressive candidates were openly saying that people were getting tired of thinking Imperially ('Well, I think we have done this long enough. It is time we began to think domestically'), tired of chasing Mad Mullahs in different parts of the world when they had plenty of Mad Mullahs at home.[4] Churchill, whose political career was bound up with Lancashire's change of heart, was the most adept at deploying against Chamberlain, whom he dismissed as 'a Birmingham man of unusual versatility and large views', the weight of Lancashire's political history. 'You will be proud in twenty years to say that we held Lancashire for Free Trade against a Birmingham attack', he said, 'that you in Manchester were true to the old cause of Cobden and Peel (long cheers).'[5] At Bury the chief piece of Liberal literature showed the statue of Peel on the cover with the caption, 'Bury is True'.[6] One Liberal candidate claimed to have stood once more 'because he could not stand by and see the work of Richard Cobden, John Bright, Peel and Gladstone ruthlessly cast aside by that more or less political adventurer from Birmingham, Mr Chamberlain'.[7] Since Birmingham contained 'all the incompetent manufacturers in the world', the tariff struggle was 'a war between the selfish interests of Birmingham, thinking only for itself, and the unselfish public spirit of Lancashire, thinking not only for itself but for the rest of the country'.[8] And the longer Lancashire resisted the more did it become 'almost a territorial war', in which 'We Manchester men are the enemy', and every General Election was 'a struggle on the one

[1] Hardie at Preston, *Lancs. D.P.*, 28 September 1900.
[2] Charles Schwann in Manchester North, *M.G.*, 1 October 1900.
[3] Snowden at Blackburn, *N.D.T.*, 22 September 1900.
[4] W. H. Carr in Preston, *Lancs. D.P.*, 25 November 1910; Oswald Partington in the High Peak, *M.G.*, 12 January 1906.
[5] Churchill in Manchester North West, *M.G.*, 5, 12 January 1906.
[6] Booklet, 'What Is the Issue?', in Bury local collection.
[7] Sir J. Leese at Church, *N.D.T.*, 12 January 1906.
[8] Hilton Young at Preston, *Lancs. D.P.*, 25 November 1910.

side to keep this city politically great and on the other to make it politically little'.[1] On polling day in January 1910 the *Guardian* published across seven columns of its main Manchester news page line drawings of the statues of Cromwell, Peel, Bright, Cobden and Gladstone (plans for whose memorial the Manchester Liberal Federation had abandoned due to lack of interest in 1898) under the heading, 'Manchester's Silent Witness'.

As a corollary, the Tariff Reformers were inevitably accused of wishing to bring back the conditions of the Hungry Forties. The old men were sought out to bring forth their memories – of bread at 8*d*. or 10*d*. a loaf at Morecambe, 10*d*. a loaf for stale bread in Manchester East, bread at 1*s*. 2*d*. a four pound loaf in Salford West; flour at 7*s*. a score in Blackpool, wheat a guinea a measure at Knutsford, where lump sugar was 10*d*. a pound, coarse brown sugar ('dark as a boot sole') 7*d*. a pound, or 8*d*. a pound 'and like sand at that', and in Manchester brown sugar 10*d*. a pound; in Knutsford, too, life on 'skimmed milk and porridge, mashed potatoes with skimmed milk poured on for dinner, and occasionally boiled cabbage', or 'porridge 21 times a week' in Blackburn.[2] These folk memories (intertwined as they were with recollections of the soup-kitchen days of the Cotton Famine) were not easily exorcised by statistics.

One of the main difficulties of the Tariff Reform position, especially in 1906, was that there was so much confusion over what was proposed. This obscurity encouraged Liberal scare-mongering. But it was a direct result of Balfour's leadership. Balfour's belief that 'high policy depends on fine distinctions' did not absolve him from the charge of 'want of candour' even from those who were accustomed to his dialectical subtlety.[3] Electorally it cut no ice. Balfour's premiership, said Scott, 'was a marvel of shiftiness, a triumph of evasion'.[4] Balfour's Liberal opponent of 1906 was able to score heavily by taking the plain man's view:

He had read all Mr Balfour's speeches on the fiscal question – (A voice: 'Are you tired?' followed by laughter.) No, he was not tired, but he was in 'a state of great philosophical doubt' (laughter). His final impression was that Mr Balfour was a Free Trade Protectionist (renewed laughter). But it was a misfortune that Mr Balfour could not give Lancashire people a straight answer to a straight question – was he for or against Mr Chamberlain's protective proposals? – (hear, hear).[5]

Those who claimed to be followers of Balfour laid themselves open to similar charges of ambiguity. But although Balfour aroused irritation and

[1] Leader, *M.G.*, 26 November 1910.
[2] See Liberal meetings at Morecambe and Blackpool, *Lancs. D.P.*, 12 December 1905, 18 January 1906; at Manchester East and Salford West, *M.G.*, 5, 12 January 1906; at Blackburn, *N.D.T.*, 5 January 1906; and Liberal address at Knutsford, *M.G.*, 6 January 1906.
[3] See Hewins, *Apologia of an Imperialist*, I, 9; Hugh Cecil to Balfour, 27 July 1907, BP 49759.
[4] Scott at Leigh, *M.G.*, 30 December 1905.
[5] T. G. Horridge in Manchester East, *M.G.*, 30 December 1905.

even distaste, he did not meet the personal bitterness which Chamberlain, Lloyd George and Churchill had to contend with, possibly because he was less successful electorally than they. 'There is', wrote the *Guardian*,

a kind of inverted craftiness about Mr Balfour, a cunning that seems always to fix him in cleft sticks, a way of aiming at two birds with one stone and only hitting himself with it. If it were based on some mystic doctrine of political self-sacrifice we should revere him, but we fear he is out for votes like many other people and differs from them only in this – that while they go at votes straight he chooses some wonderful roundabout way and then loses it.[1]

As far as the Liberals were concerned Balfour was merely putting a more sophisticated gloss upon the Chamberlainite policy. While admitting that the two approaches were distinct, they insisted that there was 'no difference in the antagonism of the two leaders...to Free Trade': a sentiment echoed by F. E. Smith when he welcomed as his allies 'first, and most warmly, every man who believes in fiscal union with our colonies', but 'also every man who will put on his armour to do battle with the fetish of Cobdenism'.[2] Since neither brand of fiscal reformer was in office after 1905 the difference between them remained academic; and the full development of Tariff Reform as a party policy waited upon Balfour's own formulation of it.

III

The four heads of Balfour's Birmingham speech of 14 November 1907 (they were the terms also of the conference motion to which he was replying) provide the best framework for an examination of the fiscal controversy. These were: the strengthening of the British position in foreign markets; colonial preference; the safeguarding of productive industries; and broadening the basis of taxation.

Securing better terms for British exports by means of retaliation was the thin end of the tariff wedge. This, of course, was an old favourite of Balfour's; it was prompted by his question, 'whether a fiscal system suited to a free trade nation in a world of free traders, remains suited in every detail to, a free trade nation in a world of protectionists', and it led to his plea ('in harmony with the true spirit of free trade') 'for freedom to negotiate that freedom of exchange may be increased'.[3] In contrast to the preferentialists, the retaliationists looked back to Cobden's ideals more in sorrow than in anger. 'Let us have Free Trade by all means', they said, 'but we have not got it now.'[4]

[1] Leader, *M.G.*, 8 December 1910.
[2] Leader, *Lancs. D.P.*, 20 December 1905; Smith at Walton, *L. Courier*, 1 December 1905.
[3] Balfour, *Economic Notes on Insular Free Trade*, paras. 10 and 63.
[4] D. McMaster at Leigh, *M. Courier*, 28 December 1905.

Balfour, it was held, was a better Free Trader than the Liberals whose policy supinely accepted foreign tariffs; England was not true to herself in allowing foreign importation without a system of retaliation. 'Mr Balfour', on the other hand, claimed one candidate, 'wished to do something to reduce tariffs, and if he could do so by making some bargain with foreign countries he (the speaker) should agree with him.'[1] Retaliation was thus a means to 'universal Free Trade' or 'Free Trade all round and no favour'.[2] But the mechanics of the process were somewhat imprecisely explained (or indeed understood) by the Balfourites. '*We* know that retaliation is a farce', the preferentialists had always asserted in private,[3] and the difficulties of implementing the policy in detail were seized on by the Liberals in public. They asked against whom retaliation was to be employed. France? ('with whom we had now such an "entente cordiale"'). Germany? ('which was absolutely our best customer except India'). America? ('Could we retaliate against the United States by putting a duty on cotton? That at least would bring them to their knees (loud cheers)'). Japan? ('I ask you, business men, would it be wise to expose £9,600,000 worth of goods to attack when you can only retaliate on £1,290,000 worth?'). Tariff wars always resulted in a loss of trade and no moderation of the tariff; like Peel they should fight hostile tariffs with free imports. 'Tell me the country against which you wish to retaliate', demanded Sir George Kemp, 'and I will show you why we could not do so with advantage to ourselves (cheers).'[4]

Colonial preference necessarily involved food taxes. The central question was, what effect would these have? The Tariff Reformers claimed that any new taxes on bread, meat or butter would be balanced by remissions of duty on tea, coffee and sugar. 'They were only going to rearrange the present burdens so that they would pay no more in the aggregate on their food than they were doing to-day.'[5] Moreover, the effect of the tax would not in any case be passed on to the consumer, for the foreigner would have to pay it; so that 'even in the first instance, owing to effective competition, there would be no increase in the price of bread'.[6] Competition was such a wonderful instrument that if they would only put a small duty on butter 'there would then be so much competition amongst our own people that the price of Irish and English butter would eventually be cheaper to the consumer, and not

[1] G. Arbuthnott at Burnley, *Lancs. D.P.*, 3 January 1906.
[2] Sir W. Tomlinson at Preston, *Lancs. D.P.*, 28 December 1905; J. G. Groves, address, Salford South, *M.G.*, 2 January 1906.
[3] Joseph Chamberlain to Austen Chamberlain, 12 November 1904, Garvin and Amery, *Life of Joseph Chamberlain*, VI, 644.
[4] See speeches by Harold Cox at Preston, *Lancs. D.P.*, 1 January 1906; Churchill and Kemp in Manchester North West, *M.G.*, 9 January 1906, 1 December 1910.
[5] E. Russell Taylor at Stalmine, *Lancs. D.P.*, 7 December 1909.
[6] Salvidge in Liverpool, *L. Courier*, 4 January 1910.

dearer (applause)'.[1] The theory rested primarily upon the prospects of expanding Colonial sources of supply, for if, as was predicted, 'by 1918 Canada would produce a sufficient quantity of wheat to supply all the British islands three times over',[2] then prices would fall commensurately.

The Liberals found themselves unable to accept these economics. They denounced as a fable the idea that bread would be as cheap under protection as under Free Trade. If, they wondered, a four per cent tax upon the brewers was vindictive, how was it that the people would not feel a six and two-thirds per cent tax upon food?[3] Germany, too, it was recalled, had started with a duty of 2s. on wheat; by 1910 it stood at 11s. 10d. Readjustment of such duties would be no boon: for fifty years the Liberals had not added to the taxation of food; the Government had reduced tea and sugar taxes without any *quid pro quo*. The price of foreign foodstuffs would not fall in order to compete with those from the Empire, which comprised only 25 per cent of the market. Instead, Canadian wheat prices would rise to the new taxed level. The Liberals asked whether the Tariff Reformers did not vitiate their case by treating raw materials separately. For, aside from the point that if raw materials were not taxed 'then the whole doctrine of Colonial Preference broke down, as it was mainly raw materials that we got from the colonies',[4] what was the reason for the distinction? Since 'the colonial ox will surely be provided with a skin, and the colonial sheep will surely grow wool on its back'[5] should not the market price be influenced by the same considerations of supply as food? Yet raw materials were to be exempted from all duties. 'If a tax on corn cheapened the price of bread', it was suggested, 'then Lancashire ought to put a small tax on raw cotton in order to lower its price (laughter)'.[6] It was calculated that '*the average Rochdale family would have to pay 3s. a week* extra as the price of so-called Tariff Reform'.[7] Taxation of food was unthinkable in such circumstances since it would inflict hardships on the poorest classes ('Hands off the people's food') and there was no compensating gain. For trade could not be diverted from its natural channels 'without very serious results to the country and the Empire'.[8]

The Tariff Reformers had despaired of the 'natural channels'; but Balfour's plan for safeguarding home industries managed to stop short of outright protection by characterising 'dumping' as 'a form of competition

---

[1] Morgan Byrne at Bradshaw, *Bolton Chron.*, 1 January 1910.
[2] Max Aitken at Ashton, *M. Courier*, 26 November 1910.
[3] A. H. Scott at Ashton, *M.G.*, 7 January 1910.
[4] Max Muspratt in Liverpool Exchange, *L. Courier*, 6 January 1910.
[5] Sir John Simon in Manchester South West, *M.G.*, 30 November 1910.
[6] F. W. Hirst at Preston, *M.G.*, 30 November 1910.
[7] 'What is the Issue?' (January 1910), Rochdale local collection.
[8] 'Who are our best customers?', leaflet in Gorst collection, Preston.

which most persons would instinctively regard as unfair'.[1] Frank protectionist sentiment, however, replaced imperialism as the mainspring of the Tariff Reform case. Even more than the case for retaliation this relied upon the practical grievance and the blank assertion. The electors must not 'be led away by the clap-trap of capitalists who have become wealthy because of free Trade, but who do not care for the larger welfare of their country or their country-men and country-women'.[2] Since unemployment existed before their eyes the remedy was only a matter of right feeling. 'If they thought it right', said one candidate, 'that people should be wearing American boots while English bootmakers walked the streets barefoot he would scorn to take their votes.'[3] And although the claim of 'work for all' was officially repudiated, the contention that 'Tariff Reform will reduce unemployment below the level at which it has maintained itself during the last two decades'[4] went some way towards it. 'Many industries now dying out', it was explained, 'would be revived and others, long since dead, would be brought to new life.'[5] The Liberals admitted that some imported goods could be made at home but held that, apart from the fact that it would raise prices to the British consumer, interference with imports would injure British trade as a whole out of all proportion.

And whatever help Tariff Reform might give to home industries in general it was difficult to see what help it could give to the cotton industry in particular. Cotton was neither dependent on the home market (in which it was secure anyway) nor was it in decline. If cotton were the only industry, the Conservatives admitted, they might possibly go on under the old system.[6] The Tariff Reformers' normal polemical technique was to seize upon an acknowledged economic problem and to claim that their policy was the solution. In the case of cotton they lacked an opening of this kind. Instead they advanced three claims. They appealed to altruism ('You can feel for people who are not as happily circumstanced as you are; you can feel for people whose industries have hardly been as fortunate as yours.').[7] They claimed that cotton could not stand alone ('The cotton industry must ultimately share the fate of all the other industries in the country. If they flourish, it will flourish. If they are injured, it will be injured.').[8] And they invoked the future ('This was the choice. Would the cotton trade secure for

[1] Balfour, *Economic Notes*, para. 55.
[2] An open letter from Cllr H. Ross Clyne (Manchester South, January 1910), Manchester broadsheet collection.
[3] H. Howell in Manchester North, *M.G.*, 25 November 1910.
[4] Henry White at Gorton, *M. Courier*, 13 November 1909.
[5] C. H. Potter at Prestwich, *M. Courier*, 4 December 1909.
[6] E.g. Arthur Taylor in Manchester North East, *M.G.*, 23 November 1910.
[7] C. B. Crisp at Oldham, *M.G.*, 11 January 1906.
[8] Leader, *M. Courier*, 3 January 1906.

ever the markets of one-fifth of the surface of the earth and one-fourth of the population of the world – that was, the British Empire – or would they go on taking their chance on a gamble for the whole, with the dice loaded against them in three-quarters of the area over which they played?').[1] On this showing, then, the cotton industry had little to gain from Tariff Reform. It did not need the security tariffs would offer it, but with eighty per cent of its production exported it had a great deal to lose. Charles Macara, who was later to describe Tariff Reform as 'an appeal to timidity', declared that 'to tax the necessaries of life, raise the cost of living, and thus enhance the cost of production, would sooner or later throw us out of the race'.[2] Since the Conservatives denied that their proposals would have this effect upon the cost of living they did not concede that cotton would suffer, even if they could not promise that it would benefit. 'If you vote for Tariff Reform', read a Liberal leaflet, 'we *shall* lose the *Cotton Trade* and by working long hours and for low wages we *may* gain the *Tin Whistle* trade.'[3] At this level Free Trade too was 'an appeal to timidity'.

The position of cotton was a more particular difficulty to Tariff Reformers in one respect – India. A Tariff Reform Government, the Liberals asserted, would be in a dilemma: 'either it must quite cynically, and for purely selfish British reasons, deny to India those very benefits of Protection which it had gained office by extolling, or it must extend them to India and thereby strike a deadly blow at the cotton industry of Lancashire'.[4] This was a real difficulty for the Tariff Reformers. Joynson Hicks overcame it in especially brutal (or as he put it 'frank and honest') fashion by saying that 'they took India for the good of England. They conquered India by the sword and they were going to hold India by the sword (cheers).'[5] India should give Lancashire a preference by raising its duties against foreign countries in return for Britain abolishing duties on Indian tea (which had to be abolished anyway to compensate for the corn tax). As Kemp said,

What the Tariff Reformers say comes to this – We refuse to give you in India what you really want, but we will give you something else which you don't want... Whether that will add to the peace of India and their ideas of our disinterested government of them we need not trouble to inquire. At any rate, Lancashire is not to suffer.[6]

[1] George Wyndham at Hale, *The Times*, 31 December 1909.
[2] Article by Macara, 'Cotton and Tariffs', *Lancs. D.P.*, 29 December 1909; cf. Macara, *Recollections*, p. 212.
[3] Leaflet in Gorst collection.   [4] Leader, *M.G.*, 15 November 1910.
[5] Joynson Hicks at Stalybridge, *M. Courier*, 16 November 1909.
[6] Kemp in Manchester North West, *M.G.*, 11 November 1910. As Viceroy, Curzon had been very dubious over the effects of any tariff proposals upon India. 'Our fiscal interests would be subordinated as they always have been (notice the Cotton duties – a most scandalous episode) to Lancashire or other British exigencies.' Curzon to Joseph Chamberlain, 13 November 1904, Garvin and Amery, *Life of Joseph Chamberlain*, VI, 641–2. The truth of this comment (which

Lancashire, of course, was not to suffer either under Liberal finance, but her lack of suffering was in that case to be borne with a better conscience.

The Tariff Reform argument from the point of view of revenue – the fourth head of the Birmingham programme – was integral to the Conservatives' social programme. Chamberlain regretted that he had been forced to abandon the idea of using preferential duties for revenue; but if the corn tax were pre-empted to provide for compensating remissions then revenue must come from protective duties. The Tariff Reformers claimed that there was anything between £100 and £200 millions of manufactured imports upon which they might levy a ten per cent duty. This taxation, it was held, '*would be paid by the foreigner*...By "Free Trade" taxation *we tax ourselves*; by "Tariff Reform" Taxation *we tax the foreigner*.'[1] This method of raising revenue combined equity and painlessness. One Conservative slogan was, 'England expects that every foreigner should pay his duty', and to the Liberal plea that this was misleading, F. E. Smith had a short answer: 'The Liberals said, "You can't tax the foreigner." The Conservatives said, "If you can't, make way for better people who can and will" (applause).'[2] The Liberals cited numerous practical examples to show that the importer not the exporter paid customs duties. And they professed not to understand how, if the Tories were successful in affording a measure of protection by 'taxing those importations of fully manufactured goods which came here as finished productions to compete with British labour',[3] they could also raise revenue from the original amount of imports. Churchill referred to these schemes as 'wonderful visions...of wealth without toil, of taxes paid by foreigners, of work for three hundred thousand people to be found by shutting out foreign imports and manufactured goods, and of a revenue of twelve millions a year to be derived from a ten per cent tax on those same imports and manufactured goods which were shut out'.[4]

In practice these four aspects of the fiscal controversy were often lumped together into generalised assertions as to the respective merits of Tariff Reform or Free Trade. The object lesson was a great standby. Kennington's

Kemp was unknowingly echoing) was borne out by the understanding Curzon came to with Austen Chamberlain in 1908. There was much to be said for leaving on the import duties while removing the excise duties but, Chamberlain concluded, 'To propose that in Lancashire would be suicide'. By adjusting only the foreign tariffs Lancashire would keep its preference; but India would be denied any measure of protection – not for its own good but for Lancashire's. See Chamberlain, *Politics from Inside*, pp. 112–14.

[1] Advertisement for the Manchester candidates, *M. Courier*, 11 January 1910. The most fully formulated tariff proposals were those published in the *Birmingham D. Post*, 8 December 1909, which was widely cited on both sides.
[2] Marshall Hall at Southport, F. E. Smith in the Wirral, *L. Courier*, 23 January 1906, 21 January 1910.
[3] D. MacIver in Kirkdale, *L. Courier*, 16 January 1906.
[4] Churchill at Accrington, *M.G.*, 8 January 1906. There are two other completely different versions of this passage in *The Times* and *N.D.T.* for the same date.

poster 'Free Trade' eloquently attributed destitution at home to the fiscal system. 'Great Britain', the Liberal bills countered, 'is the only Great Free Trade Country in the World. THAT'S WHY WE LEAD!'[1] Conversely, the example of Germany was often cited. The Tariff Reformers argued that German prosperity was due to tariffs; but they were loth to abandon their claim that British workmen should be protected against unfair competition from Germany. For the workers of Gorton – 'The concrete fact of a German made article that has done them out of work is enough', the supporters of the Tariff Reformer White maintained in 1910. But this sort of inference was to invite the riposte that 'on Mr White's own showing, SWEATED WAGES ARE PAID ABROAD UNDER TARIFF REFORM'.[2] The Liberal arguments from offal ('Protection will give you horseflesh sausages') followed from this, and the working-class prejudice in favour of white bread was ruthlessly exploited: to which the Tariff Reformers replied, somewhat uneasily, either that the Germans preferred black bread or that their prosperity was causing its consumption to fall. ('They can have it whichever way they like, but not both ways at once', reflected the *Guardian*.)[3] At its simplest, then, 'Free Trade and Prosperity' were solemnly set against 'Protection and Poverty' by the Free Traders, with the conjunctions reversed by the Tariff Reformers.

There was a further argument (Seely called it 'the main point') derived more or less directly from the American experience: 'that political corruption must come with protective duties'.[4] Powerful interests would have a sinister concern in manipulating a tariff system for their own benefit. The workingman would gain nothing; it would mean 'trusts for the rich, crusts for the poor'.[5] The grand virtue of Free Trade, on the other hand, was its combination of efficiency and impartiality. 'Free Trade', said C. P. Scott with a reverence that was not confined to economic liberals, 'was the basis on which the whole industry and commerce of the country had been built up for two generations. To touch this vast and complicated fabric was very much like touching some great organic creation of nature in the hope of building up a living structure by the art of man.'[6]

IV

In 1906 *laissez-faire* and progressivism both called themselves Liberalism. The Liberal campaign was cast in a traditional and even a conservative mould. Campbell-Bannerman, his supporters explained, stood for 'a policy

[1] Liberal leaflet in Gorst collection. For 'Free Trade' see above, pp. 132–3.
[2] *M. Courier*, 29 December 1909; Labour leaflet, 'The Black List' (December 1910) in Gorton collection.
[3] *M.G.*, 5 January 1910.   [4] Seely in Abercromby, *L. Courier*, 5 January 1906.
[5] Charles Schwann in Manchester North, *M.G.*, 1 January 1910.
[6] Scott in Manchester North West, *M.G.*, 7 January 1910.

covered by the oldest and best of political watchwords, "Peace, Retrenchment, and Reform"', and his 'insistence upon the necessity for retrenchment in our national expenditure' was held to have 'favourably impressed all classes of the people'.[1] There was a touch, but no more than a touch, of irony in one Liberal candidate's outright claim to be 'a rank Conservative for the first time in his life' because over Free Trade he wished 'to keep what they had got' and did not want 'any new-fangled ideas of taxation on the food of the people'.[2] For the most part issues like unemployment were brushed aside ('I dare say the expenditure of the late Government has been largely responsible', said Churchill)[3] in favour of unconstructive banalities that offended neither old nor new Liberals. Yet this was also a great progressive victory. Because the new elements in the Liberal appeal did not receive adequate specific recognition a great symbolic issue was invested with deeper overtones; only thus can the extraordinary furore over Chinese Labour be understood.

The introduction of indentured Chinese into South Africa by the Conservative Government was not, as its defenders were quick to point out, very different in kind from past enterprises, notably the sanctioning of indentured labour in British Guiana under a Liberal Government. The electoral context, however, was totally different. Balfour would urbanely express surprise at two prevalent and, as he contended, mistaken beliefs: that his Government had done something reprehensible and that the Liberal Government would reverse that policy.[4] The Tory case was that white labour was unsuitable and that the employment of Chinese was a necessary part of South African economic recovery. Some Liberals were ready to state that the issue had been argued too much 'as if it were merely an economic question' when it was 'a moral question as well'.[5] But, especially in the industrial constituencies where it was a leading topic, doing right by the Chinese was strictly subordinated to keeping them in their place. Chamberlain, it was said, 'had called the war a miners' war. He did not tell them it was to be a war for the benefit of Chinese miners.'[6] Even on the substantive merits of the case it was the feeling that the cause of white immigration had been betrayed that was to the fore. 'I do not care so much about the slavery', admitted Balfour's opponent, Horridge, who, as one of the leading exponents of the whiteman's-country school, indulged in fierce denunciations of the 'filthy' coolies.[7]

[1] Leaders, *N.D.T.*, 22 December 1905; *Lancs. D.P.*, 26 December 1905.
[2] Sir J. Leese at Belthorn, *N.D.T.*, 13 January 1906.
[3] Churchill in Manchester North West, *M.G.*, 10 January 1906.
[4] Balfour in Manchester East, *The Times*, 13 January 1906.
[5] Harold Cox at Preston, *Lancs. D.P.*, 29 December 1905.
[6] T. G. Horridge in Manchester East, *M.G.*, 6 January 1906.
[7] Horridge in Manchester East, *M.G.*, 3 January 1906.

The deeper significance of the question, however, lay in the extent to which it went beyond any reasonable consideration of benefit to the potential emigrant and symbolised the whole status of labour in relation to capital. It was of the essence that the Government which was responsible for Chinese Labour was the Government which would not reverse the Taff Vale judgement. The mines, explained L. W. Zimmerman, were doing well 'but they were not doing well enough for the capitalist, who wanted to reduce wages and get cheap labour'[1] – a line or argument plainly capable of extension. The Liberal George Harwood reported that: 'The largest mineowner in South Africa said to him, "We don't want any of your trade unionism over here", and that was the secret of the position.'[2] The episode, then, involved a principle ('especially for the labourers of this country')[3] which was of universal application. Whether the Liberal and Labour parties were seriously maintaining that the Unionists might introduce Chinese labour into Lancashire is a moot point. But certainly they asked, where was the inner check in the policy the Unionists defended? They declared that 'if it was right to employ Chinese in the colonial mines at a shilling a day, then it was right to bring them into Lancashire and put them into the cotton mills under similar conditions'.[4] For Liberals in industrial constituencies, like William Byles in Salford North, there was a heaven-sent opportunity to explain 'the necessary connection between Chinese Labour on the Rand and home labour in Salford' and to seize on the Unionist policy as 'a degradation to the cause of labour everywhere'.[5]

v

Since a great progressive issue did not exist it had been easy, not to invent, but to inflate one. Underlying Chinese Labour, of course, was the Liberal promise to reverse the Taff Vale judgement, just as in 1910 the Liberal

---

[1] L. W. Zimmerman in Manchester East, *M.G.*, 3 January 1906.
[2] Harwood at Bolton, *N.D.T.*, 20 December 1905.
[3] E. Hamer at Blackburn, *N.D.T.*, 23 December 1905.
[4] E. Hamer at Blackburn, *N.D.T.*, 3 January 1906. The frequent statements to this effect are only an assertion of moral equivalence: but what about the following report to its members by the Preston Spinners?

'The principal of any Government or party allowing Chinese labour to be imported into any portion of the British Empire is too unpleasant to think about as there is no knowing where it will stop; and it is not outside the limits of possibility for Chinese or other cheap foreign labour to be imported into Preston and other parts of Lancashire upon the grounds that many of the old mills in the county cannot be worked at a profit.

Remember! English ships are manned by Lascars and our coal mines in Scotland worked in many cases by Polish miners; consequently it is in no wise impossible to imagine old cotton mills being worked by cheap labour if you and public opinion will permit it; because those who voted in Parliament in favour of white men in South Africa being deprived of the chance to work there would have little or no hesitation in our opinion in doing the same thing for us when it suited their purpose or if we happened to be engaged in some big strike against a reduction in wages.' *Lancs. D.P.*, 29 December 1905.   [5] Interview with Byles, *M.G.*, 15 January 1906.

undertaking to remedy the Osborne judgement was a necessary condition of Labour support; but neither of these essentially conservative proposals fired the imagination. The issues arising from the Budget of 1909, which dominated the next two elections, substantially fused the Free Trade and progressive lines of policy. Just as the progressives' notions as to how revenue might be raised for social reform had played their part in prompting the Conservatives to seek other means of 'broadening the basis of taxation', so the prospect of a revenue tariff sharpened the Liberals' awareness that 'if it could not be proved that social reform (not Socialism) can be financed on Free Trade lines, a return to Protection is a moral certainty';[1] and the 'Free Trade Budget' in turn threw doubtful Tories back upon Tariff Reform. Tariff Reform and social reform drove each other on. The premises of the progressive social programme were really two. The first was stated by J. R. Clynes when he said: 'Free Trade was the most perfect system on earth for creating wealth. Its operation in distributing that wealth fairly was not so perfect.' The second by the *Guardian* when it affirmed 'the principle that the prime necessity of life should never be taxed till every other resource has been exhausted'.[2]

Churchill had led the defence of Free Trade in the north west and he now led the offensive in favour of the policy that developed out of it: one with which he was particularly identified. The Conservatives carped at Churchill for still imagining that he was 'a Lancashire force',[3] but he succeeded, most fully in January 1910, in imposing his own view of the issues upon the region. 'Mr Churchill seems in a peculiar sense to belong to Lancashire', wrote the *Guardian*; 'certainly Lancashire people feel towards him and listen to him as one of themselves, and they have come to regard him as the politician who is best able to interpret their economic and political convictions to themselves and to the country.'[4] When his Lancashire speeches were published he expressed the hope that they stated 'some of the main arguments upon which we may rely in forms which I hope will make them simple and plain', and offered them 'as ammunition passed along the firing line'.[5] Never was a hope better grounded. His very words were taken by others and used as their own. He had outlined the case upon which virtually every Liberal and Labour candidate was to rely.

Churchill did not pitch his claims low. 'A new strength', he asserted, 'has

---

[1] Asquith to St Loe Strachey, 9 May 1908, Gollin, *Proconsul in Politics*, p. 152. Gollin calls this 'a startling secret': a curious judgement.

[2] Clynes in Manchester North East, *M.G.*, 11 January 1906; leader, *M.G.*, 5 May 1902.

[3] *M. Courier*, 4 December 1909.   [4] Leader, *M.G.*, 13 December 1909.

[5] Churchill, *The People's Rights*, preface. This book draws upon the speeches of Churchill's Lancashire campaign of December 1909; it complements his earlier speeches reprinted in their original form in *Liberalism and the Social Problem*. Parallel citations to them will be given below where appropriate for the passages quoted from Churchill's speeches.

come into political life and has filled it with a reality and a seriousness which many were beginning to feel had departed when Mr Gladstone died.' Social problems stood in the centre of the new politics. 'When you come to look into the affairs of your own country', he challenged, 'I do not say that there is no light mingled with the shade. There is. But there is a great deal of shade.'[1] Money was needed – and would be raised by the Budget – to pay not only for Dreadnoughts and old age pensions 'but to develop large, constructive, interdependent schemes of social reorganisation (cheers)'.[2] In the forefront stood National Insurance, comprising state-aided insurance against unemployment, sickness and invalidity, with provision for widows and children deprived of a breadwinner ('the same kind of great scheme of insurance which Bismarck gave to consolidate the structure of the social life of Germany');[3] labour exchanges, which tested willingness to work, were complementary; and reform of the Poor Law to rescue the children, the incapacitated, and those at present debarred from pensions would follow. 'All that', he said, 'depends upon the Budget.'[4]

Given these objectives, the problem came down to raising the money. The Tariff Reform scheme he refused to take seriously. 'It would be a very interesting thing', he commented,

if we could raise all our revenue by taxing the foreigner. Why we could all retire (laughter). There would be no need for us to go to work any more (laughter). We should simply have to sit still and tax the German, and the Frenchman, the Italian and the American, and all these good people would come and pour their wealth into our lap.[5]

Taxing the foreigner 'would be utterly contemptible if it were not utterly absurd (cheers)... The revenue upon which we live must come from British pockets, and all other language is mere folly and deception.' There were only two courses open: to tax accumulated wealth or weekly wages. Free Trade finance must take account of – though it was not responsible for – the fact that the number of wealthy people in the country was growing whilst the income of workingmen was almost stationary.

The disproportion between the rewards of capital and labour which is now evident in every modern country, and which, I think, is not decreasing, and the uneven distribution of wealth may be a grave evil, but it will not be removed by an abandonment of our Free Trade system, and it will only be aggravated by the adoption of a Protectionist system.[6]

[1] Speech at Preston, *M.G.*, 4 December 1909; cf. *People's Rights*, pp. 111–12; *Liberalism*, pp. 368–74.
[2] Speech at Crewe, *M.G.*, 10 December 1909; cf. *Liberalism*, pp. 299 ff.
[3] Speech at Oldham, *M.G.*, 13 December 1909; cf. *People's Rights*, p. 137. And see Gilbert, *The Evolution of National Insurance in Great Britain*, pp. 252–3.
[4] Speech at Crewe.   [5] Speech at Warrington, *M.G.*, 20 December 1909.
[6] Speech at Liverpool, *M.G.*, 9 December 1909; cf. *People's Rights*, pp. 51–2; *Liberalism*, p. 389. Churchill examined these tendencies in a letter to Morley, 27 November 1909, *Companion*, II, 924–6.

Hence the Budget strategy and the 'fundamental issues' – 'They are great class and they are great economic and social issues' – which it raised. For sixty years there had been a tendency from indirect to direct taxation. The Tariff Reformers wished to arrest this. 'We', declared Churchill, 'we believe that is a beneficial tendency. We believe that it is a profoundly democratic tendency.'[1] There was, he maintained, a need for 'equality of sacrifice'.[2] The difference between indirect and direct taxation was 'the difference between the taxation of wages and the taxation of wealth – (cheers) – for indirect taxation is mainly a tax on wages, and direct taxation is mainly a tax on the accumulated profits of the capitalist'.[3] The other elements of the crisis were contingent upon the Government's deliberate decision to opt for direct taxation. 'The quarrel between a democratic electorate and a one-sided hereditary chamber of wealthy men', Churchill concluded, 'has often been threatened, has often been averted, has been long debated and long delayed, but has always been inevitable. It is now open and it is now flagrant and it must be brought to a conclusion.'[4]

This in essence was the progressive case. There were, of course, two other ways, apart from income taxes, in which the Budget raised revenue. The land taxes were welcomed by the Liberals as a step in the right direction. That unearned increment should make a contribution to the needs of the community was natural justice. In this respect too the Budget placed 'The Burden on the Right Back'.[5] The whisky and tobacco duties, on the other hand, would be paid by all – indeed Churchill justified them by saying, 'I think the working classes would have thought poorly of a Government which was afraid to come to them for their share.'[6] Although Socialists like Hyndman might cavil, arguing that it amounted to 'feeding a dog with its own tail',[7] the Labour Members accepted the progressive programme. 'Socialists supported the Budget upon its merits', declared J. R. Clynes, 'and why the people had so long and so silently borne their burdens passed his comprehension.' Speaking in Gorton, Arthur Henderson asked whether they could 'go on fighting a Government that has passed such a great social reform, when there is a responsibility for finding the money?'[8] They could not; they 'would back up Mr Lloyd George to the hilt'.[9]

[1] Speech at Warrington; cf. *People's Rights*, p. 64.
[2] Speech at Burnley, *M.G.*, 18 December 1909.
[3] Speech at Warrington.
[4] Speech at Southport, *M.G.*, 6 December 1909; cf. *People's Rights*, p. 3.
[5] Leaflet, 'The Unearned Increment Tax', Gorst collection.
[6] Speech at Bolton, *M.G.*, 8 December 1909.
[7] H. M. Hyndman at Burnley, *N.D.T.*, 23 December 1909.
[8] Clynes in Manchester North East, Henderson in Gorton, *M.G.*, 17 December 1909, 22 January 1910.
[9] James Sexton in West Toxteth, *Liverpool D.P.*, 25 November 1909.

The support of avowed socialists lent colour to the Conservative charges that the Budget was an exercise in pure socialism. There was a widespread legend that Lloyd George had framed it upon the proposals of Philip Snowden. (Snowden naturally did nothing to discourage this story.) 'They were told', said the Conservatives, 'that Socialism and Liberalism were two different things but just now they were in a working and practical alliance.'[1] They saw before them now 'the complete fusion of Radicalism and Socialism, which has been in process for some time'.[2] The Tories confided that they 'could respect a real Liberal representative of the Gladstone–Bright school',[3] but such were no longer before them. 'Even Mr Lloyd George', it was recalled, 'had said that the old Liberalism was dead.'[4] They feared that he was right. 'Was there', asked one Tory speaker, 'a real Liberal present who believed in the old principles of individualism, which were so dear to the Manchester school?'[5] The Liberal party was now imbued with socialism and 'every action of the Government seems to drive one to the conclusion that they are determined to rely on Socialistic principles rather than on any other'.[6] Lloyd George and Churchill were particularly responsible. 'Between the ideals projected by Mr Lloyd George in his lurid rhetoric and the ideals of the Right-to-Work Manifesto there is no essential difference in principle', it was asserted.[7] And the conclusion that the Conservatives drew was that 'the Liberal Unionists and their own party were the real upholders of the Gladstone and Bright principles'.[8]

By and large, the Liberals faced these charges with equanimity. John Morley himself, the biographer of both Cobden and Gladstone, declared that 'they might say they were a Socialist Government if they liked', but insisted that 'more quackery, more economic charlatanry', would come from the Tariff Reformers than from 'a hundred Mr Snowdens'.[9] They wanted to see 'an era of social reform', but, Alfred Emmott maintained, 'so far as we have gone in the direction of Socialism, so-called, whether it be in regard to free and compulsory education, whether it be in regard to old age pensions, or in respect of any other reform, we have not diminished, but rather added to the liberty of the individual'.[10] Far from revealing that it was a spent force, the years since 1906 had shown that 'Liberalism is a living system', which

[1] George Bowles at Blackburn, *N.D.T.*, 10 December 1909.
[2] London letter, *M. Courier*, 28 November 1910.
[3] Leader, *Blackburn Gazette*, 22 January 1910.
[4] G. D. White at Southport, *Lancs. D.P.*, 6 December 1910.
[5] Sir Gilbert Parker at Southport, *L. Courier*, 12 December 1910.
[6] Ian Malcolm in Salford North, *M.G.*, 5 January 1910.
[7] Leader, *L. Courier*, 9 December 1909.
[8] Gershom Stewart at Heswall, *L. Courier*, 5 December 1910.
[9] Morley at Blackburn, *The Times*, 3 December 1910. Had he lived to see Snowden at the Exchequer, doubtless he would have stood by his judgement.
[10] Emmott at Great Harwood, *Lancs. D.P.*, 8 December 1910.

'demands for the community, acting through the State, in some cases the control *of,* and in all cases equal access *to,* those gifts of nature that are essential to all'.[1] As to the Conservative charge that 'The very first result of the Budget was to set class against class',[2] some Liberal candidates revealed that they had had 'letters from rich men saying that...they could not bear Lloyd George, and that they would this time withdraw their support' and intimated that 'poor men ought to know it too (cheers)'.[3] And the well-to-do were warned that 'the welfare and security of wealth in this country will depend in the future, as in the past, on its civic and social loyalty' and that if it ever came to 'a class fight between all the rich and all the poor, the poor might be hit first, but the rich could not win'.[4]

Insofar as the Conservatives condemned Liberal policy as being socialistic it was because of the way it raised rather than the way it spent money. The Conservatives were pledged, at least *ex post facto,* to both the Dreadnoughts and the pensions. The only alternative to the Budget, everyone agreed, was Tariff Reform. The action of the House of Lords in rejecting the Budget had to be seen in this light. 'We opposed the Budget on its own account', Lord Lansdowne explained at Liverpool, 'and we also opposed it because we don't want the country to be switched off Tariff Reform and switched on to another policy which we believe to be suicidal (cheers).'[5] The Lords had acted so that the people might make their considered choice. 'Of course, if you want the Budget you can have it', Lord Curzon conceded at Burnley. 'Supposing you do not want it, the House of Lords will have provided you with a constitutional opportunity of saying so (hear, hear).'[6] On these terms, the action of the House of Lords was a mere procedural move. 'If they wanted the Budget', it was asked, 'what on earth did it matter if it was deferred a few weeks?'[7]

For the Liberals, however, great issues of representative government had been raised, and the shades of Cromwell, Pym, Hampden and Milton were summoned to battle. One aspect of the 1910 elections was this clash of historic principle. Strangely enough, the Labour candidates were among those most eager to re-fight the Civil War, asserting the need to 'safeguard the liberties their forefathers won'.[8] A Labour leaflet recalled that 'for nine years (1649 to 1658) the English Parliament was without a House of Lords'

[1] 'What Is the Issue?' (January 1910), p. 14; booklet in Rochdale local collection. All this passage was in heavy type.
[2] A. A. Tobin at Preston, *Lancs. D.P.,* 30 December 1909.
[3] W. P. Byles in Salford North, *M.G.,* 1 December 1910.
[4] Leader, *M.G.,* 21 December 1909.
[5] Lansdowne at Liverpool, *M.G.,* 6 January 1910.
[6] Curzon at Burnley, *The Times,* 22 December 1909.
[7] R. Pierpoint at Warrington, *L. Courier,* 5 January 1910.
[8] J. Macpherson at Preston, *Lancs. D.P.,* 8 December 1909.

362

and maintained that 'the nation reaped the greatest moral and material advantage at home and abroad'. 'In 1641', stated the rival Tory interpretation, 'the English House of Commons abolished the Second Chamber, and the House of Commons became the greatest tyrant to the democracy of England that there had ever been.'[1] At the heroic level the struggle was between People and Peers. In the Peers' version the great evil was a 'chance majority in the House of Commons', 'that worst of tyrannies – the tyranny of a chance majority in a Single Chamber'.[2] The hereditary element in the House of Lords, by contrast, provided a more stable influence. 'We need not trim our sails there to catching the passing gusts of popular opinion', Curzon explained.[3] In the People's version, the House of Lords, acting in its own interests, had overthrown the constitution. 'The Peers', declared Lewis Harcourt, 'have proclaimed a class war. Very well; they shall have it – (cheers) – and on their heads be the blood of the conflict they have caused.'[4]

But there was also a utilitarian aspect to the issues of the 1910 Elections which focused attention less upon constitutional machinery as such than upon its likely workings. The question was, the Tories implied, not so much what powers to allow to any British Government but what powers to allow to this particular Liberal Government. 'The House of Lords may or may not enjoy the public confidence and favour', it was admitted; 'but we are quite certain that the British nation is not going to abolish the House of Lords in order that the party led by Mr Lloyd George and Mr Winston Churchill may be free to do as they please.'[5] Those Conservatives who claimed that they 'would much sooner be governed by the Germans than by Mr Churchill'[6] were clearly in no mood to quibble at the Peers rather than the People ruling. The prime need was for an effective brake; hence the growing emphasis on reform of the House of Lords in order to strengthen it. 'A strong and fair Upper House upon the basis of Unionist Reform', read the full page advertisements in December 1910, 'would be a wise check on all parties. It means security.' Or, quite simply, in letters inches high: 'Unionism Means Safety.' Conversely, the progressive case rested upon the likely benefits to be derived from the emasculation of the House of Lords. 'All progress had been stopped by the Lords in throwing out the social welfare Budget', ran the analysis; looking to the future, 'They might bid good-bye

---

[1] 'Lords and Labour' (December 1910), Gorton collection; A. A. Tobin at Knutsford, *M. Courier*, 12 December 1910.
[2] Ian Malcolm in Salford North, *M.G.*, 10 December 1909; Lord H. Cecil at Burnley, *L. Courier*, 28 November 1910.
[3] Curzon at Oldham, *M.G.*, 16 December 1909.
[4] Harcourt at Rawtenstall, *Lancs. D.P.*, 6 January 1910.
[5] Leader, *L. Courier*, 23 November 1909.
[6] Lawrence Rawstorne at Blackpool, *Lancs. D.P.*, 5 January 1910: an eerie adumbration of 'better Hitler than Blum'.

to social legislation and social reform if they were going to let the Lords have their own way.'[1] If there was a danger of revolution, it would arise only when progressives became convinced that their reforms were always doomed. 'I don't think', said Scott, 'that there is the smallest danger in this country of our going too fast. The difficulty always is to get anything effectual done at all.'[2]

[1] J. E. B. Seely in Liverpool Exchange, *Liverpool D.P.*, 18 December 1909; A. H. Gill at Bolton, *Bolton Chron.*, 1 January 1910.
[2] C. P. Scott at the Free Trade Hall, *M.G.*, 26 November 1910.

14   *Vox populi*

One voter said he had always voted Blue because his father had, but agreed to vote the other way if Manchester went for Free Trade.

Canvasser's report from Blackpool, 1906

I

Although it is the contention of this book that election results were the manifestation of deep-seated social and political forces, it is nonetheless necessary to establish the exact chronology and immediate context of voting in some detail. Each election campaign had unique aspects; the balance of issues and the balance of advantage were in constant flux. Moreover, the possibility that the progress of the campaign itself influenced the result must be examined. In the first place, developments during the campaign assumed at the time an inflated proportion, and movements of opinion were often attributed to them; secondly, the fact that polling was spread over several weeks was commonly held to have produced a snowball effect in the voting. Whether the campaign had such a clear effect upon voting is highly doubtful. All the indications from the four General Elections 1900–10 suggest that their results are more consistent with long-term than with short-term explanations.

In the late 1890s the Conservatives were slipping slightly from their strong position of 1895, not only in Lancashire but in the country as a whole.[1] In the years 1895–9 there were nine by-elections in the north west, all in Conservative-held seats. Of these, four were not contested by the Liberals. In Liverpool Exchange in 1897 the Conservatives held the seat with a decreased majority; in Middleton in 1897 and in Southport in 1898 the Liberals gained the seats, and at a second election at Southport in 1899 they increased their majority; at the double by-election at Oldham in 1899 the Liberals gained both seats. Then the War broke out. The first test came in the solidly Nonconformist Rossendale division in February 1900, and William Mather held the seat comfortably. In May 1900, however, came the debacle in Manchester South when the 'Mafeking mania' swamped the Liberal effort. Admittedly, South, as the leaders were assured, was 'not a working class constity. – mostly clerks & small residents'.[2] But it was enough to make the

---

[1] See Dunbabin, 'Parliamentary elections in Great Britain', *E.H.R.*, LXXXI (1966), esp. Table 5, p. 93.
[2] Campbell-Bannerman to Gladstone, 28 May 1900, HGP 45987 f. 99.

365

Liberals' blood run cold at the thought of a General Election 'at which, to gain votes, candidates would have to do little more than clap masses of excited persons on the back and say that their excitement did them honour'.[1]

This was, *mutatis mutandis*, much the reasoning of the Unionists in going to the country that September. 'Political events followed one another very fast', said M'Arthur, accurately and prophetically reflecting Chamberlain's thinking, 'and if the election were left over for another year, some other subject might then occupy the mind of the country.'[2] The Liberals, of course, accused Chamberlain of snatching 'a mean advantage'; he was trying to 'take every advantage of the Jingo spirit while it exists, instead of waiting till it evaporates, as Lord Beaconsfield did'.[3] Everything centred on Chamberlain (Salisbury, indeed, at first proposed not issuing a manifesto because 'he had nothing to say').[4] At the end of September the War seemed to be over and the newspapers were printing complacent editorials about hurrying the bonfire preparations; on 25 September, for instance, the *Liverpool Daily Post*'s main headline read, 'The War: Utter Collapse of the Enemy'. This, then, was the mood a week before the first polls.

The Liberals were, on the whole, more optimistic than they had been earlier in the year. Herbert Gladstone thought that there were about seven seats to be won in the north west, in addition to by-election gains, and only two which he expected to lose – those of the pro-Boers Scott and Schwann. As a forecast this was no more accurate or less optimistic than that of his opposite number, Akers Douglas, who expected Lancashire to be one of the areas where the Conservatives would gain.[5] Gladstone's public admission during the campaign that a Liberal majority was unlikely was seized on by the Government. Much attention was focused on the contest in Oldham, the scene of the Liberal triumph the previous year. Winston Churchill was again one of the Conservative candidates and he had by this time acquired some fame as a war hero which served him well. Chamberlain made his only foray outside the Birmingham area to go and speak for Churchill on 25 September. Three days later Campbell-Bannerman, who had undertaken to speak at Rochdale, pulled in a flying visit to Oldham and was so impressed by the enthusiasm with which he was received ('comparisons made with 95 greatly to the detriment of that year')[6] that he included a warm reference to

---

[1] Leader, *M.G.*, 28 May 1900.

[2] Charles M'Arthur at Exchange, *Liverpool D.P.*, 21 September 1900; cf. Garvin and Amery, *Life of Joseph Chamberlain*, III, 606.

[3] Leader, *Lancs. D.P.*, 18 September 1900.

[4] See Sandars to Balfour, 20 September 1900, BP 49760. Salisbury issued a manifesto on 24 September.

[5] See Gladstone's list of constituencies to be won and lost, n.d. (1900), HGP 46108 f. 122; Akers Douglas to Balfour, 19 September 1900, Chilston, *Chief Whip*, pp. 285–6.

[6] Campbell-Bannerman to Gladstone, 30 September 1900, HGP 45987 f. 119.

it in his next big speech in London. But although the Liberal party was rather encouraged (and rather surprised) by the new-found unity of purpose it was daily developing, there was an undercurrent of fatalism: a belief that 'imperialism, as exemplified by the miserable African enterprise, has thrown opulent and dominant Liberals nearer to the Tory party, and they are not likely to return', and a recognition that 'there were certain Liberals who would probably vote Tory at this election'.[1]

Five boroughs polled on 1 October. The Liberals did at least as well as in 1895 in Preston, Wigan, Stalybridge and Rochdale (indeed the disappointment at Rochdale was that they did not capture the seat). Oldham, however, was an anti-climax in that, although Emmott was again returned at the head of the poll, Churchill beat the second Liberal. Emmott called it 'a bad start to the general election', although he was able to point out that the Liberals had shown a clear improvement over their 1895 position.[2] Churchill captured all the headlines, becoming, in his own words, a 'star turn'; he was asked by Balfour to cancel an engagement in London in order to help the Unionists in Stockport. Elsewhere, too, the results were mixed. Some Tories called them 'highly satisfactory' but Chamberlain would go no further than 'satisfactory but not convincing'; while the Liberals claimed to have 'no reason for desponding' and Gladstone thought 'Ashton' and Rochdale 'justifies some hope of Lancs'.[3] On 2 October Manchester and Salford went to the polls. The Liberals previously held only one of these nine seats (Schwann's) and were fearful for that; luckily for them, the swing in North was the least in any of the eight contested divisions and Schwann hung on by 26 votes. In six of the seven other divisions the swing against the Liberals was between 5 and 10 per cent. It has been suggested that the movement against the Liberals in the urban constituencies may have been due more to Irish disaffection than working-class support for the War.[4] If anything, the opposite must be true of Manchester. In the three solid working-class divisions (Manchester East, Manchester South West and Salford South) the swing against the Liberals was 9.6 per cent, 9.3 per cent and 8.0 per cent, respectively; whilst in the two Irish strongholds (Manchester North and Manchester North East) the swing was 2.6 per cent and 3.1 per cent. In suburban Manchester South it was 6.7 per cent – a distinct improvement for

---

[1] Letter from 'Churchman', *M.G.*, 22 September 1900; the Rev. W. Owen in Manchester North, *M. Courier*, 26 September 1900.

[2] Emmott at Oldham, *M.G.*, 2 October 1900.

[3] Leader, *M. Courier*, 2 October 1900; Chamberlain to his wife, 2 October 1900, Garvin and Amery, *Life of Joseph Chamberlain*, III, 602; leader, *N.D.T.*, 2 October 1900; Gladstone to Campbell-Bannerman, 2 October 1900, CBP 41216 ff. 14–15. Gladstone meant Stalybridge.

[4] See Pelling, *Popular Politics and Society*, pp. 93–4. It is a difficult point to resolve since there were large numbers of Irish in the 'working-class' divisions while the 'Irish' divisions were largely working class.

the Liberals over the by-election. Fixing its eyes upon the Liberal gains elsewhere, the *Guardian* concluded that 'the war fever in its most acute form is fast dying out except in a few of the largest cities' and disingenuously stated that in its own city 'the strength of the political parties remains unchanged'. The *Manchester Courier*, on the other hand, was 'hardly surprised to observe that the local organ of the pro-Boers does not venture to discuss the results of the various contests'. On 3 October the Conservatives slightly improved their position in Ashton. The Liberals continued to dwell upon their net gain of seats in the country to date; and it was Churchill's opinion that the election had 'shown so far the strength not the weakness of Liberalism in the country'.[1]

Thursday 4 October 1900 was the only really khaki day of the General Election. 'Tories Sweep the Boroughs', 'A Bad Day for the Liberal Party', read the headlines of Liberal newspapers which had hitherto put on a brave face. 'At last!' exclaimed Chamberlain. In the north west the Liberals captured a seat at Stockport, despite the Conservatives' special efforts and the importation of Churchill. It was, however, the Conservatives who improved their position in the other seats. At Burnley Philip Stanhope was unexpectedly defeated ('the victim of the khaki boom');[2] at St Helens the movement of opinion was unusually strong; and in the Kirkdale and Exchange divisions of Liverpool, 'not even the most sanguine Conservative anticipated the alarming shrinkage of the Liberal total'.[3] The voting in Widnes followed the Liverpool pattern, and here the Irish influence cannot be discounted.

With the shift from the boroughs to the counties, the Liberals drew breath. In the cities, they reflected, the Tories' gains had been 'tolerably small' – 'The result is a gain for the Tories, but it is not such a gain as they expected.' And Herbert Gladstone threw out the suggestion that if the election had taken place a few months earlier it would all have been much worse.[4] Chamberlain did not let up. It was at this stage that he sent the notorious telegram which, by the time that it arrived at Heywood, read: 'Every seat lost to the Government is a seat sold to the Boers.'[5] On 8 October the Liberals gained seats at Radcliffe and in the High Peak, and cut the Tory majority in Gorton; and on the next day they gained Lancaster too. Middleton, however, was lost, and Scott suffered a setback at Leigh – but it

[1] Churchill to Rosebery, 4 October 1900, *Companion*, I, 1205–6.
[2] *N.D.T.*, 5 October 1900.
[3] *Liverpool D.P.*, 5 October 1900. The swings were 10.7 per cent and 14.5 per cent.
[4] Leaders, *M.G.* and *N.D.T.*, 6 October 1900; Gladstone at Accrington, *The Times*, 8 October 1900.
[5] Chamberlain had written 'gained to the Boers'. See Garvin and Amery, *Life of Joseph Chamberlain*, III, 600. The Liberals did not believe that such an error could have crept in during transmission; see e.g. the morse transcriptions of 'gained' and 'sold', *Lancs. D.P.*, 15 October 1900.

was enough of a triumph that he held on to the constituency at all. On 10 October five cotton divisions polled and all showed a slight Liberal improvement. The tide had turned, but it was not flowing fast enough to help Sir George Pilkington at Southport on 11 October. Pilkington had renounced Home Rule and had made suitably imperialist speeches at Mafeking time, but all his 'me-tooism' could not hold the seat. And on 13 October, while Sir John Brunner lost ground in Northwich, the Liberals scored a runaway victory at Crewe that was as much a local freak as the Tory victory there in 1895 had been.

'I hoped Lancashire would have done better', wrote Sir Ughtred Kay-Shuttleworth. 'The great town-populations go sadly astray.'[1] But on the whole the Liberals were not downhearted. They thought that 'the Government had reaped the ordinary advantage of having a war to declaim about, but not the extraordinary advantage expected from the expedient of calling everybody who opposed it a traitor.'[2] The Government had preserved a large majority intact – a feat that seemed all the greater in an age that expected the pendulum to swing as a matter of course. Contemporaries were almost exclusively impressed by the seats that changed hands. The Conservatives gained four seats in the north west over the dissolution. They won Burnley in a straight fight whereas they had been beaten there in a three-cornered contest in 1895. Their three other gains, however – Oldham, Southport and Middleton – were all seats which had been Conservative in 1895; and in all three the Liberal share of the poll was higher in 1900 than it had been in 1895. On the other side, the four Liberal gains – High Peak, Lancaster, Crewe and Radcliffe – were all straightforward improvements over 1895. In addition, one of the Oldham seats captured in 1899 was retained. While it is true that the Conservatives scored a notable victory, it marked a falling away from the levels of 1895. The flood of War enthusiasm was virtually confined to the large towns. The smaller boroughs which polled first did not give a jingo lead; this came only when the results from the city divisions were known; but the county divisions which went to the polls with the force of this example before them resisted it and went their own way.

II

From the time of the Bury by-election of 1902 the Unionist Government met with a string of setbacks in by-elections, not least in the north west. There are indications that, left to himself, Balfour would have preferred a dissolution of Parliament in the autumn of 1905; in this preference, however, he was

[1] Kay Shuttleworth to Scott, 12 October 1900, MGP.
[2] Leader, *M.G.*, 15 October 1900.

supported only by William Vaudrey of Manchester among the party managers, and an autumn election was ruled out.[1] The Government was on its last legs. The question, then, was not whether but why there would be an election in the New Year: through Balfour's dissolution or resignation? Everyone was obsessed by precedents. Akers Douglas thought Balfour might resign 'as Mr G. did in '74 *before* the meeting of Parliament'. Sandars came round to the view that if 'an unmotivated resignation' was to be ruled out, 'the reputed advantage of resignation' following a parliamentary setback was 'very trifling, if indeed it is an advantage at all (1895 e.g.)'. Balfour was quite clear in his own mind that while 'the broad result of an election is not likely to be profoundly modified by any difficulties the other side may have in framing either a Government or a policy', there was a considerable advantage in forcing the Liberals' difficulties into the open just before an election – 'an election moreover', so Sandars now believed, 'in which we shall be the attacking party'.[2] Following Rosebery's clean break with official Liberalism in his Bodmin speech, Balfour therefore resigned on 4 December, hoping to profit from Liberal disunity, and Campbell-Bannerman even toyed with the idea of forcing him to carry on ('There was Disraeli's great precedent of 1873'),[3] before contracting out of this game of tactics by setting about forming an administration.

This course of action had several advantages for the Liberals. The separation of Rosebery was accepted even by his erstwhile supporters among the Liberal Imperialists. 'Such a speech as Lord Rosebery delivered to the members of the Liberal League yesterday', wrote the *Lancashire Daily Post* on 12 December, 'reconciles us to his exclusion from a Liberal ministry.' The proximity of an election militated in favour of unity at every level. The Liberals had all the advantages of a Government, yet with their clean slate they retained the advantages of an Opposition attacking the past record. After Balfour had hung on to office so long it was difficult to explain why he should now resign. 'The party retires temporarily because it has chosen to think rather than to vegetate', offered the *Manchester Courier*; when Balfour came to speak to his constituents he explained that the Government had been too 'distracted by internal controversies to go on'.[4] He now sought to bring the question of Home Rule to the fore. The Liberals, by contrast, stood by their position that though they believed in Home Rule it could not be an issue in

---

[1] See Hood's memorandum (really Sandars's), 10 August 1905, BP 49771; Fitzroy, *Memoirs*, I, 280.

[2] For Douglas's view see Sandars to Balfour, 19 October 1905, and his own in Sandars to Balfour, 16 November 1905, both in BP 49764; Balfour to Chamberlain, 2 November 1905, Garvin and Amery, *Life of Joseph Chamberlain*, VI, 737–40; Sandars's memorandum, n.d. (22 November 1905), BP 49764.

[3] Gladstone's autobiography, HGP 46118 f. 92.

[4] Leader, *M. Courier*, 5 December 1905; Balfour at Manchester East, *M.G.*, 11 December 1905.

the next Parliament, an attitude reaffirmed in Campbell-Bannerman's Albert Hall speech on 21 December. As his major policy speech this was remarkable in two respects: it contained a notable lack of policy and it was a huge success. The Tories might sneer at its 'crude and vague promises'[1] but these had not been the point of the occasion. At the Albert Hall, 'after a ten years' exile, Liberalism celebrated its restoration', reported the *Guardian*. 'A Liberal Government is in office', enthused the *Liverpool Daily Post*, 'and Liberal policy has already begun to work.' And it recognised fully and finally the ascendancy of the new Prime Minister. 'In the dark days he kept the flag flying', admitted his former detractors, 'he has fought the battle bravely, and he now sees not only the vindication of Liberal principles but enjoys a personal triumph as well.'[2]

The General Election as a whole, like all the Free Trade elections, centred largely upon Manchester, where Balfour and Churchill were candidates and where polling would take place on the first legal day. The Tory press could not keep away from Churchill; nearly every day the cartoons in the *Manchester Courier* tried to depreciate his influence, but they too called him 'Winston' while referring to other candidates by their surnames. 'He won the election as "Winston",' commented the *Guardian*. 'To add the surname was a waste of time, and to call him "Mr Churchill" was some sign of a rather unattractive pedantry of mind.'[3] Churchill's address was issued on 1 January 1906. Just as he had claimed in 1900 that a Conservative victory would be a national victory (indeed partly because this had been 'perverted to crude and paltry purposes of party') so he now claimed that a Liberal victory would 'not be merely a party victory' but 'a national victory'. Free Trade, he insisted, was the main issue since the victory of either Balfour or Chamberlain was the victory of both. Balfour's address, two days later, set out his own fiscal policy and tacitly admitted that the Liberal Government would gain a majority.

In Manchester itself all the Conservative candidates were Balfourites (some, like W. J. Galloway, with strong Free Food leanings) as were most in that part of Lancashire. Those M.P.s like Coningsby Disraeli, J. G. Groves and Edward Chapman who had been reckoned among Chamberlain's supporters now affirmed their loyalty to Balfour's policy, as did the Tory M.P.s for Preston. In the Liverpool area, by contrast, all the Conservative candidates except M'Arthur were undisguised whole-hoggers. In the north

[1] Leader, *M. Courier*, 23 December 1905.
[2] *M.G.* and *Liverpool D.P.*, 22 December 1905; leader, *Lancs. D.P.*, 6 December 1905; cf. leader, *L. Courier*, 9 January 1906 recalling that at the time of Rosebery's Chesterfield speech the Liverpool Liberals had been distinctly hostile to Campbell-Bannerman, whose leadership they now warmly welcomed.
[3] *M.G.*, 15 January 1906.

west as a whole the candidates were split about half and half. But whereas the Chamberlainites often affirmed their personal loyalty to Balfour, the Balfourites did all they could to dissociate themselves from Chamberlain. 'I have nothing to do with Mr Chamberlain; I am a follower of Mr Balfour', said Cyril Potter in Middleton. And S. W. Royse in Gorton gave his frank opinion that 'a system of preferential tariffs between the Mother Country and the Colonies would lead to great complications, and instead of consolidating the Empire would cause ill-feeling and friction'.[1]

It was not just that the Balfourite policy was a more limited version of Tariff Reform; the Balfourites were less keen on Tariff Reform at all. Consequently they tried to fight the election on other issues. In Manchester South, for instance, where the Liberal address concluded: 'It will be said that there are other issues beside Free Trade, or Protection, but this is the real issue at this election', the Balfourite Conservative's address concluded: 'All other issues must pale into insignificance before the vital ones, Religious Education and Unity of the Empire.'[2] There was, then, a fairly overt attempt by both sides to promote their own favourite issues and ignore those of their opponents. 'If he was silent upon the fiscal question', admitted John Rutherford, 'his opponent was also silent upon several other important questions such as Home Rule, and the education question.'[3] The Balfourites had a clear preference for trying to make the quasi-religious issues prominent; but so too had most of the Chamberlainites, because they happened to be standing in constituencies where Home Rule was a better card than Tariff Reform. This was most obviously true of Liverpool, where the Conservative placards proclaimed: 'Every vote given for a Liberal is a vote for Home Rule.' And the rival newspaper advertisements on the eve of the poll read: 'The Real Issue: Protection versus Free Trade', or 'The Real Issues in Liverpool', listed as: first, Home Rule; second, Religious Education; third, Tariff Reform.

Home Rule was not what it had been. One Conservative canvasser in Heywood admitted 'that the ordinary cottager here is more concerned about John Chinaman six thousand miles away than he is about Ireland sixty miles away'.[4] Chinese Labour was a great favourite on the hoardings. And the announcement of John Burns's appointment as President of the Local Government Board was undoubtedly popular with labour. Indeed, the

---

[1] See letter from a Middleton elector to Chamberlain, *M. Courier*, 12 January 1906; Royse at Gorton, *M. Courier*, 22 December 1905. On the division of Balfourites and Chamberlainites see esp. lists drawn up by Gladstone 1903 and 1904, HGP 46106 ff. 107–18; views of Manchester candidates, *M. Courier*, 6 December 1905, and list in *M.G.*, 30 January 1906.

[2] Addresses in Manchester local collection. 'Unity of the Empire' in this context was not Imperial preference but Home Rule.

[3] Rutherford at Bamber Bridge, *Lancs. D.P.*, 15 December 1905.

[4] *M. Courier*, 16 January 1906.

Government as a whole seemed to get a much better reception than might have been expected, and the recognition that the return of Balfour's Government was, in every sense, impossible, was a help to the Liberals. The electors were reminded that 'a vote given against the Liberal Government is a vote given to recall the old Government to power'.[1] Balfour professed himself struck by the extraordinary indifference his meetings showed in the opinions of the new Government as compared with their interest in the late Government. 'The remarkable rally of reactionary politicians to the Liberal banner' (as F. W. Jowett called it)[2] was another sign of this; there was as yet nothing to alarm the Unionist Free Traders. Against the Liberal cries that Free Trade was in immediate danger the Tories could only respond with the detached comment: 'We do not wish to exaggerate the importance of the issues at stake.'[3] This was hardly a call to strain muscle and thew. A vote of no-confidence in Balfour's Government was perceptibly in the offing.

On Saturday, 13 January, the *Guardian* took note of the Liberal victory in Ipswich, which had irregularly gone to the polls the previous day, but insisted that 'the real work begins to-day. For to-day Manchester, the birthplace and capital of Free Trade, votes on a clear Free Trade issue.' At the outset of the election the Liberals had expected to hold Manchester North and to gain the two prosperous divisions of North West and South; but they had no great hopes for the three working-class divisions of North East, South West and East (Balfour's seat).[4] Manchester, Salford, Rochdale, Ashton, Burnley, Bury and Stalybridge all polled on the first day. In 1900 they had elected thirteen Conservatives and one Liberal. Now they returned fourteen progressives. 'The most sanguine expectations of the Free Trade party were exceeded on Saturday', admitted the Liberals, and hastened to pay tribute to Churchill's action in standing for North West ('It was an act of splendid daring. It has had a magnificent triumph.'). The Conservatives had expected a setback: 'Few, however, can have anticipated a result so disastrous in its immediate effects.' And the Liberals at once took up the cry that 'Balfourism has been beaten in the boroughs', and that 'Manchester's verdict is decisive.'[5]

The moral force of the Manchester results, especially of Balfour's defeat, could not help but change the tone of the Unionist campaign. 'That is all the more reason why I should be returned', argued the adaptable F. E. Smith, 'because you want a few good men on the Conservative side.'[6] On 15 January there was voting in Bolton, Oldham, Preston and Warrington. In 1900 they

---

[1] Leader, *Liverpool D.P.*, 13 January 1906.
[2] Article by Jowett, *Clarion*, 12 January 1906.
[3] Leader, *M. Courier*, 13 January 1906.
[4] See forecasts, *M.G.*, 5 December 1905, *The Times*, 13 January 1906.
[5] Leaders, *Lancs. D.P.*, *Oldham Evg Chron.*, *M. Courier*, *N.D.T.*, *Liverpool D.P.*, 15 January 1906.
[6] Smith at Walton, *Liverpool D.P.*, 15 January 1906.

had elected only two Liberals; now all seven seats were captured. So, as Liverpool prepared to vote, the north west had not elected a single Conservative M.P. At a lunch to the Unionist candidates on polling day Salvidge's men hit back defiantly. 'Were they men of Liverpool to sell their birthright as citizens of the United Kingdom and a great Empire for a mess of miserable mercenary free trade pottage like Manchester?' asked R. P. Houston.[1] The Salvidge machine held five of the nine seats, a result which, the *Courier* commented, 'has greatly disappointed the confident expectations of their opponents'. It was the two business divisions which Seely and Cherry captured for the Liberals; Austin Taylor was elected as a Free Trader and T. P. O'Connor as a Nationalist. Salvidge claimed that 'in the populous parts of the city where their victories had been won, 97 per cent of the voters were workingmen, who had stood true to the traditions of the past and of their party'.[2] In the other boroughs the Liberals carried all before them, except in Blackburn and Wigan, where the Free Traders Sir Harry Hornby and Sir Francis Sharp Powell held their seats.

In the county divisions, polling from 18 January, there was an inevitable backwash from the boroughs. In Altrincham, for instance, the Tory Coningsby Disraeli had been saying in December that the Liberals 'were not wanting in courage to come forward again'; after the Manchester results he was boasting of how he himself could 'fight with his back against the wall' – and it was said that the number of Conservative workers doubled after the first pollings were known.[3] C. A. Cripps in Stretford seems to have believed that the prior announcement of the Manchester results contributed to his defeat.[4] The swing against him was 17.7 per cent; but in Manchester South, the division it most closely resembled, the swing had been 25.1 per cent. In some county divisions the Liberal advances were as great as they had been in the towns. This was true in divisions like Widnes, Wirral, Prestwich, Stretford and Altrincham, which were, at least in part, suburban. But many exhibited that greater stability which had favoured the Liberals in 1900, and which now helped the Conservatives to retain one or two seats like Darwen. North Lonsdale, polling ten days after Manchester, is an interesting case. This was Richard Cavendish's seat and he was confidently expected to retain it as a Liberal. Yet he lost. Cavendish felt 'that there had been a reaction after the wave of Liberal victories, and if their poll had been a week earlier they would have won'.[5]

[1] Houston in Liverpool, *L. Courier*, 16 January 1906.
[2] Salvidge after the poll, *Liverpool D.P.*, 17 January 1906; cf. leader, *L. Courier*, 17 January 1906.
[3] Disraeli at Sale and at Ashton-on-Mersey, *M.G.*, 20 December 1905, 20 January 1906; cf. *M. Courier*, 18 January 1906.
[4] See Parmoor, *A Retrospect*, p. 58.
[5] Cavendish after the poll, *Lancs. D.P.*, 24 January 1906.

It was largely on the experience of 1900 and 1906 that the belief in the 'bandwagon effect' was founded.[1] In particular, the impact of the Manchester results became a legend in the Conservative party ('Black Saturday') and prompted their rather desperate offensives in 1910. But a comparison of the swings day by day shows that there was no snowball gathering size and pace. It was the social character of a constituency which determined its voting, not the sequence in which it polled. Strung out on a calendar, the swings against the Conservatives of 15 to 20 per cent in Stretford, Gorton and Altrincham as late as 18, 22 and 25 January look rather out of place; plotted on a map they are immediately in context with the rest of the Manchester area. This is a factor (like the publication of opinion polls, with which it has been compared) which the activist is inclined to exaggerate. As one observer commented: 'It is experienced much more by the thick-and-thin party man than by the elector who has not yet made up his mind: and the thick-and-thin party man, while he may be elated or depressed by the first results, is unlikely to vote for the enemy merely because of an eleventh-hour emotion.'[2]

The Liberals were inclined to offer a compendious explanation of the results: to say that Lancashire 'spoke in defence of Free Trade and of its staple industries, in detestation of Chinese labour, in condemnation of the most inept and perverse Government of modern times, and in hope of better things at the hands of a Government pledged to sound finance, capable and efficient administration and progressive legislation'.[3] No doubt there is some truth in all of this. The education question is missing; and it is very doubtful whether this had much force, except perhaps among sectarian Nonconformists. Free Trade was the great umbrella; fighting negatively, the Liberals got every disaffected element underneath it. It was, of course, the Chamberlainite position – one accepted loyally by the great man's biographers – that if only the election could have been taken on fiscal reform alone the Liberals would have had a far more difficult time. 'I gained votes as a whole-hearted tariff reformer', said Seton-Karr, the defeated candidate for St Helens.[4] Now it is true that in the north west eight of the fifteen Tories returned were whole-hoggers, and to that extent the 'half-hearted' Tariff Reformers had little to show (though three other Members were Unionist Free Traders). But this is simplistic. In the first place, the Balfourite candidates were putting forward views of (as they hoped) an inoffensive nature in deference to the strong Free Trade sentiment of their consti-

---

[1] See e.g. Snowden, *Autobiography*, I, 118; Bonham Carter, *Winston Churchill as I knew Him*, p. 75; Gollin, *The 'Observer' and J. L. Garvin*, pp. 238–9.
[2] Special correspondent, *The Times*, 23 December 1909.
[3] Leader, *Oldham Evg Chron.*, 16 January 1906.
[4] Letter from Seton-Karr, *The Times*, 19 January 1906. This general verdict is endorsed by Garvin and Amery, *Life of Joseph Chamberlain*, VI, 794–5; Fraser, *Joseph Chamberlain*, p. 273.

tuencies. After the first results had shown which way the wind was blowing those candidates still in the fight retreated further and further towards Free Trade – *they* had no illusions but that Tariff Reform was a vote loser. Secondly, all of the Chamberlainites who were returned came from the Liverpool area. Salvidge told Chamberlain that 'your policy has not lost ground in Liverpool' and that 'the democratic constituencies of Liverpool... went solidly for those candidates who supported your programme in its entirety'.[1] This is disingenuous. Salvidge had, as usual, made Protestantism the issue, and to claim the result as one for Tariff Reform is nonsense (as, indeed, Salvidge's later disenchantment with Tariff Reform shows).

But it is quite true that to call 1906 a Free Trade victory does not do justice to its novel aspects. Herbert Gladstone singled out the cooperation between Liberalism and Labour as 'the chief factor in securing an unprecedented electoral triumph'.[2] Balfour came to the same conclusion. 'Chinese labour', he informed Chamberlain at once, 'was to all appearance the chief stumbling block: but the true cause must have lain much deeper.' Two days later, more confident of his diagnosis, he wrote to Acland Hood: 'My impression is that the "dear Loaf" had very little to do with Manchester: in most divisions it was mere "Labour".' And, in his final synthesis, he told Stanley that 'the constituency did not in the least want to argue any question at all except Chinese Labour, which was a convenient peg upon which to hang their programme'.[3] Stanley himself, who had been overturned by a massive swing at Westhoughton, did not believe that 'the fiscal question as such, had much effect, except in so far as the Labour organisation have for the moment accepted Free Trade as an article of faith'.[4] It is an important qualification; the Liberal candidates in Manchester were dependent on 'labour', but the Labour candidates there were equally dependent on Free Trade.[5] It was a progressive victory, then, but one achieved under the banner of Free Trade; for everyone could agree upon Free Trade, not only progressives but Nonconformists and economic liberals too.

III

There were only three by-elections in the north west during the 1906 Parliament. In September 1907 the Unionists barely maintained their position in Liverpool Kirkdale. In April 1908, in the Government's blackest

[1] Salvidge to Chamberlain, 14 February 1906, Salvidge, *Salvidge of Liverpool*, pp. 70–1.
[2] Autobiography, HGP 46118 f. 97; cf. f. 102.
[3] Balfour to Chamberlain, 15 January 1906, Garvin and Amery, *Life of Joseph Chamberlain*, VI, 790; Balfour to Hood, 17 January 1906, BP 49771; Balfour to Stanley, 27 January 1906, Churchill, *Lord Derby*, pp. 90–1. On Liverpool, cf. Seely, *Adventure*, pp. 102 ff.
[4] Fitzroy, *Memoirs*, I, 280.
[5] See R. B. Suthers, *Clarion*, 19 January 1906.

hour, Churchill lost Manchester North West. But in July 1909 Oswald
Partington held High Peak with only a marginal fall in the Liberal vote.
The Budget policy, claimed Churchill, had 'vivified and invigorated the
Liberal Party'.[1] While the fate of the Budget lay in the hands of the House of
Lords in the autumn of 1909, the Tariff Reformers prepared a propaganda
offensive upon Lancashire. The *Manchester Courier* took up the cry that in
this crisis 'the County Palatine is the keystone of the arch',[2] and at the time
of the conference of the National Union of Conservative Associations in
Manchester, Tariff Reform meetings were held in all the big centres. It was,
said Joynson Hicks, 'a kind of revival week in Manchester, and they hoped
they would soon have the penitent forms full (laughter)'.[3] By way of retaliation the Lancashire and Cheshire Liberal Federation agreed to invite
Churchill to make a tour of the region in the event of the Lords' rejecting the
Budget, and on 17 November the arrangement was made public and un-
conditional. 'I am going to make a pilgrimage about Lancashire', declared
Churchill in his first speech. The Budget had been rejected on 30 November.
Churchill's Lancashire campaign lasted from 3 to 18 December and involved
major speeches at Preston, Southport, Manchester, Bolton, Liverpool,
Crewe, Oldham, Burnley and Warrington. Asquith asked some of those who
heard them whether he had repeated himself at all and was told, 'Never'.[4]
Asquith, like most of the Liberal press, was immediately reminded of the
Midlothian campaign with which Churchill's tour was compared. 'The battle
in Lancashire has begun', echoed the Conservative newspapers, conceding
that Churchill appeared 'in the role of a serious-minded statesman rather
than that of a belligerent braggadocia'.[5] Churchill probably spoke to about
fifty thousand people throughout the region in these two weeks and the
Conservatives soon became concerned at the influence he was having. In
Manchester, while the *Guardian* thought Churchill was 'setting Lancashire
ablaze', the *Courier* had concluded that his visit was 'already an entire
failure', an opinion passed on through its owner, Northcliffe, to Balfour.[6]
This assessment was, however, contradicted by the counter-measures which
the Tories found it necessary to take; they set their leader-writers upon
Churchill; Northcliffe was rebuked for giving him so much space in the press.

[1] Speech after the 'miniature General Election', Churchill, *Liberalism and the Social Problem*,
p. 344; cf. leader, *M.G.*, 1 October 1909.
[2] London letter, *M. Courier*, 13 November 1909.
[3] Joynson Hicks at Stalybridge, *M. Courier*, 16 November 1909.
[4] Bonham Carter, *Winston Churchill as I knew him*, p. 186. Naturally Churchill drew on earlier
speeches given elsewhere. His speech at Manchester in May 1909 was the original of the Crewe
speech; his speech at Leicester in September 1909 of the Preston speech; and his speech at
Abernethy in October 1909 of the Liverpool speech.
[5] Leader, *L. Courier*, 4 December 1909.
[6] *M.G.*, 8 December 1909; *M. Courier*, 7 December 1909; Sandars to Balfour, 22 December 1909,
BP 49766.

Following Churchill's speech at Oldham Curzon went there too and made an impassioned defence of the hereditary principle; and Curzon followed Churchill also to Burnley (later complimenting him on his 'very remarkable Lancashire campaign').[1] The speeches were published as *The People's Rights* early in the New Year. They made him, at least in the north west, the central figure of the General Election.[2] F. E. Smith too set out upon a Lancashire tour, mainly in the western half of the county. But on the Unionist side the platform activities of the peers themselves, and the navy-scare articles of Robert Blatchford in the *Daily Mail* and of J. L. Garvin, the rising editor of the *Observer*, attracted most of the attention.

Asquith spoke at the Albert Hall on 10 December 1909; his speech was notable chiefly for its (misleadingly) emphatic declaration about the House of Lords, and for the reintroduction of Home Rule into practical politics. But although Home Rule was admittedly a live question in this election, the Unionists did not talk about it as much as in 1906 when it had been as dead as a doornail. No longer were they trying to direct attention from Tariff Reform; and when Balfour, who had been *hors de combat*, returned to the platform in January the Tariff Reformers rejoiced 'over the splendid way in which Arthur has put himself at the head of the fight'.[3] The Tories hoped that it was 'not too late to recover whatever ground may have been lost. The spokesmen of the Government have shot their bolt.'[4] Until the issue of the writs on 8 January 1910 the Tory peers themselves continued to present their own case, meeting with a rather mixed reception. But despite the exceptionally long campaign public enthusiasm and interest remained keen. In Liverpool much of the novelty of the later part of the election came from Balfour's undertaking that Liverpool should be a free port of the status of Hamburg if Tariff Reform were implemented. And the Unionist candidates found it necessary to calm fears on one other point; on 10 January they issued an advertisement guaranteeing that in the event of their return they would vote for the supplies necessary for the payment of old age pensions.

'Everybody', said Joynson Hicks, 'knew that this election was of vital importance to England – (cheers) – and not merely to Manchester, but

---

[1] Curzon to Churchill, 15 February 1910, *Companion*, II, 1136.

[2] The speech Lansdowne gave when he visited Liverpool illustrates this: 'I think I may take, perhaps, as the culminating point the statement which was made a few days ago by Mr Winston Churchill...I quote again the high authority whom I quoted a moment ago – Mr Winston Churchill...to use Mr Winston Churchill's expression...I am irresistibly driven back to Mr Winston Churchill because he has filled so large a space in the discussion lately...I come back again to Mr Winston Churchill (laughter). I cannot get away from him. (A voice: "He is such a liar.")' *The Times*, 6 January 1910.

[3] George Wyndham to his sister, 9 January 1910, Wyndham and Mackail, *Life and Letters of George Wyndham*, II, 646–8.

[4] Leader, *L. Courier*, 5 January 1910.

378

everyone knew that Manchester would have an enormous influence upon the surrounding constituencies in Lancashire, and that upon the result in Lancashire would depend the real result throughout the country (cheers).'¹ It was a statement which both sides could accept. Churchill, who had been plying Manchester with messages throughout the campaign, appealed on the eve of the poll for it 'to lead all England to a great Progressive victory', and, as in 1906, all eyes were fixed upon the polling there. 'Unionist Triumph in Sight', reported the *Manchester Courier*. On 15 January Manchester, Salford and six other boroughs voted. The Conservatives gained Manchester South West, where there had been a three-cornered contest, but North West was recaptured for the Liberals by Sir George Kemp. (In North West, however, there had been a shift to the Conservatives since 1906 of 7.6 per cent, a swing exceeded only by that in South (9.1 per cent), the other middle-class division.) The lack of a positive advance – and especially the loss of North West – made this a 'most dispiriting' result for the Conservatives.² They made gains elsewhere at Burnley, the scene of Hyndman's candidature, and at Staly-bridge. Unlike previous elections, the north west did not mirror the national trend, for throughout the south of England the Unionists were virtually demolishing the 1906 majority. Monday 17 January was a day of mixed fortunes in the north west. The Conservatives gained seats at Chester and Preston but lost them at Blackburn and Wigan. Both sides took some comfort, either from the mounting Conservative victories or from the reflection that the north was holding firm. On 18 January Liverpool voted. Most of the divisions there showed below-average shifts towards the Conservatives, or, in three cases, a swing to the Liberals. But Seely was rejected by the businessmen of Abercromby, and it was this that was seized upon, in congratulation by the Conservatives and in commiseration by the Liberals. 'Liverpool, as of old, stood apart yesterday from the great movement of Lancashire opinion', concluded the *Guardian*. For the rest, the results gave the Conservatives a number of seats back, like some of the divisions of rural Cheshire, but there was a handful of seats which swung towards the Liberals and even gave them the seat at Darwen.

The results made no single simple impression in favour of either party – no bandwagon. Some Conservatives, like Sandys in Bootle, asked electors to 'go with the flowing tide', but others, like the defeated candidate in Stockport, declared that 'Manchester has killed us'.³ As far as industrial Lancashire was concerned, the Conservative revival was virtually confined to Liverpool and Preston. (According to Sandars, 'Liverpool was a green oasis in the

¹ Joynson Hicks at Manchester North West, *M.G.*, 7 January 1910.
² See *M. Courier*, 17 January 1910.
³ Conservative poster in Bootle, *L. Courier*, 21 January 1910; G. E. Raine at Stockport, *Stockport Advertiser*, 21 January 1910.

desert of Lancashire.')¹ In both places the Conservatives had laid emphasis upon religious issues and in both they could still poll well enough among the workingmen. A Labour speaker at Preston lamented the support that the Tories 'had received from the poor themselves – people who were right down at the bottom, and who had everything to lose'.² But elsewhere in Lancashire the Conservatives' hopes had been dashed. Acland Hood told Balfour frankly that, 'I was mistaken as to our strength both in Lancashire and the North.'³ The *Guardian* pointed out that, apart from the two seats (Manchester South West and Burnley) lost in three-cornered fights, 'Lancashire is weaker by only one seat on the Progressive and Free Trade side than she was in 1906.' Five seats had been lost, and four gained.⁴ Not quite accurate, since Manchester North West had merely reverted to its pre-1908 allegiance; but even so it is remarkable. There are, however, two further considerations which fall outside this analysis. In Cheshire the Liberals had lost five seats, comprising three agricultural divisions plus Chester itself and the cotton seat of Stalybridge. Moreover, although the progressive vote had held up very well and much of the advantage seized in 1906 had been retained, some of the margin had been eroded. There were now eleven seats in the north west vulnerable to a swing to the Conservatives of only three per cent. Nine of them were to be lost that December.

IV

Having gained ground in so much of southern England, the Conservatives were more determined than ever to win over Lancashire. Their proposals for reform of the House of Lords had this as one objective. And throughout 1910 the Tariff Reformers continued their efforts to convert Lancashire, efforts which culminated at the time of the Tariff Reform League Conference held there from 8 November. During the week in which it took place sixty meetings were arranged throughout south east Lancashire, addressed by all the leading lights of the League; and a great 'dumping exhibition' was opened at the Midland Hotel. As it happened, this 'whirlwind campaign' formed the beginning of the election campaign, for on 10 November it was announced that the inter-party conference on the constitutional question had broken down. There was a great deal of relief, especially on the Liberal side, that no secret agreement was to prejudice the respective party positions. A further General Election was presaged; at first it was assumed that it

---

¹ See F. E. Smith to Salvidge, 4 February 1910, Salvidge, *Salvidge of Liverpool*, p. 94.
² Jos. Wallwork after the poll, *Lancs. D.P.*, 18 January 1910; cf. Sir John Gorst to Churchill, 19 January 1910, *Companion*, II, 964.
³ Hood to Balfour, 29 January (1910), BP 49771.
⁴ Leader, *M.G.*, 27 January 1910.

would take place in January but (after Asquith had extracted the necessary guarantees from the King) it was announced that the dissolution would take place on 28 November. The Liberal Whips' office, whose strategy this was, envisaged a gain of about thirty seats for the progressives in England and Wales from an immediate dissolution, and Sir Ben Johnson told the Liberal agents that nine of these ought to come from the north west. The Unionists also had high hopes of being returned to office, though Salvidge discovered that these were not shared by Balfour himself.[1]

The role of the press was unusually important in this election. For the Liberals, the *Guardian* played a large part in defining the issue and keeping up the enthusiasm of January. On the Unionist side this was, above all, J. L. Garvin's election. As one Irish leader-writer of another, it was C. E. Montague's opinion that, 'Even foaming at the mouth, in prose, is done much better by an Irishman than an Englishman – e.g. J. L. Garvin of the *Observer*.'[2] From the time that Garvin dubbed John Redmond 'the Dollar Dictator' on account of his American fund-raising and supposed influence over the Government, this became the chief Conservative catchphrase. It was a theme that lent itself to treatment in newspaper cartoons and on the hoardings, but even accomplished speakers were not ashamed to borrow it. 'I am interested to hear that Mr Asquith is coming to Burnley', said F. E. Smith, 'and would recommend you to put him a kindly sympathetic question, "Have you got Redmond's leave?"' (laughter)'. The *Guardian* called Garvin 'the brain of the Protectionist general staff', whose '"battle-cries" and "watchwords" and "fighting briefs" are rapturously reprinted and spread broadcast'.[3] The presence of Bonar Law in Manchester North West was the focal point of the Conservative effort. 'If Sir George Kemp should lose his seat on the first day of polling', ran the conventional wisdom, 'it is more than probable that several of his political colleagues and neighbours will also suffer disaster.'[4] On 25 November Churchill came to speak in Manchester and Scott took the chair for him in the Free Trade Hall. Churchill's Free Trade harangue was warmly received, but the Conservatives, who had been bitterly attacking him for not using troops against the strikers in Tonypandy, affected to believe that he was 'rather a spent force with men who admire decision and a firm hand in quelling disorder, after the "soldiers of Wales" incident'.[5]

[1] See Jesse Herbert to Elibank, 9 November 1910, EP 8802 ff. 129–30; Johnson at L.C.L.F. agents' meeting, *M.G.*, 18 November 1910; Salvidge to his wife (18 November 1910), Salvidge, *Salvidge of Liverpool*, p. 99.
[2] Montague to his brother, midnight 31 December 1909 – 1 January 1910, Elton, *C. E. Montague*, pp. 65–6; and see Gollin, *The 'Observer' and J. L. Garvin*, ch. 7.
[3] Smith at Burnley, *L. Courier*, 28 November 1910; leader, *M.G.*, 28 November 1910.
[4] Special correspondent, *The Times*, 22 November 1910. This was evidently *another* special correspondent; cf. above, p. 375 n. 2.   [5] *M. Courier*, 25 November 1910.

The position of the House of Lords was the central issue of this election, on which all other issues hinged. It was an issue which perfectly suited Asquith's talents and, unlike the previous January, he dominated the campaign. The *Guardian* called his speech at Glossop late in the campaign 'the best statement of the Liberal case that has been made during the election'; Lloyd George was to tell him that wherever he went he had found the party heartened by Asquith's 'brilliant leadership', and Churchill assured him 'that yr leadership was the main & conspicuous feature of the whole fight'.[1] The Liberal plan of suspending the Lords' veto, combined with Asquith's commitment to Home Rule, gave a real prospect of a Home Rule Bill becoming law. At a very late stage (within a fortnight of polling) the Unionists had come up with their own plan, consisting broadly of Rosebery's proposals for Lords reform plus Lansdowne's proposals for settling differences between the Houses, ultimately through a referendum. The only such deadlock envisaged was between a Conservative majority in the Lords and a Liberal majority in the Commons. The Liberals would thus have to put Home Rule to a referendum, but the Unionists would be in no such difficulty over Tariff Reform. On 28 November the *Guardian* pointedly asked whether Bonar Law would 'undertake to do his best to ensure that any Tariff Reform Budget shall be referred to the people before it becomes law?' The previous day's *Observer* had proposed just this and such a scheme was very much in the air in Manchester. There were, it is true, Conservatives who resisted such a suggestion, of whom H. E. Howell, the candidate for Manchester North, may be taken as representative. 'We must not be side-tracked away from Tariff Reform', he wrote. '...My platform from to-day to Saturday has three planks, and only three. The first is Tariff Reform, the second is Tariff Reform, and the third is Tariff Reform.'[2] It was not just that a referendum on Tariff Reform was (as the *Morning Post* characterised it) 'a dodge to sweep Lancashire': many Unionists feared that it would prove an unsuccessful dodge.

On 29 November, in his speech at the Albert Hall, Balfour said that he had 'not the least objection to submitting the principles of Tariff Reform to a Referendum'. This was a somewhat cryptic utterance. Was it a pledge? or an expression of opinion? or a pledge contingent upon the Liberals' agreeing to submit Home Rule to a referendum? The *Manchester Courier*, along with such Chamberlainite papers as the *Morning Post*, took it in the last sense. 'As things stand at present', it concluded, 'we must look on this business of the challenge as a sporting offer not likely to materialise.' The *Liverpool Courier*,

---

[1] Leader, *M.G.*, 15 December 1910; Lloyd George to Asquith, 17 December 1910, copy, EP 8802 ff. 159–60; Churchill to Asquith, 3 January 1911, *Companion*, II, 1030–3.

[2] Letter from Howell, *M. Courier*, 29 November 1910; and see above, pp. 297 ff.

on the other hand, thought that it 'must very materially affect the whole course of this election...It narrows down the issue in a way which will immensely help the cause of Unionism.' This was to take *The Times*'s view that it was an 'explicit declaration'. The Liberals naturally exploited these differences. Some mocked Balfour for having 'put his pride in his pocket and said he would try Mr Garvin's famous "dodge to sweep Lancashire"', while others admitted Balfour's good faith but insisted that 'the Protectionists would be too strong for him...The leader would go, Protection would remain.' These fears the *Manchester Courier* belatedly tried to counter by shamelessly repudiating its previous editorial line.[1] The pledge received its seal of guarantee from Rosebery, speaking to a 'non-party' meeting at the Free Trade Hall on 30 November. Even Rosebery's former supporter the *Lancashire Daily Post* now asked why, since he was 'an open and relentless foe of the progressive forces in this country', he did not become an avowed Tory. Rosebery's message was that, after the pledge, the issue was a single Chamber or two. But genuine doubts remained and spurious doubts were fostered about the referendum. In the Darwen division, for instance, all talk of it was denounced as 'rubbish' by the Liberals. And it was not until several days after the first pollings that Balfour explained how it would operate electorally.

'The field is quite gay to-day with white flags', commented the *Guardian*. 'They flap over every post that the Lords held a week since.' The tactical retreat, however, had opened up the prospect of a Home Rule election, and it was a common opinion that 'the full voting strength of the Unionist Party in Lancashire is about to be polled for the first time in ten years'.[2] Not only in Liverpool, but throughout the region, the Home Rule bogey was brought out of mothballs. There were almost frantic efforts to generate a mood of unity and confidence. The *Manchester Courier*, for example, which on Tuesday had thought a referendum undesirable, and on Wednesday had refused to believe in it, on Thursday called it 'an accepted fact' and on Saturday 'a master-stroke of policy'. Considering the seriousness of the Conservative party's assault on Manchester, their failure to get the candidate for Manchester South nominated was an extraordinary blunder. The remaining five divisions polled on 3 December and returned five Liberals, albeit with reduced majorities. Bonar Law was defeated and South West, lost in a three-cornered contest in January, was regained by the Liberals. The Conservatives gained Belloc's old seat in Salford South. In addition, F. E. Smith's brother Harold captured Warrington; Wigan was wrested from Labour; and Max Aitken

[1] Leaders, *M.G.*, *Lancs. D.P.*, 30 November 1910; cf. the editorial note to letter from 'Conservative Free Trader', *M. Courier*, 1 December 1910, stating that Balfour had 'definitely pledged' the party.
[2] Leader, *M.G.*, 2 December 1910; Lancashire survey, *The Times*, 2 December 1910.

won at Ashton. The Liberals took comfort from the Manchester results which in the circumstances ('Probably there has never before been so strenuous an effort by the whole forces of a great political party to bend one city to its will') they found creditable.[1] On 5 December Liverpool and five other boroughs went to the poll. Most of the Liverpool results were good for the Conservatives and they gained the Exchange division. They also won Birkenhead. The Liverpool area, said the *Guardian*, was 'so much pre-occupied with Anglo–Irish and inter-denominational spites that questions which absorb the rest of Lancashire seem scarcely to attract its attention'. As in Liverpool, so in Preston, where the Conservative majority, although reduced, was still formidable. 'They had heard', said its new M.P., 'a great deal about the extinct monster, the Conservative working man (laughter). But he seemed very much alive that night (cheers).'[2] Thereafter, things improved slightly for the Liberals in the north west, and nationally they began to make up the ground that had been lost. On 6 December the Conservatives lost Burnley but won St Helens, and they were to win a further mining seat at Newton the next day. On 8 December the Liberals lost Darwen and Altrincham and although they made way slightly in some of the remaining divisions they lost High Peak too on the last day of polling. 'Where now is the "solid North"?' the Tories asked, counting up the Lancashire victories.[3]

It was the opinion of those who had instigated it (Marsden, Garvin, Sandars) that the referendum pledge was responsible for the Unionists doing 'splendidly in Lancashire'.[4] The effect of the pledge is, as Austen Chamberlain recognised, 'impossible to *prove* one way or the other', but there is a lot to be said for his own view that it had very little effect.[5] In Manchester the only substantial swing to the Conservatives (7.2 per cent) was in North East where the Conservative candidate had repudiated the referendum; the worst result (the loss of the seat in South West) was attributed to it by the candidate. At Ashton Aitken had talked tariffs almost exclusively. Chamberlain declared that Wigan too (6.0 per cent swing) 'was won without the Referendum', an opinion, however, not shared by its new M.P. who called his victory 'one for the new referendum policy'.[6] At Stockport one of the defeated Conservatives stated that 'Mr Balfour's proposal of a Referendum had come too late to be of use to him'; and at Middleton W. A. S. Hewins believed that it had done

---

[1] Leader, *M.G.*, 5 December 1910.
[2] George Stanley at Preston, *Lancs. D.P.*, 6 December 1910.
[3] Leader, *M. Courier*, 8 December 1910.
[4] See Gollin, *The 'Observer' and J. L. Garvin*, p. 272.
[5] See Chamberlain, *Politics from Inside*, pp. 307–12. Chamberlain wrote a memorandum as the results came in, drawing upon his correspondence from Tariff Reform candidates. It is the source for otherwise unattributed statements below.
[6] R. J. Neville after the poll, *L. Courier*, 5 December 1910.

him harm.[1] These assertions, like those of the Garvin group, are *ex parte*, but they have considerable justification. Imperfectly understood and sprung at the last moment, the referendum was a very sophisticated weapon, likely to appeal to a sophisticated class of voters. There is reason to suppose that the great bulk of Unionist Free Traders were already prepared to vote Conservative; the small but uniform shifts in the popular vote, moreover, suggest that the old register was a more potent influence; and the larger swings in one or two mining seats were more likely to have been caused by the effects of the Eight Hours Act than (something no-one ever hinted at) pockets of Unionist Free Traders underground.[2] In so far as the referendum was effective (and Salvidge, though deploring the lack of time to explain it, firmly believed in it)[3] it was the means of staging a Home Rule election. But Home Rule was only likely to be the Unionists' best issue in those places where communal politics could still be reactivated. As Howell said of Manchester, in a letter already quoted: 'The average voter is not interested in Home Rule. He dislikes it, and is prepared to prove his dislike when it is really needed. But he does not see in it anything more than a pawn in the game of party politics.'

The advocates of the referendum had the better of the argument in one respect; they could claim a gain of eleven seats (and a net gain of nine) in the north west. But the average swing in these eleven was only three per cent. The Liberals had been lucky in retaining a number of seats by a small majority in January; now, with a small swing to the Conservatives, there was a disproportionately dramatic turnover of seats. (The Liberals lost Warrington, Darwen and High Peak on swings of less than two per cent.) The Liberals had done rather less well than they had hoped in the north west – but so had the Conservatives. There was satisfaction, both public and private, that 'the pendulum has been held up not only once but twice' and that 'our old friend – and enemy – the pendulum is smashed'.[4] The results had shown too 'that Lancashire, like Yorkshire, is politically not one county but three ridings'. The Liverpool riding, extending up to the Fylde, was 'agricultural, commercial, residential, but not manufacturing, and it is in the main Conservative'. The Manchester riding, overlapping in to Cheshire and Derbyshire, was 'almost wholly industrial in its interests, and is predominantly Liberal'.[5] And between them was, geographically and politically, the middle ground.

---

[1] R. Campbell at Stockport, *M.G.*, 6 December 1910; Hewins to Balfour, 11 December 1910, BP 49779; cf. Hewins, *Apologia of an Imperialist*, 1, 262.
[2] These considerations receive fuller treatment above, pp. 298–300, 125–6, 323.
[3] See his correspondence with Walter Long, Salvidge, *Salvidge of Liverpool*, pp. 101–4.
[4] Leader, *M.G.*, 13 December 1910; Charles Geake to Gladstone, 11 January 1911, HGP 46042 ff. 198–201.   [5] Leader, *M.G.*, 10 December 1910.

v

Between December 1910 and the outbreak of the Great War there were nine by-elections in the north west. Three were in Conservative seats and all were held; six were in Liberal seats and four were lost. Whether this performance was any worse for the Government than its record during the 1906 Parliament is, however, doubtful. These elections came thick and fast during the period up to May 1913, but in the last fifteen months of peace there was no vacancy. The first of them was more an appendage to the December elections than an episode in its own right. After Bonar Law's defeat in Manchester North West he was eventually offered the Bootle division, which he won comfortably in March 1911. The division had not been contested in December, and the swing to the Conservatives of 3.3 per cent since January 1910 was rather less than the inter-election swing in most of the comparable Liverpool seats: but then there was a new register in force.

On 2 August 1911 polling took place in the Middleton division consequent on the need of the Liberal M.P., Sir Ryland Adkins, to seek re-election. He was again opposed by W. A. S. Hewins who this time preferred to campaign not upon Tariff Reform but upon the iniquities of the National Insurance Bill. It was not unjustly said of Hewin's campaign against the Bill that he 'snatched at any and every criticism and adopted it regardless of the policy of his party and of his own consistency'.[1] His charge that the burden would fall upon the workers provoked Lloyd George to send Adkins a letter refuting him in detail, and National Insurance remained the chief topic right up to polling day despite the mounting crisis at Westminster over the Parliament Bill. There was a swing against the Government of 1.4 per cent, but Adkins was safely elected. From this time onward the National Insurance Bill produced its own cave of Adullam of all those who were discontented with the Government. It was attacked from right and left. The Ashton Trades Council, for instance, criticised its 'numerous defects and injustices' from the workers' point of view,[2] but at the Oldham by-election in November 1911 it was the Conservatives who attacked it as 'an impossible tax'.[3] The Oldham contest, though, was less a fight between the Conservatives and the progressives than one between the Liberal and Labour candidates for the right to the progressive label. Many workmen apparently believed (not without reason) that Robinson of the cotton unions was 'the better Liberal of the two'.[4] Although the Conservatives benefited from the split vote and won the seat, their share of the poll was down by nearly four per cent.

---

[1] Leader, *M.G.*, 29 July 1911.
[2] See F. C. Bowden to Aitken, 9 September 1911, Beaverbrook P.
[3] See *Oldham D. Standard*, 10 November 1911; and above, p. 317.
[4] See *M.G.*, 14 November 1911.

When Walter Long visited Manchester and Liverpool that winter on Law's behalf he found that for the time being the Insurance Act was very unpopular, although it was expected that the electoral benefits for the Conservative party would disappear once it was fully implemented. 'The Insurance Act appeals more to the working classes than "Home Rule"', Aitken heard from Ashton-under-Lyne. 'They want to discuss it & the majority are opposed to it. "Home Rule" no longer frightens them.'[1] The Unionist attempt to stump Lancashire on Home Rule at this time fell distinctly flat, and the view that 'public opinion is almost entirely occupied with the Insurance Act'[2] was accepted by the party managers on both sides. Despite the efforts of both the Manchester Liberal Federation and the Lancashire and Cheshire Liberal Federation in mounting propaganda in its favour the Bill was neither understood nor liked. When Sir Arthur Haworth had to seek re-election in Manchester South in March 1912, therefore, the Liberals realised that, for all their majority of two thousand in January 1910, it would be a stiff fight. The Conservative Glazebrook took his stand on providing a 'Better Insurance Act' for the clerks and warehousemen who comprised so much of the suburban electorate. 'The election is going better than I had dared to hope', he told Law.[3] It was, indeed, hard to persuade men who already enjoyed considerable security of employment of the virtues of the Act. Sir John Simon came to explain the alternative benefits which insured men could choose through their friendly societies if they were already covered against the standard hazards. And the *Guardian* enlarged upon the Act's bold appeal 'to all of us in this country to act as if we really believed with all our hearts that we are members one of another, and that all of us are worse off when any of us sink into destitution or disease'. It was, it argued, the insurance principle itself that the Conservatives were really attacking ('In the nature of things it has to be in some measure a helping of the weak by the generous readiness of the strong') and concluded: 'Well, tomorrow the clerks and workmen of South Manchester will be tested.'[4] For the Liberals the result was 'a bit of a staggerer'.[5] Haworth was defeated. There was a swing to the Conservatives of 11 per cent. No-one had any doubt that the unpopularity of National Insurance was entirely to blame. 'That's bad, that's very bad', said Lloyd George when he heard of it.[6]

[1] J. M. W. Morison to Aitken, 27 February 1912, Beaverbrook P.; cf. Long's memoranda on Manchester, 29 February 1911 (1912), and on Liverpool, 8 March 1912, BLP 26/1/76.
[2] Elibank memorandum, 2 February 1912, EP 8803 ff. 16–18; cf. the arrangements for a National Insurance campaign, L.C.L.F. Minutes, 24 January 1912.
[3] P. K. Glazebrook to Law, 3 March (1912), BLP 25/3/7; cf. Glazebrook broadsheets, Manchester local collection.   [4] Leader, *M.G.*, 4 March 1912.
[5] Donald Maclean to Elibank, 8 March 1912, EP 8803 ff. 23–4.
[6] Masterman, *C. F. G. Masterman*, pp. 234–5; and see Long's report, 8 March 1912, BLP 26/1/76; M.L.F. Minutes, 15 March 1912.

Going to the country

The summer of 1912, with the commencement of National Insurance contributions, was a bad time for Liberalism. In July there was the three-cornered contest at Crewe, which was tackled by the Liberals with little prospect of their being able to hold the Labour vote low enough to win themselves. The Conservative duly gained the seat on a minority vote, his share of the vote rising by about one per cent. It was fatalistically concluded that

so long as Progressive politicians who agree on nine points of ten cannot accommodate or suspend their differences about the tenth, and so long, too, as our electoral system gives human perversity of this kind the power to deprive a constituency of the representation of its own views on the sole or chief issue at an election – so long will these miscarriages happen.[1]

The Liberals hobbled from one lost cause to another. On the day the Crewe result was published the candidates issued their addresses in Manchester North West. The question here was not so much whether as how the Conservatives would win the seat. They chose to do so upon the general theme, 'We are tired of this Government', taking National Insurance as the leading illustration. The swing against the Liberals was 8.1 per cent. 'The Death-Knell of the Government', proclaimed the Conservative press.[2]

At this point, however, the Conservative advance faltered. They had damned National Insurance up hill and down dale for eighteen months, but now that the Act was in operation they found themselves on less favourable ground. The referendum pledge was publicly repudiated in mid-November 1912. Ten days later polling took place in the Bolton by-election, caused by George Harwood's death. This was a cotton-spinning constituency with a strong Labour vote; following the split vote at Oldham and the Manchester results, the Conservatives had high hopes. But this time the full progressive vote turned out for Tom Taylor, the Liberal candidate (a more impressive performance than a reciprocal arrangement when both Liberal and Labour candidates were in the field) and the two *motifs* of Free Trade and Labour ran through the campaign. It is difficult to compare the result with that of December 1910 (when there had been three candidates and each elector had had two votes) with any precision. In December 1910 the Liberals polled 54.4 per cent of all votes cast for either the Liberal or Conservative candidates; now they polled 53.1 per cent. In short, by any test the Liberal vote had held up remarkably well. 'Bolton has won', said Taylor euphorically; 'the party of progress has won, and the Government of progress will win (cheers).'[3] And, according to Lloyd George, Welsh Disestablishment had won too, since

[1] Leader, *M.G.*, 29 July 1912; and see above, pp. 327–8.
[2] *M. Courier*, 9 August 1912; and see above, pp. 304–5.
[3] Taylor at Bolton, *Bolton Chron.*, 30 November 1912.

388

Harwood had opposed the Bill but Taylor supported it. Even this is true in the sense that the Church could no longer mobilise the political support of the Bolton working class. Food taxes were held chiefly responsible. Bonar Law was warned that 'in Manchester it is now believed that the Government being thus relieved of anxiety over an election will dissolve before next March, certain to come back with a majority & carry all'.[1] The confidence of high summer had gone. By Christmas the Lancashire Tories were struggling desperately to rid the party of a policy which they believed would again drag them down to defeat.

The dropping of food taxes in January 1913 did not, however, immediately improve the Unionist position. In February there was a by-election in Lord Balcarres's old constituency of Chorley and although the Conservatives retained it comfortably their majority was cut. On a high poll there was a swing towards the Liberals of 2.8 per cent. There was further evidence that the tide had turned in the by-election at Altrincham in May. The ground there might have been mapped out for the Conservatives. The comfortable suburbs of Altrincham probably contained 'a greater share of the wealth and comfort of Manchester than any other constituency either within or without the city'.[2] It was as though Manchester South and North West were rolled into one, and the Conservative campaign was reminiscent of those triumphs. They reverted to the objectionable provisions of National Insurance, and had the platform support of the Free Traders under F. R. B. Lindsell. Home Rule too was brought to the fore. Yet the swing against the Liberals of 3.2 per cent was trifling compared with the reverses of the previous year.[3] The indications, then, are rather mixed. There was no polling in the north west after May 1913 and the impact of Lloyd George's land campaign there is impossible to gauge. All that can be said is that the Conservatives scored some impressive victories during the twelve months from the autumn of 1911; and that in the socially segregated divisions of Manchester, first the clerks and then the businessmen turned against the Liberals, a trend that found a fainter echo the following May. But, equally, the fragmentary evidence of the by-elections shows that as late as November 1912 a Liberal candidate could hold his own in an industrial constituency, and that as late as February 1913 a Liberal candidate could actually gain ground. What this might have portended for a hypothetical General Election in 1915 is an open question.

---

[1] T. G. Bowles to Law, 27 November 1912, BLP 27/4/57. Bowles was not disinterested but his contacts in Manchester were good. On the Bolton result, cf. J. C. Buckley to Aitken, 28 November 1912, Beaverbrook P.; Morgan, *Wales in British Politics*, pp. 264–7; and see above, pp. 227, 319.
[2] *M.G.*, 16 May 1913.
[3] On the Altrincham result see Edward Russell to Lloyd George, 29 May 1913, LGP C/7/6/2; L.C.L.F. Minutes, 10 June 1913; Viscount Duncannon to Law, 6 June 1913, BLP 29/5/11.

PART SEVEN
CONCLUSION

15 Edwardian Progressivism

> *A*: Who's writing the Long to-night?
> *B*: C.P.
> *A*: What is the subject?
> *B*: Saving Lloyd George's soul again.
>
> *Manchester Guardian* office, *c.* 1925

I

After 1906 the electoral prospects of the Liberal party depended upon keeping social and economic issues to the fore. The difficulties in which the Government was enmeshed just before the Great War, on the other hand, arose largely through the legacies of Home Rule and Welsh Disestablishment, from which there could be no escape. The settlement of these questions – however necessary, however overdue – held up for the time being the development of social policy. 'More than ever before', Lord Crewe had written in 1905, 'the Liberal party is on its trial as an engine for securing social reforms, – taxation, land, housing, etc. It has to resist the I.L.P. claim to be the only friend of the workers. Can it do this and attempt Home Rule as well?'[1] By 1914 it was having to try. Some of the Tariff Reformers were prepared to fight progressivism on its own terms and boldly put forward their own economic policy. 'It is quite possible, however', Bonar Law told a Manchester candidate in 1913, 'that the question of Home Rule may become so acute that all other questions will sink; and indeed, I hope this will be the case.'[2]

If the progressive impetus which Liberal policy had been given after 1906 once lost momentum the party would founder. The domestic difficulties which it faced were complex and manifold; and perhaps they would have overcome it. Much turned on the party leadership. 'Always remember that this is a Liberal League Government', the sour Gladstonian Loreburn warned Scott in 1911. And if this was so, was there scope for a working arrangement between Asquith and Lloyd George? Lloyd George himself repudiated the description; he consistently spoke of the loyal manner in which Asquith treated him, of his 'great liking for the P.M.', and of the invaluable political support he had received from him.[3] After two years of war, of course,

---

[1] Crewe to Campbell-Bannerman, 19 November 1905, CBP 41213 ff. 337–8.
[2] Law to Arthur Taylor, 1 October 1913, copy, BLP 35/5/62.
[3] See Scott's interview notes, 20, 22 July 1911, 3 February 1913, SP 50901 ff. 21–2, 23–30, 87–9; Lloyd George to Elibank, 29 November 1910, EP 8802 ff. 148–9; Masterman, *C. F. G. Masterman*,

the position was rather different. But until 1914 it was above all Asquith and Lloyd George who carried the hopes of a progressive Government. As the Master of Elibank wrote in 1917: 'Theirs has been the most formidable political combination that this country has ever known. Look what has been achieved within the last ten years.'[1] While Asquith and Lloyd George worked together, while the Cabinet retained a hold over events, while the Government majority cohered in the House of Commons, while the party was in good heart in the country – so long was there a chance of pulling off the hazardous reorientation of Liberal policy and consolidating the progressive position. 'The present Government', said Sir Ben Johnson in 1913, 'has beaten the record of all modern Governments by winning three general elections. We believe that we shall win the fourth when it comes along (cheers).'[2]

But it was the War that came along instead. 'War is fatal to Liberalism', Churchill had said;[3] and so it proved. At a difficult corner in the party's history the War discredited progressivism and the Liberal party alike. The question arises, should not a collectivist party have been able to wage a collectivist war? But for the progressives the antithesis of collectivism and individualism had always been false; ends not means had weighed with them. They had been able to make an accommodation with 'socialism' in order to tackle the problems of peace because it seemed that all that had to be sacrificed were theoretical notions of economic liberty. Many Liberals, however, found it peculiarly difficult to swallow 'war socialism' because this seemed to threaten living ideals of political liberty. The conduct of the War brought into play motives both higher and lower than those of party. The replacement of Asquith's Government by Lloyd George's was both less and more far-reaching than an ordinary change of parties. The Liberal party at Westminster split; the party in the country withered. The coalition with Labour was abandoned for other coalitions.

With Asquith a broken reed, the future rested in Lloyd George's hands. In 1917 Lloyd George was still talking of his wish 'to form a progressive Cabinet after the war'.[4] He was, however, no longer a free agent and the

---

pp. 174–5. It is an *ex post facto* myth – albeit one nurtured by both factions – to read back the split of 1916 into the pre-War period. Those loyal to Asquith found it necessary to postulate a Lloyd George plot of ignoble intent and long standing lest they be forced to admit that Lloyd George came to power on merit. The partisans of Lloyd George, on the other hand, seeking to justify working with the Conservatives against their old party, set up against official Liberalism, to which they were apparently disloyal, the higher claims of an ethereal Liberalism which the Asquithites had themselves betrayed; their excessive posthumous devotion to Campbell-Bannerman was part and parcel of this.

[1] Elibank to J. T. Davies, 25 May 1917, Murray, *Master and Brother*, p. 173.
[2] Johnson at L.C.L.F. Annual Meeting, 8 March 1913.
[3] Speech at Glasgow, 11 October 1908, Churchill, *Liberalism and the Social Problem*, p. 67.
[4] Haldane to his sister, 13 June 1917, Stephen E. Koss, *Lord Haldane, scapegoat for Liberalism* (1969), p. 231.

immediate temptations of continued office were too much for him. Unlike many of his cast of mind, Scott did not entirely despair of him. He explained to President Wilson that Lloyd George 'responded very greatly to his surroundings and could, I believed, be greatly influenced by him, but he was extremely elusive and in dealing with him you had to keep a bright look-out'. Scott wrote to Hobhouse in 1919 that Lloyd George 'may yet emerge as a shining example of Progressive statesmanship'. And even when these hopes were successively dashed Scott could still see the best in him – 'one must not forget that there's a root of rectitude in Ll.G.'.[1] But progressivism was by then beyond all redemption.

After the War there were new conditions to face; there was a new division of parties; and there was a new electorate. With the extension of the franchise the number of electors was roughly trebled. Furthermore, nearly eight years had passed without a General Election. Even if the loyalty of the 1910 voters had held it would not have been enough; and the premises underpinning a progressive vote in 1910 had by 1918 been destroyed and perhaps forgotten. The new voters acquired new habits of voting. By and large, voting Liberal was not one of them (though it is salutary to note that the total Liberal poll was bigger by a million and a half in 1923 than in 1906). Under the redistribution of seats the north west had its representation increased from 71 to 80 M.P.s, divided as follows in party allegiance:[2]

| | Conservative | Liberal | | Labour | Others[a] |
		Lloyd George	Asquith		
1918	54	9	1	15	1
1922	49	7	3	19	2
1923	28	26		24	2
1924	55	2		18	5

[a] *viz.* 1 Irish Nationalist, 1918–24; 1 Independent (ex-Coalition Liberal and effectively Conservative), 1922–4; 3 Constitutionalists, 1924.

It is not necessary to penetrate very far behind the formal statistics of seats won and lost to see the fate of progressivism. The progressives had won 49 seats at one or other of the 1910 elections. Labour had 13 of these; redistribution increased this to 14. Of these Labour won 11 in 1918 (including one Coalition Labour), and in addition two seats each from the Liberals and the

[1] Hammond, *C. P. Scott*, pp. 250, 262, 296.
[2] Because it uses party headings, of course, the table to some extent misrepresents the 1918 results, e.g. one 'Labour' member was a Coalitionist. The analysis below is based on the returns as given in F. W. S. Craig, *British Parliamentary Election Results, 1918–1949* (1969). The nearest geographical equivalents have been taken in comparisons with the 1885 constituencies.

Conservatives. It is true that in six of the 15 victories there had been no opposition from official Liberal or Conservative candidates, but that does not gainsay the fact that Labour held its seats as of right, by virtue of its strength. The Liberals, on the other hand, who had won 36 seats in 1910 (increased by redistribution to 41), held only ten in 1918. Moreover, in none of these did they face a Conservative candidate; two were unopposed and in the other eight the Liberal candidate provided the right-wing opposition to Labour. In one other seat (Salford North) where there was a straight Liberal–Labour contest, Labour won, as it did in the three-cornered contest at Burnley. Of the remaining 29 seats, Coalition Conservatives won 19 and orthodox Conservatives the other 10 – plainly the 'coupon' had little to do with it.[1] Where the people had a Conservative alternative to Labour the Liberals lost; insofar as they survived it was as a second-best alternative.

Organised Liberalism had been fatally undermined, as Herbert Gladstone, with the eye of an old Chief Whip, appreciated.

The result of 1918 [Gladstone wrote], broke the party not only in the House of Commons but in the country. Local Associations perished or maintained a nominal existence. Masses of our best men passed away to Labour. Others gravitated to Conservatism or independence. Funds were depleted, and we were short of workers all over the country. There was an utter lack of enthusiasm and even zeal.

This was no ordinary defeat, even though it might remind the veterans of the dismissal of Rosebery's Government. 'It took us ten years to make good the defeat in 1895', Gladstone recalled. 'The causes of the debacle in 1918 went much deeper.'[2] There was, it is true, a reaction, from which the Liberal party benefited. When Lloyd George's Coalition broke up around him, the prodigal son returned. The Manchester Liberals still had hopes for progressivism. The wealthy manufacturer, E. D. Simon, failed to produce pure milk commercially at his experimental farm at Leadon Court; but it became the home of the Liberal Summer School and produced the pure milk of the word for a new generation of Liberals.

In the General Election of 1923, with Free Trade at stake once again, the Liberals won more seats than Labour in the north west. Some of these were impressive gains against all-comers in industrial constituencies, as in Oldham, Rochdale, Stockport, Darwen and Royton. But too many were in the wrong kind of seat. Residential areas like Altrincham, Southport, and the Manchester divisions of Withington and Rusholme, which now went Liberal, had not been safe for progressivism before the War; and other victories were notched up in middle-class areas which had been solidly Conservative even in 1906 – Lonsdale, Blackpool, Bootle, the Wirral, and the Liverpool divisions

---

[1] Cf. Wilson, *The Downfall of the Liberal Party*, pp. 177–83.
[2] Gladstone's memorandum, 18 November 1924, HGP 46480 ff. 129–37.

of Wavertree and West Derby. This was not the new Liberalism of progressivism so much as the even newer Liberalism of suburbia: the road not to Westminster but to Orpington. Moreover, in the double-member boroughs – a good touchstone – although there had been a progressive understanding at Preston, Labour and Liberals were at loggerheads in Stockport, Bolton and Oldham; and at Blackburn there was an anti-socialist pact. Indeed in three other constituencies (Accrington, Heywood-and-Radcliffe, and Stretford) the Liberal victor was the sole anti-socialist candidate.[1] The Liberal successes, then, lacked a rationale. Insofar as the party had a new claim to support it was by way of being a better conservative party than the Conservative party. Yet this was just the claim which the Liberals' position in supporting (albeit reluctantly) a minority Labour Government did most to vitiate. 'What a party!' reflected E. D. Simon on the eve of the next election, 'no leaders, no organization, no policy! Only a summer school!'[2] The Hundred Days of 1923 were ended by the Waterloo of 1924. The Liberal vote slumped disastrously, especially in the suburban seats where a fall of over 15 per cent of the poll was commonplace.[3] In the north west only two orthodox Liberals were returned, plus three Constitutionalists who later accepted the Liberal whip. All five were elected with Conservative support. By 1924 Lancashire Liberalism could only return M.P.s on the basis of a sort of Nonconformist bastard Toryism.

And from this there was no recovery. Hobhouse observed that 'traditions and class distinctions kept many "good Liberals" outside Labour. Now Labour has grown so much that it tends to absorb them and to leave the "bad" Liberals who incline to the Tories, and a mass of traditional Liberals who can't desert a party of that name.'[4] No longer fighting on the left, no longer enjoying mass working-class support, no longer with any prospect of power, the Liberal party was plainly no longer 'the best available instrument of progress'.

II

It is very odd that historians should have neglected the term 'progressive' which has virtually been consigned to a not dissimilar period of American history. It is a classical instance of 'whig' usage. After the War, progressivism guttered on and flickered out. It was forgotten. Yet the term is hardly

[1] On Preston, Blackburn and Accrington, cf. R. W. Lyman, *The First Labour Government 1924*, n.d. (1957), pp. 63–4.
[2] Stocks, *Ernest Simon of Manchester*, p. 69. On Manchester and the Liberal Summer School, see Wilson, *The Downfall of the Liberal Party*, pp. 215 ff.
[3] E.g. Liverpool West Derby – F. E. Smith's old seat – had elected its one and only Liberal M.P. in 1923 with a poll of 54.2 per cent in a straight fight with the Tories; in the three-cornered contest of 1924 the Liberal polled 17.9 per cent.
[4] Hobson and Ginsberg, *L. T. Hobhouse*, p. 66.

strange in the 1890s, and by 1910 it starts out from every newspaper page. Its use is important because it relates to changes in the nature of politics: changes which dispose of some of the triter judgements on the Liberal revival. This is not to say that labels should be taken at their face value. All those who glibly appropriated the progressive label in 1910 were not new Liberals. (Equally the old rhetoric of Peace, Retrenchment and Reform had been applied to progressive victories like Scott's at Leigh in 1900.) But, with its connotations of social justice, state intervention and alliance with Labour, it aptly describes the basis of Liberal policy after 1906.

The Liberal revival in Lancashire really cannot be attributed to a sectional belief in Free Trade transcending class divisions. It is, for instance, a highly suspicious circumstance that the Free Traders should have gone on claiming the overwhelming support of the cotton employers on the basis of the famous declaration of 1903, the credentials of which were increasingly disputed. The most plausible reason why the cotton trade was not polled on the fiscal issue is that neither side had much to gain by it: that although the Tariff Reformers would have lost, the Free Traders would have won by a far less decisive margin than the votes of the activists suggest. It is clear, moreover, that among the Free Traders was a large number of men who, by 1910 at any rate, would under no circumstances have voted Liberal. The Liberal party in Lancashire was the party of Free Trade but not of *laissez-faire*; the extent to which it benefited from the support of economic liberals has been greatly exaggerated. They played a full part, it is true, in the party's greatest electoral triumph. In 1906, while Liberal policy offered a hint of change to those for whom politics were a matter of aspiration, it offered an impression of security to those for whom they were a matter of conservation. It was all things to all men –

> *manna to the hungry soul,*
> *And to the weary rest.*

By 1910 the ambiguity had been resolved.

Furthermore, the so-called constitutional crisis of 1909–11 was less of an anomalous episode in English electoral politics than is usually supposed. The Peers' case was much better (and much more of a party case) than is often acknowledged. 'Peers versus People' was not necessarily a winning card for the Liberals (such theoretical issues were apt to fall flat) and it was the practical issues contingent on the Lords' action which were at stake. The Liberals were by 1910 the party of social reform, and it was upon this that electoral cleavages were based. The familiar critique of the Edwardian Liberal party, of course, asserts that the party failed to go far enough in a social democratic direction and thereby lost the support of the working class.

In a suggestive essay, Henry Pelling has sought to turn this thesis on its head, arguing in general that the working class were not interested in social reform, and in particular that social reform was not the issue in 1910.[1] This is an interesting proposition: but no more than that. As far as the north west is concerned, it is demonstrably false to maintain that social reform was not the most fundamental question in 1910. The whole controversy revolved around the means of financing it. This was the core of the argument, however the separate 'issues' are compartmentalised. As to whether social reform was a vote-winner, it is quite true that schemes were most popular *after* they had been carried out, and least popular *while* they were being implemented. (National Insurance is a case in point.) But the recovery in Liberal fortunes during 1909 suggests that the *prospect* of social reform was welcomed too. In so far as measures like Old Age Pensions and National Insurance were redistributive, the state was taking as well as giving. Those who were consequently worse off, as well as those better off, not unnaturally took a keen interest in the rival proposals. By comparison, the constitutional position of the House of Lords *as such* was rather an academic matter. Paradoxically, the new Liberalism's failure was not over social democracy but political democracy. A fourth Reform Act was needed, yet the only terms on which it could come were by including woman suffrage. Asquith's failure to see either the necessity or the urgency of this is the most serious criticism that can be made of his leadership.

The themes of this book are diverse. The case it is making is capable of rigorous proof in some particulars; in many others it must rest upon the balance of probabilities. Although no more can be said of several hypotheses than that they are consistent with the evidence, those hypotheses are interrelated and interdependent, and so the whole is greater than the sum of its parts. The interpretation offered here is internally coherent. Its force would be weakened (though not fatally) by a breakdown in any particular. Conversely, alternative explanations do not fit all the known facts. It must now be asked, though, how far are the developments which took place in Lancashire consistent with what was happening elsewhere?

It has been suggested by Paul Thompson that the Liberal revival in London was less impressive than it seemed. In London, as in Lancashire, 1906 saw a broad Liberal advance over 1900. But in 1910, Thompson writes, 'the majority of lost Liberal voters must have been working class, for while

[1] 'The working class and the origins of the welfare state' in Pelling, *Popular Politics and Society in Late Victorian Britain*, esp. p. 12. B. B. Gilbert is more in the orthodox tradition in asserting that *although* social reform was popular ('the one form of legal enactment that an opposition responsible to a democratic electorate dare not fight'), nonetheless 'welfare legislation never figured as an electoral issue in the years before World War I'. See *The Evolution of National Insurance in Great Britain*, pp. 449–51.

Conclusion

the percentage of electors voting Liberal fell in working class constituencies it rose in middle class constituencies'.[1] (This is so even though the Liberal share of the *vote* fell by four or five per cent in each group.) This comparison, however, is a very partial one, and it reveals not so much that by 1910 London had ended in a different place from Lancashire as that it had started from a different place. The Liberal problem in London was sociologically different from that in Lancashire. In Lancashire politics were not class-based, and status-based politics benefited the Conservatives; whereas 'voting in London was principally decided by class divisions after 1885'.[2] The need in Lancashire was to change the rules; in London to do better under the existing rules. The London Liberal revival was *already* class-based in 1906 in a sense that the victories in Lancashire at that time were not. But the same long-term trends are visible in both. In the first chapter Lancashire voting in 1885 was compared with December 1910 in order to assess the overall trend. The same comparison for London can be made from Thompson's own figures.

TABLE 1. *Percentage of electorate voting Liberal*[3]

| | Working-class seats | | Middle-class seats |
	A	B	E/D
1885	35.8	37.1	30.0
1910	38.1	39.0	26.6
	+2.3	+1.9	−3.4

Over twenty-five years, then, the Liberal vote showed an improvement in the working-class seats but had slumped in the middle-class seats. Similarly, the two Liberal victories of 1892 and January 1910 can be compared.

TABLE 2. *Percentage of electorate voting Liberal*

| | Working-class seats | | Middle-class seats |
	A	B	E/D
1892	40.0	38.2	28.5
1910	45.7	43.0	32.9
	+5.7	+4.8	+4.4

[1] Thompson, *Socialists, Liberals and Labour*, p. 167.   [2] *Ibid.* p. 295.
[3] *Ibid.* App. A., pp. 299–303. Group A are divisions with over 90 per cent working-class electors; Group B with over 83.4 per cent in 1885 and over 80 per cent in 1910; Group E (1885–1900) and Group D (1900–10) with over 40 per cent middle-class electors. Naturally the seats in each group vary between the two periods.

400

It should be recalled that in 1892 the Liberals had made 'a remarkable recovery', one 'based on working class votes', and that this was 'a labour-based Liberal victory'.[1] Nonetheless, by 1910 the Liberals had increased their advantage by around five per cent in the working-class seats, as well as improving their position by a slightly smaller amount in the middle-class seats. Putting the comparison another way, between 1885 and January 1910 the Liberal share of the electorate increased by nearly *three* per cent in the divisions with over 40 per cent *middle-class* electors, and by nearly *ten* per cent in those with over 90 per cent *working-class* electors. This surely points to a shift in voting over a generation which is not dissimilar from the Lancashire pattern.

K. O. Morgan has suggested that in Wales the early twentieth century saw a conflict between religious politics, derived from the social structure of the countryside, and the economic issues of industrial communities. He sees this change as a direct analogue of the change from Liberalism to Labour, arguing that the Liberal party was helped to its triumphs of 1906 by the short-lived religious revival of 1904–5.[2] But this is to close too many doors. Even on the coalfield the Liberal party retained an extraordinary appearance of health right up to 1914; the Liberal performance in 1910 was as good as that of 1906, and independent Labour candidatures were doomed to defeat.[3] For a dying animal Welsh Liberalism plainly had a big kick. Perhaps it is premature to infer that the 'sociological revolution' which was pending in Wales would ineluctably have worked to the advantage of Labour. Both Thompson and Morgan believe that local Liberal party organisation was in a state of decay.[4] This may be. What is in dispute is, not so much the claim that Liberalism was dying in London or Wales or anywhere else, as the assumption that it must have been. This assumption ('We know now that time was on Labour's side')[5] is not absent from R. G. Gregory's fine study of the Miners. Gregory encounters difficulty in explaining why the miners voted for affiliation to the Labour party while preferring Liberal candidates in parliamentary elections:[6] a difficulty, of course, which largely disappears once both actions are seen within the framework of progressivism. There are no other comparable detailed studies (nothing on Yorkshire, for instance). It may be noted that, although Pelling has elsewhere attributed the Liberal collapse to 'long-term social and economic changes',[7] this is not an inference

[1] *Ibid.* p. 96.   [2] Morgan, *Wales in British Politics*, pp. 210–11, 217–18.
[3] *Ibid.* pp. 249–55.
[4] *Ibid.* pp. 166–71, 243–5; Thompson, *Socialists, Liberals and Labour*, pp. 167–79. The 'derelict' constituencies in Lancashire for which the L.C.L.F. was responsible might be held to show the same.
[5] Gregory, *The Miners and British Politics*, p. 179.
[6] *Ibid.* pp. 188 ff.
[7] 'Labour and the downfall of Liberalism', *Popular Politics and Society*, p. 120.

he draws from his survey of the whole country between 1885 and 1910. His conclusion there is that, over the period, the influence of organised religion was on the wane and that of organised labour on the increase; but that 'the question of whether the Labour Party could or would displace the Liberal Party as one of the two main parties of the State hardly seemed to arise'.[1] For the issue is, not whether the Liberal party would infallibly have overcome every political difficulty which might face it, but whether it was viable.

III

On this question the evidence from the north west is important in its own right. In studying industrial politics it is not enough to dismiss Lancashire as precocious or unrepresentative. It is not just that Lancashire was the prototype for industrial society: it was Marx's prototype too. Marx and Engels looked at the Lancashire workingmen and decided that capitalism would educate them into revolution.[2] The truth was more literal. The Church educated them into Toryism – working, of course, with the grain of socialisation of other kinds. As a prediction, the Marxist model failed, not because it distinguished the material interests of the working class incorrectly, but because during the late nineteenth century the struggle for power was institutionalised by the pre-existing parties and comprised the clash of ideal interests. And when this style of politics was overthrown in the early twentieth century it was not because of a change in the economic infrastructure. It was a political initiative which precipitated the decisive class polarisation of the electorate. Admittedly, this tendency had been latent for the best part of a generation, but the events during that time which had contrived to urge it on or hold it back (Home Rule, the Boer War, Tariff Reform, for instance) testify to the primacy of politics. And it was a change in political issues that was the clearest sign of the new politics.

After 1910 the Conservatives became more ready to commit their appeal to the old issues, notably Home Rule, because they were the ones on which they remembered doing well. The Conservatives were helped by religion: the Liberals by economics. Some Unionists, like Selborne, looking for a partisan handle with which to convince their leaders of the virtues of woman suffrage, argued that 'women will bring to the ballot boxes a deeper religious

---

[1] *Social Geography of British Elections*, pp. 433–5.
[2] Cf. Engels, *The Condition of the Working-class in England*: 'The factory operatives, and especially those of the cotton district, form the nucleus of the labour movement. Lancashire, and especially Manchester, is the seat of the most powerful Unions, the central point of Chartism, the place which numbers most Socialists. The more the factory system has taken possession of a branch of industry, the more the working-men employed in it participate in the labour movement; the sharper the opposition between working-men and capitalists, the clearer the proletarian consciousness in the working-man.' *Marx and Engels on Britain*, p. 276.

feeling and a firmer & sterner sense of patriotism than men have as a sex'.[1]
In the same vein, though from an opposite standpoint, Masterman would
expatiate in 1908 on 'how much the Churches forced political and not social
issues on a candidate' and warned them 'how a big shifting of ground in
politics is coming from the political to the social and economic'.[2] This
change, linked as it was to changes in voting behaviour, made a lifelong
impression upon Churchill, who had enjoyed an intimate acquaintance with
both parties in Lancashire. When the fiscal issue was still a novelty he
predicted that: 'The old Conservative Party, with its religious convictions
and constitutional principles, will disappear, and a new party will arise,
rich, materialist, and secular.' As a Manchester M.P. he told the Commons
that 'in the main the lines of difference between the two Parties are social
and economic – in the main the lines of difference are increasingly becoming
the lines of cleavage between the rich and the poor'. And as leader of the
Conservative party he would tell the House the same. 'More than 40 years
ago', he said in 1949,

I sat myself in a Left-wing Government with a majority even greater than that of
the present one, and I was one of their most prominent and controversial figures.
The House returned in 1906 represented, in my view, more or less the same slice
of the population, the people who elected it coming very largely from the same
homes and from the same areas, as does this majority to-day.[3]

The movement was not, of course, uniform or complete. The old patterns
of voting were under least strain where they did not openly clash with the new.
The Irish, for instance, continued to vote largely on ethnic lines – but for the
same party which they would have supported on class lines. In north east
Lancashire temperance was still accepted in its entirety by the progressives,
in the knowledge that Nonconformity was strong among the working–class
electorate there. But the old basis of Lancashire Toryism was undermined.
'It is too late in the day to begin making a song about the dear old Church',
wrote a Blackburn miner impatiently in 1909.[4] Things had changed too in
Preston, where the Tories were still the stronger party. The Labour candidate
transparently claimed that 'they had never once in the contest, of their own
accord and free will, dragged in the question of religion, excepting to reply
to their opponents'.[5] And what greater symbol could there be of the passing

[1] Selborne to Law, 13 March 1912, BLP 25/3/26.
[2] Masterman, *C. F. G. Masterman*, p. 114; cf. p. 236.
[3] Churchill, *Winston S. Churchill*, II, 63–4; Churchill, *Liberalism and the Social Problem*, p. 145;
    5 Hansard, 468, col. 174 (28 September 1949). I owe the last reference to Jenkins, *Mr. Balfour's
    Poodle*, in which see App. A, pp. 285–91 for an interesting comparison of the election results in
    1906 and 1945.
[4] Letter from 'Miner', *N.D.T.*, 8 December 1909.
[5] J. T. Macpherson at Preston, *Lancs. D.P.*, 17 January 1910.

of the great days of Tory Democracy than the candidature of Sir John Gorst as a Liberal?

Coming back to Preston after my long absence [he declared], I naturally see a great number of changes, but what change surprised me most is the great change which has taken place in the political feelings of the people (cheers). Preston in my younger days was celebrated for its Conservative working men, and I had a good deal to do with them in former days, and frequently addressed them. I now find the Conservative working men, I won't say have disappeared – (laughter) – but have become much less numerous than before (cheers). A considerable number of them have become members of the Liberal party – (cheers) – and a still greater number have become members of the Labour party – (cheers) – and here am I, who in my younger days was a disciple and a follower of Mr Disraeli, and helped him very much in the organisation of the Conservative party 30 or 40 years ago, appearing at Preston as a Liberal candidate, and in close federation with the Labour party in the borough (cheers). What is the reason of this great change? As far as I am personally concerned, I know what it is with me, and I have no doubt that with most of those who are in this altered position the change has come because of the altered attitude of the parties of the state on the question of social reform (cheers).[1]

Liverpool was more immovable. But even there the Roman Catholic James Sexton met a better reception as a Labour candidate in 1910. 'The old and bitter prejudice was on the wane', he recalled.[2] It was a slow business. Pastor George Wise was instrumental in founding a new Protestant party in 1922 and, working with the Unionists, this made it its business to oppose men like Sexton. Not until after the 1964 General Election could it be agreed 'that Liverpool must now be classed as a typical industrial city and in no way different as it was when voting was largely on religious lines', a tendency which 'probably survived as a tradition only among the older generation of Irish families up to the 1959 election'.[3]

Clearly the Liberals had no *desire* to lose their wealthy supporters. In the aftermath of the 1906 elections one socialist wrote that it was the Tories' policy

to frighten the man who has five pounds in the coffee-pot into voting Tory next time. Mr Chamberlain knows that the bulk of the Liberal Party have at least five pounds, if not five pounds and nine farthings, in their coffee-pots. Consequently, he argues, 'If the Labour Party force the Liberal Government to pass some far-reaching measure of social reform which touches, or threatens to touch, the coffee-pot of my Liberal friends, then I shall detach these men to my side.' He thinks, quite rightly, that the coffee-pots would prefer Protection to Socialism.[4]

[1] Gorst at Preston, *Lancs. D.P.*, 11 January 1910.
[2] Sexton, *Sir James Sexton*, p. 213.
[3] *The Times*, 5 January 1965; and see article by William Hamling, *Liverpool D.P.*, 16 September 1960. For the Protestant party see George Thayer, *The British Political Fringe* (1965), pp. 225–37.
[4] R. B. Suthers, *Clarion*, 26 January 1906.

The acuteness of this analysis was confirmed by events. Alfred Emmott declared in 1910 that 'he was sometimes astonished that more of the rich and well-to-do in this world did not leave the party...It might almost be said to be easier for a camel to pass through the eye of a needle than for a rich man to remain in the Liberal party.'[1] The reason more did not leave could only have been that they retained faith in Liberalism as a disinterested principle of government. It was this that Hobhouse had in mind when he justified the role of the *Guardian* in terms of its ability to strike a just balance. He thought it had some authority

because people know that we look at each question on its merits, and are prepared, if necessary, to admit faults on our side. If, indeed, Labour were always and necessarily in the right, this caution would not be required. But is not this dictum a confusion of two things? Labour is presumably suffering from the wrong of un-equal distribution, and in all its efforts commands, therefore, a certain sympathy. It does not follow that every particular effort it makes to right that wrong is wise, or even fair...[2]

This was one point at which progressivism, working in the interests of the community at large, parted company with a narrow trade-union policy.

A narrow trade-union policy, however, was the only distinctive appeal of the Labour party. In Marxist terms, there is a critical distinction between this type of 'trade union consciousness', which is developed spontaneously, and a 'socialist consciousness' which is not. The British Labour movement's 'spontaneity' – which might be defined as a propensity not to see beyond the end of one's nose – left it with little of the ideological mettle necessary 'to prevent the movement from drifting into mere reformism'.[3] Now it is perfectly consistent for the Marxists to lay the axe to reformism in general and to argue that it is an inadequate political strategy for the working class. In this respect, of course, the later Labour party is hardly less vulnerable than the Edwardian Liberal party. But those historians who adopt a sub-Marxian critique of the reformist Liberal party *from the point of view of the reformist Labour party* are sawing off the branch on which they are sitting. It is true that in their social democratic aims the progressives looked to salvation *for* rather than *by* the working class. In believing that the poor would inherit the earth, they entertained no illusion that the downtrodden would, by virtue of being downtrodden, become uniquely equipped as agents of social regeneration.

Nor, of course, was the Liberal party a perfect instrument. The grip of the past over it was necessarily strong. It was not without difficulties in

[1] Emmott at Shaw, *Oldham Chron.*, 3 December 1910.
[2] Hobhouse to Margaret Llewelyn Davies, February 1914, Hobson and Ginsberg, *L. T. Hobhouse*, pp. 64–5.
[3] E. J. Hobsbawm, *Labouring Men* (1964), pp. 334 ff.

Conclusion

attempting to redefine its social base; that party finance should be on a precarious footing was one sign of this. But other changes in the nature of politics helped to make progressivism viable. This is notably true in four important respects. In the first place, change in the criteria of political leadership could only benefit the Liberal party. When the Lancashire towns had been bossed by the millowners the Liberals were championed by the bourgeois paragons of the Manchester School – 'the individuals produced by Individualism'.[1] But under the conditions of twentieth-century politics they could no longer expect to be sustained by such influences; hence it was the Conservatives who suffered most directly when the patriarchs were toppled. Second, as the importance of religious divisions declined it was again the Conservative party which had most to lose in the north west. The mainspring of democratic Toryism was running down; and in successfully identifying with the class interests of the workingmen, the progressives were preparing for the politics of the future. Third – associated with this – the development of a coherent ideology which lay behind the rhetoric of the 1910 elections gave progressivism a cutting edge. Insofar as election issues turned increasingly on economic and social questions, this was meat and drink to the new Liberals; and although it somewhat bemused the old Liberals, it baffled the Tories completely. Lastly, all these changes interacted with a change in the ambit of politics. Tory Lancashire had been built around local politics; but in almost every sphere national influences were becoming more important. Party organisation became increasingly centralised; through a centralised organisation party orthodoxy was enforced; with greater orthodoxy, national issues counted for more; as national issues imposed themselves, it became less advantageous to have them argued by local leaders; as local leaders disappeared, so the local communities to whom they appealed lost their ascendancy. These developments, then, were not only cumulative but cumulatively favourable to progressivism.

Thus the first quarter of the twentieth century saw two sorts of change in British politics. The first sort centred upon the emergence of class politics in a stable form; the second sort upon the effective replacement of the Liberal party by the Labour party. But the first – with which this book is concerned – does not in any simple way explain the second. For one thing, the chronology is wrong. By 1910, the change to class politics was substantially complete. That from Liberalism to Labour had not really begun. Nor were there signs that it must begin. It was not a light thing to overturn one party and make another to put in its place. At the beginning of the second decade of the twentieth century it looked as though both Labour and Liberalism would be subsumed in progressivism. It seemed that social

[1] Mills, *The Manchester Guardian*, p. 96.

democracy in England was bound up with the prospects of the Liberal party; and in the generation after its downfall the social democratic record is not one of achievement. But that is another question. Tomorrow is another day. It is upon how Edwardians voted (as distinct from how Victorians voted) that the case of this book rests. For by the time of the General Election of January 1910, during which Liberals eagerly celebrated the Gladstone centenary, politics had entered a world in which the Grand Old Man would not have been at home.

APPENDICES
BIBLIOGRAPHY
INDEX

APPENDIX A

Voting in the north west

Table 1. PERCENTAGE CONSERVATIVE OR UNIONIST VOTE

1. In 2-member boroughs with 4 or more candidates the votes for the 2 Unionists have been aggregated; where there were only 3 candidates, the Unionist poll as a percentage of the votes cast for the leading candidate on either side is given in brackets (Preston 1885, 1892, 1895, 1900; Blackburn 1895, 1900; Bolton 1906, December 1910).

2. * – Unionist vote in 1886 that of the former Liberal M.P. (Barrow, Burnley, Rossendale, Bury).

3. unop. – Unionist candidate unopposed.

4. N. – no Unionist candidate.

5. n.c. – no contest, i.e. representation shared in Bolton, 1900; Austin Taylor only nominally a Unionist in Liverpool East Toxteth, 1906.

6. *50.0* – figure italicised where more than 2 candidates standing (or more than 4 in a 2-member borough).

7. Dates and figures for by-elections given under the year of the Parliament in which they occurred.

	1885	1886	1892	1895	1900	1906	Jan. 1910	Dec. 1910
1. Barrow	46.9	63.1*	53.4	*53.5*	unop.	39.7	44.8	47.1
	[86]	[90]						
	41.0	*36.6*						
2. North Lonsdale	51.4	55.5	44.9	54.4	unop.	51.1	51.0	50.5
3. Lancaster	55.4	48.7	46.1	53.4	49.8	46.4	45.9	49.5
4. Blackpool	unop.	unop.	65.2	unop.	unop.	58.9	59.3	unop.
		[86]	[95]		[00]			
		71.4	unop.		55.8			
5. Darwen	50.0	53.2	49.2	53.2	51.7	50.1	49.4	50.6
6. Preston	(60.6)	60.3	(56.6)	(65.1)	(64.9)	43.1	*53.1*	53.1
					[00]			
					unop.			
					[03]			
					57.1			
7. Blackburn	59.3	unop.	56.7	(58.3)	(61.3)	50.1	43.4	47.3
8. Burnley	46.3	50.3*	43.8	*42.5*	51.9	*32.7*	*35.2*	*37.5*
		[87]	[93]					
		47.2	47.0					
		[89]						
		N.						
9. Clitheroe	39.5	N.	41.8	N.	N.	N.	32.7	32.3
	[86]				[02]			
	N.				N.			
10. Accrington	47.6	51.1	47.6	48.6	*46.1*	N.	41.9	44.3
			[93]					
			48.9					
11. Rossendale	41.1	57.8*	41.7	N.	N.	40.4	*37.5*	44.0
		[92]		[00]	[04]			
		44.4		43.5	N.			
12. Heywood	46.6	47.2	46.2	53.3	51.2	44.2	45.0	46.1
13. Middleton	45.4	51.6	49.5	53.9	50.6	43.9	45.0	47.1
				[97]				[11]
				48.7				48.5
14. Radcliffe	47.3	49.3	49.5	52.9	49.7	43.2	44.2	46.9
15. Bolton	*52.4*	54.8	52.3	59.5	n.c.	(37.9)	38.0	(45.6)
								[12]
								46.9
16. Bury	48.8	unop.*	55.7	54.8	55.7	43.1	46.7	48.5
					[02]			
					47.4			
17. Rochdale	44.3	42.4	45.1	*46.0*	*46.1*	*34.6*	*38.6*	*40.9*
18. Oldham	49.3	51.4	48.9	51.2	49.8	40.7	40.6	44.0
				[99]				[11]
				47.1				*40.4*
19. Chorley	67.6	unop.	unop.	unop.	unop.	55.7	58.3	60.3
			[95]		[03]			[13]
			unop.		56.5			57.5
20. Westhoughton	61.6	unop.	57.9	unop.	61.7	39.8	43.2	46.8
					[03]			
					unop.			

412

	1885	1886	1892	1895	1900	1906	Jan. 1910	Dec. 1910
21. Leigh	41.5	42.2	44.9	46.5	49.4	41.9	*35.1*	44.8
22. Ince	53.4	57.2	48.7	52.2	unop.	29.8	39.4	42.8
23. Newton	52.3	55.2 [86] 54.8	55.2	58.2 [99] unop.	unop.	47.8	47.3	50.5
24. Wigan	57.2	54.8	50.8	56.2	54.7	*46.5*	47.2	53.2
25. St Helens	50.4	51.5	50.3	53.5	60.9	43.4	46.7	51.1
26. Warrington	55.4	53.6	54.1	54.6	57.5	42.3	49.3	51.2
27. Eccles	51.4	51.8 [90] 48.9	48.7	51.9	50.9	*34.8*	*38.7*	47.6
28. Salford North	51.3	51.2	48.0	50.0	55.5	43.1	45.3	48.6
29. Salford West	48.1	50.9	50.2	50.6	55.9	41.1	*37.8*	46.7
30. Salford South	49.6	50.9	*46.5*	*45.1*	58.5	44.4	47.9	51.6
31. Manchester North West	53.3	55.2	unop.	58.6	unop.	43.8 [08] 50.7	46.5	47.9 [12] 56.0
32. Manchester North	56.8	49.3	48.1	47.2	49.8	36.3	43.1	46.1
33. Manchester North East	60.0	52.3 [91] 50.9	50.7	*48.1*	54.5	35.4	41.6	48.8
34. Manchester East	55.0	54.3 [86] unop.	52.0 [95] unop.	53.8	63.4	40.9	45.5	45.7
35. Manchester South	45.2	47.4	48.9	50.4 [00] 61.4	57.1	32.0	41.1	N. [12] 52.1
36. Manchester South West	53.9	49.2	49.0	53.3	62.6	41.2	*42.4*	48.1
37. Gorton	39.4	47.4 [89] 45.5	48.9	57.9	52.4	33.6	48.4	47.8
38. Prestwich	46.4	50.7	50.7	49.6	47.3	37.2	41.4	41.0
39. Stretford	49.0	54.2	55.7	unop.	60.4 [01] 55.0	42.7	45.1	41.0
40. Hyde	46.7	52.7	51.7	*52.5*	53.2	44.7	*39.4*	48.6
41. High Peak	50.1	51.0	52.1	52.9	49.1	46.1 [09] 48.4	49.5	50.8
42. Ashton	50.4	50.0	51.0	*52.6*	*53.1*	43.7	*45.7*	51.2
43. Stalybridge	51.8	55.0	52.7	55.1	50.6 [05] 43.3	46.9	50.4	52.7
44. Stockport	52.0	53.1	49.0 [93] 52.3	52.5	49.1	38.5	44.1	46.0
45. Southport	48.9	53.3	53.4	54.0 [98] 48.6 [99] 47.3	51.0	49.1	51.4	52.3

	1885	1886	1892	1895	1900	1906	Jan. 1910	Dec. 1910
46. Ormskirk	68.7	unop.	68.7	71.7 [98] unop.	unop.	61.5	59.7	unop.
47. Widnes	62.0	56.0	51.4	53.5	69.6	54.6	55.2	unop.
48. Bootle	63.1	unop.	59.4	unop.	unop.	51.1	52.9	unop. [11] 56.2
49. Liverpool Kirkdale	55.3	58.7	57.5	60.7 [98] unop.	71.4	54.3 [07] 54.6	51.4 [10] 55.5	58.4
50. Liverpool Walton	58.3	63.1 [86] unop. [88] unop.	59.8	unop.	unop.	53.2	52.6	55.9
51. Liverpool Everton	68.7	unop. [91] unop.	64.6	unop.	unop. [05] 60.2	57.8	62.4	unop.
52. Liverpool West Derby	57.9	61.6 [88] unop.	58.4 [93] 61.5	73.3	unop. [03] 62.7	60.2	58.5	62.5
53. Liverpool Scotland	N.	33.0	34.7	41.0	42.1	28.5	20.9	21.9
54. Liverpool Exchange	50.2	48.5 [87] 49.9	49.4	52.3 [97] 50.5	65.0	48.6	48.3	51.6
55. Liverpool Abercromby	56.0	55.7	56.4	unop.	unop.	48.2	54.7	58.1
56. Liverpool East Toxteth	58.0	unop.	62.8	68.0 [95] unop.	unop. [02] 52.8	n.c.	51.8	56.7
57. Liverpool West Toxteth	67.9	unop.	59.2	68.6	unop.	56.5	57.5	61.7
58. Birkenhead	55.7	56.3	52.8 [94] 50.4	50.8	unop.	36.4	49.6	53.4
59. Wirral	59.3	unop.	64.7	unop.	54.5	44.7	53.8	56.5
60. Northwich	44.3	52.7 [87] 43.8	43.7	41.6	46.5	41.8	45.4	48.6
61. Knutsford	57.7	unop.	63.0	unop.	unop.	46.5	54.9	56.8
62. Altrincham	54.3 [86] 53.5	unop.	54.3	57.5	57.6	40.5	47.3	50.4 [13] 53.6
63. Macclesfield	46.2	54.4	56.0	unop.	unop.	46.9	49.2	48.4
64. Crewe	45.7	46.3	41.8	52.7	44.6	40.4	37.2 [10] 44.2	43.7 [12] 44.6
65. Chester	47.1	50.7	55.5	unop.	56.2	49.7	51.3	50.7
66. Eddisbury	50.7	54.2	53.1	60.6	unop.	44.1	53.2	51.4

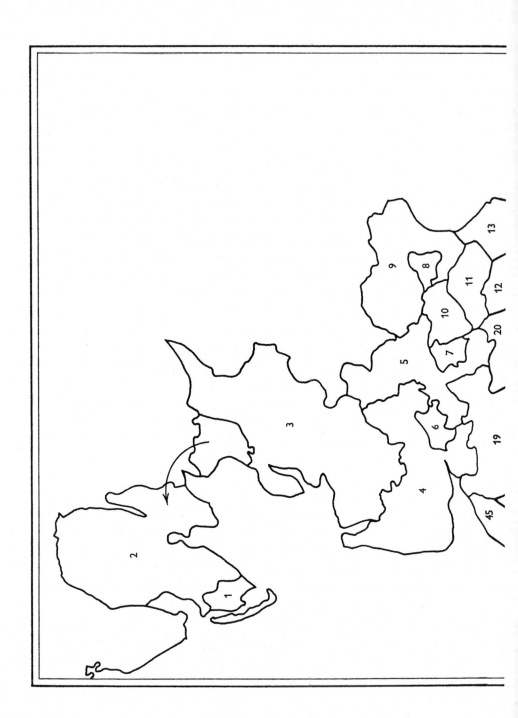

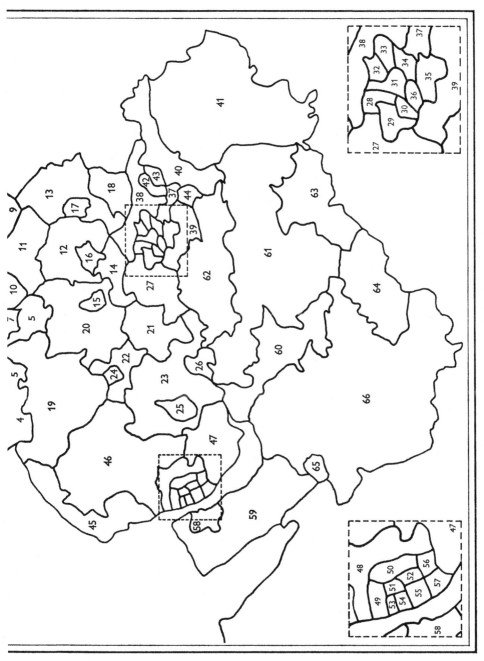

Fig. 1. Constituency boundaries in the north west

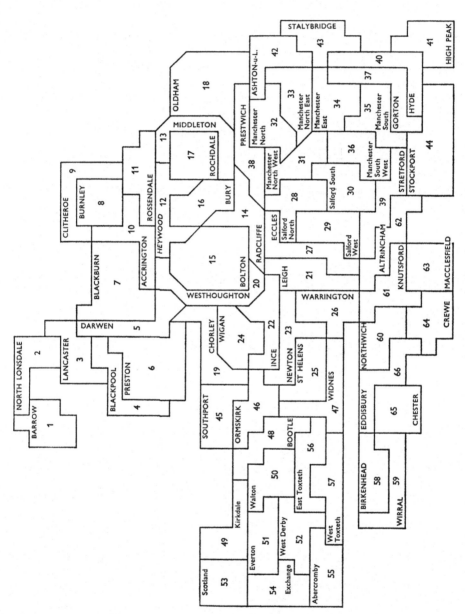

Fig. 2. Equal-area diagram of constituencies in the north west

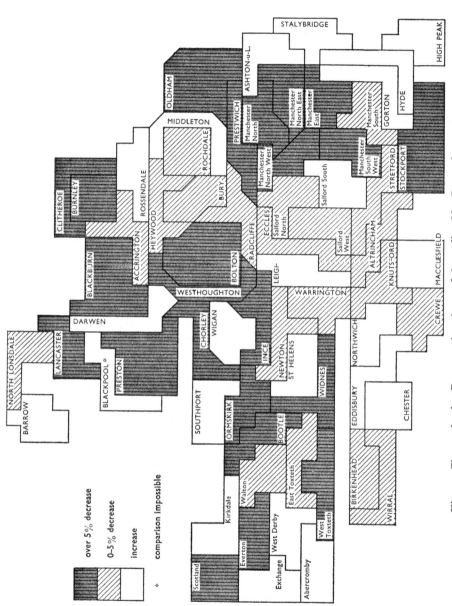

Fig. 3. Change in the Conservative share of the poll, 1885–December 1910

N.B. 1. There was no contest in December 1910 in Widnes, Bootle, Ormskirk, Liverpool Everton and Manchester South; the figure for January 1910 has been used instead.

2. There were 3-cornered contests in December 1910 at Rochdale and Burnley.

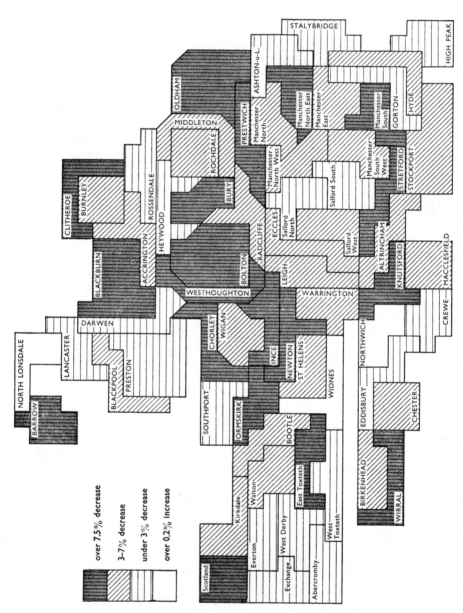

over 7.5% decrease

3-7% decrease

under 3% decrease

over 0.2% increase

Fig. 4. Change in the Conservative share of the poll, 1892–January 1910

STALYBRIDGE

HIGH PEAK

ASHTON-u-L.

OLDHAM

MIDDLETON

PRESTWICH

Manchester North East

Manchester East

ROCHDALE

Manchester North

Manchester South

GORTON

HYDE

BURY

Manchester North West

Manchester South West

STRETFORD

CLITHEROE

BURNLEY

ROSSENDALE

HEYWOOD

ACCRINGTON

Salford South

STOCKPORT

ECCLES

Salford North

Manchester South West

RADCLIFFE

Salford West

ALTRINCHAM

BLACKBURN

BOLTON

LEIGH

Salford West

KNUTSFORD

MACCLESFIELD

DARWEN

WESTHOUGHTON

WARRINGTON

LANCASTER

CHORLEY

WIGAN

CREWE

NORTH LONSDALE

PRESTON

INCE

NEWTON

NORTHWICH

BLACKPOOL

ST HELENS

BARROW

SOUTHPORT

ORMSKIRK

WIDNES

EDDISBURY

CHESTER

BOOTLE

Kirkdale

East Toxteth

BIRKENHEAD

Walton

West Derby

West Toxteth

WIRRAL

Everton

Exchange

Abercromby

Scotland

420

Note

The Elections of 1892 and January 1910 offer scope for fair comparison for several reasons – there were few unopposed returns and there are not the same local peculiarities as in 1885 and 1886 over the Irish and Unionist votes. There are, however, two difficulties.

(1) Some allowance has to be made for the effect of three-cornered contests. There was only one of these in 1892 (Salford South) and there the 1885 figures are used for comparison, as they are in Chorley and Manchester North West, which were uncontested in 1892. In the 12 cases in which there were third candidates in January 1910, the percentage fall in the Conservative vote since 1892 has been halved (on the neutral assumption that the Conservatives were losing votes equally to both opponents). This is somewhat arbitrary but it is more satisfactory for present purposes than taking the swing between the top two candidates. In several cases this would express the net advantage to the Conservatives of the intervention of a Labour candidate, while disguising an absolute drop in Conservative support. But the effect which we wish to measure is not that of Labour on the Liberal vote, but that of Liberalism (and Labour) on the Conservative vote.

(2) In those constituencies which moved strongly either way between 1885 and 1892 a comparison of the 1910 results only with 1892 may be misleading if the object is to measure the new Liberalism against the old. Thus the fall in the level of Conservative support between the two phases will be *exaggerated* if there was a big swing towards them between 1885 and 1892, since some of the drop may represent not a new pattern but the reversion to an old one; and it will be *under-estimated* in those cases where it was the Liberals who benefited from the Home Rule crisis. It is this which goes far towards explaining the results in Widnes and North Lonsdale, which at first sight appear quite anomalous. These were the only two seats in which there was a marked increase in the Conservative share of the poll 1892–January 1910 – for the reason mentioned above, *viz.* these were the two prime instances of a large Liberal gain after 1886; so, although the Conservatives improved upon their 1892 position in January 1910, they were still polling, in North Lonsdale slightly below, and in Widnes well below, their level of 1885. Similarly, in Lancaster and Liverpool West Toxteth the Conservatives polled nearly as well in January 1910 as in 1892 – but still 10 per cent below 1885; and in Manchester North East, where they were running nearly 10 per cent below 1892, they were nearer 20 per cent below 1885. The same is true to a lesser degree in the other areas where Home Rule had gained votes for the Liberals.

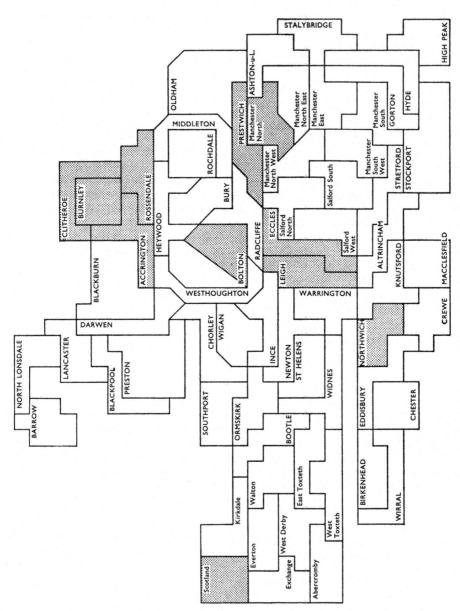

Fig. 5. General Election of 1895 (Unionist seats left unshaded)

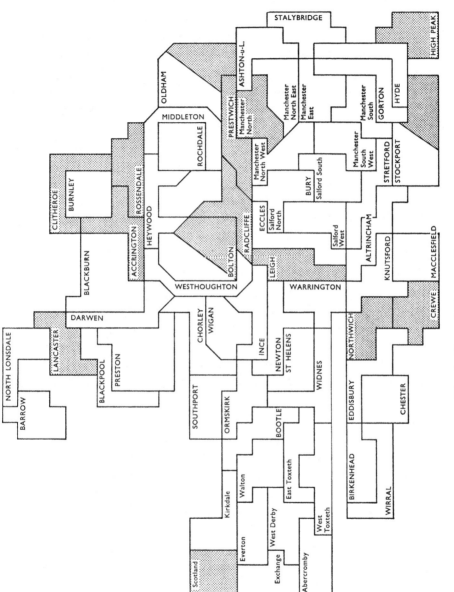

Fig. 6. General Election of 1900

423

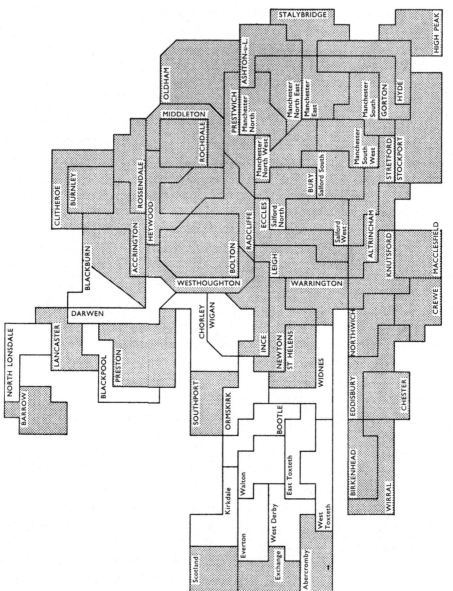

Fig. 7. General Election of 1906

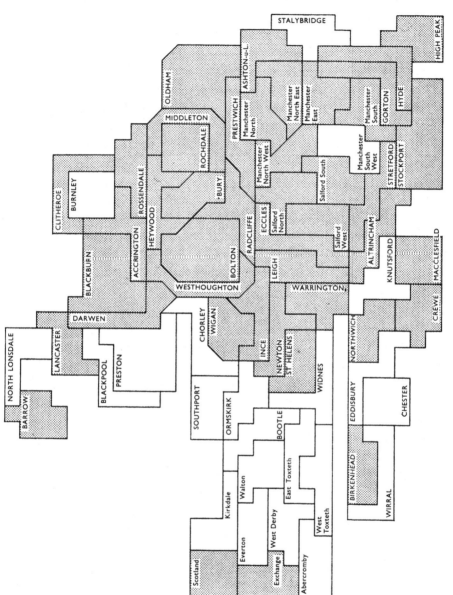

Fig. 8. General Election of January 1910

425

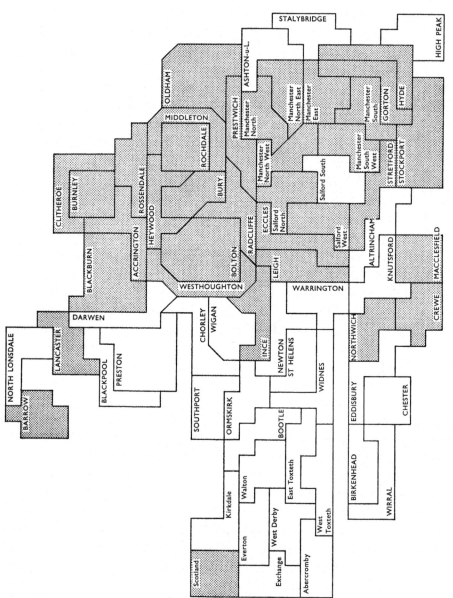

Fig. 9. General Election of December 1910

The Franchise

TABLE I. Estimated proportion (%) of adult males on the register 1901 and 1911.

	1901	1911
Barrow	45.8	54.3
North Lonsdale	72.4	76.7
Lancaster	62.9	65.1
Blackpool	61.8	63.2
Darwen	76.9	77.8
Preston	58.2	59.6
Blackburn	61.8	64.4
Burnley	60.9	60.8
Clitheroe	67.1	65.2
Accrington	65.5	66.0
Rossendale	67.3	68.3
Heywood	69.5	72.5
Middleton	71.8	69.1
Radcliffe	61.5	62.9
Bolton	59.9	59.4
Bury	60.5	64.5
Rochdale	69.0	68.9
Oldham	61.3	61.1
Chorley	61.2	61.9
Westhoughton	62.6	65.5
Leigh	57.0	55.7
Ince	56.3	58.8
Newton	54.1	55.3
Wigan	51.0	52.1
St Helens	47.9	47.8
Warrington	54.2	52.0
Eccles	62.5	63.6
Salford North	53.8	51.4
West	55.7	56.2
South	52.2	46.9
Manchester North West	64.0	63.6
North	50.9	46.8
North East	53.1	49.0
East	50.9	47.9
South	53.4	54.6
South West	51.2	46.8
Gorton	58.4	57.4
Prestwich	61.8	61.8
Stretford	83.6	77.0
Hyde	69.3	71.6
High Peak	65.5	71.2
Ashton	60.0	60.5
Stalybridge	64.2	64.2

	1901	1911
Stockport	62.5	60.1
Southport	66.1	68.8
Ormskirk	56.2	57.9
Widnes	51.3	52.1
Bootle	56.4	55.6
Liverpool Kirkdale	48.1	46.0
Walton	53.0	54.4
Everton	46.4	38.1
West Derby	52.9	46.8
Scotland	42.0	39.7
Exchange	57.1	50.2
Abercromby	59.6	56.2
East Toxteth	56.4	55.0
West Toxteth	48.6	49.3
Birkenhead	52.7	51.1
Wirral	61.7	60.0
Northwich	63.6	66.0
Knutsford	64.4	66.1
Altrincham	69.2	74.0
Macclesfield	67.5	68.9
Crewe	67.0	69.7
Chester	64.0	63.1
Eddisbury	72.2	71.4

Calculated from the Census. The figures for adult males as a proportion of all males in Lancashire as a whole (54.4 per cent in 1901; 57.8 per cent in 1911) were applied to the male population of each constituency. The Lancashire figure was used throughout since that for Cheshire was only marginally different and that for Derbyshire likely to be unrepresentative of the High Peak.

TABLE 2.   The Plural Vote.

1. Estimates of the number of outvoters in particular constituencies vary, and it is not always clear whether they refer solely to the borough freeholders, or the total plural vote or even the ownership vote as a whole. Despite the lack of precise figures, it is clear that the proportion of outvoters in the total electorate must lie within fairly firm limits.

Percentage of borough freeholders in county electorates

County division	Borough included	1900	1906	1910
Stretford	Manchester, Salford, Stockport (part)	'Nearly 30 per cent'	20	16
Bootle	Liverpool	—	5–10	11
Darwen	Blackburn	13	12	12–13
Blackpool	Preston	—	10	—
North Lonsdale	Barrow	—	—	14
Wirral	Birkenhead	7–9	14	6–7
Westhoughton	Bolton	—	—	2
Middleton	Rochdale	—	—	4–5
Clitheroe	Burnley	—	—	2
Eddisbury	Chester	—	—	10–11

The proportion for Stretford in 1900 is given by *M.G.*, 6 October 1900 and almost certainly refers to the ownership vote as a whole; that for Bootle in 1910 is given by Blewett, 'The franchise in the United Kingdom, 1885–1918', *Past & Present*, **32** (December 1965), p. 49. The rest of the figures are calculated from estimates in *M.G.* (Stretford, Bootle, Blackpool, North Lonsdale, Wirral); *M. Courier* (Westhoughton, Middleton); *L. Courier* (Eddisbury, Bootle, Wirral); *Lancs. D.P.* (Darwen, Clitheroe); *Liverpool D.P.* (Wirral). In 1911 there were 400 Rochdale freeholders (2–3 per cent) and a total of 800 non-resident voters (5–6 per cent) in Middleton; and in 1913 there were 600 Stockport freeholders (3 per cent) and a total of 1,500 non-residents (7 per cent) in Altrincham.

2. In the 1890s the Manchester Liberal Union plainly must have possessed fairly full information about the politics of the duplicate voters in the city. These voters were not plural voters because of the nice legal point that Manchester's six divisions comprised a single parliamentary borough; but they had plural qualifications. Unfortunately the numbers of duplicate voters were not recorded in a standardised form and in only two years do the figures seem to be both full and reliable.

	Liberals	Conservatives	Total
1890	1,590	1,280	2,870
1896	1,183	795	1,940

(SOURCE: M.L.U. Minutes, 18 November 1890, 13 May 1896.)

In 1890, then, it was believed that 55 per cent of these voters were Liberals, and in 1896 60 per cent. It is likely, moreover, that owing to the parties' role in registration these figures are comprehensive. It is surprising to find the Liberal element so strong, and it may be asked whether the duplicate voters are representative of the plural voters. Now it is true that these men, whose normal qualification must have been as ten-pound occupiers, were *ipso facto* not of quite the same class as the ownership voters. But it was this same occupier franchise which enabled most of the non-resident city voters to become pluralists proper; indeed, those who had more than one ten-pound franchise *were* duplicate voters as well. And, although probably to a lesser degree, outvoters too were among the duplicate voters. In the business division of Manchester North West the duplicate vote, which must have comprised much of the large plural vote there, ran to nearly 1,500 in 1896, and of this the Liberals had 60 per cent.

TABLE 3. Number of removals, December 1910.

Constituency		Removals	Electors	Ratio
Counties				
Lancaster		2,500	14,797	1:7
Accrington		4,000	16,297	1:4
Heywood		3,000	11,339	1:4
Leigh		2,000	14,150	1:7
Ince		3,000–4,000	14,107	1:4
Stretford		5,000	27,629	1:5–6
Hyde		3,000–3,500	12,166	1:4
Wirral		2,000+	14,899	1:7
Southport		4,000	13,164	1:3–4
Clitheroe	Clitheroe	300–400	18,584	Perhaps 1:10
	Nelson	500		
Darwen		2,000	15,308	1:7–8
Gorton		3,000 since Jan.	14,511	1:3–4
Prestwich		3,000	15,732	1:5
Radcliffe		3,000–4,000	12,244	1:4
Boroughs				
Bury		1,600	9,657	1:6
Bolton		7,000	21,341	1:3
Rochdale		3,500	14,909	1:4
Oldham		10,000	35,315	1:3–4
Wigan		3,000+	9,577	1:3
Blackburn		8,000	19,496	1:2–3
City divisions				
Manchester North		4,500+	10,284	1:2
	East	5,000–6,000	12,646	1:2
	South West	4,300	8,180	1:2
Manchester (all)		20,000–30,000	68,590	1:2–3
Salford North		2,500	9,850	1:4
Liverpool Exchange		'33 per cent'		1:3
Liverpool (all)		26,000	83,193	1:3

Based on estimates given in one or more of the following newspapers: *M.G., L. Courier, M. Courier, Lancs. D.P., N.D.T., Oldham Chron., Bolton Chron., Blackburn Times.*

Strength of the Irish vote

	1900	1906	1910
*Manchester North East	1,000 +	1,000	
*Manchester North		1,200	1,500
Manchester North West		400	800
Manchester East		700	
Manchester South		3-400	
*Manchester South West		1,000 +	1,500
*Salford South			(7-800)
Liverpool Kirkdale	1,200		
Liverpool West Toxteth			(over one-third)
*Liverpool Exchange			2,000
Blackburn	1,800	2,000	
Preston		1,000	800[a]
*Oldham	2,000	1,500	
Bury		600	
*Stockport			1,200
Rochdale		600[a]	800-1,000
*Ashton			(300)
Chester		3-400	
*St Helens			one-third
*Wigan	(2,000)		
*Warrington		1,000 +	
*Darwen	800		1,000
Newton	(1,600)		
*Leigh			2,000
*Widnes			2,000
Westhoughton			1,000
Bootle			1,500

[a] Size of meeting of Irish electors. Figures in brackets are for 'Roman Catholics'. Constituencies asterisked are on Herbert Gladstone's two lists of 'seats "Dominated" by Irish vote', n.d., HGP 46107 ff. 28-35. Also listed there are: Burnley, Crewe, Northwich, North Lonsdale, Radcliffe, Ince, Salford North, Birkenhead, Hyde, Salford West, and Stalybridge. (The above estimates are taken mainly from the press.)

APPENDIX D

Support given to Liberals or Conservatives by leading Unionist Free Traders (mainly from Manchester) in general elections, and in two by-elections in Manchester North West

	1906	1908	Jan. 1910	Dec. 1910	1912
Tom Garnett	L	L	L		
F. R. B. Lindsell	L	L	C	C	C
Frank Calvert	L	L	Ind.	C	
Francis Ashworth	L	L	Abst.	C	
Alfred Crewdson	L	L		C	C
E. Tootal Broadhurst	L	L	C		
E. L. Oliver		C		C	C
F. Boyd Merriman	L	L		C	
G. P. Dewhurst		L		C	C
J. A. Hutton	L	L	L		
Henry Bell (Preston)	L		Ind.		
Robert Clayton (Darwen)	L*		C	C	
H. H. Owtram (Lancaster)	L		Ind.		
F. C. Danson (Liverpool)	L*		C	C	

L* – supported retaliationist Conservative as well as Liberal
Ind. – *viz.* Harold Cox
Abst. – refused to make views known

432

Analysis of the poll in 2–member boroughs, 1900–10

PRESTON

1900 (*Lancs. D.P.*, 2 October 1900)

Hanbury (Cons.)	236	8,944
Tomlinson (Cons.)	220	8,067
Hardie (Lab.)	3,453	4,834
Hanbury/Tomlinson	7,586	
Hanbury/Hardie	1,120	
Tomlinson/Hardie	261	

1906 (*Preston Guardian*, 20 January 1906)

Macpherson (Lab.)	nearly	2,000	10,181
Cox (Lib.)		150	8,538
Kerr (Cons.)	about	50	7,303
Tomlinson (Cons.)	about	50	6,856
Cox/Kerr	some	180	
Cox/Tomlinson	about	80	
Macpherson/Kerr		450	

Enough figures are given here to calculate the rest but unfortunately there is some discrepancy. If, however, Macpherson's plumpers of 'nearly 2,000' – the most imprecise figure here – are assumed to be the erroneous element the following would explain the result:

Macpherson	1,500
Cox	150
Kerr	50
Tomlinson	50
Macpherson/Cox	8,130
Macpherson/Kerr	450
Macpherson/Tomlinson	100
Cox/Kerr	180
Cox/Tomlinson	80
Kerr/Tomlinson	6,620

1910 Not available

BLACKBURN

1900 (*Blackburn Wkly Telegraph*, 6 October 1900)

Coddington (Cons.)	87	9,415
Hornby (Cons.)	280	11,247
Snowden (Lab.)	5,335	7,096
Coddington/Hornby	9,267	
Coddington/Snowden	61	
Hornby/Snowden	1,700	

1906 (*N.D.T.*, 17 January 1906)

Drage (Cons.)	10	8,932
Hamer (Lib.)	311	8,892

433

BLACKBURN (*cont.*)

Hornby (Cons.)	94	10,291
Snowden (Lab.)	1,504	10,282
Drage/Hamer	86	
Drage/Hornby	8,751	
Drage/Snowden	85	
Hamer/Hornby	624	
Hamer/Snowden	7,871	
Hornby/Snowden	822	

January 1910   (*Blackburn Wkly Telegraph*, 22 January 1910)

Barclay (Lib.)	409	12,064
Bowles (Cons.)	56	9,112
Cecil (Cons.)	71	9,307
Snowden (Lab.)	415	11,916
Barclay/Bowles	163	
Barclay/Cecil	253	
Barclay/Snowden	11,239	
Bowles/Cecil	8,807	
Bowles/Snowden	86	
Cecil/Snowden	176	

December 1910   (*Blackburn Wkly Telegraph*, 10 December 1910)

Boyd-Carpenter (Cons.)	54	9,814
Norman (Lib.)	327	10,754
Riley (Cons.)	46	9,500
Snowden (Lab.)	449	10,762
Carpenter/Norman	307	
Carpenter/Riley	9,262	
Carpenter/Snowden	191	
Norman/Riley	95	
Norman/Snowden	10,025	
Riley/Snowden	97	

BOLTON

1900   No contest

1906   (*Bolton Chron.*, 16 January 1906)

Harwood (Lib.)	2,317	10,953
Gill (Lab.)	1,818	10,416
Goschen (Cons.)	5,115	6,693
Harwood/Gill	7,828	
Harwood/Goschen	808	
Gill/Goschen	770	

January 1910   (*Bolton Chron.*, 22 January 1910)

Ashworth (Cons.)	52	7,326
Gill (Lab.)	425	11,864
Harwood (Lib.)	542	12,275
Mattinson (Cons.)	89	7,479
Ashworth/Gill	71	
Ashworth/Harwood	213	
Ashworth/Mattinson	6,990	
Gill/Harwood	11,244	
Gill/Mattinson	124	
Harwood/Mattinson	276	

BOLTON (*cont.*)

December 1910   (*Bolton Chron.*, 10 December 1910)

Gill (Lab.)	550	10,108
Harwood (Lib.)	525	10,358
Hesketh (Cons.)	7,870	8,697
Gill/Harwood	9,282	
Gill/Hesketh	276	
Harwood/Hesketh	551	

STOCKPORT

1900   2 Libs. v. 2 Cons. (analysis incomplete)

1906   (*Stockport Advertiser*, 19 January 1906)

Duckworth (Lib.)	317	6,544
Wardle (Lab.)	642	7,299
Barnston (Cons.)		4,591
O'Neill (Cons.)		4,064
Duckworth/Wardle	6,000	
Barnston/O'Neill	3,843	
Barnston splits	742	
Wardle splits	657	
Duckworth splits	227	
O'Neill splits	215	

11,781 votes recorded (about 20 spoilt)

January 1910   (*Stockport Advertiser*, 21 January 1910)

Wardle (Lab.)	312	6,682
Hughes (Lib.)	264	6,645
Raine (Cons.)	39	5,268
Rankin (Cons.)	33	5,249
Wardle/Hughes	6,239	
Wardle/Raine	67	
Wardle/Rankin	64	
Hughes/Raine	76	
Hughes/Rankin	66	
Raine/Rankin	5,086	

December 1910   (*Stockport Advertiser*, 9 December 1910)

Hughes (Lib.)	368	6,169
Wardle (Lab.)	348	6,094
Lort-Williams (Cons.)	78	5,234
Campbell (Cons.)	70	5,183
Hughes/Wardle	5,575	
Hughes/Williams	132	
Hughes/Campbell	94	
Wardle/Williams	88	
Wardle/Campbell	83	
Williams/Campbell	4,936	

OLDHAM

1900   (*Oldham Evg Chron.*, 2 October 1900)

Churchill (Cons.)	155	12,931
Crisp (Cons.)	6	12,522
Emmott (Lib.)	95	12,947
Runciman (Lib.)	35	12,709

OLDHAM (*cont.*)

Churchill/Crisp	12,478
Churchill/Emmott	214
Churchill/Runciman	54
Crisp/Emmott	28
Crisp/Runciman	10
Emmott/Runciman	12,610

1906 (*Oldham Evg Chron.*, 16 January 1906)

Bright (Lib.)	55	16,672
Crisp (Cons.)	147	11,989
Emmott (Lib.)	162	17,397
Hartley (Cons.)	27	11,391
Bright/Crisp	202	
Bright/Emmott	16,331	
Bright/Hartley	84	
Crisp/Emmott	632	
Crisp/Hartley	11,008	
Emmott/Hartley	272	

January 1910 (*Oldham Chron.*, 22 January 1910)

Barton (Lib.)	130	18,840
Emmott (Lib.)	200	19,252
Hilton (Cons.)	352	13,462
Stott (Cons.)	33	12,577
Barton/Emmott	18,539	
Barton/Hilton	154	
Barton/Stott	17	
Emmott/Hilton	471	
Emmott/Stott	42	
Hilton/Stott	12,485	

December 1910 (*Oldham Chron.*, 10 December 1910)

Barton (Lib.)	99	16,941
Denniss (Cons.)	100	13,281
Emmott (Lib.)	171	17,108
Wrigley (Cons.)	146	13,440
Barton/Emmott	16,397	
Barton/Denniss	301	
Barton/Wrigley	144	
Denniss/Emmott	135	
Denniss/Wrigley	12,745	
Emmott/Wrigley	405	

Max Aitken and the Ashton Trades Council, December 1910

A. H. Scott certainly had a long and creditable record as a Manchester Progressive, working closely with Labour. Moreover, as M.P. for Ashton he had several times voted against the Government on Labour questions, notably on the Right-to-Work Bill. 'The Labour Party', claimed one of his trade union supporters, 'had regarded Mr. Scott as practically "one of their own".'[1] In the election the Trades Council had appointed a deputation of three to question the candidates and report back to it. It consisted of H. Cocker, its Vice-President, and the secretaries of the local Weavers and Spinners, S. T. Goggins and Edward Judson. It met the candidates on the Wednesday before the Saturday of polling and seems to have discussed three matters. While Scott declared himself in favour of the Right-to-Work Bill and the Minority Report of the Poor Law, Aitken merely asked for more time to consider them; but on the Osborne Judgement Scott made it clear that although he supported the Labour party Bill he would welcome provision for contracting out, while the untutored Aitken promised to support it *sans phrase*. Cocker later apparently held Aitken up to ridicule, saying: 'Yon fellow will promise to vote for anything, but he doesn't understand what he's promising. He asked us not to be too hard on him, as he'd "only been in politics a week"!' The deputation did not, however, report back to the Trades Council, since the secretary had empowered them to send the answers to the press direct: which done, Judson and Gobbins washed their hands of the affair.

At about this point one of the leading members of the S.D.F., F. E. Featherstone, who had earlier been a 'Tariff Tripper' to the Continent, met Aitken in an hotel room and agreed to help him. Now Cocker too was a Socialist of uncompromising views. On the Thursday evening the Executive of the Trades Council met. Judson and Goggins were not members and, having no reason to believe that further action was contemplated, they did not attend; nor did the Liberal trade unionists who were out electioneering for Scott. Only seven members out of sixty were present, and Cocker seized his chance. After making a one-man report he moved, 'That a letter be drafted, signed by the Secretary and President, to draw the attention of the trade unionists to the questions and answers and appeal to them to use their judgment and vote accordingly.' Although the Chairman had qualms about this, he was, as he confessed, inexperienced, and neither he nor the Secretary voted. The motion was carried by three votes to two. But this was not the form in which the resolution appeared in the minutes nor in which it was sent to the press (a discrepancy for which Cocker later admitted responsibility); in its final form the

---

[1] This account is based on the report of the deputation and the letters accompanying it, *Ashton Evening Reporter*, 3 December 1910; Judson's statement and the meeting of the Trades Council, *Ashton-under-Lyne Herald*, 10 December 1910; F. E. Featherstone to Aitken, 22 May 1911, Beaverbrook P.

resolution was an unvarnished recommendation of Aitken. Although a counter-circular from some Liberal members of the Trades Council was issued as soon as they discovered what had been done in their name, Aitken was the immediate beneficiary. At the next meeting of the Trades Council after the election there was a full attendance and, despite Cocker's vigorous defence, the motion was cere-monially expunged from the minutes on a vote of 32 to 18.

It is unlikely that Aitken had been privy to these machinations. 'I admit that I am an amateur in politics', he later wrote to Featherstone, 'and that I know very little of the objects and aims of the Trade Unions.'[1] His answer on the Osborne Judgement had been ingenuous, not machiavellian. His relations with the Labour party remained good after 1910, and his chairman kept in touch with Carr of the Cardroom Workers' and Judson of the Spinners', who were the leading figures. Aitken seems to have entertained them both on a visit to London in 1912, after which they professed themselves ready to support him at the next General Election in preference to any Liberal candidate: a considerable testimony to Tory Demo-cracy at so late a date. It seems quite likely, however, that a Labour candidate would have been run with Liberal support.[2]

[1] Aitken to Featherstone, 26 September 1911, copy, Beaverbrook P.
[2] This is based on letters between Aitken and J. M. W. Morison, December 1911–July 1912; J. C. Buckley to Aitken, 12 July 1912, Beaverbrook P.

Bibliography

Place of publication London unless otherwise stated.

Material from the public libraries in Blackburn, Burnley, Bury, Liverpool, Manchester, Preston, Rochdale, St Helens, Stockport, Warrington and Wigan was consulted. Asterisks indicate availability in the appropriate local collection.

1. PRIVATE PAPERS

Balfour Papers, B.M. Add. MSS 49693–4, 49708, 49737, 49743, 49758–67, 49771, 49776–7, 49853, 49858.[1]

Beaverbrook Papers (relating to Ashton-under-Lyne, 1910–17), Beaverbrook Library.

Augustine Birrell collection, Liverpool University Library.

Campbell-Bannerman Papers, B.M. Add. MSS 41213–17, 41231, 41234–6, 41241, 41252.

Viscount Cecil of Chelwood Papers, B.M. Add. MSS 51071–2, 51075, 51085, 51156–60.[1]

Elibank Papers, National Library of Scotland, MSS 8802–3.

Viscount Gladstone Papers, B.M. Add. MSS 45986–8, 45996–7, 46017, 46020–6, 46042, 46057–63, 46105–11, 46118, 46480–5.

Bonar Law Papers, Beaverbrook Library.

Lloyd George Papers, Beaverbrook Library.

Rosebery Papers, National Library of Scotland.[1]

Correspondence between Rosebery and Sir Edward Russell, 1888–1901, Liverpool University Library.

C. P. Scott Papers: (i) B.M. Add. MSS 50901.
(ii) in the possession of the *Guardian*, Manchester.

St Loe Strachey Papers, Beaverbrook Library.[1]

Minutes of the Manchester Liberal Union Federation, in the possession of the City of Manchester Liberal Party.

Minutes of the Lancashire and Cheshire Liberal Federation, formerly in the possession of the North West Liberal Federation.

2. OFFICIAL PUBLICATIONS

Return for each Parliamentary Borough and Division of Borough in England and Wales, the number of Voters on the Register for 1888, distinguished according to Qualifications, and in the case of Occupation Voters and Freemen, Freeholders,

[1] Arrangement only provisional at the time consulted.

Bibliography

and other *Ancient Rights, setting forth those Resident and Non-Resident in the constituency*, 1888 (394–5) lxxix, 907, 919.

Copy of the shorthand writers' notes of the evidence and judgements at the trial of Election petitions, 1893–4, lxx, 805.

List of School Boards and School Attendance Committees in England and Wales, 1902 (Cd. 1038) lxxix, 559.

Return of Diagrams showing the Parliamentary and Municipal Boroughs and the Parliamentary County Divisions, 1903 (280) liv, 315.

List of Schools under the Administration of the Board, 1901–2, 1902 Cd. 1277, lxxix, 1.

Board of Education Special Report on the School Training and Early Employment of Lancashire Children, 1904 (Cd. 1867) xix, 681.

List of Boroughs and Urban Districts in England and Wales, with a population of 5,000 and upwards, in which there are no Council Schools, 1906 (Cd. 3054) lxxxix, 1.

Return showing, with regard to each Parliamentary Constituency in the United Kingdom, the Total Number, and Number in each class of Electors on the Register now in force; also showing the Population and Inhabited Houses in each Constituency, 1900 (116) lxvii, 445; 1906 (Cd. 2807) xciv, 837; 1910 (Cd. 4975) lxxiii, 685 (and for by-elections).

Return of Charges made to candidates, total expenses of each candidate and the number of votes polled for each candidate, 1901 (352) lix, 145; 1906 (302) xcvi, 19; 1910 (272) lxxiii, 701; 1911 (299) lxii, 705 (and for by-elections).

Home Office *List of Mines* (1900, 1914).

Census 1901

County Reports: 1902, cxviii and cxix; General Report: 1904, cviii; Summary Tables: 1903, lxxxiv.

Census 1911

Vols III, IV, IX, X: 1912–13, cxii, cxiii; 1913, lxxviii, lxxix; 1914–16, lxxxi; 1917–18, xxxv.

3. NEWSPAPERS

The following were used exhaustively for the period of election campaigns:

The Cotton Factory Times — *Manchester Courier*
Lancashire Daily Post — *Manchester Guardian*
Liverpool Courier — *Northern Daily Telegraph*
Liverpool Daily Post (and Mercury) — *The Times*

Also consulted:

(Ashton) Evening Reporter — *Bolton Chronicle*
Ashton-under-Lyne Herald — *Bolton Evening News*
Blackburn Advertiser — *Catholic Times and Opinion (Manchester)*
Blackburn Catholic News — *Clarion*
Blackburn Labour Journal — *Cheshire Observer*
(Blackburn) Weekly Standard and Express — *Liverpolitan*
Blackburn Weekly Telegraph — *Liverpool Catholic Herald*

Liverpool Echo	*St Helens Newspaper*
Manchester Catholic Herald	*St Helens Reporter*
Morning Post	*Spectator*
Oldham Chronicle	*Standard*
Oldham Daily Standard	*Stockport Advertiser*
Oldham Evening Chronicle	*Stockport Chronicle*
Preston Guardian	*Tablet*
Preston Herald	*Textile Mercury*

4. *ELECTION LITERATURE

Bury: Collection of pamphlets.

Liverpool: Some literature in cuttings series.

Manchester: Broadsides dates and numbered; cards and addresses, 1895–1912, in Folders 12–17; leaflets etc. from Gorton elections of 1910.

Preston: Gorst collection for January 1910, numbered (1) to (65).

Rochdale: Some pamphlets.

Warrington: Roberts collection of letters.

5. REFERENCE WORKS

I. GENERAL

The Annual Register.

George W. Bacon, *New Large Scale Atlas of the British Isles from the Ordnance Survey, with plans of towns* (1889).

David Butler and Jenny Freeman, *British Political Facts, 1900–1960* (1963).

The Catholic Directory.

The Constitutional Year Book.

Debrett's Peerage (1914).

Dictionary of National Biography.

Dod's Parliamentary Companion.

Michael Kinnear, *The British Voter. An atlas and survey since 1885* (1968).

Lancashire Biographies, Rolls of Honour, intro. W. Ralph Hall Caine (1917).

Liverpool and Birkenhead in the Twentieth Century, intro. W. T. Pike (1911).

Men of the Period. Lancashire. Part First (The Biographical Publishing Company), n.d. (1895).

Philips' *Atlas of the British Isles* (1904).

Rogers on Elections. Vol. I, *Registration,* 17th edn by Maurice Powell (1909). Vol. II, *Parliamentary Elections and Petitions,* 18th edn by C. Willoughby Williams (1906).

Who's Who (1908).

II. *LOCAL (place of publication not given where uncertain, but presumably local).

A. Directories

Kelly's *Directory of Lancashire* (1905, 1913).

Bibliography

P. Barrett and Co., *General and Commercial Directory of Blackburn, Accrington, Darwen, Clitheroe*, etc. (Preston 1900, 1903, 1906, 1909, 1912, 1915).

P. Barrett and Co., *General and Commercial Directory of Burnley, Nelson, Colne, Padiham*, etc. (Preston 1899, 1902, 1905, 1908, 1911, 1914).

Slater's *Manchester Trades Directory* (Manchester 1900).

P. Barrett and Co., *General and Commercial Directory of Preston, Blackpool, Fleetwood, Lytham St Annes*, etc. (Preston 1898, 1901, 1904, 1907, 1910, 1913).

St Helens Trade Directory (1914).

James Clegg, *Commercial Directory of Rochdale* (Rochdale 1907–8, 1916).

J. G. Duncan, *Rochdale and District Commercial and Postal Directory* for 1899–1900 (Bolton 1899).

New Cheshire County News Co., *The Stockport Directory* (Stockport 1899, 1902, 1905, 1907, 1910).

Warrington Guardian Directory and History of Warrington and Environs (Warrington 1908).

R. Seed and Sons, *Wigan and District Directory* (Preston 1909).

Wigan Printing Co., *The '20th Century' Directory for the Wigan Union and Postal Areas* (Wigan 1903).

B. Town Year Books

County Borough of Burnley, *The Year Book* (Burnley 1899–1915).

County Borough of Blackburn Year Book (Blackburn 1900–15).

The Liverpool and Birkenhead Official Red Book (Liverpool 1901–3, 1906–7, 1909–15).

The Official Handbook of Manchester and Salford (Manchester 1900–15).

County Borough of St Helens, *Year Book* (St Helens 1900–14).

Lancashire County Council Year Book (1900–1).

Cheshire Year Book (1897, 1905–7, 1909–13).

Crompton's *Bury Union and Parish Historic Almanack* (1901–2, 1905).

Vickerman's *Bury Almanack and Diary* (Bury 1907–14).

Bury Times Annual (1906), continued as *Bury and Radcliffe Annual* (1907, 1912, 1913).

James Clegg's *Domestic Almanack* (Rochdale 1901–14).

Stockport and District Express Annual and Guide (1907–14).

Stockport Record (1903, 1907–10, 1912).

Warrington Guardian Year Book (Warrington 1900–14).

Wigan Almanac (1897–1914).

Wigan Standard Year Book (Wigan 1901).

C. Other Year Books

Almanack for the Diocese of Salford (1900, 1914).

Manchester Diocesan Directory (1900).

Year Book of the Lancashire and Cheshire Association of Baptist Churches (1900–1).

Lancashire Congregational Year Book (1900–14).

Blackburn and District Free Church Council, *Annual Reports* (1908–11).

Stockport Labour Church Official Handbook (1907).

Warrington and District Band of Hope Union, *Annual Reports* (1901–10).

Warrington Chamber of Commerce, *Annual Reports* (Warrington 1900–14).

Warrington Conservative Association, *Pocket Book and Vade Mecum* (1914).

6. OTHER CONTEMPORARY WORKS

J. M. Baernreither, *English Associations of Working Men* (1889).
A. J. Balfour, *Economic Notes on Insular Free Trade* (1903).
Winston Churchill, *Liberalism and the Social Problem* (1909).
— *The People's Rights, selected from his Lancashire and other recent speeches* (1910).
A. G. Gardiner, *Prophets, Priests and Kings* (1908).
L. T. Hobhouse, *The Labour Movement* (1893).
— *Democracy and Reaction* (1904).
— *Liberalism* (1911).
A. Lawrence Lowell, *The Government of England*, 2 vols (1908).
Charles W. Macara, *Social and Industrial Reform, some international aspects* (8th edn Manchester 1920).
Karl Marx and Frederick Engels on Britain (2nd edn Moscow 1962).
M. Ostrogorski, *Democracy and the Organisation of Political Parties*, 2 vols (1902).
S. Rosenbaum, 'The General Election of January 1910 and the bearing of its results upon some problems of representation', *Jnl. Roy. Stat. Soc.*, LXXIII (1910).
Brougham Villiers, *The Opportunity of Liberalism* (1904).
Graham Wallas, *Human Nature in Politics* (1908; new edn 1924).
Robert Spence Watson, *The National Liberal Federation* (1907).
Sidney and Beatrice Webb, *The History of Trade Unionism* (1894; new edn 1920).
— *Industrial Democracy* (1896; new edn 1920).

7. BIOGRAPHICAL WORKS

A. J. Ashton, *As I Went on My Way* (1924).
Lord Askwith, *Industrial Problems and Disputes* (1920).
H. H. Asquith (Lord Oxford), *Fifty Years of Parliament*, 2 vols (1926).
— *Memories and Reflections, 1852–1927*, 2 vols (1928).
— *H.H.A.: Letters of the Earl of Oxford and Asquith to a friend*, 2 vols (1933–4).
   Roy Jenkins, *Asquith* (1964).
A. J. Balfour (Lord Balfour)
   Blanche E. C. Dugdale, *Arthur James Balfour*, 2 vols (1936).
   Alfred M. Gollin, *Balfour's Burden. Arthur Balfour and Imperial Preference* (1965).
   Kenneth Young, *Balfour* (1963).
Sir Thomas Barclay, *Thirty Years. Anglo-French Reminiscences, 1876–1906* (1914).
H. J. P. R. Belloc
   Robert Speaight, *The Life of Hilaire Belloc* (1957).
C. C. Bigham (Lord Mersey), *A Picture of Life, 1872–1940* (1941).
Augustine Birrell, *Things Past Redress* (1937).
Robert Blatchford
   Laurence Thompson, *Robert Blatchford. Portrait of an Englishman* (1951).
W. B. Brocklehurst
   Mary Crozier, *An Old Silk Family, 1745–1945. The Brocklehursts of Brocklehurst-Whiston Amalgamated, Limited* (Aberdeen 1947).

15-2

Bibliography

William Byles, *William Byles by his youngest son*, private printed (Weymouth, 1932).

Henry Campbell-Bannerman
  J. A. Spender, *The Life of the Rt. Hon. Sir Henry Campbell-Bannerman*, 2 vols (1923).

Lord Robert Cecil (Lord Cecil of Chelwood), *All the Way* (1949).

Austen Chamberlain, *Politics from Inside* (1936).

Joseph Chamberlain
  Peter Fraser, *Joseph Chamberlain. Radicalism and Empire, 1868–1914* (1966).
  J. L. Garvin and Julian Amery, *The Life of Joseph Chamberlain*, 6 vols (1932–69).

F. J. Chavasse
  H. Gresford Jones, *Francis James Chavasse, 1846–1928, Bishop of Liverpool*, n.d. (1928).
  J. B. Lancelot, *Francis James Chavasse, Bishop of Liverpool* (Oxford 1929).
  Francis James Chavasse. Impressions by five of his friends... (Oxford 1928).

W. S. Churchill, *My Early Life* (1930; Fontana edn 1965).
— *Great Contemporaries* (1937; Fontana edn 1959).
  Violet Bonham Carter, *Winston Churchill as I Knew Him* (1965).
  Randolph S. Churchill, *Winston S. Churchill*, vols 1 and 2 and companion vols (1966–9).
  Oskar K. Rabinowicz, *Winston Churchill on Jewish Problems* (London and New York 1960).

J. R. Clynes, *Memoirs*, 2 vols (1937).
  Edward George, *Mill Boy to Minister* (1919).

Lord Courtney
  G. P. Gooch, *Life of Lord Courtney* (1920).

Lord Crewe
  James Pope-Hennessy, *Lord Crewe, 1858–1945. The likeness of a Liberal* (1955).

C. A. Cripps (Lord Parmoor), *A Retrospect. Looking back over a life of more than eighty years* (1936).

Lord Cromer
  Marquess of Zetland, *Lord Cromer* (1932).

Duke of Devonshire
  Bernard Holland, *The Life of Spencer Compton, eighth Duke of Devonshire*, 2 vols (1911).

A. Akers Douglas (Lord Chilston)
  3rd Viscount Chilston, *Chief Whip. The political life and times of Aretas Akers Douglas, 1st Viscount Chilston* (1961).

Almeric Fitzroy, *Memoirs*, 2 vols, n.d. (1925).

James Fraser
  John W. Diggle, *The Lancashire Life of Bishop Fraser* (1889).
  Thomas Hughes, *James Fraser, second Bishop of Manchester. A Memoir*, new edn (1888).

J. L. Garvin
  A. M. Gollin, *The 'Observer' and J. L. Garvin, 1908–1914. A study in great editorship* (1960).

Herbert Gladstone (Lord Gladstone)

    Charles Mallet, *Herbert Gladstone, a memoir* (1932).

Lord Goschen

    A. D. Elliot, *The Life of George Joachim Goschen, 1st Viscount Goschen*, 2 vols (1911).

R. B. Haldane (Lord Haldane), *An Autobiography* (1929).

E. Marshall Hall

    Edward Marjoribanks, *The Life of Sir Edward Marshall Hall* (1929).

Keir Hardie

    Emrys Hughes, *Keir Hardie* (1956).

    David Lowe, *From Pit to Parliament. The story of the early life of James Keir Hardie* (1923).

A. G. C. Harvey

    Francis W. Hirst, *Alexander Gordon Cummins Harvey. A Memoir*, n.d. (1926).

Arthur Henderson

    Mary Agnes Hamilton, *Arthur Henderson* (1938).

W. A. S. Hewins, *The Apologia of an Imperialist. Forty years of Empire Policy*, 2 vols (1929).

Edward Lee Hicks

    J. H. Fowler (ed.), *The Life and Letters of Edward Lee Hicks* (1922).

W. Joynson Hicks (Lord Brentford)

    H. A. Taylor, *Jix, Viscount Brentford. Being the authoritative and official biography of the Rt. Hon. William Joynson-Hicks, first Viscount Brentford of Newick* (1933).

F. W. Hirst, *In The Golden Days* (1947).

L. T. Hobhouse

    Ernest Barker, 'Leonard Trelawney Hobhouse', *Proceedings of the British Academy*, xv (1931).

    J. A. Hobson and Morris Ginsberg, *L. T. Hobhouse, his life and work* (1931).

S. G. Hobson, *Pilgrim to the Left. Memoirs of a modern revolutionist* (1938).

John Hodge, *Workman's Cottage to Windsor Castle* (1931).

Robert Hudson

    J. A. Spender, *Sir Robert Hudson, a memoir* (1930).

S. Leigh Hughes, *Press, Platform and Parliament* (1918).

H. M. Hyndman, *Further Reminiscences* (1912).

    Chushichi Tsuzuki, *H. M. Hyndman and British Socialism* (Oxford 1961).

E. A. Knox, *Reminiscences of an Octogenarian, 1847–1933*, n.d. (1935).

A. Bonar Law

    Robert Blake, *The Unknown Prime Minister. The life and times of Andrew Bonar Law, 1858–1923* (1955).

John Lea

    Frank Elias, *John Lea, citizen and art lover. A sketch*, n.d. (Liverpool 1928).

W. H. Lever (Lord Leverhulme)

    2nd Viscount Leverhulme, *Viscount Leverhulme by his son* (1927).

    Charles Wilson, *The history of Unilever. A study in economic growth and social change* (1954).

Bibliography

C. W. Macara, *Recollections* (1921).
  W. Haslam Mills, *Sir Charles W. Macara, Bt. A study of modern Lancashire* (Manchester 1917).
C. F. G. Masterman
  Lucy Masterman, *C. F. G. Masterman, a biography* (1939; new edn 1968).
Sir William Mather
  Loris Emerson Mather (ed.), *Sir William Mather*, n.d. (1925).
Lord Milner
  Alfred M. Gollin, *Proconsul in Politics, a study of Lord Milner in opposition and power* (1964).
A. M. Mond (Lord Melchett)
  Hector Bolitho, *Alfred Mond, first Lord Melchett* (1933).
C. E. Montague
  Oliver Elton, *C. E. Montague, a memoir* (1929).
James Moorhouse
  Edith C. Rickards, *Bishop Moorhouse, of Melbourne and Manchester* (1920).
John Morley (Lord Morley), *Recollections*, 2 vols (1918).
  D. A. Hamer, *John Morley, liberal intellectual in politics* (1968).
Alexander Murray, Master of Elibank (Lord Murray)
  Arthur C. Murray, *Master and Brother. Murrays of Elibank* (1945).
T. P. O'Connor, *Memoirs of an Old Parliamentarian*, 2 vols (1929).
  Hamilton Fyfe, *T. P. O'Connor* (1934).
Richard Pilkington
  Now Thus – Now Thus, 1826–1926. (*Pilkington Brothers Ltd.*) private printed, n.d. (St Helens 1926).
  T. C. Barker, *Pilkington Brothers and the Glass Industry* (1960).
Sir F. S. Powell
  H. L. P. Hulbert, *Sir Francis Sharp Powell, Baronet and Member of Parliament* (Leeds 1914).
William Rathbone
  Eleanor F. Rathbone, *William Rathbone, a memoir* (1905).
Lord Rosebery
  Robert Rhodes James, *Rosebery, a biography of Archibald Philip, 5th Earl of Rosebery* (1963).
  E. T. Raymond, *The Man of Promise: Lord Rosebery* (1923).
William Royle
  William Royle of Rusholme, by his daughter (Manchester 1924).
Edward Russell, *That Reminds Me –* (1899).
J. C. Ryle
  Marcus L. Loane, *John Charles Ryle, 1816–1900. A short biography* (1953).
Archibald Salvidge
  Stanley Salvidge, *Salvidge of Liverpool. Behind the political scene, 1890–1928* (1934).
C. P. Scott
  J. L. Hammond, *C. P. Scott of the Manchester Guardian* (1934).
  C. P. Scott, 1846–1932. The making of the 'Manchester Guardian' (1946).

J. E. B. Seely (Lord Mottistone), *Adventure* (1930).

James Sexton, *Sir James Sexton, Agitator. The life of the dockers' M.P. An auto-biography* (1936).

E. D. Simon (Lord Simon of Wythenshawe)
  Mary Stocks, *Ernest Simon of Manchester* (Manchester 1963).

F. E. Smith (Lord Birkenhead), *Contemporary Personalities* (1924).
  2nd Earl of Birkenhead, *F.E. The Life of F. E. Smith, first Earl of Birkenhead by his son* (1959).

Philip Snowden (Lord Snowden), *An autobiography*, 2 vols (1934).
  Colin Cross, *Philip Snowden* (1966).
  C. E. Bechofer Roberts, *Philip Snowden, an impartial portrait* (1929).

Harold Spender, *The Fire of Life, a book of memories*, n.d. (1922).

Lord Stanley (Lord Derby)
  Randolph S. Churchill, *Lord Derby, 'King of Lancashire'. The official life of Edward 17th Earl of Derby, 1865-1948* (1959).

J. St Loe Strachey, *The Adventure of Living, a subjective autobiography* (1922).
  Amy Strachey, *St. Loe Strachey, his life and his paper* (1930).

R. P. W. Swift
  E. S. Fay, *The life of Mr Justice Swift* (1939).

T. C. Taylor
  George A. Greenwood, *Taylor of Batley. A story of 102 years* (1957).

Ben Tillett, *Memories and Reflections* (1931).

Beatrice Webb, *My Apprenticeship* (1926; Penguin edn 1938).

— *Our Partnership* (1948), and *Diaries, 1912-24* (1952) edited by Barbara Drake and Margaret I. Cole.

J. H. Whitworth
  W. L. Mackennal, *The life of Major JohnHaworth Whitworth* (Manchester 1918).

E. Crawshay Williams, *Simple Story. An accidental autobiography* (1935).

George Wyndham
  J. W. Mackail and Guy Wyndham, *Life and Letters of George Wyndham*, 2 vols n.d.

Some works of a more personal character are also useful.

B. Bowker, *Lancashire under the Hammer* (1928).

Neville Cardus, *Autobiography* (1947).

Katherine Chorley, *Manchester Made Them* (1950).

Stella Davies, *North Country Bred. A working-class family chronicle* (1963).

Kingsley Martin, *Father Figures: a first volume of autobiography* (1966).

Geoffrey Mitchell (ed.), *The Hard Way Up. The autobiography of Hannah Mitchell, suffragette and rebel* (1968).

*C. E. Montague, *A Hind Let Loose* (1910; Penguin edn 1936).

George Orwell, *The Road to Wigan Pier* (1937).

E. Sylvia Pankhurst, *The Suffragette Movement* (1931).

Charles Rowley, *Fifty Years of Ancoats, loss and gain*, n.d. (1899).

— *Fifty Years of Work without Wages* (1912).

* Novels.

Bibliography

F. B. Smith, *Parsons and Weavers, a study in Lancashire clerical work* (1897).
Joseph Stamper, *So Long Ago* (1960).
*Robert Tressell, *The Ragged Trousered Philanthropists* (Panther edn 1965).

8. UNPUBLISHED THESES

Leslie Bather, 'A history of the Manchester and Salford Trades Council', Manchester Ph.D. (1956).

Neal Blewett, 'The British General Elections of 1910', Oxford D.Phil. (1967).

John Brown, 'Ideas concerning social policy and their influence on legislation in Britain, 1902–1911', London Ph.D. (1964).

P. F. Clarke, 'Elections and the electorate in north west England: an inquiry into the course of political change, 1900–1910', Cambridge Ph.D. (1967).

J. O. Foster, 'Capitalism and class consciousness in earlier 19th century Oldham', Cambridge Ph.D. (1967).

R. G. Gregory, 'The miners and politics in England and Wales, 1906–14', Oxford D.Phil. (1963).

Grace A. Jones, 'National and local issues in politics: a study of East Sussex and the Lancashire spinning towns, 1906–1910', Sussex Ph.D. (1965).

Anthony S. King, 'Some aspects of the history of the Liberal party in Britain, 1906–1914', Oxford D.Phil. (1962).

B. David Rubinstein, 'The decline of the Liberal party, 1880–1900', London Ph.D. (1956).

A. K. Russell, 'The General Election of 1906', Oxford D.Phil. (1962).

G. R. Searle, 'The development of the concept of "national efficiency" and its relation to politics and government, 1900–1910', Cambridge Ph.D. (1966).

Roland Smith, 'A history of the Lancashire cotton industry between the years 1873 and 1896', Birmingham Ph.D. (1954).

Philip Whitaker, 'The growth of Liberal organisation in Manchester from the 1860s to 1903', Manchester Ph.D. (1956). But see above, p. 201 n. 3.

9. WORKS PRIMARILY CONCERNED WITH THE NORTH WEST

*William Astle (ed.), *Centenary History of Stockport, 1822–1922* (Stockport, 1922).

Hartley Bateson, *A Centenary History of Oldham* (Oldham 1951).

Frank Bealey, 'The Northern Weavers, independent labour representation and Clitheroe, 1902', *Manchester School*, xxv (1957).

*Eustace B. Beesley, *The History of the Wigan Grand Lodge*, privately printed (Manchester 1920).

*Arthur Bennett, *Warrington, its history, industrial growth and present advantages and resources* (Warrington 1929).

W. Bennett, *The history of Burnley from 1850* (Burnley 1951).

A. H. Birch, *Small Town Politics. A study of political life in Glossop* (Oxford 1951).

* Novels.

A. H. Birch and Peter Campbell, 'Politics in the North West', *Manchester School*, XVIII (1950).

*Blackburn Independent Labour Party, *Bazaar Handbook* (March 1908).

A. L. Bowley and A. R. Burnett-Hurst, *Livelihood and Poverty. A study in the economic conditions of working class households in Northampton, Warrington, Stanley, and Reading* (1915).

*Sir Charles Brown, *Origins and Progress of Horrockses, Crewdson & Co.*, n.d. (Preston 1921).

H. Campion, 'Pre-War fluctuations of profit in the cotton-spinning industry', *Journal of the Royal Statistical Society*, XCVIII (1934).

W. H. Chaloner, *Social and Economic Development of Crewe, 1780–1923* (Manchester 1950).

S. J. Chapman, 'Some policies of the cotton spinners' trade unions', *Economic Journal*, X (1900).

— *The Lancashire Cotton Industry. A study in economic development* (Manchester 1904).

S. J. Chapman and T. S. Ashton, 'The sizes of businesses, mainly in the textile industries', *Journal of the Royal Statistical Society*, LXXVII (1913–14).

S. J. Chapman and F. J. Marquis, 'The recruiting of the employing classes from the ranks of the wage-earners in the cotton industry', *Journal of the Royal Statistical Society*, LXXV (1912).

P. F. Clarke, 'British politics and Blackburn politics, 1900–1910', *Historical Journal*, XII (1969).

*Clayton (Manchester) Divisional Labour Party, *Memorial Souvenir to the Late Charles Priestley*, n.d. (1927).

H. W. Clemesha, *A History of Preston in Amounderness* (Manchester, 1912).

C. Stella Davies (ed.), *A History of Macclesfield* (Manchester 1961).

George E. Diggle, *A History of Widnes* (Widnes 1961).

N. J. Frangopulo, *Rich Inheritance. A guide to the history of Manchester* (Manchester 1963).

P. Harnetty, 'The Indian cotton duties controversy, 1894–1896', *English Historical Review*, LXXVII (1962).

John R. Harris and Theodore C. Barker, *A Merseyside Town in the Industrial Revolution. St Helens, 1750–1900* (Liverpool 1954).

G. B. Hertz, *The Manchester Politician, 1750–1912* (1912).

H. R. Hikins, 'The Liverpool general transport strike, 1911', *Transactions of the Historic Society of Lancashire and Cheshire*, CXIII (1961).

John Jewkes and E. M. Gray, *Wages and Labour in the Lancashire Cotton Spinning Industry* (Manchester 1935).

R. Lawton, 'Population trends in Lancashire and Cheshire from 1801', *Transactions of the Historic Society of Lancashire and Cheshire*, CXIV (1962).

J. M. Lee, *Social Leaders and Public Persons. A study of county government in Cheshire since 1888* (1963).

A. Marcroft, *Landmarks of Local Liberalism* (Oldham 1913).

T. R. Marr, *Housing Conditions in Manchester and Salford* (1904).

Thomas Middleton, *The History of Hyde and its neighbourhood* (Hyde 1932).

Bibliography

George C. Miller, *Blackburn. The Evolution of a Cotton Town* (Blackburn 1951).

William Haslam Mills, *The Manchester Reform Club, 1871–1921*, privately printed (Manchester 1922).

— *The Manchester Guardian, a centenary history* (1921).

R. W. Moffrey, *A Century of Oddfellowship, being a brief record of the Manchester Unity of the Independent Order of Oddfellows* (Manchester 1910).

H. W. Ogden, 'The geographical basis of the Lancashire cotton industry', *Journal of the Textile Institute*, XVIII (1927).

*E. Omar Pearson, *Wesleyan Methodism in Blackburn* (Blackburn 1913).

W. Pilkington, *Flashes of Preston Methodism* (Preston 1916).

*Preston Conservative Working Men's Club Bazaar, *Official Handbook* (October 20–3, 1909).

Arthur Redford, *A History of Local Government in Manchester*, 3 vols (1939–40).

— *Manchester Merchants and Foreign Trade*, II, *1850–1939* (Manchester 1956).

Nesta Roberts, *Manchester University Settlement. Diamond Jubilee, 1895–1955*, n.d. (1955).

W. Gordon Robinson, *A History of the Lancashire Congregational Union, 1806–1956* (Manchester 1955).

R. Robson, *The Cotton Industry in Britain* (1957).

Rochdale in the Coronation Year of His Majesty King Edward (Rochdale 1902).

Rochdale Reform Association, 1834–1934, n.d. (1934).

*St Helens Congregational Church, *A Handbook to the Bi-centenary Celebrations* (1910).

Ian Sellers, 'The Pro-Boer movement in Liverpool', *Transactions of the Unitarian Historical Society* October 1960.

— 'Nonconformist attitudes in later nineteenth century Liverpool', *Transactions of the Historical Society of Lancashire and Cheshire*, CXIV (1962).

Shena D. Simon, *A Century of City Government. Manchester 1838–1938* (1938).

*Stockport Labour Church, *Our Winter Work* (1908–9, 1909–10).

H. A. Turner, *Trade Union Growth Structure and Policy* (1962).

James Vickers, *History of Independent Methodism* (Newton-le-Willows 1920).

J. R. Vincent, 'The effect of the Second Reform Act in Lancashire', *Historical Journal*, XI (1968).

J. E. W. Wallis, *A History of the Church in Blackburnshire* (1932).

History of Warrington Conservative Club n.d.

J. Brierley Watson, *The Member for Eccles* (Eccles 1964).

Brian D. White, *A History of the Corporation of Liverpool, 1835–1914* (1951).

W. T. Whitley, *Baptists of North West England, 1649–1913* (Preston 1913).

W. Ogwen Williams, 'The Platts of Oldham', *Transactions of the Caernarvonshire Historical Society*, XVIII (1957).

George Henry Wood, *The History of Wages in the Cotton Trade in the past hundred years* (1910).

10. OTHER SECONDARY WORKS

R. Page Arnot, *The Miners. A history of the Miners' Federation of Great Britain, 1889–1910* (1949).
— *The Miners. Years of Struggle* (1953).
Frank Bealey, 'The electoral arrangement between the Labour Representation Committee and the Liberal Party', *Journal of Modern History*, XXVIII (1956).
Frank Bealey and Henry Pelling, *Labour and Politics, 1900–1906. A history of the Labour Representation Committee* (1958).
A. H. Birch, 'The habit of voting', *Manchester School*, XVIII (1950).
Neal Blewett, 'The franchise in the United Kingdom, 1885–1918', *Past & Present*, **32** (December 1965).
— 'Free Fooders, Balfourites, Whole Hoggers. Factionalism within the Unionist party, 1906–10', *Historical Journal*, XI (1968).
A. L. Bowley, *Wages and Income in the United Kingdom since 1880* (Cambridge 1937).
Asa Briggs, *Victorian Cities* (1963).
Asa Briggs and John Saville (eds), *Essays in Labour History, in memory of G. D. H. Cole* (1960).
John Cotton Brown, 'Local party efficiency as a factor in the outcome of British elections', *Political Studies*, VI (1958).
D. E. Butler, *The Electoral System in Britain, 1918–1951* (Oxford 1953; 2nd edn 1963).
H. A. Clegg, Alan Fox and A. F. Thompson, *A History of British Trade Unions since 1889*, vol. I, *1889–1910* (Oxford 1964).
G. D. H. Cole, *British Working Class Politics, 1832–1914* (1941).
James Cornford, 'The transformation of Victorian Conservatism', *Victorian Studies*, VII (1963).
Maurice Cowling, *1867. Disraeli, Gladstone and Revolution. The passing of the Second Reform Bill* (Cambridge 1967).
Michael Craton and H. W. McCready, *The Great Liberal Revival, 1903–6*, Hansard Society pamphlet (1966).
George Dangerfield, *The Strange Death of Liberal England, 1910–1914* (New York 1935; Capricorn edn 1961).
Hirendra Lal Dey, *The Indian Tariff Problem in relation to industry and taxation* (1933).
J. P. D. Dunbabin, 'Parliamentary elections in Great Britain, 1868–1900. A psephological note', *English Historical Review*, LXXXI (1966).
R. C. K. Ensor, *England, 1870–1914* (Oxford 1936).
E. J. Feuchtwanger, *Disraeli, Democracy and the Tory Party. Conservative leadership and organization after the Second Reform Bill* (Oxford 1968).
Peter Fraser, 'Unionism and Tariff Reform: the crisis of 1906', *Historical Journal*, V (1962).
John S. Galbraith, 'The pamphlet campaign on the Boer War', *Journal of Modern History*, XXIV (1952).
B. B. Gilbert, *The Evolution of National Insurance in Great Britain. The Origins of the Welfare State* (1966).

Bibliography

John Glaser, 'English Nonconformity and the decline of Liberalism', *American Historical Review*, LXIII (1958).

Roy Gregory, *The Miners and British Politics, 1906–1914* (Oxford 1968).

William B. Gwyn, *Democracy and the Cost of Politics in Britain* (1962).

Elie Halevy, *A History of the English People in the Nineteenth Century*, vol. V, *Imperialism and the Rise of Labour, 1895–1905*; vol. VI, *The Rule of Democracy, 1905–1914* (1929, 1934; new edn 1961).

H. J. Hanham, *Elections and Party Management. Politics in the time of Disraeli and Gladstone* (1959).

Janet Howarth, 'The Liberal revival in Northamptonshire, 1880–1895. A case study in late nineteenth century elections', *Historical Journal*, XII (1969).

K. S. Inglis, *Churches and the Working Classes in Victorian England* (1963).

— 'English Nonconformity and social reform, 1880–1900', *Past & Present*, **13** (April 1958).

John Archer Jackson, *The Irish in Britain* (1963).

Roy Jenkins, *Mr. Balfour's Poodle. An account of the struggle between the House of Lords and the Government of Mr. Asquith* (1954).

Grace A. Jones, 'Some further thoughts on the franchise, 1885–1918', *Past & Present*, **34** (July 1966).

R. B. Jones, 'Balfour's reform of party organisation', *Bulletin of the Institute of Historical Research*, XXXVIII (1965).

G. Kitson Clark, *The Making of Victorian England* (1962).

H. W. Lee and E. Archbold, *Social Democracy in Britain. Fifty years of the socialist movement* (1935).

Trevor Lloyd, 'Uncontested seats in British General Elections, 1852–1910', *Historical Journal*, VIII (1965).

A. M. McBriar, *Fabian Socialism and English Politics, 1884–1918* (Cambridge 1962).

H. W. McCready, 'The revolt of the Unionist Free Traders', *Parliamentary Affairs*, XVI (1963).

Barry McGill, 'Francis Schnadhorst and Liberal party organisation', *Journal of Modern History*, XXXIV (1962).

R. T. McKenzie, *British Political Parties. The distribution of power within the Conservative and Labour parties* (2nd edn 1963).

R. T. McKenzie and Allan Silver, *Angels in Marble. Working class Conservatives in urban England* (1968).

Ralph Miliband, *Parliamentary Socialism. A study in the politics of Labour* (1961).

Kenneth O. Morgan, *Wales in British Politics, 1868–1922* (Cardiff 1963).

Homer Lawrence Morris, *Parliamentary Franchise Reform in England from 1885 to 1918* (New York 1921).

C. A. Moser and Wolf Scott, *British Towns. A statistical survey of their social and economic differences* (1961).

Cornelius O'Leary, *The Elimination of Corrupt Practices in British Elections, 1868–1911* (Oxford 1962).

Henry Pelling, *The Origins of the Labour Party, 1880–1900* (1954; 2nd edn 1965).

— *Popular Politics and Society in Late Victorian Britain* (1968).

— *Social Geography of British Elections 1885–1910* (1967).

E. H. Phelps Brown, *The Growth of British Industrial Relations. A study from the standpoint of 1906–14* (1959).

Philip P. Poirier, *The Advent of the Labour Party* (1958).

Donald Read, *The English Provinces, c. 1760–1960. A study in influence* (1964).

— *Cobden and Bright. A Victorian political partnership* (1967).

J. H. Stewart Reid, *The Origins of the British Labour Party* (Minneapolis 1955).

B. C. Roberts, *The Trade Union Congress, 1869–1921* (1958).

R. Robson (ed.), *Ideas and Institutions of Victorian Britain. Essays in honour of George Kitson Clark* (1967).

Constance Rover, *Women's Suffrage and Party Politics in Britain, 1866–1914* (1967).

Benjamin Sacks, *The Religious Issue in the State Schools of England and Wales, 1902–1914. A nation's quest for human dignity* (Albuquerque, New Mexico, 1961).

Bernard Semmel, *Imperialism and Social Reform. English social-imperial thought, 1895–1914* (1960).

R. T. Shannon, *Gladstone and the Bulgarian Agitation 1876* (1963).

Paul Smith, *Disraelian Conservatism and Social Reform* (1967).

Peter Stansky, *Ambitions and Strategies. The struggle for the leadership of the Liberal Party in the 1890's* (Oxford 1964).

A. J. P. Taylor, *The Trouble Makers. Dissent over British foreign policy, 1792–1939* (1957).

— *English History, 1914–1945* (Oxford 1965).

F. M. L. Thompson, *English Landed Society in the Nineteenth Century* (1963).

Paul Thompson, *Socialists, Liberals and Labour. The struggle for London, 1885–1914,* (1967).

Frank Tillyard, 'The distribution of the Free Churches in England', *Sociological Review* (January 1935).

Chushichi Tsuzuki, 'The "Impossiblist Revolt" in Britain', *International Review of Social History*, I (1956).

John Vincent, *The Formation of the Liberal Party, 1857–1868* (1966).

— *Pollbooks. How Victorians voted* (Cambridge 1967).

A. P. Wadsworth, 'Newspaper circulations, 1800–1954', *Transactions of the Manchester Statistical Society* (1954–5).

Robert F. Wearmouth, *The Social and Political Influence of Methodism in the twentieth century* (1957).

Trevor Wilson, *The Downfall of the Liberal Party, 1914–1935* (1966).

Index

454

Banner, J. S. Harmood, 50
Baptists, 64
Barbour, George, 250
Barclay, Thomas, 29
Barlow, J., 136
Barnston, Harry, 250
Barron, J. W. D., 199, 266
BARROW-IN-FURNESS, 12, 38, 111
  Liberals and Labour, 315, 324, 333
Beach, Michael Hicks, 301
Beamers', Twisters' and Drawers' union, 317
Beazley, J. H., 283
Bell, Henry, 283, 292, 432
Bellairs, Carlyon, 242
Belloc, Hilaire, 168, 235, 249, 259, 291, 298
  as anti-suffragist, 119-20
  as constituency member, 146-7, 220, 270
  as Catholic, 255, 257, 264, 267
Bennett, Arthur, 57
Bigham, C. C., 232
Bimetallic League, 86, 134, 282
BIRKENHEAD, 12, 21, 120, 242-3, 267, 307, 384
  franchise in, 111
  and Labour, 336-7
  electioneering in, 135, 139, 141
  and Protestants, 265
  and Free Trade, 283
Birley family, 34 n., 64
Birmingham, 70, 278
  and Nonconformity, 54-5
  and Liberal organisation, 204, 205
  and Chamberlain's policy, 275, 277, 347
  and Balfour speech (1907), 284, 286, 287, 288, 349 ff.
Birrell, Augustine, 37, 57, 134, 168, 190, 200
  and Manchester, 141, 176-7, 184, 234
BLACKBURN, 12, 56, 90, 225, 230, 245 n., 333, 347, 374, 379
  cultural politics in, 34, 59-60, 259, 261-2, 263, 266, 267, 268-9, 403
  and Free Trade, 280, 287, 288, 300, 306, 348
  socialism in, 40, 329, 339
  progressivism in, 315, 316, 319, 332
  and candidates, 237; Hornby, 224, 241; Snowden, 200-1, 312; Cecil, 289-290, 292
  electioneering in, 133, 135, 139-40, 149
  franchise in, 23, 104 n., 125, 128
Blackburn Weavers' case, 91
BLACKPOOL, 12, 135, 267, 348, 365
  and landed interest, 249, 251
Blatchford, Robert, 41-2, 171, 378
Blayney, J. J., 100
Blewett, Neal, 114 n.
Bliss, Joseph, 135, 231
Blundell, W. B., 222
Boer War, 122, 142, 151, 155, 167, 168, 173, 197, 205

effect on Liberal party, 18, 173, 176, 181, 312, 402
  as electoral issue, 242-3, 343-6, 365-9
Boilermakers' union, 324
BOLTON, 12, 77, 84, 100, 115, 124, 373-4
  by-election (1912), 319, 388-9
  religion and politics in, 41, 69, 261-2, 265, 267-8
  style of politics in, 227, 245
  and Free Trade, 281, 298
  Liberals and Labour in, 93, 314, 316, 318-19
Bolton Evening News, 131
Bolton, William, 269-70
BOOTLE, 12, 200, 236, 379
  by-election (1911), 386
  Catholic issue in, 67, 266
  and franchise, 105, 110
Bourne, Archbishop (of Westminster), 255
Bowles, George, 288, 290, 292, 304, 361 n.
Bowles, Thomas Gibson, 304, 308-9, 389
Bowring, F. C., 232 n., 236
Bowring, William, 216, 232
Boyle, D., 254
Bradford Observer, 156-7
Brailsford, H. N., 120, 168, 181
brewers, 351
  and Conservative party, 225, 226, 234, 269-70
  and Liberal party, 232, 270
Brewers' Central Association, 271
bribery, *see* corruption
Bright, Allan, 231, 236, 242
Bright, J. A. (Albert), 57, 178, 179, 231, 240, 245
Bright, Jacob, 32, 37-8, 60, 158, 166 n., 167, 213, 234
Bright, John, 28-9, 58, 153, 163, 172, 173, 223, 240, 306 n., 347, 348, 361
Bright, Ursula, 166 n.
Brimelow, William, 57, 231
British Cotton Growing Association, 75-6
Broadhurst, Edward Tootal, 294, 432
  and Free Trade organisations, 276, 285, 288, 293
  and Churchill, 281-2, 285-6
Brocklehurst, Fred, 147
  as I.L.P.er, 175, 311, 312, 314, 315
  and Boer War, 181 n., 183
  as turncoat, 242
Brooklands Agreement (1893), 81-2, 83
Broughton, Delves, 250, 252
Brunner, John Tomlinson, 144, 188
  as pro-Boer, 181, 369
  and Liberal organisation, 214-15, 230, 231, 323
  as patriarch, 222-3, 228, 231, 245
Brunner, J. F. L., 117, 188, 228, 322
Bryce, James, 158, 160-1, 176

Index

Gladstone (*cont.*)
  and Labour, 92, 185, 311, 313–16, 319, 321, 329, 376
  and khaki election, 122, 184–5, 366, 367, 368
  and Unionist Free Traders, 276, 277, 278
  on Liberal downfall, 396
Gladstone, Robert, 299
Gladstone, W. E., 3–4, 28, 29, 31, 58, 134, 136, 166, 178, 227, 252, 299, 347, 348, 359, 361, 370, 407
Gladstone Liberal Club, 159
Gladstone–MacDonald, pact, 313–16, 329
Glazebrook, P. K., 387
Glover, Thomas, 148, 245, 257, 321, 322
God, 147
Gorst, John, 119, 242, 291
  as social reformer, 39, 404
  pamphlet collection, 132, 351 n., 353 n., 355 n.
GORTON, 13, 199, 214, 220, 240, 368, 372
  Irish in, 11, 37, 258
  dirty contests in, 144, 148–9
  and Labour, 211, 243, 263, 312, 331–2
  Liberal–Labour relations, 162, 166, 315, 316, 324, 338
  and Free Trade, 277, 278, 283
  Liberalism in, 267, 323
  Conservatives in, 237, 261 n., 332
  issues in, 355, 360, 363 n.
Goschen, George, 280
Gould, F. Carruthers, 132
Goulding, Edward, 295
Grant, Corrie, 191
Green, Rev. S. F., 61, 62–3
Green, T. H., 172
Greenall family, 226, 230, 269–70
Greenall, Thomas, 321, 322–3
Gregory, R. G., 401
Gregory, Theodore, 176 n., 185, 203
Gretton, R. H., 168
Grey, Edward, 140, 160, 180, 195, 278, 345
Griffith, Ellis, 346 n.
Groves, J. G., 234, 269, 270, 350 n., 371
Guthrie, Edwin, 106–7, 159
  and Labour, 164, 174–5
  and Boer War, 178, 180, 182
  and reorganisation of M.L.U., 203–5
  death, 186

Haig, Douglas, 49
Haldane, R. B., 185
halfpenny papers, 130–1, 156, 187
half-time system, 87–8
Hall, E. Marshall, 147, 344 n., 354
Hall, Leonard, 163
Hamer, Edwin, 57, 357
Hamilton, Mary Agnes, 5
Hammond, J. L., 154 n., 181, 194

Hanbury, R. W., 344 n.
Hanley by-election (1912), 328
Harcourt, Lewis, 120, 238, 363
Harcourt, William, 3, 4, 167, 238, 345
Hardie, J. Keir, 253 n., 269, 312, 313, 347
Harford, Austin, 252–3
Harker, John, 315
Harmsworth, Alfred, *see* Northcliffe, Lord
Harrop, J., 209 n.
Hartington, Lord, *see* Devonshire, Duke of
Hartley, E. L., 100 n., 243
Hartley, J. H., 290, 292
Harvey, A. G. C., 29, 230
Harwood, George, 69, 119, 225, 388
  as patriarch, 227, 245
  and Labour, 319, 357
Hatch, E. F. G., 220, 268, 316, 338
  as Free Trader, 276, 277, 278, 279, 297
Haworth, Arthur, 189, 213, 219, 231, 235, 287, 303, 308
Helme, Norval, 57, 229, 231, 258
Hempsall, John, 243, 312–13
Henderson, Arthur, 326, 327, 337, 360
Henry, Charles, 157
Herbert, Jesse, 223, 257
  as Gladstone's assistant, 138, 206, 208–9, 237, 314
  head of Liberal machine, 207, 209
Hesketh, G., 100, 298
Hewart, Gordon, 304
Hewins, W. A. S., 36, 302, 384–5, 386
HEYWOOD, 12, 123, 243, 245, 368, 372
  and Kemp, 86, 277, 278
Hibbert, Rev. Fred, 56, 147
Hibbert, John, 86
Hicks, Edward Lee, 71–2, 74, 154, 268
Hicks, William Joynson, 143, 144, 254, 260, 281, 282
  as Evangelical, 72, 73, 264, 268
  and Tariff Reform, 285–7, 289, 293, 353 n., 377, 378–9
High Churchmen, 50, 62–3, 227, 264, 266; *see also* Ritualism
HIGH PEAK, 9, 12, 110, 118, 147, 249, 250, 368, 369, 384, 385
  by-election (1909), 377
  style of politics in, 53, 228–9, 243, 245
Higinbottom, S. W., 47
Hill, John, 50–1
Hill-Wood, Samuel, 228–9
Hilton, James, 95
Hindle, F. G., 14, 118, 136, 337
Hirst, F. W., 168, 172, 181, 351 n.
Hobhouse, L. T., 151, 153, 156, 157, 171, 180, 188, 214, 227, 276, 395
  as progressive, 44, 171–2, 189–90, 195, 405
  and *Guardian*, 167, 168, 169, 170 ff.

Index

Law, Andrew Bonar, 49, 99, 143, 150, 155, 198, 199, 233, 288
 and Manchester, 235, 295–7, 299, 300–1, 381, 383
 and Bootle, 236, 266, 386
 as Conservative leader, 302, 304, 305–7, 387, 389, 393
Lawrence, C. N., 240
Lawton, J. E., 141
Laymen's League, 46, 263–4, 265
Lea, John, 57, 71, 236
Lee, James Prince, 1st Bishop of Manchester, 58–9
Leeds Mercury, 156
Lees, Elliott, 242–3, 283
Leese, Joseph, 209–10, 231, 240, 245, 344 n., 356
Legh of Lyme, Lord, 250
LEIGH, 12, 185, 228, 237, 327
 franchise in, 115, 124, 125
 Co-operative movement in, 36
 Nonconformity in, 55–6, 64, 69, 267
 electioneering in, 134
 and Free Trade, 283, 293
 Scott and, 163, 167, 187–8, 398
 1900 election, 184–5, 368–9
 expenses in, 198, 199, 220–1
 Welsh in, 260
 Liberal–Labour relations in, 267, 322–3
Lever, W. H., 119, 149, 231, 240, 345
 as social leader, 133, 222–3
 and Liberal organisation, 211, 214–16, 230, 245
Lewis, Henry, 290, 292, 300
Liberal Central Association, 122, 205, 206, 207
 fund, 208, 214–15
Liberal Imperialism, 180–1, 205, 312
 and press, 130, 184
 and party unity, 185–6, 241, 370–1, 383, 393–4
 Conservative attacks on, 345
 electoral appeal of, 369
Liberal party, 27 ff., 127, 138
 problems in 1890s, 3–5, 160
 Edwardian revival of, 7–9, 398–402
 organisation: party machine, 201–7; 217–19, 321–3; and Whips, 174–7, 189, 207–11; and funds, 200, 201, 212–17; and register, 105–9, 111, 128; and electoral system, 117–21, 122–3, 125, 129
 policy of: and *laissez faire*, 274, 279, 282, 355; and War issue, 345; and fiscal issue, 350–5; and House of Lords, 362–4; alleged socialism of, 287, 289, 299, 300, 309, 338, 361–2
 in relation to status politics: and Irish, 253–4, 256; and Catholics, 257; and Non-

conformity, 57, 257, 267–8; and Jews, 259–60; and Protestants, 264; and temperance, 268–9; and drink trade, 270–1; Churchmen as candidates, 262–3, 267
 in relation to class politics: and wealthy men, 115–17, 201, 212–16, 222–4, 309–10; and Unionist Free Traders, 276–7, 278, 285, 288, 290, 294; defections from, 293, 303 n.; and working-class voters, 33–6, 112–13; relations with Labour, 44, 92, 95, 153, 159, 160–1, 162–6, 166 n., 174–5, 177, 181, 184, 185, 186–7, 203–4, 205, 223, 311–12, 386–9; and Labour alliance, 314, 316–20, 324–8, 336–9, 356–8, 376, 394–6; and S.D.F., 329, 331–2
Liberal Publication Department, 132, 216
Liberal Unionism, 38–9, 56, 225, 276, 333, 361
Liberalism (Hobhouse), 173
Liberalism and the Social Problem (Churchill), 191
Lib–Lab candidates, 215, 316, 318, 328, 334
 at Gorton, 311–12, 316
 in coal seats, 320–1
 at Burnley, 329–30, 336
 bitterness over, 336–7
Licensing Bill, 271; *see also* drink
Lindsay family (Earls of Crawford), 249
Lindsell, F. R. B., 276, 286, 294, 389, 432
Liquor Trades confederation, 271
Liverpool, 9, 55, 69, 362
 Conservative party in, 38, 46–9, 122, 124, 217, 219, 232–3, 237, 271–2, 341, 379–80
 and Tariff Reform, 302–3, 306, 371, 372, 374, 376, 378
 Liberal party in, 56, 208, 231, 232, 236, 253, 267
 Labour seats in, 315, 324
 peculiar politics of, 14, 40, 45–52, 272–3, 384, 404
 extent of participation, 122, 123, 124, 128, 135–6, 136–7
 transport strike (1911), 40, 49
 cultural groups in: Catholics, 257, 258; Welsh, 260; Anglicans, 261, 262; Orangemen, 265–6, 272; Irish, 37–8, 252, 253, 254
 style of politics in, 127, 141, 232–3, 235–6, 237
LIVERPOOL ABERCROMBY, 13
 plural vote in, 114
 businessmen in, 299–300
 and Free Trade, 236, 279, 283, 299, 303, 379
Liverpool Constitutional Association, 46, 48
Liverpool Courier, 56, 116, 131, 149, 378 n.
 and referendum pledge, 306, 382–3
 quoted, 72–3, 140, 254, 279, 283, 299, 363, 374

Index

Index

old age pensions (*cont.*)
  and Tory Democracy, 233
  and economic liberals, 289, 291, 292
  as electoral issue, 345, 359, 361, 362, 378, 399
OLDHAM, 12, 30–1, 57, 69, 77, 103, 123, 127, 264, 268, 345, 366–7, 369, 373–4, 378
  by-elections (1899), 42–4, 71, 85, 365; (1911), 317, 386
  electioneering in, 133, 136, 139–40
  Liberalism in, 207–8, 239, 240
  Conservative party in, 217
  and Churchill, 238, 241, 277–8, 378
  and fiscal issue, 86, 275, 298
  Labour in, 93, 94, 95, 100, 314, 316–17
Oldham Evening Chronicle, 375 n.
Oliver, E. L., 286, 304, 306–7, 432
Operative Conservative Societies, *see* Tory Democracy
Orangemen, 36, 40, 50, 51, 52, 265
Ord, Alderman, 291
ORMSKIRK, 12, 243, 245
  and franchise, 105 n., 111
  Lever in, 222–3
  and landed interest, 221, 249
  and Protestants, 264
Osborne, W. V., 330
Osborne judgement, 95, 332, 335, 337, 358
Ostrogorski, M., 200
Oswald, James, 86
outvoters, *see* plural voters
Overlookers' union, 94
Owtram, H. H., 292, 432

Pankhurst, Christabel, 19, 121
Pankhurst, Emmeline, 166 n., 194
  inept tactics of, 119, 120, 121, 195
Pankhurst, Dr R. M., 41, 161, 163, 166, 194
Parker, Gilbert, 361 n.
Parnaby, Rev. Henry, 56
Parnell, Charles Stewart, 11 n., 37
Partington, Edward, 228
Partington, Oswald, 228–9, 231, 243, 347 n., 377
party organisation, ch. 8 *passim*
  importance in registration, 105–7, 111, 126, 129
  and removals, 122, 124
  and turnout, 128
passive resistance, *see* Nonconformity
Pateson, J. W., 283
Paul, Herbert, 176
Pease, J. A., as Chief Whip, 206, 217 n., 219, 325
Peel, Lord, Report on temperance, 268
Peel, Robert, 28, 347, 348
Peel, W. R. W., 183, 184, 243, 277

Pelling, Henry, 399, 401–2
Penny, John, 313, 315
People's Rights, The (Churchill), 378
People's Suffrage Federation, 120
Perks, R. W., 170
Permewan, Dr, 52, 236
personation, *see* corruption
Peto, Basil, 305
Petrie, Charles, 49, 236
Pierpoint, Robert, 226, 244, 362 n.
Pilcher, Jesse, 231
Pilkington family, 56, 225, 230, 231
Pilkington, George, 241, 369
Pilkington, Richard, 222, 225, 344 n.
Pilling, Walter, 100
Platt family, 30–1, 231
Platt-Higgins, F., 141
plumping, 145, 318–19
plural voters, 103, 113, 117
  distribution of, 109–10, 114–15
  politics of, 23, 115–17
  Liberal attacks on, 117–18
Ponsonby, Arthur, 192, 193
Poor Law, 134
  disqualification for franchise, 104, 117, 118
  reform of, 335, 359
  overseers and registration, 104, 107, 109, 111
Postal Workers' union, 332
Potter, Beatrice, *see* Webb, Beatrice and Sidney
Potter, C. H., 352 n., 372
Powell, Francis Sharp, 344 n., 374
  as Tory Democrat, 31–2
  as patriarch, 225, 244, 245
  and Free Trade, 29, 280, 288, 374
Prentice, Archibald, 153
Presbyterianism, 57
press, *see* newspapers *and* halfpenny papers
pressure groups, in elections, 134, 249 and Part 5 *passim*
PRESTON, 13, 90, 125, 221, 230, 231, 367, 373–4
  by-elections (1881), 29; (1903), 93–4, 319
  Conservatism, 46 n., 261 n., 332, 333
  Labour in, 95, 263, 312, 339, 357 n.
  Liberal–Labour relations in, 145, 315, 316, 320
  Free Trade in, 291, 293, 300
  Calvert and, 276, 279, 282–3, 287, 371
  Cox and, 238, 279, 281, 291–2
  cultural politics in, 373, 379–80, 384, 403–4
  electioneering in, 127, 132, 135, 141, 142
  political leaders in, 237, 244, 245 n.
  and cotton, 77, 99
  and drink, 268, 269, 270
  religious influences in, 36, 64, 66, 258–9, 262, 267, 272

Index

Index

Siegfried, André, 14
Simon, E. D., 196, 396
Simon, John, 197, 308, 351 n., 387
Simpson, Albert, 96–7, 98
Smith, Albert, 94–5
Smith, Arthur, 293
Smith, F. E., 50, 51, 103, 124, 143, 145, 150,
 235, 277, 310, 345, 373
 and religious issues, 73, 266
 as charismatic leader, 135–6, 345 n., 378
 as Liverpool M.P., 233, 258, 272
 and fiscal issue, 292, 349, 354
Smith, F. H., 232
Smith, Harold, 226–7, 244, 383
Smith, J. Fulton, 270
Smith, Tom, 144, 302, 334, 335
Smith, Thorley, 120
Snowden, Philip, 41, 55, 241, 268, 347
 on old register, 122–3, 125
 on atheism, 147
 on Hornbyism, 224
 and Blackburn, 312, 319, 332
 and Liberalism, 313, 326, 337, 361
Social Democratic Federation (Party), 40–1,
 144, 315
 electoral strategy of, 312–13, 314, 329–32,
 337
social leaders, 220, 241–2, 244–5
 employers as, 221–3
 in Liberal party, 222–4, 230–2, 239–40,
 406
 as M.P.s, 224–30, 232–4, 237
socialism, 40–2, 43
 in north east Lancashire, 90, 92, 94, 312–13,
 337, 339
 Labour and, 339, 405
 Conservative view of, 333
 attacked as atheistic, 50–1, 147
 progressive view of, 171–3, 189–90
Southern, Ald., 180, 185
SOUTHPORT, 13, 105 n., 115, 139, 261 n., 264,
 369
 by-elections (1898), 365; (1899), 46, 365
 electioneering in, 135, 137, 147, 149–50
 expenses in, 199
 and Pilkington, 241
 and landed interest, 251
 Catholics in, 257
 temperance in, 268
Sowler, Harry, 141, 154
Sowler, Thomas, 154
Spectator, 287, 292
Spender, Harold, 168, 181, 191–2
Spinners' trade unions, 42, 80–1, 98, 318
 politics of, 84–5, 90, 93, 94, 357 n.
 see also United Textile Factory Workers'
 Association

STALYBRIDGE, 13, 95, 100, 200, 236, 242, 367,
 373, 379, 380
 by-elections (1871), 32; (1905), 241–2
 corruption in, 138
Stalybridge dispute (1891), 81
Stamford, Earl of, 250
Standard, 133, 334
Stanhope, Philip, 22, 92, 205, 346, 368
Stanley family, 49, 221, 249
Stanley, Lord, *see* Derby, 17th Earl of
Stanley, A. Lyulph, 232, 250, 251–2, 317
Stanley, Arthur, 221, 223, 250, 264
Stanley, George, 384
Stanley of Alderley, Lord, *see* Sheffield, Lord
status politics, 6, 16–19, 20, 400, 401
 in 19th century, 36–7, 88–9, 247
 persistence of, 50–1, 379–80, 384, 385,
 403–4
 essentially local, 241–2, 406
 and electoral issues, 393, 402–3, 406
 see also religion
Steadman, W. C., 174
Steel-Maitland, Arthur, 116, 217 n., 219, 235,
 307
Stephens, William, 232
Stewart, Gershom, 293, 361 n.
STOCKPORT, 12, 14–15, 77, 240, 245, 367, 368
 and Labour, 41, 315, 316, 317–18
 M.P. crosses floor, 71
 Tory clergy in, 261
 drink trade in, 271
 and bandwagon effect, 379
 and referendum, 384
Stockport Advertiser, 318
Stott, P. S., 95–6, 100
Strachey, J. St Loe, 274, 285, 287, 289, 291
STRETFORD, 12, 57, 231
 outvoters in, 110, 115–16
 lodger voters in, 111
 registration expenses in, 208
 and Nuttall, 244
 Tory clergy in, 261–2
 and bandwagon effect, 374
suburbs, 30–1, 54
 voting in, 11, 13, 389, 396–7
Sully, Daniel, 95
Sunday Chronicle, 41
Sunday Schools, 55, 59, 65
Sutton, J. E., 117, 245 n., 325–7
Swift, Rigby, 244
Symonds, A. G., 154, 163, 165, 205, 206, 213–15
 and labour representation, 161–2, 165
 and candidates, 198, 237

Tablet, 255
Taff Vale cases, 9, 332, 357; *see also* Trades
 Disputes Bills

Index